Historia Patria

Politics, History, and National Identity in Spain, 1875–1975

CAROLYN P. BOYD

Beginning with the Restoration of the Bourbon monarchy in 1875 and ending with the death of General Francisco Franco in 1975, this book explores the intersection of education and nationalism in Spain. Based on a broad range of archival and published sources, including parliamentary and ministerial records, pedagogical treatises and journals, teachers' manuals, memoirs, and a sample of over 200 primary and secondary school textbooks, the study examines ideological and political conflict among groups of elites seeking to shape popular understanding of national history and identity through the schools, both public and private.

A burgeoning literature on European nationalisms has posited that educational systems in general, and an instrumentalized version of national history in particular, have contributed decisively to the articulation and transmission of nationalist ideologies. The Spanish case reveals a different dynamic. In Spain, a chronically weak state, a divided and largely undemocratic political class, and an increasingly polarized social and political climate impeded the construction of an effective system of national education and the emergence of a consensus on the shape and meaning of the Spanish national past.

HISTORIA PATRIA

HISTORIA PATRIA

POLITICS, HISTORY, AND NATIONAL IDENTITY IN SPAIN, 1875–1975

Carolyn P. Boyd

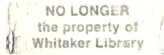

PRINCETON UNIVERSITY PRESS   PRINCETON, NEW JERSEY

Library of Congress Cataloging-in-Publication Data

Boyd, Carolyn P., 1944–
Historia patria : politics, history, and national identity in
Spain, 1875–1975 / Carolyn P. Boyd.
p.   cm.
Includes bibliographical references (p.   ) and index.
ISBN 0-691-02656-4 (cl : alk. paper)
1. Nationalism and education—Spain—History.   2. Education and
state—Spain—History.   3. Politics and education—Spain—History.
4. Spain—History—Study and teaching—Spain.   5. Nationalism—
Study and teaching—Spain.   I. Title.
LC93.S7B69   1997
320.54′0946—dc21   96-45261
                                                                    CIP

This book has been composed in Sabon

Princeton University Press books are printed on acid-free paper and
meet the guidelines for permanence and durability of the Committee
on Production Guidelines for Book Longevity of the Council on
Library Resources

10 9 8 7 6 5 4 3 2 1

To My Parents and My Children

_____

Contents

_____ *Illustrations* _____

_ Abbreviations Used in the Text and the Notes _

ACN de P	Asociación Católica Nacional de Propagandistas
AGMEC	Archivo General de la Administración. Ministerio de Educación y Ciencias
BILE	*Boletín de la Institución Libre de Enseñanza*
BOE	*Boletín Oficial del Estado*
BOMIP	*Boletín Oficial del Ministerio de Instrucción Pública*
BRAH	*Boletín de la Real Academia de la Historia*
BUP	Bachillerato Unificado Polivalente
C	Circular
CEDA	Confederación Española de Derechas Autónomas
CP	*Cuadernos de Pedagogía*
CSIC	Consejo Superior de Investigaciones Científicas
D	Decree
DGIP	Dirección General de Instrucción Pública
DSC	*Diario de las sesiones de las Cortes españolas*
DSCC	*Diario de las sesiones de las Cortes constituyentes*
EGB	Educación General Básica
EM	*Enseñanza Media*
ES	*El Sol*
FAE	Federación de Amigos de la Enseñanza
FET y de las JONS	Falange Española Tradicionalista y de las Juntas de Ofensiva Nacional-Sindicalista
FETE	Federación Española de Trabajadores de la Enseñanza
I	Instruction
ILE	Institución Libre de Enseñanza
Gaceta	*Gaceta de Madrid*
LE	*La Enseñanza*
Leg.	Legajo
LGE	Ley General de Educación
MEC	Ministerio de Educación y Ciencia
MEN	Ministerio de Educación Nacional
O	Order
OC	Circulating Order
OC	*Obras completas*
PSOE	Partido Socialista Obrero Español

RD	Royal Decree
RO	Royal Order
ROC	Royal Circulating Order
RE	*Revista de Educación*
REP	*Revista Española de Pedagogía*
RP	*Revista de Pedagogía*
RSE	*Revista de Segunda Enseñanza*
RyF	*Razón y Fé*
UP	Unión Patriótica

Preface

> The history that interests us socially is not that
> which professors know, but that which is
> known by the Spaniard who walks down the
> street, who, by virtue of his knowledge of the
> past, often intervenes in contemporary history
> as an actor and collaborator.
> (*Rafael Altamira*)[1]

LIKE THE INFLUENTIAL Spanish historian and educator Rafael Altamira, elites in modern or modernizing societies have generally considered a communal sense of the national past to be an essential component of national solidarity and civic consciousness. Centrally relevant to ideologies of nationhood and national identity, national history can be invoked either to legitimize or to subvert the existing political order. In democratic as well as authoritarian states, a shared understanding of the past potentially serves an integrative function by building a sense of group origins and destiny, authorizing (or disauthorizing) the nation's present fortunes, and defining collective values and behaviors. It also implicitly sets an agenda for the future by explaining the trajectory of the national community from the past through the present and by setting the parameters of legitimate change.[2]

In Europe preoccupation with popular understanding of the past emerged in the mid-nineteenth century as states—particularly those

---

[1] Rafael Altamira y Crevea, "Direcciones fundamentales de la historia de España en el siglo XIX," *BILE* 47, no. 759 (30 June 1923): 179.

[2] On the role of history in the construction of nationalism and national identity, see especially Bernard Lewis, *History Remembered, Recovered, Invented* (Princeton: Princeton University Press, 1975); Eric Hobsbawm and Terence Ranger, eds., *The Invention of Tradition* (Cambridge: Past and Present Publications, 1984); Eric Hobsbawm, *Nations and Nationalism since 1780: Programme, Myth, Reality* (New York: Cambridge University Press, 1990); Marc Ferro, *The Use and Abuse of History, or How the Past Is Taught* (Boston: Routledge and Kegan Paul, 1984); J. H. Plumb, *The Death of the Past* (New York: Houghton Mifflin, 1971); and Josep Fontana, *Historia: Análisis del pasado y proyecto social* (Barcelona: Editorial Crítica, 1982); On nationalism more generally, see Benedict Anderson, *Imagined Communities: Reflections on the Origins and Spread of Nationalism* (London: Verso, 1983); John Breuilly, *Nationalism and the State* (Manchester: Manchester University Press, 1982); Anthony D. Smith, *National Identity* (Reno: University of Nevada Press, 1991); and Liah Greenfeld, *Nationalism: Five Roads to Modernity* (Cambridge: Harvard University Press, 1992).

with formal democratic institutions—endeavored to inculcate "patriotic" or "national" values in their citizens by including national history among the core disciplines taught in their expanding systems of primary and secondary education. In the French Third Republic, for example, a republican version of French history played a key role in creating a spirit of *revanchisme* against Germany and, together with instruction in "civics," aided the conversion of "peasants into Frenchmen." In Germany, at the urging of Emperor Wilhelm II, the classical secondary school curriculum was revised in the 1890s to include more German language and history in order to produce "young Germans, and not Greeks or Romans."[3] In the same decade across the Atlantic, both the American Historical Association and the National Educational Association recommended four years of history instruction as the indispensable basis for intelligent citizenship in a nation whose population was composed of immigrants originating in many different parts of the world.[4] National history, in other words, was central to the cultural construction of the nation, conceived as an "imagined community" whose members shared a common past and, by extension, a common present and future.

To instill a collective sense of history and identity, advanced Western societies extended their systems of public education during the last quarter of the nineteenth century. Economic expansion, urbanization, state consolidation, and the spread of liberal democratic political institutions made apparent the utility of mass primary education as a way both of increasing the productivity of the labor force and of assuring popular allegiance to the political and social order, particularly in the context of heightened international tension. In response to the demands of the new entrepreneurial and bureaucratic classes, state-supported secondary education expanded at the same time, although not to the same extent, since it remained the preserve of the elite groups, old and new.[5]

[3] For France, see Eugen Weber, *Peasants into Frenchmen: The Modernization of Rural France, 1870–1914* (Stanford, Calif.: Stanford University Press, 1976); Fritz K. Ringer, *Fields of Knowledge: French Academic Culture in Comparative Perspective, 1890–1920* (New York: Cambridge University Press, 1992); and Mona Ozouf, *L'École, l'Église et la République, 1871–1914* (Paris: Armand Colin, 1963); for Germany, see James C. Albisetti, *Secondary School Reform in Imperial Germany* (Princeton: Princeton University Press, 1982).

[4] American Historical Association, Committee of Seven, *The Study of History in the Schools: Report to the American Historical Association* (New York: Macmillan, 1899); N. Ray Hiner, "Professions in Process: Changing Relations between Historians and Educators, 1896–1911," *History of Education Quarterly* 12, no. 1 (1972): 34–42.

[5] Margaret S. Archer, *Social Origins of Educational Systems* (London and Beverley Hills, Calif.: Sage Publications, 1979); Mary Jo Maynes, *Schooling in Western Europe: A Social History* (Albany, N.Y.: SUNY Press, 1985).

It would be a mistake to overschematize the process of "nationalization," however. Even in the modern states whose historical experience has provided the models for recent theorizing about nationalism, the ingredients of national identity and the contours and significance of the collective past were themselves the subject of bitter debate, and the dispute over the right to define and transmit the meaning of history was an important component of a larger political and social struggle. The contested past was not merely a product of political conflict but also an explanation of it, an independent phenomenon that perpetuated and intensified ideological and social cleavages. Furthermore, the emergence of state educational systems did not automatically guarantee the hegemony of the ruling elites. Private schools, by successfully advertising their social superiority, continued to educate a substantial fraction of the propertied classes, often inculcating a system of values at odds with the values of the state.

What was ultimately at issue in the conflict over *who* should educate was the selection of curricula, textbooks, and pedagogical methods. School curricula encapsulate those cultural elements deemed most worthy of preservation and transmission to new generations; they establish a hierarchy of knowledge that in distilled and systematic form explains and gives meaning to the natural and social world. In modern schools this systematized knowledge is usually transmitted through textbooks, whose contents and format shape the students' understanding of both the subject matter and the real world issues with which the subject purports to deal. Teaching methods are likewise developed in accordance with identifiable assumptions about human nature, psychology, and potentiality. By setting behavioral limits and expectations for children, classroom culture—the so-called hidden curriculum—gradually establishes patterns of thought and activity that are meant to carry over into adult life. Curricula, textbooks, and teaching methods are, in other words, partly ideological constructs; through them, modern societies provide children with a framework for understanding and living in the world.

Starting from this insight, both functionalist and Marxist theorizing about education has stressed the role of the schools in cementing and perpetuating prevailing relations of social and economic power. As agents of social and cultural reproduction, the schools logically cannot serve as effective instruments of revolutionary change; indeed, Marxist critics have insisted that, to the extent that they deflect attention from the class struggle, efforts to transform society through the schools are not only utopian, but also counterproductive.[6] Once again, however,

---

[6] For functionalist analyses, see Émile Durkheim, *Education and Sociology*, trans. Sher-

one should avoid defining the relationship between schools and society in an excessively mechanical way. In defiance of the theory, educational systems and economic structures have historically been rather imperfectly correlated, and school curricula have been notoriously riddled with contradictory aims and values, reflecting the weight of inertia, tradition, and compromise in shaping educational practice.[7] Moreover, as the Marxist theoretician Antonio Gramsci first noted, traditional Marxist theory denies subordinate groups the power to resist the dominant ideology or to respond creatively with an alternative set of cultural values, whereas in practice, schooling has been an important arena of ideological struggle among groups competing for social and political power, particularly where educational systems have been weak or decentralized. Whether by attempting to capture the state in order to transform cultural values through the public schools or by challenging the ideological hegemony of ruling elites from outside the system, intellectual leaders of subordinated groups have acted on Gramsci's thesis concerning the relative autonomy of the cultural sphere. To dismiss their struggles as utopian is to neglect an important source of the ideological conflicts and political instability that have plagued

---

wood D. Fox (Glencoe, Ill.: Free Press, 1956); Talcott Parsons, *The Social System* (Glencoe, Ill.: Free Press, 1959); Peter Berger and Thomas Luckmann, *The Social Construction of Reality* (New York: Doubleday, 1966); Clifford Geertz, *The Interpretation of Cultures: Selected Essays* (New York: Basic Books, 1973). Influential Marxist analyses include Louis Althusser, "Ideology and the Ideological State Apparatuses," in *"Lenin and Philosophy" and Other Essays*, trans. Ben Brewster (New York: Monthly Review Press, 1971); and Raymond Williams, *The Long Revolution* (New York: Columbia University Press, 1961). For further development of these approaches, see also Michael F. D. Young, ed., *Knowledge and Control: New Directions for the Sociology of Education* (New York: Collier-Macmillan, 1971); Basil Bernstein, *Class, Codes and Control*, vol. 3, *Towards a Theory of Educational Transmission* (Boston: Routledge and Kegan Paul, 1975); J. Eggleston, *The Sociology of the School Curriculum* (Boston: Routledge and Kegan Paul, 1977); Michael W. Apple, *Ideology and Curriculum* (Boston: Routledge and Kegan Paul, 1979); and Martin Carnoy, "Education and Theories of the State," *Education and Society* 1, no. 2 (1983): 3–25; 2, nos. 1–2 (1984): 3–19. A thoughtful critique is in Henry A. Giroux, "Theories of Reproduction and Resistance in the New Sociology of Education: A Critical Analysis," *Harvard Educational Review* 53, no. 3 (1983): 257–93. For schools as instruments of cultural reproduction, see Pierre Bourdieu and Jean-Claude Passeron, *Reproduction in Education, Society and Culture*, trans. Richard Nice (London and Beverley Hills, Calif.: Sage Publications, 1977); and *The Inheritors: French Students and Their Relation to Culture*, trans. Richard Nice (Chicago: University of Chicago Press, 1979). For Marxist analyses of the Spanish case, see Carlos Lerena Alesón, *Escuela, ideología y clases sociales en España: Crítica de la sociología empirista de la educación* (Barcelona: Ariel, 1976); and Manuel Tuñón de Lara, *Medio siglo de cultura española (1885–1936)* (Madrid: Tecnos, 1973).

[7] See Fritz K. Ringer, *Education and Society in Modern Europe* (Bloomington: Indiana University Press, 1979).

the modern history of most European nations, including modern Spain.[8]

Twentieth-century Spain has been marked by continuous debate over the meaning of national history and identity and over the scope and function of history in the schools, reflecting and contributing to an ongoing crisis of legitimacy that has only recently been resolved with the consolidation of democratic, constitutional government. Although scholars have analyzed literary discourse on national identity and history, they have often failed to explore its broader political and cultural significance, while its repercussions in the realm of schooling have received almost no attention at all.[9] Yet it was at the level of popular understanding that the stakes were the highest, once it became clear that political authority in the modern world required popular assent. By seeking to monopolize the transmission of collective representations of national history and identity to Spanish schoolchildren, both the right and the left aspired to validate their pretensions to power. Ironically, however, the chief result was to divide further a bitterly divided society. Rather than forge consensus, national history became yet another

[8] See Antonio Gramsci, *Prison Notebooks*, ed. and trans. Joseph A. Buttigieg and Antonio Callari (New York: Columbia University Press, 1991); also, Henry A. Giroux, *Ideology, Culture and the Process of Schooling* (Philadelphia: Temple University Press, 1981); and "Hegemony, Resistance and the Paradox of Educational Reform," *Interchange* 12, nos. 2–3 (1981): 3–26; and Paul Willis, "Cultural Production Is Different from Cultural Reproduction Is Different from Social Reproduction Is Different from Reproduction," *Interchange* 12, nos. 2–3 (1981): 48–67.

[9] On the cultural debate, see, for example, Pedro Laín Entralgo, *España como problema*, 2 vols. (Madrid: Aguilar, 1962); Juan López-Morillas, *Hacia el 98: Literatura, sociedad, e ideología* (Barcelona: Ariel, 1972); José-Carlos Mainer, *La edad de plata (1902–1931): Ensayo de interpretación de un proceso cultural* (Barcelona: Ediciones Asenet, 1975); and Edward Inman Fox, *La crisis intelectual del 98* (Madrid: EDICUSA, 1976). The few studies of schoolbook history have dealt mainly with the nineteenth century or with the Franquist period. See Horacio Capel et al., *Ciencia para la burguesía: Renovación pedagógica y enseñanza de la geografía en la revolución liberal española, 1814–1857* (Barcelona: Universitat, 1983); Eduardo Fey, *Estudio documental de la filosofía en el bachillerato español (1807–1957)* (Madrid: Consejo Superior de Investigaciones Científicas, Instituto de Pedagogía San José de Calasanz, 1975); José Luis Peset et al., *Ciencias y enseñanza en la revolución burguesa* (Madrid: Siglo XXI, 1978); Gregorio Cámara Villar, *Nacional-catolicismo y escuela: La socialización política del franquismo, 1936–1951* (Jaén: Hesperia, 1983); Rafael Valls Montés, *La interpretación de la historia de España y sus orígenes ideológicos en el bachillerato franquista (1938–1953)* (Valencia: Instituto de Ciencias de la Educación de la Universidad Literaria, 1984); Fernando Valls, *La enseñanza de la literatura en el franquismo (1936–1951)* (Barcelona: Antoni Bosch, 1983); Clementina García Crespo, *Léxico e ideología en los libros de lectura de la escuela primaria (1940–1975)* (Salamanca: Ediciones Universidad, Instituto de Ciencias de la Educación, 1983); and José-Luis Haro et al., "La historia en los textos de bachillerato (1938–1975): Proyecto de investigación y análisis de un tema: La Segunda República," *Revista de Bachillerato* 2, no. 9 (January-March, 1978): 2–18.

obstacle to political stability and social integration. By analyzing competing discourses on national history and the efforts to disseminate them through the medium of the schools, this study hopes to illuminate certain features of Spain's modern political and cultural history—especially the low levels of civic engagement, the conspicuous absence of a mass nationalist movement, and the weak attraction of Spanish, as opposed to regional or local, identity.

The organization of this study is chronological, reflecting my understanding of the successive regime changes of the past century in Spain as elements in a single process of ideological and political conflict. The first two chapters analyze the gradual deterioration of the Restoration political settlement after 1875 and the concomitant rise of the debate over "national" education. Once the liberal state had been consolidated, the traditional political elites neglected popular education because they preferred an inert to an engaged citizenry. The weak, decentralized state educational system invited competition from a dynamic private sector that sought to create the cultural conditions needed for a radical transformation of state and society. Although the dynastic parties finally acknowledged the link between national regeneration and national educational policy in the aftermath of the Spanish-American War, the political class ultimately proved too divided over the meaning and purpose of "the nation" to agree upon a common program of educational reform. This ideological rift was most clearly visible in the continuing neglect of national history as a school subject, whose content and methods comprise the subject of chapter 3.

In contrast, both integrist Catholic and liberal democratic critics of the Restoration monarchy sought to mobilize a particular interpretation of the national past in defense of their assertions about national identity and purpose. Chapters 4 and 5 contrast the historical discourse of Catholic integrists and progressives and their competing models of how national history should be conceptualized and taught. Chapters 6 and 7 analyze the successive efforts of the military dictatorship of 1923–30 and the left republican regime of 1931–36 to implement these opposing projects. The contest to define national history and identity culminated in the civil war of 1936–39 and the eventual triumph of the authoritarian right. Chapter 8 is devoted to the first fifteen years of the Franco regime, which claimed to represent "authentic" Spanish values and traditions and, accordingly, made transmission of the national Catholic interpretation of Spanish history the keystone of its program of political and cultural "nationalization." Chapter 9 describes how economic and educational modernization during the second phase of the regime rendered national Catholicism increasingly anachronistic; the regime's decision to abandon national history as a principal tool of ideological legitimization cleared a space for the emergence of new historical paradigms derived from contemporary European scholarship. By the early 1970s, a cultural foundation had been laid for the consensual evolution toward political democratization that occurred after the death of General Franco.

Describing and explaining the contested meaning of the national past and its transmission to successive generations of young Spaniards has involved several separate, but interrelated, areas of investigation. The first task was to identify the ideologies and objectives of the political and cultural elites who protagonized the conflict. There was no lack of sources for this part of the project; the debate was carried out in books, journals of opinion, the national press, pedagogical publications, and the Cortes. The second task was to understand how competing discourses on history and identity were transmitted to Spanish schoolchildren. The intent of policy makers could be traced by consulting the relevant legislation, but knowing how much of this legislation actually affected what teachers taught was more problematic. Clichés about the excessive centralization of the Spanish state and the cultural hegemony of the ruling elites notwithstanding, historically the weak Spanish state could neither provide a sufficient number of public schools (leaving a deficit filled primarily by private Catholic schools) nor effectively impose uniform standards on its own schools and teachers. Regardless of the regime in power, official mandates and prescriptions were honored most often in the breach and thus do not afford a reliable guide to actual classroom practice.

What became clear during the course of my research, however, was that textbooks have been the privileged medium of instruction in most Spanish schools right up to the present. Analysis of the textbooks used in the schools thus provides a reasonably reliable way of capturing the ideas and images that Spanish political and cultural elites wished to impress upon the nation's youth. Unfortunately, identifying the most widely adopted history books among the hundreds published since 1875 posed substantial difficulties. Although legally required since 1857 to regulate and approve textbooks and to inspect public and private schools, the Spanish state generally lacked the financial resources or the political will to do so until the 1930s. Since the 1930s, lists of approved texts have been published regularly, but in the absence of centralized inspection records or publishers' data on edition sizes and sales, it has been difficult to identify which books were most widely used. Nevertheless, I have made an informed judgment by inferential use of scattered evidence in official, pedagogical, literary, and commercial sources and have compensated for the lack of precision by examining a relatively large sample of texts from each period.

In addition to opening a window on Spanish classroom processes, the textbooks dramatically illustrate the ideological cleavages that have divided Spanish elites in the past century. History textbooks convey more than facts about the past; through value judgments, selection and omission of topics, emphasis, imagery, and format they suggest notions about national character and destiny, historical agency and motivation, and the relationship between past and present. Thus, history textbooks reflect the multiple and conflicting messages about national character and development with which competing groups of elites have attempted to forge popular support for their respective political projects.

What this book has not attempted to do is to assess their impact on popular perceptions of the national past. Like everyone else, Spaniards have acquired a sense of the past from sources other than school and schoolbooks—from local and national festivals and monuments, religious rituals and sermons, folktales and ballads, and increasingly in the twentieth-century, from radio, films, comics, and television. Although exploration of these sources would undoubtedly be fruitful, they lie outside the scope of this study. Within the limits of this investigation, moreover, it has been impossible to ascertain how much schoolbook history was retained by the average student. Given the "memoristic" instructional methods, the aridity of the texts, and the rapidity with which the subject was surveyed during most of the century, it might be concluded that students absorbed little, if any, of the history they crammed at exam time. But if this was undoubtedly true of the many historical facts and details in the textbooks, it is nonetheless likely that the broad themes and attitudes toward the past in the texts left a residue. In any event, both the ineffectuality of the medium and the lack of agreement on the message that this study documents help explain why creating a consensual political culture eluded successive Spanish regimes and why effective transmission of a common definition of national history and identity was thought to be so important.

In Spain today, the struggle among intellectual elites to define the national past has lost much of its virulence but not its relevance, and the value and purpose of history education are still the subject of debate. If the transition to democracy since 1975 has seemingly resolved the crisis of political legitimacy that has beset the nation since 1808, the new state rests on secure foundations only to the extent that a political culture congenial to democratic institutions and to the competing claims of peripheral nationalisms and national integration can be cultivated. With this in mind, educational reformers have rewritten social studies and history curricula, publishers have commissioned new textbooks, and teachers have experimented with new approaches to teaching about the past in order to encourage tolerance, pluralism, and national solidarity. At the very least, this book may help place such efforts in histori-cal perspective.

But Spain is not the only society now confronting the role of history in the education of the young. In Western Europe, the former Soviet Union, and the United States, interest in history as a school subject has revived among intellectuals, educators, historians, and policy makers. Cultural and social fragmentation, and the accompanying rise of iden-tity politics, the increasingly analytical and self-referential character of academic history, and the enormities of twentieth-century history itself have all made history teaching both controversial and inescapable. Where there is no consensus on national history and identity, the im-pulse to use coercion or to abandon the field to the forces of disaggrega-tion is strong. The Spanish example, however, illustrates the potentially perilous outcome of either course.

In the years since I first began work on this project, I have been gener-ously assisted by many individuals and institutions. The American Council of Learned Societies and the University Research Institute of The University of Texas at Austin provided support for research, travel, and writing. I am grateful for the courteous and knowledgeable assis-tance of the staff at the Biblioteca Nacional, the Hemeroteca Municipal, the Ministerio de Educación y Ciencia, and the former Instituto de San José de Calasanz in the Consejo Superior de Investigaciones Científicas in Madrid, the Ministerio de Educación y Ciencia archive of the Archivo General de la Administración Central in Alcalá de Henares, the Hispanic Section of the Library of Congress, and the Perry-Castañeda Library at the University of Texas. I am especially indebted to the fol-lowing friends and colleagues who read all or portions of the manu-script and offered helpful suggestions for its improvement: Richard Herr, James Boyden, José Álvarez Junco, Nicolas Shumway, David Ring-rose, Stanley Payne, Joan Connelly Ullman, and Standish Meacham. Needless to say, all remaining errors of fact or interpretation are exclu-sively my own, as are all translations, unless otherwise indicated. My research assistants, José Antonio Fernández, John-Marshall Klein, Joe Ridout, Charles Frago, and Kristin Tegtmeier have contributed to the completion of this project in ways both large and small. I am also thankful for the kindness of many friends in Madrid, who over the years have provided shelter, sustenance, advice, and friendship. I will always be grateful for their kindness. My husband, Frank, and my sons, Peter and Michael, shared a wonderful six months in Madrid with me in 1985 and have lived with this project almost continuously ever since. For their love, patience, and support, I am most grateful of all.

HISTORIA PATRIA

CHAPTER 1

The Spanish Educational System and Its Critics, 1857–1900

> The question of education is a question of
> power: the one who educates, dominates; for to
> educate means to form men, . . . molded
> according to the views of the one who
> instructs them.
> (*Antonio Gil de Zárate*)[1]

> Con quien pasces, no con quien nasces.
> (Nurture, not nature.)
> (*Spanish proverb*)[2]

A NATIONAL SYSTEM of education developed in tandem with the consolidation of the liberal state in nineteenth-century Spain. Realizing that the battle for cultural hegemony between liberalism and Catholic traditionalism involved both institutional and ideological power, liberals prepared draft legislation as early as 1814 creating a national educational system that would reinforce the claims of the liberal state to the primary allegiance of Spaniards.[3] Public instruction, liberals believed, "creates good family men, honorable citizens, and faithful, zealous, and illustrious servants of the State; inspires in all respect for the law and submission to legitimately constituted powers, and thus tightening social bonds, assures the internal peace of nations."[4] Despite several decades

---

[1] A. Gil de Zárate, *De la instrucción pública en España* (1855), quoted in Antonio Viñao Frago, *Política y educación en los orígenes de la España contemporánea: Examen especial de sus relaciones en la enseñanza secundaria* (Madrid: Siglo XXI, 1982), 348.

[2] See the "Refranero pedagógico" in Rufino Blanco y Sánchez, *Bibliografía pedagógica de obras escritas en castellano o traducidas a este idioma*, 5 vols. (Madrid: Tip. de la Revista de Archivos, Bibliotecas y Museos, 1907–12), 4:873.

[3] "Dictamen sobre el Proyecto de Decreto de arreglo general de la enseñanza pública de 7 de marzo de 1814" and "Proyecto de Decreto para el arreglo general de la enseñanza pública de marzo de 1814," in *Historia de la educación en España: Textos y documentos*, 5 vols. (Madrid: Servicio de Publicaciones del Ministerio de Educación y Ciencia, 1979–90), 2:357–401.

[4] "Dictamen de la comisión nombrada para informar sobre el Proyecto de Ley de Instrucción pública," quoted in Federico Sanz Díaz, *La segunda enseñanza oficial en el siglo*

of legislative effort, however, it was not until 1857 that a durable law of national education (subsequently known as the Ley Moyano for its author, the Moderado liberal Claudio Moyano) was approved by the Spanish Cortes.[5] Like its French counterpart, the Loi Falloux of 1850, the Ley Moyano was a pragmatic compromise between the competing claims of church and state. After four decades of civil conflict and popular unrest, the Moderado oligarchy was eager to forge a stable system that would safeguard the victory of the liberal state without relinquishing the benefits to the social order that religious control over popular education had traditionally provided. Reflecting the liberals' faith in education as a "fountain of prosperity," the law assigned responsibility for public instruction to the minister of development (*fomento*), who was given authority to regulate personnel, curricula, textbooks, examinations, and degrees at all levels in the educational pyramid. Implementation and enforcement of ministerial policy was entrusted to ten university rectors, state appointees who exercised jurisdiction over all public and private schools in their districts. To balance this affirmation of state supremacy, the law conceded to the church the right to review the moral and doctrinal content of teaching and textbooks, mandated religious instruction for primary and secondary students, and recognized the right of private individuals to establish primary and secondary schools, albeit subject to state regulation. In this sense, the law was a sequel to the Concordat negotiated in 1851 by a socially conservative elite alarmed by the democratic revolutions of 1848 elsewhere in Europe. Although the compromise failed to satisfy the church completely, it was nevertheless a significant step away from the total secularization advocated by progressive anticlericals.

As was the case nearly everywhere in Europe, the three-tiered Spanish

XIX (Madrid: Ministerio de Educación y Ciencia, Dirección General de Enseñanzas Medias, 1985), 36.

[5] Law of 9 September 1857, in *Historia de la educación* 2:244–302. For the origins of the modern Spanish educational system, see Julio Ruíz Berrio, *Política escolar de España en el siglo XIX (1808–1833)* (Madrid: Consejo Superior de Investigaciones Científicas, 1970); Viñao Frago, *Política y educación*; Àngels Martínez Bonafé, *Ensenyament, burgesia i liberalisme: L'ensenyament secundari en els orígins del País Valencià contemporani* (Valencia: Diputació Provincial, 1985); Mariano Peset and José Luis Peset, *La universidad española (Siglos XVIII y XIX): Despotismo ilustrado y revolución liberal* (Madrid: Taurus, 1974); and José Luis Peset et al., *Ciencias y enseñanza en la revolución burguesa* (Madrid: Siglo XXI, 1978). A good overview of modern Spanish educational history is provided by Manuel de Puelles Benítez, *Educación e ideología en la España contemporánea (1767–1975)* (Barcelona: Editorial Labor, 1980). Also useful is Jordi Monés i Pujol-Busquets, *El pensament escolar i la renovació pedagògica a Catalunya (1833–1938)* (Barcelona: Edicions de La Magrana, 1977). For collections of documents, see Sanz Díaz, *Segunda enseñanza*; and *Historia de la educación*.

system was vertically segmented, reflecting and reinforcing in its structure the Spanish social hierarchy.[6] Primary education was deemed sufficient to serve the limited educational needs of the popular classes; secondary education, only formally separated from the universities in 1845 and still conceptualized as preparation for advanced studies, was, like the universities, reserved for the social elites. The financial resources of the state being limited, responsibility for school finance was distributed among municipal, provincial, and state authorities. All towns of more than five hundred inhabitants were required to provide obligatory and—in the case of the poor—free primary instruction for all children between the ages of six and nine. In provincial capitals and large cities, the law also mandated a public upper primary school (*escuela primaria superior*) for boys and girls ages ten through thirteen. Each administrative province was required to provide an *instituto* of secondary education to dispense general and practical education and to prepare students for university study. Only the ten universities (definitively organized in 1857 to include faculties of natural sciences and philosophy in addition to the traditional schools of theology, law, and medicine) were to be maintained at state expense.

The administrative bureaucracy provided avenues for the expression of competing professional, political, and social interests at all levels, with the degree of independence from the tutelary function of the ministry growing progressively down the educational ladder. Serving in an advisory capacity to the minister on personnel and policy matters was the Royal Council of Public Instruction, whose members included political and ecclesiastical dignitaries, appointed representatives from the three levels of public instruction, and distinguished members of "society" at large. At the provincial and municipal levels, committees (*juntas*) composed of governmental and ecclesiastical representatives and "fathers of families" were given responsibility for monitoring local school finance, administration, and pedagogy and for reporting on needed improvements to the higher authorities. At this level, local autonomy was nearly absolute, and the provisions of the Ley Moyano were freely interpreted or ignored altogether. Proposals to reassert the policy-making authority of the state by centralizing the financial structure, expanding the state school inspection corps, or providing a national certification standard for primary school graduates met with op-

[6] For social segmentation in nineteenth-century European school systems, see Fritz K. Ringer, *Education and Society in Modern Europe* (Bloomington: Indiana University Press, 1979); and Detlef K. Müller et al., *The Rise of the Modern Educational System: Structural Change and Social Reproduction, 1870–1920* (New York: Cambridge University Press, 1987).

position from both fiscal conservatives and defenders of local and clerical interests.

The state jealously guarded its monopoly over the granting of degrees at the university and secondary levels, reflecting the liberal view that the competition was keenest—and the political stakes, highest—in the education of elites. As a corollary, the Ley Moyano stipulated ministerial regulation of textbooks and course content, but these provisions were allowed to lapse in the last quarter of the century because there was no consensus on their implementation. Inspired initially by the threat to liberalism from the clerical right, state control over teachers and textbooks became politically divisive in the 1860s as the Moderados used ministerial power to silence professors sympathetic to democratic radicalism. In response, during the revolutionary sexennium of 1868–74, the Progressives included both the "freedom to teach" (*libertad de enseñanza*, that is, the right to establish a school) and the "freedom to profess" (*libertad de cátedra*, or academic freedom in the classroom) among the fundamental "conquests" of the Constitution of 1869. When the Conservative heirs of the Moderados attempted to reimpose ideological conformity on progressive professors after the restoration of the monarchy in 1875, they triggered a protracted crisis that threatened the fragile consensus upon which the Restoration monarchy rested. In the interest of political stability, after 1881 university rectors no longer possessed the right to sanction professors accused of political or religious heterodoxy, and both Liberal and Conservative governments abstained from exercising their theoretical right to approve textbooks and establish course content.[7]

Despite numerous modifications and even more numerous criticisms, as a compromise between conflicting political forces the Ley Moyano survived until well into the twentieth century. But as a blueprint for creating an economically productive, politically integrated and enlightened citizenry, the law was less successful. Whereas in the last decades of the nineteenth century, educational systems in France, Germany, and England underwent expansion and articulation in interaction with de-

[7] RD and ROC of 26 February 1875, signed by the marqués de Orovio; ROC of 3 March 1981, signed by José Luis Albareda. Educational legislation for the period before 1890 is in *Colección legislativa de España*; for the period 1890–1910, in Ministerio de Instrucción Pública y Bellas Artes, *Anuario legislativo de Instrucción Pública*; for 1910–36 and the period after 1940, in Ministerio de Instrucción Pública y Bellas Artes, *Colección legislativa de Instrucción Pública*. Major legislation is also in the *Gaceta de Madrid* or, after 1940, the *Boletín Oficial del Estado*. The "second university question" and its precursor in the mid-1860s are discussed in Puelles Benítez, *Educación e ideología*, 169–72, 194–213; and Yvonne Turin, *La educación y la escuela en España de 1874 a 1902: Liberalismo y tradición*. Trans. Josefa Hernández Alfonso (Madrid: Aguilar, 1967), 295–97.

mocratization and growing social and occupational complexity, in Spain public education stagnated.[8] As with Spanish liberalism in general, liberal educational legislation antedated the full development of the social and economic structures to support it. On the one hand, the agricultural and financial elites that controlled the constitutional monarchy at both the national and the local levels did not have a strong economic interest in expanded educational opportunities for their children or in the creation of an educated labor force. On the contrary, education was frequently viewed with suspicion, since it might encourage social discontent or insubordination.[9] At the same time, because the immature Spanish economy did not as yet place a premium on literacy, demand from "below" was frequently absent as well. For most urban workers and landless peasants, a child in school still represented not an economic opportunity but a sacrifice of family income; few poor children attended school beyond the age of nine or ten, if at all. Demand for expanded public educational services came chiefly from the urban middle classes, who viewed education as the key to preserving or enhancing their social and economic independence.

By the end of the century, demand for education began to expand as an industrial bourgeoisie on the periphery confronted the lack of a skilled labor force and the working classes began to perceive the liberating potential of education. But the nature of the Spanish political system frustrated the ready translation of this demand into political action. Indeed, the insulation of the Restoration political parties after 1875 from political pressure—the result of their ability to invalidate democratic politics through electoral manipulation—was another reason why the political elites displayed so little interest in education. The rotation of the Liberal and Conservative parties in office was dependent upon royal consent, interparty agreement, and the mechanisms of *caciquismo* (political bossism), rather than on shifts in public opinion.[10] When working-class challenges to the system in the form of strikes and uprisings began to appear in the 1880s and 1890s, the ruling elites found it more convenient to meet them with force rather than to organize an educational system that would integrate marginalized groups into the political and social order. Nor did the incentives that international rivalries lent to other European nations come into play; Spain's diplomatic isolation

---

[8] For a useful summary of recent scholarship on European education, see Mary Jo Maynes, *Schooling in Western Europe: A Social History* (Albany, N.Y.: SUNY Press, 1985).

[9] See the recollections of Federico Rubio, *Mis maestros y mi educación: Memorias de niñez y juventud* (Madrid: Imp. encuad. de V. Tordesillas, 1912), 113–14.

[10] The classic analysis of the Spanish political system during the Restoration is José Varela Ortega, *Los amigos políticos* (Madrid: Alianza Editorial, 1977).

and shaky hold on the remnants of her American empire made it easy to ignore the urgings of a handful of nationalist politicians to "nationalize" the citizenry. Thus, although universal education had seemed to be an unavoidable corollary of liberal state-building at the beginning of the century, habitual electoral falsification and repression made it practically expendable. To add insult to injury, the dynastic politicians often pointed to the ignorance and apathy of the electorate to justify their continuing resort to caciquismo. In response, critics came to view popular education as a precondition of political reform.

A final explanation for the failure of the state educational system lies in the continuing influence of the church in Spanish political and social life. The Spanish church remained suspicious of all schooling not firmly under its control, preferring the as yet unproved dangers of ignorance to the known perils of heterodoxy. Through its influence in the Conservative party, the church managed to stave off proposals for a larger state role in education until the turn of the century; through its network of schools, it isolated the middle class from the deficiencies of the public school system and thus curtailed demand for its reform. Moreover, in a confessional state like Spain, the ideological role of the church in maintaining the social order rendered a large fraction of the political elite unappreciative of the potential for ideological control through the schools until late in the century.

For the foregoing reasons, the quality and extension of Spanish schooling at the end of the nineteenth century were dismal, and its contribution to the creation of a uniform national culture was nearly nil. Forty years after passage of the Ley Moyano, adult illiteracy was still estimated at 55–60 percent, a global figure that masked major differences by sex and region. Although Spanish literacy rates were comparable to those elsewhere in southern and eastern Europe, Spain's failure to keep pace with Great Britain, Germany, and France (where illiteracy had been nearly eradicated by the end of the century) was the despair of progressive reformers.[11]

---

[11] The first important study of Spanish illiteracy was undertaken by the educational reformer Lorenzo Luzuriaga, *El analfabetismo en España* (Madrid: J. Cosano, 1926). For a review of the literature, see Mercedes Samaniego Boneu, *La política educativa de la Segunda República durante el bienio azañista* (Madrid: Consejo Superior de Investigaciones Científicas, 1977), 141–54. Two detailed and methodologically sophisticated recent studies are Clara Eugenia Núñez, *La fuente de la riqueza: Educación y desarrollo económico en la España contemporánea* (Madrid: Alianza Universidad, 1992); and Mercedes Vilanova Riba and Xavier Moreno Julià, *Atlas de la evolución del analfabetismo en España de 1887 a 1981* (Madrid: Centro de Publicaciones del Ministerio de Educación y Ciencia, CIDE, 1992). For comparative data, see Clara Eugenia Núñez and Gabriel Tortella, eds., *La maldición divina: Ignorancia y atraso económico en perspectiva histórica* (Madrid: Alianza Universidad, 1993). Only a third of adult women were literate in 1900; literacy rates for both sexes were 20 to 30 points higher in the north than in the south.

Critics of the state attributed illiteracy to the chronic deficit of schools and teachers, which by 1900 was substantial and growing larger; perhaps as many as ten thousand additional public schools were needed to fulfill the minimum requirements of the Ley Moyano.[12] According to official estimates, in 1895 over 68 percent of children were not in school, in many cases, for lack of school places.[13] The deficit would have been greater without the contribution of the private sector. By 1900 there were close to six thousand private primary schools, most of them operated by the religious orders, which educated almost 20 percent of all children—a practical reason why liberal governments tolerated the growing clerical influence in education.[14] Not reflected in the official statistics was the deplorable state of many existing school buildings, which, having been converted from other uses, often lacked proper ventilation, heat, light, sanitation, or equipment.[15]

[12] For varying estimates of the number of schools in Spain at the end of the century, see Ricardo Macías Picavea, *El problema nacional: (Hechos, causas y remedios)*, ed. José Esteban (Madrid: Fundación Banco Exterior, 1992), 98; Puelles Benítez, *Educación e ideología*, 310; Turin, *Educación*, 86; Enrique Bernad Royo, *La instrucción primaria a principios del siglo XX: Zaragoza, 1898–1914* (Zaragoza: Institución "Fernando el Católico," 1984), 62–64; Rafael Altamira, "Problemas urgentes de la primera enseñanza en España," *BILE* 36, no. 625 (30 April 1912): 97–105; Rafael Shaw, *Spain from Within* (London: T. Fisher Unwin, 1910), 270; Enrique Guerrero Salom, "La Institución, el sistema educativo y la educación de las clases obreras a finales del siglo," *RE* 23, no. 243 (1976): 66.

[13] Manuel B. Cossío, "La reforma escolar" (1899), quoted in *Historia de la educación* 3:341. For those actually enrolled, the attendance rate for 1916 was estimated at 67 percent. United States Department of the Interior, Bureau of Education, *Biennial Survey of Education, 1916–1918* (Washington, D.C.: Government Printing Office, 1921), 13. The school attendance rate in Madrid is estimated at about 83 percent for boys in 1903 by Alejandro Tiana Ferrer, *Maestros, misioneros, y militantes: La educación de la clase obrera madrileña, 1898–1917* (Madrid: Centro de Publicaciones del Ministerio de Educación y Ciencia, CIDE, 1992), 142. The case of a single rural school in the province of Soria exemplifies both the lack of school places and the erratic attendance of enrolled students: José Andrés Gallego, "Una escuela rural castellana: Fuencaliente de Burgo, 1847–1901," *REP* 120 (1972): 401–15.

[14] Turin, *Educación*, 86; Luis Morote, *Los frailes en España* (Madrid: Imp. de Fortanet, 1904), 12–26. For the distribution of public and private schools in Zaragoza, see Bernad Royo, *Instrucción primaria*, 139–40; for Seville province, see Eugenio Pérez González, *El magisterio sevillano a comienzos del siglo XX* (Seville: Servicio de Publicaciones del Ayuntamiento, 1982), 36; for Barcelona, *Anuario estadístico de la ciudad de Barcelona* (Barcelona: Ayuntamiento, 1905), 275–81; for Madrid, Tiana Ferrer, *Maestros*, 133–72. Catholic education had also provided an important supplement to French public schools in the early years of the Third Republic, according to Raymond Grew and Patrick J. Harrigan, "The Catholic Contribution to Universal Schooling in France, 1850–1906," *Journal of Modern History* 57, no. 2 (June 1985): 211–47.

[15] Aniceto Sela y Sampil, *La educación nacional: Hechos y ideas* (Madrid: Librería general de Victoriano Suárez, 1910), 50, 92–96. One survey in 1885 found that only 59 percent of all public primary schools were housed in buildings owned by the municipality. An evaluation of all 23,300 public schools categorized 22 percent as "good," 50 percent

Even had there been sufficient public classrooms, there were not enough trained teachers (*maestros*) to occupy them. According to one estimate, the ratio of schoolteachers to students nationally was 1:154; it was even higher in some urban areas.[16] To redress the chronic shortage, towns filled public schoolrooms with religious personnel, the untrained, and the barely literate, and tolerated extremely high student-teacher ratios.[17] Most primary schools typically consisted of a single room in which seventy to eighty children between the ages of six and thirteen studied together under the direction of a solitary, overworked, and underpaid teacher.

Teachers' salaries and status were so low that competent personnel could not be attracted to the profession. "If the allocations for primary instruction are not modified immediately," one reformer wrote, "only two kinds of persons will be able to teach: those possessed of a vocation bordering on madness and those who cannot do anything else."[18] Although salaries for experienced teachers in the larger cities were not much inferior to those paid elsewhere in Europe, in 1900, 62 percent of all primary teachers (two-thirds of them men) earned 500 pesetas or less annually; in the more remote villages, teachers earned as little as 125 pesetas a year.[19] Even when supplemented by provision of a dwelling

as "fair," and 27 percent as "bad." Manuel B. Cossío, "La enseñanza primaria en España," *BILE* 22, no. 454 (31 January 1898): 11. See also U.S. Department of Interior, *Biennial Survey,* 15; Andrés Gallego, "Escuela rural"; Tiana Ferrer, *Maestros,* 165–72; and Alvaro Figueroa y Torres, conde de Romanones, *Notas de una vida* (Madrid: Renacimiento, 1928–29), 2:88–90 n. 1. Luis Bello, *Viaje por las escuelas de España,* 4 vols. (Madrid: various publishers, 1926–29) documents in rich detail the miserable condition of many schools in the 1920s.

[16] Angel Marvaud, *La Question sociale en Espagne* (Paris: Félix Alcan, 1910), 354. The average ratio in the Zaragoza public schools around 1900 was l:131. Bernad Royo, *Instrucción primaria,* 69–72.

[17] A law of 11 July 1871 established the procedures for hiring those without degrees. In 1880, 23 percent of public school teachers had only an upper primary certificate, and another 9 percent possessed no diploma of any kind. Carlos Groizard y Coronado, *La instrucción pública en España: Discursos y notas* (Salamanca: Ramón Esteban, 1897), 114. For 1890, see Comisión de Reformas para el Mejoramiento de la Clase Obrera, *La clase obrera a finales del siglo XIX,* 2d ed. (Bilbao: Zero, 1973). See also Guerrero Salom, "La Institución," 67. Many of those without diplomas were members of religious orders. See the complaint from the primary school inspector of the district of Barcelona, dated 20 August 1862, against the French nuns teaching in the Barcelona public schools in AGMEC, leg. 6354. Foreign members of the Piarist Fathers also taught in public schools. See Cossío, "La enseñanza primaria en España," *BILE* 22, no. 456 (31 March 1898): 65. In Barcelona in 1902 the municipality subsidized 43 private schools (not all of them religious), which were attended by 6,500 working-class children and adults. *Anuario estadístico de la ciudad de Barcelona.*

[18] Sela, *Educación nacional,* 83.

[19] To make matters worse, many municipalities failed to pay on time; the amount in

and auxiliary payments from wealthier students and provincial authorities, these meager salaries were insufficient to support a family, and many teachers were obliged to augment their income with secondary employment as sextons, town clerks, or handymen.

The penury of the profession was prefigured in the undemanding routine of the normal schools, whose course of studies scanted both pedagogical theory and practice teaching.[20] After two years at normal school, students were qualified to teach in the lower grades; an additional two years were required for a post in an upper primary school or a well-paying urban school. In 1880 only 16 percent of teachers nationwide held the higher degree.[21] Most of those who resigned themselves to teaching did so with little enthusiasm or skill. Fortunately for them, the curriculum prescribed for the lower primary schools in the Ley Moyano was an undemanding one, aimed at producing docile, useful workers; until 1901 the official elementary program consisted of religious doctrine, sacred history, and the three Rs, together with "notions" of agriculture, industry, or commerce for boys and embroidery for girls. Only in the larger towns did upper primary schools provide education beyond basic literacy training to aspiring children of the popular classes.

Given their lack of preparation, the impoverishment of both students and schools, and the high student-teacher ratios, schoolmasters relied on pedagogic techniques that maximized efficiency and discipline. The basis of instruction at all levels was memorization and oral recitation of a catechism, textbook, or reader; in the poorest schools, children brought papers or family documents from home to practice reading. Discipline was achieved through violence, both physical and psychological; a famous Spanish proverb advises, "La letra, con sangre entra" (Letters are learned with blood.).[22] Although state inspection of both

---

arrears nationwide amounted to over eight million pesetas by 1900. Cossío, "La enseñanza primaria en España," *BILE* 22, no. 456 (31 March 1898) 65–84; Turin, *Educación*, 91.

[20] For normal schools during the Restoration, see Manuel B. Cossío, "Carácter y programa de las escuelas normales," *BILE* 13, no. 297 (30 June 1889): 177–82; and "La enseñanza primaria en España," *BILE* 22, no. 460 (31 July 1898): 198–207; Agustín Escolano Benito, "Las escuelas normales, siglo y medio de perspectiva histórica," *RE* 30, no. 269 (1982): 55–99; Miguel A. López, *La Escuela Normal de Granada, 1846–1970* (Granada: Universidad, 1979); and María del Mar del Pozo Andrés et al., *Guadalajara en la historia del magisterio español, 1839/1939: Cien años de formación del profesorado* (Alcalá de Henares: Universidad, 1986).

[21] Jordi Monés i Pujol-Busquets, *La llengua a l'escola (1714–1939)* (Barcelona: Barcanova, 1984), 72.

[22] A large number of the proverbs cited by Rufino Blanco in his "Refranero pedagógico" associate learning with violence: Blanco y Sánchez, *Bibliografía pedagógica* 4:872–76. See also the recollections of Rubio, *Mis maestros*; and Pedro Martínez Baselga, *Sociología y pedagogía* (Zaragoza: Tip. de Emilio Casañal, 1909).

public and private schools had been mandated in principle since 1849, conservative and clerical resistance to state authority over education kept funding so low that rural schools were visited perhaps once every three or four years. In any event, inspectors were charged primarily with reviewing school records and were not expected to monitor teaching techniques or textbooks, or to provide professional advice.[23]

Most of the structural deficiencies of the primary school system originated in the lack of money. In 1898 total expenditures at the municipal, provincial, and national levels for primary instruction totaled only 27,577,000 pesetas, or about 12 pesetas per child. (In contrast, France was spending the equivalent of 52 pesetas a child; Italy, 44; Greece and Bulgaria, 26.)[24] Nearly all (94 percent) of this amount was spent at the local and provincial level to pay for teachers' salaries and school maintenance. Raising by decree the admittedly miserable amounts spent in the smallest localities would have imposed an unbearably heavy tax burden on those least able to pay.[25] Equity demanded transferring financial responsibility for primary education to the central government, which in 1898–99 budgeted only 13 million pesetas (1.5 percent of total expenditures) for public instruction.[26] But this crucial reform was postponed throughout the Restoration, in part because of strenuous resistance by the clerical right to the assumption of a state obligation for primary education. Equally important, however, was the lack of sufficient motivation on the part of the political elites, who until the end of the century perceived no compelling political or economic advantage in the expansion of state schooling.

The state system of secondary education also failed to develop along the lines envisioned by its creators. Under the old regime, secondary education as a separate level of instruction lying between primary (popular) and university (elite) education had not existed, although private academies and seminaries offered preparatory training in classical languages and literature.[27] Interest in an alternative, secular form of educa-

[23] See U.S. Department of the Interior, *Biennial Survey*, 17; Turin, *Educación*, 89–90. There was one inspector for each province in the nineteenth century. No travel funds were provided.

[24] Sela, *Educación nacional*, 51; Bernad Royo, *Instrucción primaria*, 100–101.

[25] Cossío, "La enseñanza primaria en España," *BILE* 22, no. 456 (31 March 1898), 68. The school tax burden of a resident of a village of a few hundred inhabitants was already three to five times greater than that imposed on the inhabitant of a large town.

[26] *DSC*, 30 March 1898 (no. 32), 928.

[27] For the early history of secondary education, see Viñao Frago, *Política y educación*; Peset, *Universidad*; Sanz Díaz, *Segunda enseñanza*; Martínez Bonafé, *Ensenyament*; John R. Perz, *Secondary Education in Spain* (Washington, D.C.: Catholic University, 1934); Manuel Utande Igualada, "Un siglo y medio de segunda enseñanza," *RE* 30, no. 271 (1982): 7–41; and Matilde García y García, "Orientaciones legislativas de las enseñanzas

tion stressing "modern" and "practical" subjects—natural sciences, modern languages, geography, and history—had originated with enlightened reformers in the eighteenth century and was transmitted to their liberal heirs in the nineteenth. The creation of a new, intermediate stage of schooling—with separate institutions, professors, and curriculum—for a new kind of student seemed a fitting way to proclaim the accession of the "middle classes" to political power, to establish a new elite based on talent rather than birth, and to consolidate the new political and social order, as well as to promote economic progress through cultivation of the practical arts. This progressive vision could still be detected in 1845, when secondary education was definitively institutionalized by the Moderados. The decree signed by the marqués de Pidal broadly defined secondary education (la segunda enseñanza) as "that appropriate to the middle classes, whether they wish only to acquire those elements of knowledge which are indispensable in society for any moderately educated person, or whether they wish to prepare the way for higher studies whose acquisition is more difficult."[28]

In practice, however, Spanish secondary education did not experience the kind of internal articulation and differentiation typical of post-primary schooling elsewhere in Europe after 1875. The Spanish state lacked incentives to develop a multitrack system of secondary education because Spanish society remained relatively undifferentiated until the turn of the century and even beyond. Instead, the 58 institutos established in the provincial capitals retained a near monopoly on public post-primary schooling and served a relatively narrow segment at the top of the social hierarchy. In purpose, methods, and content, secondary education continued to be conceptualized as a downward extension of the university rather than as an upward extension of the primary school, and the curriculum of the new, single-track degree program (the bachillerato) was less the embodiment of the general culture needed for productive and responsible citizenship than an unsystematic amalgam of modern and traditional subjects whose sole purpose was preparation for advanced study.[29] The bachillerato and the university degree (the

---

del bachillerato en el presente siglo," *Educadores* 6, no. 30 (1964): 855–85. Secondary education during the Restoration is described in Enrique Díaz de la Guardia, *Evolución y desarrollo de la enseñanza media en España de 1875 a 1930: Un conflicto político-pedagógico* (Madrid: Ministerio de Educación y Ciencia, CIDE, 1988).

[28] The general plan of studies of 17 September 1845 was written by the director of public instruction in the Development Ministry, Antonio Gil de Zárate, who published an exposition of liberal educational philosophy: *De la instrucción pública en España*, 3 vols. (Madrid: Imprenta del Colegio de Sordomudos, 1855).

[29] For the argument that the liberal educational system did embody a new "bourgeois" culture, see Peset et al., *Ciencias*.

licenciatura) were the credentials that regulated access to administrative and professional careers, which together with landholding still supported the bulk of the Spanish middle and upper classes. As long as the existing system of higher education effectively safeguarded the privileges of these groups by providing a litmus test of eligibility for political and social preferment, they possessed little incentive to press for change. With the majority of the population still lacking primary education, pressure for increased vocational opportunities was absent as well— except on the periphery, where the industrial and commercial bourgeoisie sponsored the creation of applied and technical schools.[30]

In the absence of alternatives, the institutos expanded to include a growing number of students of "mesocratic" social origin.[31] By 1891– 92, 2 percent of the male population ten to fourteen years of age was studying for the bachillerato in public and private schools throughout Spain, a relatively large percentage, given the small size of the Spanish middle class.[32] (The first girls did not seek degrees until the 1890s and did not begin to enroll as official students until after the turn of the century. In 1910 only 353 girls were studying for degrees nationwide.)[33] The greater social inclusiveness was partly a result of the comparatively low tuition and fees in Spain, which remained stable at about 55 pesetas a year until the turn of the century. In facilitating access to the bachillerato for the urban middle class, low fees contributed to social and political stability in an economy that offered few opportunities for middle-class employment outside the bureaucracy and the professions. At the same time, the direct and indirect cost of secondary schooling— especially once the expense of books and foregone employment was taken into account—was sufficiently high to discourage working-class competition for scarce places. When population growth began to create pressures on these traditional sources of employment for the middle classes, demands for a more diversified system of secondary schooling

[30] See the figures in Viñao Frago, *Política y educación*, 459–60.

[31] This assertion is based on somewhat impressionistic evidence gleaned from the voluminous literature on secondary education that began to appear at the end of the century. See, for example, Eloy Luis-André, *La educación de la adolescencia: Estudio crítico del estado de la segunda enseñanza y de sus reformas más urgentes* (Madrid: Imp. de "Alrededor del Mundo," 1916), 237. Data on the social origins of instituto students are not available.

[32] Degree programs valid for university entrance enrolled 2.7 percent of German boys and 2.56 percent of French boys. Müller et al, *Rise*, 81, 193; John E. Talbott, *The Politics of Educational Reform in France, 1918–1940* (Princeton: Princeton University Press, 1969), 31.

[33] Rosa María Capel Martínez, *El trabajo y la educación de la mujer en España (1900– 1930)* (Madrid: Ministerio de Cultura, Dirección General de Juventud y Promoción Cultural, 1982), 381, 387, 420.

would start to emerge. Until then, however, the audience for a reform program was minimal because the middle-class consumers of secondary education did not much care what kind of education they received, as long as it could be completed quickly and cheaply and as long as it performed, however inefficiently, its purpose of social reproduction.

The "credentialist" character of the bachillerato was reflected in its brevity and its curricular incoherence. The 1880 plan of studies admitted boys age nine or ten to a single-option, five-year program that led to a degree and eligibility for university entrance at age fourteen or fifteen.[34] (In contrast, the norm for secondary students elsewhere in Europe was entrance at age eleven, eight or nine years of study, and completion at age eighteen or nineteen.) Suggestions to raise the minimum age or to extend the length of the bachillerato were resisted by middle-class parents eager for their sons to graduate to secure "careers" in the state administration as quickly as possible. As one critic observed, "We work in order to achieve in a short and fixed period a diploma that will excuse us from having to work ever again."[35]

Functionally serving as a restraint on the pool of potential competitors for scarce middle-class jobs, the bachillerato did not serve the additional purpose of maintaining status distinctions among middle-class strata and thus was not internally differentiated into classical and modern sides. To put it another way, its function was social, rather than cultural, reproduction. As a kind of neutral middle ground between opposing ideological viewpoints, the secondary curriculum was instead a composite of traditional and modern, general and specialized subjects. Although somewhat greater emphasis was given to classical-humanistic studies, these were never stressed to the same degree as they were in elite schools elsewhere in Europe, and seem to have persisted primarily out of inertia or institutional conservatism. After 1867 Latin was taught only during the first two years of study, while Greek was dropped altogether.[36] Most of the fourteen academic courses in the long-lived 1880 curriculum were taught for only one or two years on alternate days of the week; even the foundation courses, Latin and Castilian grammar

[34] Plan of studies of 13 August 1880. All secondary "plans of studies" through 1964 may be found in Manuel Utande Igualada, ed., *Planes de estudio de enseñanza media* (Madrid: Ministerio de Educación Nacional, Dirección General de Enseñanza Media, 1964).

[35] Luis-André, *Educación de la adolescencia*, 237.

[36] In the French lycées students studied Latin for six years, Greek for five. The contrast with the Prussian *gymnasia* and the British public schools was even more pronounced. For the curricula of secondary schools around the world at the turn of the century, see the report prepared by the Museo Pedagógico Nacional, "Situación actual de los estudios secundarios," dated 8 October 1894, in Ministerio de Fomento, *Boletín Oficial: Reforma de la segunda enseñanza* 2, no. 3 (1894): 361–436.

and literature, were not taught at all in the last two years of study—that is, to children over age twelve. As a result, none of the subjects, classical or modern, was even tenuously assimilated by the students; in Spain, possession of "culture" did not imply an intimate relationship with certain venerated texts, but merely possession of a diploma.[37] University professors complained incessantly that, despite its declared "preparatory" function, the bachillerato did not prepare students for advanced work; most students spent a year or two after receipt of the bachillerato studying independently for the entrance exams to the various university schools.

Absent from the curriculum were courses aimed at developing other than purely intellectual abilities—art, music, religion, civics, physical education, or modern foreign languages. Since students paid by the course, extending the prescribed course of studies meant extra tuition, matriculation and examination fees, and textbooks for hard-pressed parents. Opposition to curricular expansion also came from the small private academies, most of which were ill prepared to offer a "modern" curriculum, and the religious *colegios*, which opposed state usurpation of the "educative" or "formative" (as opposed to the "instructional") function of schooling. The striking inhibition of the state with regard to the formation of political and personal values in the students reflected both the complacency of Spanish elites and the ideological disagreements that divided them.

In contrast to elite schooling elsewhere, which placed as much or more emphasis on the socialization of the young as on their instruction in the disciplines, the Spanish institutos accorded near total freedom to both students and professors. Receipt of the bachillerato did not depend on class attendance or participation in school life; students were required only to register and to submit to official annual examinations conducted by the faculty in the institutos. In fact, the state recognized three types of matriculation: official (those attending classes in the institutos); incorporated (those studying in legally affiliated and regulated private colegios); and *libre*, or independent (those studying in unaffiliated academies, with private tutors, or on their own). By the 1890s only one-third of all secondary students were officially enrolled in the 58 institutos, while 57 percent were pursuing the bachillerato in one of 511 *colegios incorporados*, and another 20 percent were registered as "li-

---

[37] Cf. the conception of "general culture" in France and Germany. See Fritz K. Ringer, *Fields of Knowledge: French Academic Culture in Comparative Perspective, 1890–1920* (New York: Cambridge University Press, 1992); and *Education and Society*; and James C. Albisetti, *Secondary School Reform in Imperial Germany* (Princeton: Princeton University Press, 1982).

bres"—a much higher percentage of privately educated students than anywhere else in Europe.[38] In 1894–95, the ratio of private to officially matriculated students was over 6:1 in Seville, nearly 4:1 in Barcelona, Madrid, and several southern provincial capitals, and 2:1 or better in many other cities.[39]

The physical setting of the institutos contrasted sharply with the cloistered elite state secondary schools in France and Germany. Many were housed in structurally inadequate former convents; only fifteen new institutos were constructed during the last third of the century.[40] Officially registered students received no more attention than those studying independently, for the methods generally employed in the institutos were the impersonal, unsupervised routines of the university, in which professors spoke ex cathedra to dozens of inattentive boys. Although most institutos had laboratories and libraries, there were no gymnasiums, playgrounds, or study halls. And even though the location of the institutos in the provincial capitals forced children to live apart from their families, there were no dormitories, dining halls, or tutors to monitor their conduct and academic progress.

The professors, or *catedráticos*, consciously modeled themselves on their namesakes in the university and jealously guarded their reputations as scholars. Appointment to a chair in an instituto was achieved, as it was throughout the state instructional system, by state competition (the famous *oposiciones*) in which scholarship was, at least in theory, the sole criterion for selection. Most catedráticos held doctorates; many were corresponding members of Spanish and foreign scholarly societies; and a few eventually earned professional advancement to a university chair through the publication of scholarly monographs and textbooks. Few, if any, had been exposed to courses on pedagogy. Although some undoubtedly possessed a vocation for teaching, many taught because university training in sciences or the humanities had few other prestigious occupational outlets. Catedráticos generally proved reluctant to encumber their relatively light schedules with the homework, study sessions, and frequent evaluations that would have made secondary education more meaningful. Underpaid and thus financially strapped, many held additional employment elsewhere, and in the most notorious cases never appeared in the classroom, abandoning their responsibilities to ill-paid assistants.[41]

[38] Viñao Frago, *Política y educación*, 410–11; Díaz de la Guardia, *Evolución*, 317, 504–7, 512.
[39] Ministerio de Fomento, *Reforma de la segunda enseñanza*, 332–41.
[40] Díaz de la Guardia, *Evolución*, 455–58.
[41] The salary scale for instituto professors ranged from the entry-level salary of 3,000 to

In the classroom, the individual catedrático enjoyed complete autonomy. Although official responsibility for issuing uniform course syllabi and for authorizing textbooks had been entrusted to the Royal Council of Public Instruction in 1890, the Council almost never exercised its prerogatives because of the opposition to state limitations on academic freedom on both right and left. Thus, each professor was free to develop his own syllabus and to select or write a textbook for his course. In general, only a fraction of the syllabus would actually be covered during the academic year, which, by one estimate, comprised little more than one hundred instructional days once vacations and national and local holidays were subtracted.[42] Apart from infrequent recitations of assigned lessons from memory, even officially matriculated students had no contact with their professors, and student absenteeism was predictably high.

All students, whether officially registered or studying privately, were assigned grades on the basis of a single final oral examination in each subject, administered at the end of the academic year by an examination board of three instituto catedráticos. The examinations were the mechanism by which the state exercised its monopoly over degrees and were thus potentially a means of enforcing ideological conformity. But in practice, the state did not monitor the examination process, which was in any case too cursory to guarantee effective assimilation of the subject matter by the students. Since at the larger institutos there might be several hundred examinees in each subject, professors did not administer written exams or even conduct extended oral examinations, although they collected an examination fee of 2.5 pesetas from each student.[43] The standard examination format required each student to answer three questions selected at random from the list of topics on the professor's syllabus. The surest way to prepare was simply to memorize the textbook assigned by the professor in order to be able to regurgitate the paragraphs in the text that corresponded to the topics on the syllabus. Once out of the examination room, the pupil could safely forget what he had "learned" from memory.

---

a maximum of 4,500 pesetas a year. The average salary was 3,500 pesetas per year, well below that of senior civil servants, although roughly equivalent to the average for university catedráticos.

[42] Eduardo Benot, *Errores en materia de educación y de instrucción pública*, 4th ed. (Madrid: Librería de Hernando, 1899), 43, 189. On 2 December 1896 the general director of public instruction complained to the directors of the institutos that students had already begun their Christmas vacations.

[43] The reforming general director of public instruction, Eduardo Vincenti, acknowledged in 1895 that a system of written exams, however desirable, could not be implemented immediately because students were unaccustomed to writing. RO of 12 January 1895.

More effective education would have required an extended school year, a longer course of study to permit concentration in the basic disciplines, and frequent assignments and evaluation. It would also have required more money in the form of higher tuition fees, which currently contributed only 20 percent of the actual cost of education.[44] But proposals for reform were unpalatable to the majority of middle-class parents and students. The existing system, although stressful at exam time, enabled students with good memories, good tutors, or quick wits to graduate with minimum effort and maximum speed. Especially in the provinces, catedráticos seem to have recognized the real social function of the system by tailoring their oral exams to the students' inevitably scanty knowledge of the course material. Students able to pay for their travel often enrolled in several institutos simultaneously in order to be examined by the professor with the greatest reputation for leniency in each subject. (According to one critic, an agency in Madrid brokered this information for a fee.)[45] The larger private schools paid for examining boards to come to them, believing (correctly) that a warm reception and a good meal would soften the hearts of the examiners. Nationwide, failure rates averaged less than 10 percent, compared to over 30 percent in the classical lycées in France.[46]

The competition from the growing private sector established an educational hierarchy that in some ways paralleled the socially differentiated multitrack systems elsewhere in Europe. But whereas in those systems prestige was measured by the value of the cultural capital acquired—with the least utilitarian tracks conveying the greatest status— in Spain prestige was more crudely measured by the actual cost of education. High-quality private education was not cheap. In addition to their tuition and boarding fees in the colegios, students wishing to earn state diplomas—the only valid diplomas for university entrance—had

[44] Díaz de la Guardia, *Evolución*, 458–68. Public revenues for secondary education derived from three sources: income-producing property transferred to the provincial deputations after the ecclesiastical disentailments of mid-century; taxes levied on the municipalities by the deputations; and student fees. In 1887 the state assumed budgetary responsibility for the institutos, and the fees and income from the disentailed properties was transferred to the state, but the remaining financial obligation still rested with the impoverished deputations, which were required to transfer funds to the Ministry of Development for disbursement.

[45] Apostolado de la Prensa, *La segunda enseñanza en España y fuera de España: Algunas consideraciones sobre los últimos decretos del Ministerio de Fomento* (Madrid: Agustín Avrial, Imp., 1899), 24–25.

[46] See the figures in Viñao Frago, *Política y educación*, 463–64, and Díaz de la Guardia, *Evolución*, 508–9. At the instituto in the Canary Islands in 1900–1901, there were only ten failures out of 1,109 exams administered. AGMEC, leg. 6941. For France, see Müller et al., *Rise*, 192.

also to pay the full matriculation, examination, and diploma fees at the instituto in which they were to be examined. In the 1890s this amounted to 276.5 pesetas for the full five years, exclusive of textbooks, which might total another 150 pesetas.

Those who could afford it were attracted to the religious colegios, whose numbers grew by 50 percent between 1880 and 1900, as the church launched its campaign to recapture the allegiance of Spanish elites. Many families, however, were obliged to turn to one of the hundreds of small private academies (the so-called *escuelas de piso*) that were operated, in entrepreneurial fashion, by poorly prepared "professors" who eked out a living coaching students to pass the state examinations.[47] Such instruction was worse than that offered in the institutos or the religious colegios, but it allowed students in small towns without an instituto to study inexpensively at home. The alternative of a differentiated private sector partially deflected criticism from the institutos, which by the end of the century were primarily attended by marginally middle-class students, and enabled the dynastic politicians to avoid the political controversy and expense that would have inevitably surrounded an energetic effort to develop a comprehensive state educational system.

The absence of a vigorous state educational agenda for nationalizing the masses invited criticism at the same time that it offered opportunities for effective challenge. For the opponents of the Restoration monarchy, the illegitimacy of the state was the result of its divorce from a nation abandoned to ignorance and apathy; education would liberate the potential vitality of the nation and awaken it to the need for political and social reform. But although opposition groups agreed that education was the solution to the problem, their views on the appropriate content, methods, and control of the educational process diverged as widely as did their prescriptions for national regeneration. The right urged a return to the Catholic values historically and indissolubly linked with the nation and allegedly betrayed by the liberal state; the democratic left

---

[47] In 1900 there were 387 private secular colegios; of the 2,555 lay professors, only 1,042 held a degree. Pío Zabala y Lera, *Historia de España y de la civilización española en la edad contemporánea*, 2 vols. (Barcelona: Sucesores de Juan Gili, 1930), 2:211; Luis-André, *Educación de la adolescencia*, 243. According to the republican Miguel Morayta, there were 105 colegios incorporados attached to the two institutos in Madrid, many enrolling just one or two students. *DSC*, 15 January 1900 (no. 105), 3502. The interests of these private professors were represented from 1899 on by the periodical *La Enseñanza*, published in Madrid. For enrollments in Badajoz, see Felicidad Sánchez Pascua, *El instituto de segunda enseñanza de Badajoz en el siglo XIX (1845–1900): (Orígenes, tratamiento estadísticos del alumnado y bibliométrico de los profesores)* (Badajoz: Diputación Provincial, 1985).

adamantly insisted that it was precisely those anachronistic values, in conjunction with the shortcomings of a corrupt and illiberal state, that had enervated the most dynamic social groups and retarded national economic growth.

Although part of a European-wide phenomenon, the faith in education was particularly fervent in Spain, where other nonviolent agencies of social and political change were as yet poorly developed. Education, or "pedagogy," involved the communication of knowledge—*ciencia*, in Spanish usage—which was, in nineteenth-century terms, the equivalent of power and, thus, of autonomy. Both a *philosophy*, positing certain assumptions about human nature and human knowing, as well as a *method*, uniting both science and art, pedagogy set parameters for behavior and guided efforts to acquire and evaluate knowledge. By shaping the individual's view of himself and his way of relating to the world around him, pedagogy transmitted ideological and cultural values with the power to confirm, transform, or subvert the social and political order.

In pursuing their counterhegemonic projects, critics of the Restoration monarchy followed two strategies. On the one hand, they established independent private schools under the aegis of the "freedom to teach" clause in article 12 of the Constitution of 1876, a gradualist approach that would produce the desired results only in the relatively distant future, if at all. Thus, they simultaneously attempted to bring direct pressure to bear on the policies of the two parties that controlled the Spanish state. The nature of the Restoration political system, which existed primarily to conciliate and integrate political groups that might otherwise have posed a threat to the monarchy, encouraged the factions that occupied the unstable fringes of the Liberal and Conservative parties to demand changes in educational policy as the price for their allegiance to the system. Occupancy of the Ministry of Development (or later, of Public Instruction)—traditionally an entry-level portfolio—became a kind of escape valve through which the dynastic parties co-opted dissidents who threatened the stability of the regime.[48]

The obvious difficulty with the political strategy was that it produced few durable results. Although integrist Catholics were able to win concessions for confessional schools during periods of Conservative rule, and the bourgeois left successfully pressed Liberal governments for some of the pedagogic reforms championed by the Institución Libre de Enseñanza, none of these political minorities possessed sufficient politi-

---

[48] Prominent examples of this phenomenon include the appointment of the neo-Catholic Alejandro Pidal y Mon in the Cánovas government of 1884; of the *institucionista* Segismundo Moret in the Sagasta government of 1892; and of the left-liberal Santiago Alba in the Canalejas government of March 1912.

cal weight to overcome the inertia of a system whose purpose was to maintain the balance of political forces in support of the status quo. Measures unacceptable to either extreme were automatically undone by succeeding ministers, leaving an impression of great legislative activity but little actual movement. In this paradoxical fashion, educational issues became a significant point of differentiation in the community of interest that united the two dynastic parties while the educational system itself remained disastrously inadequate.

Given the legal privileges accorded the church by the Moderados and their successors in the Conservative party, it may seem extravagant to characterize the church as a dissident within the Restoration system. Nevertheless, the truce between the Spanish church and the liberal state was an uneasy one. Badly scarred by the liberal attack on ecclesiastical property and authority early in the nineteenth century and again by the aggressive anticlericalism of the "revolutionary sexennium" of 1868–74, the church never fully overcame its defensive mentality. The Spanish church was never a monolith, of course. By the 1880s a majority of Catholics in Spain had come grudgingly to accept collaboration with the Conservative party as the best way of protecting Catholic interests. The Carlists, defeated militarily in 1879 and systematically excluded from ecclesiastical appointments by the Conservative leader, Antonio Cánovas del Castillo, also edged into a tentative modus vivendi with the constitutional regime. But an influential minority of Catholics, including the religious orders and the dissident Carlists who founded the Integrist party in 1888, remained stridently opposed to any form of compromise with liberalism, the political manifestation of a broader social and cultural secularization that they were determined to resist. In compensation for the church's loss of material power, they intransigently defended the absolute spiritual authority it had traditionally wielded over the lives of the faithful and rejected the articles in the liberal Constitution of 1876 that guaranteed religious toleration and freedom of thought (articles 11 and 13). Although they lacked *political* influence outside the traditionalist strongholds of rural Catalonia and the Basque provinces, through the press and the pulpit they spearheaded the Catholic revival of the 1880s and 1890s and prevented any real rapprochement between the church and the liberal state.[49]

---

[49] On the mentality of the Catholic right during the Restoration, see Frances Lannon, *Persecution, Privilege, and Prophecy: The Catholic Church in Spain, 1875–1975* (New York: Oxford University Press, 1987), especially chap. 5; Teódulo García Regidor, *La polémica sobre la secularización de la enseñanza en España (1902–1914)* (Madrid: Fundación Santa María, 1985); Stanley Payne, *Spanish Catholicism: An Historical Overview* (Madison: University of Wisconsin Press, 1984), 97–121; María Victoria López-Cordón

The centerpiece of their campaign to reassert Catholic cultural hegemony was education. Catholic educators were the shock troops in a
valiant struggle against "an enemy army [that] has armed itself against
them and combats and harasses them in a thousand ways."[50] For the
most intransigent polemicists, the church's traditional monopoly over
education was an "absolute, superior and inalienable right"; beneath
the "apparently simple" debate over who should teach, the Marists acknowledged, lay "a question of sovereignty."[51] At best, state schools
were a temporary remedy to a social deficiency; until "society" (that is,
the private sector) was able to redress that deficiency, their mission
should be restricted to "instruction"—that is, the provision of literacy,
formalized knowledge, and professional training. "Education"—the
formation of character, the shaping of values, beliefs, and behaviors—
was, on the other hand, the exclusive responsibility of the family and
society and of their representative, the church.[52] Illiteracy and ignorance
were preferable to instruction that could not be reconciled with the basic tenets of the faith.

Clerical interests interpreted broadly the prerogatives assigned to the
church in the Concordat, the Ley Moyano, and the Constitution of
1876, arguing that the official status of the Catholic faith necessarily
implied the interdiction of contrary beliefs and ideas—that is, an inherent limitation on academic freedom that the state was obligated to enforce in its own schools. Unable to press this interpretation on the dynastic parties successfully after 1881, the church did not abandon its
absolute claim to censorship rights, but as a practical matter focused its
attention on expanding and eliminating state interference in its own
schools on the grounds that state regulation violated the constitutionally guaranteed "freedom to teach."

At the beginning of the Restoration the number of religious schools
was small. There was no tradition of diocesan schools in Spain, and of
the male teaching orders, only the Piarist Fathers (or Escolapians, as
they were known in Spain) had been exempted from the decree that

---

Cortezo, "La mentalidad conservadora durante la Restauración," in José-Luis García Delgado, ed., *La España de la Restauración* (Madrid: Siglo XXI, 1985), 71–110; and Joan C.
Ullman, *La Semana Trágica: Estudio sobre las causas socioeconómicas del anticlericalismo en España (1898–1912)* (Barcelona: Ariel, 1972).

[50] F.T.D., *Guía del maestro para uso de los Hmnos. Maristas de la Enseñanza: Redactada según las reglas y enseñanzas de su venerable fundador* (Barcelona: Editorial F.T.D.,
1928), 170.

[51] Apostolado de la Prensa, *La verdadera regeneración de España* (December 1898), 26;
F.T.D. *Guía del maestro*, 170.

[52] These arguments were recapitulated by Pius XI in the 1929 encyclical *Divinis Illius
Magistri*.

dissolved most of the religious orders in 1837.[53] During the last quarter of the century, however, the number of religious congregations of all kinds expanded prodigiously, with the aid of a loophole in the Concordat. Both Liberal and Conservative governments either formally sanctioned or turned a blind eye to the founding of new communities, partially as a conciliatory gesture to the church, partially in recognition of the state's inability to respond adequately to the growing demand for social services, including education. After the turn of the century, when French and Portuguese anticlericalism drove religious communities across the borders to a more sympathetic environment, their numbers would grow even more rapidly.[54] By 1904, there were reportedly 509 male religious communities in Spain, 294 of them dedicated to teaching; of the 2,656 female communities, 910 were from the teaching orders.[55] The schools of the religious orders not only provided catechistic opportunities, but also generated revenues for communities whose financial base had been destroyed by the disentailment legislation earlier in the century.

Like the state educational system, Catholic schools were socially segmented. Most of the congregations provided primary education (often with the aid of municipal subventions) to the working classes as part of their charitable and apostolic mission. The number of such schools rose dramatically as the orders increased in number and evangelical fervor and as anticlericals began to establish their own schools in the 1880s. As the Marist teachers' manual observed, "thanks to the religious indifference of certain parents, children have become the most valued prize in a preliminary combat between the Catholic and the a-Catholic or laic school on the common ground of non-religious instruction."[56] By 1900 nearly 20 percent of elementary-age children attended one of the nearly six thousand religious colegios, and many others attended municipal schools in which the schoolmaster or mistress was a religious. Some

---

[53] In France the Piarist Fathers are known as the Brothers of the Christian Doctrine. In 1870 the order was teaching 14,000–15,000 poor boys in Spain and nearly 45,000 worldwide. Severiano Giner, *Escuelas Pías: Ser e historia* (Madrid: Ediciones Calasancias, 1978), 286.

[54] In 1900 some 6,400 boys were studying in 79 religious colegios incorporados throughout the peninsula, a figure that does not include colegios offering professional and vocational training and finishing schools for girls. By 1906 there were approximately 3,800 foreign monks and nuns in Spain, concentrated particularly in the large cities of the Basque provinces and Catalonia. Díaz de la Guardia, *Evolución*, 487–92; Luis-André, *Educación de la adolescencia*, 245; Zabala y Lera, *Historia de España* 2:211.

[55] Morote, *Frailes en España*, 12–26; see also José Manuel Castells, *Las asociaciones religiosas en la España contemporánea: Un estudio jurídico-administrativo (1767–1965)* (Madrid: Taurus, 1973), 325–26.

[56] F.T.D., *Guía del maestro*, 170.

orders offered Sunday schools and night classes for adult workers as well.[57]

The dynastic politicians found it convenient to tolerate the expansion of religious primary schools in newly urbanizing areas, not only because of the tax savings involved, but because the kind of education dispensed in the religious colegios reinforced the social order by stressing class harmony and Christian resignation in the face of social inequality. In the words of the Marist teachers' manual, the main purpose of Catholic primary education was "to give the child the means to achieve his natural destiny in this world and his supernatural one in the next, that is, the salvation of his soul"; each child should receive the instruction "appropriate to his needs and his social position."[58] The backbone of the curriculum in religious primary schools was the catechism, from which students learned to read and which they committed to memory through incessant repetition of the question-and-answer format. Inherently dogmatic and authoritarian, the catechisms were also explicitly antiliberal.[59] As in the state schools, the meager academic curriculum was also taught catechistically. Memorization of easily assimilated textbooks provided structure for large groups of children of varied abilities and relieved teachers whose own mastery of the material was often slight. A common learning technique since the Middle Ages, memorization also reflected the orders' orientation toward inherited, as opposed to created, knowledge.[60]

A few teaching orders deviated from this methodological traditionalism. The LaSalleans and Piarists, for example, were early exponents of "mutualism"—that is, of cooperative or group learning, an effective system that permitted them to expand the size of their schools without increasing the number of teachers.[61] More radical in his innovations, if also more idiosyncratic, was the Granadan priest Andrés Manjón, whose Escuelas del Ave María would be lionized as a model of Catholic

[57] See the list of free religious schools for the poor in Barcelona in Ana Yetano, *La enseñanza religiosa en la España de la Restauración (1900–1920)* (Barcelona: Anthropos, 1988), 362–66. LaSallean free schools educated nearly 9,400 boys in 1903. See Saturnino Gallego, *Sembraron con amor: "LaSalle," centenario en España (1878–1978)* (San Sebastián: Industria Gráfica Valverde, 1978), 224.

[58] F.T.D., *Guía del maestro*, 9, 12.

[59] The most famous and widely used of these was the catechism of Father Gaspar Astete (1537–1601), *Doctrina cristiana* (1599), which went through six hundred Spanish editions.

[60] See Mary J. Caruthers, *The Book of Memory: A Study of Memory in Medieval Culture* (New York: Cambridge University Press, 1990); Ramón Ruiz Amado, *La educación intelectual*, 3d. ed., rev. (Barcelona: Editorial Librería Religiosa, 1942), 277–89.

[61] Ramón Ruiz Amado, *Historia de la educación y de la pedagogía*, 5th ed. (Barcelona: Gustavo Gili, 1930), 236.

pedagogy when the ideological struggle over education heated up after the turn of the century. A professor of canon law, Manjón created his first primary school for the very poor in 1889 in a cave near the Sacromonte district in Granada. In his open-air experimental school, Manjón channeled the natural energies of his pupils through "active methods" borrowed from progressive pedagogy. Memorization was not banished, but made more palatable through games, role-playing, singing, and manual exercises; names and dates were chanted while skipping rope or playing hopscotch, for example.

But however superficially progressive the methods of the Ave María schools and seminaries (which numbered over three hundred at Manjón's death in 1923), their political and philosophical foundations were avowedly Catholic, dogmatic, and antiliberal—or, as the founder insisted, "Spanish." Conceived as a "labor of regeneration and reconquest," Manjón's aims were to recover Spain from the clutches of the "foreign" heresies propagated by liberalism in all its guises. In learning to "know truth and love the good," the "modest classes" would abandon their "ridiculous pretensions to rise above their sphere" and return to the Christian virtues of traditional Spain.[62]

If primary education in Catholic colegios was generally no better than in the public schools, at the secondary level the religious colegios consciously strove to outperform the state institutos. The most socially exclusive orders—the Jesuits, Augustinians, Marianists, and Benedictines for boys and the Ursulines and Sacred Heart for girls—specialized in providing primary and secondary schooling to the well-to-do, although they often also offered separate sections for selected "disadvantaged" day students, who earned their scholarships by winning high marks on the state examinations.[63] Their imposing buildings were generally erected in affluent neighborhoods in the expanding cities, although the Jesuits also selected provincial towns for their boarding schools. In 1886 the Jesuits created the first university for Catholic laymen in Deusto, near Bilbao, which offered studies (but not official degrees) in law and engineering to a significant portion of the Basque elite. The Piarists, LaSalleans, Salesians, and Marists, on the other hand, attracted lower-middle- and working-class students by offering vocational training in

[62] Andrés Manjón, *Hojas históricas del Ave María* (Granada: Escuela de Ave-María, 1915), 55, 72. See also his *Hojas catequistas y pedagógicas del Ave María: Libro 3º* (Granada: Imprenta-Escuela de Ave María, 1921); José Manuel Prellezo García, *Manjón, educador: Selección de sus escritos pedagógicos* (Madrid: Editorial Magisterio Español, 1975); and José Luis Sastre, *El Magisterio Español: Un siglo de periodismo profesional* (Madrid: Editorial Magisterio Español, 1966), 32–86.

[63] For the reminiscences of one such student see Arturo Barea, *The Forging of a Rebel*, trans. Ilsa Barea (New York: Viking Press, 1972).

accounting, drafting, the manual arts, and other technical skills in addition to the bachillerato.[64]

Until the end of the nineteenth century the cultural and social atmosphere in the elite Catholic colegios was still heavily "aristocratic," concerned with shaping taste, attitudes, and behavior. (In Castilian the "educated person" [persona educada] is not known as such for his academic accomplishments, but for his good manners.)[65] To be sure, their academic curriculum was increasingly identical in content to that of the institutos, because most of their students were pursuing official degrees. The Jesuits, for example, were obliged to abandon teaching the Ratio studiorum in Latin when the official curriculum was temporarily enlarged in 1894, since Catholic parents were unwilling to pay for the additional years of schooling that retaining the Ratio would have required.[66] Because it interfered with their traditional programs, the colegios resisted the extension of the official curriculum. In addition, many of the proposed new subjects, like the natural and social sciences and "formative" subjects like ethics and civics, were potentially incompatible with Catholic teaching, which insisted on the impossibility of an independently derived morality and on the essential unity of all knowledge.

Since the state abstained from stipulating course content or prescribing textbooks, the colegios were free to present each subject in their own way. Religious instruction was not one subject among many; it saturated the entire curriculum.[67] Philosophy was taught from a neo-Thomist perspective; natural history followed pre-Darwinian models; textbook illustrations of the human anatomy were discreetly covered. The antiliberal and antiempirical dogmatism of the colegios could pose

---

[64] One of the most prestigious Jesuit colegios is described in Luis Fernández Martín, S.J., *Historia del Colegio San José de Valladolid, 1881–1981* (Valladolid: Colegio San José, 1981). The novel by Father Zenón Aramburu, *Higinio Roca*, is set in this colegio, as is the famous anticlerical novel by Ramón Pérez de Ayala, *A.M.D.G.* For the Spanish Marianistas, see *Breve reseña histórica de la Compañía de María (Religiosos marianistas)* (Madrid: n.p., 1935), 213–24; for the Sacred Heart, see Frances Lannon, "The Socio-Political Role of the Spanish Church—A Case Study," *Journal of Contemporary History* 14, no. 2 (April 1979): 193–210. For the Brothers of the Christian Schools (LaSalleans), see Gallego, *Sembraron con amor*; for the Piarists, Giner, *Escuelas Pías*; and Valentín Caballero, *Aportaciones pedagógicas de las Escuelas Pías* (Madrid: Consejo Superior de Investigaciones Científicas, Instituto San José de Calasanz, 1950); for the Marists, María Ángeles Dorado Soto, *El pensamiento educativo de la Institución Marista* (Barcelona: Nau Llibres, 1984); and F.T.D., *Guía del maestro*.

[65] "Adornment" classes, including foreign languages, music, and art, were offered for an extra fee. In the colegios for girls, these subjects, along with embroidery and other handwork, occupied a large part of the curriculum.

[66] Fernández Martín, *Colegio San José*, 26–29.

[67] See J. M. Aicardó, "Misión de la Iglesia en la enseñanza," *RyF* 4 (1902): 428–46.

potential problems, since their survival depended upon student success in oral examinations conducted by catedráticos whose approach might be radically different.[68] To offset this difficulty, the colegios prepared easily memorized, bowdlerized summaries of the textbooks assigned in the institutos, monitored the study habits of their pupils, and kept track of notoriously lenient examiners. The extra attention and vigilance— which presented a stark contrast to the totally unsupervised atmosphere in the institutos—usually did pay dividends in the form of low failure rates, although lasting comprehension or retention of the memorized material was probably equally lacking in both groups of students.[69]

Catholic pedagogy rested on authoritarian and paternalistic assumptions that were incompatible with the fundamental liberal principles of individual autonomy, toleration, and free debate. Although the colegios cultivated the intellect through memory exercises and emulative techniques,[70] formation of the spirit (often defined as the "heart" or the "will") was their chief goal. The underlying assumption in all Catholic education was the reality of original sin; without education the child, like the savage, would remain a prisoner of his baser instincts. Education meant overcoming a corrupt human nature: "Education (from *educare*) is lifting man as much as possible out of weakness into strength, from frailty to health, from ignorance to wisdom, from vileness to dignity, from inertia to activity, from unreflective action to properly guided, premeditated, and conscious action, from impotence to power, from the yoke and slavery of the passions and sin to the domination of oneself, from quasi-embryonic and animal life to rational, moral, human and Christian life."[71] Accordingly, the path to self-control, and thus, moral freedom lay through the apprehension and practice of the Christian principles of obedience, piety, and virtuous conduct.[72]

These Christian values, along with humility, self-denial, and morality (defined primarily as chastity), were reinforced through incessant prayer, devotions, pious commemorations, and other elaborate religious observances. In the elite colegios an effort was made to create a clois-

---

[68] For the exams, see the testimony of P. M. Quera, S.J., *La estela de una institución centenaria*, in Yetano, *Enseñanza religiosa*, 327.

[69] For a general critique of the methods of the religious colegios by a catedrático, see Mariano Domínguez Berrueta, *Ante una campana injusta: Notas para la defensa de la enseñanza oficial, de la libertad de enseñanza y del profesorado de los institutos nacionales* (Ávila: Tip. y Enc. Senén Martín, 1925); for the reminiscences of a resentful student, see Manuel Azaña Díaz, *El jardín de los frailes* (Madrid: Alianza, 1982).

[70] See Ramón Ruiz Amado, *Educación intelectual*; Caballero, *Aportaciones pedagógicas*; Dorado Soto, *Pensamiento educativo*; Fernández Martín, *Colegio San José*.

[71] Quoted in Sastre, *Magisterio Español*, 82–83.

[72] Ramón Ruiz Amado, in Luis Sánchez Sarto, ed., *Diccionario de pedagogía* (Barcelona: Editorial Labor, 1936), 2:2818.

tered environment uncontaminated by temptation or worldly values; boarders (the majority) were educated separately from the day students. Silence, discipline, ritual, and constant vigilance constituted the self-contained world of the colegio, where the Spanish bourgeoisie acquired loyalties and habits of thought and behavior that were not easily abandoned.[73]

Given the socialization function of Catholic education, it is understandable that Catholic educators stressed the "sacred mission" of the teacher. Their conception of the teacher-student relationship was essentially "charismatic"; the successful educator taught through the power of example and the pull of affection. As the French founder of the Marist Brothers observed, "the child will belong, generally speaking, to the one who first conquers his heart."[74] Given this outlook, it is not surprising that most of the teaching orders provided their members with little training in either subject content or pedagogical techniques. This indifference to the science (as opposed to the "art") of teaching was sanctioned by the state, which did not require members of the religious orders to pass the state primary teachers' examinations, even if they were teaching in public schools, and did not require professors in religious colegios offering the bachillerato to hold university degrees until 1894.[75] The few exceptions to this general indifference to academic rigor—the Jesuits, Marianists, and Augustinians for boys and the Company of Mary and the Institución Teresiana for girls—only confirmed the rule.

Even as it fought the premises of the liberal state, the Catholic right was willing to use its influence in the Conservative party to secure decrees favorable to its interests—that is, to use the power of the state to eliminate state authority over Catholic schools. The Conservatives, for their part, were not only ideologically sympathetic to the goals of the religious orders, but also found concessions on education to be an effective way of limiting Catholic disaffection from the Restoration system.[76]

---

[73] In the longer run, however, the insistence on such unworldly—indeed, "unbourgeois"—values may have turned many middle-class Spaniards against the church later in life. See Gaziel [Agustín Calvet], *Tots el camins duen a Roma* (Madrid: Editorial Aedos, 1959); Pedro Gual Villalbé, *Memorias de un industrial de nuestro tiempo* (Barcelona: Sociedad General de Publicaciones, 1922); Yetano, *Enseñanza religiosa*, 269.

[74] F.T.D., *Guía del maestro*, 170.

[75] Even thereafter, a degree in theology from a pontifical seminary was held to fulfill the letter, if not the spirit of the law. See the letter of 23 February 1895 from the Junta Directiva of the Sociedad Facultativa de Ciencias y Letras de Barcelona to the minister of development, in AGMEC leg. 6939.

[76] Examples include the RDs of 28 February 1879, 18 July 1885, 1 September 1910, and 25 May 1915, which allowed private school teachers to sit on state examination boards, and the RDs of 27 October 1875, 28 February 1879, 20 July 1900, and 27 May 1915, which authorized traveling examination boards. This Conservative legislation was

But when the Liberals took the offensive against the orders after the turn of the century, the natural limits to the strategy of defending Catholic education through the good offices of the Conservative party became apparent. Catholic suspicion of, if not hostility to, liberalism and the constitutional monarchy thus increased, rather than diminished, with time.

Both the inadequacies of state schooling and the aggressive expansion of the Catholic colegios alarmed Spanish progressives, who saw them as impediments to the creation of a modern democratic society. Their response was the Institución Libre de Enseñanza (ILE), a private school founded in Madrid by a group of university professors, most of them veterans of democratic and republican politics in the revolutionary period 1868–74. The ILE's statutes stressed its independence of all political, religious, or philosophical dogma and its allegiance to the principle of academic freedom.[77] Initially conceived as a "free university" complemented by a preparatory school, its focus soon shifted to younger children as the founders became convinced that creating a political environment congenial to independent inquiry was possible in Spain only if preceded by a profound cultural reform. In 1878, a primary school was added and the university classes suspended; a few years later, the secondary school relinquished its "incorporated" status because its educational aims could not be reconciled with the official curriculum at the institutos. After 1881, the Institución was exclusively dedicated to political and cultural reform through the application and dissemination of the principles of modern pedagogy. Although the number of students it enrolled was small, its ideology and methods profoundly influenced Spanish educational policy—and indirectly, Spanish politics—during the fifty years that preceded the civil war of 1936–39.

The history and philosophy of the Institución Libre de Enseñanza have received substantial scholarly attention, making necessary only a relatively brief summary here.[78] The guiding spirit of the school was

---

systematically revoked by intervening Liberal ministers. See chap. 2 for further discussion of this phenomenon.

[77] Article 15 of the statutes was reproduced on every masthead of the biweekly *Boletín de la Institución Libre de Enseñanza*, published between 1877 and 1937.

[78] See Vicente Cacho Viu, *La Institución Libre de Enseñanza* (Madrid: Rialp, 1962); Antonio Jimenez-Landi, *La Institución Libre de Enseñanza y su ambiente* (Madrid: Taurus, 1973); Turin, *Educación*; Dolores Gómez Molleda, *Los reformadores de la España contemporánea* (Madrid: Consejo Superior de Investigaciones Científicas, Escuela de Historia Moderna, 1966); Fernando Millán Sánchez, *La revolución laica: De la Institución Libre de Enseñanza a la escuela de la República* (Valencia: Fernando Torres, 1983); María Nieves Gómez García, *Educación y pedagogía en el pensamiento de Giner de los Ríos* (Seville: Publicaciones de la Universidad, 1983); Juan Ángel Blasco Carrascosa, *Un*

Francisco Giner de los Ríos (1839–1915), catedrático of the Philosophy of Law at the University of Madrid. Like other young intellectuals of his generation, he had been converted to the doctrines of the German philosopher Karl Friedrich Krause after studying law at the university in the 1850s under Julián Sanz del Río. Sanz and his disciples, many of whom later won university chairs of their own, found in Krausism an idealist philosophy of law and history with which to critique neo-Thomist orthodoxy and upon which to build an intellectual foundation for a more humane, productive, and ethical society.[79]

The Spanish Krausists defined man as a rational and moral being whose evolving nature was shaped by ongoing processes of self-discovery and self-creation. Although author of the universe and immanent within it, God did not actively intervene in the world; man's progress toward knowledge of the divine presence (in the world and in himself) was an autonomous activity with its origins in man's own nature. Discovery of the natural foundations of moral law and the moral basis of ethical conduct was thus a purely human undertaking, dependent upon individual experience and rational reflection, just as the religious sense was a reasoned response to the unity of God's creation, rather than a formalistic adherence to an authoritarian dogma.

For intellectuals in a society that had largely escaped the intellectual and cultural repercussions of the Reformation and the Enlightenment, Krausism served as an ideology of both protest and renewal. Krausist ideals were a prescriptive for social and cultural change, illuminating the path toward a nation modernized and ennobled by the industry, sobriety, and rationality of its members. Its individualism and reformism made it congenial to successive generations of Spanish middle-class intellectuals, who were influenced by its moral and intellectual idealism and its implications for individual conduct long after Krausism as a formal system of thought had lost its vitality.

The Krausist intellectuals, including Giner de los Ríos, had enthusiastically embraced the democratic revolution of 1868 and the republican experiment of 1873.[80] But Giner's faith in "political" solutions had

---

arquetipo pedagógico pequeño-burgués: (Teoría y praxis de la Institución Libre de Enseñanza) (Valencia: Fernando Torres, 1980); Carlos Lerena Alesón, Escuela, ideología y clases sociales en España: Crítica de la sociología empirista de la educación (Barcelona: Ariel, 1976); and Juan López-Morillas, The Krausist Movement and Ideological Change in Spain, 1854–1874, trans. Frances M. López-Morillas (New York: Cambridge University Press, 1981).

[79] For Krausism, see especially López-Morillas, Krausist Movement; Pierre Jobit, Les Éducateurs de l'Espagne contemporaine: Les krausistes (Paris: E. de Boccard, 1936); and Elías Díaz, La filosofía social del krausismo español (Madrid: EDICUSA, 1973).

[80] In 1868 Giner had helped write legislation guaranteeing academic freedom (RDs of 21 and 25 October); in 1873 he authored a secondary school reform plan that embodied

died with the First Republic. Political remedies, he concluded, could not produce the "profound and intimate transformation in every social order" that was necessary to lift the nation out of its backwardness. The truly revolutionary task was "to make men" (*hacer hombres*)—"sincere, natural, sober, magnanimous, creative, manly, modest men, healthy in body and soul, invincible friends of the good and implacable enemies of evil."[81] For Giner, education was a reformist means to a revolutionary end: the nurturing of a new elite to rid Spanish society and culture of stagnation, frivolity, and inauthenticity. "We are going to redeem the Patria and return it to its destiny," he promised.[82]

"Pedagogy anticipates what man ought to be," José Ortega y Gasset, a friend of the ILE, once remarked, "and then seeks those instruments that enable man to become what he ought."[83] With a clear vision of what the educated man ought to be, Giner and his former student and closest collaborator, Manuel B. Cossío, developed an intensely personal method of teaching that drew inspiration from Krausist idealism and Romantic pedagogic theorists like Rousseau, Froebel, and Pestalozzi, as well as from theorists of the "new pedagogy" then in vogue in Europe and America.[84] Taking as a given the innate curiosity, intelligence, and creativity of the individual child, the *institucionistas* preached a child-centered "intuitive" or "active" method that was opposed in spirit and practice to the authoritarian, memory-based, "bookish" techniques employed in both public and Catholic schools.

Like Catholic educators, the institucionistas believed that mere "instruction" was insufficient to create an educated person, but their diametrically opposed conception of human nature and of human potential implied a radically different kind of classroom. In Cossío's words, "The educated man is not the one who knows, but rather the one who knows how to do. . . . And how to do is learned only by doing."[85] The role of the teacher was not to impose a predigested body of approved knowledge upon a passive, silent child, but rather to liberate the creative forces within him. Through active exploration, engagement, and

the Spencerian notion of "integral" education (RD of 3 June). See Juan López-Morillas, *Racionalismo pragmático: El pensamiento de Francisco Giner de los Ríos* (Madrid: Alianza Universidad, 1988), 13–21.

[81] Ibid., 18, 42.

[82] Manuel Tuñón de Lara, *Medio siglo de cultura española (1885–1936)* (Madrid: Tecnos, 1973), 46.

[83] José Ortega y Gasset, "La pedagogía social como programa político" (1910), in *BILE* 50, no. 678 (30 September 1916): 257–68.

[84] For the methods of the ILE, the *BILE* is a rich source. See also Manuel B. Cossío, *De su jornada: (Fragmentos)* (Madrid: Imp. de Blass, 1929).

[85] M. B. Cossío, quoted in Ángel García del Dujo, *Museo Pedagógico Nacional (1881–1941): Teoría educativa y desarrollo histórico* (Salamanca: Ediciones Universidad, Instituto de Ciencias de la Educación, 1985), 100.

work, the child would learn about the world firsthand, acquiring the knowledge, the habits of thought, and the self-confidence needed to master and transform his environment. By implication, such methods would develop the kind of active, engaged citizenry that could lead Spain out of its current misery and lethargy into the fraternity of modern civilized nations. That is, the goal was not only individual, but also social improvement.

Classroom culture in the Institución Libre de Enseñanza supported these aims. Textbooks and rote memorization were banished; things— and the process of learning about them—not words lay at the heart of each lesson. Classrooms were equipped with maps, laboratories, animal and mineral specimens, and artistic reproductions to permit children to see and do, rather than merely to read. Students observed and took notes, read original sources, visited museums, monuments, offices and factories, sketched and drafted from life, and worked with their hands. For the lecture ex cathedra the teachers in the ILE substituted the Socratic method and the dialogue. Examinations, prizes, and competition were eliminated altogether, replaced by a system of continuous evaluation and feedback by the professors and of cooperative group learning by the pupils.

Highly critical of the compartmentalization of primary and secondary instruction and the preprofessional orientation of the latter, the institucionistas viewed secondary schooling as a natural extension of the primary school, in which children acquired the general culture needed for intelligent participation in modern society.[86] This meant knowledge of national language, literature, history, and art, along with manual training, music, and games. Derived in part from Giner's admiration for the English public school ideal, in part from the Spencerian concept of "integral education," and in part from the French republican project for secondary school reform,[87] this regimen also reflected his preference for practical subjects that would enable the middle classes to be productive, independent citizens, whether or not they chose to pursue university studies. The central defect of official education, he frequently asserted, was that it only produced more worthless members of the "pessimistic, restless and disastrous mob of 'proletarians in frock coats.'"[88]

At the Institución, education was more than mere instruction; it was

[86] See ibid. and Francisco Giner, "Nota sobre la segunda enseñanza," *BILE* 17, no. 385 (28 February 1893): 49–53; Manuel B. Cossío, "La segunda enseñanza y su reforma," in Cossío, *De su jornada*, 43–59; and José de Caso, "Relación de la segunda enseñanza con la primaria," *BILE* 16, no. 380 (15 December 1892): 357–62.

[87] See Ringer, *Fields of Knowledge*.

[88] Francisco Giner, "Problemas de la segunda enseñanza," *BILE* 16, no. 370 (15 July 1892): 196. See also the continuation in *BILE* 16, no. 371 (30 July 1892): 209–15; and "El decreto de segunda enseñanza" (1899), *BILE* 45, no. 731 (28 February 1921): 33–38.

preparation for life. The environment in the school therefore encouraged the development of values and behavior that would enable the individual to live harmoniously and productively among others in a liberal democratic society: freedom of inquiry and opinion, mutual toleration and respect, personal morality and religious sincerity (as distinct from the dogmatism and external morality of Spanish Catholicism), equality and respect between the sexes (coeducation was a novel—and, by Catholic critics, vigorously condemned—feature of the Institución), artistic sensibility (including appreciation of Spanish popular arts), healthful habits and exercise, and an indifference to luxury and ostentation. Both Giner and Cossío made these values their own, believing that personal example lay at the heart of the most effective pedagogy (a "charismatic" conception of teaching that they shared with the religious orders). The hallmark of their teaching style was a prolonged, intimate contact with their students that communicated an approach to life based on intellectual curiosity, rectitude, and freedom.[89]

Life as Giner believed it ought to be was not, however, life as it was generally lived in late-nineteenth-century Spain. At times his despair over the deep roots—in the family, in the culture, in the schools—of the false or outmoded values he was trying to eradicate overcame his customary serenity. Yet he persisted in his campaign against the tyranny of history and society. Until "what ought to be" had become "what is," he insisted, "there will not be a real and true Spain, that is, a people worthy of being included in the civilized humanity of the future; an educated people, in love with the ideal, sincere, serene, measured, at once both gentle and energetic, honorable, patient, sensible, well fed, and even clean, instead of this horde of epileptics that the majority of us are now."[90]

This hostility to their social milieu had some unfortunate consequences for the institucionistas. Their idealistic critique of traditional teaching methods was accompanied by blindness to the realities of Spanish society: many students at the ILE could not afford to dispense entirely with official examinations and degrees and were thus obliged either to study for the official examinations while simultaneously enrolled at the Institución or to transfer to an instituto in order to pursue a degree.[91] More important, the high pedagogical standards of the institucionistas frequently limited their impact among those most needing assistance, for their methods presupposed material and human re-

---

[89] For memories of Giner, Cossío, and the ILE, see J. Pijoán, *Mi don Francisco Giner, 1906–1910* (San José de Costa Rica: Repertorio Americano, 1927); and Jimenez-Landi, *Institución.*

[90] In López-Morillas, *Racionalismo pragmático,* 55–56.

[91] "La segunda enseñanza en la Institución," *BILE* 53, no. 831 (31 July 1929). See the intelligent discussion in Turin, *Educación,* 218–20.

sources not often available to teachers in the overcrowded, poorly endowed state schools.[92]

Other criticisms, arising from threatened class or corporate interests, were less warranted. Defensive maestros, unprepared in many cases to absorb the lessons of the new pedagogy or to translate them to their own impoverished milieu, dismissed the institucionistas as arrogant or irrelevant.[93] Catedráticos, jealous of their standing as scholars, resented suggestions that the instituto should be an extension of the primary school and that knowledge of child psychology mattered more than erudition. The austere model of personal comportment of Giner and Cossío, which became the hallmark of the institucionista "style," also irritated outsiders, who labeled it condescending or hypocritical.

The most vituperative critics, however, were the church and its supporters on the right. Catholic critics equated the undogmatic and tolerant spirituality of the institucionistas with atheism and replied to the institucionista criticism of traditional Catholic culture with charges that the ILE was promoting "foreign" values alien to Spanish history and beliefs. However unfair this characterization, it is true that the ILE's rejection of religious formalism and its insistent defense of scholarly and scientific objectivity implicitly challenged the ideological authority of the church in Spanish society. As the struggle to chart the future of that society intensified after the turn of the century, Catholic attacks on the ILE, as a tangible symbol of the forces of secularization, would increase in venom and scope.[94]

In evaluating the influence of the ILE, it is important to distinguish between its direct and its indirect impact. Giner's most immediate goal was the formation of a new cultural and political elite to provide leadership for the broader social transformation he envisioned for the future. In this he was dramatically successful. Although at its peak the ILE never enrolled more than 200–250 students a year—most of them from progressive professional families of relatively modest means—many former students achieved prominence in left-Liberal, republican, and Socialist circles. Alongside them were university professors, teachers, political allies, and sympathizers who would later collectively be referred to as the "extended Institución."[95] Connected by a web of personal, intel-

[92] See the trenchant criticism of Father Manjón, quoted in Sastre, *Magisterio Español*, 83–84.

[93] Luis Batanaz Palomares, *La educación española en la crisis de fin de siglo: (Los congresos pedagógicos del siglo XIX)* (Córdoba: Diputación Provincial, 1982), 187–98.

[94] The most virulent of the Catholic critiques of the ILE appeared just before and after the civil war. See chap. 9 below. For a more recent and measured Catholic evaluation, see Gómez Molleda, *Reformadores*.

[95] The phrase was coined by Luis de Zulueta at Giner's death in 1915: "Lo que nos deja," *BILE* 39, no. 658 (1 January 1915): 48–56. For the "extended Institución," see

lectual, and political bonds and recognizable as a group to both their friends and their enemies, they rallied around the ILE as the embodiment of a liberal democratic cultural alternative to the dominant values of traditional Spain. Serving as vehicle of communication among them was the *Boletín de la Institución Libre de Enseñanza*, a journal of political and pedagogical opinion that appeared every two weeks between 1877 and 1937.[96]

Within a few years of its founding, however, the institucionistas began to conceive of the problem—and their own role in finding a solution—more broadly. Not only was it essential to shape a modern, Europeanized elite, it was also necessary to create a people capable of responding positively to its leadership. In the words of Cossío, "in Spain there are scholars who are the equal of foreign scholars . . . ; what is lacking is a people [*pueblo*]; a people that lives with freedom of thought, with its own independent opinion; what is lacking is a 'country'; that country that we admire in England as in no other place and that, in backward nations, if it is not formed in the schools, which today are their only civilizing force, where do you think it can be formed?"[97] In other words, the educational program of the Institución represented the cultural component of the democratization process in Spain. Seen from this perspective, only a radical restructuring of the state educational system would do, beginning with the thousands of ill-educated, impoverished primary teachers. Thus, from 1881 on, the institucionistas began to use their network of influential supporters to promote state action during periods of Liberal government. This conversion to state action was reluctant and never complete, but it was clear to Cossío, and even clearer to the third generation of institucionistas, many of whom were active in republican and liberal democratic circles, that it would be possible to implement the new methods at the local level only if the resources of the state could be brought to the task of improving the material and professional circumstances of the thousands of primary teachers.[98]

As the party of attraction of the left, the strategic function of the Liberal party was to blunt the threat of republicanism by co-opting its best issues—and its most able spokesmen—whenever possible. The def-

Gómez Molleda, *Reformadores*; and León Esteban Mateo, *La Institución Libre de Enseñanza en Valencia* (Valencia: Editorial Bonaire, 1974).

[96] For a chronological index, see León Esteban Mateo, *Boletín de la Institución Libre de Enseñanza: Nómina bibliográfica (1877–1936)* (Valencia: Departamento de Educación Comparada e Historia de la Educación de la Universidad, 1979).

[97] Luis Palacios Bañuelos, *Instituto-Escuela: Historia de una renovación educativa* (Madrid: Ministerio de Educación y Ciencia, Centro de Publicaciones, 1989), 17.

[98] For the "generations" in the Institución, see Tuñón de Lara, *Medio siglo*, 44–46.

icit in popular education and the inadequacy of public secondary schooling, both ably exploited by the critics of the monarchy, were causes naturally suited to the party's "democratic" identity. So was anticlericalism, which could be focused against the rising number of teaching orders. By the 1890s additional arguments in favor of popular education were supplied by the "regenerationists"—social pundits whose prescriptions for economic and political renovation were inevitably prefaced with a devastating analysis of the state educational system—and by the rise of working-class unrest, which suggested the need for the conscious construction of social solidarity through the schools.

The collaboration of the institucionistas and the Liberal party produced some durable achievements. In 1882 the first Liberal government of the Restoration established a resource center in Madrid for apprentice teachers and practicing maestros seeking access to new ideas and methods. Under the directorship of Cossío, the Museo Pedagógico Nacional sponsored courses and lectures, published books and pamphlets, created a circulating library and an exposition of teaching aids.[99] Other successful programs included the summer camps (*colonias escolares*) for working-class children, funded by the state from 1887 until 1929, and the University Extension movement, a cultural outreach program initiated at the University of Oviedo in 1898 by a group of socially conscious professors sympathetic to the Institución.[100]

More sweeping proposals to "nationalize" public education failed to prosper, however. Liberal efforts in the 1890s to create an independent Ministry of Public Instruction and to transfer financial responsibility for maestros' salaries to the state collapsed in the face of fiscal stringency and clerical opposition.[101] A major reform of secondary schooling was no more successful. Intended to reinvigorate Spain's "anemic" middle class by educating it for productive citizenship, the draft proposal prepared in 1893 by the Liberal minister Segismundo Moret, a founder and president of the ILE, reflected the institucionista faith in the power of education to remodel society. Moret proposed a two-part bachillerato divided into a four-year general degree and an optional two-year course of advanced study for the minority preparing for university entry. The general degree was intended for "those numerous youth, the real sinews of the fatherland, who will later fulfill the technical and professional functions of the industrial professions, commercial offices, factories, farms, workshops." Moret nearly tripled the number of required courses

[99] Created by royal decree on 6 May 1882 as the Museo de Instrucción Primaria, the center changed its name in 1894. See García del Dujo, *Museo Pedagógico Nacional*.

[100] See Guerrero Salom, "La Institución."

[101] See Juan Uña, "La discusión parlamentaria," *BILE* 19, no. 427 (30 October 1895): 296–300.

by including more sciences and "formative" subjects such as civics and physical education and by mandating "cyclical"—that is, annual—instruction in the basic academic courses such as languages and math.

While granting institutos greater administrative autonomy, Moret proposed a greater "tutelary mission" for the state in the internal affairs of both public and private schools. In order to standardize course content, the decree briefly defined the parameters and objective (or "pedagogic idea") for each subject in the curriculum. It also reaffirmed the responsibility of the Council of Public Instruction to review and approve the format and price of all textbooks. This partial abridgment of the cherished principle of academic freedom reflected the Liberals' growing belief in an overriding state interest in national educational outcomes.

Opposition to the reform, which was signed into law in 1894 after considerable alteration by the Council of Public Instruction, came from several quarters.[102] Most outspoken was the clerical right, which rejected the implicit assumption of a greater "educative" role for the state, as well as the "naturalist" and secularizing tendencies in the curriculum; in particular, they objected to the civics course, which seemed to elevate loyalty to the state above loyalty to the church. Although the Liberals subsequently agreed to "balance" the curriculum by introducing the voluntary study of religion,[103] integrist opinion was unrelenting. When the Conservatives returned to office in 1895, they bowed to the clerical wing of the party by setting aside the new plan and reinstating the totally antiquated five-year classical curriculum prescribed in the Ley Moyano, which included an obligatory class in religion for all students.[104] The Conservative repeal of the Liberal plan of 1894 was not motivated exclusively by ideology, however, but also responded to the protests of indignant middle-class parents, who failed to perceive the value of a general bachillerato that did not lead to the professions and who objected to the additional expense, time, and effort required to attain the university bachillerato under the new plan.[105]

For democratic reformers within the Liberal party, the dilemma was apparent. To the extent that the weak political system was unable to move much ahead of public opinion, the "top-down" approach was limited. Conversely, the inadequacy of public schooling and the hostility of the church hindered the emergence of an informed middle-class pub-

[102] RD of 16 September 1894. The complete documentation on this reform is in Ministerio de Fomento, *Reforma de la segunda enseñanza*.

[103] RD of 25 January 1895.

[104] D of 12 July 1895.

[105] See the comments of Julián Calleja, in Ministerio de Fomento, *Reforma de la segunda enseñanza*, 149.

lic supportive of educational reform. Altering the status quo became more compelling in the decade of the 1890s, however, as emerging new opponents of the Spanish state sought to create a climate for change through alternative kinds of schooling.

One challenge came from political Catalanism, whose roots lay in the Romantic linguistic and cultural revival of the mid-nineteenth century. By the 1880s political and economic grievances against the Restoration system had convinced the Catalan industrial bourgeoisie that the cultural distinctiveness of their region could be translated into a political movement for which they would provide the "natural" leadership. Among their objectives was a system of public instruction adapted to the "needs and character of the civilization of Catalonia."[106] Local control over all levels of schooling would not only restore Catalan as the language of high culture and politics in the region, but would also "Catalanize" a growing immigrant labor force and provide technical and vocational alternatives to the classical bachillerato In the meantime, early organizers of the Catalanist movement created a Foundation for Catalan Education to promote the opening of Catalan-language schools. It was not until 1898, however, that the first such school was established.[107]

Equally threatening to the Restoration system was the upsurge of social conflict and the emergence of working-class political movements. However divergent their ultimate political goals, populist republican and anarchist groups saw the deficit of public education as an opportunity for political recruitment and social change. Viewing ignorance and oppression as two sides of the same coin, they believed that disseminating knowledge was a revolutionary act. The schools they opened for adults and children in clubs, atheneums, and party headquarters responded to the small but growing demand for schooling among the working classes. Basic literacy and training in marketable urban skills such as accounting and drafting comprised the curriculum in their day and night schools, as they did in the colegios run by their competitors in the religious orders. For the republicans the challenge was primarily political: by providing a social service that would attract workers to their precincts, they hoped to build a solid base in the urban working class with which to break the grip of caciquismo. But like the anarchists, republicans also sought to subvert the perceived ideological hegemony of Catholic conservatism. From the 1880s on a growing number

[106] The Memorial de Greuges (1885) and the Bases de Manresa (1892) are reproduced in Albert Balcells, *Cataluña contemporánea, 1900–36*, 2 vols. (Madrid: Siglo XXI, 1976) 1:214–19, 228–31.

[107] Jordi Monés i Pujol-Busquets, *La llengua a l'escola (1714–1939)* (Barcelona: Barcanova, 1984).

of laic schools appeared, particularly in the Catalan region, which although nominally "neutral," were militantly anticlerical and anti-Catholic.[108]

The reflexive response of the dynastic parties to the challenges posed by Catalanists, radical republicans, and anarchists was frequently repression. But the counterhegemonic challenge of the religious orders and the institucionistas was more difficult to answer, particularly since many dynastic politicians shared their faith in the potential power of education to cultivate a spirit of social harmony. What ultimately hindered official efforts to improve state schools was the lack of ideological consensus among the governing classes; whereas Conservatives inclined toward the church and traditional values, Liberals favored the secular, progressive cultural project of the ILE. Fearing that a more effective system of national education might fall into the hands of an ideologically uncongenial faction, the dynastic parties took refuge in inaction.

---

[108] On republican and anarchist schools for workers before 1900, see Joaquín Romero Maura, *La rosa de fuego: El obrerismo barcelonés de 1899 a 1909* (Barcelona: Grijalbo, 1975); Diana Velez, "Regeneration and Pacification: Modernization and the Agents of Social Control, Spain, 1895–1917" (Ph.D. diss., Princeton University, 1977); Tiana Ferrer, *Maestros*; José Álvarez Junco, *La ideología política del anarquismo español* (Madrid: Siglo XXI, 1976), 515–46; Antoni Jutglar Bernaus, "Notas para el estudio de la enseñanza en Barcelona hasta 1900," *Anales de Sociología* 2, no. 3 (1967): 7–39; Carolyn P. Boyd, "The Anarchists and Education in Spain, 1868–1909," *Journal of Modern History* 48 (1976): 125–72; Turin, *Educación*, 264–71; and Clara E. Lida, "Educación anarquista en la España del ochocientos," *Revista de Occidente* 97 (1971): 33–47.

CHAPTER 2

National Regeneration and Educational Reform, 1898–1923

> Pedagogy is the science of transforming societies. We used to call this politics: thus, for us, politics has become social Pedagogy and the Spanish problem, a pedagogical problem.
> (*José Ortega y Gasset*)[1]

WHAT FINALLY IMPELLED educational reform into the arena of national debate was the defeat in Cuba and the Philippines in 1898. The disaster was widely viewed as an indictment of the Restoration politicians who had staked so much on the retention of the empire, but also, more broadly, of the society and culture that had shared their illusions and pretensions. Many agreed with Giner that "our catastrophe is not that of the year '98. What happened then is a sign, and nothing more, of a spiritual and material dissolution that goes way back."[2] By exposing the incompetence of the elites, the technological backwardness of the army and navy, and the misery and alienation of the masses, the war enabled dissidents to link the popular demand for national regeneration to educational reform at all levels, just as critics had done in Prussia in 1806 and France in 1870. The ambitious young regenerationist politician Santiago Alba articulated the judgment of many when he affirmed that "rational, humane, flourishing Yankee schools have conquered primitive, routine-ridden and poor Spanish schools."[3] As the nation searched for an explanation for the defeat and a prescription for national renewal, broad social support for educational reform materialized almost overnight. Conservatives who had previously dismissed the ILE's project for educational reform as "Krausist nonsense" now agreed that a "na-

---

[1] José Ortega y Gasset, "La Pedagogía social como programa político" (1910), in *BILE* 40, no. 678 (30 September 1916): 264.

[2] Francisco Giner, "El decreto de segunda enseñanza" (1899), *BILE* 45, no. 731 (28 February 1921): 38.

[3] Prologue to Eduardo Demolins, *En qué consiste la superioridad de los anglosajones* (1899), quoted in Luis Palacios Bañuelos, *Instituto-Escuela: Historia de una renovación educativa* (Madrid: Ministerio de Educación y Ciencia, Centro de Publicaciones, 1989), 46.

tional Pedagogy . . . would work the miracle of renovating our soul, and in renovating it, would automatically bring the rest along with it: culture, wealth, power, confidence in our own worth and our own means."[4] "Our epoch," Cossío could claim with satisfaction, "especially current times, are saturated . . . with pedagogy."[5]

To be sure, the recipes for pedagogical reform varied as widely as the definitions of regeneration; the disaster that progressives attributed to Spain's failure to modernize, conservatives interpreted as God's punishment for national apostasy. Partly because there was no coherent elite leadership on the issue, middle-class enthusiasm for educational reform eventually subsided. Nevertheless, political mobilization in favor of educational reform endured long enough to provoke a response among the dynastic politicians, who achieved consensus on a number of essential reforms that reflected their awareness of the potential power of state schooling to reinforce the existing order. From 1900 on, as challenges to the regime mounted, the dynastic parties sought to reassert the authority of the state over education. But as state activity intensified, the groups contesting power correspondingly increased their efforts to influence, directly or indirectly, what children learned in the classroom.

At the center of the revitalized educational reform movement after 1898 were regenerationist politicians and intellectuals, many of them members of the "extended Institución," who perceived that the moment had arrived to overcome the stalemate of the 1890s. Chiefly responsible for carrying their message beyond the confines of the Cortes and the press to the nation at large was Joaquín Costa. A Krausist and erstwhile professor at the ILE, Costa was a legal historian, journalist, and reformer whose lifelong battle to modernize and revitalize Spanish society culminated in his successful, if temporary, mobilization of the urban and rural middle classes against the prevailing political and social order in the aftermath of the disaster.[6]

---

[4] César Silió Cortés, *La educación nacional* (Madrid: Francisco Beltrán, 1914), 9.

[5] Manuel B. Cossío, *De su jornada: (Fragmentos)* (Madrid: Imp. de Blass, 1929), 140. For the sudden national interest in education after 1898, see Yvonne Turin, "1898, el desastre, ¿fué una llamada a la 'educación'?" *RE* 23, no. 240 (September–October 1975): 23–29; and Alberto del Pozo Pardo, "Año 1898: Llamada de esperanza a una regeneración pedagógica de España," *REP* 36, no. 140 (1978): 103–16.

[6] Of the substantial literature by and about Costa, see especially his own writings on education, erratically collected in *Maestro, escuela y patria: (Notas pedagógicas)*, vol. 10 (Madrid: Biblioteca Costa, 1916); and in Eloy Fernández Clemente, *Educación y revolución en Joaquín Costa y breve antología pedagógica* (Madrid: EDICUSA, 1969). For two influential interpretations, see Rafael Pérez de la Dehesa, *El pensamiento de Costa y su influencia en el 98* (Madrid: Sociedad de Estudios y Publicaciones, 1966); and Enrique Tierno Galván, *Costa y el regeneracionismo* (Barcelona: Editorial Barna, 1961). Also useful are George J. G. Cheyne, *Joaquín Costa, el gran desconocido: Esbozo biográfico* (Bar-

A complex, contradictory figure, Costa shared the ambivalence of many middle-class Spanish progressives who understood the necessity of popular mobilization but who believed democratic reform was potentially perilous unless preceded by educational reform to prepare the popular classes for the responsible exercise of self-government. Thus, for Costa, national regeneration could be summed up in the slogan School and Larder (*Escuela y despensa*): what Spain needed to escape from the misery and ignorance that imprisoned her was a thorough reform of schooling at all levels, from the primary school to the university, "with the certainty that the redemption of Spain is in them or it is nowhere."[7] Echoing Giner and Cossío, Costa insisted that more schooling implied not only "instruction"—the reduction of illiteracy and the improvement of technical education (although these were of course necessary)—but "education"—the formation of industrious, democratic citizens willing to assume responsibility for themselves and the nation: "We must remake the Spaniard; perhaps it might be better to say, make him."[8]

By 1899, Costa had managed to rally a large portion of the economically and politically active sectors of the nation behind his proposals for state-sponsored educational reform, especially those plans that promised to improve national productivity and technical competence.[9] In fact, the demand for educational reform was only the most prominent feature of a broader program of state-sponsored political and economic modernization, or "Europeanization," as Costa and other regenerationists usually called it.[10] But while his program of irrigation schemes, agricultural modernization, and political democratization found an echo among the Spanish middle classes, translating their response into concrete action proved impossible within a political system impervious to public opinion. Within a few years the regenerationist movement was dead, and Costa, after suggesting that only an "iron surgeon" could cut the Gordian knot of caciquismo, retired to his native Aragon in bitterness and frustration.

In the meantime, however, the dynastic parties could not completely

---

celona: Ariel, 1972); and *El legado de Costa: Huesca, septiembre de 1983* (Madrid: Ministerio de Cultura, Subdirección de Archivos, Diputación General de Aragón, Departamento de Cultura y Educación, 1983).

[7] Joaquín Costa, *Reconstitución y europeización de España* (1900), quoted in Fernández Clemente, *Educación y revolución*, 107.

[8] Quoted in Gumersindo de Azcárate, "Educación y enseñanza según Costa," *BILE* 44, no. 720 (31 March 1920): 68.

[9] Pozo Pardo, "Año 1898," summarizes the demands of the National League of Producers organized by Costa in 1899.

[10] The key text is *Reconstitución y europeización de España* (1900).

ignore the public demand for accountability and reform. The defeat called into question the legitimacy of the entire Restoration system, including the two institutional pillars upon which it rested, the army and the church. It also breathed new life into working-class and regionalist movements, which after 1898 redoubled their efforts to win adherents by opening schools. Moreover, the demand for educational reform was a political weapon that could be effectively exploited by factions seeking to control the dynastic parties, left leaderless by the assassination of Cánovas in 1897 and the death of Sagasta in 1903. Whereas the political stability of the Restoration settlement had earlier favored inaction, after the turn of the century it counseled action to restore national unity and political authority.

The corpus of legislation produced by the Spanish state after 1900 was therefore a fundamentally defensive response in which economic modernization and political stability were the chief goals. This minimal consensus was reached, however, only after it became clear that a more ambitious program of cultural and political integration was impossible, given the inability of the dynastic parties to come to an agreement on national purposes and values. The depth of the ideological divide was exposed during the Conservative "regenerationist" ministry of Francisco Silvela, a devout Catholic who initially entrusted the renovation of Spanish education to an prominent integrist, the marqués de Pidal. Pidal's prescription for national regeneration was not state-sponsored educational expansion nor economic development, but rather a return to "traditional Spanish values" under the auspices of the religious colegios.[11] Accordingly, his reform program involved not only the liberation of the colegios from the tutelage of the state, but the infusion of state schooling with Catholic cultural values by means of a new seven-year, rigorously classical bachillerato, the preparation of official syllabi for each course, and state revision of textbooks to eliminate "error."[12] So anachronistic was this interpretation of regenerationism in the context of the general demand for political democratization and economic modernization that Silvela was forced to dismiss Pidal in order to avoid a political crisis.

On 31 March 1900 Silvela announced the creation of an independent Ministry of Public Instruction and Fine Arts, a step long resisted by the clerical right. To head the new ministry he appointed Antonio García Alix, a former military lawyer and Conservative party regular with little

---

[11] See María Victoria López-Cordón Cortezo, "La mentalidad conservadora durante la Restauración," in José Luis García Delgado, ed., *La España de la Restauración* (Madrid: Siglo XXI, 1985), 81.

[12] RD's of 26 May and 24 July 1899.

previous experience or known enthusiasm for educational matters. Nevertheless, García Alix soon proved himself to be an able direct descendent of the centralizing Moderado ministers of the previous century. "One of the principal purposes of the State is education and instruction," he averred. "I do not want the State to abandon it in order to surrender it to the institutions on the right or the left."[13] During his year in office, he laid the foundation for a reinvigorated state presence in national education upon which his successors in the Liberal party found they could comfortably build when they returned to office in 1901.[14]

Primary schools (symbolically renamed "national schools" in 1910) benefited most from the regenerationist anxiety after 1898 and, later, from the crisis atmosphere that followed the end of the world war.[15] In 1901, under the Liberal minister, the conde de Romanones, the state finally assumed full financial responsibility for the salaries of primary teachers.[16] Other landmarks were the adoption of a graduated pay scale for teachers, based on training and seniority, in 1910 and the approval of a General Statute for Primary School Teachers in 1917.[17] Significant increases in average salaries were slow to materialize, however. By 1914 the median salary of the 25,700 public schoolteachers was still only 1,100 pesetas a year, despite the rise of the entry-level salary to 1,000 pesetas in 1911. Ten years later, when prices had more than doubled, teachers would still average little more than 2,000 pesetas a year, less than the average annual wage of a manual laborer.[18] As a consequence, normal school enrollments continued to fall, even as their admission standards and degree requirements were gradually raised.[19] A major breakthrough was the Liberal creation of the Escuela de Estudios Supe-

[13] Manuel de Puelles Benítez, *Educación e ideología en la España contemporánea (1767–1975)* (Barcelona: Editorial Labor, 1980), 260.

[14] For the politics of educational reform in this period, Yvonne Turin, *La educación y la escuela en España de 1874 a 1902: Liberalismo y tradición*, trans. Josefa Hernández Alfonso (Madrid: Aguilar, 1967) remains the standard work.

[15] The schools were renamed in an RD of 8 June 1910.

[16] RD of 26 October 1901. For a justification of his activism in the ministry, see Álvaro de Figueroa y Torres, conde de Romanones, *Las responsabilidades del antiguo régimen* (Madrid: Imp. Cervantina, 1924).

[17] RDs of 7 January 1910 and 12 April 1917. The statute was revised in an R.D. of 18 May 1923.

[18] RD of 25 February 1911; Enrique Bernad Royo, *La instrucción primaria a principios del siglo XX: Zaragoza, 1898–1914* (Zaragoza: Institución "Fernando el Católico," 1984), 219; Luis de Zulueta, "La reforma de la enseñanza," *BILE* 48, no. 773 (31 August 1924): 233–40. For an overview in 1912, see Rafael Altamira, "Problemas urgentes de primera enseñanza en España," *BILE* 36, no. 624 (31 March 1912): 65–69.

[19] RDs of 6 July 1900 and 30 August 1914 modified the regimen at the normal schools. For an overview, see Agustín Escolano Benito, "Las escuelas normales, siglo y medio de perspectiva histórica," *RE* 30, no. 269 (1982): 55–99.

riores del Magisterio in 1909 to provide advanced training for future state inspectors and normal school professors.[20] Tangible results at the level of local schools could be expected only in the long term, however, since the better trained graduates naturally gravitated to the urban areas and the state inspection corps remained understaffed.

As always, the root cause of the problem was financial. The amount allocated in the national budget for education climbed slowly, never amounting to more than 10 percent of total spending except briefly during the world war. Expenditure per elementary student in 1911 was still less than one-fourth that in France and slightly more than one-fourth that in Italy.[21] In response to the postwar crisis of 1918–23, however, expenditures began to rise more sharply, with primary schools receiving the bulk of the new spending.[22]

Although the state's assumption of responsibility for salaries theoretically freed local funds for school construction and other improvements, in practice only larger cities with progressive city councils seem to have seized the opportunity.[23] Urban areas were also the principal beneficiaries of the accelerating growth in the number of religious colegios. Thus, although illiteracy declined nationally by 25 percent (to 44 percent) by 1920, the decrease was less noticeable in impoverished rural areas, especially in the south.[24] In 1912 it was estimated that an additional nine thousand schools were needed just to reduce the national student/teacher ratio to 50:1.[25]

[20] An RD of 3 June 1909 created the Escuela Superior del Magisterio (renamed the Escuela de Estudios Superiores del Magisterio on 10 September 1911). Its curriculum was diversified and extended to three years on 30 August 1914. See Salvador Ferrer C. Maura, *Una institución docente española: La Escuela de Estudios Superiores del Magisterio (1909–1932)* (Madrid: Imp. CEDESA, 1973).

[21] Santiago Alba, "Política pedagógica española," *BILE* 37, no. 638 (31 May 1913): 132.

[22] Clara Eugenia Núñez, *La fuente de la riqueza: Educación y desarrollo económico en la España contemporánea* (Madrid: Alianza Universidad, 1992), 301–9.

[23] For a comparison of schools in urban areas, see Bernad Royo, *Instrucción primaria*; José María Hernández Díaz, *Educación y sociedad en Béjar durante el siglo XIX* (Salamanca: Ediciones Universidad, Instituto de Ciencias de la Educación, 1983); Antoni Jutglar, "La enseñanza en Barcelona en el siglo XX," *Anales de Sociología* 2, no. 3 (1967): 7–39; and Alejandro Tiana Ferrer, *Maestros, misioneros, y militantes: La educación de la clase obrera madrileña, 1898–1917* (Madrid: Centro de Publicaciones del Ministerio de Educación y Ciencia, CIDE, 1992).

[24] Mercedes Vilanova Ribas and Xavier Moreno Julià, *Atlas de la evolución del analfabetismo en España de 1887 a 1981* (Madrid: Centro de Publicaciones del Ministerio de Educación y Ciencia, CIDE, 1992), 166. Núñez, *Fuente*, who provides an extended study of regional and sex differences in literacy, puts the national illiteracy rate in 1920 at 39 percent.

[25] Rafael Altamira, "Problema urgentes de la primera enseñanza en España," *BILE* 36, no. 625 (30 April 1912): 97–105.

As a result of these constraints, the enriched and expanded primary school curriculum enacted by the conde de Romanones in October 1901 remained an expression of an ideal rather than a description of reality in most schools.[26] Clearly inspired by the Institución, the new curriculum—optimistically graded into a preschool period, an elementary period of three years, and an upper primary period of five years—prescribed annual, or "cyclical," study of such practical and "formative" subjects as "notions of law" (i.e., civics), national history, natural sciences (including hygiene and agriculture), drawing, singing, and physical education. Despite a Liberal mandate in 1911, however, as late as 1926 only 641 of the twenty seven thousand public primary schools in Spain were graded.[27] The 1901 decree also reaffirmed the principle of obligatory and free school attendance for children between the ages of 6 and 12, but in practice families were required to contribute one-third of the teacher's salary until 1913, and school attendance rates remained low because of economic hardship and lack of school places.[28] Given the sporadic school attendance of most children, full implementation of the new primary curriculum was a challenge that rural teachers found "terrifying."[29]

Under the Liberals, oversight of the content and methods of primary school teaching was entrusted to an expanded educational bureaucracy. Although funding was never adequate to ensure an effective state presence, the corps of state primary school inspectors was removed from local control and its jurisdiction extended to include the "morality and hygiene" of private schools.[30] In 1911 the Liberals created the General Office of Primary Instruction as a technical unit within the ministry with responsibility for collecting statistical data on primary schools and disseminating the latest findings of "scientific pedagogy" among the state teacher corps. They also reorganized and "depoliticized" the advisory Council of Public Instruction by reducing its ecclesiastical membership and increasing the participation of public school teachers and other professionals.

[26] RD of 26 October 1901.

[27] *RP* 5, no. 5 (May 1926): 211–12; Antonio Viñao Frago, *Innovación pedagógica y racionalidad científica: La escuela graduada pública en España (1898–1936)* (Madrid: Ediciones Akal, 1990).

[28] An RD of 14 March 1913 relieved parents of the obligation to pay teachers. Slightly more than half the school-age population was enrolled in 1916–17. Rosa María Capel, "La enseñanza primaria femenina en España: Su evolución histórica," in José Luis López-Aranguren et al., *Infancia y sociedad en España* (Jaén: Editorial Hesperia, 1983), 97–116. The school-leaving age was officially raised to fourteen in the Estatuto General del Magisterio de Primera Enseñanza of 1923 (RD of 18 May).

[29] See Juan Antonio Onieva, "El libro de lectura," *RP* 1, no. 12 (December 1922): 449.

[30] RDs of 12 April 1901; and 1 July, 1 September, and 9 October 1902.

These reforms, inspired and in many cases implemented by the institucionistas, were intended to make the Ministry of Public Instruction and its subsidiary organizations an "apolitical"—that is, purely technical—administrative agency. But it was either naive or disingenuous to view these reforms as politically neutral in a nation in which "scientific pedagogy" implied a concrete political and cultural agenda highly threatening to traditional interests. As the young José Ortega y Gasset candidly admitted to his students in the Escuela Superior del Magisterio in 1910, politics and pedagogy were functionally interchangeable in the Spanish context.[31] Thus, the Liberals' successive attempts to transform the Council of Public Instruction into a consultative body of politically neutral professionals were rejected by Catholics who contended—not wholly without justification—that the "professionals" were generally unsympathetic to their interests.[32] Moreover, misgivings about surveillance of classroom teachers by state inspectors were not confined to the clerical right; they were harbored as well by republicans, anarchists, and—despite their influence in the ministry—institucionistas.

Even the Liberals proved reluctant to assert an aggressive state presence in the classroom. Although theoretically supportive of making education an instrument of national integration and modernization, in practice they shied away from any direct interference with the academic freedom of professors, whether public or private. Clinging to a kind of pure liberalism, they preferred simply to establish a level ideological playing field, primarily by reducing church privileges. Romanones captured the essentially negative character of the Liberal position: "If it is true that the State should not shape characters, it is also important that it prevent others from shaping them."[33]

In fact, the Conservatives, loud champions of the "freedom to teach" when religious schools were involved, were less fastidious about the academic freedom of republican and anarchist schools, whose numbers increased after the turn of the century. Most famous of these was the Modern School, founded in Barcelona in 1900 by Francisco Ferrer Guardia, a radical educator whose progressive pedagogy served a revolutionary anarchist agenda.[34] The Conservatives closed Ferrer's school,

[31] See the quotation that opens this chapter.
[32] Liberals "reformed" the Council of Public Instruction in 1898, 1900, 1902, 1911, 1913, and 1914.
[33] Puelles Benitez, *Educación*, 260.
[34] See Francisco Ferrer Guardia, *La Escuela Moderna* (1912) (Gijón: Ediciones Júcar, 1976); Pere Solà Gusiñer, *Françesc Ferrer i Guardia i l'escola moderna* (Barcelona: Curial, 1978); Jordi Monés i Pujol-Busquets et al., *Ferrer Guardia y la pedagogía libertaria: Elementos para un debate* (Barcelona: Icaria Editorial, 1977); and Carolyn P. Boyd, "The Anarchists and Education in Spain, 1868–1909," *Journal of Modern History* 48 (1976):

along with other laic and anarchist schools, after an unsuccessful assassination attempt on the king's life in 1906. The following year, they expanded state inspection rights over private schools to include their "ethical and civic teaching,"[35] a provision employed by the Conservative government of Antonio Maura two years later in the aftermath of the so-called Tragic Week in Barcelona, when angry crowds protesting the Moroccan war burned Catholic schools and convents. On the grounds that their subversive teaching had contributed to the prerevolutionary mood in the city, the government closed dozens of leftist schools and tried and executed Ferrer for his alleged role in the revolt.[36]

Almost as worrisome to the dynastic parties was the growth of the Catalan regionalist movement, which included, as we have seen, a demand for instruction in Catalan. Romanones prohibited maestros from teaching the catechism in other languages in 1902; the Castilian language, he asserted, was the "most valuable bond of union among all the provinces of the Kingdom."[37] But the electoral successes of the Catalan regionalist parties after 1906 led eventually to the concession of partial autonomy to the four Catalan provinces joined in the Mancomunitat in 1914. Thereafter, the Barcelona city government, the provincial deputation, and the Mancomunitat exercised their expanded authority over all levels of schooling to subsidize pedagogical publications, teacher training schools, textbooks in Catalan, technical institutes, and historical and linguistic scholarship. Although Catalanism before 1923 was dominated politically by a conservative Catholic industrial bourgeoisie unsympathetic to democratic social reform, its educational project was increasingly shaped by those sympathetic to the progressive methods of "scientific pedagogy." It was thus viewed as a potential ally by those working to modernize Spanish state and society.[38]

Alarmed by these challenges to the declining authority of the dynastic parties and the parliamentary monarchy, rightist politicians, like the Maurist Conservative César Silió, called stridently for a more assertive program of national education "to socialize the largest possible number of individuals, as intensively as possible, into the group within which

---

125–72. For rationalist schools more generally, see Pere Solà Gusiñer, *Las escuelas racionalistas en Cataluña (1909–39)* (Barcelona: Tusquets, 1976).

[35] RD of 18 November 1907.

[36] RD of 3 February 1910. The standard work on the Tragic Week is Joan C. Ullman, *La Semana Trágica: Estudio sobre las causas socioeconómicas del anticlericalismo en España (1898–1912)* (Barcelona: Ariel, 1972).

[37] RD of 21 November 1902.

[38] See Jordi Monés i Pujol-Busquets, *La llengua a l'escola (1714–1939)* (Barcelona: Barcanova, 1983), 83–156; Joan Gay, *Societat catalana i reforma escolar* (Barcelona: Laia, 1973), 1–40; and Cèlia Cañellas y Rosa Toran, *Política escolar de l'Ajuntament de Barcelona, 1916–1936* (Barcelona: Barcanova, 1982), 24–96.

they live, so that this group can confront the competition from rival groups." Only aggressive state action could forge "a community of ideals" and mold youths "who put love of the Patria above all the interests and conveniences of the moment."[39] The difficulty of course lay in agreeing upon which ideals to instill. From 1900 on, "'neo-Catholicism' and anticlericalism constituted the warp and the woof of the political struggle," with the Liberals adopting anticlericalism as the keystone of their modernizing project and the Conservatives defending clerical interests as they had always done.[40] Thus, even though mounting class conflict and the growing electoral strength of republican, regionalist, and Socialist candidates in the cities suggested the desirability of forging bonds of national and social solidarity, the dynastic parties were unable to agree upon the political and moral values upon which national unity might be built. Furthermore, the still-limited reach of public schooling made it an unreliable bulwark against social disorder. Elite divisions and the weakness of the state thus guaranteed the survival of caciquismo and military repression as instruments of political and social control.

Given this ideological fault line, the Spanish state was unable to develop or impose a national primary and secondary curriculum with a strong cultural or political orientation. Clearly, religion could no longer play the socialization role earlier assigned to it by the Ley Moyano. Arguing that dogmatic religious training discouraged scientific innovation, violated individual freedom of conscience, and inculcated a restrictive, artificial, and hypocritical morality, the Liberal party abolished religion as a required subject for non-Catholics studying the bachillerato in 1901 and extended the exemption to nonpracticing primary school children in 1913.[41]

Finding an alternative source of moral authority that could command the respect of all Spaniards and produce the desired social harmony was not so simple, however. A similar dilemma in the French Third Republic had inspired the introduction of French geography, language, civics, and history as a substitute for religion and monarchical tradition in the

---

[39] Silió, *Educación nacional*, 24, 239.

[40] Joan C. Ullman, "The Warp and Woof of Parliamentary Politics in Spain, 1808–1939: Anticlericalism versus 'Neo-Catholicism,'" *European Studies Review* 13 (1983): 151. For the church-state struggle in this period, see José Manuel Castells, *Las asociaciones religiosas en la España contemporánea: Un estudio jurídico-administrativo (1767–1965)* (Madrid: Taurus, 1973); and José Andrés Gallego, *La política religiosa en España, 1889–1913* (Madrid: Editora Nacional, 1975).

[41] ROC of 21 March and RD of 12 April 1901; RD of 25 April 1913. Romanones was minister of public instruction in 1901 and prime minister in 1913.

1870s and 1880s.[42] But none of these was easily adaptable to the Spanish situation. As the following chapters will show, the meaning of Spanish history was politically divisive and thus not easily exploited for patriotic ends. With nationalist sentiment rising in the linguistically diverse peripheral regions, forging unity through the Castilian language was equally doubtful. Instruction in civic responsibilities in a system grounded in electoral falsification and popular demobilization was inherently contradictory. Furthermore, the very legitimacy of the Restoration system was contested by significant portions of the nation's political and cultural elites. The democratic left insisted that caciquismo had opened an unbridgeable gulf between "official" and "real" Spain—that is, between the "state" and the "nation"; the same distinction was sustained by the neo-Catholic right, which still labeled liberalism an "antinational" heresy that betrayed national tradition and values.[43] Even an (ultimately unsuccessful) attempt to require daily classroom recitation of a poem honoring the Spanish flag raised reservations in the mind of one Conservative minister, who feared the practice would elevate the poem to the same status as "sublime religious petitions."[44] Not surprisingly, then, the civics requirement (disguised as "notions of law") in the 1901 primary school curriculum was most often honored in the breach.[45]

The dynastic parties were more comfortable with the concept of "patriotism," which had fewer troublesome connotations. In 1913, a Liberal government instructed local juntas to ensure that public education "have an eminently patriotic character and that maestros and maestras not lose the opportunity to inculcate moral precepts in their students and awaken in them a sense of duty."[46] Following the successful example set in France by the "patriotic" reader *Le Tour de France par deux enfants*, by G. Bruno, in 1921 the Maurist minister of public instruction, César Silió, announced a remunerative competition for a "Book of

---

[42] See Eugen Weber, *Peasants into Frenchmen: The Modernization of Rural France, 1870–1914* (Stanford, Calif.: Stanford University Press, 1976); Mona Ozouf, *L'École, l'Église et la République, 1871–1914* (Paris: Armand Colin, 1963).

[43] José Ortega y Gasset, "Vieja y nueva política," *OC* (Madrid: Alianza Editorial/Revista de Occidente, 1983), 1:265–308; Ramón Ruiz Amado, *Educación cívica* (Barcelona: Librería Religiosa, 1918), 6.

[44] RO of 13 August 1907, signed by Faustino Rodríguez San Pedro. The poem, by Sinesio Delgado, may be found in G. M. Bruño, *Epítome del párvulo* (Madrid: Administración Bruño, 1915), 121; and Pascual Santacruz Revuelta, *España sobre todo: Páginas patrióticas para la infancia* (Madrid: Imp. Viuda y hijos de Jaime Ratés, 1926), 155.

[45] In 1911 the Council of Public Instruction reiterated the importance of "moral and civic education" in the primary grades. RO of 28 May 1911.

[46] RD of 5 May 1913.

the Patria" to teach children "what Spain is and represents and make them love her."[47] Copyright of the winning entry would pass to the state, which would prepare an inexpensive edition for mandatory use in the public schools. But in March 1923 a Liberal government announced that no award would be made.[48] Ideological deadlock between the Conservative jury selected to choose the winner and a government committed to political democratization and academic freedom seems the most probable cause. The ideological—and political—deadlock was broken a few months later, however, by the *pronunciamiento* of General Miguel Primo de Rivera. Under the dictatorship a large number of these "patriotic" texts would be published.

A major transformation of secondary education after 1898 was similarly thwarted by financial constraints, ideological disagreement, and the persistent credentialist mentality of the middle classes. The first minister of public instruction, García Alix, accepted the democratic premise that secondary education should be "an extension of the primary school" when he argued, in the preamble to his decree of 1900, that an acceptable reform must "strengthen state schools; relate, for cultural purposes, the past with the present in order to prepare a future of more beneficial and practical results; and give education, as its greatest and principal objective, the maintenance and, if it is necessary, the creation of the national character."[49] But in its final form, after two years of debate and concessions, the bachillerato of 1903 strongly resembled its predecessors, particularly in its narrow conception of secondary schooling as preparation for university study. The new curriculum tilted slightly more toward modern subjects like history, geography, and the sciences, and made room for new subjects like ethics, law, and physical education, which were supposed to prepare students for civic and social

---

[47] RD of 9 September 1921. See Alberto del Pozo Pardo, "El Libro de la Patria, un concurso escolar vacío, de matiz regeneracionista (1921–1923)," in Julio Ruiz Berrio, ed., *La educación en la España contemporánea: Cuestiones históricas. Libro homenaje a Ángeles Galiño* (Madrid: Sociedad Española de Pedagogía, 1986), 195–202, for a brief discussion of this competition; and Carolyn P. Boyd, " 'Mother Spain': Patriotic Travel Books in Spain, 1900–1950" (manuscript). G. Bruno was the pseudonym of Augustine Fouillée, the wife of the French philosopher Alfred Fouillée. The book was first published in 1877 and eventually reached eight million copies in print. See Aimé Dupuy, "Les livres de lecture de G. Bruno," *Revue d'histoire économique et sociale* 31, no. 2 (1953): 128–51; Ozouf, *L'École et l'Église*, 138–40; Dominique Maingueneau, *Les Livres d'école de l'école libre, 1870–1914: (Discours et idéologie)* (Paris: Le Sycomore, 1979); and Jacques Ozouf and Mona Ozouf, "*Le tour de France par deux infants*: Le petit livre rouge de la République," in Pierre Nora, ed., *Les Lieux de mémoire* (Paris: Gallimard, 1984), 2:291–321.

[48] RO 27 March 1923. The jury was appointed in an RO of 27 July 1922.

[49] RD of 20 July 1900.

life. But remnants of the classical curriculum survived because of inertia and vested interests, and a proposal to require annual intensive study of language, literature, and mathematics was overruled by middle-class objections to greater expense. Thus, the six-year curriculum finally consolidated in 1903 was only slightly more demanding and no more internally coherent than its predecessors.[50]

The initial intention to make secondary schooling more practical failed for lack of interest or comprehension. An attempt in 1901 by the conde de Romanones to enhance the status of technical careers by merging vocational and technical schools with the provincial institutos (correspondingly renamed Institutos generales y técnicos) failed to attract the middle classes away from their fixation on the bachillerato and drew fire from the instituto catedráticos, who felt diminished by their association with trade schools.[51] Between 1903 and 1914 the schools of agronomy, industry, commerce, education, and fine arts gradually reverted to independent status and continued to struggle. Meanwhile, other proposals to make the bachillerato more "formative" or demanding failed for political or financial reasons. The only durable material improvements were the organization of an official corps of teaching assistants and the elimination of the unseemly direct payments of examination fees to the catedráticos.[52]

Under these circumstances the institutos remained at a disadvantage in competing with the religious colegios for middle- and upper-class students. Although the number of secondary students rose 82 percent between 1890 and 1923 (including a dramatic increase in the number of women students, who by then comprised 12 percent of the total)[53], only a third of them were officially matriculated in the institutos. Secondary education, traditionally a marker of social identity for the Spanish middle classes, now increasingly divided them. Attendance at the institutos was devalued in the marketplace of prestige and connections, undermining its traditional purpose of an avenue of social mobility for the urban

[50] García Alix's secondary school plan was modified by Romanones in RDs of 17 August 1901 and 6 September 1903.

[51] Álvaro de Figueroa y Torres, conde de Romanones, *Notas de una vida* (Madrid: Renacimiento, 1928–29), 2:84.

[52] The Cuerpo de Auxiliares de Institutos was created on 24 December 1909. The catedráticos were partially compensated for the loss of the examination fees by the organization of a new pay scale that ranged from a high of 8,000 pesetas a year to a beginning salary of 4,000. The majority of catedráticos earned 5,000–6,000 pesetas annually. Salaries were raised further in 1913 and again in 1919, when the median salary was 8,000.

[53] The number of women receiving secondary schooling of all kinds grew by 230 percent between 1910 and 1920. Rosa María Capel Martínez, *El trabajo y la educación de la mujer en España (1900–1930)* (Madrid: Ministerio de Cultura, Dirección General de Juventud y Promoción Cultural, 1982), 415.

and rural middle classes. In 1905, Eloy Luis-André, an instituto professor of philosophy and frequent commentator on educational issues, warned against the ideological, social, and cultural cleavages that separated the educated classes: "The result is a deep, an enormous separation in the behavior and beliefs of today's youth. Youths who so live in the bosom of the Nation cannot feel solidarity. Thus, there will be, as indeed in reality there already are, two *estates* in a Nation, two *sovereignties* in a state. . . . When the youth of a nation live divided, fighting stupidly among themselves, destroying themselves barbarously, they are condemned to die. If the Nation is old, only youth can rejuvenate it. And if youth is uselessly wasted, from whence shall come the remedy?"[54] Like conservatives in France and Germany, Luis-André deplored the emergence of a socially uprooted "intellectual proletariat" driven by envy and frustration into radicalism or reaction.[55] Unlike many of them, however, he was no champion of the religious colegios, but instead favored the extension of state secondary schooling to create an authentically "Spanish," "civically unanimous" youth.

Few Conservatives were willing to allow the state to define the national interest at the expense of the autonomy and privileges of the colegios, however. After an initial attempt by the regenerationist Conservative minister García Alix to render private schools more accountable by placing them under the supervision of the provincial institutos, the Conservative/clerical alliance reasserted itself, and it was left to the Liberals to try to bolster state authority over the private sector. Within a month after taking office in 1901, the conde de Romanones issued a decree on state examinations that took away many privileges that the colegios incorporados had extracted from Conservative ministries in the previous two decades; most importantly, he eliminated traveling state examiners and prohibited private school professors from participating as voting members on examination boards, on the grounds that the exams represented the only official check on the education delivered in the colegios.[56] The state exams, in fact, lay at the heart of the debate over the "freedom to teach."[57] Accordingly, over the next twenty years

[54] Eloy Luis-André, *La educación de la adolescencia: Estudio crítico del estado de la segunda enseñanza y de sus reformas más urgentes* (Madrid: Imp. de "Alrededor del Mundo," 1916), 247–49.

[55] For a discussion of the debate on the "intellectual proletariat," see Fritz K. Ringer, *Fields of Knowledge: French Acadmic Culture in Comparative Perspective, 1890–1920* (New York: Cambridge University Press, 1992), 127–40.

[56] RDs of 12 April 1901 and 25 April 1913. For the decrees that created these privileges, see chap. 1 n. 76.

[57] See Ramón Ruiz Amado, "La inspección de la enseñanza privada," *RyF* 4 (1902): 136–53; and "La reforma de la segunda enseñanza: El examen final," *RyF* 20 (1908): 288–302.

Conservatives would extend the examination privileges of the colegios and Liberals would take them away.[58]

A related battle was fought over the textbooks that governed success in the examinations. Whereas textbooks had at one time been welcomed as an improvement on the brutal rote methods of the dominie, by the end of the nineteenth century they had come to symbolize all that critics found wrong with state schooling. Catedráticos were free to choose the number and kind of texts for use in their courses; many, in fact, wrote their own texts to supplement their salaries and to serve as "merits" for promotions in the civil list. Frequently lengthy, arid, and pedantic, occasionally inaccurate or out-of-date, many texts underwent numerous editions with only minor revisions to prevent incoming students from borrowing or buying used editions. Progressive reformers found them odious because they stood for all that was "verbalistic," passive, and stagnant in the existing system; the right, not averse in principle to highly codified and unchanging distillations of knowledge,[59] hated the officially assigned texts because their content, to the extent that it was scientific and up-to-date, was often inevitably in conflict with the reactionary mentality of Spanish Catholicism. Middle-class parents, even if indifferent to the ideological controversy, complained strenuously and unremittingly of their expense and length. The only consistent defenders of the texts were the authors themselves.[60]

However valid the criticisms of the textbooks, their central role in the Spanish educational process made it utopian to consider prohibiting them altogether, as the Institución Libre de Enseñanza advocated and, in its own classrooms, practiced. At the primary level, textbooks were an indispensable aid to overtaxed and ill-prepared teachers, who relied on them to convey the essentials of the state-mandated curriculum, structure the learning process, and occupy the students during the long periods when the teachers were occupied with others in the room. The textbook played the same functional role in many small private academies whose professors relied on textbooks to supplement their deficient knowledge. Most important, textbooks supplied privately edu-

[58] The prohibition on traveling examination boards was reaffirmed by a Liberal government in 1911; the traveling boards were reinstated by the Conservatives in 1915, restricted heavily by the Liberals in 1918, and abolished altogether in 1919. Conservatives restored the right of private professors to participate, with a vote, in official examinations in 1910, but the Liberals took away the vote in 1912 and 1914, only to have it restored when the Conservatives returned to office in 1915.

[59] See, for example, Ramón Ruiz Amado, *La educación intelectual*, 3d ed., rev., 2 vols. (Barcelona: Editorial Librería Religiosa, 1942).

[60] For a persuasive defense of the texts, see Juan Carandell, "El libro de texto y el catedrático español," *RSE* 5, no. 29 (1927): 72–76. See also Manual Prat Alcalde, "Nuestras espinas," *RSE* 4, no. 23 (1926): 200–201.

cated students with the facts, viewpoints, and emphases considered significant by the instituto professors responsible for state examinations. Since "learning the book" was the cultural norm, the extension and level of detail typical of many texts was a particular source of irritation. In 1902 aggrieved parents, adroitly encouraged by the entrepreneurial owners of private academies and the religious colegios, formed an association to exchange "textbook horror stories."[61]

Given the functional and ideological centrality of the textbooks in the educational process, it is not surprising that they had been the object of continuous (and contradictory) legal dispositions, particularly in the early years of liberal state consolidation. As we have seen, the Ley Moyano mandated periodic government authorization of bachillerato texts in each subject, supplemented by ecclesiastical review of primary readers and religious manuals. The democratic revolutionaries of 1868, however, had extended complete freedom to professors to design courses and select texts "in harmony with their beliefs."[62] The reassertion of ministerial control over course content by the Conservatives in 1875 was justified by citing "the Government's duty to guard morality and healthy doctrine"; the Liberals' revocation of the 1875 decree, by affirming that "speculative reason must be independent."[63] Although professors were supposed to submit their textbooks to the Council of Public Instruction for approval, the Council's authority over their content was restricted in 1890 to flagrant cases of scholarly inadequacy, moral deviance, or excessive cost or length. Even this limited responsibility was rarely exercised; Council approbation was sought primarily by catedráticos seeking to justify a merit step increase in the salary schedule.[64]

By the 1890s, however, the two parties had begun to converge on the issue. The Liberals' earlier enthusiasm for total deregulation was tempered by the results of a survey of existing practice in the institutos, which revealed a proliferation of lengthy, poorly conceptualized, expensive, and occasionally inaccurate texts: nationwide, there were 212 different texts in use in humanities courses alone.[65] The Liberals' view of

---

[61] See *LE 5*, nos. 104 and 121 (1903): 1.

[62] The Moderado legislation on textbooks included RDs of 17 September 1845 (art. 48), 11 August 1849, 28 August 1850 (art. 39), 10 September 1852 (art. 70), and 9 September 1857 (arts. 86–93). The Progressive decree was signed on 21 October 1868.

[63] RDs of 26 February 1875 and 3 March 1881.

[64] The Law of 27 July 1890 reorganized the Council and reasserted its prerogative over texts, but it was not implemented until 1895, and then with unhappy results. The Council was reorganized in 1898, 1900, 1902, and 1911.

[65] The ministry asked for two copies of every textbook in use in a circular of 15 December 1893; the recommendations of the director general of public instruction to the minister of development were published on 20 October 1894. The complete statistics may be found in AGMEC, leg. 6940. See also Eduardo Benot, *Errores en materia de educación y de instrucción pública*, 4th ed. (Madrid: Librería de Hernando, 1899), 26–38.

education as a tool for cultural modernization could not be easily reconciled with complete academic freedom for professors. As one reformer observed, "Public instruction proposes a great goal: national development. And this progress is unattainable if everyone does whatever he wants."[66] But Liberal attempts in the 1890s to exercise greater control through publication of a standard syllabus for each course had succumbed to ministerial instability. In 1898 another Liberal minister again demanded controls to curb the "truly awesome multiplication" of texts that "corrupted literary taste" and "exploited official positions."[67]

As the Liberals inched toward greater state regulation, the Catholic right countered with their own solutions to the "poison" of the textbooks, which they labeled "one hundred times worse than the separatists or the Yankees."[68] One strategy involved strict ecclesiastical and political control over course content and textbooks. The church never tired of reminding the state that the Ley Moyano had given bishops responsibility for monitoring the moral and doctrinal content of textbooks. But although secondary texts occasionally incurred episcopal condemnation, ecclesiastical censure was not sufficient to remove offending books from state classrooms unless backed by state sanctions.[69] As minister in 1899, the neo-Catholic marqués de Pidal began state textbook censorship and proposed to establish a standard syllabus for all courses.[70] But it soon became clear that state intervention was acceptable only if permanent Catholic control of the ministry were assured; when political expediency led to Pidal's abrupt dismissal, the clerical right was forced to reconsider its support for state controls. The uncertainty of Catholic ideological hegemony also curbed its enthusiasm for the favorite panacea of penny-pinching parents—the so-called *texto único*, a single authorized text for each subject, published by the state.[71]

A safer strategy for clerical interests was to insulate private school students from the pernicious doctrines dispensed in the state institutos. In early 1900 a group of Catholic deputies introduced a bill in the Cortes that would have allowed students to be examined on the basis of

[66] Benot, *Errores*, 32.

[67] RDs of 16 September 1894, signed by Alejandro Groizard, and 13 September 1898, signed by Germán Gamazo. The list of texts in use in all institutos in 1898 is in AGMEC, leg. 6940.

[68] Pedro Pidal, "¡Español, deifícate!" *Vida Nueva* 24 (20 November 1898): 1.

[69] For examples of the limits of ecclesiastical censure, see AGMEC, libro 655, Actas de la Junta Consultiva de Instrucción Pública, Sec. 2a, session of 3 June 1895; and *La Enseñanza Católica* (Madrid) 11 (July–August 1921): 325–26.

[70] RD of 26 May 1899. See above, p. 44. A Junta Superior Consultativa was appointed by an RO of 26 May 1899 to write the syllabi. Highly detailed programs for the first two years appeared on 24 July. The curriculum and programs are discussed further in chap. 4.

[71] See *LE* 4, no. 98 (22 November 1902); and 5, no. 104 (3 January 1903): 1.

any text or syllabus of their own choosing.[72] But most dynastic politicians, whatever their ties to the church or their allegiance to the principle of academic freedom, did not need to be reminded that the official exam was "the only effective intervention of the State in the intellectual direction of the mass of Spanish students."[73] In its final form the law they approved in 1901 was a casuistic compromise that (1) instructed the Council of Public Instruction to write standard syllabi (or *cuestionarios*) setting the "purpose, character and extension" of each subject; (2) confirmed the professor's right to total freedom in "course design, methodology, and doctrine"; and (3) asserted the student's right to study any textbook he wished.[74] This was a right that students already possessed and were unlikely to exercise as long as the catedráticos controlled the exams. Privately educated students taking official exams would always hedge their bets by buying the text recommended by the examining professor.

Since the Council of Public Instruction thereafter continued to evade its responsibility to review texts and write course cuestionarios, the state had no real control over what students learned, other than the exams themselves, which were of course independently administered by an ideologically diverse group of catedráticos.[75] This was a slim reed indeed upon which to hang the burden of forging a national consensus. With privately educated students amounting to nearly 70 percent of the total, what Spanish students learned was therefore largely a function of where and with whom they chose to study. This heightened the competition for the allegiance of Spanish youth, even as it intensified the ideological differences that divided them. While religious colegios railed against even the frail curbs on their autonomy, Liberals and republicans denounced clerical influence over middle-class youth. Institutional pluralism, social segmentation, and the weakness of the liberal state combined to fuel the ideological conflicts that increasingly characterized Spanish society, particularly as the parliamentary regime entered its crisis after 1917.

The contrast with France, where church-state rivalry and educational

[72] Proposición de ley of 15 January 1900. *DSC*, no. 113, app. 1 (24 January 1900).
[73] Mariano Domínguez Berrueta, *Ante una campaña injusta: Notas para la defensa de la enseñanza oficial, de la libertad de enseñanza y del profesorado de los institutos nacionales* (Ávila: Tip. y Enc. Senén Martín, 1925), 60–61.
[74] Law of 1 February 1901. A previous RD of 6 July 1900 had already outlined the terms of the compromise.
[75] Repeated orders to prepare the mandated cuestionarios and to review textbooks reveal the continuing failure of the Council to perform its duties. See RDs of 12 April 1901 and 21 February 1902; RO of 24 July 1902; ROC of 7 October 1905; RO of 28 February 1908; RDs of 18 January 1911 and 23 October 1913.

and social segmentation were equally divisive, dramatizes the inefficacy of the Spanish state. After the monarchist resurgence of the mid-1870s, French republicans acted decisively to "republicanize the Republic," first by strengthening state authority over education, secularizing public school teachers and curricula, expanding free public school places, regulating minutely the content and form of classroom instruction, prohibiting the use of textbooks critical of republican values and institutions, and, eventually, by denying the religious orders the right to teach or open schools. These measures halted the earlier expansion of Catholic schooling and created the conditions for an energetic program of political socialization through the curriculum and the approved texts.[76] A stronger, more democratically organized state coupled with greater fears of the international consequences of an ideologically divided population seem to explain this difference in outcomes.

The role of the Institución Libre in the debate over the state's role in education was ambivalent. Although the younger institucionistas were eager to harness state authority to their campaign for educational reform, they remained faithful to the original commitment of the ILE founders to academic freedom and institutional autonomy, not least because the Spanish state continued to prove particularly resistant to democratization.

On the other hand, they persisted in using their influence in the Liberal party to support their long-term project for political and cultural reform through the creation of a "Europeanized" elite. At their urging in 1907 a Liberal government created the Junta para Ampliación de Estudios e Investigaciones Científicas, an official but independently administered foundation that awarded scholarships to students and teachers for study abroad and supported scientific investigation within Spain.[77]

---

[76] On the educational policies of the Third French Republic, see Ozouf, *L'École et l'Église*; Ringer, *Fields of Knowledge*; Weber, *Peasants into Frenchmen*; John E. Talbott, *The Politics of Educational Reform in France, 1918–1940* (Princeton: Princeton University Press, 1969); and Jacqueline Freyssinet-Dominjon, *Les Manuels de l'histoire de l'école libre, 1882–1959: De la loi Ferry à la loi Debré* (Paris: Armand Colin, 1969). For the decline in Catholic primary school enrollment, see Raymond Grew and Patrick J. Harrigan, "The Catholic Contribution to Universal Schooling in France, 1850–1906," *Journal of Modern History* 57, no. 2 (June 1985): 211–47; for secondary schools, see Harrigan, "The Social Appeals of Catholic Secondary Education in France in the 1870s," *Journal of Social History* 8 (spring 1975): 122–41.

[77] Between 1908 and 1936 the Junta awarded some 1,700 scholarships, distributed primarily among those seeking advanced study abroad in pedagogy, medicine, the physical sciences, art history, and law. Alfonso Ruiz Miguel, "La Junta para Ampliación de Estudios," *Historia 16* 5, no. 49 (May 1980): 85–93; Luis Palacios Bañuelos, *Castillejo, educador* (Ciudad Real: Diputación Provincial, 1986); Carmela Gamero Merino, *Un*

In 1910 the Junta inaugurated two autonomous centers for research, scholarly publication, and training—the Centro de Estudios Históricos and the Instituto Nacional de Ciencias Fisico-Naturales—both of which quickly assumed intellectual leadership in the nation.[78] The same year it opened the Residencia de Estudiantes, a highly successful experiment modeled on the English university colleges and dedicated to the formation of "the student rich in public and civic virtues, capable of fulfilling . . . whatever the historical destinies of the race may require of him."[79] A women's residence was added in 1915.

The governing board of the Junta was carefully selected to represent a broad spectrum of Spanish intellectual and political opinion. The Catholic integrist Pedro Sainz Rodríguez, no friend of the Institución, later called the Junta "a kind of middle ground, in the scientific area, in that division between left and right that always disturbed Spaniards in all aspects of their national life together."[80] Nevertheless, its scientific, "Europeanist" program, administered with dedication and enthusiasm by the permanent secretary of the Junta, José Castillejo (a protégé of Giner's), and the institutional independence of its subsidiaries marked it clearly as an offspring of the Institución and earned it the enmity of the Catholic right as well as the resentment of the less well endowed university faculties.

Under its auspices developed the only notable effort to revitalize public secondary schooling under the parliamentary regime, the Instituto-Escuela. Authorized by the left-Liberal Santiago Alba in 1918, three years after the death of Giner de los Ríos, the Instituto-Escuela was a memorial to the influence Giner's ideas had achieved in official circles.

---

modelo europeo de renovación pedagógica: José Castillejo (Madrid: Consejo Superior de Investigaciones Científicas, Instituto de Estudios Manchegos, 1988); José Castillejo, *The War of Ideas in Spain* (London: H. Milford, 1937); and the entire issue of *Arbor* (Madrid) 126, no. 493 (January 1987).

[78] On the Centro de Estudios Históricos, see chap. 5; and Justo Formentín and María José Villegas, "Altamira y la Junta para la Ampliación de Estudios e Investigaciones Científicas," in Armando Alberola, ed., *Estudios sobre Rafael Altamira* (Alicante: Instituto de Estudios "Juan Gil-Albert," Caja de Ahorros Provincial de Alicante, 1988), 175–208; Rafael Lapesa, "Menéndez Pidal, creador de escuela: El Centro de Estudios Históricos," in *¡Alça la voz pregonero!: Homenaje a Don Ramón Menéndez Pidal* (Madrid: Corporación de Antiguos Alumnos de la Institución Libre de Enseñanza y Cátedra-Seminario Menéndez Pidal, 1979), 43–79; and Javier Varela, "La tradición y el paisaje: El Centro de Estudios Históricos," in José Luis García Delgado, ed., *Los orígenes culturales de la II República* (Madrid: Siglo XXI, 1993), 237–74.

[79] From the introductory brochure prepared by Alberto Jímenez Fraud, quoted in Luis García de Valdeavellano, "La 'Residencia de Estudiantes' y su obra," *RE* 23, no. 243 (1976): 57.

[80] Pedro Sainz Rodríguez, *Testimonios y recuerdos* (Barcelona: Editorial Planeta, 1978), 34.

An experimental secondary school chartered to test new methods for application in other institutos and to train prospective catedráticos in modern pedagogy, the Instituto-Escuela provided "education" as well as "instruction" leading to the bachillerato. In organization and methods it approximated the milieu of the Institución: self-discipline, industry, and moral development were encouraged through active methods, small classes, games, and excursions; textbooks, annual examinations, and competition were banned. It soon proved necessary to add a primary school to prepare prospective students adequately for the independence and rigor of the secondary program. Attended by the children of many of Spain's progressive elites, the Instituto-Escuela became another center of irradiation of the democratic "European" cultural alternative long associated with the ILE.[81]

By 1923 the original strategy of Giner de los Ríos—to train a new cultural elite capable of redirecting Spanish political and social life— appeared to have been at least partially justified. The institucionistas had been remarkably successful in capturing the strategic heights of the expanded central administration, at least during periods of Liberal rule. Their dominance was uninterrupted in the Museo Pedagógico and its publications and subsidiaries, and was substantial, although not uncontested, in the various organisms sponsored by the Junta and the Escuela de Estudios Superiores del Magisterio, whose students had graduated to influential positions in the inspection corps and the normal schools. Their successful appropriation of the mantle of scientific objectivity and modernity gave them an advantage over their conservative Catholic rivals in setting the tone and terms of discourse on educational policy. In 1922 their hegemony was further consolidated with the appearance of a new professional journal, the *Revista de Pedagogía*, edited and published by Lorenzo Luzuriaga, a former student and teacher in the Institución and a close collaborator of Cossío in the Museo Pedagógico. Through the *Revista* (which was published continuously until 1936) a whole generation of maestros absorbed the principles of democratic, child-centered, active pedagogy.[82]

The Catholic rivals of the institucionistas accused them of unfairly

[81] See Junta para Ampliación de Estudios e Investigaciones Científicas, *Un ensayo pedagógico: El Instituto-Escuela de segunda enseñanza de Madrid: (Organización, métodos, resultados)* (Madrid, 1925); J. Rogelio Sánchez, "El Instituto-Escuela," *RSE* 3, no. 17 (1925): 511–16; Palacios Bañuelos, *Instituto-Escuela*; and for a negative view, Luis Hernández y González [Eloy Luis-André], *El espíritu nuevo en la educación: Un informe y un voto sobre el Instituto Escuela. Reformas urgentes en la segunda enseñanza* (Madrid: Sucesores de Rivadeneyra, 1926).

[82] See Eloisa Mérida-Nicolich, *Una alternativa de reforma pedagógica: "La Revista de Pedagogía" (1922–1936)* (Pamplona: Ediciones Universidad de Navarra, 1983).

taking over the inspection corps and normal schools "with bribery and monopoly . . . with all the rules of the centralizing, liberal and bureaucratic art, and with the cunning and tenacity of sectarians."[83] But this was a distortion of reality. Catholic points of view were always well represented in the Junta, the Council of Public Instruction, and the faculty of the Escuela de Estudios Superiores del Magisterio. If the ideals and methods of the Institución were increasingly dominant, it was owing to their association with a modern, progressive political and cultural agenda that grew in strength as the parliamentary regime plunged further into crisis. Those hoping to save the monarchy by modernizing it, as well as those hoping to replace it, viewed the new pedagogy as a potential instrument of defense or attack.

On the other hand, at the local level the impact of the Institución was still barely perceptible in 1923. The capture of the strategic heights could not produce the cultural transformation envisioned by the institucionistas as long as the financial and political resources of the Spanish state remained as scarce as they were under the parliamentary monarchy and as long as the social and economic development of the nation limited the audience for educational reform. Educating an elite could produce a new political class willing to change the direction of the Spanish state, but it could not produce the broad cultural transformation necessary to support it.

In any event, the clerical right was determined to prevent the institucionistas from monopolizing pedagogic discourse. In response to the growing professionalism of primary teachers, the expansion of the state educational bureaucracy, and the visible presence of the ILE within it, Catholic conservatives, led by the religious orders, launched a pedagogic counteroffensive designed to mold a Catholic elite capable of defending the nation against decadent "foreign" ideas.[84] In 1902 the Jesuits launched *Razón y Fé*, a journal conceived as a Catholic alternative to the *Boletín* of the ILE. That same year the Catholic Congress held in Santiago de Compostela focused exclusively on educational issues, particularly the secularizing and centralizing decrees of the conde de Romanones. The Sociedad Española de Pedagogía, founded in 1906 by collaborators of the conservative Catholic professional periodical, *El Magisterio Español*, encouraged pedagogic innovation that aimed at harmonizing "active" methods and Catholic values. Father Manjón's Escuelas del Ave María became the prototype for this allegedly modern-

[83] Andrés Manjón, *Hojas históricas del Ave María* (Granada: Escuela del Ave María, 1915), 43. See also Hernández y González, *Espíritu nuevo*.

[84] See the comments of Rufino Blanco y Sánchez, *Bibliografía pedagógica de obras escritas en castellano o traducidas a este idioma* (Madrid: Tip. de la Revista de Archivos, Bibliotecas y Museos, 1907–12), 1:lxvi.

ized Catholic pedagogy, while Manjón himself became an outspoken critic of secular education, whether public or private.[85] Among his best-known followers was the Catholic philanthropist Manuel Siurot, who, along with archbishop of Huelva, founded the Escuelas del Sagrado Corazón de Jesús in 1907. By 1916 Siurot was promoting Manjonian methods through a nationally circulated journal, *Cada Maestrito*, and had started a teachers' training college.[86]

Believing that isolated individual initiatives alone could not combat the growing influence of the ILE, in 1910 another disciple of Manjón, Father Pedro Poveda, proposed an Institución Católica de Enseñanza to coordinate and promote Catholic schooling. This was followed by other analogs to the Institución Libre and its subsidiaries—a teacher training academy in Gijón in 1911, and in 1914, a Catholic residence for students studying at the Escuela de Estudios Superiores del Magisterio in Madrid. Poveda's most enduring foundation, however, was the Institución Teresiana, established in Jaén in 1911. Lay sisters dedicated to higher education for women within a Catholic context, the Teresians established secondary schools and university residences that set a high standard of academic excellence that was disseminated throughout the peninsula by Poveda's journal, *Academia Teresiana*.[87] As the Catholic right tried to match the pace set by the ILE, the volume of pedagogical literature mounted; by 1909 the Catholic bibliographer Rufino Blanco could count 1,154 new titles published or translated into Spanish since the turn of the century, more than double the number published in the previous decade.[88]

Like their progressive rivals, Catholic educational activists alternated between opposition to and manipulation of the liberal state. As the parliamentary regime entered into crisis, beset by the social and economic tensions that it proved incapable of moderating or resolving, its weakness was both a temptation and a frustration for reformers seeking to transform Spanish society and culture through education. On the one hand, the reticence of the state to establish a hegemonic discourse on national values and identity allowed its challengers a free field in which

[85] See Turin, *Educación*, 287–88.

[86] Manuel Siurot, *Cada maestrito: Observaciones pedagógicas de uno que no ha visto en su vida un libro de pedagogía* (Seville: El Correo de Andalucía, 1912).

[87] See Pedro Poveda Castroverde, *Itinerario pedagógico* (Madrid: Consejo Superior de Investigaciones Científicas, Instituto de Pedagogía Aldus, 1964).

[88] Blanco y Sánchez, *Bibliografía pedagógica* 1:xiii. This figure underrepresents the reality, because Blanco included books in Castilian dealing only with pedagogical theory and methods, thereby excluding the sizable bibliography in Catalan and the huge corpus of textbooks, programs, legislative compilations, policy treatises, and so on. On the other hand, the bibliography included books published in the Americas, which generally did not circulate widely in Spain.

to promote their rival visions of national regeneration. On the other, the crisis of the parliamentary regime, which intensified after 1917, exposed the perils of unmediated ideological conflict for the social order and strengthened the resolve of both right and left to reform the state in order to enlist its resources in the battle for social and ideological dominance.

CHAPTER 3

History Invented: History Education and the Liberal State

> The History of Spain is of lively interest and
> great utility for us, because it informs us, along
> with the glorious deeds of our fathers, about the
> character, ideas, institutions, customs and all the
> social elements of our pueblo; and therefore the
> study of national history constitutes a patriotic
> duty for the citizen at both the primary and
> secondary level of instruction.
> (*Alfonso Moreno Espinosa*)[1]

WHAT CRITICS unanimously deplored about the Restoration system was its divorce from the pueblo, or nation. The fault lay as much with the pueblo as with the state: in an age of mass politics, Spain lacked a "people," or at least a self-aware, vital people capable of creating a state in its own image. Critics also agreed that cultural renewal, by awakening the nation to its own destiny and infusing it with moral and intellectual vigor, could overcome the national crisis. Where the critics parted company was in their definition of "the nation," the causes of its decadence, and the political solution to its ills.

The political elites who controlled the Restoration system of course denied the existence of a state/nation dichotomy; it was no coincidence that in its 1884 edition of the Dictionary of the Castilian Language, the Royal Academy officially conflated the two concepts for the first time.[2] In their view, the liberal monarchy was the culmination of the historical

---

* The titles of this chapter and of chapters 5 and 6 have been borrowed from Bernard Lewis, *History Remembered, Recovered, Invented* (Princeton: Princeton University Press, 1975).

[1] Alfonso Moreno Espinosa, *Compendio de historia de España distribuído en lecciones y adaptado a la índole y extensión de esta asignatura en la segunda enseñanza*, 12th ed., rev. (Barcelona: Tip. el Anuario de la Exportación, 1912), 16.

[2] Lluis García i Sevilla, "Lengua, nació i estat al diccionari de la Real Academia Espanyola," *L'Avenç* 16 (May 1979): 50–55. The dictionary defined *nation* as "a State or political body which recognizes a supreme center of common government" and "the territory constituted by that state and its individual inhabitants considered as a whole."

development of the nation and, thus, the embodiment of national sovereignty. This defense was perfected in the opening years of the Restoration by its architect, Antonio Cánovas del Castillo, but its roots lay earlier in the century, when conservative critics of the progressive constitution of 1837 had introduced the concept of an "internal constitution" whose fundamental principles set the natural limits of constitutional legitimacy. In contrast to voluntaristic, majoritarian conceptions of popular sovereignty, like Rousseau's "general will" or Renan's "daily plebiscite," which might or might not at any given moment faithfully reflect the "true" spirit of the nation, Cánovas invoked a more enduring national will whose essential spirit and mission were visible in the institutions through which the nation had organized itself over time. Because the oldest historical expressions of the internal constitution of the Spanish nation were the monarchy and the Cortes, it followed that their investment as co-sovereigns in the Constitution of 1876 was the greatest proof of that document's legitimacy and viability.[3]

This appeal to history allowed Cánovas to dismiss alternative proposals for political organization as utopian or illegitimate: "A nation may very well wish to be what it is not, but the change or transformation does not depend on its own pleasure, just as it not under the control of the ugly man to be handsome."[4] This reproof was aimed not only at republicans but also at traditionalists who, unrealistically in his view, wished to restore the absolute monarchy. Absolutism had been rendered obsolete by history, whereas politics was the art of the possible. In 1876, historical possibility pointed exclusively to the constitutional monarchy.

But Cánovas's resort to history to define the internal constitution, which lent a fictive empirical base to an essentially a priori definition of "the nation," opened a Pandora's box that was not easily closed. Legitimating the Restoration monarchy by claiming that it was the necessary outcome of national historical development encouraged oppositional political groups to invoke alternative historicist theses. As the stability of the Restoration settlement gave way to class and regional conflict,

---

[3] See Luis Sánchez Agesta, *Historia del constitucionalismo español (1808–1936)*, 4th ed., rev. (Madrid: Centro de Estudios Constitucionales, 1984), 181–91, 311–14; Richard A. H. Robinson, "Political Conservatism: The Spanish Case, 1875–1977," *Journal of Contemporary History* 14, no. 4 (1979): 567–71; and Andrés de Blas Guerrero, *Sobre el nacionalismo español* (Madrid: Centro de Estudios Constitucionales, 1989), 32–34. For a critique of Cánovas's position, see José Luis López-Aranguren, *Moral y sociedad: Introducción a la moral social española del siglo XIX*, 2d ed. (Madrid: EDICUSA, 1966), 165–68.

[4] Antonio Cánovas del Castillo, *Problemas contemporáneos* (1884), quoted in Sánchez Agesta, *Historia del constitucionalismo*, 313.

Cánovas's assertion that the political system engendered in 1876 reflected the "historical principles" and "secular facts" of national existence was challenged from the right by those who argued that the parliamentary monarchy represented a betrayal of the national past and from the left by those who argued that it was based on a misreading of it.[5] By the turn of the century—and especially after the defeat of 1898—there was a quickening of interest in historical studies and in the teaching of history to the nation's youth, cultural activities whose political implications were clearly visible to all parties in the national debate.

In a contest of ideologies aimed at mobilizing the literate middle-class public, the liberal state in Spain was ultimately the loser, not because it rested on a fiction, but because it declined to promote that fiction aggressively, in the end fearing the consequences of political mobilization more than the cultural offensive mounted by its enemies. Having refused to engage its opponents in the struggle for the hearts and minds of the middle-class young, the liberal state would be left without defenders when General Primo de Rivera rose against it in 1923.

With the definition of the "nation" and its relationship to the state at the center of the contested ideological ground, national history was inevitably the subject of vigorous intellectual and pedagogical debate. The development of history, especially national history, as a scholarly discipline and as a school subject, was a generalized phenomenon that accompanied the formation and consolidation of the liberal state in nineteenth-century Europe. The newly ascendant classes required an interpretation of the national past to legitimate and celebrate their access to power, as well as a shared set of myths and cultural values to unite citizens to the new nation-states in common bonds of empathy and pride. National history provided a justification for the new order of things—in the words of Josep Fontana, "a genealogy of the present"[6]—that explained the inevitable historical process by which the liberal state and its new ruling class had come into being and defined their historical mission. As the century progressed, political democratization and international rivalries expanded the functional role of national history. With the introduction of universal public schooling, history became an important part of state curricula, charged with helping to create an "imagined community" of citizens often hitherto separated by language, ethnicity, or regional loyalties. By cultivating belief in a common history and identity, democratizing political systems were able to blunt desta-

---

[5] Cánovas del Castillo, quoted in Sánchez Agesta, *Historia del constitucionalismo*, 311.
[6] Josep Fontana, *Historia: Análisis del pasado y proyecto social* (Barcelona: Editorial Crítica, 1982), 9.

bilizing social and political forces and to strengthen sentimental attachments to the nation-state.[7]

The liberal revolution in Spain only partially followed this pattern. To be sure, the middle decades of the nineteenth century saw the appearance of a new historiography, whose purpose was to legitimate and celebrate the recent victory of the liberal state over the forces of the old regime and to create a civic consciousness of the contours of the "Spanish" nation and identity. The most typical product of this historiography was the national narrative, or "general history of Spain." As José-María Jover has pointed out, the general history was "a kind of secularized Bible, the national book par excellence, called to occupy a preferential place in the offices and libraries of the upper and middle classes."[8] By far the most influential of this genre was the thirty-volume *Historia general de España desde los tiempos más remotos hasta nuestros días*, published between 1850 and 1867 by the former priest, Progressive politician, and journalist, Modesto Lafuente.[9] Lafuente's history was "one of the most read books during the second half of the nineteenth century and in the first years of this one." Its success inspired a host of imitations and rebuttals in the years following its initial publication, but its hegemony remained undiminished until the emergence of

---

[7] On the rise of history and its incorporation into the school curriculum in the nineteenth-century, see inter alia, George Peabody Gooch, *History and Its Historians in the Nineteenth Century* (Boston: Beacon Press, 1959); Eric Hobsbawm, *Nations and Nationalism since 1780: Programme, Myth, Reality* (New York: Cambridge University Press, 1990); and with Terence Ranger, *The Invention of Tradition* (Cambridge: Past and Present Publications, 1984); Bernard Lewis, *History Remembered, Recovered, Invented* (Princeton: Princeton University Press, 1975); Marc Ferro, *The Use and Abuse of History, or How the Past Is Taught* (Boston: Routledge and Kegan Paul, 1984); Eugen Weber, *Peasants into Frenchmen: The Modernization of Rural France, 1870–1914* (Stanford, Calif.: Stanford University Press, 1976); John Breuilly, *Nationalism and the State* (Manchester: Manchester University Press, 1982); Jacqueline Freyssinet-Dominjon, *Les Manuels de l'histoire de l'école libre, 1882–1959: De la loi Ferry à la loi Debré* (Paris: Armand Colin, 1969); Victor G. Kiernan, "Class and Ideology: The Bourgeoisie and Its Historians," *History of European Ideas* 6, no. 3 (1985): 267–86; Fontana, *Historia*; Francisco Murillo Ferrol, *Estudios de sociología política* (Madrid: Tecnos, 1963); and Benedict Anderson, *Imagined Communities: Reflections on the Origins and Spread of Nationalism* (London: Verso, 1983). More generally on the growth of nationalism, see Ernest Gellner, *Nations and Nationalism* (Ithaca: Cornell University Press, 1983); Anthony D. Smith, *National Identity* (Reno: University of Nevada Press, 1991); Pierre Nora, ed., *Les Lieux de mémoire*, vol. 2, *La Nation* (Paris: Gallimard, 1986); and Liah Greenfeld, *Nationalism: Five Roads to Modernity* (Cambridge: Harvard University Press, 1992).

[8] José-María Jover Zamora, "Caracteres del nacionalismo español, 1854–1874," *Zona Abierta* 31 (1984): 8. See also his *La civilización española a mediados del siglo XIX* (Madrid: Espasa-Calpe, 1991), 140–91.

[9] Modesto Lafuente, *Historia general de España, desde los tiempos más remotos hasta nuestros días*, 30 vols. (Madrid: Establecimiento Tipográfico de Mellado, 1850–67).

professional, archivally based histories at the end of the century. The publication in 1890 of the multivolume *Historia general de España*, edited by Cánovas del Castillo under the aegis of the Royal Academy of History and composed of contributions from leading specialists in each period, signaled the passing of an era.[10]

The outpouring of "general histories of Spain" in the 1850s and 1860s was not completely novel, for it had been preceded by a similar wave of enthusiasm for national history among the enlightened public in the eighteenth century.[11] Like their predecessors, the new national histories were written by Spaniards; "a Spanish book, for Spain," the young Cánovas del Castillo called his *Historia de la decadencia de España* when it appeared in 1854.[12] Since the publication of Father Juan de Mariana's *Historia general de España* in 1605, many of the most authoritative histories of Spain had been published by foreigners, some of them highly critical of Spanish institutions and values; indigenous products, on the other hand, had been marred by the inclusion of fabulous legends and impossible deeds. The histories published during the years of Moderado and Liberal Union rule aimed at rescuing the Spanish past from foreign contempt and domestic mythmaking. While acknowledging the evils associated with the so-called Black Legend, liberal historians hastened to vindicate the Spanish past by documenting Spanish preeminence on the world-historical stage and by unearthing historical antecedents for the liberal revolution so recently achieved. In this way they meant not only to justify and purify the past, but also to legitimate their claims for a place among the great nation-states of Europe.

Many eighteenth-century historians were clerics, but the new Spanish historians were typically liberal lawyers, politicians, and journalists

[10] Ciriaco Pérez Bustamante, *Primer centenario de la muerte de Don Modesto Lafuente: Discurso leído en la junta solemne conmemorativo del 29 de enero de 1967* (Madrid: Imprenta y Editorial Maestre, 1967), 7. See also Manuel Moreno Alonso, *Historiografía romántica española: Introducción al estudio de la historia en el siglo XIX* (Seville: Servicio de Publicaciones de la Universidad, 1979); Jover Zamora, "Caracteres"; Paloma Cirujano Marín et al., *Historiografía y nacionalismo español, 1834–1868* (Madrid: Consejo Superior de Investigaciones Científicas, Centro de Estudios Históricos, 1985); Alfonso Orti, "Regeneracionismo e historiografía: El mito del carácter nacional en la obra de Rafael Altamira," and Juan Sisinio Pérez Garzón, "El nacionalismo historiográfico: Herencia del siglo XIX y dato precedente de la obra de R. Altamira," both in Armando Alberola, ed., *Estudios sobre Rafael Altamira* (Alicante: Instituto de Estudios "Juan Gil-Albert," Caja de Ahorros Provincial de Alicante, 1988), 275–368.

[11] Richard Herr, *The Eighteenth-Century Revolution in Spain* (Princeton: Princeton University Press, 1958), 337–47.

[12] Antonio Cánovas del Castillo, *Historia de la decadencia de España desde el advenimiento de Felipe III al trono hasta la muerte de Carlos II*, 2d ed. (Madrid: Librería de Gutenberg de José Ruiz, 1910), 3.

whose approach to the discipline was more political and patriotic than professional. This orientation was evident in the composition of the Royal Academy of History, a creation of the Spanish Enlightenment that was reorganized in 1847. Throughout the nineteenth century the thirty-six "numerary" members, as well as the far larger number of corresponding members in Spain and abroad, were primarily "patrons, collectors, bibliophiles, scholars, litterateurs, and amateurs" (including twelve prime ministers), drawn from the traditional elites. Under the Constitution of 1876, the Academy was represented in the Senate by a member elected from among its senior ranks. Although the emergence of history as an academic discipline was registered by the creation of the Escuela Superior Diplomática in 1856 and the chairs of Spanish history in the Faculties of Law and Philosophy and Letters in the Ley Moyano of 1857, professional historians did not comprise the majority of the membership until after 1900.[13]

Historical production in the nineteenth century rested on an eclectic methodology derived from Enlightenment philosophy, Romantic idealism, and empiricism.[14] The excavation and publication of original documents and greater attention to corroborative detail bolstered the conclusions of liberal historians locked in ideological combat with their Catholic rivals. Historical substantiation of liberal political claims was important because Catholic traditionalists condemned liberal institutions and values precisely on the grounds that they were "un-Spanish"—that is, foreign to the Spanish historical tradition. For traditionalists, liberals were not merely utopian schemers wedded to abstract and impractical theories, they were traitors to the unalterable elements of the internal constitution—Catholic unity, divine right monarchy, and customary local rights. In contrast to the new liberal historiography, Catholic historiography relied less on recourse to the "facts" of historical development than on invocations of divine and natural law.[15] To liberal arguments that the historical evolution of the nation demanded a reconfiguration of the state, traditionalists replied that the historical path down which the nation had been led by the state since the eighteenth century constituted a lamentable departure from both providential design and national identity.

[13] Antonio Rumeu de Armas, "Real Academia de la Historia," in *Las Reales Academias del Instituto de España* (Madrid: Alianza, 1992), 105–69. The RAH was founded in 1735 and awarded royal patronage three years later.

[14] Paloma Cirujano Marín, "Aproximación sociológica al panorama historiográfico español, 1844–1874," in *Estudios de historia social: Homenaje a Manuel Tuñón de Lara* (Madrid: Universidad Internacional Menéndez Pelayo, 1981), 2:697–711; Moreno Alonso, *Historiografía romántica*, 459–81.

[15] Andrés Ollero Tassara, *Universidad y política: Tradición y secularización en el siglo XIX español* (Madrid: Instituto de Estudios Políticos, 1972).

To be sure, there was a strong streak of apriority in liberal historiography as well, nowhere more evident than in its identification of an unchanging "Spanish" national character evident since prehistoric times. Liberal historians derived the alleged elements of this national character from the same sources mined by the traditionalists—the historical literature of the Habsburg era, much of which had been reissued in the eighteenth century to meet the demand for history among the new reading public. Reflecting the international rivalries and prejudices of the age of Spanish imperial power, as well as the essentially conservative character of Moderado liberalism, the identities and counteridentities alleged to be typically "Spanish" embodied values that were fundamentally aristocratic and premodern. Lafuente, subsequently the source for countless other historians, included among the innate characteristics that Spaniards had inherited from their "Celtiberian" ancestors "bravery, . . . the tendency toward isolation, the conservative instinct and attachment to the past, confidence in their God and love of their religion, constancy in disaster and suffering in misfortunes, bravado, indiscipline, the daughter of pride and of the high opinion of oneself, that kind of arrogance that, although it sometimes benefits collective independence, too often impairs it because it leads too often to individual independence, a fertile seed of heroic and fearless acts, . . . sobriety and temperance, which lead to dislike of work.[16] This archetypical national identity was for liberals both normative and cautionary—a source of national unity, but also potentially hazardous to political and social integration. In the historical trajectory of the nation, however, it was the bond "that eventually united the inhabitants of Spanish soil in a single great family, governed by a single scepter, under a single religion and a single faith."[17]

As José María Jover has pointed out, the nationalist historiography produced by the dominant Moderados was essentially retrospective and conservative; it invoked the national past from a position of "arrival," of general satisfaction with present arrangements.[18] Led by Lafuente, it represented Spanish history as a teleological journey toward territorial, political, and religious unity whose culmination was the constitutional monarchy of the Isabelline era.[19] Consequently, it privileged those periods when progress toward state consolidation had been greatest: the Visigothic monarchy of the sixth century; the seven-century Reconquest of the peninsula from the Moors; the reign of the Catholic Kings, whose

[16] Lafuente, *Historia general* 1:12.

[17] Ibid. 1:11.

[18] Jover, *Civilización*, 165–69.

[19] Jover, "Caracteres," 12. See Jocelyn N. Hillgarth, "Spanish Historiography and Iberian Reality," *History and Theory* 24, no. 1 (1985): 23–43, on the "quest for unity" as an enduring theme in Spanish historiography.

marriage in 1469 had reunited the fragmented peninsular principalities; the reigns of the first Habsburgs, who centralized the monarchy and defended religious unity; and the "War of Independence" against Napoleon in 1808, which had expelled the foreign invader and produced the liberal Constitution of 1812.[20] At the same time, it emphasized the continuities between the present and the past by valorizing the historical persistence of the underlying principles of Spanish nationhood, especially the unitary monarchy. That is, Moderado historians legitimated the constitutional monarchy not by dramatizing its differences from the old order, but rather its affinities with it.

Although inspired by the Romantic liberal historiography of contemporary Europe, Spanish liberal historiography departed from it in its limited enthusiasm for "the people" as historical protagonists and in its lack of a national project. The antidemocratic orientation of Moderado liberalism and its indifference to expansionism and imperialism drew fire from progressives, who responded with their own interpretation of the national past. As champions of the democratic rights of the pueblo, progressives exalted the Middle Ages, when municipal liberties (fueros), religious tolerance, and representative assemblies made Spain the cradle of democracy and popular sovereignty. Conversely, they regarded the accession of the absolutist Habsburg dynasty in 1516 as a deviation from Spain's natural historical trajectory, a deviation that had led to religious fanaticism, cultural isolation, and political absolutism. Progressives also expanded the concept of the nation and its mission to include Portugal (sometimes within an Iberian federation) and rejected the Moderado definition of the Isabelline and Restoration monarchies as the expression of the national will.[21]

The Spanish liberal state also deviated from the European pattern by failing to convert instruction in national history into an effective instrument of political socialization and national integration. After 1870 in France, national history occupied an increasingly large place in the schools; both secondary and primary students studied history every year, and what they learned was subject to rigorous state surveillance.[22] In Germany both classical and modern schools revised their curricula in the 1890s to emphasize the history of the Germans and, especially, of the Prussian state, in response to an exhortation from the emperor to "raise young Germans, not young Greeks and Romans."[23] Similarly, a

---

[20] See José Álvarez Junco, "La invención de la Guerra de la Independencia," *Studia Histórica: Historia contemporánea* 12 (1994): 75–100.

[21] Jover, *Civilización*, 171–91.

[22] Before 1880 the French Commission of Public Instruction published lists of approved texts; after 1880, it published lists of proscribed books.

[23] James C. Albisetti, *Secondary School Reform in Imperial Germany* (Princeton: Prince-

special Committee of Seven of the American Historical Association in 1896 recommended four years of history study to prepare the student "for a comprehension of the political and social problems that will confront him in everyday life, . . . for social adaptation and for forceful participation in civic activities."[24]

The new enthusiasm for instruction in national history was a startling departure from previous practice. Until the last quarter of the nineteenth century, students receiving a secondary education learned ancient history as an adjunct to the classics, in deference to Cicero's dictum that "History is the mother of morality" (alternatively, he calls it the *magister vitae*).[25] By providing uplifting examples of heroism, virtue, and statesmanship, history built individual character and provided a guide to personal conduct. A secondary advantage of studying history was thought to be its utility in cultivating the powers of memory, through daily recitations of Latin tags, chronologies, dynastic successions, and noteworthy events.[26] To these acknowledged benefits to the individual, the nation-states of the West now added the *social* task of instilling national consciousness and patriotic allegiance in citizens who might be called upon to defend the nation against its enemies, foreign and domestic.

Early in the century, Spanish liberals had seen history education as an essential element in the nation-building process. As the royal academician José Zaragoza explained in 1852, "since kings are no longer the

---

ton University Press, 1982), 140. See also Ministerio de Fomento, Dirección General de Instrucción Pública, *Boletín Oficial: Reforma de la Segunda Enseñanza* 2, no. 3 (1894): 369–483; Freyssinet-Dominjon, *Manuels d'histoire*; Frédéric Tourneur, "L'Enseignement historique a l'étranger, principalement en Alemagne," in Charles Seignebos et al., *L'Enseignement de l'histoire: (Conférences du Musée Pédagogique, 1907)* (Paris: Imprimerie Nationale, 1907), 79–115; and Ricardo Becerro de Bengoa, *La enseñanza en el siglo XX* (Madrid: Edmundo Capdeville, Librero, 1900), 68–69.

[24] American Historical Association, Committee of Seven, *The Study of History in the Schools: Report to the American Historical Association* (New York: Macmillan, 1899), 18. According to the bibliographer Rufino Blanco y Sánchez, the report of the Committee of Seven was translated into Spanish in 1904 as *El estudio de la historia en las escuelas: Informe a la Asociación Americana de Historia por La Comisión de los Siete*, trans. Edgar C. Courtaux (Buenos Aires: Taller Tipográfico de la Penitenciaría Nacional, 1904). See Blanco y Sánchez, *Bibliografía pedagógica de obras escritas en castellano o traducidas a este idioma*, 5 vols. (Madrid: Tip. de la Revista de Archivos, Bibliotecas y Museos, 1907–12) 2:141–44. The citation includes the entire table of contents and an excerpt from the text of the report.

[25] See Antonio Viñao Frago, *Política y educación en los orígenes de la España contemporánea: Examen especial de sus relaciones en la enseñanza secundaria* (Madrid: Siglo XXI, 1982).

[26] See the pedagogical treatise by the baron de Bielfeld, *Curso completo de erudición universal o análisis abreviado de todas las ciencias buenas, artes y bellas letras* (Madrid, 1803), quoted in Moreno Alonso, *Historiografía romántica*, 273.

only arbiters of the nations, since the people have also aspired to be absolute, history should be written for everyone, because everyone has to learn from it."[27] National history was introduced as a required subject in the secondary curriculum as early as 1836, when a Progressive minister, the duque de Rivas, proposed two years of geography and two years of Spanish history, followed by two years of "universal" history in a reform plan that fell victim to the political instability of those years.[28] The following year geography and national history became part of the required course of study in the Central Normal School in Madrid and in 1843, in all the provincial normal schools in the peninsula.[29] With the Pidal plan of 1845 geography and Spanish history were definitively incorporated into the plan of studies at both the secondary and the university levels. "It is shameful that there are people from the distinguished classes of society who do not know what this society has been and how it was formed," observed Antonio Gil de Zárate, one of the chief architects of the secondary school system.[30]

But as the Moderados consolidated their power, the amount of required history and geography shrank, along with the rest of the course of studies. By 1880 the secondary curriculum allotted just a single year of classes meeting three days a week in which to cover the entire span of Spanish history, with all of "universal" (actually, European) history covered the following year.[31] Despite several short-lived attempts by progressive reformers in the 1890s to expand the number of hours or enhance the "educational" value of history in the secondary curriculum, the dynastic parties' fundamental resistance to popular mobilization and the traditional pressures to minimize the scope and duration of the bachillerato prevailed. After the wave of regenerationist tinkering with

[27] José Zaragoza, *Discursos leídos en la Real Academia de la Historia, el 12 de abril de 1852* (Madrid, 1852), quoted in Cirujano Marín, *Historiografía*, 33

[28] See Manuel Utande Igualada, ed., *Planes de estudio de enseñanza media* (Madrid: Ministerio de Educación Nacional, Dirección General de Enseñanza Media, 1964). For geography as a nation-building discipline, see Horacio Capel et al., *Ciencia para la burguesía: Renovación pedagógica y enseñanza de la geografía en la revolución liberal española, 1814–1857* (Barcelona: Universitat, 1983).

[29] María del Mar del Pozo Andrés, *Guadalajara en la historia del magisterio español, 1839/1939: Cien años de formación del profesorado* (Alcalá de Henares: Universidad, 1986).

[30] Quoted in Moreno Alonso, *Historiografía romántica*, 271.

[31] The Moyano Law of 1857 prescribed two years of geography and history combined, taught on alternate days of the week. Two subsequent modifications of the curriculum separated the two subjects and required one year of each. The Orovio plan of 1866 specified a year of geography and world history combined, followed by a year of Spanish history. The 1880 plan of Fermín Lasala ordered them sequentially, over the first three years of the program, with Spanish history preceding universal history. Utande, *Planes*, passim.

the curriculum receded, the bachillerato of 1903 once again required only one year each of geography, national history, and universal history.

History was not even mentioned in the elementary school curriculum mandated in the Ley Moyano, an omission that underscored the restricted definition of "the nation" under the Moderado order. To be sure, primers often included historical anecdotes or themes because of their "useful moral and educational lessons."[32] Civic-minded authors also produced simplified Spanish history textbooks for the elite private colegios and the upper primary schools.[33] Regenerationist concerns motivated the expansion of the primary school curriculum in 1901, which mandated "cyclical"—that is, yearly and comprehensive—instruction in national history and geography. For the reasons described earlier, however, primary instruction changed little in most schools, where history was taught in a haphazard fashion, if at all.

The essentially defensive political strategy of the dynastic parties also explains their lack of interest in promoting civic or national consciousness by regulating the content of history teaching and textbooks. What an individual child read about his country's history and identity was highly contingent upon the book assigned in the instituto in which he was examined. Even before the Liberals reinstated the "freedom to teach" in 1881, texts other than those on the official lists were in use in the institutos; afterward, the reality was one of the most absolute laissez-faire. A ministerial survey of secondary school textbooks in 1894 revealed that twenty-three different history texts were in use in the fifty-eight institutos nationwide. In over one-third of the institutos catedráticos had assigned history or geography textbooks written by themselves.[34] Only the state monopoly on exams acted as a brake on the number of books in use.

Given the centrality of the exams as instruments of ideological control, it is remarkable that the state did not exercise its authority to regulate their content. But disagreement over political and cultural goals frustrated repeated attempts by both neo-Catholic and left-Liberal ministers to write standardized syllabi or to review textbooks. Thus, a few of the books in the 1894 survey had been submitted for review twenty

---

[32] Article 29 of the Law of Primary Instruction of 2 June 1868, signed by the marqués de Orovio.

[33] A partial list from mid-century may be found in Moreno Alonso, *Historiografía romántica*, 259–62.

[34] AGMEC, leg. 6940; *Memoria sobre el estado del Instituto de Segunda Enseñanza de Lérida durante el año escolar de . . .* (1859–92); and *Memoria para la apertura del curso académico de . . . en el Instituto Provincial de Segunda Enseñanza de Barcelona* (1862–95). I am grateful to Stephen Jacobsen for collecting the data on textbooks used in Lérida and Barcelona.

years earlier; others had been evaluated by the Council of Public Instruction exclusively for purposes of the author's professional advancement; and still others had received no scrutiny whatsoever. As the director general of public instruction remarked in a position paper to the minister, "However fertile we might suppose the terrain to be and however careful the cultivation, where there is so much abundance, it is obvious that we must find a likely field for growing and propagating parasitic and poisonous plants."[35]

The total autonomy enjoyed by instituto catedráticos explains the two chief characteristics of secondary-school history textbooks under the parliamentary monarchy: their ideological diversity and their indifference to their audience. Without state guidelines as to content, length, or structure, the books reflected the professional priorities and political values of their authors, among whom were represented the entire range of political options. Nearly all textbooks were written by instituto or, occasionally, university catedráticos, who had earned licentiates in Philosophy and Letters at one of the regional universities and doctorates in Philosophy or Law at the Central University in Madrid. Founders of local atheneums and literary academies, correspondents of the Royal Academy of History and other scholarly associations, contributors to the press and to local antiquarian societies, they were sometimes also active in local or national politics as city council members, parliamentary deputies, or members of the Council of Public Instruction.[36]

Seven textbooks that long enjoyed popularity in the institutos exemplify the range of political views that young middle-class Spaniards might encounter.[37] At one end of the spectrum were the books by Felipe

[35] Exposition of 20 October 1894, reproduced in Ministerio de Fomento, *Boletín Oficial: Contestaciones de los rectores a las Reales Ordenes circulares de 19 y 20 de mayo de 1893, referentes a los libros de texto de los catedráticos* 2, no. 2 (1894): ii.

[36] The conclusions in this paragraph are based on data compiled from a variety of sources: the 1894 survey of textbooks in AGMEC, leg. 6940; seniority lists of catedráticos, such as *Escalafón de antigüedad de los catedráticos numerarios de los institutos generales y técnicos* (1908, 1923) and *Escalafón de los catedráticos numerarios de Institutos Nacionales de Segunda Enseñanza* (1934–36); *Guía oficial de España* (1873–1930); *Guía del estudiante, 1918–19* (Madrid: S.I., 1918); the card catalog of the Biblioteca Nacional in Madrid; and the textbooks themselves. See also Joaquín García Puchol, *Los textos escolares de historia en la enseñanza española (1808–1900): Análisis de su estructura y contenido* (Barcelona: Publicacions Universitat de Barcelona, 1993) for a useful inventory of nineteenth-century textbooks.

[37] The seven texts most frequently cited in the 1894 survey included Felipe Picatoste Rodríguez, *Compendio de historia de España* (Madrid: Librería de la Viuda de Hernando, 1884) (5th ed. 1892); Moreno Espinosa, *Compendio*; Félix Sánchez Casado, *Prontuario de historia de España y de la civilización española*, 16th ed. (Madrid: Lib. Hernando, 1896) (1st ed. 1867; last edition 1917); Eduardo Orodea e Ibarra, *Curso de lecciones de historia de España*, 6th ed. (Valladolid: Imp. y Lib. de Hijos de Rodríguez, 1875) (1st ed.

Picatoste, a radical journalist and civil servant with close ties to the republican Manuel Ruiz Zorrilla and, later, to the democratic wing of the Liberal party, and by Alfonso Moreno Espinosa, a "second-wave" Krausist republican active in Cadiz municipal politics and catedrático in the instituto there from 1867 until 1905. At the opposite end was the textbook by Felix Sánchez Casado, an antiliberal Catholic integrist who held the chair at the prestigious Instituto de San Isidro in Madrid until his death in 1896. Between these two extremes were those by Rufino Machiandiarena, a progressive sympathizer with the regional liberties and traditions of his native Basque country; Eduardo Orodea, a social Catholic at the instituto in Santander; Bernardo Monreal, a conservative Catholic teaching at the huge Instituto de Cardenal Cisneros in Madrid; and the more moderate Conservative Manuel Zabala Urdániz, first catedrático in Valencia and, then, successor to Sánchez Casado in Madrid.

Among this group, three textbooks commanded a national market. The manual by Moreno Espinosa, which went through twenty-two editions, was in use in thirteen of the fifty-eight institutos in 1894; the two-volume text by Zabala was read by thousands of students in Madrid and elsewhere until the 1930s. The slim volume by Picatoste was also widely adopted, probably because its publisher, Casa Hernando, dominated the national schoolbook market until the end of the century.[38] The other textbooks in the sample enjoyed regional popularity, reflecting the political, personal, or professional prestige of their authors among their colleagues in neighboring provinces.[39]

Despite the disparate political and ideological commitments of these widely read textbooks, they tended to conform to a standard type. The demands of the academic calendar, Spanish classroom culture, and the examination system dictated the internal structure of the texts, while the desire for political harmony curbed the impulse to editorialize. Furthermore, most catedráticos aimed at a "scientific" approach to their subject, which demanded the restraint of the authorial voice: the facts, once established, could speak for themselves, their meaning evident and

---

1867; 13 editions altogether); Rufino Machiandiarena, *Ensayo de historia de España* (San Sebastián: Imp. de Pozo, 1893) (1st ed. 1884); Bernardo Monreal y Ascaso, *Curso de historia de España*, 2d ed., rev. (Madrid: Aribau [Sucesores de Rivadeneyra], 1875) (1st ed. 1867; 5th ed. 1890); and Manuel Zabala Urdániz, *Compendio de historia de España*, 17th ed., rev., 2 vols. (Madrid: Imp. de Jaime Ratés Martín, 1922) (1st ed. 1883).

[38] Jean-François Botrel, *Libros, prensa y lectura en la España del siglo XIX*, trans. David Torra Ferrer (Madrid: Fundación Germán Sánchez Ruiperez, 1993), 385–470.

[39] For example, the manual by Rufino Machiandiarena, catedrático at San Sebastián, enjoyed considerable vogue in the institutos in northern and northwestern Spain; the text by Eduardo Orodea, catedrático in Santander, was adopted in several institutos in Old Castile.

unmediated by the biases of the writer. Finally, academic authors tended to paraphrase or even plagiarize (usually without attribution, although sometimes with quotation marks) the work of earlier historians when constructing their own narratives. Identical phrases and interpretations thus echoed through the pages of the most diverse texts.

Such borrowing was part of the display of erudition that was considered de rigueur among instituto catedráticos, who wrote their textbooks to impress their professional colleagues rather than to accommodate the interests and abilities of the twelve-year-old boys who felt obliged to purchase and read them in order to pass the exam. Two-thirds of Moreno Espinosa's massive tome, for example, was consumed by his 1,521 discursive footnotes; another strategy was to insert extended discussions of professional controversies in small print throughout the narrative. Inclusion of the apparatus of historical scholarship—footnotes, annotated bibliographies, primary sources, references to the "auxiliary sciences," such as numismatics, archaeology, paleography, and the like—increasingly counted for promotion in the eyes of the scholars on the Council of Public Instruction (or after 1901, in the Royal Academy of History) who reviewed the texts for "merit."[40]

The logorrhea that plagued the history texts was thus only a symptom of the much-lamented conceptualization of the bachillerato as a preliminary to university training rather than as an extension of the general education of the average citizen. The most widely adopted history text, by Moreno Espinosa, filled 531 densely printed pages, and the average length of the seven most frequently assigned history books in 1894 was 457 pages. Since the entire span of Spanish history had be to covered in a one-year class meeting three times a week, these lengthy, arid tomes were the despair of students "learning the book" in preparation for the annual exams.[41] It seems doubtful, however, that exam-oriented students read the books cover to cover. As if in recognition of this, authors usually subdivided their texts into sections and chapters (or "lessons"), and further into numbered "topics," and added chapter summaries to facilitate memorization (see plate 1).[42] Some authors also

[40] The Council was assigned the task of determining the merit of textbooks submitted by academic authors in an RD of 24 May 1895. Article 29 of the RD of 12 April 1901, and a subsequent RD of 28 February 1908 transferred this responsibility to the Royal Academy of History, which soon thereafter began publishing reports on submitted textbooks in its *Boletín* (*BRAH*).

[41] See the comments reproduced in Eduardo Benot, *Errores en materia de educación y de instrucción pública*, 4th ed. (Madrid: Librería de Hernando, 1899), 26–28.

[42] The average number of annual "lessons" was a bit more than fifty in the 1860s and around seventy under the 1880 degree plan (which left at least a month at the end of the academic year for review).

4. **Destierro de D. Alvaro.** — Nuevamente ex-
citados los nobles por la suprema autoridad que ejercía
D. Alvaro, mientras el rey se distraía en juegos y diver-
siones, formaron una gran coalición, que pidió al rey
separara del gobierno al condestable, a lo cual, aunque
mal de su grado, accedió el monarca en vista de la ac-
titud del rey de Aragón y del infante de Castilla D. Enrique.

Esto no obstante, concertado en breve el rey de Castilla con su favorito, dió lugar a una guerra civil, en la
que se declararon por los rebeldes el príncipe de Asturias y hasta las reinas de Castilla y Navarra, siendo si-
tiados el rey y D. Alvaro en *Medina del Campo*, de donde logró fugarse D. Alvaro, siendo respetado el rey, a
quien obligaron a decretar el destierro del favorito por
espacio de seis años.

5. **Guerra civil: combate de Olmedo.** — Esto
no obstante, como el rey no pudiera prescindir de su
favorito, origináronse nuevas discordias, que termina-
ron con un combate cerca de *Olmedo* (1445), en donde
D. Juan II y D. Alvaro derrotaron a sus enemigos, ha-
ciendo huir a sus Estados al rey de Navarra y a Calata-
yud al infante D. Enrique, en donde murió luego.

Esta victoria sirvió, como no podía menos, para que
el condestable ejerciera una gran influencia, de la que
se valió para concertar el segundo matrimonio del rey
con Doña Isabel de Portugal, matrimonio que fué el
principio de la decadencia del poder de D. Alvaro.

Las bodas se celebraron en Madrigal, pueblo de la provincia de Avila, a cuya ciudad confirmó Juan II el antiguo
privilegio del *Pote*, esto es, el patrón para las medidas de
áridos. La vasija de hierro o *pote*, se conserva aún en el
Ayuntamiento de Avila.

6. **Decadencia, prisión y muerte de D. Alvaro de Luna.** — Celosa la reina del influjo que sobre

el rey ejercía el condestable, inclinó el ánimo de su es-
poso en contra de D. Alvaro. Al mismo tiempo, los nobles, disgustados de la energía y crudeza con que el va-
lido los trataba, se coligaron contra él, y cuando Don
Alvaro se aprestaba a la lucha fué cercado en la casa
en donde paraba en Burgos y reducido a prisión me-
diante una cédula del monarca, en la que éste empeña-
ba su fe y palabra real de que no recibiría daño ni en
su persona ni en su hacienda. Procesado luego y sen-
tenciado a pena de muerte, D. Alvaro de Luna fué eje-
cutado en Valladolid el día 2 de Julio de 1453 (1).

Don Alvaro dícese que mostró una gran serenidad de
ánimo al subir al cadalso. Se arrodilló delante de un cru-
cifijo, y después de orar, como viera a un caballerizo del
príncipe D. Enrique, llamado Barrasa, le dijo: «Ven acá,
*Barrasa; tú ves la muerte que me dan; di, pues, al príncipe tu
señor, que dé mejor galardón a sus criados que el rey mi señor
mandó dar a mí.*»

Al año siguiente bajó al sepulcro el rey, sufriendo
el castigo de su inconsciencia para con D. Alvaro
(año 1454).

7. **Guerras contra los árabes.** — En tanto, acaecía
en Granada que, nuevamente destronado *Mohamed* por su
sobrino *Aben-Osmín* y levantándose contra éste *Aben-Ismail*
(otro sobrino de Mohamed) con auxilio de Castilla, se cro-
yó el primero en el caso de entretener a los suyos empe-
ñándolos en una guerra contra Castilla, aprovechándose de
las discordias que la dividían, talando las campiñas de
Huéscar, Galera, Castilleja y los Vélez, llegando hasta los
campos de Murcia, donde cerca de Lorca tuvo una comple-
ta derrota, que ocasionó la caída de Aben-Osmín, reempla-
zándole Aben-Ismail (año 1452), que agradecido al rey de
Castilla por los auxilios que le prestara, se reconoció su
vasallo y tributario.

(1) Puede consultarse, para estudiar debidamente la vida de D. Alvaro de
Luna, la obra siguiente: *Juicio crítico y significación política de D. Alvaro de Luna*,
por Nido y Ramírez, obra premiada por la Academia de la Historia.
  Don Alvaro había sido llevado a la corte por su tío D. Pedro de Luna, arzobis-
po de Toledo; sirvió de paje en la corte de Juan II, y entre ambos hubo siem-
pre gran amistad y confianza.

Plate 1. Pages 374 and 375 of volume 1 of Manuel Zabala Urdániz,
Compendio de historia de España, 17th ed., rev., 2 vols. (Madrid: Imp.
de Jaime Ratés Martín, 1922). This two-volume bachillerato textbook,
first published in 1883, was widely used in Spanish secondary schools
for more than forty years. The selection is taken from lesson 37, which
details the political history of the reign of Juan II of Castile (1406–54).
The lesson is divided into eight numbered subtopics. Facts of secondary
importance, bibliographic references, and anecdotal material are set in
small font or consigned to the footnotes.

distinguished between principal events and supporting detail and interpretation by printing the latter in small type. Despite these concessions
to credentialism, students and their parents nevertheless complained
strenuously about the length of the manuals and their excessive cost.

Partly to keep costs down, few illustrations and fewer maps interrupted the endless pages of text in most of these books. Four of the
seven in the sample group, including the highly regarded Moreno Espinosa, had none at all. The two-volume survey by Manuel Zabala contained only a few murky engravings and croquis of famous battles. Major exceptions to this rule were the relatively brief surveys by Sánchez

Casado and Picatoste, which were enlivened by engravings of historical tableaux, royal portraits, maps, and drawings and photographs of paintings, architecture, and material culture. It is easy to imagine the relative delight these books must have inspired, and equally easy to envision the dread with which young boys must have addressed the unrelieved texts of Moreno Espinosa or Zabala.

Perhaps in unacknowledged recognition of the limited appeal of these books, it was conventional to open the narrative by reciting the benefits to be derived from the study of the national past. Chief among these were patriotism and a sense of national identity. "The present is a consequence of the past and will in its turn give birth to the future. . . . He who is ignorant of the History of his patria, is a stranger in it," Zabala reminded his readers, and the warning was echoed by Picatoste: "No one loves what he does not know."[43] Not explicitly stated, but underlying all the texts, was also a "therapeutic" conception of national history as an antidote to negative stereotypes concocted by jealous or ignorant foreigners. The tone of these narratives was thus in places both boastful and defensive. Republicans in particular were acutely conscious of accusations that Spain had contributed little to human progress. "Spain is one of the peoples that has done most in the work of civilization and that has exercised the greatest influence in Universal History," Moreno Espinosa argued: "She placed her generous breast between the heart of Europe and the scimitar of the Arabs . . . ; completed the geographical and anthropological unity of the Globe with the discovery of America and Oceania; . . . and saved Europe from the Caesarism of Napoleon."[44] To validate Spain's "modernity," liberal and republican authors offered lists of "Spanish contributions to civilization" that invariably included constitutionalism, the development of the scientific method, and the creation of "the richest and most fertile" literature in Europe.[45]

Another reason offered for studying history was that it provided the key to national identity. In Spain, where obvious unities of language, "race," or ethnicity were lacking, it was only too easy to ask, "Where is the history of the Spaniards . . . ? upon seeing it disappear among the history of the Carthaginians, the Romans, the Goths, the Arabs, and the foreign dynasties."[46] One solution, to which all authors, following Lafuente, subscribed uncritically, was to point to the alleged fusion of the Celts and the Iberians in the central *meseta* to produce the "Celtiberian race"—a solution that had the additional advantage of prefiguring the

[43] Zabala, *Compendio* 1:24; Picatoste, *Historia*, 5. See also Moreno Espinosa, *Compendio*, 16.

[44] Moreno Espinosa, *Compendio*, 15.

[45] Picatoste, *Historia*, 273–74.

[46] Ibid., 7.

later leadership of Castile in the consolidation of the nation. The disadvantage was that pressing claims of racial or cultural purity in a peninsula with a long history of invasion and conquest was patently absurd. Thus, textbook authors made Spanish history itself the central element in the formation of the national character. National history and identity were inseparable; to be familiar with one was to define and comprehend the other. Invasion, conquest, domination, resistance, the struggle for unity against foreign and domestic enemies—these had shaped the national character. National identity was thus both immutable and historically determined. For Catholic authors, in particular, the persistence of national character was fundamental: "There is no other pueblo in the world whose national character has been conserved more tenaciously through the centuries," averred the neo-Catholic Sánchez Casado.[47]

Because their authors cribbed shamelessly from earlier historians, Restoration textbooks defined the elements of the Spanish national character in remarkably similar terms. Echoing Modesto Lafuente and the Golden Age historians from whom Lafuente had borrowed, they depicted the Spanish character in essentially aristocratic terms. "Arrogant, chivalrous, courageous to the point of heroism, and an unparalleled lover of his independence,"[48] the Spaniard was distinguished by his "ingenuity, typical of the Southern races; his boundless imagination . . . and the grandeur of his soul in misfortune."[49] Beneath the consensus lurked subtle differences of emphasis, however. Conservative Catholic authors celebrated the Spaniard's "religious sentiment, without which Spain would have ceased to be a nation" and his "genius of resistance," stressing his instinctive rejection of everything foreign.[50] Progressives, in contrast, viewed cultural pluralism as a constituent component of Spanish nationality itself; Spaniards were "a synthetic race, capable of adaptation, like no other, to all climates and all customs, and of assimilation of all ideas."[51] Whereas all authors agreed on Spanish disdain for manual labor and material prosperity, progressives regarded this as regrettable, while integrists interpreted disregard for material values as a laudable sign of preoccupation with "the kingdom of God."[52]

In theory, national character was essential to understanding the historical trajectory of the nation. The formal definition of history in Spanish textbooks varied only slightly from author to author: history was

[47] Sánchez Casado, *Prontuario*, 3.
[48] Zabala, *Compendio*, 29. See also Orodea, *Historia*, 13.
[49] Picatoste, *Historia*, 11.
[50] Sánchez Casado, *Prontuario*, 2, 3.
[51] Moreno Espinosa, *Compendio*, 33.
[52] Sánchez Casado, *Prontuario*, 357.

"the scientific narration of the deeds realized by free and intelligent human activity, developed with a tendency toward fulfillment of its destiny," or the "true and orderly exposition of the important deeds realized by the Spanish pueblo in all the periods of its life and in all the spheres of its activity."[53] All tended to interpret history teleologically and genetically, as the unfolding of a story in which each phase was the necessary prelude to its successor. But beneath this apparent agreement lay divergent assumptions about historical causation and epistemology. The providentialist and authoritarian orientation of Catholic authors contrasted sharply with the liberal and progressive emphasis on human agency and the "scientific" foundations of historical knowledge. In both, however, the character or spirit of the Spanish people was assumed to play a determining role. Following the example of the German practitioners of *Kulturgeschichte*, Spanish textbook authors routinely insisted that "true" history must encompass not only "external history" (a narration of political and military events), but also "internal history," or the history of "civilization" (a description of the laws, institutions, art, and literature embodying the particular genius of the people and exemplifying its "progress").

In practice, however, every textbook "history of Spain" was little more than a political and military chronicle, conventionally divided into ancient, medieval, and modern "ages." Periodization was determined first by the succession of conquering peoples or ruling dynasties in the peninsula, and second by royal reigns. Terse descriptions of social and cultural institutions, unrelated to any general thesis about Spanish national identity, were usually printed in small type at the conclusion of the political narrative or in the footnotes, where they could safely be ignored by students studying for the exam.

Striking by their absence were discussions of popular culture as the embodiment of the national spirit. For most progressives, Spanish popular culture was too regionally diverse, on the one hand, and too intertwined with Catholic culture, on the other, to fit their idealized vision of a unified, modern nation. For Moderado liberals and Catholic traditionalists, any effort to promote the pueblo to the foreground of Spanish history represented a subversive challenge to the established social order.

All textbook authors followed liberal historiography in portraying Spanish history as an ineluctable progression toward national unity—specifically, toward the consolidation of a unitary Spanish state. A common formula (again, borrowed from Lafuente) defined Spanish "nationality" in terms of three underlying "principles": "the religious principle, which has saved it in tremendous crises, the love of the patria, by which

[53] Zabala, *Compendio* 1:9; Moreno Espinosa, *Compendio*, 15.

it has defended always its independence, and the monarchical principle, which has given its history days of glory and has contributed in an efficacious way to the formation of our nationality."[54] Even republican authors conceded the *operational* value of church and monarchy in overcoming the centrifugal tendencies that threatened national unity, even though these essential, and historically determined, "principles" of Spanish nationality implicitly legitimated the Restoration monarchy.

Beyond these commonalities, the seven books most frequently read by Spanish youth during the Restoration represented national history in mutually contradictory ways. Written in the 1880s or even earlier, they all dealt summarily with "primitive times," not only for lack of knowledge about the early inhabitants of the peninsula (other than the Celtiberian "national character"), but also perhaps because for both liberals and conservatives prehistory possessed little intrinsic interest or ideological utility. Reluctant to relinquish a venerable myth of common descent, and unfettered by scientific skepticism, the neo-Catholic Sánchez Casado repeated the ancient claim that Túbal and Tarsis (the grandsons of Noah) were the first inhabitants of the peninsula. But most books displayed little interest in early cultures. For liberals, "primitive" societies existed primarily to demonstrate human progress, while in Catholic circles archaeology was a suspect science that challenged biblical accounts of human origins.[55] By the end of the century, however, progressive authors like Moreno Espinosa would begin to revise their texts to incorporate recent archaeological findings. Meanwhile, a Catholic congress in 1892 had called for a chair in "true Catholic prehistory."[56]

Conservative Catholic writers devoted considerable space in their books to what was conventionally known as the "Ancient Age," for several reasons. First, the "national" rebellion of the Lusitanian leader, or *caudillo*, Viriatus and the martyrdoms of Sagunto and Numancia illustrated enduring elements in the Spanish national character—love of independence and hatred of foreigners. Second, under Rome, Spaniards had achieved political and cultural unification. Most importantly, the Roman age had witnessed the "greatest of historical events, the birth of the SAVIOR OF THE WORLD" and the rapid Christianization of Spain, "the patria of holy martyrs."[57]

[54] Zabala, *Compendio* 1:29. See also Sánchez Casado, *Prontuario*, 2–3; Moreno Espinosa, *Compendio*, 263.

[55] For a discussion of the debate on ancient history, see Manuel Núñez Encabo, *Manuel Sales y Ferré: Los orígenes de la sociología en España* (Madrid: EDICUSA, 1976), 74.

[56] María Victoria López-Cordón, "La mentalidad conservadora durante la Restauración," in *La España de la Restauración*, ed. José Luis García Delgado (Madrid: Siglo XXI, 1985), 105.

[57] Monreal, *Historia*, 15; Sánchez Casado, *Prontuario*, 36.

Progressives, on the other hand, were more partial to the "Middle Age," the constituent period of Spanish nationhood when "Spaniards succeeded in victoriously creating their nationality, their independence, their language and their religion; singular example in the history of Europe."[58] Encompassing the thousand years from the fall of Rome through the Reconquest and the unification of the Spanish monarchy in 1469, the Middle Age occupied up to 60 percent of the narrative in progressive manuals. The story was a potentially dramatic foundation myth of sin and redemption, beginning with the political and religious unification of the nation under a strong Visigothic monarchy, its decay and subsequent collapse during the Arab invasion of 711, and its gradual restoration under Castilian leadership during the Reconquest. In most texts, however, the drama was dissipated in endless political detail and in laborious discussions of the legal and institutional advances so dear to the hearts of nineteenth-century liberals, such as the Germanic law codes, the Councils of Toledo (precursors of medieval Cortes, in the liberal view), and the municipal fueros.

Despite their embrace of this myth, progressives viewed the Reconquest with ambivalence. On the one hand, they celebrated the triumph of freedom-loving Spaniards over a backward people who lacked comprehension of concepts like "pueblo, nation and political rights."[59] On the other, the undeniable brilliance of "Hispano-Arabic" civilization and the religious and cultural pluralism of the high Middle Ages were a source of patriotic pride. To reduce this tension, they often found it convenient to nationalize the invaders, transforming them into "*moros españoles*," who could be comfortably assimilated into a tradition of national greatness. For Catholic conservatives, however, the significance of the Reconquest was unambiguous: it was a religious and cultural war against foreign heretics. "How unlikely that Providence should allow the pure and humanitarian religion of the Crucified One to succumb to the lascivious and cruel code of the voluptuous apostle from Arabia."[60]

Conservatives and progressives alike hailed the reign of the Catholic Kings as "the most brilliant and glorious epoch of Castile's history."[61] As this quotation suggests, from the Modern Age onward, Restoration textbooks conflated the history of "Spain" with that of Castile, completely disregarding the continuing institutional autonomy and internal development of the other peninsular kingdoms. Diplomatic triumphs, military victories, and state-building activities of the monarchs dominated the narrative, but all authors felt obliged to address three sensitive

---

[58] Picatoste, *Historia*, 10.
[59] Ibid., 70.
[60] Sánchez Casado, *Prontuario*, 85.
[61] Picatoste, *Historia*, 187.

issues that had sullied Spain's reputation abroad: the Inquisition, the expulsion of the Jews, and the conquest and colonization of the Americas. Under the guise of patriotism, embarrassed liberal authors offered several excuses: that the Catholic Kings had acted under popular pressure; that, despite "abuses," the religious purges and the expulsion had achieved "the great work of ethnic and religious unity"; or that other nations had treated Jews and religious dissidents even worse.[62] Moreno Espinosa eased his Krausist conscience by praising Jewish contributions to Spanish culture and reassuring his readers that religious intolerance was a thing of the past: "The noble spirit of human fraternity maintains the doors of the country open to all people, whatever their religion: because freedom of conscience is a principle stated in the fundamental laws of all civilized peoples."[63] According to Sánchez Casado, however, the list of services rendered to the nation by the Inquisition was long: "1°, the preservation of Catholic unity, cornerstone of national unity and greatness; 2°, the defense of the faith, motive of the loftiest undertakings, among others that of discovering and civilizing a New World, and that of defending Catholicism on the seas and fields of Europe; 3°, the incalculable benefit of having spared us in the sixteenth and seventeenth centuries the bloody revolutions, shadowy conspiracies and cruel punishments that other countries in Europe witnessed, preventing, with an insignificant number of trials, the horrors of the religious wars."[64]

As for the American empire, Restoration textbooks focused exclusively on the "Discovery." Echoing the first historian of the New World, Francisco López de Gomara, Sánchez Casado labeled it "the most important event in history, after the Redemption, and at the same time the reward to the nation that more than any other had fought against the enemies of religion and the Christian reputation."[65] Hailing Columbus as "the most extraordinary and glorious man" in history, Moreno Espinosa predicted his eventual canonization.[66] It was conventional to lament that Columbus had died unappreciated and in poverty, a myth given wide circulation earlier in the century by Washington Irving and congenial to progressive critics of Spanish obscurantism.[67] But the Americas after Columbus received short shrift. Most authors were con-

---

[62] Moreno Espinosa, *Compendio*, 299.

[63] Ibid., 297.

[64] Sánchez Casado, *Prontuario*, 235.

[65] Ibid., 239. Francisco López de Gomara's *Crónica de la Nueva España* (pt. 2 of his *Historia general de las Indias*) was published in Zaragoza in 1552. A modern edition is López de Gomara, *Conquista de México*, ed. José Luis Rojas (Madrid: Historia 16, 1987).

[66] Moreno Espinosa, *Compendio*, 317.

[67] Carla Rahn Phillips, "Sources for the Life of Christopher Columbus," Society for Spanish and Portuguese Historical Studies *Bulletin* 17, no. 1 (1992): 13.

tent to observe that Spain had brought "civilization" and religion to the New World, and had received little economic benefit in return; indeed, like Columbus himself, Spain had been a victim of her own generosity and spirituality.

Where progressives and conservatives of various stripes really parted company was in their evaluations of the Habsburgs, whose adventitious accession to the Spanish throne in 1516 marked, for progressives, the beginning of Spanish decadence. The authoritarianism and religious fanaticism of the new dynasty had fostered "a kind of divorce between the crown and the people"[68]—that is, between the state and the nation. Just as Charles V had suppressed the gallant defense of Castilian liberties by the Comuneros, so Philip II had triggered a similar defense of local liberties in the Netherlands and the Crown of Aragon. In contrast, conservatives applauded the Habsburg crusade to preserve the religious unity of Europe and attributed the undeniable "decline" in Spanish prestige and power in the seventeenth century to the insufficient authority of the last three Habsburg monarchs. Where progressives and conservatives found common ground was in condemning the Habsburg pretensions to "universal monarchy," which had distracted them from *national* interests.

They also shared a positive view of the eighteenth-century Bourbons, whose foreign origins and absolutist pretensions were forgiven because of their devotion to administrative unification, economic development, public instruction, and freedom of thought; even the Moderado Monreal noted with pleasure that under the Bourbons the pueblo was "satisfied, submissive and docile."[69] Only the neo-Catholic Sánchez Casado expressed outrage at Bourbon regalism and at the "cycle of reforms that, in the religious field, almost reached schism, and that prepared that of the revolutions that fill our century and that have not renewed the nation's way of being except in order to corrupt and pervert it."[70]

Restoration history textbooks rarely extended the national story into the nineteenth century. For some, recent history was by definition off-limits to the historian committed to "objectivity"; for all, recent Spanish history was a political minefield that was perhaps best avoided. The textbooks in this sample that ended in 1808 or 1833 dedicated only a few pages to a terse chronicle of wars, invasions, revolts, conspiracies, pronunciamientos, and revolving-door ministries.[71] Thus sketchily de-

---

[68] Picatoste, *Historia*, 223.

[69] Monreal, *Curso*, 430.

[70] Sánchez Casado, *Prontuario*, 459, 418.

[71] Authors who carried the narrative into the nineteenth century included three liberals—Moreno Espinosa, Picatoste, and Zabala (a Conservative party stalwart)—and one integrist, Sánchez Casado.

scribed, the constant upheaval appeared to be mere "factionalism," an evil universally decried in late-nineteenth-century Spain. The Krausist republican Moreno Espinosa attributed the endemic political instability to the failure to educate the pueblo to its civic responsibilities;[72] the Conservative Zabala, to the absence of a strong monarchy. For Sánchez Casado, the Catholic integrist, instability proved the illegitimacy of the liberal state. But none of the three examined the ideological struggle that underlay the civil conflicts, and none related those conflicts to present concerns. By omitting discussion of the recent past, authors deprived their readers of any knowledge of the historical process by which the liberal state had taken shape and discouraged children from seeing the present as a continuation of the past. Few of the books attempted to draw young readers into a national tradition in which they might imagine themselves as historical actors. Why did they neglect the opportunity to explain and celebrate the triumph of liberalism?

The answer lay in the long century of civil war and political crisis, which had not produced a clear victory for liberalism or democracy. The Restoration monarchy was a negotiated compromise whose survival depended on elite co-optation and popular demobilization. Juridically liberal but neither "bourgeois" nor democratic, the parliamentary monarchy was unable to define itself clearly either as the continuation of or the successor to the old regime. Whereas in France, republicans could exalt their revolutionary heritage, in Spain the revolutionary tradition was discredited by the recent upheavals of the Sexenio. The defense of religion, routinely asserted to be one of the "principles" defining Spanish nationality, could not be enthusiastically invoked by liberal authors, given the persistent hostility of the church toward liberalism. The pueblo, an occasional shadowy protagonist in the texts of the progressive authors, frequently lacked any real historical agency beyond loyally supporting its kings, repelling foreign invaders, and exercising its (unspecified) rights through representative institutions. The schoolbooks did not explain how the rights had been won or examine the social and economic forces that motivated "the people" to act. To do so would have undermined the notion of a "community" without conflict and invited reflection on the limitations of democracy under the parliamentary monarchy.

Another solution might have been to celebrate the historic origins of established national symbols, but symbols acceptable to the liberal state (as opposed to traditional Catholic symbols like Santiago or Saint Teresa) were only in the process of "invention" and lacked historical resonance. Only one of the history textbooks even included a map of the

[72] Moreno Espinosa, *Compendio*, 514.

national territory. The Spanish flag, of relatively recent origin, was for many a partisan and, thus, divisive symbol, and none of the textbooks even depicted it.[73]

Moreover, the opportunity to create a foundation myth for the liberal state around the proclamation of the Constitution of Cádiz of 1812 was clouded by its siting within the War of Independence against France, the very birthplace of modern constitutionalism. Catholic traditionalists could argue that, true to their national identity, in 1808 the Spanish people fought for independence and absolutism and against foreign heresy. For liberals, the war was harder to situate. If France was the enemy, why did patriotic Spaniards adopt liberalism? If liberal constitutionalism meant freedom, why did the pueblo rise up against the French, and why were the *afrancesado* supporters of José I and the Constitution of Bayona condemned as traitors? The simplest solution was to reduce the War of Independence to (yet another) struggle against a foreign invader and to minimize the significance of the liberal revolution. Lack of consensus and ambivalence thus neutralized the possibility of creating a potent national myth around the war and the birth of liberal constitutionalism. Instead, the foundation myth of the Spanish state was situated in the Reconquest (or "Restoration"), and its protagonists were the chivalrous kings and knights whose deeds exemplified the "Spanish" virtues of honor, valor, and independence. However inspiring, this national identity was seemingly irrelevant, if not actually dysfunctional, in late-nineteenth-century Spain and did not invite emulation. Readers of these history texts—like the Spanish polity itself—were instead encouraged implicitly to sit back and enjoy the show.

The structure of the texts was of a piece with the authoritarian credentialism of the school system as a whole. Only one text among the most popular (that of Orodea) was organized as a series of questions to be debated rather than as set responses to the anticipated queries of an imaginary examining tribunal. (Moreno Espinosa's conception of history as a continuous process of development and of historical scholarship as a dialectic was apparent only if one read the footnotes—an unlikely prospect.) In the rest, history was presented as a collection of facts to be learned, like theorems or verb conjugations. Spaniards could be counted on to recall, years later, the list of the Visigothic kings, which they had chanted like a mantra as students: "Ataulfo, Sigerico, Walia, Teodoredo," and so on, through Egica, Witiza, and Rodrigo.

[73] The flag was devised in 1785 to distinguish Spanish warships from other ships flying the Bourbon flag. It was declared the emblem of the Spanish monarchy and extended to the army by the Moderados only in 1843 and was not flown over public buildings until 1908.

An emphasis on the retention of dates and stock phrases character-ized history education in most countries at the end of the century, and even beyond.[74] What distinguished Spanish schooling was not its "mem-orism" or positivism but the relatively inert quality of the material to be learned. Despite repeated declarations about the value of history in character formation, Spanish history texts provided little in the way of moral guidance. To be effective as a guide to individual character for-mation, history must be a rather more "conative" than "cognitive" dis-cipline, training the heart and will rather than the intellect.[75] History instruction of this type aims to capture the moral imagination of the reader, either by dramatizing a hero's resolution of a moral quandary or by structuring his life to exemplify a desirable character trait or virtue, particularly in public life. But although the pantheon of Spanish heroes was remarkably uniform among the authors here considered, the writers failed to bring them to life or to present them in a moral conflict. As Manuel Azaña later recalled, "History tired me because of its inhuman dryness. Although succinctly embodied in a few dozen great persons, the countenance of these heroes was not that of a man. They had arrived on earth with the task of reciting a role learned from memory and to fulfill the decrees of Providence. We didn't learn what they did; it rather seemed that they came forward to fulfill what was written."[76]

Restoration history textbooks limited themselves to brief moral judg-ments about the personal strengths and weaknesses of kings and a few notable warriors routinely lauded for their martial prowess. Profession-ally and politically interested in the history of institutions, the authors ignored the heroes of popular legend and myth, like Guzmán el Bueno or Santiago Matamoros, as well as the great saints and mystics of the sixteenth century. Even the Cid, protagonist of the national epic, re-ceived no more than a passing mention from most authors, possibly because recent scholarship based on Arabic sources (by the Dutch histo-rian Reinhardt Dozy) had effectively attacked the historicity of the *Poema del Cid* and the image of the loyal and patriotic Christian knight portrayed therein.[77]

---

[74] See the memories of George Orwell in "Such, Such Were the Joys," in *Collected Essays, Journalism and Letters of George Orwell*, ed. Sonia Orwell and Ian Angus (New York: Harcourt, Brace and World, 1968) 4:337.

[75] Joseph A. Diorio, "The Decline of History as a Tool of Moral Training," *History of Education Quarterly* 25, no. 21 (spring–summer 1985): 76–77.

[76] Manuel Azaña Díaz, *El jardín de los frailes* (Madrid: Alianza Editorial, 1982), 94–95.

[77] Reinhardt Dozy, "Le Cid d'après de nouveaux documents," in *Recherches sur l'his-toire et la littérature de l'Espagne pendant le moyen age*, 3d ed. (Leiden: E. J. Brill, 1881) (1st ed. 1849).

Thus, apart from the stock definitions of national character and the "principles of Spanish nationality" in the opening pages of some of the manuals, most liberal textbooks did not give young readers a sense of who "Spaniards" were or what higher purposes their nation had historically served. Instead they portrayed the history of "Spain" as a disembodied process of territorial, legal, and institutional unification. But establishing Spain's credentials as a juridical nation-state could not automatically instill a sense of nationalism; that is, the legal abstraction that liberals called the "nation" and identified with the parliamentary monarchy lacked the emotional resonance associated with the term "patria" (which liberals tended to concede to the Catholic right), or the sense of participatory democracy connoted by the progressive term "pueblo."[78] Nor did the texts identify a clearly defined enemy or set of competing national principles against which Spaniards might define themselves as a nation; although the texts described endless military encounters against foreigners and invaders, they did not dichotomize in moral terms.[79] The absence of any real external threat to Spain in the present eliminated this inducement to national self-definition, as did the transactional character of the Restoration settlement, which eliminated the option of vilifying the internal enemies of the liberal regime.

When, in 1898, Spain did briefly face a formidable external enemy, Spaniards were psychologically unprepared for the contest. On the one hand, uncritical glorification of the heroic martial deeds of the Reconquest and the Empire inclined them to dismiss the United States as an arriviste nation with no history. On the other hand, the dynastic parties' failure to nationalize the masses deprived them of popular support when the illusion of an easy victory vanished.

If the nation is a socially constructed "imagined community" that confers meaning on and solidarity among its members, then Restoration history texts were surely inadequate to the task. To convince young Spaniards to identify with "Spain" as they identified with their local communities, the history texts might have drawn explicit parallels between the known and the new, and evoked images, myths, and symbols familiar to their readers.[80] But since the history of the Spanish state was

[78] For a discussion of these distinctions at the opening of the liberal era, see Pierre Vilar, "Patria i nació en el vocabulari de la Guerra contra Napoleó," in *Assaigs sobre la Catalunya del segle VIII* (Barcelona: Curial, 1973), 133–71.

[79] The oppositional character of nationalism is stressed in R. D. Grillo, ed., *"Nation" and "State" in Europe: Anthropological Perspectives* (New York: Academic Press, 1980); and in Peter Sahlins, *Boundaries: The Making of France and Spain in the Pyrenees* (Berkeley and Los Angeles: University of California Press, 1989).

[80] Growing up in Alcalá de Henares at the end of the last century, Manuel Azaña commented on the patriotism of his fellow *alcalaínos*: "their patriotism was local. We were

still very much a struggle against localism and decentralization, this recourse was, quite intentionally, ignored. With the exception of the Basque Machiandiarena, authors made few references to local heroes, shrines, or monuments, and never drew upon experiences presumably familiar to young adolescents, whether rural or urban. The texts did not adapt to their readers, but rather forced their readers to meet them on their own terms. It seems doubtful that they succeeded.

With Spanish history defined exclusively as a progression toward unity, once that historic task had been realized, the future mission of the nation became problematic. Having ignored or trivialized the constitutional struggles of the recent past, the texts could not help students identify still unresolved political issues. Nor did any of the books prepare middle-class students intellectually or psychologically for the challenges that would increasingly face the constitutional monarchy after the turn of the century. The Castilian focus of the national story made the emergence of national feeling in Catalonia and the Basque provinces seem mystifying, when not perverse,[81] and the total absence of any consideration of social and economic issues and the reduction of contemporary politics to "factionalism" left the younger generation unequipped to deal constructively with the labor movement and social unrest.

The preponderant message of the Restoration history books was one of passivity, complacency, and obedience to constituted authority. In this basic sense, Restoration history textbooks reinforced the political and social status quo. But the texts did not invite even middle-class youth to identify strongly with the nation or to accept responsibility for its destiny. Under the laissez-faire conditions that prevailed from 1881 on, they did not even convey a uniform message about the meaning and direction of the Spanish historical process. Small wonder, then, that those who believed national regeneration must begin with the education and mobilization of the young often targeted history education as one part of the curriculum most urgently in need of reform.

To be sure, the fraction of the population studying the bachillerato was very small. A few young Spaniards undertook professional and technical studies; the vast majority, none at all beyond the primary level. Any

---

only persuaded of the greatness of Alcalá, not of Spain. . . . History was intelligible if we could give it a [local] face and accent; if not, it fell into the shadowy exterior." Azaña Díaz, *Jardín*, 90–91. On the incorporation of the familiar and the local into general history, see, for example, John Ahier, *Industry, Children and the Nation: An Analysis of National Identity in School Textbooks* (London: Falmer Press, 1988).

[81] Zabala explicitly rejected regionalist proposals: "To think about a federal organization after having constituted the nation, is to think about an absurdity that both History and Logic reject." *Compendio* 1:27.

attempt to evaluate history education during the Restoration must therefore examine, however briefly, the textbooks and instructional patterns that prevailed in the primary schools. As we have seen, formal instruction in history was confined to the upper primary schools until 1901, when curricular reform mandated national history for all children. Even then, most children were not systematically exposed to the history of their country; limited resources, erratic attendance, and low expectations stood in the way.

Given the diversity of schools, teachers, and textbooks, generalizations about primary history education must be tentative. Nevertheless, it is clear that history was taught "catechistically," like other subjects in the curriculum, in large measure because most teachers were ill equipped to employ any other method. History training in the normal schools lasted but one year and was far from uniform, as the ministerial survey of textbooks in 1894 revealed. Free to choose from the available manuals, faculties varied widely in their preferences, perhaps reflecting the degree of preparation of their students as well as the political inclinations of their directors or the influence of local catedráticos. In any case, the scholarly level and ideological diversity of books in use was striking. Although seventeen men's teachers' colleges assigned the text by the erudite Krausist republican Moreno Espinosa, another eighteen reported using the antiquated manual by Manuel Ibo Alfaro y Lafuente, a private school professor and popular writer best known for his sympathetic chronicle of the revolution of 1868.[82] First published in 1864 as a textbook for the bachillerato but restricted to the normal schools in 1880, it was a long political and military account that stressed the centrality of monarchy and religion in national unification and that uncritically narrated legends, myths, and apocrypha that instituto catedráticos had since excised from the bachillerato texts. Thus, for example, Alfaro reported as fact the settlement of the peninsula by Túbal and Tarsis, the birth of Christ 4,004 years after the Creation, the betrayal of "Spain" to the Arabs by the vengeful Count Julián, Guzmán el Bueno's patriotic refusal to surrender to the enemy in order to save his son's life, and so forth. If it was too old-fashioned to be acceptable in the institutos by the 1880s, its uncritical methodology and romantic

---

[82] Manuel Ibo Alfaro y Lafuente, *Compendio de la historia de España*, 11th ed., rev. (Madrid: Lib. de la Viuda de Hernando, 1889) (1st ed. 1863; 15th ed. 1908). Alfaro (1828–85) was variously a professor of mathematics, logic, and psychology in a number of private academies in Madrid and a well-known writer of light fiction. See Carmen Simón Palmer, *La enseñanza privada seglar en Madrid, 1820–1868* (Madrid: Instituto de Estudios Madrileños, 1972), 380. His progressivism is patent in his *Historia de la interinidad española, escrita en presencia de documentos fidedignos*, 2 vols. (Madrid: Est. tip. de la Viuda e Hijos de M. Álvarez, 1871).

content (and its publication by Casa Hernando) were probably what made it attractive to the normal schools, whose graduates were largely destined to teach a rural population for whom such religio-historical myths and legends might constitute the foundation of patriotism.

Another text widely used in the women's normal schools was a short manual originally written in 1846 for upper primary students by the progressive educator Ángel María Terradillos.[83] Also part of the Hernando list, this text was written as a series of questions and answers, a format that intentionally invoked the familiar dialogic style and authoritative voice of the catechism. Terradillos defined history as "the true exposition of events that have occurred in our patria, for the instruction of the living and those to come," without, however, explicitly drawing the lessons to be learned.[84] A book only 125 pages long permitted little elaboration or anecdote, but the author assumed a lively, moralizing tone, particularly when delineating the personal virtues and vices of the Spanish monarchs or commemorating milestones in the march toward national unity and popular liberty. Terradillos was quick to condemn "excessive zeal" in religious matters, as well as regal ineptitude or indifference.[85] Symbolizing his exclusive focus on great men, engraved portraits (some wholly imaginary, as in the case of Viriatus and don Pelayo) comprised the only illustrations in the book. In addition to the usual chronological tables of dynasties and kings, the end matter included a history in verse by the eighteenth-century Jesuit satirist José Francisco Isla, author of *Fray Gerundio.*

Spanish history textbooks written for primary students were relatively scarce before the turn of the century. Some of the most durable, like that of Terradillos, had been written by normal school teachers and other professional educators early in the liberal period, when aspirations to create a universal system of primary instruction had been high and the patriotic and civic rewards of history instruction had been accepted as an article of faith. Others had been written to satisfy older notions of history as a "formative" discipline. But a review of a selected sample of upper-primary history textbooks from the late-nineteenth

---

[83] Ángel María Terradillos, *Prontuario de historia de España*, 18th ed. (Madrid: Librería de la Viuda de Hernando, 1890) (lst ed. 1846; 22d ed. 1911). The author, a prolific writer of textbooks and pedagogical treatises, was a professor of rhetoric and geography at the university and in various institutos and colegios in Madrid until his death in 1879. A biography of Terradillos may be found in Capel, *Ciencia para la burguesía*, 317. His treatise *Los deberes de los niños*, written in 1846, was in its seventieth edition in 1926.

[84] Terradillos, *Prontuario*, 5.

[85] For example, in discussing the "fanaticism" of the Reconquest, the "excessive zeal" of Philip II, and the "crudest superstition" of the late-seventeenth century. Ibid., 76, 92, 99.

century suggests that most suffered from the same lack of pedagogical insight and confusion of purpose that blunted the "educational" value of history books for the bachillerato.

These textbooks fell into three basic types: narrative histories; "catechistic" surveys; and readers (*libros de lectura*) that included national history as one of the formative subjects in the primary curriculum.[86] Least common were the narratives, which resembled the bachillerato textbooks and, like them, presupposed a reasonably high level of literacy and sufficient economic ease to permit an extended period of schooling; not surprisingly, they were used primarily in elite colegios whose pupils were not pursuing the bachillerato. In contrast, the catechistic texts and the readers were well adapted to the situation in most primary schools, where books were rare, advanced students mingled with beginning readers, and all learning was conducted by rote recitation. But in every context and format, the book was the cornerstone of the educational process.

Diverse as they were in length, intended audience, and aims, the primary texts defy easy characterization. In most cases, however, they were merely miniature versions of the bachillerato history books, from which everything had been extracted but a schematized chronology of political and military events. The question-and-answer mode, coupled with a general tendency toward genteel euphemism (one author, for example, referred to the Arab invasion as a "contretemps"),[87] further deadened the inherently dry recounting of reigns and battles and reduced all events to the same level of insignificance. National history in these texts was a set of seemingly incontestable "answers" to be committed tempo-

[86] The sample includes eleven texts. Narratives: Teodoro Baró, *Historia de España*, 4th ed., rev. (Barcelona: Lib. de Antonio J. Bastinos, 1891) (1st ed. 1876); catechistic histories: Pedro de Diego, *Lecciones familiares de historia de España. Libro de lectura* (Madrid: Librería de Hernando, 1878); María Orberá y Carrión, *Nociones de historia de España* (Valencia: Imp. de R. Ortega, 1878); Esteban Paluzie Cantalozella, *Historia de España para los niños* (Barcelona: Hijos de Paluzie, 1908) (1st ed. 1871); Prudencio Solís y Miguel, *Nociones de historia de España, para uso de escuelas y colegios* (Valencia: Libs. de Juan Mariana y Sanz, 1875); Carlos Yeves, *Programas de primera enseñanza: Historia de España*, 8th ed., rev. (Madrid: Lib. de los Sucesores de Hernando, 1908) (1st ed. 1879); Saturnino Calleja y Fernández, *Nociones de historia de España*, 65th ed. (Madrid: Editorial Saturnino Calleja, 1915) (1st ed. 1886); and Terradillos, *Prontuario*; readers: Edmundo de Amicis, *Corazón: (Diario de un niño)* (Madrid: Hernando, 1956) (1st Spanish ed. 1887); Luigi A. Parravicini, *Juanito: Libro de lectura* (Barcelona: Imprenta Elzeviriana y Librería Camí, 1948) (1st Spanish ed. 1848; 34th ed. 1916); Pilar Pascual de Sanjuán, *Flora, o la educación de una niña* (Barcelona: Imp. y Lit. de Faustino Paluzie, 1881); and Ezequiel Solana, *Lecciones de historia de España: Primer grado o curso preparatorio*, 6th ed. (Madrid: El Magisterio Español, 1907).

[87] Solís y Miguel, *Nociones*, 30.

rarily to memory and then forgotten. Since the responses were frequently factually inaccurate or even patently false (the fabulous Túbal and Tarsis were staples of the primary texts, for example), this was perhaps not a bad thing.

Almost the only historical actors to appear in these books were kings and warriors, just as the monarchy was the only political institution given any attention and battles were the only historical events consistently recorded. Most primary textbook authors did not even pay lip service to the importance of "internal history" as a key to understanding the "genius of the race"; indeed, even the national character was only hinted at through unsystematic and infrequent allusions to national unity or resistance to foreign invaders. The past did not transmit a heritage or outline a mission for young Spaniards to embrace; at most, it lent authority to a unified politico-spatial entity known as "Spain" and inhabited by "Spaniards."

If the patriotic value of these books was thin, they were often saturated with moral and religious values. A text by María Orberá y Carrión, an administrator in the Higher Normal School for Women in Valencia and the sister of the archbishop of Almería, interpreted the Spanish past as a morality play in which the wicked were punished and the virtuous rewarded.[88] The "effeminacy . . . degradation and vice" that infected the Visigothic monarchy were the cause of its downfall: "people as well as individuals who stray from the path of virtue are unfailingly headed toward vilification and ruin."[89] In contrast, Queen Isabel I had been a "superior woman, of magnanimous heart, elevated intelligence and highest piety," whose husband "had never put on a shirt that was not woven and sewn by her hands."[90]

After the curricular reform of 1901, the number of primary school history books increased, but in the absence of state intervention or guidance, the new books were often no more "formative" or attractive than the old. Within the dominant catechistic format, a wide range of opinion was allowed to flourish, including the overt antiliberalism of the religious orders, whose texts will be discussed in the next chapter. At the other end of the spectrum were radically democratic and federalist texts, like those published in Barcelona by the militant Progressive educator and schoolbook publisher Esteban Paluzie. In 1908 Paluzie published a profusely illustrated and much abbreviated version of a manual he had written in 1871 for upper primary students, which managed to

---

[88] Orberá y Carrión, *Nociones de historia.*
[89] Ibid., 15.
[90] Ibid., 63–64.

condense into a small space an unusually pluralistic and "popular" perspective on the national past.[91] In service to his federalist conception of the nation Paluzie emphasized the independent and equal political development of the various Christian monarchies in the peninsula during what he called the "Arab" period—a divergence from the usual Castilocentric narrative. A further distinction was his attention—within the limits imposed by brevity—to the arts and to social and economic organization. Paluzie assigned an active role to "the pueblo" at moments of national crisis and denounced his enemies in vivid terms, especially the bloodthirsty, fanatical, and oppressive Habsburgs and the ambitious and greedy Moderados. Whether because of his radicalism or in spite of it, Paluzie's little textbooks sold well, especially in Catalonia.

Most primary texts, however, betrayed a moderate liberalism in which the highest political values were the least controversial: respect for the monarchy, national unity, established religion, and civil order. The same pressure to conform to the status quo defeated attempts at methodological innovation. Carlos Yeves, a professor at the School of Arts and Trades in Madrid who initially challenged the passive question-and-answer structure by writing "narrations" that might cause children "to become fond of history instruction" or that might "excite and develop in them the sentiment of love of country," acknowledged defeat in subsequent editions of his works by providing things to memorize: cuestionarios (lists of questions to be answered), chronologies, and easily learned summaries of major events.[92]

Perhaps the author who came closest to infusing conventional forms with a warm appeal to the patriotic and religious sentiments of children was Saturnino Calleja, whose Nociones de historia de España was in its sixty-fifth edition in 1915.[93] A popular publisher who supplanted Casa Hernando as the leading distributor of schoolbooks after 1900, Calleja illustrated his text with engravings of battles and other epic episodes in the history of the nation and lost no opportunity to teach his readers "how much love the madre patria deserves and needs from her sons and . . . how many sacrifices it has cost to create her." A major theme was the temporal and spiritual identity of Spain and Catholicism: just as the "social mission" of the catechism was to "form good and patriotic citizens," so too were Spain's "strength and importance" the result of the "protective shadow of the Catholic Religion." Another was the superi-

---

[91] Historia de Espana para los ninos (Barcelona: Hijos de Paluzie, 1908). A short biography of Paluzie (1806–73) may be found in Capel, Ciencia para la burguesía, 316.

[92] Yeves, Programas, 3.

[93] For a brief recollection of the cultural significance of Saturnino Calleja, see Dionisio Pérez, "Cuentos de ayer, realidad de hoy," Nuevo Mundo 26, no. 1300 (6 December 1918): n.p.

ority of Spanish culture; the highly praised artistic monuments of the Arabs, he pointed out, were actually "works executed by Spaniards and Greeks."[94] Almost uniquely, he called attention to the contemporary symbols of the nation, like the flag, and urged children to remember their civic duties, especially military service. But Calleja's little survey, like the popular storybooks he distributed free to thousands of rural schoolchildren, was an exception among the generally dreary primary level textbooks that prevailed at the turn of the century.

That children responded more enthusiastically to narratives inhabited by real people with whom they might identify is suggested by the vast popularity enjoyed by two readers that stayed in print well into the twentieth century: *Juanito*, by Luigi A. Parravicini, and *Corazón (Diario de un niño)*, by Edmundo de Amicis, both of them originally penned by liberal Italian authors prior to the Risorgimiento.[95] The enormous popularity of the Spanish edition of *Juanito* (first published in Spain in 1848) encouraged the translation and publication of de Amicis's text in 1887 and the publication in 1881 of *Flora*, a companion volume for girls written by a Spanish normal school teacher, Pilar Pascual de San Juan. Each of these books was protagonized by a child whose daily life in school and at home was recounted in vignettes designed to encourage morality, good manners (*urbanidad*), patriotism, and civic virtue. Although the effulgent praise for Italian national symbols, heroes, and history in *Juanito* and *Corazón* must have lacked resonance for Spanish children, this drawback was apparently offset by the authors' lively, affective language and their recourse to settings and experiences accessible and familiar to children.

Flora's success seems to have been owing to the lack of appropriate texts for girls rather than to its inherent charm. In *Flora*, history was presented as a distant and morally neutral pageant, to be observed and respected, but not made. The dry chronology of political and military events in Flora's notebook was no substitute for the patriotic odes to Garibaldi or the dramatizations of civic virtue in action in *Juanito* and *Corazón*; it might "instruct," but it could not "educate." The "education" of *Flora* was in fact entrusted to the lessons on religion—missing, of course, from the Italian liberals' secularized morality plays for boys—and to the anecdotes about Flora's daily life, where she learned the behaviors and attitudes appropriate to a young girl of "good customs."

[94] Calleja, *Nociones*, 8, 114, 182.

[95] For evidence of their continuing popularity, see Víctor García Hoz, *La educación en la España del siglo XX* (Madrid: Rialp, 1980), 230–32; and Francisca Montilla Tirado, *Selección de libros escolares de lectura* (Madrid: Consejo Superior de Investigaciones Científicas, Instituto San José de Calasanz, 1954), 207–10. The last Spanish editions of *Juanito* and *Flora* were published in Madrid in 1954; the last of *Corazón* in 1956.

The primary and secondary school history books examined in this chapter were in many ways well adapted to the political aims and aspirations of the Restoration monarchy, in that they implicitly reinforced the status quo. Like the political settlement of 1876 itself, the books discouraged popular mobilization in defense of national ideals by representing those ideals in a finished state, and by distancing readers from their own past in a variety of ways. Given the essentially immobilist aims and apparent institutional and social stability of Restoration political life, the dynastic parties were generally uninterested in proposals to modify the school system—including, or even especially, the history curriculum—to create a different kind of citizen, a different kind of nation, or a different kind of state.

But the weakness and complacency of the liberal state, although intended to conserve the status quo, was equally an invitation and an opportunity to alter it. From the moment of its creation, but increasingly after the system began to enter in crisis after the turn of the century, groups on both left and right began to contest the state in a number of ways, including attempting to modify the history curriculum. Challenging the assumption of a necessary coincidence between the Restoration monarchy and the Spanish nation, the critics turned to history to define a different nation as a precondition of constructing an alternative state. But if left and right fought over the meaning of the Spanish past and its relation to the present and future, they agreed that history teaching and textbooks were central to revitalizing the nation and thus the state. The following chapters analyze the way in which both history and history teaching were instrumentalized by oppositional groups seeking to transform Spanish political life.

CHAPTER 4

History Remembered: Catholic Integrism and the Sacralization of the National Past

> History . . . is nothing more than the testament
> of the centuries written by God and men.
> (*Father Andrés Manjón*)[1]

LIBERAL HISTORIOGRAPHY had been devised in the first instance partly to contest the traditionalist interpretation of the national past. But the traditionalists' proprietary grip on Spanish history was not easily broken. Unless they were willing to repudiate the national past altogether, even republican historians were forced to admit the undeniable alliance of church and monarchy during much of the history of the peninsula. But whereas progressives viewed this association as opportunistic, developmentally pernicious, and, in the contemporary context, anachronistic, the Moderados and their Conservative successors largely accepted the Catholic equation of national identity and Catholic unity as part of their rapprochement with the church from the 1850s on. The Concordat of 1851 and the Constitution of 1876 implicitly endorsed the Catholic interpretation of the national past by declaring Catholicism to be the state religion.

But Catholic traditionalists were not prepared to meet the Conservatives halfway, either politically or historiographically. They rejected the liberal premise that the state was responsible for the organization and direction of civil society (the "nation") and that its claims should thus supersede those of the church, and they framed that rejection in historical terms. If, as Conservatives themselves argued, the state should reflect the internal constitution of the nation, then the Restoration monarchy was by definition illegitimate, because the freedom of thought and belief central to liberal doctrine (and incorporated in articles 11 and 13 of the Constitution of 1876) was incompatible with the religious unity and orthodoxy historically characteristic of the Spanish people and defended

---

[1] Quoted in José Manuel Prellezo García, *Manjón, educador: Selección de sus escritos pedagógicos* (Madrid: Editorial Magisterio Español, 1975), 454.

by the Spanish monarchy. Abandoning that tradition represented nothing less than an abandonment of national identity itself.[2]

Catholic traditionalists invoked essentialist arguments to justify their claims about the past, appealing to a higher historical truth discernible beneath the "accidents" of history. Not all history was historically "true"; some historical events or even whole epochs might be factually verifiable but might nonetheless be "false" to the spirit or legitimate historical trajectory of the nation. The epistemological foundation of historical knowledge of this kind was metaphysical and intuitive, rather than empirical, but both Cánovas and the Catholic polemicists typically deployed historical evidence to lend a spuriously scientific cast to their arguments.[3]

The champions of Spanish Catholic integrism in the 1870s were the Jesuits and the Dominicans, both orders ultramontane in their loyalties, neo-Thomist in their philosophical allegiance, and theocratic in their politics.[4] Like the French traditionalists whom they strenuously admired, Spanish integrists proclaimed Catholicism to be intrinsic to the Spanish soul or "race," transcending accidents of political organization or circumstance, and to be uniquely responsible for the historic moments of grandeur and sacrifice that inspired national pride and constituted the best hope for a future resurgence of national glory. Integrist historiography located the origins of the Spanish nation in the conversion of the Visigothic king Reccared to Catholicism in 589 A.D., which initiated both the Catholic unity of the nation and the historic alliance of throne and altar. The subsequent decadence of the Visigothic monarchy had attracted divine retribution in the form of the Arab invasion; through the Reconquest, however, the nation had atoned for its sins.[5] The pinnacle of national culture had been achieved in the Middle Ages; thereafter, they argued, philosophy and literature had been infected by Renaissance "paganism," and the monarchy had gradually surrendered

[2] See the constitutional debates in 1855 and 1876, discussed in Luis Sánchez Agesta, *Historia del constitucionalismo español (1808–1936)*, 4th ed., rev. (Madrid: Centro de Estudios Constitucionales, 1984), 250–52, 325. See also María Victoria López Cordón, "La mentalidad conservadora durante la Restauración," in José Luis García Delgado, ed., *La España de la Restauración: Política, economía, legislación y cultura* (Madrid: Siglo XXI, 1985), 71–110.

[3] For a discussion of "metaphysical" vs. "empirical" or "naturalist" history in Spain, see Rafael Ninyoles, *Madre España* (Valencia: Prometeo, 1979).

[4] The views of Spanish traditionalists on national history and politics are collected in Juan Rey Carrera, S.J., *El resurgir de España previsto por nuestros grandes pensadores: Donoso, Balmes, Aparisi, Menéndez y Pelayo, Vázquez de Mella* (San Sebastián: Editorial Española, 1938).

[5] Peter Linehan, *History and the Historians of Medieval Spain* (New York: Oxford University Press, 1993), traces the elaboration of the "myth" of the Reconquest.

its authority to foreign ideas and enemies. Spanish political power, of course, had reached its apex in the sixteenth and seventeenth centuries, when the nation had spent its wealth and power in the struggle against foreign heresy and in the evangelization of the Americas. Integrists attributed the impotence and loss of moral compass that characterized contemporary Spain to the perfidy of a state that had deflected the nation from its natural path from the eighteenth century onward and insisted that only a return to absolute monarchy and religious uniformity could restore the medieval fusion of nation and state.[6]

In the 1870s integrist historiography was simultaneously reinforced and challenged by the meteoric rise to intellectual and academic eminence of Marcelino Menéndez y Pelayo, a brilliant young literary scholar who achieved notoriety after a series of polemical exchanges with Gumersindo de Azcárate, Manuel de la Revilla, and other Krausist intellectuals over the impact of the Inquisition on the development of Spanish science and philosophy.[7] Revilla's assertion that "the country in which every despotism, every intolerance and every superstition prevailed could never give life to scientific thought, which can only be stimulated by freedom" had drawn a spirited retort from Menéndez y Pelayo, who argued that Spanish contributions to modern science had been overlooked by Spanish intellectuals slavishly enthralled by foreign ideas.[8] Somewhat in defiance of Thomist orthodoxy, he made a special plea for the existence of an indigenous *modern* philosophy, whose greatest luminary was the Renaissance humanist Luis Vives. Above all, he dismissed

---

[6] Marta M. Campoamor Fornieles, "Menéndez Pelayo y los problemas del intelectual católico de la Restauración," in Ciriaco Morón Arroyo et al., *Menéndez Pelayo: Hacia una nueva imagen* (Santander: Sociedad Menéndez Pelayo, 1983), 73–100; Pedro Laín Entralgo, *España como problema*, 2 vols. (Madrid: Aguilar, 1962) 1:54–64; Peter Linehan, "Religion, Nationalism and National Identity in Medieval Spain and Portugal," in Stuart Mews, ed., *Religion and National Identity* (New York: Oxford University Press, 1982), 161–99.

[7] For an introduction to the life and work of Menéndez y Pelayo, see Adolfo Bonilla y San Martín, *Marcelino Menéndez y Pelayo (1856–1912)* (Madrid: Est. Tip. de Fortanet, 1914); Vicente Palacio Atard, *Menéndez Pelayo y la historia de España* (Valladolid: Escuela de Historia Moderna de CSIC, 1956); Pedro Sainz Rodríguez, *Marcelino Menéndez Pelayo, ese desconocido* (Madrid: Fundación Universitaria Española, 1975); Laín Entralgo, *España como problema*; Morón Arroyo, *Menéndez Pelayo*; and Douglas W. Foard, "The Spanish Fichte: Menéndez y Pelayo," *Journal of Contemporary History* 14 (1979): 83–97. An abbreviated anthology of Menéndez y Pelayo's principal works is Miguel Artigas, ed., *La España de Menéndez Pelayo: Antología de sus obras, selección y notas*, 2d ed. (Valladolid: Cultura Española, 1938).

[8] Ernesto García Camarero and Enrique García Camarero, *La polémica de la ciencia española* (Madrid: Alianza Editorial, 1970), 203. This volume contains part of the exchange between Menéndez y Pelayo and his Krausist adversaries, including the essay by Manuel de la Revilla in *Revista Contemporánea* in May 1876.

the notion that the Inquisition had been a source of intellectual and cultural decadence: "I understand, and I applaud, and I even bless the *Inquisition* as a prescription of the philosophy of *unity* that has ruled and governed national life through the centuries, as the daughter of the genuine spirit of the Spanish people, and not an oppressor of it except in a few individuals and on very rare occasions."[9]

Appointed at age twenty (with the considerable aid of Cánovas and the neo-Catholic leader Alejandro Pidal) to the chair of Spanish literature at the Central University in 1877, Menéndez y Pelayo elaborated this patriotic defense of the national past—and particularly of its "modern" history—with what was to become his most famous work, the three-volume *Historia de los heterodoxos españoles*, published between 1880 and 1882.[10] Menéndez y Pelayo's principal themes in this polemical essay were the consubstantiality of the Spanish nation and the Catholic faith and the instinctive Spanish rejection of foreign ideas and heresy. The young scholar's definition of national identity depended on an unresolved mixture of essentialist and historico-cultural arguments: on the one hand, Spaniards formed a "race" or "caste" intrinsically inclined toward religious orthodoxy; on the other hand, their religious and cultural unity had been won dearly and against great odds.[11] That unity sprang from the universalistic culture of classical civilization, enriched by the equally universalistic values of Christianity. "Unity of belief," rather than legal or institutional unity, had made Spain a "great nation, instead of a crowd of assorted peoples."[12] It had enabled the nation to overcome invasion and occupation by "Germanic barbarians" and Muslim infidels and to emerge victorious and all-powerful in the modern age, when Spaniards carried the truths of classical civilization and Christianity around the world: "Spain, evangelizer of half the globe; Spain, hammer of heretics, light of Trent, sword of Rome, cradle of St. Ignatius . . . ; that is our greatness and our unity: we do not have any other."[13]

In the third volume of his essay, published after the Liberals' guarantee of academic freedom in 1881, Menéndez y Pelayo launched upon an extended denunciation of Spanish history since the eighteenth century. First, French rationalism and, later, German pantheism (in the form of

[9] Marcelino Menéndez Pelayo, *Revista Europea* 8 (24 September 1876), quoted in Garcia Camarero, *La polémica*, 241.

[10] Marcelino Menéndez y Pelayo, *Historia de los heterodoxos españoles*, 3 vols. (Madrid: Librería Católica de San José, 1880–81).

[11] This contradiction forms the basis of Laín Entralgo's analysis of Menéndez Pelayo's thought in *España como problema* 1:113–347.

[12] In Artigas, *España de Menéndez Pelayo*, 139.

[13] Ibid., 141.

Krausism), had artificially introduced revolutionary ideas that by the 1870s had destroyed the unity and authenticity of Spanish culture: "Everything bad, everything anarchic, everything debauched in our character is preserved and comes to the surface, with more force everyday. . . . We no longer have our own science, nor a national politics, nor even our own art and literature. Whatever we do is a poor imitation and weak copy of what we see praised elsewhere." Menéndez y Pelayo did not explain why Spaniards who were both intrinsically and historically hostile to everything foreign had suddenly become easy prey for heterodox ideas.[14] But he did acknowledge that the disease had so far infected only the minority in the cities, leaving "the Catholic spirit" intact among the rural masses. His implication was clear: those who had succumbed to foreign heresy were not really Spaniards, did not really form part of the Spanish pueblo, at all.

The audacity and elegance of Menéndez y Pelayo's attacks on Krausism, and his Catholic and nationalist interpretation of the Spanish past, secured him the patronage of the Conservative party and the Catholic right. In 1884 he joined Pidal's "possibilist" Catholic Union and served twice in the Cortes as a Conservative deputy, a compromise with the parliamentary monarchy that earned him the enmity of the Carlists.[15] From the 1890s on, however, Menéndez y Pelayo distanced himself from politics and from the polemics of his youth, preferring to serve the patria by recuperating and vindicating its literary heritage. As editor of the first collection of Spanish literary classics and as director of the National Library, his influence extended far beyond the circle of his devoted disciples, who absorbed his dedication both to scholarship and to traditional "Spanish" values. Until his death in 1912, he continued to insist on the validity and relevance of traditional Catholic culture to the future of the nation: "Where the inheritance of the past, poor or rich, great or small, is not piously preserved, let us not hope for the birth of an original thought or a compelling idea. . . . An old people cannot renounce its [intellectual culture] without extinguishing the most noble part of its life and falling into a second childhood very near to senile imbecility."[16]

During his lifetime, Menéndez y Pelayo's relationship with the Catholic right was ambivalent. Although they cherished the antiliberal po-

---

[14] Ibid. For a discussion of the contradictions in Menéndez Pelayo's work, see André Barón, "Lo francés y *La Historia de los heterodoxos españoles*" in Morón Arroyo, *Menéndez Pelayo*, 122–60.

[15] A useful discussion of Menéndez y Pelayo's place in the Catholic politics of the Restoration is Campoamor Fornieles, "Menéndez Pelayo," in Morón Arroyo, *Menéndez Pelayo*, 73–100.

[16] In Bonilla y San Martín, *Menéndez Pelayo*, 171.

lemics of his youth, the integrist press and the teaching orders (who preferred to celebrate Spain's antithetical relationship to modern thought and values) objected to his willingness to compromise with the constitutional monarchy, his respect for the neutrality of scholarship, and his campaign to establish the "modernity" of Spanish culture. Their effort to recapture Spain for the church took a variety of forms—sermons, commemorations, newspapers and journals, pilgrimages, and congresses—but their message was remarkably uniform: "the nation [was] a creation of Christianity," whose historic identity had been betrayed by secularizing rulers from the eighteenth century onward, and especially by the liberal state.[17] As the regenerationist literature of the 1890s revived familiar liberal indictments of Spain's inquisitorial and crusading past, Catholic publicists redoubled their efforts to defend their version of the national trajectory. In 1889, in counterpoint to centennial commemorations of the French Revolution, Catholic publicists celebrated the thirteen hundredth anniversary of King Reccared's conversion; in 1892 they hailed the four hundredth anniversary of Columbus's voyage with paeans to Spain's evangelical mission in the New World and with reminders of the common cultural and religious bonds that united the Ibero-American world. Whereas progressives reacted to the disaster of 1898 with laments over Spain's failure to modernize, the Catholic right attributed the defeat to the dilution of the traditional spiritual values that had raised the nation to the heights of imperial power in the Golden Age.[18]

Catholic integrists were particularly attentive to the place of history in secondary schooling, where the nation's elite was formed. In their view the inclusion of national history in the bachillerato could be justified only if it reinforced Catholic doctrine and enlisted the young in a national community defined by religious belief; to the extent that history instruction undermined that belief by encouraging critical thinking or the rejection of authority, it was to be condemned as the product of the "evil teachings" of foreign Protestants and domestic unbelievers.[19] Fearing the corrosive effects of a liberal and secular view of Spanish history on the religious unity of the nation and on the privileged place

[17] Juan Vázquez de Mella, quoted in José Pemartín Sanjuán, *Los valores históricos en la dictadura española*, 2d ed. (Madrid: Editorial Arte y Ciencia, 1929), 43.

[18] López Cordón, "Mentalidad conservadora," in García Delgado, *España de la Restauración*, 79–95; Frederick B. Pike, *Hispanismo, 1898–1936: Spanish Conservatives and Liberals and Their Relations with Spanish America* (Notre Dame, Ind.: University of Notre Dame Press, 1971), 35–36; and Frances Lannon, *Privilege, Persecution and Prophecy: The Catholic Church in Spain, 1875–1975* (New York: Oxford University Press, 1987), 136.

[19] Manuel Merry y Colón and Antonio Merry y Villalba, *Compendio de historia de España: Redactado para servir de texto en los seminarios y colegios católicos* (Seville: Imp. y Lit. de José María Ariza, 1889), 11.

of the church in the Spanish state, they campaigned relentlessly against the textbooks assigned by catedráticos in the institutos, accusing them of both incompetence and impiety. As we have seen, few Restoration textbooks were intensely hostile to the church or religious belief; nevertheless, the positivist assumptions imbedded in most of the schoolbooks did challenge Catholic conceptions of Providence and the human condition. Liberal evolutionism and its corollary, faith in human progress, were incompatible with the Catholic conviction that history was instructive because "the soul is always the same and phenomena identical."[20] In Catholic eyes, the purpose of history was to promote understanding of "the motives that guide human actions and the *limitation* of human possibilities in the face of natural obstacles," particularly, original sin.[21]

Catholic integrists criticized history instruction in the institutos not only for what it was, but for what it was not—"educational." The modern curriculum, of which national history was an integral part, did not recognize that the educated man was distinguished by his possession of knowledge superior to the practical arts.[22] Catholic educators were particularly impatient with what they called "culturalist history"—the endless narratives of dates and facts that they considered to be the product of a misguided effort to make history "scientific." The problem was not its memoristic methodology—which Catholics favored themselves— nor its focus on "external history": "War," declared one prominent Jesuit educator, ". . . is the most intense manifestation of the life of a pueblo. Epochs of military aggrandizement tend to coincide with commercial, industrial, scientific and literary prosperity."[23] Rather, the defect of official history instruction lay in its neglect of the "formative" value of history. Defenders of the ancient dictum that "history is philosophy teaching by examples," Catholics charged instituto textbooks with turning children into "warehouses of useless erudition."[24] They advised teachers and textbook writers to focus on only "the great principles of

[20] Francisco Apalátegui, S.J., "Del estudio de la historia en la segunda enseñanza," in *Asociación Española para el Progreso de las Ciencias: Congreso de Valladolid* (Madrid: Imp. de Eduardo Arias, 1917) 8:327. Apalátegui was professor of history at the elite colegio de San José in Valladolid. See also Jean Guibert, *A los maestros cristianos. El educador apóstol: Su preparación y ejercicio de su apostolado*, trans. Antolín Saturnino Fernández, 14th ed. (Barcelona: Imp. Moderna de Buinart y Punolar, 1908).

[21] Ramón Ruiz Amado, S.J., *La educación intelectual*, 3d ed., rev., 2 vols. (Barcelona: Editorial Librería Religiosa, 1942), 419.

[22] Apalátegui, "Del estudio," 315.

[23] Ibid., 317.

[24] Enrique Herrera Oria, S.J., *La enseñanza de la historia en el bachillerato: Orientaciones sobre planes y métodos. El material escolar y los museos escolares* (Valladolid: Tip. de Andrés Martínez Sánchez, 1926), 15. The maxim is from Dionysius de Halicarnassus (30–7 B.C.).

history" and the small number of transcendentally important events that illuminated "the character or physiognomy of an epoch."[25] For Father Ruiz Amado, the chief Jesuit commentator on educational issues at the turn of the century, the immutability of human nature meant that "the child can understand the motives that guided the conduct of Alexander the Great, just as he can understand those that inspired Napoleon I."[26] The traditional Catholic regard for ancient history lay in its lessons for personal development and the public weal; thus, one Catholic critic in the 1920s located the roots of Spain's political crisis in her neglect of the classics.[27]

Without ceasing to champion ancient history, Catholic integrists increasingly acknowledged the "patriotic" value of national history—that is, its potential to bind Spaniards to their particular conception of national tradition. Unlike the Moderados, however, who tended to deploy history in defense of the status quo, the Catholic opponents of the liberal state structured their version of national history to demonstrate where things had gone wrong, where state and patria had parted company. This was a viewpoint they shared with progressive critics. But whereas for progressives, the main point of understanding the past was to be able to overcome it, for Catholic integrists, patriotism demanded total identification with the "national soul" and its history of "glory and misfortune."[28] The future republican prime minister, Manuel Azaña, recalled that the Spanish history he had learned from the Augustinian friars at El Escorial was infused with nostalgia, resentment, and fatalism. "The crime against Spain" perpetrated by "barbarians" inside and outside the patria was the theme of countless diatribes; so, too, was the friars' insistence that "Spain *is* insofar as she realizes the Catholic plan." Tenaciously adhering to *casticismo* and *españolismo*, the true Spanish patriot was the one who learned "to participate in a tradition and to strive to restore it." The historic institutions of Spain were not "symbolic forms nor memorable trophies that [might] be exchanged for others"; they possessed "an active, sacramental quality. . . . Spain [was] the Catholic monarchy of the sixteenth century." In consequence, the subsequent history of the monarchy must be seen as a betrayal of "Spain" herself.[29]

---

[25] Teodoro Rodríguez, *La enseñanza en España* (Madrid: Imprenta Helénica, 1909), 90. Father Rodríguez was the director of the Augustinian Real Colegio Alfonso XII in El Escorial.

[26] Ruiz Amado, *Educación intelectual*, 419.

[27] Enrique Herrera Oria, *Educación de una España nueva* (Madrid: Ediciones FAX, 1934), 45–50.

[28] Apalátegui, "Del estudio," 324; Ramón Ruiz Amado, *El patriotismo* (Madrid: Razón y Fé, 1910).

[29] Manuel Azaña Díaz, *El jardín de los frailes* (Madrid: Alianza Editorial, 1982), 101,

The corollary to this patriotism of passionate nostalgia was an equally strong conviction that contemporary liberal historiography, like liberalism itself, had undermined the national traditions that were the wellspring of patriotism. Quoting de Maistre, Catholic integrists accused modern history of being "a great conspiracy against the truth"[30] and resolved to put it right by restoring the traditional Catholic interpretation of the national past to the schools. Their first opportunity to put their convictions into practice arrived when Silvela included the neo-Catholic marqués de Pidal in his regenerationist government of 1899. During his brief tenure in the Ministry of Development, Pidal undertook to make the bachillerato truly educational by lengthening the course of study to seven years and imposing a classical curriculum. Stripping away most "modern" subjects, Pidal spared only national history, which he recast as a six-year course integrating Spanish history with universal history and geography.[31] The course descriptions included in the 1899 reform plan divided Spanish history into six chronological periods, one for each year of study beginning in the second year of the bachillerato. Ignoring prehistory entirely and slighting modern and contemporary history, Pidal's history curriculum emphasized the classical and Christian roots of Spanish nationhood. Its center of gravity was Rome and the Middle Ages, which were allotted three of the six years of study.

As noted in chapter 2, Pidal also appointed a Higher Consultative Committee of three distinguished intellectuals to write a single syllabus for each subject and to review textbooks for appropriate length, format, and price. The syllabus for the first-year history course, released on 24 July 1899, must have disappointed those who had expected the committee (whose membership included Menéndez y Pelayo) to prescribe a narrowly Catholic interpretation of the past.[32] By and large, the syllabus was a carefully neutral list of political and military topics, with a few nods to the "history of civilization," especially that of Greece. On this occasion, as on several others, Menéndez y Pelayo's refusal to subordinate scholarship to politics made him an unreliable ally of the integrist right.

Thus, the following year a group of Catholic deputies took their campaign for ideological control a step further by proposing state adoption

---

106. Chapter 12 is devoted entirely to the teaching of history at the Augustinian colegio where the author studied.

[30] Ignacio Ramón Miró, *La enseñanza de la historia en las escuelas* (Barcelona: Antonio J. Bastinos, 1889), 120.

[31] RD of 26 May 1899.

[32] RO of 26 May 1899. The other members of the committee were the writer and engineer Eduardo Saavedra and the republican mathematician and playwright José Echegaray.

of a single text for each subject. Ardent opponents of state education in theory, the Catholic right proved in practice to be only too willing to extend state power in pursuit of Catholic objectives. But as noted in chapter 2, the Catholic proposal to write a single text for each subject—or failing that, to allow students to be examined on texts of their own choosing—met with no greater success than the Pidal curriculum. By 1902, history was once again merely one of many modern subjects in an "encyclopedic" curriculum, and Catholic colegios found themselves still obliged to teach from the textbook assigned by the instituto catedrático if their students were to pass the state exams. The Liberal party's proscription of the practice of transporting students to several different institutos to be examined by catedráticos known for their ideological congeniality made the task of protecting Catholic youth from the perils of liberalism even more difficult. One common recourse was to prepare short summaries of the instituto texts for exam preparation, a strategy that permitted the colegios to excise offensive language and interpretations. There was little incentive to publish Catholic textbooks to supplement the official ones, however, since it was wholly unrealistic to expect students to read two books or their parents to pay for them.

Occasionally, the instituto textbook was written from an integrist perspective. Such was the case of the *Prontuario de historia de España*, by Felix Sánchez Casado, which in the 1890s was assigned not only by the author in his classes at the Instituto de San Isidro in Madrid, but also by catedráticos in Cuenca, Guadalajara, Córdoba, Salamanca, and Santiago de Compostela, and in various normal schools throughout the peninsula.[33] Integrist Catholic history textbooks were more often assigned in schools whose students were not preparing for the bachillerato—principally, seminaries, normal schools, and colegios for girls. Starting from the assumption that history was a discipline of the heart, not the intellect, these Catholic textbooks deployed language several degrees warmer than that typically found in liberal instituto textbooks, whose authors prided themselves on their allegiance to "cold" fact.[34]

Widely used in Catholic seminaries and colegios during the Restoration was the Spanish history textbook by Manuel Merry y Colón and Antonio Merry y Villalba. At the time of its publication in 1889, Merry y Colón was catedrático of Spanish history at the University of Seville and the author of a recently published six-volume general history of Spain. The purpose of both the general history and the textbook was to

---

[33] Ministerial surveys of 1894 and 1898 in AGMEC, leg. 6940. See chap. 3 for a discussion of Sánchez Casado's textbook.

[34] Severiano Doporto, a republican professor in Teruel, in a petition to the Ministry of Development for approval of his world history syllabus, in early 1898 or early 1899. AGMEC, leg. 6940.

purge "our History of the series of errors with which Protestantism, Philosophism, and Rationalism have tried to obscure our national glories, which, insofar as they have been great and many, have been eminently Catholic." Merry's text was the antithesis of the liberal histories that he condemned for "falsifying the truth and obscuring our glorious traditions with the dark hues of denial or error."[35] Because his goal was ideological persuasion (not encyclopedic coverage of content or erudition), Merry's narrative was selective, fluent, and succinct. By incorporating traditional legends, homely anecdotes, and editorial comment, and by adopting ardent and inclusive language, Merry sought to instill a shared sense of divinely inspired identity and purpose in his readers.

Merry y Colón defined the history of Spain as "the science that narrates the deeds realized by the Spanish nation in fulfillment of its providential destiny."[36] "Spain" (that is, the national spirit), not "Spaniards," was the real protagonist of the national saga that followed, although "Spaniards" appeared occasionally in a protective role, expelling foreigners and anti-Spanish ideas from the patria.[37] In contrast to liberal identification of the "nation" with the state or the national territory, here the nation was conceived as a community of believers; indeed, Merry's history of Spain was in many ways a history of the communal faith in its institutionalized forms, a history of the church in a national context. Like his liberal counterparts, Merry associated the trinity of "God, patria, and king" with Spanish nationhood, but unlike them, he clearly subordinated the second two terms of the triad to the first. Liberal historians viewed religious unity as an auxiliary to political and territorial unity; for Merry, kings and states existed to preserve the faith.

The distribution of pages in Merry's text mirrored this fundamental assumption: the Reconquest ("those centuries of religiosity, bravura and heroism") occupied nearly 40 percent of the whole (two pages of which discussed Muslim Spain). Another 25 percent was devoted to the Catholic Kings (who dedicated Spain to "the triumph of the Catholic idea") and the Habsburgs (who "subordinate[d] all their acts to religion, who submit[ted] social life to it, and who present[ed] themselves to the

[35] Merry y Colón and Merry y Villalba, Compendio, 7. Before his appointment in Seville, Merry y Colón (sometimes spelled "Colom") was catedrático of history at the instituto in Osuna and the University of Granada . López Cordón discusses several of his textbooks in "Mentalidad conservadora," in García Delgado, España de la Restauracion, 85–91.

[36] Merry y Colón and Merry y Villalba, Compendio, 9.

[37] The same observation about the protagonist of French Catholic history manuals is made by Jacqueline Freyssinet-Dominjon, Les Manuels de l'histoire de l'école libre, 1882–1959: De la loi Ferry à la loi Debré (Paris: Armand Colin, 1969), 106.

world as the true standard-bearers of Catholicism"). The period from the eighteenth century until the revolution of 1868, in contrast, merited only 15 percent of the text. After the Bourbons ("sophistically resorting to a distinction between politics and religion") had signed the death warrant of "genuinely Christian Spanish politics," the pueblo had become "the faithful repository of our beliefs." Although betrayed by kings and ministers, the pueblo had preserved that faith and in 1814 had welcomed Fernando VII with cries of "Down with the Constitution! Long live the Holy Office!" As for the revolution of 1868, it was the "logical consequence of that series of outrages that Spain had witnessed in prior years, *such as the aforementioned massacre of friars, the despoilment of the property of the Church, the exile of Bishops, the persecution of the Nuncio, the beginning of the Schism and the discussion sustained with the Vicar of Jesus Christ; the favor shown to atheist and rationalist propaganda, and the other errors condemned by the Roman Pontiff and the recognition of the usurpation of the Patrimony of St. Peter.*"[38]

In his narrative Merry highlighted events that exemplified the intertwining of the sacred and the secular in Spanish history. His contempt for those who cast doubt on "tradition" as a source of historical truth was unbounded: to deny the patriotic and pious value of national traditions, however fabulous or miraculous, "would be in us extreme cowardice." Thus, he unhesitatingly described the settlement of the peninsula by Túbal and/or Tarsis (sacred authorities disagreed); the evangelization of the peninsula by Saint James; his visitation on the banks of the Ebro by the Holy Virgin, "who in person promised to look with singular favor on the Spanish nation," and his return at the head of the Christian forces during the Reconquest.[39] By inserting these legends uncritically into the narrative, Merry not only sacralized the national past, but also implicitly elevated tradition and authority over scientific evidence as sources of truth.

Identifying Túbal and Tarsis as the first inhabitants of Spain served an additional function for Catholic authors, who would cling to the tradition well into the twentieth century. Túbal provided a powerful "origin myth" in a nation whose origins and character were contested. Even when they affirmed the existence of a national character or an "internal constitution," conservative liberals and progressives fundamentally saw the nation as the culmination of an historical *process* (although they disagreed about the nature of that process and its end result). The Catholic right, on the other hand, took an essentialist position that situated

[38] Merry y Colón and Merry y Villalba, *Compendio*, 119, 127, 146, 181, 207, 213–14.
[39] Ibid., 49, 18.

national identity outside the processes of historical change. Making Túbal the progenitor of the nation was a way of materializing Catholic arguments about the Spanish "race" that were otherwise impossible to sustain.

Merry's text also celebrated the alliance of throne and altar in Spain— ecclesiastical and religious milestones like church councils and papal intercessions, the evangelization of the Americas, the wars against Protestantism, and of course, the establishment of the Inquisition, "so hated by Protestants and the impious, so celebrated and praised by the faithful sons of the Catholic church." Responsibility for the Inquisition lay with the Jews and *conversos*, whom Merry condemned with remarkable ferocity for their heresy, antipatriotism, and greed. The success of the Inquisition in dealing with religious and civil disunity merited the highest praise: "The Holy Office is the most faithful portrait of our character; it is Spanish political thought put into practice."[40]

Merry frequently interrupted his story to praise the heroes who embodied the ideals of the nation, particularly the "gigantic figure of the Cid Campeador," whose very existence foreign and even a few national historians had dared to doubt: "It is enough for him to have been a man of ardent Faith and a glory of the patria, for Protestants and freethinkers to want to uproot him from the national soil."[41] Naturally, Merry's portrait of the Cid omitted his service to Muslim rulers during his years of exile from Castile. The Cid, like Cardinal Cisneros, the astute Fernando of Aragon and the pious Isabel of Castile, Charles V, Philip II, and Fernando VII, deserved respect and emulation not as state-builders, but as defenders of the faith. Their patriotism and national identity, like their personal virtues, emanated from the wellspring of their religion.

Exclusively targeting seminaries and Catholic colegios, Merry y Colón was able to indulge in the purest form of integrism. To reach a wider audience, however, Catholic authors were obliged to adopt a less combative, more "objective" tone. A case in point is the manual for primary teachers published in 1916 by the Catalan Jesuit Ramón Ruiz Amado.[42] A vocal opponent of state education and a strident advocate of integrist pedagogy, Ruiz Amado hoped to provide a counterweight to the growing influence of progressive methods among the nation's maestros. In form, his manual resembled the official texts to which maestros were accustomed: it was reasonably (if not exhaustively) comprehen-

---

[40] Ibid., 129, 160.
[41] Ibid., 67, 68.
[42] Ramón Ruiz Amado, S.J., *Compendio de historia de España desde las más remotas épocas hasta la guerra europea de 1914* (Barcelona: Librería Religiosa, 1916).

sive, conventional in periodization, and organizationally congruent with
the liberal model of the Spanish past. It was also more cautious with
respect to "national traditions" that lacked historical substantiation,
like the evangelization of the peninsula by Saint James, and cool in its
portraits of national heroes. While affirming the historicity of the Cid,
for example, Ruiz Amado attributed his renowned knightly virtues to
the idealization of popular poetry.[43]

At the interpretative level, however, Ruiz Amado's history of Spain
was no less traditionally Catholic and antiliberal than Merry y Colón's.
Objectivity, he noted in his prologue, "should not be confused with
amoral *indifference*, which . . . treats with strict impartiality virtuous
heroes of the fatherland and immoral men whose crimes have been the
cause of our sad disasters."[44] A follower of the German educator Jo-
hann Herbart and his neo-Thomist disciple Otto Willmann, Ruiz Amado shared their belief in the educational value of history. But whereas
the Germans had emphasized individual character formation, the Spaniard was more sensitive to the social and political function of history.
History must aim to "to stimulate in our youth the sacred fire of *patriotism*, so necessary for the resurgence of our patria and so weakened,
unfortunately, by the political discussions that have occupied and ster-
ilized us during the entire nineteenth century."[45]

Like Merry y Colón, Ruiz Amado defined nationality in terms of religious (as opposed to political) unity. In his view, national history had
really begun with the Reconquest. Before the invasion of the Arabs, the
peoples of the peninsula had been divided; afterward, "we find only
Christians." If Christianity and nationality were historically coter-
minous in Spain, it followed that threats to that union—whether in the
form of Jews, conversos, or Protestants—warranted an energetic and
intransigent response. Contrary to progressive allegations, religious intransigence had not caused the so-called decadence of the seventeenth
century: "*Religion*, far from accelerating our decadence, contained it,
lending a solid base to our national character, and serving as a *bond*
among all Spaniards, in other things so disunited." By placing spiritual
well-being before economic advantage, the Habsburgs had indeed courted
political and economic disaster, but at least they had died out "in the
sad but majestic light of a setting sun," and had not, like their Bourbon

---

[43] Ibid., 20, 56.

[44] Ibid., v.

[45] Ibid., vi. On Herbart and Willmann, see Gino Ferretti, "La historia, el espíritu filo-
sófico y la educación moral," in Instituto de Ciencias de la Educación, Geneva, *El espíritu
internacional y la enseñanza de la historia: Estudios presentados al tercer Congreso Internacional de Educación Moral* (Madrid: Ediciones de La Lectura, Espasa-Calpe, 1932),
97–98.

successors, "tied Spain to the triumphal chariot of France, from whose imitation and fatal dependence it has not been able completely to dissociate itself up to our own day."[46]

In claiming a unique spirituality for Spain, Ruiz Amado fashioned a national identity antithetic to those of the "modern" nations to which she was so often invidiously compared. Spain's virtues—austerity, liberality, spirituality, and abnegation—gave her a claim to "universality" that the "godless" French or the money-grubbing English lacked. If those qualities had not led to material prosperity, they nonetheless established Spain's right to a preeminent place among the civilized nations of the West.[47]

Unlike many integrist Catholic authors, Ruiz Amado devoted a large fraction of his narrative to history since the eighteenth century. Since the accession of the Bourbon dynasty, he argued, Spain had endured "two periods of *afrancesamiento,* which have turned almost the entire volume of Spanish life away from the channels of our ancient tradition." In the eighteenth century, the Bourbons had introduced "*absolutism* of the French variety"; Spanish regalism was but "an imitation of the *Gallicanism* with which the French sovereigns had succeeded in enslaving the church in France." Since 1808 French revolutionary ideas had held sway, "producing a general skepticism united to the most refined immorality." The Constitution of 1812 was "a fictitious juridical scaffolding" imposed on a pueblo that "was spilling its blood" in defense of its "homes and altars." Ruiz Amado's scarcely veiled antiliberalism permeated his discussion of the Carlist wars, the liberal disentailment of church lands by "the Jew Mendizábal," and the "pettiness of . . . domestic politics" during the Restoration. His narrative closed with a rare burst of passion, an invocation that looked backward to the Golden Age of Spanish imperial power for its inspiration: "God save our patria! And let us, its children, each one working in his place, in faithful fulfillment of his duty, strive to restore it to its former grandeur!"[48]

National regeneration, from the integrist perspective, implied a restoration, a journey backward in time to recapture the nation's true self, which had been lost in the intervening centuries of "foreign" interests and ideas. To progress, the nation must regress; to save itself from an ignominious present and future, it must first return to the point of deviation from its "true" history. When contrasted with the glories of the

---

[46] Ruiz Amado, *Compendio,* 46, 145–46, 159.

[47] See the discussion of identities and counter identities in Orest Ranum, "Counter-Identities of Western European Nations in the Early-Modern Period: Definitions and Points of Departure," in Peter Boerne, ed., *Concepts of National Identity: An Interdisciplinary Dialogue* (Baden-Baden: Nomos Verlagsgesellschaft, 1986), 63–78.

[48] Ibid., 165, 168, 171, 175, 203, 217, 222.

past, the baseness of the present was thrown into high relief. As Ruiz Amado remarked on another occasion, "We should turn to the past and remember what those Spaniards learned who did not lose colonies, but who conquered empires."[49]

Where Catholic educators could fully inculcate children with their views on national history and identity, unfettered by the restraints imposed by the state examination system, was in the primary schools— both their own and the many public schools where priests and teaching brothers and sisters served in the absence of state teachers. Properly taught, history could fruitfully supplement religion and sacred history in teaching Christian morals: it illustrated "the intervention of Providence in the world, the beneficial consequences of virtue and the pernicious results of vice."[50] Bereft of its Christian underpinnings, however, "the History of humankind lacks meaning; one doesn't know from where man has come nor where he is going." Indeed, improperly conceived, history harbored grave dangers: "Few subjects present so many and so well-disguised means for inoculating the tender understanding of children with error or corrupting the innocence of their hearts."[51]

Assuming the existence of a universal moral law and an essential human nature, the history in Catholic textbooks was often extremely reductionist. A reader entitled *La moral de la historia*, by the maestra Pilar Pascual de Sanjuán (author of *Flora*), presented world history as a reservoir of "sketches" exemplifying desirable moral principles, such as brotherly love, respect for teachers and elders, love of work, and humility. The first chapter, entitled "The Customs of the Indians," did not describe Indian religion or culture. Readers learned, however, that religion permeated every aspect of Indian life; thus, even though Indian religion was a "monstrous tissue of errors," this aspect of Indian society could be emulated by Christian children, who had the added advantage of a "divine law from the lips of God himself." The "historical" lesson to be committed to memory was "Be pious and devout above all." The remaining sketches were equally stingy with concrete historical information and equally replete with ahistorical moralizing. From the life of a

[49] Ramón Carbonell [Ramón Ruiz Amado], *Los dos bachilleratos*, quoted in Yvonne Turin, *La educación y la escuela en España de 1874 a 1902: Liberalismo y tradición*, trans. Josefa Hernández Alfonso (Madrid: Aguilar, 1967), 352.

[50] F.T.D., *Guía del maestro para uso de los Hmnos. Maristas de la Enseñanza: Redactada según las reglas y enseñanzas de su venerable fundador* (Barcelona: Editorial F.T.D., 1928), 234.

[51] Miró, *Enseñanza de la historia*, 129, 18. See also *Programa de enseñanza para las escuelas elementales* (Sarriá-Barcelona: Escuela Tipográfica y Librería Salesiana, 1904), 29–30, a guide prepared for schools operated by the Holy Society of San Francisco de Sales.

Roman slave, children learned to be faithful even in misfortune; from Saint Louis of Gonzaga, to be satisfied with their station in life. A lesson on Antoninus concluded, "Philosophy is truth, and as the greatest truth, the only truth, is Christian, we may thereby deduce that all so-called philosophers have usurped this title, professing and propagating doctrines that are more or less sophistical and more or less exaggerated."[52] The cumulative message conveyed to young readers was that good Catholics, obedient subjects, and docile workers would earn a heavenly reward; private, not public, virtue was the goal of this kind of history.

A similar quietist strain ran through a manual on history teaching published in 1889 by Ignacio Ramón Miró. To be fully effective as an instrument of social discipline, Miró contended, history should be taught selectively; the skilled and prudent teacher knew when "to choose, tell, veil and keep silent." Prehistory, for example, should not be discussed apart from the revealed history of Creation in Genesis. Contemporary history was not only difficult to extract from the "dense cloud formed by the vapors of passion," but might "wound the susceptibilities of parents," even when dispassionately taught. Moreover, contemporary history involved politics, and Miró reminded his readers that most Spanish Catholics agreed with the French traditionalist Monsignor Dupanloup, that the only lesson in politics appropriate for children was that which taught them "to love, respect, and obey."[53]

However well suited to the antidemocratic sentiments of the Catholic right, this political quietism had to be modified after 1890 to accommodate the shifting political and social landscape in Spain. Universal suffrage, rising social tension, and the growing influence of the Institución Libre de Enseñanza shifted the emphasis of Catholic history education from molding passive and obedient workers to shaping patriots committed to preserving Spain's Catholic identity. The fact that most of the new teaching orders were refugees from French anticlericalism only added to their zeal. After the inclusion of national history into the primary curriculum in 1901, Catholic schools paid greater attention to the patriotic dimension of history teaching. Correctly focused, national history would teach children that "the History of Spain is the history of the Spanish church and the greatness of Spain is the delicious fruit of Christianity."[54] Filled with "noble sentiments of filial love, *hidalguía* [nobility], and sacrifice both towards the madre Patria and toward the

[52] Pilar Pascual de Sanjuán, *La moral de la historia: Colección de cuadros históricos con su aplicación moral al alcance de los niños*, 6th ed. (Barcelona: Lib. de Juan y Antonio Bastinos, 1881), 7–9, 103–4.

[53] Miró, *Enseñanza de la historia*, 160, 161–62, 191. See also Pascual de Sanjuán, *Moral*, 3.

[54] *Programa de enseñanza*, 29.

church," and endowed with models from the past with which "to judge current events, institutions and personages," children would become patriots burning with "the sacred fire of love of the patria."[55]

To ensure that patriotic loyalty did not shade into an unhealthy exaltation of the state, the Catholic orders elaborated guidelines for teaching national history. The youngest children were to be taught orally, by means of stories about great men or interesting events, "drawing consequences that stimulate children to love virtue and diligence and to make themselves worthy sons of such a glorious patria."[56] Children in the upper grades were to study from textbooks that had been carefully vetted for doctrinal and moral orthodoxy.[57] Catholic educators warned that, as in France, apparent neutrality was as tendentious as outright liberal bias: "There are some [texts] in whose pages *impiety* is *cleverly disguised*; in others a criminal and intentional *silence* omits everything related to the supernatural and the Christian religion."[58] It was important, too, that students memorize lesson summaries accurately and that they understand the meanings of unfamiliar, and thus potentially dangerous, terms. In his teachers' manual, Miró prudently included correct definitions of the thorniest concepts: progress, liberty, equality, fraternity, patriotism, rights, civilization, enlightenment, fanaticism, superstition, and so forth. His definition of liberty, for example, drew heavily on the papal encyclical *Libertas* of 1888: "Unlimited liberty for the individual would mean the dissolution of society; liberty that is not circumscribed to its just limits produces disorder, and disorder is always a sickness more or less grave for the social body."[59]

Despite the admonition to teach young children orally, after 1900 some of the orders began to publish textbooks for the primary grades. The Brothers of the Christian Schools of La Salle, which had originally translated their French books for use in Spain, began to publish in Barcelona in 1896. Subsequently opening offices in Madrid and Gijón, their Bruño imprint was publishing at least three million volumes annually by 1928.[60] F.T.D. (later, Edelvives), the publishing house of the Marist

---

[55] F.T.D., *Guía del maestro*, 234, *Programa de enseñanza*, 29. See also Ángel Rojí de Echeñique, *El educador en acción* (Pamplona: Imp. de la Viuda de Román Velandia, 1910). The author was a teaching brother in a Piarist school.

[56] *Programa de enseñanza*, 50; see also F.T.D., *Guía del maestro*, 234–35.

[57] See the recommendations in *Programa de enseñanza*, 69–72.

[58] F.T.D., *Guía del maestro*, 149.

[59] Miró, *Enseñanza de la historia*, 73. See also F.T.D., *Guía del maestro*, 149; *LE* 5, no. 121 (2 May 1903): 956–57.

[60] Saturnino Gallego, *Sembraron con amor: "LaSalle," centenario en España (1878–1978)* (San Sebastián: Industria Gráfica Valverde, 1978), 230–31, 339, 477–78. For the texts and pedagogical methods of the Brothers of the Christian Schools in France, see Henri-Charles Rulon and Philippe Friot, *Un siècle de pédagogie dans les écoles primaires*

Brothers, also flourished in Spain after the "textbook wars" in France led to the prohibition of its history texts there.[61] Other orders gradually established their own lines of primary schoolbooks as the market for them expanded and the battle to capture hearts and minds intensified: the Salesians (Librería Salesiana), the Piarist Fathers (E.P.), the Marianist Fathers (S.M.), and the Jesuits (Razón y Fe and later, Miñón) all launched their own presses.

An early example of these Catholic primary history texts was the *Epítome del párvulo*, published by Bruño in 1915. The *Epítome*, a forerunner of the "encyclopedias" that would dominate the Spanish textbook market after the civil war, included a brief overview of every subject in the official curriculum, which reduced textbook expenditures substantially for families in straitened circumstances. Both the reading skills of the students and the brevity of the text dictated that each section should be very short; in 23 pages and 189 questions and answers the text covered the history of Spain from prehistory to the present.[62] The answers, never more than one sentence long, were primarily unadorned factual responses to questions such as "From where did the Carthaginians come?" or "Who were the most celebrated kings of the House of Austria?"

But even in this austere compilation of events and personages there was room for the integrist staples. Children learned that Túbal (son of Jafet and grandson of Noah) and Tarsis (Noah's great-grandson) were the first settlers in the peninsula, that Saint James evangelized Spain and led the Christian troops against the Moors at Clavijo, and that don Pelayo's hearty band defeated 200,000 Arabs at Covadonga. Seven questions were allotted to the Christianization of the peninsula, seven more to Christopher Columbus, but only one to the final three Habsburgs. Charles III was acclaimed for placing Spain under the patronage of the Immaculate Conception, but rebuked for expelling the Jesuits ("with great damage to Spanish science and letters") on the advice of "impious ministers." The text noted that Ferdinand VII was "hailed with enthusiasm" on his return to Spain in 1814, but was silent on the Constitution of Cádiz (and all other constitutions).[63] The Carlist war was mentioned without hinting that the Carlists had lost. A final question about famous men of recent times elicited a short catalog of intransigently Catholic luminaries—Zorrilla, Balmes, Verdaguer, Clavé, Donoso Cortés, and Menéndez y Pelayo, among others.

(1820–1940): Histoire des méthodes et des manuels scolaires utilisés dans l'Institut des Frères de l'Instruction chrétien de Ploermel (Paris: J. Vrin, 1962).

[61] See Freyssinet-Dominjon, *Les Manuels d'histoire*, 39.

[62] G. M. Bruño, *Epítome del párvulo* (Madrid: Administración Bruño, 1915), 97–121.

[63] Ibid., 115, 116.

The usual themes of liberal history books—national unification, in particular—were striking by their absence from the texts of the religious orders. Monarchs appeared not as agents of state consolidation, but as personifications of Christian virtues and vices and as the figures personally responsible for national glories and misfortunes, as they were defined by the church. Absent, too, was any definition of national character or identity, apart from religious communion; on the contrary, the texts encouraged children to place their identity as Spaniards at the service of their identity as Catholics. The Spanish nation was a community of like believers; accordingly, non-Catholics were ipso facto not part of the nation, and the patriotic duty of "true" Spaniards was to preserve the unity of the faith.

Although this message was imbedded in the catechistic histories published by the orders, it was not expressed emphatically or even explicitly. Like the liberal textbooks of the same era, these histories generally presented the national past as a colorless chronology fundamentally unrelated to the lives, present concerns, or secular responsibilities of their readers. History was not about "us," but about remote individuals or a disembodied group, "the Spaniards," whose glorious deeds were to be passively applauded and committed to memory, but whose human dimension or patriotic significance was not made real. Linking patriotism and national glory primarily to war, both Catholic and liberal textbooks suggested that the fundamental civic duty was to die for the nation. Politics, especially recent politics, was disruptive and unedifying, the resort of scoundrels, factions, and antipatriots.

These Catholic textbooks shared another characteristic with their liberal counterparts: their reliance on rote memorization. This was congruent with the essentially passive role that both Catholics and conservative liberals envisioned for the Spanish masses, but for that very reason, it attracted the ire of progressives who equated "active education" with democratic political reform. The Catholic response to progressive educators was spearheaded by Father Andrés Manjón, whose open-air schools and active methods were given wide publicity by integrist Catholic publicists.[64] National history played a major role in Manjón's Escuelas del Ave María, where it was assigned the function of preparing children for "practical life, not only individual, but collective and national."[65] Like all subjects, history was taught through play, rather than textbooks. Children dramatized the colonization of the peninsula and martial episodes from the Spanish past and, most famously, played hopscotch on a diagram of Spanish history while reciting the succession of

---

[64] For Father Manjón, see chap. 1.

[65] *El pensamiento del Ave-María*, pt. 3, quoted in Ángel Benito Durán, "Manjón," *Atenas* 10, nos. 89–90 (1939): 94; and in Prellezo García, *Manjón, educador*, 454.

ruling peoples and dynasties. As progressive critics were quick to note, games and role-playing did not eliminate memorization, they only facilitated it. (In a teacher training course sponsored by the ministry in 1913, the institucionista Rafael Altamira likened children in Manjón's schools to "trained dogs.")[66] Active educational methods that required children to think for themselves were conspicuously absent from Manjón's schools.

But however "memoristic" or predigested, Manjónian history education could not be accused of neglecting the "formation" of the child; on the contrary, formation in the Catholic sense of the word lay at the core of his enterprise. History was, in Manjón's view, the supreme magister vitae, enabling children to understand the present and providing them with "models to imitate and ideals and destinies to fulfill" in the future. The lesson plans, games, and activities that Manjón recommended to Catholic educators in a series of widely admired publications were infused with integrist values and with determined indifference to the achievements of recent historical scholarship (labeled the "vain erudition of dilettantes" by the master).[67] The historical episodes he selected for dramatization, which always began with the arrival of Túbal in 2200 B.C., exemplified the moral and patriotic virtues of the nation. Even the hopscotch diagram, intended as an aide-mémoire, was a visual exposition of the integrist vision of the national past (plate 2).

Through fidelity to national tradition, children would become true patriots. Patria was what Spain was and had been, not what revolutionaries and atheists wished it might be. Real patriots would never wish to replace the historic Spain with a new one modeled on French or English examples, or to repudiate her providential mission to defend the faith. With history as guide and restraint, the patriot would confidently reject the innovators, revolutionaries, and Europeanizers whose promises of a new Spain could lead only to betrayal and oppression.[68]

For Manjón and other integrists, the word *patria* captured best their concept of the nation. Love of the patria was like the love that bound children to their mothers—a primordial bond forged by blood, birth, and belief. Children inherited their patria as they inherited their families, not out of choice, nor with an eye to their improvement, but out of sentiment and necessity. Indeed, the "honorable, Christian and well-organized patriotic family" was the patria "in embryo."[69]

[66] Rafael Altamira, "Una lección de metodología histórica," *Ideario pedagógico* (Madrid: Editorial Reus, 1923), 162.

[67] Quoted in Prellezo García, *Manjón, educador*, 455.

[68] Andrés Manjón, *Hojas catequísticas y pedagógicas del Ave María: Libro 3°* (Granada: Imprenta-Escuela de Ave María, 1921), leaflet 12.

[69] Manuales Manjón, *Historia de España: Breve resumen con dos gráficos*, 14th ed. (Granada: Imprenta-Escuela de Ave-María, 1940), 179.

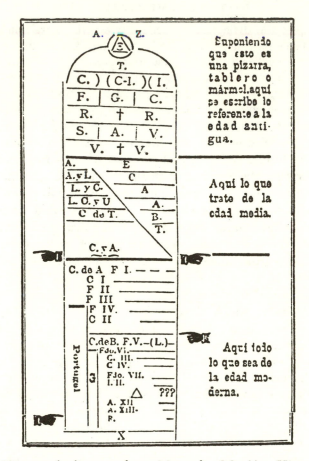

Plate 2. Hopscotch diagram from Manuales Manjón, *Historia de España: Breve resumen con dos gráficos*, 14th ed. (Granada: Imprenta-Escuela del Ave-María, 1940), 5. Under the eye of Providence, the Spanish nation, starting with its progenitor, Túbal, and the Celtiberian "race," unfolds toward its destiny. United politically and religiously under Rome (R.) and then again under the Visigoths (V.), its history is interrupted by the Arab invasion but gradually reconstructed under the leadership of Castile. With the merger of the crowns of Castile and Aragon, the nation expands westward to the Americas and eastward to the Mediterranean until, with the dynasty of the Bourbons, the European and American empires are lost. Symbols on the diagram remind children of painful episodes like the loss of Portugal and Gibraltar or the (alleged) Masonic conspiracy that forced the abdication of Isabel II. Manjón's contempt for the Bourbons is registered in the small type with which their names are recorded. In this version of the diagram, published in the 1930s, the Republic is followed by X, the unknown future.

On the other hand, what distinguished Manjón from other integrist Catholic educators was his conception of history as a spur to political engagement; history as nostalgia and resentment was not enough. Manjón insisted that classroom instruction should not dwell on ancient history, but on the recent past and its lessons for current and future affairs. Instead of the passive obedience the teaching orders (and most of the Restoration politicians) aspired to instill, Manjón aimed at mobilizing Catholic opinion—not just among the elites, but in the "nation" as well. Acutely aware of the link between national identity and perceptions of the national past, Manjón made the case for history as the key to political and social transformation in an age of mass politics: "Those called to govern nations learn history, so let us all learn it, for if the former need it to guide from above, we need it to guide from below; because leadership, including social leadership, is the mission of education."[70]

Although Manjón's pedagogical innovations were publicized enthusiastically by the Catholic press and even imitated in a handful of schools,[71] until his death in 1923 his methods served Catholic education primarily as a propagandistic counterweight to the pedagogical offensive of the Institución Libre de Enseñanza. The traditionalist right would only gradually come to share his activist views on the need to mobilize the masses behind the Catholic banner; during the Restoration, their posture was more one of passive lament than of political counteroffensive. Manjón's integrist conception of history, however, was typical of Catholic colegios in general during the Restoration. In Catholic classrooms children were exposed to a national story that was openly subversive of the version that validated the liberal state. Catholic textbooks portrayed Spanish history since the eighteenth century as a sorrowful tale of betrayal, invasion, and bondage to foreign ideas and institutions. According to this story, the freedoms guaranteed in the liberal constitution were false; true freedom lay in liberating the nation from her captors and restoring her cultural and religious identity. Since the colegios educated a large and growing fraction of Spanish secondary and primary students, and integrist Catholic teachers and professors taught many more in public classrooms and private academies, the political implications for liberal parliamentary government were not promising.

---

[70] Quoted in Prellezo García, *Manjón, educador*, 456.

[71] See, for example, Manuel Siurot, *Cada maestrito: Observaciones pedagógicas de uno que no ha visto en su vida un libro de pedagogía* (Seville: El Correo de Andalucía, 1912).

CHAPTER 5

History Recovered:
Rafael Altamira and National Regeneration

> I have the firm belief that, among the essential
> conditions for our national regeneration, the
> following two are inescapable: (1) Restore the
> credit of our history, with the goal of returning
> to the Spanish people their faith in their native
> qualities and their aptitude for civilized life, and
> of taking advantage of the useful elements that
> the knowledge and conduct of past times offer
> us; (2) Wisely avoid allowing this to lead us to
> the resurrection of past forms, to an
> archaeological regression. Our reform must be
> realized in the direction of modern civilization,
> in contact with which our national spirit will be
> enlivened and purified.
> (*Rafael Altamira*)[1]

CHALLENGES to the Moderado interpretation of national history were
of course not restricted to the Catholic right. Since the debate was really
over the shape of the future, not of the past, critics across the political
spectrum constructed alternative interpretations of the national past to
legitimate their proposals for political and social reform. Like conservatives and Catholic integrists, progressives generally acknowledged the
need to marshal history in support of their political projects. But the
historical longevity of the institutions to which they were most opposed—the church and the monarchy—problematized the search for a
serviceable past. For many progressives the easiest answer lay in the
simple repudiation of national history, or at least those parts progressives found difficult to assimilate into their vision of national regeneration. By blaming history for the failings of the present, the path lay
open to overcoming it. Thus, much of what passed for politically progressive historical discourse during the Restoration involved little more

[1] Rafael Altamira y Crevea, "La universidad y el patriotismo" (1898), in *Ideario pedagógico* (Madrid: Editorial Reus, 1923), 268.

than the inversion of the accepted verities of the Catholic and Moderado traditions. What integrists or conservatives held dear, democrats and republicans reflexively debunked. Thus, whereas neo-Catholics blamed the Bourbons for forcibly separating Spain from her true identity, progressives accused the Habsburgs. The great republican orator Emilio Castelar scandalized traditionalists with his oratory in 1868: "There is nothing more frightful, more abominable than that great Spanish empire that was a shroud that extended over the planet. We have no agriculture, because we expelled the *moriscos* . . . ; we have no industry, because we threw out the Jews. . . . We have no science, we are an atrophied member of modern science. . . . We lit the bonfires of the Inquisition, threw our thinkers in them, burnt them and thereafter of the sciences in Spain there was no more than a pile of ashes."[2]

As we have seen, reprises of this theme in the 1870s provoked the retaliatory defense of "Spanish science" by the brilliant young Catholic apologist, Marcelino Menéndez y Pelayo. With the restoration of academic freedom in 1881, the polemic extended to the universities. The colorful and unrelenting attacks on Philip II and the Inquisition (delivered "with no less ill-will than if they had personally suffered grievances at their hands")[3] by the two republican catedráticos who successively taught the history of Spain in the School of Philosophy and Letters at the University of Madrid, Miguel Morayta and Juan Ortega y Rubio, delighted or infuriated students, depending on their political allegiances, well into the twentieth century.[4] From the late 1880s on, much of the prescriptive regenerationist literature also took as its starting point a condemnation of the imperial past. The stunning defeat of 1898 lent added urgency to the historical analysis of "the national problem." The explanation of "our national ruin," insisted Ricardo Macías Picavea, lay in the "de-nationalization" of Spain by Teutonic foreigners. Despite their "pseudo-españolismo," the Habsburgs in fact had destroyed the thriving municipal democracy and the indigenous Hispano-Arabic civi-

[2] Quoted in Pedro Sainz Rodríguez, *Evolución de las ideas sobre la decadencia española y otros estudios de crítica literaria* (Madrid: Ediciones Rialp, 1962), 119.

[3] José de Deleito, *La enseñanza de la historia en la universidad española y su reforma posible: Discurso leído en la solemne apertura del curso académico de 1918 a 1919 en la Universidad Literaria de Valencia* (Valencia: Tip. Moderna, 1918), 18. For additional comments on the politicization of the history *cátedras* during the Restoration, see Pedro Sainz Rodríguez, *Testimonios y recuerdos* (Barcelona: Editorial Planeta, 1978), 29; and José Jorro de Miranda, *Nuestros problemas docentes*, vol. 1, *La Administración* (Madrid: Sucesores de Hernando, 1919), 541–43.

[4] Both were the authors of general histories of Spain—Miguel Morayta de Sagrario, *Historia general de España desde los tiempos ante-históricos hasta nuestros días*, 9 vols. (Madrid: González Rojas, 1886–96); and Juan Ortega y Rubio, *Historia de España*, 8 vols. (Madrid: Bailly-Baillière, 1908–10)—as well as of manuals for their students.

lization of the Middle Ages and the Renaissance. "Good-bye nationality! Good-bye tradition! Good-bye progress!"[5]

The ultimate target of these attacks was, of course, the constitutional and political settlement of 1875, whose compromises with traditionalism were grounded in organicist discourse about the "internal constitution." In answer to Cánovas's claims to "continue the history of Spain," progressives retorted that his version of the past was but one of many possible readings, and one, moreover, that marginalized the achievements of the revolutionary Sexenio. By demonstrating that the universalistic "Spanish" values held by Cánovas and his Catholic allies were both anachronistic and particularistic, progressives hoped to historicize the Restoration settlement and clear the way for the secularization and democratization—that is, the "nationalization"—of the Spanish state.

At the same time, progressives perceived that mere political action was insufficient to overcome the legacy of the past. What was needed was not merely reform of the state, but reform—or even improvisation—of the nation.[6] Only when the pueblo had been revitalized—that is, when it had acquired (or recovered) a sense of itself as a nation— could it create a democratic state reflective of its highest ideals. The intense interest in educational reform at the turn of the century can be understood only in this context.

Progressive intellectuals thus viewed the pueblo with ambivalence; it was at once the repository of their hopes and the source of their despair and frustration. Giner de los Ríos, for example, took a grim view of the social and cultural burdens inherited from the past. Habsburg intolerance and martial vanity had gradually distorted the national character, transforming Spaniards into a superstitious, hypocritical, rigid, indolent, and frivolous people.[7] Similar pessimistic assessments of the national character echoed through the writings of the regenerationists in the 1890s, reaching their climax after 1898.[8] According to Joaquín

---

[5] Ricardo Macías Picavea, *El problema nacional: (Hechos, causas y remedios)*, ed. José Esteban (Madrid: Fundación Banco Exterior, 1992) (1st ed. 1899), 215.

[6] The phrase is from Joaquín Costa, *Reconstitutión y europeización de España* (1900), quoted in Frederick B. Pike, *Hispanismo, 1898–1936: Spanish Conservatives and Liberals and Their Relations with Spanish America* (Notre Dame, Ind.: University of Notre Dame Press, 1971), 56.

[7] For Giner de los Ríos, see chap. 1. Giner's views on history are discussed in Juan López-Morillas, *Racionalismo pragmático: El pensamiento de Francisco Giner de los Ríos* (Madrid: Alianza Universidad, 1988), 33–42.

[8] For regenerationist analyses of the past, see, in addition to Macías Picavea, *El problema nacional*; Lucas Mallada, *Los males de la patria y la futura revolución española* (Madrid: Tip. de M. Ginés Hernández, 1890); Luis Morote, *La moral de la derrota* (Madrid: G. Juste, 1900); Pompeyo Gener, "La decadencia española: De la incivilización de España" (1888), quoted in Sainz Rodríguez, *Evolución de las ideas*, 120; and Manuel

Costa, from the sixteenth to the eighteenth centuries Spain had experienced a kind of "reverse selection" that, "owing to the excess of convents, the religious Inquisition and the colonization of America" eliminated "the superior and most generous elements of the race."[9] At present, he insisted, "the Spanish soul has as its fundamental character a spirit made into dogma, rigid, incapable of evolution . . . , bound to the past . . . , subjected to a necromantic regime."[10]

The portrait of the national character that emerged in regenerationist discourse invoked both identities and counteridentities. Although the "aristocratic" moral qualities long associated with the Spanish were not disputed, they were found, upon closer examination, to be vices: honor was in fact arrogance; hidalguía, sloth and aversion to useful labor; religiosity, fanaticism; monarchism, servility; generosity, ostentation.[11] Bad enough in themselves, these vices derived additional force when compared with the much-admired "European" virtues of industry, tolerance, and sobriety. Thus defined in opposition to "Europe," Spaniards looked more like other groups similarly defined—like Africans, or Arabs. The occasional critic held "Arabic" or "Semitic" blood accountable for the Spanish addiction to routine and fatalism, but such biological explanations were relatively rare, particularly because progressives were inclined to value positively the cultural pluralism of the Middle Ages.[12] In any case, progressives generally shunned deterministic biological theories in favor of historicist models that suggested continuing evolution of the national character. Admittedly, historical evolution was not necessarily synonymous with progress. According to the progressive historian José Deleito, for example, Spain had only become "an African country" in the nineteenth century, as a result of the cultivation of "barbaric hyper-Spanishness" among traditionalists. But like Costa's exhortation to expel "the Africa that has invaded us," Deleito's explanation

---

Sales y Ferré, "Psicología del pueblo español," *Nuestro Tiempo* 2, no. 13 (1902), 9–20. For discussions of this literature, see Pike, *Hispanismo*, especially chap. 5; Sainz Rodríguez, *Evolución de las ideas*; and Julián Juderías, *La leyenda negra: Estudios acerca del concepto de España en el extranjero*, 13th ed. (Madrid: Editora Nacional, 1954).

[9] From *Los siete criterios de gobierno* (1899), quoted in Eloy Fernández Clemente, ed., *Educación y revolución en Joaquín Costa y breve antología pedagógica* (Madrid: EDICUSA, 1969), 111.

[10] Ibid., 46.

[11] The cultural critique based on counteridentities had a venerable history in Spain, going back to the *arbitristas* of the seventeenth century. See Julio Caro Baroja, *El mito del carácter nacional: Meditaciones a contrapelo* (Madrid: Seminarios y Ediciones, 1970), 87.

[12] See Pompeyo Gener, *Cosas de España: Herejías nacionales. El renacimiento de Cataluña*, cited in Alberto del Pozo Pardo, "Año 1898: Llamada de esperanza a una regeneración pedagógica de España," *REP* 36, no. 140 (1978): 103–16.

of national character made it the historico-cultural product of human agency, and thus subject to restoration, invention, or renewal.[13]

It was not easy to see, however, how the Spanish pueblo could recover the path of progress and prosperity if its history had left it so structurally degraded. The answer for many lay in simply shrugging off the dead weight of the past. Joaquín Costa's famous exhortation to "double-lock the tomb of the Cid!" was nothing more than a prescription for a forward-looking cultural modernization unencumbered by links with a self-destructive past. "History can deceive us greatly," Miguel de Unamuno observed in 1902, "by showing us not the native aptitudes of a people, but rather only those that have been allowed to develop."[14] "We ought to forget all our history," added Ramiro de Maeztu, still in his Europeanizing phase, "and place our eyes only on the supreme ideal, there in the future."[15] Conveniently forgetting that they had condemned the Habsburgs for rupturing an earlier national tradition, progressives now concluded that a break with the "tyranny of the past" was essential to restore the nation to its better self—to reconcile, in the words of Giner, "what ought to be and what is."[16] Costa, always adept at coining memorable phrases, expressed it succinctly: "The only way to honor the past is to put an end to it."[17]

This revolt against history led progressive reformers to refuse to commemorate occasions that they associated with the pernicious past, like the quatercentenary of Columbus's voyage or the centennial of the 1808 uprising against the French. But this only lent substance to the accusations of the Catholic right, who labeled the Europeanizers as "anti-Spanish," "imitative," or "patrio-masochistic." Progressives complained bitterly about this reflex: "We have a national history that, while unknown, is taken out to shine like an arm of combat every time someone questions our exaggerated greatness."[18] And they counterattacked by pointing out that "nothing is more deceptive than tradition. With it you can defend anything, even the return to paganism."[19] The

[13] José de Deleito, *El aislamiento de España en el pasado y el presente: Conferencia dada en el Círculo Instructivo Reformista de Valencia el día 17 de marzo de 1919* (Valencia: n.p., 1915), 16; "Africa that has invaded us," quoted in Manuel de Puelles Benítez, *Educación e ideología en la España contemporánea (1767–1975)* (Barcelona: Editorial Labor, 1980), 243.

[14] Miguel de Unamuno, OC 3:716.

[15] Quoted in Pike, *Hispanismo*, 50. Maeztu's Europeanist essays are collected in *Hacia otra España* (Madrid: Fernando Fé, 1899).

[16] Quoted in López-Morillas, *Racionalismo pragmático*, 54.

[17] Fernández Clemente, *Educación*, 49.

[18] Deleito, *Aislamiento*, 21.

[19] Miguel de Unamuno, "Más sobre el crisis del patriotismo español" (1906), in OC 3:875.

young Ortega y Gasset, dismissing the "quietistic and voluptuous patriotism" of triumphalists who wished to rest on Spain's laurels, argued that real patriotism meant refusing to be satisfied with the past or the present: "In order to know what our patria should be tomorrow, we have to weigh what has been and overemphasize the defects of our past. True patriotism is criticism of the land of the fathers and construction of the land of the sons."[20]

Ortega's own contribution to this patriotic task was published in 1921 under the title *España invertebrada*. Lamenting the "particularism" that was tearing the nation apart, Ortega lay the blame on a failure of leadership and national purpose. Since the sixteenth century, Castile—or more specifically, the monarchy and the church—had mistaken their particular interests for those of the nation, thereby hastening the process of disintegration that was now reaching its climax. But Ortega's diagnosis went beyond the familiar indictment of the Habsburgs: the roots of the national malaise, he argued, lay in the Visigothic invasion of the fifth century. Unlike the robust Franks to the north, the German tribes who conquered the Iberian peninsula were overly civilized by long exposure to the Romans and were therefore too inert to articulate a dynamic feudal society. Deprived of healthy leadership, Spain's masses had never learned to recognize or to follow the natural elites that infuse great nations with "historical vitality." But although historically imbedded in the national culture, this defective relationship between the "select minority" and the pueblo did not necessarily condemn Spain to permanent chaos and mediocrity; all that was needed was a resolute effort to shrug off the burden of the past and to commit the nation to a better future.[21]

But progressives were forced to recognize that, in simply dismissing the past as irrelevant or prejudicial to the present, they were in danger of ceding the field of popular historical discourse to the Catholic right. Not only did this deprive the left of an important tool of legitimation, but, equally important in their eyes, it left intact the national myths that were "one of the great obstacles that prevent the improvement of our life."[22] In an early issue of the *Boletín* a professor of history at the Institución had argued that revision, not rejection, of the past was the key to future reform: "Since the direction of our national history has been false for a long time, we should admit it frankly and try to avoid it energetically from here forward. To achieve this result, nothing would

[20] José Ortega y Gasset, "La pedagogía social como programa político" (1910), *BILE* 40, no. 678 (30 September 1916): 259.
[21] José Ortega y Gasset, *España invertebrada: Bosquejos de algunos pensamientos históricos* (1921) in OC 3:35–128.
[22] Ibid., 111.

be more proper than a rectification of the ideas called national, many of which are, in reality, great *national* prejudices, and nothing [would be] more convenient than the free and serene examination of our past life, brought before the tribunal of reason and truth. In this way we will see how without ceasing to be Spanish, and very Spanish, we may become active members of humanity."[23]

Recovery of a serviceable national past—a past not only held captive, but actually lost or unknown—thus became a major task for patriotic regenerationists and democratic reformers at the turn of the century.[24] By identifying an alternative past from which they could claim ancestry, progressives sought to find exemplars, models, and neglected or truncated traditions that might point toward new directions for the nation and reestablish its links to the more progressive and cultivated Europe they perceived beyond the Pyrenees. They also hoped to uncover underappreciated elements in the national character that might support some degree of optimism about the future. What they were looking for in the past of course depended in large measure on their diagnosis of the nation's current ills and their projects for the future. If Ortega felt the absence of elite leadership, others believed that regeneration must come from below. But whatever their perspective on the present, they agreed that the past must be made to yield memories distinct from the usual "hymns to Otumba, Ceriñola, and Pavía" that recalled the centuries of Spanish military might; they ransacked the past for models and precedents that might help identify the "means most able to correct our vices and set us upon better paths."[25] History, in short, must be both pedagogic and therapeutic, an instrument of regeneration, not a vehicle for nostalgia.

As several commentators have observed, the reformers, regenerationists, and cultural critics of the generations of 1898 and 1915 shared a set of assumptions that constrained their vision of both the past and the

---

[23] Ángel Storr, "Indicaciones sobre un programa de historia de España aplicado a los estudios de segunda enseñanza," *BILE* 2, no. 45 (31 December 1878): 186. The first two parts of this essay were published in no. 39 (30 September 1878): 143–44 and no. 44 (16 December 1878): 174–75.

[24] Among the many works dealing with the historical views of the generation of 1898, see, for a sampling of contrasting perspectives, Pedro Laín Entralgo, *España como problema*, 2 vols. (Madrid: Aguilar 1962); Dolores Gómez Molleda, *Los reformadores de la España contemporánea* (Madrid: Consejo Superior de Investigaciones Científicas, Escuela de Historia Moderna, 1966); Edward Inman Fox, *La crisis intelectual del 98* (Madrid: EDICUSA, 1976); Manuel Tuñón de Lara, *Medio siglo de cultura española (1885–1936)* (Madrid: Tecnos, 1973); José-Carlos Mainer, *La edad de plata (1902–1931): Ensayo de interpretación de un proceso cultural* (Barcelona: Ediciones Asenet, 1975); and Rafael Ninyoles, *Madre España* (Valencia: Prometeo, 1979).

[25] Giner de los Ríos, quoted in López-Morillas, *Racionalismo pragmático*, 42.

future of Spain.[26] Most important was their sense of "the nation" as a unified cultural and historical community that shared a common past and that must, in order to survive, devise a common ideal. Frustrated by the corruption and inertia of the parliamentary regime and troubled by the real fissures along lines of class and region that had begun to appear in Spanish society, they sought a "Spanish" identity that might transcend such differences and bring the nation together in a common enterprise. With linguistic, ethnic, or even territorial unity contested by regionalists on the periphery, history promised to be the most fruitful source of revelation about the nation's character, spirit, and destiny. History could provide an ideal representation of the nation not only to contrast with traditionalist ideology and the Canovite state but also to transcend the internal conflicts that divided Spanish society.

The invocation of the past in support of a national identity was facilitated by the philosophical idealism characteristic of many turn-of-the-century intellectuals with roots in or affinities with the Krausist tradition. Even those also substantially influenced by positivism were inclined to fall back on idealist assumptions about the national character or the meaning of "Spain"—precisely, of course, because empirical observation of past or contemporary Spain and Spaniards provided little incontrovertible evidence of such transcendent identities. In this resort to metaphysics, progressive intellectuals resembled the Catholic right. But it is misleading to suggest, as some critics have done, that the generations of '98 and '15 were therefore the precursors of the "National Catholics" and fascists of the 1930s and 1940s. The differences that separated the political and cultural reformers at the turn of the century from their rightist interlocutors then and later were at least as great as their similarities. Whereas the right's image of "the Spaniard" was fixed, progressives argued that the national character was the product of history itself and, thus, in continuous creation. For the right, national identity, like all truth, was unchanging; for the left, truth emerged and deepened in the process of evolution. For neo-Catholics, national identity and culture were bastions against unwelcome political and social change. Progressives, in contrast, sought to resuscitate and transform national identity in order to create an active, engaged citizenry committed to democratic reform. Far from prefiguring the authoritarian right, these "civic nationalists" would ultimately become its victims.

[26] For example, Ninyoles, *Madre España*; Mainer, *La edad de plata*; Francisco Villacorta Baños, *Burguesía y cultura: Los intelectuales españoles en la sociedad liberal (1808–1910)* (Madrid: Siglo XXI, 1980); Antonio Elorza, "Nacionalismo económico y renovación política, 1914–1923," in José Luis García Delgado, ed., *España, 1898–1936: Estructuras y cambio. Coloquio de la Universidad Complutense sobre la España contemporánea* (Madrid: Universidad Complutense, 1984), 161–75;

Progressive critics blamed traditional historiography, with its obsession with kings, battles, and diplomacy, for the distorted image that Spaniards harbored of their past. The "real Spain" could be discovered only in what the Krausist historians had called "internal history," the Germans called *Kulturgeschichte*, and the French, the "history of civilization." Internal history revealed the "state of the national spirit";[27] it took as its object not the ephemeral activities of the state, but the cultural achievements of the pueblo. The young essayist and philosopher Miguel de Unamuno called it *intrahistoria*, "the sub-historic facts that endure and are stratified in deep layers" in the daily lives of the masses.[28] The cultural groundwork for this refocusing of the historical optic was laid by the great Spanish novelist Benito Pérez Galdós, whose monumental *Episodios Nacionales*—forty-six novels published between 1868 and 1912—recounted the contemporary history of Spain from the battle of Trafalgar in 1805 through the early years of the Restoration.[29] Against the backdrop of the epic events of the nineteenth-century struggles for national independence, liberal constitutionalism, and finally, popular democracy, Galdós depicted the ordinary men and women whose daily lives provided the truest insight into the "spirit of an age." Galdós expressed his philosophy of history (and literature) in one of his early novels: "If History were only battles; if its only actors were famous people, how insignificant it would be! It is in the slow and almost always sorrowful life of society, in what everyone does and in what each one does."[30]

The *Episodios Nacionales*, sold serially in inexpensive editions, were denounced by the right and initially ignored by the literary establish-

[27] José de Castro, "D. Federico de Castro," *BILE* 52, no. 813 (31 January 1928): 17.

[28] Miguel de Unamuno and Ángel Ganivet, "El porvenir de España (1898–1912)," in Unamuno, *OC* 3:662.

[29] For Galdós and the contemporary significance of his historical novels, see especially Hans Hinterhauser, *Los 'Episodios Nacionales' de Benito Pérez Galdós* (Madrid: Editorial Gredos, 1963); Brian J. Dendle, *Galdós: The Early Historical Novels* (Columbia: University of Missouri Press, 1986); Peter Bly, ed., *Galdós y la historia* (Ottawa: Dovehouse Editions, Canada, 1988); "Homenaje a Galdós," *Cuadernos Hispanoamericanos: Revista mensual de cultura hispánica*, nos. 250–52 (1970–71); and José María Jover Zamora, *La imagen de la primera república en la España de la Restauración: Discurso leído el día 28 de marzo de 1982 en el acto de su recepción pública; y contestación del Excmo. Sr. D. José Antonio Maravall Casenoves* (Madrid: Real Academia de la Historia, 1982); and "El siglo XIX en la historiografía española contemporánea (1939–1972)," in Jover Zamora, ed., *El siglo XIX en España: Doce estudios* (Barcelona: Editorial Planeta, 1974), 9–151. José Luis López-Aranguren has called the *Episodios* "the best book of democratic political education of the Spaniards and the epic of our liberal destiny." *Moral y sociedad: Introducción a la moral social española del siglo XIX*, 2d ed. (Madrid: EDICUSA, 1966), 32.

[30] From *El equipaje del rey José* (1875), quoted in Vicente Llorens, "Historia y novela in Galdós," in "Homenaje a Galdós," 74.

ment, but they were instantly popular with young intellectuals and reformers. The publication of a handsome edition of the *Episodios* in 1880, followed by appointment to a safe Liberal seat in the Cortes and election to the Royal Academy, measured the progress of Galdós's literary and political success.[31] His popularity can be explained by the values and assumptions he shared with his contemporaries—first, his belief in a durable and unique "national physiognomy" that persisted beneath the surface disturbances of national life and, second, his conviction that the redemption of Spain lay in moral, rather than radical political reform, an attitude he absorbed from Giner.[32] Nevertheless, it was Galdós who resurrected the popular and democratic experience of the First Republic from the "antinational" purgatory to which it had been consigned, making it possible to think positively about a second.[33] Reflecting contemporary social reality, his novels provided an inspiration for others to explore history at the level of the pueblo.

The concern with history from below did not necessarily imply democratic politics; in fact, the commitment to "intrahistory" often led straight to conservatism, as the cases of Azorín, Ángel Ganivet, and—after their youthful progressivism had faded—Unamuno and Maeztu clearly demonstrated. But Galdós's popular progressivism did find a strong and consistent echo among those associated with the Institución Libre de Enseñanza and its offshoots, where the search for a usable past was led by the indefatigable and extraordinarily influential Joaquín Costa.

Costa's efforts to revitalize the nation and, thereby, the state began in the 1880s with his legal scholarship, which aimed at clarifying the historical relationship between the two.[34] Enemy of the omnipotent and arbitrary state, Costa argued that law must follow custom—or to put it another way, law must be understood sociologically and historically: "the only true laws are those that the pueblo knows and endorses by obeying them, translating them into deeds."[35] At a time when critical historical scholarship of the kind earlier developed in German university seminars was almost unknown in Spain, Costa devoted his considerable

[31] For biographical details, see H. Chonon Berkowitz, *Pérez Galdós: Spanish Liberal Crusader* (Madison: University of Wisconsin Press, 1948).

[32] See Llorens, "Historia y novela," in "Homenaje a Galdós"; Dendle, *Galdós*; Eamonn Rodgers, "Teoría literaria y filosofía de la historia en el primer Galdós," in Bly, *Galdós y la historia*, 36–37.

[33] Jover Zamora, *Imagen*, 88–119.

[34] See Jesús Delgado Echeverría, "Costa y el derecho," in *El legado de Costa: Huesca, septiembre de 1983* (Madrid: Ministerio de Cultura, Subdirección General de Archivos, Diputación General de Aragón, Departamento de Cultura y Educación, 1983), 101–10.

[35] In Fernández Clemente, *Educación*, 33.

scholarly talents to the excavation and analysis of archival and literary sources for customary law.

In Costa's work political and scholarly purposes commingled. His influential study of traditional communal agriculture, *Colectivismo agrario en España* (1898), supplied the foundation for his municipal and agricultural reform proposals after 1898. In the same way, his regenerationist call for popular mobilization grew out of an earlier historical investigation, commissioned by the Ateneo of Madrid in 1895, when Costa was president of its Section of Historical Sciences. The assigned subject reflected the mood in the nation: "the doctrine of the 'dictatorship' as a tutor of new pueblos or retarded, fallen or infirm pueblos, incapacitated, through defects of age or accidental regress or decline, for governing their own life."[36] Costa's search for relevant historical models led him to dramatic reinterpretations of the staples of Catholic and liberal historiography: in the Lusitanian shepherd, Viriatus, he revealed the "liberator of a pueblo crushed by a capitalist nobility"; in the Cid, he found the embodiment of constitutionalism, especially "the limited character of royal power";[37] and in Isabel the Catholic, he discovered the sponsor of economic growth and national education and the head of a "popular party" that had defeated the "armed caciquismo" of the feudal lords. Far from supporting dictatorship as a remedy for decline, Costa's historical research suggested the opposite: that effective reformers were those with social support. Costa's oft-repeated exhortations to bury the past were thus directed at traditional interpretations and historical currents he considered tendentious or unproductive, not at history in its entirety. His pathbreaking critical scholarship showed a younger generation of historians that the recovery of a usable past offered a "means to assist at the birth of the great social movement of our time."[38]

In Costa the connection between historical scholarship and a concrete program of political and economic "Europeanization" was visible and direct. In the younger generation of professional historians who rose to prominence at the turn of the century, the link was sometimes less obvious, but no less certain. By applying the scientific methods of European historiography to the study of the Spanish past they hoped to accomplish several objectives: to accommodate Spanish historical practice to that of "Europe"; to critique scientifically the "false traditionalism"

---

[36] Joaquín Costa y Martínez, *Tutela de pueblos en la historia* (Madrid: Imp. de Fortanet, 1917), vi.

[37] Ibid., pp. 10–11, 159.

[38] Quoted in Gómez Molleda, *Reformadores*, 340 n. 3.

of conservative and Catholic discourse; and to capture the real Spain through the careful study of archival, archaeological, and anthropological evidence. Like other European historians of the positivist school, they believed that their empirical methods would bring to light the process of national development without recourse to a priori assumptions. But the lingering influence of Krausism also convinced them that those methods would reveal an essential national identity whose discovery would reawaken and rechannel popular energies.

Critical historical scholarship was slow to take root in Spain. In Germany, archivally based historical scholarship had accompanied and legitimated the formation of the German state; in France, the defeat of 1870–71 and the creation of the Third Republic had fostered a similar enthusiasm for university history seminars, public archives, and scholarly historical journals, in which the roots of the French nation were explored.[39] In contrast, in Spain the wave of historical writing that accompanied the triumph of liberalism at mid-century did not evolve much beyond the literary "general histories." In 1888 Costa could still deplore the "lamentable backwardness" of historical studies—the absence of university training in philology and other modern methodologies, the disorganization and poverty of national archives and libraries, and the consequent ignorance of the national past.[40] A few isolated figures had made important contributions to the historical sciences—most notably, Manuel Milà y Fontanals (and his student, Menéndez y Pelayo) in literary criticism, Francisco Codera in Arabic studies, and Eduardo de Hinojosa in legal history. But it was not until the beginning of the twentieth century, inspired by Costa and the "Krauso-positivists" Gumersindo de Azcárate and Manuel Sales y Ferré, and in response to the stimulus of the regenerationist movement of the 1890s, that a *school* of modern historical scholarship emerged. The contrast with the German and French experience was significant. Whereas the revitalization of national history through excavation and analysis of archival sources was part of the state-building process in those two nations, in Spain much of

---

[39] For France, see Louis Halphen, "France," in *Histoire et historiens depuis cinquante ans: Méthodes, organisation et résultats du travail historique de 1876 à 1926* (New York: Burt Franklin, 1971), 148–66; William R. Keylor, *Academy and Community: The Foundations of the French Historical Profession* (Cambridge: Harvard University Press, 1975); and Pierre Nora, "*L'Histoire de France* de Lavisse," in *Les Lieux de mémoire*, vol. 2, *La Nation* (Paris: Gallimard, 1986), 315–73. For a comparison of French and German historical scholarship, see Fritz K. Ringer, *Fields of Knowledge: French Academic Culture in Comparative Perspective, 1890–1920* (New York: Cambridge University Press, 1992).

[40] Joaquín Costa, *Introducción a un tratado de política sacado textualmente de los refraneros, romanceros y gestos de la península* (1888), quoted in Fernández Clemente, *Educación*, 115–17.

the impetus came from critics whose interests lay less in legitimation than in transformation of the liberal state.[41]

The long-term political and cultural significance of their efforts to modernize their discipline was foremost in the minds of the young generation of scholars, many of whom were closely associated with the Institución Libre de Enseñanza. Like their French counterparts, who were equally engaged in rescuing the past from the grips of the Catholic and monarchist right, they saw modern historical scholarship as a kind of moral and civic calling, an attitude that fit well with the almost monastic asceticism cultivated by Giner and his disciples.[42] For no one was this more true than for Rafael Altamira, who indefatigably promoted the renovation of both the teaching and the writing of history from the 1890s until his death in exile in 1951.

Born to a middle-class liberal family in Alicante in 1866, Altamira first encountered the "extended Institución" while studying law at the University of Valencia (plate 3).[43] In 1886, he transferred to Madrid, where he attended Giner's lectures and completed a doctorate in law

[41] As a discipline, Spanish historiography is in its infancy. For an introduction to the origins of professional historical scholarship in Spain, see Paul Guinard, "Espagne" in *Histoire et historiens depuis cinquante ans*, 107–38; Jover Zamora, "El siglo XIX," in *El siglo XIX*, 9–151; Mariano and José Luis Peset, "Vicens Vives y la historiografía del derecho en España," in *Vorstudien zur Rechthistorik* (Frankfurt: Vittorio Klosterman, 1977), 176–262; Gonzalo Pasamar Alzuria and Ignacio Peiró Martín, *Historiografía y práctica social en España* (Zaragoza: Secretariado de Publicaciones de la Universidad, 1987); Gumersindo de Azcárate, "Carácter científico de la historia," *BILE* 34, no. 601 (30 April 1910): 125–28; no. 602 (31 May 1910): 153–60; no. 603 (30 June 1910): 178–92; Juan Ruiz de Obregón Retortillo, "Nuevas orientaciones de la historia," *La España Moderna* 26, no. 307 (July 1914): 5–17; Alfredo Marcos Oteruelo, *El pensamiento de Gumersindo de Azcárate* (León: Institución Fray Bernardino de Sahagún, 1985); and Manuel Núñez Encabo, *Manuel Sales y Ferré: Los orígenes de la sociología en España* (Madrid: EDICUSA, 1977).

[42] For the "moral austerity" of the French republican historians, see Nora, "*L'Histoire de France*," in *Les Lieux de mémoire*, 318.

[43] Generally neglected during the Franco regime, Altamira has subsequently attracted renewed attention. See, in addition to the works by Altamira cited in the text, John E. Fagg, "Rafael Altamira (1866–1951)," in S. William Halperin, ed., *Essays in Modern European Historiography* (Chicago: University of Chicago Press, 1970), 3–21; Luis García de Valdeavellano, "Don Rafael Altamira, o la historia como educación," in *Seis semblanzas de historiadores españoles* (Seville: Publicaciones de la Universidad, 1978), 75–106; Vicente Ramos, *Rafael Altamira* (Madrid: Alfaguara, 1968) and *Palabra y pensamiento de Rafael Altamira* (Alicante: Caja de Ahorros de Alicante y Murcia, 1987); Armando Alberola, ed., *Estudios sobre Rafael Altamira* (Alicante: Instituto de Estudios "Juan Gil-Albert," Caja de Ahorros Provincial de Alicante, 1988); Irene Palacio Lis, *Rafael Altamira: Un modelo de regeneracionismo educativo* (Alicante: Publicaciones de la Caja de Ahorros Provincial, 1986); and the commemorative volume *Rafael Altamira (1866–1951)* (Alicante: Diputación Provincial, Instituto de Estudios "Juan Gil-Albert," 1987).

Plate 3. Rafael Altamira y Crevea (1866–1951) (Photo courtesy of Agencia Efe, Madrid)

under Azcárate. Influenced both by the historical school of law founded by Hinojosa and by his growing friendship with Joaquín Costa, Altamira wrote his thesis on the history of communal property, using evidence drawn not only from "positive law," but also from "everything that might have influenced it or contributed to its evolution, from education and popular feeling to the discussions of the practitioners and the philosophers; from the conditions which the physical environment may impress on the social constitution, to the disposition of intelligence and spirit, tradition and interests, that may have led a minister or a parliament to adopt a certain legislative or governmental measure."[44] Law, in other words, was a product of human activity in its social dimension, changing in response to historical circumstance.

This global and evolutionary conception of history, which Altamira, following the lead of the French (and the German historian Karl Lamprecht), preferred to call the "history of civilization," would set the tone for all of his subsequent work. As both practitioner and proselytizer, he

[44] *Rafael Altamira*, 39.

would campaign tirelessly for the addition of social, institutional, and cultural history to the traditional "external history" of politics, warfare, and diplomacy, which, because they involved the activities of a state long alienated from the life of the nation, offered little of educational value to the contemporary Spaniard. Altamira would later refer to Galdós as the "best historian of modern Spain," reflecting his appreciation of the novelist's search for historical truth beneath the surface of events.[45] Only by conveying the "unity of human experience" could history reveal and thereby unharness the strengths of the Spanish pueblo.

For Altamira, the task of the historian was thus twofold: not only to expand the fund of reliable historical knowledge, but also to communicate it to a people hitherto ignorant of their own past, and thus of their own potential. What the man in the street knew of his nation's history was more important than what the scholars knew—or more accurately, what the scholars knew was socially significant only when it had acquired social agency. By the same token, since historical memory was inseparable from the human condition, it was important for men to have an undistorted view of their past to keep from going astray. Scholarship and pedagogy were thus two sides of the same coin, just as past and present were indissolubly linked. And in Spain, both were in need of modernization.

Like his mentor, Giner de los Ríos, Altamira believed that the renovation of both scholarship and national culture must begin at the level of the primary school, and in 1888 he accepted a dual appointment as secretary of the Museo de Instrucción Pública (later, Museo Pedagógico Nacional) under Costa and as director of the *Boletín de la Institución Libre de Enseñanza*. For the next decade he divided his time and considerable energy among the Institución, the Museo, journalism, historical research, and the centrist republican party of Nicolás Salmerón.[46] A trip to Paris in 1890 brought him firsthand acquaintance with the French historians who shared his conviction that writing and teaching history could be an act of patriotism, including Ernest Lavisse, Gabriel Monod, Charles Seignebos, and the Hispanist Alfred Morel-Fatio.[47] Seignebos's course on historical pedagogy at the Sorbonne inspired Altamira's own

---

[45] Ibid., 160.

[46] In 1895, inspired by the example of the *Revue historique*, founded by Gabriel Monod in 1875, Altamira established the *Revista crítica de historia y literatura españolas, portuguesas y hispano-americanas*, a journal of historical and literary criticism that attracted the collaboration of distinguished Spanish and foreign scholars until its demise, for financial reasons, in 1910.

[47] Ramos, *Rafael Altamira*, 63. On the French historians, see Nora, *"L'Histoire de France,"* in *Les Lieux de mémoire*; Ringer, *Fields of Knowledge*, 257–83.

lectures on the subject in the Museo Pedagógico later that year.[48] Published under the title *La enseñanza de la historia* in 1891 (with a second edition in 1895), Altamira's lectures called for the reconceptualization of historical methodology and pedagogy at all levels, beginning with the university. The first manifesto of ideas that would dominate Altamira's published work throughout his life, the book established a paradigm for the teaching and writing of history in the schools that shaped reformist discourse on the subject for the next forty years.[49]

La enseñanza de la historia was shaped by several contemporary developments in Europe. One was the transformation of historical studies. In contrast to Spanish historiography, "full of fables, calumnies and false patriotisms," the new history was characterized by a search for "the indifferent voice of reality" through neutral examination of the evidence. Its foundation was a "genetic" conception of history that recognized both continuity and change: "all history is an ascendent, continuous and accumulated march towards the development of the energies and qualities of the social subject." The new history shunned the biography of great men in order to study the biography of social groups, on the grounds that the individuals "who appear as executors and directors of national life are such only to the degree that they . . . agree with and adapt themselves to the collective spirit they wish to influence." The modern historian's task was thus to understand and explain "pueblos as social units, organically, in all aspects of their activity and in all the functions of their energy," recognizing that the fundamental psychology of a nation was the result of the interaction of its constant qualities and evolving historical circumstance.[50] To understand those circumstances and the products of the collective spirit, the historian must draw on new methodologies and disciplines—geography, folklore, and sociology. To understand their effects, he must rely on the comparative method. But while searching for historical patterns, he must also avoid the pitfall of determinism, for human history was essentially the record of progressive human mastery over environmental and cultural constraints.

As with other progressive intellectuals of his generation, Altamira's positivism was moderated by Krausist idealism.[51] This intermediate po-

---

[48] See Charles Seignebos, "L'Enseignement de l'histoire comme instrument d'éducation politique," in Charles Seignebos, Charles-V. Langlois et al., *L'Enseignement de l'histoire. (Conférences du Musée Pédagogique, 1907)*, 1–24. See also Gordon H. McNeil, "Charles Seignebos, 1954–1942" in Halperin, *Essays in Historiography*, 352–69.

[49] *La enseñanza de la historia*, 2d ed. (Madrid: V. Súarez, 1895). For another statement, see, among others, *Cuestiones modernas de historia* (Madrid: Daniel Jorro, 1904). A complete bibliography may be found in Ramos, *Rafael Altamira*, 341–85.

[50] Altamira, *Enseñanza*, 10, 12, 128, 124, 95.

[51] For a critique of Altamira as an historian, see especially Alfonso Orti, "Regenera-

sition—usually labeled "Krauso-positivism"—made him wary of both positivist historical "laws" and totalizing philosophies of history, even as it directed his empirical research toward the search for the fundamental psychology of the nation and his historiographical practice toward works of synthesis and interpretation. His instrumentalist view of history convinced him that the achievements of modern historical scholarship must be made accessible to the pueblo to become operative in the political and cultural spheres. But his repeated attempts to write a general history of Spain were undermined by his positivist conviction that interpretation should occur to the reader only as "a consequence of the narration and factual exposition," and not of the historian's own vision.[52]

A second influence on *La enseñanza de la historia* was Altamira's encounter with Seignebos and other historians in France, where national history played an important role in socializing youth to republican and national values in both primary and secondary schools.[53] According to Seignebos, the pedagogical purpose of history was to provide concrete illustrations of the abstract principles taught in civics; by studying distinct societies in the past, the student would master the terminology of political discourse and become a conscientious and informed citizen.[54] Echoing Seignebos, Altamira stressed that history— "because of its link with questions that are immediate and real at all times for the student, as a man and as a citizen"—had an important role to play in the formation of civic consciousness and national unity.[55] In Spain, as in France, the meanings resident in political terminology could not be taken for granted; on the contrary, they were the subject of bitter dispute. And in Spain, where civics was not a formal school subject, it was even more important than in France to enlarge students' knowledge of the *recent* past. Like Seignebos and Lavisse, Altamira stressed that the civic value of history did not lie in its value for individual character development, as the advocates of the classical curriculum supposed, but in the way it taught students to think critically about the differences between past and present civilizations and prepared them to see present institutions as the outcome of historical evolution. Unfor-

cionismo e historiografía: El mito del carácter nacional en la obra de Rafael Altamira," and Juan José Carreras, "Altamira y la historiografía europea," both in Arbeloa, *Estudios*, 275–353, 395–415.

[52] Altamira, *Enseñanza*, 355.

[53] See Mona Ozouf, *L'École, l'Église et la République, 1871–1914* (Paris: Armand Colin, 1963); Jacqueline Freyssinet-Dominjon, *Les Manuels d'histoire de l'école libre, 1882–1959: De la loi Ferry à la loi Debré* (Paris: Armand Colin, 1969).

[54] See Ozouf, *L'École et l'Église*, 126–30; Ringer, *Fields of Knowledge*, 180–83.

[55] Altamira, *Enseñanza*, 6.

tunately, as currently taught in Spanish schools, history left the student ignorant of contemporary reality and blunted his critical faculties, making him "the slave of the official or supposed truth of his day."[56]

A third influence on *La enseñanza de la historia* were the principles of active pedagogy upheld in France by republican reformers and in Spain by the institucionistas. Altamira insisted that, properly taught, history was a discipline uniquely suited to shape active, responsible citizens. By engaging the student in the discovery of past societies, the historian/educator made him a creator rather than a passive recipient of knowledge and, by extension, a productive contributor to national life. Like his colleagues in the Institución, Altamira privileged the teacher in the educational process and was correspondingly critical of textbooks, "the most likely archives of errors in all the historical literature." Most textbooks were "third- or fourth-hand works, written hastily, without scruples, for commercial rather than scientific purposes" and suffered from the "dogmatic, closed and dry" manner in which they tried to "answer the questions on the syllabus."[57] Nevertheless, following the French example, Altamira recognized the utility of well-written textbooks for primary and secondary students. These he divided into two categories: "manuals" to provide a factual account of the "direction and march of the evolution of our pueblo," and "historical readings" to capture the imaginations of young readers. As works of reference, history manuals should contain (in addition to accurate, objective text) maps, bibliographies, illustrations, and selections from primary documents to help the student comprehend past civilizations. Interpretation and synthesis, however, should be left to the classroom teacher. As models, Altamira recommended two manuals by Seignebos, Spanish examples being entirely lacking.

The exchange of ideas between Altamira and the Institución was reciprocal. As political progressives, the institucionistas had initially harbored a certain animus toward history, to which they attributed the popular prejudices and self-congratulation that made cultural transformation so difficult. Furthermore, contemporary educators were divided over the value of teaching history to children too psychologically immature to conceptualize the past or to think abstractly about institutional change.[58] The traditional association of history teaching with the stale

---

[56] Ibid., 13.

[57] Ibid., 325.

[58] Altamira reviewed this debate in *Enseñanza*, 361–64. Two recent discussions are Roy Hallam, "Piaget and the Teaching of History," *Educational Research* 12 (1969): 3–12; and Mario Carretero et al., "Comprensión de conceptos históricos durante la adolescencia," *Infancia y aprendizaje* 23 (1983): 55–74.

dogmatism of textbooks, whether in the service of civic or religious indoctrination, was an additional cause for suspicion.[59]

Under the influence of Altamira and Cossío, however, history acquired an important place in the Institución, where it was structured so as to instill the habits of firsthand observation and responsible citizenship that were at the heart of its educational project. In the classroom and during excursions to museums and monuments, the history of human culture was explored in an "unsystematic and fragmentary" way through images and artifacts that reflected the spirit of the pueblo in ways that conventional history could not. Students observed, took notes, wrote, and, as they grew older, read selections from epic poems and ballads. The purpose was "to awaken (without saying so) the idea that everything there is, is the achievement *of all* and that the real subject in History is not the *hero* but the *entire pueblo*." From direct engagement with the achievements of human civilization, especially through the history of art, the child would discover "the idea of the evolutionary process of culture," the "relativity of the concept of *civilization*," and the social context of individual existence.[60]

Conservatives were infuriated by the institucionistas' disdain for martial exploits and imperial glory and accused them, unfairly, of lack of patriotism. A more legitimate criticism might have been that institucionista neglect of the public sphere was inconsistent with their long-range goal of democratic reform. Unlike Galdós, who had depicted the pueblo actively struggling for freedom and democracy, the institucionistas, like many in the literary generation of '98, had a tendency to aestheticize national identity by locating it in the popular arts or the Castilian landscape. If their ultimate aim was to awaken the pueblo to its civic responsibilities, then their apparent disregard for politics only widened the gulf that they were trying to bridge between the nation and the state.

Altamira seems to have understood the conservative implications of the historicist approach. In a speech delivered at the opening of the 1898–99 term at the University of Oviedo (where a year earlier he had won the chair in the history of law), he delivered an extended analysis of the ills besetting the nation and the university's role in their remedia-

[59] See Manuel Sales y Ferré, "Sobre métodos de enseñanza," *BILE* 11, no. 248 (15 June 1887): 164–68; and R. A. [Rafael Altamira], "La enseñanza oral y los libros segun Max Müller," *BILE* 14, no. 328 (15 October 1890): 292–94. An article in the *BILE* by J. Bryce, professor at Oxford University, advocated separating civics from history since the latter was so hard to teach well. *BILE* 18, no. 417 (31 December 1894): 353–58.

[60] Manuel B. Cossío, "La enseñanza de la historia en la Institución," in *De su jornada: (Fragmentos)* (Madrid: Imprenta de Blass, 1929), 26–27 (also in *BILE* 28, no. 532 [31 July 1904]: 203–05). The piece was originally written at the request of Altamira, who included it in *Cuestiones modernas*, 263–69.

tion.[61] In his view, the problem was both social and cultural: Spaniards not only lacked education, but also self-confidence, as a result of centuries of foreign and domestic criticism of the Spanish character. In the revival of national self-esteem, historians had an essential role to play, by restoring luster to the tarnished national reputation and by convincing the Spanish people of their historic capacity for constructive collective action.[62] But appreciation of national virtues, although essential, was not a license for complacency, nor should it be confused with stubborn preservation of the "particular and variable forms of each [historical] epoch, whose retention would be madness when times have changed."[63] On the contrary, recovery of the past was the first step toward liberation from it; once they understood this, the Spanish people would find the confidence to build a new future, adapting the best from their more advanced neighbors without destroying national identity. By the same token, recuperation of the achievements of the past would repair Spain's damaged reputation abroad. In no part of the world was this more important than in "Hispanic America," where the Black Legend of Spanish colonialism still prevailed. Foreshadowing his subsequent career as an ardent advocate and ambassador for *hispanismo*, Altamira in 1898 proposed a program of cultural cooperation and educational exchange to reestablish the broken bonds between Spain and her spiritual daughters.

To aid the process of self-discovery, Altamira had begun an investigation into the national character during the summer of 1898, "between tears of grief and stirrings of indignation" over the loss of the American empire. Not coincidentally, he also undertook the translation of Fichte's *Discourse to the German Nation*. With his book *Psicología del pueblo español*, Altamira hoped to produce a patriotic reaction similar to the German national revival after the defeat at Jena—an "internal regeneration, the correction of our faults, the vigorous effort that would lift us out of the deep national decadence, seen and marked some time ago by many of our thinkers and politicians, denied by exaggerated patriots and egoists, and highlighted before the eyes of the whole nation, with the eloquence of the lessons that adversity teaches."[64]

Altamira's essay was less a characterization of Spanish "national psy-

---

[61] Rafael Altamira, "La universidad y el patriotismo" (1898), in *Ideario pedagógico*, 265–324.

[62] Ibid., 268. See the epigraph that opens this chapter.

[63] Ibid., 283, 279.

[64] Rafael Altamira, *Psicología del pueblo español*, 2d ed., rev. (Barcelona: Editorial Minerva, [1917]), 27–28. The first edition of 1902 included three essays originally published separately: the inaugural address at the University of Oviedo in 1898, and two articles published in *La España Moderna*: "El problema actual de patriotismo," in no. 118 (1898), and "La psicología del pueblo español," in no. 119 (1899).

chology" (for which he concluded there was insufficient documentation at present to define) than a review and refutation of the negative qualities falsely attributed to Spaniards over the centuries. Altamira enumerated Spain's positive contributions to humanity, especially its "civilization" of the American continent, to illustrate his contention that national regeneration was possible if both the nation and the state so willed. As he saw it, the principal defect in the national character was the lack of national self-consciousness and solidarity among Spaniards. The extension and modernization of national education would correct this and other flaws and enable Spain to commit herself to active participation in the modern world.

Psicología del pueblo español revealed the tensions in Altamira's thought, between his positivist respect for documentary evidence and his idealist faith in the existence of a transcendent national character, and between scholarly objectivity and his desire to place his scholarship at the service of the nation. Resolution of these tensions was difficult, often inclining him to frame his historical analyses in negative terms, as refutations of popular misconceptions and politically manipulated myths. Thus, in his lecture series at the newly created University Extension in Oviedo in 1898, entitled "Legends of the History of Spain," Altamira demolished four myths that he believed stood in the way of national self-knowledge: the richness of the national territory, the natural decadence of the "race," the legend of the resistance of Sagunto, and the exclusively religious character of the Reconquest. Altamira's point was that historical interpretations had political repercussions; conversely, accurate historical knowledge could defeat both pessimism and self-satisfaction by denying them the legitimation that myth had conferred.[65]

What Altamira as a scholar was unwilling to do, however, was to elaborate an equally powerful national myth to replace the old ones he endeavored to destroy. His tentative conclusions and careful objectivity could exasperate contemporaries who understood the value of myth and symbol in mobilizing the masses.[66] Furthermore, because Altamira's effort to document historically a shared national identity could only be maintained in defiance of both historical and contemporary reality, it could not address the structural or political causes of regional and social conflict. His exhortations on behalf of a unique national personality thus failed to unite Spaniards in a common program of national reform.

[65] The lectures are summarized in Aniceto Sela y Sampil, *La educación nacional: Hechos y ideas* (Madrid: Librería General de Victoriano Suárez, 1910), 284–88.

[66] See, for example, the letter from the Krausist Eduardo Soler, his former mentor at the University of Valencia, commenting on *La psicología del espíritu nacional (sic)* in 1902, quoted in *Rafael Altamira*, 86.

Altamira would publish a second revised edition of *Psicología del pueblo español* in 1917 (another moment of social and regional conflict and "renovationist" sentiment), but as in 1898, its reformist and nationalist message offered no solution other than a change of heart.

During the opening years of the new century, Altamira dedicated much of his professional life to transmitting a modern vision of historical study and the national past to the educated public—"the minority who read, study, think and reason about great national problems."[67] At the same time, he played an increasingly active international role, representing Spain in the first international historical congresses,[68] endeavoring to combat the Black Legend through a more balanced presentation of Spanish history, and from 1909 on, ardently pursuing a program of hispanismo in Latin America. In *Cuestiones modernas de historia*, published in 1904, he recounted his adventures as the lone Spanish delegate at European historical congresses in a tone that alternated between exhilaration at the progress occurring elsewhere and frustration at the stagnation of historical teaching and writing in Spain. Particularly depressing to him was the reluctance of professional Spanish historians to venture beyond the narrow monograph and to communicate their findings to a wider audience: contrary to general opinion, their sin was not being excessively rhetorical, but too "dry and tied to their sources."[69]

Altamira's greatest contribution to popular historical knowledge was his influential manual *Historia de España y de la civilización española*, published in four volumes between 1900 and 1911.[70] Originally written as a textbook for university and secondary students, the manual reached a much wider audience, eventually going through three editions and serving as the standard introduction to Spanish history for a whole generation of educated Spaniards and foreign Hispanists. Writing in a "sober style" that avoided rhetorical flourishes, Altamira attempted to meet the demanding standards for history manuals that he had outlined in 1891 in *La enseñanza de la historia*. What especially won him praise from his contemporaries (Menéndez y Pelayo called it "the best book of its kind published up until now") was its balance between political, institutional, and cultural history and its careful scholarship, based on Altamira's monumental grasp of the monographic literature on a multitude of topics.[71]

---

[67] Rafael Altamira, "La universidad y el patriotismo," in *Ideario pedagógico*, 319.

[68] In Paris in 1900, Rome in 1903, and Berlin in 1906.

[69] Altamira, *Cuestiones modernas*, 231. A second revised edition was published in 1935.

[70] Rafael Altamira y Crevea, *Historia de España y de la civilización española*, 3d ed., rev. 4 vols. (Barcelona: Herederos de Juan Gili, 1913).

[71] *Rafael Altamira*, 79, which also includes additional contemporary comments on the *Historia*. Even the determined reviewer in the Jesuit educational journal *Razón y Fé* could

The first volume opened with a detailed discussion of the relative disadvantages of peninsular geography, not as a determinant of Spanish history, but as a constant challenge that the Spanish people had had historically to overcome and that had thus decisively shaped the national character.[72] In the sections that followed, Altamira broke with the conventions of both textbooks and general histories of Spain by emphasizing the evolution of social institutions (especially the family, law, education, and religion) and by including engravings and photographs of the artistic monuments whose aesthetic elements captured the spirit of an age and a people. Historical periods and cultures traditionally neglected in older history texts—Islamic Spain, the individual kingdoms of the Crown of Aragon, the Bourbon monarchy, and the society and culture of the Americas—were discussed with the same degree of erudite detail as the history of Castile or the reign of the Catholic Kings. Altamira's tone was neither apologetic nor exculpatory when discussing the Inquisition, the reign of Philip II, the expulsion of the Jesuits, or other controversial episodes in the Spanish historical record; instead, his tone was matter-of-fact, descriptive rather than judgmental. His goal was to present the results of modern research in such a way that the reader could form his own conclusions. The facts, he believed, would speak for themselves.

As an instrument of national regeneration, and as a textbook, the *Historia de España* suffered some limitations. Even though Altamira had repeatedly stressed the value of contemporary history in creating civic consciousness, for a variety of reasons—including the sheer volume of primary and secondary sources to be consulted—his final volume ended in 1808.[73] Equally important, Altamira failed to solve the technical problem of how to integrate his rich discussions of social and

---

find little substantively to criticize in the third and fourth volumes; see P. Enrique Portillo, in *RyF* 20 (January–April 1908): 113–18 and 31 (September–December 1911): 246–50. For a modern appreciation, see Fagg, "Rafael Altamira."

[72] See also Altamira, "La educación patriótica" (1922), in *Ideario pedagógico*, 169–71. For the relationship between geography and regenerationism, see Josefina Gómez Mendoza and Nicolás Ortega Cantero, "Geografía y regeneracionismo en España (1875–1936)," *Sistema* 77 (March 1987): 77–89.

[73] In the late 1920s the publishers commissioned the Conservative Maurist historian Pío Zabala y Lera—catedrático at the University of Madrid and son of Manuel Zabala—to bring the survey up to the present: Pío Zabala y Lera, *Historia de España y de la civilización española en la edad contemporánea*, 2 vols. (Barcelona: Sucesores de Juan Gili, 1930). Altamira expressed his views on contemporary history in a lecture delivered at the University of Valencia in 1922, published in *BILE* 47, no. 759 (30 June 1923): 178–85; no. 760 (31 July 1923): 218–56; and no. 762 (30 September 1923): 282–86. See also his *Manual de historia de España*, vol. 14 of *Obras completas de D. Rafael Altamira* (Madrid: M. Aguilar, 1934).

cultural institutions with the political and diplomatic history that provided the framework for his narrative. By discussing each separately, he
failed to illuminate the interconnections and influences among them.
Finally, the "patriotic" impact of Altamira's history was partly diluted
by his rhetorical restraint and by his unwillingness to incorporate his
liberal democratic convictions into a sweeping reinterpretation of national character and history. But Altamira was not a demagogue: for
him, the political value of history lay in its contribution to national self-
awareness, not in its ability to stir the emotions of the masses. It was
not his job to create new myths, but to free people for rational choice.
In the context of this "democratic elitism," the pedagogical limitations
of his text perhaps become more understandable.

Altamira, like other institucionistas, harbored a profound ambivalence
toward the state. On the one hand, like Ortega, they viewed the Restoration monarchy as a moribund organism "situated outside and apart
from the central currents of the Spanish soul of today";[74] on the other,
they recognized that the defects of the state in large measure reflected
the feebleness of "the nation." Thus, believing that only the expansion
and modernization of the public school system could create the democratic public culture they envisioned, they set aside their natural distrust
of the state in order to extend their reach. Altamira was no exception.
Although a republican in his youth, he frequently made common cause
with the democratic wing of the Liberal party. As secretary of the
Museo Pedagógico, as the first director general of primary instruction
from 1911 to 1913, and as a Liberal senator representing the University
of Valencia in 1916, 1919, and 1923, Altamira tirelessly promoted the
expansion of the public school system and the modernization of the
curriculum, including, of course, the transformation of both the content
and methods of history teaching at all levels of instruction.

It was a "regenerationist" Conservative, Antonio García Alix, however, who signed the decree creating the first formalized degree programs in history at selected Spanish universities. Echoing Altamira, García Alix indicated that history should be understood "as the consecutive
development of the Spanish national personality, in its own terms and in
its relationship to other nations."[75] The goal of the new degree programs was to train professional historians to teach the critical methods
of modern historical science in the institutos and universities. The three
years of specialized study were to include systematic training in the
"auxiliary sciences" of geography, archaeology, paleography, numisma-

[74] José Ortega y Gasset, "Vieja y nueva política" (1914), in OC 1:272.
[75] RO of 18 August 1900; RD of 20 July 1900.

tics, and epigraphy (courses previously taught at the Escuela Superior Diplomática, which was to be closed). At the doctoral level (offered only at Madrid), the decree prescribed courses in sociology, the history of Jews, Muslims, and the Americas, and "neo-Latin" languages and literatures. Seminars and research activities were to be required of all students.[76]

What the decree did not specify, as Altamira pointed out at the time, was where to find the faculty to teach the new curriculum.[77] Even at the Central University several of the professors newly appointed to the chairs in history were practitioners of the old "literary" history. At the provincial universities, the proportion unprepared to teach the prescribed courses and investigative techniques was even greater.[78] Moreover, professionalization of history education in the universities implied restricting higher education to the best prepared and motivated, a policy for which there was no precedent or political support.[79] The poorly structured curriculum asked unprepared students to conduct research before they had been given the professional tools to do so and repeated much of the work previously undertaken in the bachillerato. Most important for the long-term goals of the proposal, students completing the licenciatura were not required to take a course in pedagogy, in contrast to the practice elsewhere in Europe.[80]

By 1918, the failure of the García Alix reform was apparent to all. From his chair in universal history at the University of Valencia, Al-

[76] The curriculum was partially modified by the Liberals in 1913 (while Altamira was still serving as director general of public instruction). RD of 15 August and RO of 3 September 1913.

[77] Rafael Altamira, "La reforma de los estudios históricos en España," *BILE* 24, no. 489 (31 December 1900): 353–57, first published in the December 1900 issue of the *Bulletin hispanique*.

[78] An RO of 19 September 1900, which appointed the faculty for the Central University, included both practitioners of positivistic scholarship like Eduardo de Hinojosa and Manuel Sales y Ferré and representatives of the older romantic school of liberal historiography like Miguel de Morayta and Juan Ortega y Rubio. An RO of 19 November 1900 named the faculties at Barcelona, Granada, Oviedo, Salamanca, Santiago, Seville, and Valencia. For a list of the chairholders at the Central University between 1900 and 1908, see Pasamar and Peiró, *Historiografía*, 37.

[79] Eduardo Ibarra y Rodríguez, "Como debe ser enseñada la historia," in *Asociación Española para el Progreso de las Ciencias: Congreso de Zaragoza (1908)* (Madrid: Imprenta de Eduardo Arias, 1910), 6:59–74. See also Ibarra's *Meditemos: (Cuestiones pedagógicas)* (Zaragoza: Biblioteca Argensola, 1908). A Maurist Conservative, Ibarra was dean of the School of Philosophy and Letters and a catedrático of modern and contemporary universal history at the University of Zaragoza.

[80] An RO of 6 August 1921 established courses in the history and practice of pedagogy in the Faculty of Philosophy and Letters for those future catedráticos who wished to take them.

tamira's protégé, José de Deleito, lamented "how much there is of the artificial, rhetorical, incongruent, incomplete, and arbitrary in the existing system of historical studies in our official centers of instruction." Like his mentor, Deleito believed history should "form spirits," teaching students that "the world marches on" and that "the utopia of today can be the triumphant reality of tomorrow." Among the few catedráticos familiar with modern historical methods, however, the pendulum had swung too far in the other direction, passing from "Castelar to Ranke," with nothing in between. The result was antiquarianism, "a cold, parchment-like, sickly history, without soul, without life." At the same time the students' lack of preparation made serious research and seminars impossible. Deleito confessed that he himself had been reduced to teaching his students what they should have learned during the bachillerato.[81]

In contrast to this desolate panorama, Deleito pointed to the Centro de Estudios Históricos, created in 1910 under the auspices of the Junta para Ampliación de Estudios y Investigaciones Científicas. Like other offspring of the Junta (and the Institución), the Center was intended to modernize and revive Spanish culture by introducing European methods and standards to historical research; in its organization and purposes it resembled the École Pratique des Hautes Études, founded in France forty years earlier. According to the Liberal minister who signed the degree, the "duty not to allow foreigners to monopolize the discovery of the sources for Spanish history" and "the desire for solidarity that the Spanish-speaking peoples of America now feel" had motivated the foundation of a center dedicated to historical scholarship.[82]

---

[81] Deleito, *Enseñanza*, 7, 109–10, 87.

[82] RD of 18 March 1910, signed by the conde de Romanones. The mission of the Center was as follows:

1°. To investigate sources, preparing the publication of critical editions of unpublished or defectively published documents . . . , [as well as] of glossaries, monographs, and philosophical, historical, literary, philological, artistic, or archaeological works.

2°. To organize scientific missions, excavations, and explorations for the study of monuments, documents, dialects, folklore, social institutions, and in general, whatever may be a source of historical knowledge.

3°. To initiate a small number of students into research methods, having them take part, whenever possible, in the above-mentioned tasks, for which special laboratory exercises will be organized.

4°. To communicate with those receiving grants for historical study abroad or within Spain, in order to help them and at the same time to collect their projects, and to prepare, for those who are so disposed, work and resources so that that they are able to continue working on their return.

5°. To create a library for historical studies, and to establish relations and exchanges with similar foreign scientific centers.

The creation of the Center was an implicit indictment of the university *cátedras*. Accordingly, it attracted the envy and resentment of more traditional academics as well as the hostility of the Catholic right, which viewed all programs of the Junta as hotbeds of institucionista propaganda. But in fact the Center, like the Junta, invited participation from scholars on the basis of their professional achievement, not their politics. Among those originally asked to participate were Menéndez y Pelayo and Costa, although both declined for personal reasons. Institucionistas like Altamira, Ortega y Gasset, the art historian Manuel Gómez Moreno, and later, the literary historian Américo Castro were active collaborators, but so were neo-Catholics like Eduardo de Hinojosa and the Arabist Miguel Asín Palacios, and Conservatives like Julián Ribera and Hinojosa's disciple, Claudio Sánchez Albornoz.[83] Symbolic of this determinedly nonpartisan atmosphere was the appointment in 1915, as the first president of the Center, of the distinguished philologist Ramón Menéndez Pidal, a conservative whose scholarly work exemplified the Center's premise that professional scholarship could be an act of patriotism.

A former student of Menéndez y Pelayo and the Arabist Francisco Codera, Menéndez Pidal had made his mark as a literary scholar in the 1890s with his carefully documented claims for the historical accuracy of Castilian epic poetry.[84] To rebut the attacks of French scholars on the

[83] A complete list of the participating scholars may be found in Carmela Gamero Merino, *Un modelo europeo de renovación pedagógica: José Castillejo* (Madrid: Consejo Superior de Investigaciones Científicas, Instituto de Estudios Manchegos, 1988), 103–5. See also Sainz Rodríguez, *Testimonios*, 33–34. For the Center, see Javier Varela, "La tradición y el paisaje: El Centro de Estudios Históricos," in José Luis García Delgado, ed., *Los orígenes culturales de la II República* (Madrid: Siglo XXI, 1993), 237–74; and Justo Formentín and María José Villegas, "Altamira y la Junta para Ampliación de Estudios e Investigaciones Científicas," in Alberola, *Estudios*, 175–207. For a hostile assessment by a professor at the University of Madrid, see Ángel González Palencia, "El Centro de Estudios Históricos," in [Miguel Artigas and Miguel Allué Salvador], *Una poderosa fuerza secreta: La Institución Libre de Enseñanza* (San Sebastián: Editorial Española, 1940), 191–95.

[84] For Ramón Menéndez Pidal, see José Antonio Maravall, "Menéndez Pidal y la renovación de la historiografía," in *Menéndez Pidal y la historia del pensamiento* (Madrid: Ediciones Arion, 1960); Dámaso Alonso, *Menéndez Pidal y la cultura española* (La Coruña: Instituto "José Cornida" de Estudios Coruñeses, 1969); Diego Catalán, "España en su historiografía: de objeto a sujeto de la historia," introduction to Ramón Menéndez Pidal, *Los españoles en la historia* (Madrid: Espasa-Calpe, 1982); Rafael Lapesa, "Menéndez Pidal, creador de escuela: El Centro de Estudios Históricos," in *¡Alça la voz pregonero! Homenaje a D. Ramón Menéndez Pidal* (Madrid: Corporación de Antiguos Alumnos de la Institución Libre de Enseñanza y Cátedra-Seminario Menéndez Pidal, 1979); Richard Fletcher, *The Quest for El Cid* (New York: Alfred A. Knopf, 1990), chap. 12; José-Carlos Mainer, "De historiografía literaria española: El fundamento liberal," in *Estudios de historia social: Homenaje a Manuel Tuñón de Lara* (Madrid: Universidad

historicity of the medieval epic and, more especially, to revise the unflat-
tering portrait of the Castilian epic hero, the Cid, drawn by the Dutch
scholar Reinhardt Dozy in 1849, Menéndez Pidal had deployed the
methods of modern philological criticism in support of his thesis that a
thread of historical truth linked the earliest known versions of the *Poem
of the Cid* (and other romances) to the chronicles of the later Middle
Ages. Appointed to the chair of Romance Philology at the University of
Madrid in 1899 and to the Center for Historical Studies in 1910, Menéndez Pidal inducted a generation of students into modern textual
scholarship.

What Menéndez Pidal shared with his mentor, Menéndez y Pelayo,
was a conception of literature as the expression of national consciousness. But whereas Menéndez y Pelayo had identified Spanish national
culture with the classical Christian tradition, as exemplified in the
Golden Age, his disciple located the heart of the national tradition in
the Germanic elements of medieval popular culture. And whereas his
mentor had insisted on the unchanging character of the national spirit,
Menéndez Pidal was interested in the evolution of its expression. Menéndez Pidal thus straddled the conflicting claims of traditionalists and
progressives. Appreciation for historical continuity did not imply, in his
mind, the preservation of fossilized and obsolete customs and beliefs,
but it did suggest a way of overcoming the centripetal and disaggregat-
ing forces in Spanish life. *La España del Cid*, published in 1929, was a
scholarly but accessible rehabilitation of the "myth" of the Castilian
hero, who emerged not as an aristocratic warrior, but as the embodiment of a national ideal of peninsular political and cultural unity linked
firmly to a Christian and Romano-Germanic tradition. The author confessed to his concern for national unity in his prologue: he wished to
resurrect one of "the great historical memories that most bind us to the
essence of the pueblo to which we belong and that can most strengthen
that union of spirits—the collective soul—that inspires social cohesion."[85]

All the work of the Center for Historical Studies was "patriotic" in
this vein, although not always as overtly interpretative as Menéndez
Pidal's mature work. Blessed with state subsidies that expanded during
periods of Liberal government, the Center established research seminars, prepared critical editions of Castilian chronicles and literary texts,
accumulated a respectable working library, published journals of philol-

---

Internacional Menéndez Pelayo, 1981) 2:439–72; and Varela, "Tradición y paisaje," in
García Delgado, *Orígenes culturales*, 237–74.

[85] Ramón Menéndez Pidal, *La España del Cid*, 2 vols. (Madrid: Editorial Plutarco,
1929) 1:iii.

ogy and institutional history, sponsored exchanges with European and Latin American scholars, conducted courses for foreign students, and, most important, provided professional training to a generation of young scholars. Predominant were archaeological, philological, legal, and medieval studies, not only because of the positivist preference for dealing with a manageable number of artifacts and/or documents, but also because of the clues they seemed to hold to the origins of the Spanish nation. Binding together the disparate activities of the Center was the "persistent search for the tradition, spirit, or differential character of Spanish culture."[86]

Altamira was affiliated with the Center as director of a seminar on historical methodology from 1911 to 1918. In contrast to the other sections in the Center, his seminar focused on contemporary history, whose characteristics he found so relevant to current concerns, but so poorly understood.[87] Several of his students there went on to distinguished careers as historians (among them, José de Deleito), instituto catedráticos (including Antonio Jaén), and educational reformers (especially Lorenzo Luzuriaga). Although his seminar on historical methodology disappeared with his departure from the Center in 1918, his spirit of patriotic yet disinterested scholarship continued to flourish there until the civil war.

Institucionista efforts to transform history teaching at the secondary level paralleled their experience with the universities: after an initial attempt to channel official institutions into new paths, they ultimately turned to an autonomous, although state-supported, model school as a way of diffusing new ideas from the top down. Like their Catholic interlocutors, progressives first endeavored to enlarge the place of history in the official secondary curriculum and to render it more "formative." If the universities were to become centers of specialized training, then the institutos must assume the task of consolidating the general historical knowledge of the average citizen. Proposals sponsored by Liberal ministers in the 1890s typically suggested the integration of Spanish and universal history to clarify the commonalities between Spain and the European world and, within the school year, revision of the curriculum to emphasize modern and contemporary history.[88] The Moret/Groizard reform of 1894, the Gamazo plan of 1898, and the García Alix reform of

[86] Varela, "Tradición y paisaje," in García Delgado, Orígenes culturales, 262.

[87] The program for the seminar is in Rafael Altamira; a list of students and their paper topics is in Formentín and Villegas, "Altamira y la Junta," in Alberola, Estudios, 199–204.

[88] See, for example, Segismundo Moret y Prendergast, "Consideraciones sobre la historia contemporánea," BILE 2, no. 5 (17 June 1877); Ricardo Becerro de Bengoa, La enseñanza en el siglo XX (Madrid: Edmundo Capdeville, Librero, 1900), 105–300.

1900 each added an additional year of universal history to the bachillerato, in an effort to allow professors enough time to reach the end of the syllabus. These relatively modest proposals were, of course, contemporaneous with the neo-Catholic Pidal plan of 1899, which stipulated six years of history (especially ancient history) within the classical curriculum. Such radical disagreements on the conceptualization of history, together with the usual parental pressures to minimize the effort required to earn the bachillerato, torpedoed regenerationist efforts to make history education more relevant and "educational." The compromise curriculum of 1903, which survived until 1926, required only one year each of Spanish and universal history and made no stipulations as to their content or pedagogy.[89]

The creation of the Instituto-Escuela in Madrid in 1918 responded to this inertia. Designed as a laboratory school, the Instituto-Escuela implemented many of the methods of the Institución, including Altamira and Cossío's ideas about the teaching of history. In both the preparatory and secondary sections of the school, history was taught cyclically— that is, from beginning to end annually, with greater depth and sophistication as the student progressed through the grades—and with emphasis on "the march of culture." The bachillerato, which built on the primary curriculum, was divided into three cycles: the first two-year period was devoted to an overview of Western history; the second, to the development of social and cultural institutions; and the third, to contemporary history. Although special emphasis was given to Spanish history in each cycle, the basic framework was the "history of humankind" as a whole.

The conception of history as a training ground for the active, informed citizen was imbedded in its pedagogy. In each two-hour class, students divided their time among reading, analysis of primary texts, discussion, and participatory activities such as mapmaking, note taking, and excursions to museums. As students grew older they visited historic sites throughout Spain. With the help of slides, albums, and visits to the Prado, special attention was given to the history of art as the best means of "entering the spirit of the society that created it." Translations of textbooks by Lavisse, Seignebos, and, for contemporary history, Albert Malet and Jules Isaac supplemented the individual and group work of students and teachers, but "the memoristic effort" required of students was kept to a minimum.[90]

---

[89] For curricular reform, see chaps. 1 and 2.

[90] For the Instituto-Escuela, see chap. 2; Luis Palacios Bañuelos, *Instituto-Escuela: Historia de una renovación educativa* (Madrid: Ministerio de Educación y Ciencia, Centro de Publicaciones, 1989); and the official report of the Junta para Ampliación de Estudios y Investigaciones Científicas, *Un ensayo pedagógico: El Instituto-Escuela de segunda en-*

Despite the hostility of the Catholic right and of some catedráticos in the regular institutos,[91] the Instituto-Escuela survived the Primo de Rivera dictatorship and finally obtained permanent approval of its charter in 1930. During the Second Republic, similar model schools were established in Barcelona and Valencia. But their curriculum and methods were not easily imitated in other official institutos, for reasons amply illustrated by the example of the history curriculum. The number of required classroom hours at the Instituto-Escuela was much higher than in the regular institutos, and the labor required of professors, much more intense. The costs to the student and the state were proportionately higher, not only for personnel, but for modern teaching aids and equipment. In addition, students faced the expense of field trips and extra supplies. Moreover, the history syllabus was far too ambitious; except in the final cycle of the bachillerato, recent history continued to receive short shrift.

It is not surprising, then, to find that the Instituto-Escuela's impact on history teaching in most institutos was slight. Catedráticos continued to lecture from the podium and to ask nothing more of their students than memorization of the textbooks they themselves had written. In the early 1920s, approximately 40 percent of the professors of geography and history in the fifty-eight institutos were the authors of one or more textbooks. With the exception of the book by Manual Zabala, who continued to teach at the Instituto San Isidro in Madrid until 1927, and the equally durable text by Alfonso Moreno Espinosa, which, in revised form, continued to enjoy popularity long after the death of its author in 1905, most of these textbooks were intended only for local distribution and often reflected the strictly utilitarian (and chrematistic) spirit in which they had been written.[92] Cheaply printed, illustrated sparsely (if at all), and still structured so as to facilitate memorization of essential facts, bachillerato history manuals as a genre remained generally impervious to the pedagogical exhortations of Altamira and the institucionistas.

A few adjustments had been made. By the 1920s all the texts had

---

señanza de Madrid. (Organización, métodos, resultados) (Madrid: author, 1925). The report on history teaching at the primary level was written by Teresa Recas, Amalia de la Fuente, and Margarita Rodríguez; at the secondary level, by Francisco Barnés Salinas. Quoted material on pp. 170, 172.

[91] See Luis Hernández y González [Eloy Luis-André], Un espíritu nuevo en la educación: Un informe y un voto sobre el Instituto Escuela. Reformas urgentes en la segunda enseñanza (Madrid: Sucesores de Rivadeneyra, 1926).

[92] The 17th edition of Zabala's text was published in 1922; the 23d edition of Moreno Espinosa's, revised by Francisco Morán López (the catedrático at the Instituto Cardenal Cisneros in Madrid), appeared in 1923.

abandoned the references to Túbal and Tarsis in favor of a sketchy over-view of "prehistory" that at least tacitly accepted current evolutionary hypotheses about the origins of humanity. Nineteenth-century political and military history now received attention (although rarely more than 15 percent of the total text). But ideological diversity still characterized the offerings. Among the older generation of catedráticos, there were still antiliberal Catholics like Juan Fernández Amador de los Ríos, a professor first in Pamplona, later in Zaragoza, whose textbooks were an eccentric jumble of facts, legends, and unsupported assertions, and Marcos Martín de la Calle, in Murcia, whose rambling, disorganized books also projected Catholic and xenophobic values.[93] At the other end of the spectrum were leftists like Antonio Jaén, a former student in the Centro de Estudios Históricos, who published a three-volume Spanish history text for his students at the instituto in Córdoba in 1923.[94] While incorporating the results of recent scholarship on the Spanish past, Jaén's highly personal account was fundamentally the work of a politi-cal and pedagogical activist with an instrumentalist view of history. Much more emphatically than his mentor Altamira, Jaén denied histori-cal agency to monarchs and statesmen and stressed the gulf that had separated state and nation since the beginning of the Habsburg era. Most textbook authors, however, continued to rehash in routine fashion the liberal version of the Spanish past. Although they nodded per-functorily in the direction of social and cultural history, most texts were primarily dull, shapeless political narratives without interpretative or stylistic distinction.[95]

If bachillerato textbook authors had not responded to their critics, it was probably because they lacked real incentives. With a captive reader-ship, their market was secured, and the state had still made no effort to prescribe changes in content or presentation. In 1901 the "merit" re-

[93] Juan Fernández Amador de los Ríos was also a well known antiseparatist publicist and philologist whose principal work was a *Diccionario Vasco-Caldiaco-Castellano*, which purported to prove that Basque was both the original Iberian language and the same as the Chaldean of Abraham. *RSE* 4, no. 25 (August 1926): 519–20.

[94] Antonio Jaén Morente, *Historia de España*, 3 vols. (Seville: Imp. de Eulogio de las Heras, 1923). Jaén was active first in the Radical Republican and, then, in the Socialist party.

[95] The conclusions in this paragraph are based on a review of the following texts: Juan Fernández Amador de los Ríos, *España en la edad media* (Pamplona: Imp. lib. y enc. de Nemesio Aramburu, 1911) and *Historia moderna y contemporánea de España*, 4th ed. (Zaragoza: Imprenta Editorial Gambón, 1933); José Lafuente Vidal, *Compendio de histo-ria de España*, 2 vols. (Salamanca: Est. Tip. de Calatrava, 1924); Marcos Martín de la Calle, *Compendio de historia de España* (Logroño: Imp. y Lib. de Carlos Gil, 1906); and Gabriel María Vergara Martín, *Nociones de historia de España*, 3d ed. (Madrid: Her-nando, 1927).

view of secondary-level history textbooks was entrusted to the Royal Academy of History, whose members shared responsibility for evaluating the texts submitted by professors seeking career advancement. Their reports, published in the *Boletín* of the Academy, suggest how difficult it was to overcome the inertia built into the system. Although the academicians frequently found much to criticize—factual inaccuracies, defects of composition or construction, shabby editions—books were invariably found to be "meritorious" for the bureaucratic purposes that had justified the review in the first place. Occasionally, ideological affinities seem to have played a role, as in the case of the sympathetic review by José Ramón Melida of six textbooks by Fernández Amador de los Ríos.[96] More often, however, the academicians seem merely to have been reluctant to damage the professional interests of the authors, even those whose work they found clearly deficient.[97]

In contrast to this gloomy picture of stasis, a few secondary-school professors clearly absorbed the influence of Altamira and the "scientific" history emanating from the Centro de Estudios Históricos. One of the most influential was Pedro Aguado Bleye, catedrático at Bilbao from 1912 until his transfer to Madrid in 1932. Trained in modern historiographical methods in Zaragoza and Madrid and, later, at the School of the History and Archaeology of Spain in Rome, Aguado Bleye published a series of historical monographs on the thirteenth century. But his most durable contribution to the development of historical studies in Spain was the erudite two-volume *Manual de historia de España*, first published in 1915 and continuously revised and reprinted through the 1970s. The *Manual* was what Altamira and others called a *libro de consulta*, a reference work that synthesized recent scholarship for advanced students and professionals. For the use of his own students at the instituto, Aguado Bleye also published several "textbook" versions of the *Manual*: the first, a "summary" of 629 pages, was published in 1914. By the 1930s the text had expanded to two volumes.[98]

Aguado Bleye's purpose was expressly professional; the goal of history, he contended, was not to teach morality or patriotism, but to train historians to search for the truth using the methods of historical science. The two-volume bachillerato textbook published in 1929 was lavishly

---

[96] *BRAH* 66 (1915): 387–94.

[97] See, for example, Ricardo Beltrán y Rózpide's evaluation of Rafael Montes Díaz, *Resumen de historia de España*, in *BRAH* 70 (1917): 131–34, or Adolfo Bonilla San Martín's review of Ángel Bellver y Checa, *Lecciones de historia de España* (and two other texts) in *BRAH* 73 (1918): 405–7.

[98] Pedro Aguado Bleye, *Manual de historia de España*, 4th ed., 2 vols. (Madrid: Editorial Eléxpuru Hmnos., 1925); *Resumen de historia de España* (Bilbao: Imp. y Lib. Hijos de Pérez Malumbres, 1914); *Compendio de historia de España*, 3d ed., 2 vols. (Madrid: Espasa-Calpe, 1933).

illustrated and scrupulously documented, with updated bibliographies and thorough discussion of points still unresolved by scholars. Geography and prehistory occupied a large section at the beginning of the text. While politics provided the organizational framework, ample space was devoted to social, economic, and cultural history. In the manner of Menéndez Pidal, Aguado Bleye analyzed the historicity of popular myths and legends and traced their evolution as cultural artifacts. The subtext of the entire work was respect for established fact, combined with skepticism about all unsubstantiated "truths."

Aguado Bleye's manuals reflected the assumptions typical of Altamira and other progressive historians at the turn of the century. The subject of his work was an indivisible historical entity called "Spain," territorially defined, shaped through the mutual influence of the many civilizations that had occupied the peninsula, and only fully unified in the modern age. Rejecting providentialism, he embraced the "genetic" method, which viewed each historical moment as the logically conditioned outcome of previous moments. The subject of history could only be the pueblo, "because everyone participates in the development of [the nation's] institutions and its manner of being."[99] He preferred to emphasize Spain's positive contributions to world civilization and to explain, rather than merely to condemn, the apparent errors of past centuries.

Through Aguado Bleye's textbooks it was possible to acquire a sympathetic understanding of the complexities of Spanish history and, perhaps more importantly, to encounter a method of inquiry that lay at the heart of the Europeanizers' project for national regeneration. Whether they helped his students in the instituto acquire a sense of national identity and purpose is debatable. His textbooks ran from six hundred to eleven hundred pages in length, much of it erudite discussions of historiographical controversies printed in small type. It seems unlikely that students read these or the informative captions that accompanied the hundreds of illustrations.[100] Reluctant students and their parents probably did not share the enthusiasm of the professional historians and educated lay audience who provided a steady market for the *Manual* for decades. Certainly, the two-volume textbook provided an easy target for the Catholic right, which seized the opportunity to denounce the "consequences for the nervous system" of the twelve-year-olds obliged to read it.[101]

[99] Aguado Bleye, *Compendio*, 4th ed. (1933), 8.

[100] The owner of the copy of the two-volume textbook analyzed for this study had diligently enclosed in parentheses the essential phrases in each large-font sentence, presumably as an aide-memoire.

[101] Federación de Amigos de la Enseñanza, quoted in Mariano Pérez Galán, *La enseñanza en la segunda república española* (Madrid: EDICUSA, 1977), 301–2.

Of all the Spanish catedráticos committed to the professionalization of their craft, Rafael Ballester y Castell perhaps came closest to achieving a text potentially attractive and intelligible to a wider audience. Having completed his doctorate in history at Madrid in 1907 with a thesis on geographical methodology, Ballester had subsequently received a scholarship from the Junta to study at the Collège de France with the Hispanist Morel-Fatio. On returning to Spain, he began a teaching career that took him to institutos in Palencia, Gerona, and Valladolid. In 1913 he published *Clio: Iniciación al estudio de la historia*, a four-volume history of Western civilization that went through six editions and was translated into French and English. A shorter textbook version followed in 1917.[102] Progressive, secular, and optimistic, but at the same time more radically skeptical of the reality of national unity than either Altamira or Aguado Bleye, Ballester was also more selective in his display of erudition, more conversational in tone, more elementary in his explanations, and more willing to criticize and condemn the follies of the past, particularly when religious hypocrisy or fanaticism was in evidence. Ballester y Castell mercilessly punctured hallowed myths and venerated icons: "Celtiberia" was a geographical expression, not a fusion of peoples; Viriatus was but one of many isolated resisters of Roman authority, not a champion of "Spanish" independence; the sacred paintings of the seventeenth-century artist Bartolomé Murillo were the "expression of the superficial and mundane religiosity of the masses."[103] Rejecting, like Altamira and Aguado Bleye, the traditional conception of history as a source of moral guidance for individuals, he shared their view (in turn, absorbed from Seignebos) of its social value as "the great educator of the pueblo."[104] An invitation to teach at the Instituto-Escuela brought his work the wider recognition it deserved.

It was at the level of the primary school that Altamira expended his greatest efforts to enlarge popular historical knowledge. Owing in large part to his proselytizing, history became a required subject for all primary students for the first time in 1901. Because meaningful curricular reform was a chimera in the absence of a well-paid and well-trained corps of teachers, Altamira agreed to serve as head of the General Office of Primary Instruction created by the Liberals on 1 January 1911.[105]

---

[102] Rafael Ballester y Castell, *Clio: Iniciación al estudio de la historia*, 5th ed., 4 vols. (Tarragona: Editorial R. Ballester, 1933, 1935); *Curso de historia de España*, 2d ed. (Barcelona: Talleres Gráficas Lux, 1921). For a brief biography of Ballester, see *RSE* 4, no. 23 (1926): 204–6.

[103] Ballester, *Curso*, 347.

[104] Ballester, *Clío* 1:31.

[105] On Altamira's service as director general of public instruction, see Ramos, *Rafael Altamira*, 156–75; and the commemorative volume *Rafael Altamira*, 131–50.

On Giner's advice, he accepted only on condition that the new unit be defined as a technical and advisory body insulated from political pressures. In Spain, however, educational issues were by definition political; what modernizers defined as purely professional questions, the Catholic right interpreted as insidious efforts by the state to undermine the "natural" educational rights of the church and the family. Altamira's initiatives as director general were seemingly unobjectionable: the elevation and standardization of the salaries and status of maestros, the creation of the initial grade-schools and kindergartens, the addition of more state inspectors, and the modernization of teacher training, including the addition of four years of history study in the normal schools.[106] Nevertheless, his ambitious program was barely underway when he was forced to resign in September 1913, his credibility eroded by the incessant criticism from the right, who were already incensed by the decision to make study of the catechism optional for primary students. The right's attack on Altamira was triggered by his authorization of books proscribed by the Index for inclusion in the new lending libraries.[107] But Altamira was not vigorously defended by progressives, either, some of whom seem to have preferred a more overtly partisan approach to educational issues.[108]

Despite his frustration with the politicization of educational issues, as social and regional tensions mounted in Spain, Altamira became more than ever convinced of the need for greater state activism. In an address to primary teachers in May 1918, he stressed the integrative function of a uniform, "national" education for all Spaniards: "The primary school should be the solvent of all our historical differences, of all our regional oppositions and indifferences, in order to intensify the formation of the spirit of unity, of *Spanish patriotism*, the only [patriotism] in which a secure base from which to confront our present problems and future dangers is possible."[109] Particularly alarming was the Wilsonian-inspired renewal of cultural nationalism in Catalonia, where the Mancomunitat and the municipal government of Barcelona were actively encouraging the growth of regional identity and loyalty through the sponsorship of

[106] RD of 30 August 1914.

[107] For a Catholic evaluation of Altamira's tenure as director general, see Gómez Molleda, *Reformadores*, 478–82.

[108] Altamira blamed both the right and the left for attacking his "impartial policies." Ramos, *Rafael Altamira*, 165. Ramiro de Maeztu, in a scathing article written immediately after his resignation, commented: "For intellectuals, he is a bureaucrat, a politician, and for politicians, an intellectual." *Nuevo Mundo*, 16 October 1913, quoted in Ramos, *Rafael Altamira*, 166–67. Altamira published what he had hoped to accomplish in the General Office in December 1913. "Programa de gobierno para la primera enseñanza nacional," in *Ideario pedagógico*, 199–203.

[109] Altamira, "La escuela nacional," in *Ideario pedagógico*, 171.

Catalan schools, professional journals, and schoolbooks, including a number of textbook histories of Catalonia.[110] Altamira was no longer confident that the mere possession of accurate historical knowledge was sufficient to stimulate collective identity. Spain was in fact "a country of divisions and historic heterogeneity. . . . History [is] the least national thing we have."[111] The national crisis demanded greater historical selectivity to overcome the excessively individualistic tendencies inherited from the past. When a Conservative government announced in 1921 a competition to select a "Book of the Patria" for mandatory use in the public schools, Altamira urged that it emphasize those parts of the Spanish past that were "comforting and expressive of virtues and excellences that humanity needs today as it did in the past." Read "again and again in our schools, generation after generation," such a book would reawaken the "atrophied" patriotism that Spaniards had lost because "they were led to believe that we are worth nothing and have only produced ignorance and tyranny in History."[112]

Altamira was no less distressed by the international hatreds that had led to war in 1914, and he campaigned ardently in the postwar years for world peace. In recognition of his contributions, in 1921 he was elected one of eleven permanent judges on the Court of International Justice at The Hague, a position he held until the outbreak of the Second World War. Convinced, like other educators of the day, that chauvinistic schoolbooks were partially responsible for the outbreak of war, he was a prominent participant in the international congresses convened during the 1920s and early 1930s to encourage the revision of history textbooks.[113] It was not enough, he believed, to eliminate the negative language and judgments from existing texts; history books must be written to promote "ideas and sentiments favorable to the peaceful and concerted co-existence of all."[114] The recommendations adopted in these

[110] For a list of titles, see Rosa Mut i Carbasa and Teresa Martí y Armengol, *La resistencia escolar catalana en llibres (1716–1939): Bibliografía* (Barcelona: Ediciones 62, 1981).

[111] Altamira, "La escuela nacional," in *Ideario pedagógico*, 172.

[112] In "Los medios de la educación patriótica," in *Ideario pedagógico*, 169.

[113] See Instituto de Ciencias de la Educación, Geneva, *El espíritu internacional y la enseñanza de la historia: Estudios presentados al tercer Congreso Internacional de Educación Moral*, which covers the Congress of Geneva in 1922; and Museo Pedagógico Nacional, *La enseñanza de la historia en las escuelas*, vol. 1 (Madrid: Imp. de E. Maestre, 1934), which was the by-product of a meeting of the International Committee of Historical Sciences in Oslo in 1928. The Eighth International Congress of Secondary Education, held in Geneva in 1926, also addressed the teaching of history; see *RSE* 4, nos. 22 and 25 (1926): 262–63, 299–301, 315–16. An overview of the many international congresses of the 1920s may be found in Amaranto A. Abeledo, *La enseñanza de la historia* (Buenos Aires: Librería y Editorial "El Ateneo," 1945).

[114] "Valor social del conocimiento histórico," induction speech at the Royal Academy of History, December 1922, quoted in *Rafael Altamira*, 188.

congresses were those Altamira had long endorsed: reduction of political and military history to make room for the history of civilization; situation of national history within a comparative framework; and definition of the individual as a member of a national and human community.[115] If they were to have faith in international cooperation, students must perceive the "indisputable guiding thread of History"—human progress—beneath the undeniable record of human folly and corruption.[116]

Not all representatives at these congresses shared Altamira's enthusiasm for international perspectives on national history. At the third Congress of Moral Education in Geneva in 1922, delegates heard the Catalan educator Pau Vila extol the virtues of national history in the liberation of "oppressed" peoples from centralizing or imperialist states. Universal history, he asserted, was a luxury reserved for those nations whose rights as independent states were already secure.[117] Of course, Altamira had always maintained that national history was potentially liberating. As he pointed out, Spanish history texts and teachers' manuals generally suffered not from nationalistic excess, but rather from the absence of any kind of shaping intelligence or social purpose. Ideally, history textbooks should encourage appreciation for national difference along with reverence for the common bonds of all humankind.

Altamira came closest to realizing his ideal in an *Epítome de historia de España* he published in 1927 for maestros and secondary school professors. Into this relatively brief volume, Altamira poured the generalizations about national identity that he had so assiduously avoided in his four-volume *Historia de España*. Admitting that the professional historian might wish for more evidence before drawing conclusions, he nevertheless observed that "pueblos do not wait to form an idea of themselves until science can given them a definitive answer."[118] Because a nation's future depended upon its understanding of its own past, it was urgent to replace mistaken ideas with more positive models for historical action.

In his list of the fundamental characteristics of "Spanish civilization," Altamira combined familiar clichés about the Spanish character with

[115] See the reports of M. P. Capra, "La enseñanza de la historia en las escuelas primarias," and of Rafael Altamira, "La enseñanza de la historia en España," in Museo Pedagógico Nacional, *Enseñanza de la historia en las escuelas* 1:13–57, reprinted in *BILE* 47, no. 876 (30 April 1933): 103–8, and no. 877 (31 May 1933): 131–34. This volume also contains reports from the Latin American republics.

[116] Altamira, "La historia en la educación moral," *BILE* 55, no. 854 (30 June 1931): 167–71, and no. 855 (31 July 1931): 201–5.

[117] Pau Vila, "El internacionalismo y el nacionalismo en la enseñanza de la historia," in Instituto de Ciencias de la Educación, Geneva, *Espíritu internacional*, 203–14.

[118] Rafael Altamira, *Epítome de historia de España: (Libro para los profesores y los maestros)* (Madrid: Ediciones de La Lectura, 1927), 64.

the "European" and "popular" attributes cherished by his generation of reformers: variety and diversity (particularly racial and geographical), austerity, a tradition of communal and customary law, an intuitive approach to knowledge, pragmatism, original adaptation of borrowed culture, and the equality of women before the law and in public life. His catalog of Spanish contributions to world civilization included artistic and literary realism, the preservation of classical culture in Europe after the fall of Rome, contributions to applied science, and especially, the "civilization" of the Americas. Without being excessively smug, Altamira sought to make a reasonable case for moderate optimism about the Spanish potential for moral and material progress. In the hands of the nation's teachers, this knowledge could become a potent instrument of national liberation and solidarity.

Less successfully attuned to its audience was the brief text for beginning-level primary students that Altamira wrote at the request of the Royal Academy of History in 1930. Reflecting his institucionista ambivalence about "bookish" learning, the manual was a short and rather lifeless account whose chief virtues were its factual reliability and thematic unity.[119] Profusely illustrated with maps, drawings and photographs, and written in a simple, clear style, the narrative intentionally omitted the biographies, legends, and myths young children were supposed to enjoy; Altamira expected teachers to supply these in their oral presentations to their pupils. But teachers, accustomed to relying heavily on textbooks, responded with little enthusiasm to one that expected them to do most of the work.[120]

Nevertheless, Altamira's ideas on historical pedagogy slowly trickled down, from his immediate colleagues and disciples in the ministry, the Escuela de Estudios Superiores del Magisterio, the Centro de Estudios Históricos, and the Instituto-Escuela, to normal school teachers, primary school inspectors, and maestros. Better trained and increasingly more professionally active, at least in the urban areas, some of them in turn incorporated his precepts into their own teaching and proselytizing. What distinguished the new generation of educators from their older mentors in the Institución was their determination to shape the masses, rather than selected elites, and their full appreciation of state

[119] Real Academia de la Historia [Rafael Altamira], *Historia de España, para uso de las escuelas primarias. Primer grado* (Madrid: Cía. Gral. de Artes Gráficas, 1930); and *Indicaciones a los maestros para la enseñanza de la historia de España* (Madrid: author, 1930), reprinted in *BILE* 45, no. 850 (28 February 1931): 45–48, and no. 851 (31 March 1931): 67–72.

[120] See the reservations expressed in *LE* 32, no. 2605 (31 May 1930): 740, and the criticism in *Atenas* 2, no. 8 (15 March 1931): 273–74.

schooling as a potential instrument of political socialization and popular mobilization.

Subscribing to Altamira's project for modernizing the writing and teaching of history, his younger colleagues sought to translate his conclusions into practical tools for the nation's teachers. The second issue of the *Revista de Pedagogía*, a new journal founded in 1922 by Lorenzo Luzuriaga (a former student of Altamira's in the Center of Historical Studies), carried an essay on history teaching by Rodolfo Llopis, a normal school teacher and Socialist party militant. For Llopis, the proper subject of history was the "peaceful conquests of peoples"; its purpose was to give students an "historical sense of life"—that is, a sense of continuing human processes—rather than an antiquated "fetishism of facts." Outlining a model curriculum, he reduced Spanish history to ten synthetic "moments," culminating in the reign of Charles III (who "synchronizes Spain with the world"), the Cortes of Cadiz (a "moment of national affirmation"); and the years since 1898 (when "Spain begins a new existence").[121]

Progressive educators demanded not only the renovation of content, but of methods. Children would develop into engaged citizens of the nation and the world only when history ceased to be taught as a spectacle or passive entertainment. As Teófilo Sanjuán, a graduate of the Escuela de Estudios Superiores del Magisterio, argued in a teachers' guide published in 1923, traditional patriotic history had struck only "the epic chord, with which it helps to form a crippled and static patriotism, pure contemplation, an aesthetic pleasure of a smiling and witless order that produces . . . tenderness and adhesion to the venerable grandeurs of yesterday, and which translates in terms of conduct, into docile conservative quietism; when, on the contrary, what is needed . . . is an agile, creative, constructive, and consequently critical and renovationist, patriotism of tomorrow." History should focus not on the deeds of great men, but on "the evolutionary process of the forms of existence, . . . the uninterrupted flow of scientific, artistic and moral problems that human impulses coordinate, domesticating the planet and bettering life."[122] Following the French educational theorist Roger Cousinet, Sanjuán advocated a "history of things" and of "social goods." By studying the progressive evolution of human civilization in its material and moral dimensions (in sequences, such as "cave-hut-mansion" or "violence and cruelty–hierarchy and inheritance–convention and solidarity"), children would learn that the "patria is not only the past . . . finished and defini-

[121] Rodolfo Llopis, "La enseñanza de la historia," *RP* 1, no. 2 (February 1922): 47–52.

[122] Teófilo Sanjuán, *Cómo se enseña la historia* (Madrid: Publicaciones de la Revista de Pedagogía, 1923), 7–8.

tive in breadth and height, patria for habit and memory," but a "laborious product of coexistence, in which we all participate."[123]

The model history curriculum devised by Sanjuán suggested that putting these dicta into practice was not easy. While the "history of things" naturally occupied center stage in prehistoric times, once the Roman period began, it became harder to avoid mentioning great warriors, statesmen, and artists. The strength of established periodization and coverage proved impossible to overcome, even for a determined reformer; by the time he reached the nineteenth century, Sanjuán's syllabus was littered with allusions to reigns, wars, and other political landmarks. The syllabus also reflected the tensions between Sanjuán's desire to emphasize collective achievements in the social and cultural sphere and his natural inclination as a teacher to personalize and dramatize the past to make it intelligible to young children.[124]

More adept at confronting these practical difficulties was the elaborate teachers' guide and syllabus published by Félix Martí Alpera in 1925. Martí Alpera had encountered Altamira and Cossío at the Museo Pedagógico Nacional in the 1890s. After successfully directing Spain's first graded school in Cartagena and traveling abroad with a study grant from the Junta para Ampliación de Estudios, Martí Alpera was appointed director of a laboratory school subsidized by the municipality of Barcelona.[125] In *Historia*, published in 1925, he offered maestros structured programs for three grade levels that steered teachers away from the routines of traditional pedagogy and professional historiography.[126] Following the practice in his own schools, he insisted that all instruction be oral, with student notes replacing textbooks in the advanced grades. In order to show maestros concretely how to teach orally, Martí Alpera wrote a sample lesson for each recitation topic in his syllabus, which illustrated the tone, vocabulary, and content appropriate for each level of student. An admirer of Cousinet, he occasionally inserted chats on the "history of things"—on interior illumination or eating utensils, for example—and showed teachers how to lead their pupils in a discussion of the evolution of material culture. For the

---

[123] Ibid., 19, 9–10. For a brief summary of Cousinet's ideas, see his paper "Los principios del trabajo histórico en la escuela primaria," in Instituto de Ciencias de la Educación, Geneva, *Espíritu internacional*, 114–23.

[124] Similar difficulties can be observed in the programs published by José Xandri Pich, *Programas graduados de enseñanza primaria, divididos en seis grados con instrucciones didácticas para su desarrollo* (Madrid: Yagües, [1925?]).

[125] Juan Benimeli, "Notas biográficas de D. Félix Martí Alpera," in Pedro Cuesta Escudero, ed., *Félix Martí Alpera (1875–1946): La seva contribució a l'escola pública. En motiu del seu homenatge* (Barcelona: GRAO, 1979), 28–34.

[126] Felix Martí Alpera, *Historia* (Madrid: Publicaciones de la Revista de Pedagogía, 1925). This teachers' guide went through four editions.

youngest children, Martí emphasized legends and myths, the adventures of great men, and even of horses like Bucephalus or Babieca. Ortega y Gasset, he reminded readers, had taught us that myths nurture the vital life of men and nations.

In the programs for the upper grades, Martí Alpera drew his readers' attention to the geographical and cultural context in which political events had occurred. For each grade at least one lesson was left open to allow the teacher to introduce a personage or event from local history, preferably by means of a visit to a local monument. The thematic unity of all the lessons was the gradual material and moral progress of the Spanish people from a state of incivility to one of material well-being, popular sovereignty, and religious toleration in the modern age.

In 1930 Martí published a first-grade "encyclopedia"—a one-volume textbook containing all the subjects in the official primary school curriculum—whose history chapter faithfully observed the principles he had laid out in his teachers' guide. In forty pages he covered the entire span of Spanish history without falling into the usual trap of mere recitation of unelaborated "facts." Omitting most political history to save room for "lessons of things," he invited children to realize that their familiar world was the product of time, experiment, and collective effort. But, with the exception of the Cid, Martí left out the great national heroes and myths that he had recommended in his teachers' guide. However much they might agree with Ortega in principle that myths embodied the creative spirit of the pueblo, progressive educators were too conscious of the reactionary values imbedded in most Spanish myths to wish to perpetuate them. Their interest in mythic heroes and events was more anthropological than vitalist; national myths might be enlisted to illustrate the psychology of Spaniards in the past, but they were problematic as a source of inspiration in the present and future. Martí and the progressive textbook authors who followed his example in the 1930s preferred to ignore them altogether.[127]

The publication of teachers' guides and model syllabi in the *Revista de Pedagogía* was part of a conscious strategy to disseminate the teacher-intensive, child-centered methods of the Institución and its offshoots among a wide audience of teachers and school inspectors at a moment when the number of teachers and schools, both public and private, was expanding rapidly. It was a form of continuing education that aimed to extend and reinforce the lessons conveyed at the Escuela Normal Central and the Escuela de Estudios Superiores del Magisterio

---

[127] For a defense of myth and "vitalism," see Alfredo Jara Urbano, "La historia en la escuela: (Notas y sugestiones)," *RP* 5, no. 71 (November 1927): 515–23 and no. 72 (December 1927): 558–66.

in Madrid. By 1930 the number of pedagogical publications listed by the bibliographer Rufino Blanco had doubled from a decade earlier.[128] That history had migrated from the periphery to a place of central importance in the new progressive curriculum was a tribute to the unflagging labor of its greatest advocate, Rafael Altamira.

[128] Claudio Lozano Seijas, *La educación republicana, 1931–1939* (Barcelona: Universidad, Departamento de Pedagogía Comparada e Historia de la Educación, 1980), 186.

CHAPTER 6

The Primo de Rivera Dictatorship, 1923–1930: The Origins of "National Catholicism"

> Religion and the Patria today more than ever
> need men of ideals and firm will. . . . History is
> neither the only nor most effective measure, but
> certainly one of the most effective,
> to achieve them.
> (*Enrique Herrera Oria*)[1]

IN SEPTEMBER 1923, the captain general of Barcelona, General Miguel Primo de Rivera, announced his intention to save the nation from the evils of social disorder and caciquismo by assuming temporarily the direction of the state. Promising a swift resolution to the multiple problems facing the nation, he assured his countrymen that his personal rule would represent only a "brief parenthesis in the constitutional life of the nation," clearing the way for the emergence of "virile" and patriotic leaders untainted by the corruption and egotism of the traditional political class.[2] His pronunciamiento was opposed only by that class, whose failure to address forcefully the postwar political and social crisis—especially the costly stalemate in northern Morocco—had alienated a broad spectrum of Spaniards, including the army, from the parliamentary regime and inclined them to seek messianic solutions to the nation's woes. Despite his promise to respect the Constitution of 1876, Primo de Rivera eventually attempted to institutionalize his military dictatorship

---

[1] Enrique Herrera Oria, *La enseñanza de la historia en el bachillerato: Orientaciones sobre planes y métodos. El material escolar y los museos escolares* (Valladolid: Tip. de Andrés Martínez Sánchez, 1926), 30.

[2] For the Primo de Rivera dictatorship, see especially, Shlomo Ben-Ami, *Fascism from Above: The Dictatorship of Primo de Rivera in Spain, 1923–1930* (New York: Oxford University Press, 1983); James Rial, *Revolution from Above: The Primo de Rivera Dictatorship in Spain, 1923–1930* (Fairfax, Va.: George Mason University Press, 1986); María Teresa González Calbet, *La dictadura de Primo de Rivera: El directorio militar* (Madrid: Ediciones El Arquero, 1987); José Luis Gómez-Navarro, *El régimen de Primo de Rivera: Reyes, dictaduras y dictadores* (Madrid: Ediciones Cátedra, 1991); and Gabriel Maura Gamazo, duque de Maura, *Bosquejo histórico de la dictadura, 1923–1930*, 5th ed., rev. (Madrid: Tip. de Archivos, 1930). The manifesto of Primo de Rivera is in *La Correspondencia Militar* (Madrid), 13 September 1923, 1–2.

as a Catholic, corporatist, one-party state before finally losing the essential support of the army and the confidence of the king in early 1930. Subsequent efforts by the former dynastic politicians to prepare the way for a resumption of the parliamentary system proved unsuccessful. In municipal elections held in April 1931, republican candidates won decisively in major urban centers, convincing the king and his advisers that they no longer controlled the political situation. With the peaceful proclamation of the Second Republic, Spain entered a brief period of democratic government, an experiment that was soon interrupted by the outbreak of civil war in July 1936.

Thus, after 1923 the opponents of the parliamentary monarchy on both the right and the left, each claiming to represent "the nation," captured the state in short-lived succession. With the gridlock of the parliamentary regime broken, each side attempted to implement its project for national regeneration. Since both right and left assumed that Spain's problems derived as much from cultural as from social or economic conflict, it is not surprising that both assigned a high priority to educational reform. Both the dictatorship and the Republic would claim a more activist and tutelary educational role for the state than the liberal politicians, paralyzed by dissension and indifference, had thought desirable or possible; both would attempt to institutionalize a "formative" *national* education that could overcome the cleavages in Spanish society and imbue Spaniards with a sense of common values, purpose, and destiny. Where they differed, of course, was in their definition of national identity and purpose and, as a corollary, in the degree of latitude they were willing to concede to the church and its educational agenda.

Neither the dictatorship nor the Republic survived long enough to establish its hegemony, nor did either possess sufficient will or power to suppress its enemies; thus the heated controversy between left and right over the ends and content of education persisted throughout the 1920s and 1930s. Within that debate, the meaning of Spanish history, and its place within a national curriculum designed to forge a sense of national community, excited more interest than ever. Historians and educators, stimulated by the new activism of the state, sought to help shape the nation's future by offering radically conflicting interpretations of the nation's past. It would take a much more determined and repressive state—the dictatorship of General Francisco Franco that emerged from the civil war in 1939—to silence the debate and impose a uniform vision of Spanish history on the nation.

General Primo de Rivera envisioned himself as a regenerationist, the incarnation of Costa's "iron surgeon," with a providential mission to sweep away the obstacles to national progress. In 1923 those obstacles seemed to him—and to many Spaniards—to be susceptible to effective challenge by men of steady purpose, firm hand, and patriotic intent. His quarrel lay not with the parliamentary monarchy per se, but rather with the "caciques," "separatists," and "terrorists" who pursued particular and selfish ends at the expense of the national interest. With the aid of the army, he intended to destroy their power to obstruct the harmonious and orderly resolution of the problems facing the nation; once he had cut the Gordian knot, disinterested patriots could restore the constitutional monarchy to its intended functions.

Shortly, however, Primo de Rivera's goals began to shift. Instead of relinquishing power after ninety days, as promised, he began to institutionalize his military dictatorship and to encourage the formation of a new civilian party to mobilize political support for his regime. Although claiming to be "above party," he acknowledged frankly that his values were essentially those of the right. The various rightist formations that had emerged during the previous decade of political and social disintegration contested for leadership of the new party, the Patriotic Union (UP). Dominating the process and the outcome in the early stages was the National Catholic Association of Propagandists (ACN de P), a conservative, social Catholic lay organization founded by the Jesuits in 1909 to "re-Catholicize" the nation. Led by Ángel Herrera, the editor of the Association's influential daily, *El Debate*, and deploying modern techniques of communication and organization in pursuit of conservative goals, the *propagandistas* had created an impressive network of laymen's groups, educational missions, and peasant credit associations before uniting with other social Catholic activists to form the Popular Social Party in 1922. At the same time, *El Debate* had begun to call stridently for an authoritarian solution to the mounting political and social crisis and, along with the rest of the Catholic right, had greeted the military dictatorship with relief and expectation in September 1923. The ACN de P's networks enabled it to win the initial battle for control of the Patriotic Union when it became the official party of the dictatorship in April 1924.

With the entrenchment of the Patriotic Union in all levels of the state administration after the "civilianization" of the dictatorship in December 1925, the party swelled with opportunistic recruits from the traditionalist right, the army, and even the former dynastic parties. The initial dominance of the propagandistas was soon challenged by ideologues of various stripes, including radicalized Maurists, right-wing nationalists, and protofascists. For these groups, the supreme political value was "the nation," although they usually allowed that the nation was consubstantial with the church and the monarchy.[3] The values,

---

[3] See Raúl Morodó, *Los orígenes ideológicos del franquismo: Acción Española* (Ma-

symbols, and rhetorical conventions of these competing interests shaped the characteristic discourse of the regime and defined the program of political and cultural nationalism later known as "National Catholicism." More a mentality than a formal ideology, it blended the reactionary cultural values of traditional Spanish Catholicism with strident authoritarian nationalism and a smattering of corporatist ideas of mixed lineage.[4] National Catholicism legitimated the authoritarian state as the form of political organization best equipped to defend the economic interests and religious and cultural values associated with national unity and power.

The conviction that national greatness depended upon a common sense of purpose and identity explains the importance that regime supporters attached to reforming the state educational system. Catholic integrists had not abandoned their traditional opposition to state interference in what they considered to be the "natural" educational rights of family and church; on the contrary, the growth of democratic opinion after 1917 had strengthened their opposition to the schools of the liberal state and their (at least theoretical) embrace of free discussion and cultural pluralism. But the postwar crisis had also increased Catholic interest in an authoritarian regime that might exercise state power to halt the encroachment of secular values. Thus, by the 1920s integrist Catholics had modernized traditionalist nostalgia for the union of throne and altar in defense of a dictatorship committed to the preservation of Catholic cultural unity.

Equally interested in educational reform was the heterogeneous assortment of authoritarian nationalists, whose numbers had grown along with the deepening fissures in Spanish society. Nationalism in Spain was an elite rather than a mass movement whose roots lay in the ideological and political anxieties generated by the loss of the colonial empire and in the uneven but growing impact of modernization on traditional social and economic structures.[5] "Nationalists," loosely defined, could be found across the political spectrum; as we have seen, even progressive regenerationists like Altamira were "civic nationalists" preoccupied

---

drid: Alianza Universidad, 1985). For an overview of the Spanish right in this period, see Martin Blinkhorn, "Conservatism, Traditionalism and Fascism in Spain, 1898–1937," in *Fascists and Conservatives: The Radical Right and the Establishment in Twentieth-Century Europe* (London: Unwin Hyman, 1990).

[4] On the ideological origins of National Catholicism, see Alfonso Botti, *Cielo y dinero: El nacional-catolicismo en España (1881–1975)* (Madrid: Alianza Editorial, 1992); Juan González-Anleo, *Catolicismo nacional: Nostalgia y crisis* (Madrid: Ediciones Paulinas, 1975); and Juan Álvarez Bolado, *El experimento de nacional-catolicismo, 1939–1975* (Madrid: EDICUSA, 1976).

[5] On Spanish nationalism, see Andrés de Blas Guerrero, *Sobre el nacionalismo español* (Madrid: Centro de Estudios Constitucionales, 1989).

with overcoming Spain's internal cleavages and with establishing her place in the community of modern democracies. As a political movement, however, nationalism drew its strength from the authoritarian right, which insisted that national resurgence lay in creating a state grounded in the traditional "Spanish" values of religion, social hierarchy, and order. In contrast to the counterrevolutionary mentality of Catholic integrism, authoritarian nationalists cast national regeneration in political and economic as well as religious terms, and generally advocated state intervention in economic and social life in pursuit of material progress and international stature.

Without abandoning their sympathy for Catholic schooling, the nationalist right accepted the premise that expansion of state education was indispensable for national recovery. Starting with the appointment of the Maurist Conservative César Silió to the Ministry of Public Instruction in 1919, Conservative governments had sponsored moderate increases in state funding for primary education and had begun to explore ways to make the state schooling more "patriotic." As noted in chapter 2, however, proposals to transform public schools into effective agents of political socialization foundered on the usual discord between Liberals and Conservatives over which values, if any, the state should promote.

It was precisely this kind of parliamentary stalemate that Primo de Rivera intended to suppress. In his decidedly regenerationist view, educational reform was fundamental to national progress, not only to make the Spanish people more productive, but also to prepare them for active citizenship in a society freed from the bondage of caciquismo.[6] By the time of his resignation in 1930, nearly 8,000 new public schools had been built, the number of primary teachers had risen by nearly 20 percent, and minimum annual salaries had risen to 2,500 pesetas.[7] Over 387,000 more children were in school than in 1922–23, an increase of 23 percent. Literacy had risen correspondingly; by 1930, the nation had passed through the "literacy transition," reaching a national average of 73 percent. Even in the traditionally backward south, 50 to 60 percent of the population could claim at least minimal literacy.[8]

---

[6] See his letter to Enrique Gómez Carrillo on 2 April 1926, quoted in Carlos Seco Serrano, *Militarismo y civilismo en la España contemporánea* (Madrid: Instituto de Estudios Económicos, 1984), 323.

[7] Salaries were increased in an RD of 28 January 1924.

[8] Cf. the statistics provided by José Pemartín Sanjuán, *Los valores históricos en la dictadura española*, 2d ed. (Madrid: Editorial Arte y Ciencia, 1929), 422–24, with Clara Eugenia Núñez, *La fuente de la riqueza: Educación y desarrollo económico en la España contemporánea* (Madrid: Alianza Universidad, 1992), 94, 108; Rial, *Revolution from Above*, 214–22; Victor García Hoz, *La educación en la España del siglo XX* (Madrid:

The expansion of schooling in the 1920s was the result of rising demand as well as state investment. Reflecting local demographic pressures, municipal support for new schools increased measurably during the 1920s, particularly in urban areas, where grade schools appeared in greater numbers.[9] Female enrollment in public schools, both single-sex and coed, was another source of demand. By 1930, female literacy had risen to 60 or 65 percent nationally, up almost 10 points from a decade earlier.[10]

These positive trends require qualification, to be sure. Access and literacy rates still varied considerably by sex and region. The Spanish state remained unable or unwilling to provide public school places for all children; only slightly more than 50 percent of children ages six to twelve were enrolled in public schools by the late 1920s, with another 20 to 25 percent in nationally or municipally subsidized private schools.[11] The extended reportage by the republican journalist Luis Bello revealed the persistence of unhygienic, overcrowded, and ill-equipped schools;[12] closure of some of the most inadequate locales only reduced the net gain of school places produced by new construction. And at both local and state levels, the Spanish educational pyramid was still top-heavy, with a larger fraction of state education budgets going to secondary and university education than in other European nations.[13]

Rising literacy, however desirable economically, represented a potential threat to social and political stability unless schooling also involved political socialization. Under the influence of the Catholic right, Primo de Rivera surrendered most of the responsibility for ideological control to the church, inverting the relationship between public and private

Rialp, 1980), 121; and Mercedes Vilanova Ribas and Xavier Moreno Julià, *Atlas de la evolución del analfabetismo en España de 1887 a 1981* (Madrid: Centro de Publicaciones del Ministerio de Educación y Ciencia, CIDE, 1992), 166.

[9] By 1929, however, there were still only 784 grade schools in Spain, representing only 2.5 percent of all public schools. Claudio Lozano Seijas, *La educación republicana, 1931–1939* (Barcelona: Universidad, Departamento de Pedagogía Comparada e Historia de la Educación, 1980), 82 n. 84. See also Antonio Viñao Frago, *Innovación pedagógica y racionalidad científica: La escuela graduada pública en España (1898–1936)* (Madrid: Ediciones Akal, 1990).

[10] See Núñez, *Fuente*, 94; and Rosa María Capel, "La enseñanza primaria feminina en España: su evolución histórica," in José Luis López-Aranguren et al., *Infancia y sociedad en España* (Jaén: Editorial Hesperia, 1983), 97–115.

[11] Religious schools received 25 percent of the state funds distributed locally. Enrique Díaz de la Guardia, *Evolución y desarrollo de la enseñanza media en España de 1875 a 1930: Un conflicto político-pedagógico* (Madrid: Ministerio de Educación y Ciencia, CIDE, 1988), 410.

[12] Luis Bello, *Viaje por las escuelas de España*, 4 vols. (Madrid: various publishers, 1926–29). The reports were first published in the liberal daily *El Sol*.

[13] See Nuñez, *Fuente*, 292.

schools that had gradually been established by the liberal state, although he continued to insist on the ultimate authority of the state to monitor the content of public education. Since in practice their political and cultural values were congruent, the church welcomed the heightened vigilance of the state over classroom teachers. An order of 12 February 1924 directed primary school inspectors to close schools or suspend teachers who taught "doctrines opposed to the unity of the Patria, offensive to Religion, or of a dissolvent character."[14] In October 1925 Primo de Rivera again instructed inspectors to ferret out doctrines harmful to social order or national unity by carefully monitoring teachers, pupils, and textbooks. As beneficiaries of the state, he pointed out, teachers were obligated to set "a public example of civic virtue inside and outside the classroom."[15] A later circular ordered teachers to attend mass, regardless of their personal beliefs, on pain of dismissal.[16]

To supplement the state inspectors, army officers serving as "governmental delegates" in each municipality promoted national and patriotic values in the schools and the community.[17] As members of the Patriotic Union began to colonize the municipal administration, they scrutinized the conduct of maestros and maestras exactly as Conservative local notables had done during the Restoration. From their vantage point in the local bureaucracy, they made strategic decisions about school construction, teaching materials, personnel, and subsidies to private colegios.[18]

In this atmosphere progressive educators faced an uphill struggle to propagate their ideas. Catalanist schools and textbooks, which were closely identified with the methods of active education, were outlawed shortly after the dictator seized power, and the progressive pedagogical journal edited by the Mancomunitat and the Diputació, *Quaderns d'Estudi*, ceased publication.[19] Institucionista influence over state educational policy was curbed by restricting the autonomy of the Junta para

---

[14] RO of 12 February 1924.

[15] RO of 13 October 1925.

[16] Circular quoted in Rodolfo Llopis, *La revolución en la escuela: Dos años en la Dirección General de Primera Enseñanza* (Madrid: M. Aguilar, 1933), 233.

[17] See the remarks on their efforts to improve schooling in E.T.L., *En la dictadura. Por pueblos y aldeas: De las memorias de un delegado gubernativo* (Madrid: Editorial Católica Toledana, 1928), 145–82.

[18] An RO of 29 January 1926 signed by Primo de Rivera ordered municipalities of fewer than six thousand inhabitants to organize Sunday lectures on "the knowledge and completion of civic duties and on professional topics," to be delivered by "cultivated persons in the locality." Local notables thus collaborated in the "sowing of moral and patriotic ideas in humble minds," among adults as well as children.

[19] An RD of 18 September 1923 prohibited the expression of separatist ideas in schools. An ROC of 20 October 1923 and an RD of 11 June 1926 forbade Catalanist schools and books.

Ampliación de Estudios and reconfiguring the membership of the Council of Public Instruction to give greater weight to conservative and Catholic corporate interests.[20] Although Luzuriaga's *Revista de Pedagogía* offered its readers progressive ideas and teaching materials throughout the decade, *Avante*, an alternative journal combining active pedagogy with social Catholicism, began to compete for readers in 1928. Sensitive to the changing atmosphere, editorial houses reissued traditional readers, like *Flora* and *Juanito*, along with new "patriotic" readers and textbooks. In response to the growing number of grade schools, they also began producing "encyclopedias" that offered students and teachers cheap, compartmentalized, and easily memorized digests of each subject in the curriculum.[21] Insofar as the encyclopedias reflected any values at all, they were the implied values of respect for received authority and passive obedience. The routine traditionalism of primary education thus belied the dictator's quasi-regenerationist professions of faith in popular mobilization and civic awakening; Spanish schools under the dictatorship resembled their predecessors far more than the "fascistizing" Italian schools of the same decade.[22]

If primary education still received a comparatively small share of state resources and attention, it was because Primo de Rivera's base of support, like his liberal predecessors', lay in the middle and upper classes, whose demand for post-primary education expanded along with the economy during the 1920s. The regime authorized the creation of seven new institutos, the first in four decades, and after 1928, twenty-four "local institutos" offering the new, three-year "elementary bachillerato" opened in the smaller provincial cities.[23] By 1930, there were ninety-six institutos altogether, a 50 percent increase over the previous figure, but still insufficient to educate adequately the 50 percent increase in students. Between 60 and 70 percent of the 71,000 students nationwide were registered as *libres*—that is, they did not attend classes in the institutos.[24] Among their numbers were a growing number of middle-class female students, now seeking the necessary credentials for state employment (opened to women in 1918). By 1930, women comprised almost 12 percent of total enrollment, although only a quarter of them attended classes as officially matriculated students.[25] In 1930

[20] RDs of 26 May and 25 June 1926. A list of the new members of the Council is in *RSE* 4, no. 26 (November 1926): 369.

[21] See the discussion in García Hoz, *Educación*, 230–37.

[22] For Italy see Tracy H. Koon, *Believe, Obey, Fight: Political Socialization of Youth in Fascist Italy, 1922–1943* (Chapel Hill: University of North Carolina Press, 1985).

[23] An RD of 7 May 1928 authorized the local institutos.

[24] Díaz de la Guardia, *Evolución*, 451–55, 514–15; García Hoz, *Educación*, 126.

[25] Rosa María Capel Martínez, *El trabajo y la educación de la mujer en España (1900–*

two institutos for women opened in Madrid and Barcelona, but most women wishing to avoid coeducation and prepare for university entrance were obliged to study in religious colegios or at home.[26]

Rising demand and the shortage of official school places created an opportunity that was exploited by the religious orders with the encouragement of the dictatorship. To meet women's demand for a serious secondary education without exposing them to the perils of coeducation, Father Poveda of the Institución Teresiana created the first of several "Catholic Feminine Institutos" in 1922.[27] Overall, the number of Catholic colegios rose 41 percent between 1925 and 1931. Most of the new schools were founded in the major urban centers and the larger provincial cities, where they catered to those social groups able to pay the substantial fees.

Since fully half of all secondary students went on to professional studies, a similar upward trend was apparent in the universities. Enrollment rose to 37,000 students by 1930 (5 percent of them women). With fifteen university students per 10,000 inhabitants, Spain enrolled almost as many as France and more than twice as many as Italy. The relative weakness of technical and scientific studies, at both the university and the secondary levels, persisted through the decade, despite Primo de Rivera's regenerationist rhetoric, and was both cause and effect of Spain's uneven economic development.[28] It was precisely in these technical fields, where employment prospects were precarious, that student protests arose in 1929 against the new policy allowing private (i.e., Catholic) universities to award advanced degrees. Economic insecurity, as well as ideological opposition, fed the student disorders that eventually helped to bring down the dictator in January 1930.[29]

Only two months after seizing power, Primo de Rivera asked the Council of Public Instruction to prepare recommendations for a reform

---

1930) (Madrid: Ministerio de Cultura, Dirección General de Juventud y Promoción Cultural, 1982), 381; Díaz de la Guardia, *Evolución*, 516–17; María Rosa Domínguez Cabrejas, "El acceso de la mujer a la Universidad de Zaragoza: Proceso histórico (1900–1934), in *Mujer y educación en España, 1868–1975* (Santiago de Compostela: Departamento de Teoría e Historia de la Educación de la Universidad, 1990), 407–19. See Antonio Viñao Frago, "Espacios masculinos, espacios femininos: El acceso de la mujer al bachillerato," in *Mujer y educación* for a discussion of the awkward accommodation of women in the institutos.

[26] The local institutos Infanta María Cristina (Barcelona) and Infanta Beatriz (Madrid) were created by an RD of 14 November 1929, opened in February 1930, and achieved regular status on 1 October 1930.

[27] *Revista de la Institución Teresiana* 35, nos. 318–19, extra issue (October–November 1944): 1–2.

[28] Nuñez, *Fuente*, 292–93; Diaz de la Guardia, *Evolución*, 518.

[29] Ben-Ami, *Fascism*, 350–53.

of the bachillerato, including a solution to the textbook "abuses" so frequently denounced by the Catholic right.[30] Two months later the Council (whose members still included many institucionistas, among them Cossío) submitted its report, which suggested major alterations to enhance the prestige, educational value, and selectivity of the bachillerato as well as to resolve the competing claims of the state and the religious colegios. Its principal features included lengthening the course of study, dividing it into two periods of general and specialized course work, reducing the number of courses and teaching them cyclically, and placing the colegios under the "tutelage" of the institutos in exchange for allowing qualified private professors to participate in the state exams. The principal goal was to deepen all students' general cultural formation and at the same time to prepare students more adequately for their future university work. In an accompanying report the Council decisively rejected a single, state-approved textbook (*texto único*) for each subject as a remedy for possible textbook abuses, suggesting as an alternative government-prepared lists of approved texts.[31]

The secondary-school reform finally approved in August 1926, however, incorporated almost none of the Council's suggestions.[32] Primo de Rivera, who had personally repudiated the Council's recommendations as impractical and insensitive to the economic pressures facing the middle class, seems to have taken an active role in shaping its provisions, as did the minister of public instruction, Eduardo Callejo, an undistinguished conservative catedrático and UP organizer from Valladolid who held deep reservations about the state's right to educate.[33] The 1926 bachillerato was neither longer, cyclical, nor "formative" in the sense understood by both progressives and Catholics. It established a three-year "elementary bachillerato"—apparently conceived as a substitute for post-primary vocational schooling—that included a jumble of modern and technical subjects and excluded Latin and Castilian language and literature altogether. Religion, "ethical and civic formation," his-

[30] RO of 29 November 1923, signed by the marqués de Magaz, in the absence of Primo de Rivera.

[31] A complete copy of the report, together with the amendments offered by Cossío, may be found in *BILE* 48, no. 769 (30 April 1924): 108–20. It is discussed in Díaz de la Guardia, *Evolución*, 368–73.

[32] RD of 26 August 1926. This decree and others may be found in Ministerio de Instrucción Pública y Bellas Artes, Sección de Informaciones, Publicaciones y Estadística, *Institutos nacionales de segunda enseñanza. La reforma de 1926. Estado actual de la enseñanza en España* (Madrid: Talleres Espasa-Calpe, 1928). The official name of the institutos had been changed by a decree of 30 June 1924.

[33] Callejo's views were evident in his defense of the reform before the National Assembly in 1927, quoted in Enrique Herrera Oria, S.J., *Modernas orientaciones en la enseñanza superior y secundaria* (Madrid: Editorial Razón y Fé, 1929), 14.

tory, and geography shared the task of socializing young Spaniards into national life. The second stage of secondary schooling, a three-year "university bachillerato" bifurcated into humanities and sciences, was structured to facilitate speedy completion by students studying as libres and was therefore too abbreviated to permit intensive preparation in any subject.

The overall effect of the Callejo plan of 1926 was to diminish the prestige of the bachillerato and of the catedráticos teaching in the institutos. Responding to Catholic resentment of the "tyranny" of the state examinations, it allowed private school professors to participate in the exams for the elementary bachillerato and transferred the final exams for the university bachillerato to examination boards composed of three university catedráticos, one instituto catedrático, and one degree-holding private professor.[34] As critics quickly pointed out, by completely separating the exams from the teaching function, the decree devalued official attendance at one of the institutos and reduced instituto catedráticos to the status of exam coaches.

Most egregiously, Callejo adopted Primo de Rivera's favorite nostrum, the texto único.[35] Noting that "mercantilistic" interests had forced students to endure lengthy, pedantic, and expensive books, Callejo nevertheless defended textbooks as essential for all but the brightest students, and especially for those studying as libres. A single state-approved text would "alleviate the burden on the middle class" and improve books both pedagogically and doctrinally.[36] Behind this apparent altruism was the dictator's conviction that "all youth, in their first steps, should be educated under a single official criterion."[37] As Primo de Rivera had explained to the Council of Public Instruction many months before:

> The young boy cannot exercise his free will with regard to different theories. . . . In adolescence, the State should channel the mind of the youth in order to strengthen it and give him an education that in its moral, religious, patriotic and civic characteristics not only possesses homogeneity, but also that discreet orientation which is distant not only from the exaggerations of those who, by virtue of an extreme optimism, present Spain as the nation bestowed with every providential gift, but also from those who, to the contrary, by virtue of an accentuated pessimism, dispossess her of everything good.[38]

---

[34] The decree implementing the examination provisions was signed on 23 May 1927.
[35] RD of 23 August 1926.
[36] Note of 20 August 1926, in *El Siglo Futuro*, 20 August 1926, 2.
[37] Ibid.
[38] In Díaz de la Guardia, *Evolución*, 374.

The ministry promised that official cuestionarios, or "topical indices," for each course would soon appear and that a competition to select the best book conforming to these official syllabi would follow.

Criticism of the texto único came from all quarters, with the exception of the Catholic colegios. However pernicious the existing textbooks, most commentators agreed that the remedy was worse than the disease. The institucionistas of course reiterated their fundamental objection to textbooks as "the very negation of the formative sense of a culture . . . and the nullification of professional dignity."[39] To the detriment of national culture, Spaniards were obsessed with "the illusion of unity" and the idea that "all Spaniards should be cut from the same pattern, decreed beforehand from some Sinai."[40] Liberal critics interpreted the texto único as a victory for the Catholic colegios in their campaign against the state schools. The colegios, they charged, had systematically manipulated the anxieties of a poorly educated and economically insecure middle class that longed for cheap, easily memorized primers.[41] Observers from across the political spectrum pointed out that the publication of an official text would not necessarily prevent professors from publishing their own "supplementary" books that, in turn, would be viewed as obligatory by insecure students.[42] And the Cámara Oficial del Libro formally protested the decree as an attack on the interests of the publishing industry as well on as the "purest and highest interests of national culture."[43]

The Catholic response to the texto único was in fact mixed. On the one hand, the religious colegios perceived that it promised greater success on the exams for their students. Speaking for the Augustinians, Father Jesús Delgado noted that the single text would bring relief from "nervous tension," academic insecurity, and economic distress by freeing students from the "individualistic battles among professors for hegemony in their respective subjects."[44] Whatever the advantages for the colegios, however, the integrist Catholic press expressed reservations

---

[39] Gabriel Alomar, "Contra el texto único," *BILE* 48, no. 767 (29 February 1924): 54.

[40] E. Gómez de Baquero, *RSE* 4, no. 24 (September 1926): 245–46.

[41] Ibid., 246. See also *ES*, 3, 8, and 10 September 1926, 1, and *LE* 28, no. 2,232 (4 September 1926): 1073. See also Camilo Chousa, *La reforma de la segunda enseñanza* (Antequera: Imp. de Francisco Ruiz, 1930).

[42] *ES*, 3 September 1926, 1; *LE* 28, no. 2,236 (18 September 1926): ll47; *El Siglo Futuro*, 28 August 1926, 1; *RSE* 4, no. 24 (September 1926): 245–47.

[43] *LE* 28, no. 2,231 (30 August 1926): 1072; see also no. 2,236 (18 September 1926): 1146–47.

[44] P. Jesús Delgado, "Cuestiones pedagógicas de actualidad," *RSE* 5, no. 28 (January 1927): 11.

about the texto único, recognizing its potential for unwelcome state indoctrination.[45]

If the texto único attracted the most criticism, other aspects of the Callejo plan also came under attack. The Catholic right objected to the short shrift given to religion and the classics;[46] all educators criticized the organization and distribution of subjects in the elementary bachillerato, particularly the almost total absence of national language and literature, the "foundation of nationality and of intellectual education."[47] They also reacted with indignation and disbelief to the "monstrous" official syllabi (cuestionarios) approved in December 1927, which were universally decried as too long, comprehensive, and sophisticated.[48] After a global denunciation of the Callejo plan was delivered at the opening of the National Assembly in November 1927 by Pedro Sainz Rodríguez, a conservative Catholic professor of literature at the University of Madrid, it became increasingly clear that the Callejo plan must inevitably undergo modification.[49]

The opportunity to reassess the Callejo reform came with the abrupt resignation and exile of the dictator in late January 1930. On 24 February, Elías Tormó, the new minister of public instruction in the government of General Dámaso Berenguer, asked the Council of Public Instruction to prepare recommendations for a future reform of the bachillerato in consultation with the professional association of instituto catedráticos, who had recently organized to defend their corporate interests. Faced with the certainty of revision, the Catholic right also began to organize to defend and, if possible, to extend the privileges granted to Catholic colegios by Callejo. Their association of lay and religious activists, the Federación de Amigos de la Enseñanza, or FAE,

---

[45] For examples of the antitextbook campaign led by the orders, see the articles collected in Enrique Herrera Oria, *Educación de una España nueva* (Madrid: Ediciones FAX, 1934). For reservations about the texto único, see the debate in *El Siglo Futuro* in late August 1926, and *Primer Congreso Nacional de Educación Católica, Madrid, 21–26 de abril de 1924* (Madrid: Tipografía de la "Revista de Archivos," 1925).

[46] See Ramiro de Maeztu in *ES*, 21 and 29 January 1924, and 5 and 12 October 1926; and Alejandro Diez Blanco, "El porqué del clasicismo," *RSE 5*, no. 29 (February 1927): 59–61. For a rebuttal see Eduardo Ibarra, *Los problemas fundamentales de la segunda enseñanza* (Madrid: Huelves y Cía., [1929]).

[47] *ES*, 31 August 1926, 5; *LE* 28, no. 2,234 (10 September 1926): 1107; *El Liberal*, 4 September 1926, 1.

[48] See the evaluation of the cuestionarios by a German *gymnasium* professor in *RSE 5*, no. 32 (May 1927): 199–203 and the editorial in no. 29 (February 1927): 49–55.

[49] Sainz Rodríguez's speech, in which he labeled the syllabi "monstrous," is in Pedro Sainz Rodríguez, *Testimonios y recuerdos* (Barcelona: Editorial Planeta, 1978), 357–62. A summary of the debate on the Callejo reform is in Díaz de la Guardia, *Evolución*, 391–93.

conceived of itself as the Catholic counterpart to the "extended Institución."[50] Through the coordination of interest groups, the organization of Catholic opinion, and the publication of *Atenas*, a journal for educators, it would provide aggressive representation for Catholic educational interests for the next thirty years. Also joining the battle in 1930 were Catholic pressure groups like the ACN de P, the National Federation of Catholic Students, and the newly created National Catholic Confederation of Fathers of Families.[51]

Although the Council of Public Instruction and the minister, Tormó, obligingly acceded to every Catholic demand, a draft proposal that Tormó floated for public comment in August 1930 provoked so much controversy in the heated climate that preceded the calling of new elections that the government was forced to postpone its implementation.[52] During 1930 the debate over the educational prerogatives of the church, particularly in secondary education, had polarized. Emboldened by the headway made during the dictatorship and by the recent reaffirmation of the church's claims to educational supremacy by Pope Pius XI,[53] the Catholic right was now on the offensive, demanding complete liberation of its "50,000" students from the "most violent, unjust, and uneducational regime of LEGAL OPPRESSION in Europe (except Russia)."[54] Catholic colegios wanted total freedom to implement the curriculum as they saw fit, without official texts, syllabi, or examinations by state-appointed catedráticos (demands in fact acceded to in the stillborn Tormó plan). The only functions that Catholic integrists were now willing to concede to the state were the regulation of "hygiene" and the allocation of state funding to private schools.

The concession of legal parity to Catholic colegios was fiercely attacked by the instituto catedráticos and by the democratic left in gen-

[50] Enrique Herrera Oria, "La FAE—Sus origenes. Su actuación ante la lucha escolar. Su posición actual," in *Cuestiones actuales de pedagogía*, 4 vols. (Madrid: Federación de Amigos de la Enseñanza, 1934) 3:339–66.

[51] For the recommendations of the FAE and the Fathers of Families, see "En torno a una Asamblea," in Herrera Oria, *Educación*, 197–221. The reports of the Asamblea de Doctores y Licenciados Catedráticos de Institutos Generales de Segunda Enseñanza are in *LE* 32, nos. 2,567 and 2,596 (10 January and 22 April 1930): 19–23, 564–65. See also Chousa, *Reforma*. The rebuttal of a leading member of the FAE is Enrique Herrera Oria, *La asamblea de catedráticos de instituto* (Madrid: Editorial Razón y Fé, 1931). For an overview of the debates on educational reform in 1930, see Díaz de la Guardia, *Evolución*, 417–50.

[52] For the reports of both the special commission and the "permanent commission" of the Council and the draft proposal of Tormó, see *Atenas* 1, no. 3 (15 October 1930): 78–99.

[53] Piux XI, *Divini Illius Magistri* (31 December 1929).

[54] Petition of the FAE to the government of General Dámaso Berenguer, 13 June 1930, quoted in Herrera Oria, *Educación*, 32.

eral, who were theoretically committed to the "freedom to teach." Seizing on this inconsistency, the Catholic right contrasted the extensive freedoms enjoyed by the British public schools with the "centralizing monopoly" claimed by the Spanish state and accused the catedráticos of defending "caste interests." But although a few liberals like Gregorio Marañón continued to defend the freedom to teach as an "untouchable" liberal principle,[55] most of the democratic and revolutionary left argued that, given the superior resources and the less rigorous academic programs of the religious schools, complete freedom to teach would quickly produce not parity, but the "absolute rule of the religious orders, who would thus in the future spiritually mold all of the well-to-do in Spain."[56] Liberal republicans like Manuel Azaña had warned against the trend and its pernicious consequences for liberal constitutional government shortly after the coup of 1923:

> It is . . . undeniable that the decadence of liberalism among the governing classes was hastened with growing rapidity in proportion to the arrival of new waves of penguins, fresh offspring of the confessional teaching establishments. In 1868 the brothers had not taught the young either philosophy or history for thirty years; but the cream of the Spanish bourgeoisie—the nursery of parliamentarians—has now for forty years received the elements of its culture from proselytizing lips. The current official education perhaps does not infuse its students with civic spirit or liberal sentiments; but it could infuse them. The luxurious private institutos, which preserve, or wish to preserve the young from the corruption of the cities, not only do not infuse that spirit, those sentiments, but incapacitate their students for acquiring them, except at the expense of the most sorrowful internal drama.[57]

The difference between Britain and Spain was thus that private schooling in the former nation reinforced the liberal constitutional order, whereas in Spain it conspired to undermine it.

Both left and right could agree that secondary education should not only "instruct" but "educate." But whereas the Catholic right stressed those subjects and methods that taught self-discipline, obedience to authority, and respect for tradition, the left favored those that taught self-reliance, creative thinking, and receptivity to change. At one point in the curriculum, however, their divergent values intersected—in the study of history. Both left and right considered history to be essential to the formation of patriotic, productive citizens, primarily because both

[55] Interview in *El Heraldo*, quoted in Herrera Oria, *Educación*, 65.

[56] *ES*, 2 July 1930, 1.

[57] Manuel Azaña, "La universidad y los colegios" (1924) in *OC*, ed. Juan Marichal, 4 vols. (México, D.F.: Ediciones Oasis, 1966) 1:495.

defined the nation and national unity in moral, or spiritual, terms: through history Spaniards could acquire a common sense of identity and a common way of approaching the world. Led by Altamira, the left believed historical study should liberate Spaniards from the hoary myths and habits that condemned them to perpetual backwardness; the right, in contrast, believed history should validate the traditional "Spanish" virtues that they deemed inextricable from national greatness.

Altamira and other progressives had developed a distinctive historical discourse that laid particular emphasis on scientific methodology and pedagogy. In response, the National Catholic right developed a counter-discourse that was generally (although not exclusively) antipositivistic in its epistemology. Its roots lay in the traditionalist interpretation of the national past, but it also drew on Marcelino Menéndez y Pelayo's literary scholarship and on emerging currents of irrationalism and vitalism.

National Catholic discourse on Spanish identity took as its point of departure the work of the diplomat and journalist Ángel Ganivet, whose *Idearium Español* was published in 1896, the year before his untimely death in Riga by suicide.[58] The *Idearium* was not, however, an integrist manifesto; its themes were much more complex, lending themselves to multiple interpretations. Like other regenerationists of the 1890s, Ganivet believed that the discovery of the "natural constitution of the race" was essential to understanding the present decadence of the nation. Unlike his Europeanist contemporaries, Ganivet did not wish to reshape the Spanish character, but to "restore" its originality, rescuing it from the "false" and inauthentic modalities into which it had been channeled at decisive moments by invasions, conquests, and misguided rulers. Like progressives, however, Ganivet pinpointed the victory of the German Charles V at Villalar in 1519 as the juncture at which Spain had abandoned her essential self; henceforth, Spaniards had pursued materialistic goals incompatible with their particular genius for idealistic enterprises. Rejecting Europeanist solutions, Ganivet insisted that regeneration lay in purification of the national essence and adherence to tradition: "A restoration of the sound life of Spain cannot have any other starting point than the concentration of all our energies within our territory. We must seal with locks, keys and padlocks all the doors through which the Spanish spirit escaped from Spain to scatter itself over the four points of the compass, and from which today it is hoped

---

[58] Ángel Ganivet, *Idearium español. El porvenir de España*, 11th ed. (Madrid: Espasa-Calpe, 1981). For a penetrating discussion of Ganivet's work, see Manuel Azaña, "El 'Idearium' de Ganivet," (1921–30) in *OC* 1:568–619. In much the same vein: José Antonio Maravall, "Ganivet y el tema de la autenticidad nacional," *Revista de Occidente*, 2d ser., 3, no. 33 (1965): 389–409.

that salvation will come."[59] Only after Spain had lived "a purely Spanish historical period" might she then look outward once again to reestablish her "natural" hegemony in Africa and America.

The key to Ganivet's analysis lay in his idealist definition of national identity and history. Although *Idearium español* took the form of an essay on Spanish history, his argument was essentially ahistorical.[60] Ganivet denied the legitimacy of positivistic historical methodology: "Of what purpose is a series of exact facts, supported by authenticated proofs, if one gives them all equal weight, if one presents them all on the same plane, and does not note which are concordant with the spirit of the nation, which are opposed, which are favorable, and which contrary to the natural evolution of each territory, considering its inhabitants as an historical personality?"[61] Using this kind of litmus test, Ganivet rejected most of Spain's modern history as "false," "a political contradiction,"[62] because it was incongruent with his a priori definition of the Spaniard as ascetic, spiritual (but not metaphysical), individualistic, intuitive, artistic, and bellicose. By the same reasoning, he could condemn contemporary striving to modernize and secularize the nation while still holding out the promise of a "spiritual empire" based on Hispanic ideals in Spain's natural spheres of influence.

This intuitive, "metahistorical" definition of national identity was congenial to those eager to transcend Spain's insignificant status in the modern world.[63] It offered a hopeful contrast to the cautious objectivity of the positivists, the pessimistic appraisals of the regenerationists, and the gloomy implications of "racialist" theories like those Ortega y Gasset's expounded in his essay *España invertebrada*, which attributed Spain's incapacity for national progress to remote historical fatalities that no one could do anything to remedy.[64] Ganivet promised rebirth through mere fidelity to what he asserted was most peculiarly, even perversely, "Spanish." He was the inspiration for a triumphalism that proclaimed national greatness to be a function of belief and will rather than of "external" action, although there was an equally strong element of determinism in his insistence on a static national character that must not be violated.

It is not surprising that Ganivet enjoyed an enormous vogue among the architects of the National Catholic worldview in the 1910s and

[59] Ganivet, *Idearium*, 123–24.
[60] This point is made by both Azaña, "'Idearium,'" in *OC* 1:568–619 and Maravall, "Ganivet."
[61] Ganivet, *Idearium*, 76.
[62] Ibid., 120.
[63] Azaña, "'Idearium,'" in *OC* 3:569–71.
[64] See chap. 5 above.

1920s, although the title to his ancestry did not go unchallenged by the left, who claimed Ganivet and Costa as the spiritual forefathers of their own critique of "official Spain." When the dictatorship arranged for the return of Ganivet's body from Finland for burial in Granada in 1925, it provoked a series of demonstrations and counterdemonstrations, as well as a journalistic debate between left and right as to who might legitimately hold proprietary rights to his intellectual legacy.[65] But progressives were fighting for a lost cause. By the 1930s, the National Catholic right had made Ganivet a fixture of its discourse on the national past.

An early, highly influential essay in the development of that discourse was *La leyenda negra: Estudios acerca del concepto de España en el extranjero*, published in 1914 by Julián Juderías, a gifted linguist and former student of Menéndez y Pelayo.[66] Expanded in 1917 and dedicated to Alfonso XIII, the essay earned Juderías the patronage of the king and election to the Royal Academy of History, an honor he scarcely had time to enjoy before his untimely death in June 1918. Juderías wrote to remedy the lamentable lack of a popular and accurate historical synthesis, *written by Spaniards*, to "give the Spanish pueblo an exact idea of what it was and therefore also what it can be."[67] His essay began with a defense of the "Catholic conception of life" that had inspired the Spanish idealism of the imperial age; next came a reasoned critique of the political motivations of the foreign and Spanish historians who had invented the Black Legend (a phrase coined by Juderías for the occasion). Juderías asked not for "triumphalism" but for balance: "we were, yes, an intolerant and fanatical nation in an epoch in which all the peoples of Europe were intolerant and fanatical." Citing Ganivet extensively, Juderías also urged retention of the "dreams and follies of Don Quijote" as an antidote to the violence, "industrialism," and "plutocracy" prevalent elsewhere in Europe.[68]

This determination to turn Spain's apparent decadence into the sign of her moral superiority inspired the growing cult of Don Quijote as a symbol of national identity, which surfaced in 1905 with the three hundredth anniversary of the first part of Cervantes's great novel. It culminated in a royal decree of 1920 that mandated daily reading of a pas-

---

[65] See *ES* in the month of March 1925.

[66] Julián Juderías Loyot, *La leyenda negra: Estudios acerca del concepto de España en el extranjero*, 13th ed. (Madrid: Editora Nacional, 1954) (1st ed. 1914; 2d ed., rev. 1917).

[67] Julián Juderías Loyot, *La reconstrucción de la historia de España desde el punto de vista nacional: Discursos leídos ante la Real Academia de la Historia en el acto de su recepción pública por . . . y por el Excmo. Sr. D. Jerónimo Becker y González el día 28 de abril de 1918* (Madrid: Imp. Clásica, 1918), 14.

[68] Juderías, *Leyenda*, 401, 402–3.

sage from *Don Quijote* in all public primary schools.[69] It was also visible in the speech Pedro Sainz Rodríguez delivered at the inauguration of the academic year 1924–25 at the University of Madrid.[70] A disciple of Menéndez y Pelayo and a specialist on the mystics of the Golden Age, Sainz Rodríguez was an outspoken defender of traditional Catholicism and monarchism.[71] Spain's "decadence," he argued, had originated in the eighteenth century, when Spain's ruling classes had abandoned the Catholic ideal that had bound them to the pueblo in a common enterprise. Since then, generations of liberals and foreigners had robbed Spaniards of pride in their own history by anachronistically judging the past against the standards of the present. Following the example set by Menéndez y Pelayo, however, scholars had recently begun to recover the documents that made possible a sympathetic appreciation of Spain's singular history. Sainz Rodríguez urged a voluntary fusion of the "two Spains" to achieve "the definitive affirmation of our national conscience," based on a common understanding of the national past: "We should feel moral solidarity with our dead, explaining to ourselves in historical terms the motives behind their acts. The past belongs to all and we have a right to it: to love it and interpret it in our fashion, feeling the roots of our spirit grounded in the entrails of our race."[72] As it was for Altamira, for Sainz Rodríguez historical scholarship was a patriotic act, because accurate knowledge of the past was a precondition of national regeneration.

Most of the National Catholic manifestos published in the 1920s were, however, less concerned with empirical investigation than with feeling, belief, and will.[73] Subjectivity, not objectivity, was the key to national unity and collective action. National Catholic recourse to history to validate essential beliefs about the patria and the "race" usually

---

[69] RD of 6 March 1920, signed by Natalio Rivas.

[70] In Pedro Sainz Rodríguez, *Evolución de las ideas sobre la decadencia española y otros estudios de crítica literaria* (Madrid: Ediciones Rialp, 1962), 41–235.

[71] For Sainz Rodríguez's activities in the 1920s and beyond, see his memoirs, *Testimonios y recuerdos*.

[72] Ibid., 136, 139–40.

[73] The following paragraph is based on the following selected sources, in addition to Juderías and Sainz Rodríguez: Miguel Herrero García, *Ideas de los españoles del siglo XVII*, 2d ed. (Madrid: Editorial Gredos, 1966) (1st ed. 1927); José de Lequerica, "El pasado español," quoted in Sainz Rodríguez, *Testimonios*, 361–63; Pemartín Sanjuán, *Valores históricos*; Ramiro de Maeztu, *Defensa de la hispanidad*, 4th ed. (Madrid: Gráfica Universal, 1941) (1st ed. 1932); Ernesto Giménez Caballero, *Genio de España*, 3d ed. (Zaragoza: Ediciones Jerarquía, 1938) (1st ed. 1932); Zacarías García Villada, S.J., *El destino de España en la historia universal*, 2d ed., rev. (Madrid: Cultura Española, 1940) (1st ed. 1935); Manuel García Morente, *Idea de la hispanidad*, 2d ed. (Buenos Aires: Espasa-Calpe, 1938); and José-María Salaverría, *La afirmación española: Estudios sobre el pesimismo español y los nuevos tiempos* (Barcelona: Gustavo Gili, 1917).

involved deductive reasoning based on a priori definitions of national character. Where historical fact and ideal type diverged, history was made to give way, dismissed as "anti-Spanish," "inauthentic," or "false." As one conservative member of the Royal Academy of History remarked: "historical reconstitution does not have to involve pillage, motivated by cold skepticism, in the field of our traditions, so as to mow down, impiously, everything not supported by documents, exaggerating their value and converting them into the only source of historical knowledge."[74] Positivist historians, distracted by events on the surface, too often missed the permanent traditions that lay beneath them. They were also too critical, too "cold," to nurture the patriotic fervor the right wished to cultivate. A favorite trope in this literature was that of "Mother Spain," an image that conveyed involuntary and primordial obligations of respect, loyalty, and uncritical love. As Cánovas himself had observed, "One is with the Patria with reason and without it, as one is with one's father and one's mother."[75]

History for National Catholics was thus the memory of a common descent and a common home; it was a story that privileged ancestors, tradition, and homeland and equated citizenship with filiopiety. The claim of the dead upon the living was a common theme: according to the self-proclaimed fascist Ernesto Giménez Caballero, "The solution to a national life is always in death, in the dead."[76] Or, as one civics text instructed its readers, "On your knees, before that cemetery from which arose, like a rose on a vast boneyard, the Spanish Nation, you must solemnly promise to know her in order to love her, and repay with your daily sacrifice on their altars, the centuries-old sacrifice of millions of admirable compatriots."[77] The demands of history, like those of family, were primordial and ineluctable; for that reason, National Catholics gave precedence to symbolic historical myths, like Numancia, Lepanto, and Otumba, over more contemporary symbols of the nation, like the flag, the map, or even the monarchy, which were associated with voluntaristic notions of citizenship. At bottom, this distinction between nationality and citizenship was the same one that separated Catholic and progressive concepts of "education" or "formation"; whereas Catholics stressed that education (including history education) involved subduing and shaping the individual for his duties to God and patria, progressives

[74] Jerónimo Becker, response to the induction address of Julián Juderías in the Royal Academy of History in 1918, in Juderías, *Reconstrucción*, 56.

[75] Quoted in Pascual Santacruz Revuelta, *España sobre todo: Páginas patrióticas para la infancia* (Madrid: Imp. Viuda y hijos de Jaime Ratés, 1926), 11.

[76] Giménez Caballero, *Genio de España*, 135.

[77] Santacruz Revuelta, *España sobre todo*, 11.

defined education (including history education) as a liberating process that freed the individual to choose rationally for himself and his nation.

At their most optimistic, Altamira and other progressives turned to history for confirming evidence of the contributions of the Spanish people to the forward march of humanity. National Catholics preferred to emphasize the particular "genius" of the Spanish "race," its spiritual difference from the prevailing values in the modern world. What was distinctive about Spaniards—their Catholic spirituality, radical egalitarianism, individualism, and antimaterialism—in fact proved their superiority. Condemning the progressives' desire to supersede the past in order to improve the present, the Catholic right instead measured the present by the degree of its fidelity to the past.

Most of the National Catholic right in the 1920s did not share Ganivet's assertion that the purest essences of the national character were to be found in the Christian Middle Ages. On the contrary, they agreed with Menéndez y Pelayo that the truest model of Spanish nationality appeared in the sixteenth century, a century "which possesses an imperial ethic proportionate to its will to empire."[78] The qualities traditionally associated with the Spaniard—courage, veracity, sobriety, impulsivity, and nobility—which, for progressives in a pessimistic mood, represented an impediment to cultural modernization, for the right constituted the spiritual core of the Spanish soul and the foundation of her future resurgence. Supposedly superior "European" virtues were not relevant because not authentically Spanish: "we lose our soul trying to be what we are not."[79] Efforts to transform or modernize the Spanish pueblo were thus not only futile, but immoral and unpatriotic.

The references to empire revealed the right's preoccupation with Spain's second-class status as a modern nation and its sense that a great past demanded an equally great future. Unwilling to settle for mere nostalgia or jeremiads against a sinful world, the National Catholic right of the 1920s fought back, insisting that the Great War had demonstrated the bankruptcy of "European" values while proving the "universality" of Spanish ideals. The return of the empire—this time defined in spiritual terms—was accordingly not far off.[80] By the 1920s *hispanismo*, a movement of transatlantic cultural cooperation initially favored by both progressives and conservatives, was increasingly the exclusive preserve of the right, who recast it as *hispanidad*, a spiritual community of Hispanic nations united by the Catholic, universalist principles that were

[78] Herrero García, *Ideas*, 61.
[79] Maeztu, *Defensa*, 26.
[80] See Martin Blinkhorn, "Spain: The 'Spanish Problem' and the Imperial Myth," *Journal of Contemporary History* 15, no. 1 (January 1980): 5–25.

the legacy of Mother Spain to her daughters.[81] The most emphatic and influential exponent of this ideology was Ramiro de Maeztu, a repentant Europeanizer converted to hispanidad by Saínz Rodríguez and by his sojourn as ambassador to Argentina in the late 1920s. In *Defensa de la hispanidad*, published in 1932, Maeztu disguised unseemly (and unrealistic) yearnings for imperial glory with rhetoric that converted defeat into victory by standing history on its head. Spain had lost her empire in the eighteenth century by turning her back on the evangelical principles of the "Catholic monarchy"; she would regain it by returning to those principles and thereby rescuing the American republics from the twin perils of Yankee and Soviet materialism. What was needed in Spain was an authoritarian state, led by a selfless and patriotic elite, to communicate the values of their history and of hispanidad to unenlightened pueblos on *both* sides of the Atlantic.

National Catholics in the 1920s overcame their intrinsic distrust of state power by reviving the traditionalist conception of monarchy as the embodiment of national virtues and as the servant and support of the faith. So defined and limited, state power might be comfortably deployed in defense of national unity and in pursuit of national goals. Although Catholic monarchists like Sainz Rodríguez might resist the subordination of Catholic identity to political interests,[82] others evolved toward a position of authoritarian nationalism that in effect instrumentalized religion in the service of national unity.[83] Whereas National Catholics were nationalists because they were Catholics, these "protofascists" were Catholics because they were nationalists.

Given the importance of history to the National Catholic definition of the patria, it should not be surprising that the dictatorship attempted to make it the centerpiece of its educational project. From his initial meeting with the Council of Public Instruction, Primo de Rivera expressed his desire for a "unanimous and patriotic criterion" and his dissatisfaction with the "lamentable exaggerations" he perceived in history teaching.[84] In the Callejo plan of 1926 history was one of the few subjects selected for annual study. In the elementary bachillerato, students were to begin with universal history and geography, followed in the second year by American history and geography, and in the third, by Spanish history and geography. Students pursuing the university bachillerato

---

[81] A thorough survey of this movement may be found in Frederick B. Pike, *Hispanismo, 1898–1936: Spanish Conservatives and Liberals and Their Relations with Spanish America* (Notre Dame, Ind.: University of Notre Dame Press, 1971).

[82] Saínz Rodríguez, *Testimonios*, 194.

[83] See, for example, Pemartín Sanjuán, *Valores históricos*.

[84] Interview with *La Prensa*, reprinted in *ES*, 21 January 1924, 1.

would continue with the "history of Spanish civilization in its relations with world history."

Apart from the illogical sequencing of these courses, what was striking was the addition of the course on Hispanic America; an emphasis on hispanidad was equally evident in the official syllabi published in 1927. Led by Eduardo Pérez Agudo, a catedrático in the University of Barcelona, the right had campaigned hard for inclusion of American history and geography in the curriculum, arguing that Spaniards must overcome their ignorance about their former colonies in order to combat the creeping materialism and cultural dilution that were widening the gulf between Spain and the American republics.[85] Refuting the Black Legend was of course as appealing to *hispanistas* like Altamira as it was to the right, but it was only the latter who based dreams of renewed empire upon it, as if only the legend, and not serious deficiencies of resources and power, stood in the way of a restoration of Spanish greatness.

The Callejo plan, which was in effect during only four academic years, did not—indeed, could not—produce the "unanimous and patriotic criterion" that Primo de Rivera had aimed for. The inertia in the system, together with Catholic reservations about extending state power, defeated pretensions to establish a uniform interpretation of the national past. The new syllabi, for example, were shaped more by professional conventions than by the undoubtedly conservative ideology of the catedráticos who prepared them; accordingly, they bore a striking resemblance to their predecessors.[86] Official textbooks for the courses on American history and Spanish civilization were not published until 1929 (and were abandoned in 1931), while those for the courses on universal history and Spanish history never appeared at all. Thus, throughout the 1920s instituto catedráticos continued to publish their own textbooks for the "guidance" of both official and privately educated students, who continued to buy them as a hedge against failure on the examinations. As noted in the previous chapter, those textbooks represented a wide range of viewpoints. Leftist professors like Antonio Jaén, integrists like Fernández Amador de los Ríos, progressives like Moreno Espinosa, Ballester y Castells, and Aguado Bleye, and conservatives like Lafuente Vidal or Zabala certainly did not speak with a unanimous voice. And in most cases, their books displayed the traditional

[85] Eduardo Pérez Agudo, "Lamentable olvido en la enseñanza: Los estudios hispano-americanos," *RSE* 4, no. 19 (April 1926): 6–13.

[86] RO of 7 December 1926. The commission included Eduardo Ibarra Rodríguez, Ricardo Beltrán y Rózpide, Antonio Ballesteros Beretta, Pío Zabala y Lera, and Ciriaco Pérez Bustamante, all well-known Conservative catedráticos.

indifference toward their audience that limited their effectiveness as instruments of political socialization.

Nor were the official textbooks, when they appeared, much different from the older texts in length, tone, and format. For the course on the history of Spanish civilization, the ministry chose a survey written by Juan Francisco Yela Utrillo, a former seminarian who was professor of Latin at the instituto in Lérida. A staunch Catholic, Yela Utrillo was nonetheless a trained practitioner of historical positivism; his text, 518 pages long and profusely illustrated, was a somewhat pedantic, but generally evenhanded compendium of the latest research in Spanish social, institutional, and cultural history. Although his Thomist allegiance was evident, the author refrained from polemics and expressed polite skepticism about topics mandated in the official syllabus (like the inherent "Senequism" of the Spanish race) for which empirical support was lacking.[87] His moderate defense of the Habsburgs was followed by a balanced appraisal of the Bourbons and a thorough, if somewhat slanted, discussion of nineteenth-century Spanish culture. Following the indications of the syllabus, Yela concluded with a dispassionate discussion of the Black Legend, the Inquisition, and Menéndez y Pelayo. Yela Utrillo's textbook demonstrated that imposition of a texto único did not necessarily guarantee that national history would become a powerful tool of political socialization. As long as professionally trained scholars wrote the books, professional values and conventions, not political goals and techniques, would tend to shape the final product.

The difficulty of overcoming entrenched habits and professional loyalties, despite the apparently greater activism of the state, was frustrating to Catholic educators, whose demands for "formative" education grew more strident as the number of students at all levels grew. In an age of rising literacy, urbanization, and secularization, they were increasingly aware of the limitations of traditional methods for maintaining a swiftly deteriorating Catholic culture; to survive, the church needed not just conformity, but active commitment from the educated classes. The need to inspire emotional engagement intensified Catholic interest in history as a formative discipline and altered its place in their secondary schools. The classics were still valued for their ability to shape individual character, but the religious orders now placed greater emphasis on national history "to sow in the spirit of the students the seed of the most exalted patriotism." Religion could then share in the emotional warmth generated by love of the patria, since "Spanish deeds

---

[87] The idea that Seneca, the Roman statesman and Stoic philosopher born in southern Spain in 4 B.C., represented the essence of the Spanish spirit gained wide currency among the right through the influence of Ganivet. See *Idearium*, 9–11.

cannot be conceived without the faith that inspired them."[88] Defense of the patria, that is, would require defense of its Catholic soul. Nationalism would be the savior of the faith.

But if the patria—and the faith—were to inspire such devotion in the young, history teaching would have to be revolutionized. Religious and patriotic values had to be deeply felt, rather than memorized; books and teachers would have to appeal to the heart, not the head. During the 1920s and 1930s, the leading Catholic exponent of reform was Enrique Herrera Oria, younger brother of the editor of *El Debate* and a history professor at the elite Jesuit Colegio San José in Valladolid.[89] Outraged by the "rationalism" and liberalism he found in most textbooks, Herrera Oria published articles and books condemning history as taught in the institutos from a perspective that provided a counterpoint to the well-publicized ideas of Rafael Altamira.

Herrera Oria was a prolific scholar who had published historical monographs and edited a collection of documents on the Invincible Armada. Nevertheless, he rejected erudition and impartiality as the goals of historical *pedagogy*, whose purpose was to "guide the child" and "shape the moral common sense of the pupil according to the norms of the religion he professes." Objectivity merely confused children, whose psychology was uncongenial to dispassionate discourse; besides, "not everything that is true should be learned," because objectively true facts could sometimes undermine the "substantive" truths taught in religion class. Herrera Oria suggested that history should be tendentious, "in the good sense of the term," in order "to create intellects that are not tangled and vacillating, but rather clear and firm." As an example of what he meant, he cited Prussian schools, where teachers were instructed explicitly to teach children to appreciate the "supreme authority of the nation" and to understand the present through the past. In French schools, he pointed out, all national history was filtered through the "Masonic slogan, Liberty, Equality, and Fraternity." If other nations could distort history "for perverse ends, why cannot it be employed in Spain for a noble end, which is to educate the child in the love of the true religion and a great and Catholic Spain?" Herrera had little enthusiasm for the bland humanitarianism of Altamira: "Let us not forget . . . that in order to love humanity a little, first one must love the Patria a lot, the region, very much, and the family very, very much."[90] An

---

[88] Mirabal, "La enseñanza de la historia de España," *El Siglo Futuro*, 3 September 1926, 1.

[89] Luis Fernández Martín, S.J., *Historia del Colegio San José de Valladolid, 1881–1981* (Valladolid: Colegio San José, 1981), 185–87.

[90] Herrera Oria, *Enseñanza*, 21, 25, 22, 25, 22; *Atenas* 2, no. 8 (15 March 1931): 273–74.

activist in the FAE, he agitated for the liberation of the colegios from the tutelage of the state, so that they might be free to make history the formative subject they understood it to be.

There were even fewer changes to the traditional ways of teaching and learning history in the public primary schools, despite the dictator's professed concern. As we have seen, the regime had taken immediate action against Catalanist, laic, and anarchist schools and textbooks, and in 1925 instructed school inspectors to monitor carefully books and teachers who might try to introduce "nefarious doctrines into the souls of their students, either by omitting essential facts in their presentation of Geography and History, or by giving them ambiguous explanations."[91] But these were defensive measures to root out sources of dissent. Otherwise, the regime took no action to transform the way history was taught in the schools. By the end of the decade, however, the rapid growth in the number of schools and schoolchildren, especially in urban areas, along with the reemergence of political and social protest, made a more proactive policy of political socialization seem imperative. Primo de Rivera thus asked the Royal Academy of History to prepare a graded series of history texts for mandatory use in the nation's primary schools. As we saw in chapter 5, the Academy asked Altamira to write the books, the most elementary of which was published shortly after the dictator's resignation in early 1930. Reflecting the evolving political situation, the Royal Academy concurrently expressed its view that mandatory textbooks were incompatible with the restoration of constitutional liberties. Nevertheless, the new minister, Tormó, informed the nation's maestros that henceforth Altamira's manual would serve as the "only basis" for teaching national history in the primary schools.[92]

Of course, Altamira's little survey was not the patriotic primer that the right had in mind. Even sympathizers with its mild progressivism expressed reservations about its appeal for young children;[93] unrestrained by sympathy, the FAE's educational journal, *Atenas*, described the book's physical appearance as "an insult to aesthetics and good taste and a gesture of disrespect toward children."[94] The Catholic right preferred books like *La emoción de España*, by Manuel Siurot, a disciple of Father Manjón. Siurot had written the book in 1921 for the competition sponsored by the Maurist minister César Silió to select a "Book of the Patria"; after the jury had failed to choose a winner, he published it commercially. By 1927 it had gone into a third edition. In

[91] RO of 13 October 1925.
[92] RO of 15 April 1930. For Altamira's *Historia de España*, see chap. 5.
[93] *LE* 32, no. 2,605 (31 May 1930): 740.
[94] *Atenas* 2, no. 8 (15 March 1931): 273.

the meantime, other readers like it had begun to appear as the market for them expanded.[95]

Following the "travelogue" format specified in the competition (and for which the French patriotic reader, *Le tour de France par deux enfants*, by G. Bruno, had served as a model),[96] Siurot introduced his readers to a quartet of adolescent boys whose superior academic performance had earned them a tour of the provinces of Spain. Each boy represented a particular Spanish (i.e., Castilian) type: Juanito Menéndez ("who is thirsty for readings and books"); Pepe Velásquez ("a dreamer fond of paintings, statues, and monuments"); Miguel Saavedra ("witty, frank, and popular"); and most Spanish of all, Fernando Cid ("whose characteristic is the natural elegance of his carriage, consonant with his prevailing strength and agility in physical exercises and who, along with a clear mind, has a noble heart that beats rapidly when he sees soldiers on parade and whose noble and expressive eyes become cloudy when the red and yellow flag passes")[97] Spanish children were expected to make the connection between these young heroes and their illustrious namesakes: Menéndez y Pelayo, Diego Velázquez, Miguel de Cervantes Saavedra, and the Cid Campeador.

Eschewing the tedious cataloging of local monuments and economic activities typical in this kind of literature, Siurot led his young patriots on a pilgrimage to the sites sacred to the traditionalist version of the Spanish past. At every stop the ardent young patriots entered churches and monasteries to hear mass and pray. At the Archive of the Indies in Seville, "the sacred repository that bears witness to the greatness of Spain," the boys stood awestruck before the documents that comprised the "Civil Register of the great Ibero-American family." And in Zaragoza they paid homage to the heroes of the War of Independence and to Our Lady of the Pillar, "the mother of Spain."[98] Throughout their journey the travelers encountered wise Spaniards who treasured the customs of their particular corner of the patria, who deplored the follies and iniquities of the modern world, and who taught the boys that

---

[95] For example: Alfredo Gil Muñiz, *Hispania mater: Lecturas escolares escogidas*, 3 vols. (Burgos: Hijos de Santiago Rodríguez, 1923–31); Federico Torres, *Viajes por España: Manuscrito*, 8th ed. (Barcelona: Salvatella, [1942]); Santacruz Revuelta, *España sobre todo*; Julio Cejador y Frauca, *Tierra y alma española* (Madrid: Sucs. de Rivadeneyra, [1924]); Gabino Enciso Villanueva, *Mi patria: Lo que ha sido, lo que es, y lo que puede ser España* (Burgos: Hijos de Santiago Rodríguez [1920, 1929]); and José Xandri Pich, *Del solar hispano: (Notas geográficas e históricas, costumbres y folklore)* (Palencia: Ediciones Justicia y Caridad, n.d.).

[96] See chap. 2, n. 47.

[97] Manuel Siurot Rodríguez, *La emoción de España: Libro de cultura patriótica popular* (Madrid: Talleres Voluntad, 1927), 7.

[98] Ibid., 30, 265.

true patriots did not wish to change the patria, but merely to love her: "It is a good son, who, with affectionate sacrifice, tries to remedy the deficiencies of his mother. But those who, sometimes because of real defects and more often because of imaginary defects, detract from august old age and violate her wrinkles and gray hairs, not only sadden themselves searching for the remedy but also deliver the inviolable maternity of the Patria to ridicule and mockery."[99] At the conclusion of their journey, the boys committed themselves to the regeneration of the nation, which they had come to understand lay in the defense of its most cherished traditions.

Catholic authors could attack with incredible ferocity those who wished to "de-Hispanize" or deny "the power, hidalguía, and glory of Spain."[100] In *Tierra y alma española*, Julio Cejador y Frauca, a former Jesuit and catedrático of philology at the University of Madrid, appealed to the natural idealism and self-esteem of his young readers in order to whip up outrage at the malevolence of "anti-Spanish" intellectuals and politicians:

> Schemers and opportunists, corrupt and bad rulers, separatist traitors, step on her [Spain] and trample her piteously. Some of her children, who call themselves intellectuals, even pour out against her I don't know what kind of poison that they brought from their travels through Europe; they fill her with vituperation and injuries; they repeat to her in every variant the black legend invented by her enemies; they accuse her of cruelty, laziness, and ignorance in the past and the present; convert her glories either into legends or into the horrors of a cruel, reactionary, clumsy, and obscurantist people, enemy of liberty and culture, incapable of colonization, and wrapped in crude superstitions; a people gross, hungry, ragged, and dirty, who did not know how to do anything for humanity and thus worthy of history's disdain.[101]

In the hands of Catholic traditionalists like Siurot and Cejador, the venerated past was a counterrevolutionary stick with which to beat the advocates of secularization and modernization. In contrast, for authoritarian nationalists who sought to unify and strengthen the state, it was a spur to action. The enemy, they argued, was not just deracinated intellectuals, but also apathetic and inert masses who had lost the will to prevail so characteristic of Spaniards in the Golden Age. Nationalists attributed this *abulia* (a national vice first identified by Ganivet) to an exaggerated reverence for tradition; even National Catholic ideologues

[99] Ibid., 114–15.
[100] *La Enseñanza Católica* 14, no. 347 (June 1924): 7.
[101] Cejador y Frauca, *Tierra y alma*, 394.

like José-María Pemán acknowledged that "it is necessary to avoid the easy and loose ajudication of the honorable title 'traditional' to superficial things, manners and forms that later become obstacles and brakes on the natural development of life."[102] Secular nationalists like the outspoken catedrático Eloy Luis-André condemned more emphatically the debilitating weight of reactionary ideas. A tireless proponent of educational reform and a disciple of Wilhelm Wundt, the German theorist of national psychology and biological vitalism, Luis-André aimed to modernize and invigorate Spanish culture without making it any less Spanish. Reformers must look to the past "to capture its spirit, not to slumber in it, because to do so is to stagnate and to substantivize tradition at the expense of progress; it is to wish, at bottom, to assassinate the living and resuscitate the dead."[103] A considerable gap separated an essentially forward-looking nationalist like Luis-André from National Catholics and traditionalists who insisted that Spain was built "on the illustrious tombs [of the dead]."

A basically secular nationalism also animated *El muchacho español*, a patriotic reader published in 1917 by José-María Salaverría, a self-taught disciple of Nietzsche and a regular columnist for the monarchist daily, *ABC*.[104] Like other innovative authors discovering the key to "formative" literature, Salaverría addressed his readers directly, in passionate, stirring language: "Your Patria needs to revive, transform itself and become greater. It needs to become an empire as powerful as it once was. You can be the modern hero that Spain is asking for!"[105] Patria, for Salaverría, was a tradition of great deeds and adventures that only foreign scoffers and bad Spaniards would wish to deny. What had distinguished the great captains and explorers of the past was their will and their courage, qualities essential for national greatness. Patriotic Spaniards had a duty to live up to that tradition, not just by revering it, but by adding new and different pages of glory to it, whether in industry, science, or letters. For nationalists, rather more than for Catholics, the Spanish past validated ambitions of national projection in the wider world. But both were increasingly committed to mobilizing the nation's youth behind the defense and perpetuation of their version of the *historia patria*.

[102] José María Pemán, *El hecho y la idea de la Unión Patriótica* (Madrid: Imprenta Artística Saez, 1929), 139.

[103] Eloy Luis-André, *Españolismo. Prasología. Pueblo y conciencia nacional* (Madrid: Sucesores de Rivadeneyra, 1931), 155.

[104] See Francisco Caudet Roca, *Vida y obra de José María Salaverría* (Madrid: Consejo Superior de Investigaciones Científicas, 1972).

[105] José-María Salaverría, *El muchacho español* (Madrid: Editorial Calleja, 1917), 97.

CHAPTER 7

History and the Creation of a Republican Civic Culture, 1931–1936

All revolutions take refuge in Pedagogy.
(*Rodolfo Llopis*)[1]

WITH THE ADVENT of the Second Republic the debate among Spanish intellectuals over educational means and ends reached its peak of intensity. Although the terms of the debate had not altered since the early years of the Restoration, the context was different and the stakes seemed higher to the coalition of bourgeois democrats, Socialists, and liberal intellectuals who formed the first Provisional Government on 15 April 1931. All shared the belief that the success of democratic government would depend on the ability of Spaniards to adopt unfamiliar political values and behaviors. Rational discourse, compromise, and civic responsibility were, in their minds, not merely ideal but absolutely essential modes of thought and action in a democratic polity. Thus, the battle for hearts and minds must precede all others. Educating Spaniards in the values appropriate to a republican civic culture was the bedrock on which the Republic must be erected: "As long as education does not change, all the political reforms and regime changes will be sterile: Spanish life will continue the same as before."[2]

The conviction that their political revolution would survive only if accompanied by a profound cultural transformation underlay the republicans' relative neglect of social and economic reform during the first biennium. Manuel Azaña, the leading figure in the republican coalition, had once explained the failure of Costa's economic regenerationism by observing that men die for ideas, not material progress: "No one sustains civil wars nor faces the innumerable penalties of persecution under the banner of 'Reservoirs or death!'" Writing just after the pronunciamiento of Primo de Rivera, Azaña had continued: "Let us imagine the

---

[1] Rodolfo Llopis, *La revolución en la escuela: Dos años en la Dirección General de Primera Enseñanza* (Madrid: M. Aguilar, 1933), 10.

[2] Lorenzo Luzuriaga, quoted in Eloisa Mérida-Nicolich, *Una alternativa de reforma pedagógica: "La Revista de Pedagogía" (1922–1936)* (Pamplona: Ediciones Universidad de Navarra, 1983), 153.

horrendous nightmare of the permanent accession to power of the Spanish right. Would they blow up the dams, block the canals, prohibit the use of chemical fertilizers? In no way. They would close the paths of spiritual progress, brutalize (even more) the sensibility of the pueblo, in order to avoid its arriving at the point where an attack on the liberal conscience is less tolerable than death itself."[3]

During the dictatorship Azaña's "horrendous nightmare" had been temporarily, if not permanently, realized. Fulfilling his prediction, the right had indeed given priority to education by favoring the Catholic colegios, whose reactionary political and social values were consonant with their authoritarian aspirations. In 1931, there was no doubt in the minds of Azaña and his colleagues in the Provisional Government and the Constituent Cortes that they must either use state power to inculcate democratic values or else acquiesce in the continuing subversion of the Republic by Catholic schools whose fundamental beliefs represented "everything contrary to the principles upon which the modern State rests."[4]

It is not clear that their decision was the correct one. Azaña's opinion notwithstanding, it is arguable that social and economic reform would have been more likely to consolidate mass support for the Republic. Furthermore, in betraying the venerable liberal principle of the "freedom to teach," the anticlerical policies of the first biennium gave the Republic's enemies an issue with which to mobilize the Catholic middle classes. Finally, the reversal of those policies by the center-right coalition after its electoral victory in 1933 exposed the limits of democracy to transform the political culture of a conflicted society through the

[3] Manuel Azaña Díaz, "¡Todavía el 98!" (1923), in OC, ed. Juan Marichal (México, D.F.: Ediciones Oasis, 1966), 1:559.

[4] Azaña, speech in the Cortes, 13 October 1931, OC 2:57. For an introduction to the Second Republic, see Gerald Brenan, The Spanish Labyrinth (New York: Cambridge University Press, 1961); Gabriel Jackson, The Spanish Republic and the Civil War (Princeton: Princeton University Press, 1965); Manuel Tuñón de Lara, La II República, 2 vols. (Madrid: Siglo XXI, 1976); Stanley Payne, Spain's First Democracy: The Second Republic, 1931–1936 (Madison: University of Wisconsin Press, 1993); Paul Preston, The Coming of the Spanish Civil War: Reform, Reaction and Revolution in the Second Republic, 1931–1936 (New York: Harper and Row, 1978); José Luis Ramírez, ed., Estudios sobre la Segunda República (Madrid: Tecnos, 1975); and the two volumes of essays from the Coloquios de Segovia sobre Historia Contemporánea de España edited by José Luis García Delgado: La II República española: El primer bienio (Madrid: Siglo XXI, 1987); and La II República española: Bienio rectificador y Frente Popular, 1934–1936 (Madrid: Siglo XXI, 1988). A thoughtful analysis is Juan J. Linz, "From Great Hopes to Civil War: The Breakdown of Democracy in Spain," in Juan J. Linz and Alfred Stepan, eds., The Breakdown of Democratic Regimes (Baltimore: Johns Hopkins University Press, 1978). A sympathetic scholarly study of Azaña is Santos Juliá, Azaña: Una biografía política (Madrid: Alianza Editorial, 1990).

schools, convincing many that the only sure path to reform lay in revolution.

To condemn the "educational utopianism" of the republican left, however, is to ignore the decades of political debate in which both right and left had identified education as the key to national regeneration. Both defined "the nation" in essentially spiritual terms, as a collective project legitimated by history and a common vision of the future. After 1923, the dialectic was no longer conducted exclusively in abstract terms, but in the political arena itself. First, the dictatorship had endeavored, unsuccessfully, to create an educational system that would resurrect in the nation's youth the traditional virtues of the Spanish race. Similarly, the republicans of 1931 framed their mission in terms of awakening and cultivating a long-suppressed national aptitude for democracy and progress. The insistence on cultural renovation through education, in other words, was not a "utopianism" exclusive to the left. The radical attempt at political socialization undertaken by the Franco regime in the 1940s would be sufficient proof of that.

"We have the Republic; now we must make the Revolution."[5] In the logic of the Provisional Government, the popular revolution that had brought it to power amounted to a mandate for a total transformation of state and society. Not only must Spain be given a new constitutional and administrative framework, but the traditional obstacles to popular sovereignty, economic progress, and social justice must be uprooted. On this much the republican coalition could agree; where they began to part company was in defining the content of the revolution to come. Whereas the middle-class republican parties tended to define the revolution in juridical, political, and moral terms, and thus viewed the Republic as an end in itself, the Spanish Socialist Workers' party (PSOE), with a strong working-class base, aspired to a radical social and economic transformation alongside which the form of government was "accidental." This discrepancy, which destroyed first the coalition and ultimately the Republic, was evident in every area of policy making during the first biennium, including education.

The most significant influence on republican educational policy was of course the Institución Libre de Enseñanza, whose liberal-democratic conception of education as individual moral and intellectual emancipation had defined the progressive educational project since the 1880s. Since the second decade of the new century, however, other influences had entered the country from abroad, primarily through the Socialist party. One was the international New School movement, whose child-

[5] Llopis, *Revolución*, 8.

centered pedagogical principles emphasized liberation from all dogma and preparation for "life" through cooperation, coeducation, and active methods: its mission statement promised that the New School "will develop in the child not only a future citizen capable of fulfilling his duties to others, his nation and humanity in general, but also a man conscious of his dignity as a human being."[6] The first Spanish New School had opened in the Socialist Casa del Pueblo in Madrid in 1910; by 1922 there were forty-seven schools nationwide, and a Spanish branch of the League of New Education had been founded under the presidency of the institucionista Lorenzo Luzuriaga, the editor of the *Revista de Pedagogía*.

Luzuriaga was the author of the "Bases for a Program of Public Instruction" adopted at the eleventh congress of the PSOE in 1918, which introduced the Spanish left to the concept variously known as the *escuela unificada* or *escuela única*.[7] The terminological imprecision reflected the multiple meanings attached to the concept, which dominated political discourse on schooling in Germany and France after the Great War, when educational democratization could no longer be postponed.[8] The fundamental goal of the "unified school" was to overcome the class-based segmentation typical of nineteenth-century state educational systems by integrating primary and secondary schools into a single *national* system, which determined access to higher education by ability, not economic or social status. In Spain Luzuriaga combined the democratic pedagogy of the New School with the sociological critique inherent in the proposals for an escuela unificada into a project for a free, ideologically neutral (laic), and democratic system of public schools based on the values of work and social cooperation. He also provided a nexus between this "socialist" project and the idealist individualism of the Institución, a union whose internal tensions were not always easy to keep in balance.[9]

A number of those serving in the Ministry of Public Instruction after 1931 were also personally connected to both the liberal and socialist pedagogical projects: the first four education ministers of the Republic

[6] *RP* 6, no. 67 (July 1927): 400. The mission statement was published in every issue of *RP*.

[7] The bases are reproduced in *CP* 1, no. 11 (November 1975): 25–26.

[8] Antoine Prost, *L'Enseignement en France, 1800–1967*, 2d ed., rev. (Paris: Librairie Armand Colin, 1968), 405–20.

[9] Mérida-Nicolich, *Alternativa de reforma*; Hector Barreiro Rodríguez, *"Lorenzo Luzuriaga" y la política educativa de su tiempo: Ponencias* (Ciudad Real: Diputación Provincial, Área de Cultura, 1984), and *Lorenzo Luzuriaga y la renovación educativa en España, 1889–1936* (La Coruña: Ediciós do Castro, 1989). Luzuriaga was a prolific author whose many articles and books included two specifically devoted to the unified school: *La escuela unificada* (1922) and *La escuela única* (1931).

(Marcelino Domingo, Fernando de los Ríos, Domingo Barnés, and Francisco Barnés) and the first director general of primary education, Rodolfo Llopis, were all affiliated to a greater or lesser degree with both the Institución and the Radical Socialist or Socialist parties. Again, not without some tension, they committed the state to the expansion and democratization of the state school system at all levels in order to make Spain "a free, progressive nation, open to all the challenges of civilization."[10] The election to the Constituent Cortes in June 1931 of a large group of intellectuals and educators (including sixty-four catedráticos, professors, and maestros) insured legislative support for their program until the collapse of the republican-Socialist coalition and the victory of the center right in late 1933.[11]

The inclusion of relatively specific educational principles in the text of the new constitution was a measure of the political significance that the left republican coalition attached to educational reform. During the constitutional debates, Socialist pressure altered the draft document, which emphasized the freedom to teach, in the direction of greater responsibility for the state.[12] Article 48 in its final form established "the provision of national culture" as "an essential attribute of the state" and identified the escuela unificada as the means by which it should be delivered. Primary education was to be free, obligatory, and laic; it "will make work the focus of its methodological activity and will be inspired by ideals of human solidarity."[13] Article 49 reserved for the state the right to regulate private education and to award degrees; article 26 dissolved the Society of Jesus and prohibited the remaining religious orders from teaching. Manuel Azaña's impassioned defense in the Cortes of article 26, which he defined as "a question of public health," made him the unanimous choice for prime minister after the cabinet crisis provoked by the adoption of the article in October 1931.[14]

The educational reform program of the first biennium has been studied elsewhere and will only be summarized briefly here.[15] It was carried

[10] Marcelino Domingo, quoted in Llopis, *Revolución*, 22.

[11] Manuel Tuñón de Lara, "La política cultural del primer bienio republicano: 1931–1933," in García Delgado, *II Republica: Primer bienio*, 267.

[12] See Mariano Pérez Galán, *La enseñanza en la segunda república española* (Madrid: EDICUSA, 1977), 61–96; Mercedes Samaniego Boneu, *La política educativa en la segunda república durante el bienio azañista* (Madrid: Consejo Superior de Investigaciones Científicas, 1977), 63–84; Carlos Alba Tercedor, "La educación en la segunda república," in Ramírez, *Estudios*, 61–66.

[13] These provisions were added at the suggestion of Llopis. *DSCC*, no. 59 (20 October 1931): 1820–24.

[14] Speech in the Constituent Cortes, 13 October 1931, in Azaña Díaz, *OC* 2:57. The constitution was approved on 9 December 1931.

[15] See, in addition to the works cited in n. 12, Claudio Lozano Seijas, *La educación*

out primarily under the direction of Domingo Barnés and Llopis, in consultation with the advisers they installed in the ministry and in the Council of Public Instruction, which in August 1932 was rechristened the National Council of Culture and restructured to eliminate most corporate representatives.[16] Not surprisingly the appointees to the Council, as well as to the ministry, the Junta para Ampliación de Estudios and its subsidiaries, and to the new local and provincial educational advisory councils, came almost entirely from the ranks of educators sympathetic to the ideals of the Institución. To the right's charges of "politics" and "nepotism," the republicans responded that the criteria for appointment were not political, but "technical." Accordingly, when the right came to power in December 1933, most councillors refused to resign on the somewhat disingenuous grounds that they had been appointed for their expertise rather than for their political affiliation.[17]

As the popular base of the instructional pyramid, primary education presented the problems of greatest magnitude and urgency. Using the formula established in 1857 by the Ley Moyano, ministerial estimates placed the deficit of schools at 27,000. The projected closure of religious schools was expected to increase the number of needed school places by 350,000. Before leaving office in late 1933, the republicans created 9,325 classrooms (unitary and graded combined); an additional 5,500 were added during the second biennium. The obstacles to even more rapid creation were both financial and political, for the right refused to vote money that might be used to replace religious schools. In 1936 some 2 million children still lacked access to public schooling.[18]

---

republicana, 1931–1939 (Barcelona: Universidad, Departamento de Pedagogía Comparada e Historia de la Educación, 1980); *Historia de la educación en España: Textos y documentos*, vol. 4, *La educación durante la segunda república y la guerra civil (1931–1939)* (Madrid: Servicio de Publicaciones del Ministerio de Educación y Ciencia, 1991) contains useful documents. Two firsthand accounts are Llopis, *Revolución*; and Marcelino Domingo, *La escuela en la república: La obra de ocho meses* (Madrid: M. Aguilar, 1932).

[16] The Council was actually restructured twice, in RDs of 4 May 1931 and 27 August 1932. The reform of 1931 was the fifty-eighth reform of the Council since 1857. For its membership in 1931, see Miguel de Castro Marcos, *El ministerio de Instrucción Pública bajo la dominación roja: Notas de un espectador imparcial* (Madrid: Lib. Enrique Prieto, 1939), 10.

[17] The integrist Catholic Romualdo de Toledo demanded elimination of credits for the Council in 1935 on the grounds that thirty-seven of the fifty-seven councillors were ideologically hostile to the current government. See *DSC*, no. 212 (27 June 1935): 8613; and Castro Marcos, *Ministerio*, 29–30.

[18] On schools needed and created, Llopis, *Revolución*, 34. For the number of students enrolled in religious schools, *BOMIP* 48 (25 April 1933): 785–811. Figure for 1936 in Pérez Galán, *Enseñanza*, 338, and Alba Tercedor, "Educación," in Ramírez, *Estudios*, 67. The budget discussions in June 1934 and June 1935 were the occasion for extensive debates on republican educational policy.

As important as expanding access to primary education was the transformation of its content and methods "to liquidate a mentality and a past dominated by the Catholic church."[19] The laic, or "neutral," school (as republicans preferred to call it) was one that "respected the conscience of the child," allowing him to "live, grow and develop without impositions" by the state or the church.[20] Obligatory religious instruction in the primary schools was prohibited in May 1931, as were religious symbols, images, and observances.[21] With the exception of the immediate expropriation of the Jesuit colegios in 1932, however, the constitutionally mandated closure of the colegios run by the religious orders was delayed until passage of the implementing legislation in May 1933. A deadline of 1 January 1934 was set for closure of the primary schools, despite the lack of public schools with which to replace them.[22]

Strict confessional neutrality did not imply an environment of amorality; on the contrary, like the French republicans who were their models, the Spanish republicans assumed the existence of self-evident moral principles that were simultaneously universal and evolutionary. Just as sacred history and Catholic dogma had once provided ethical guidance, in republican schools children would absorb "civic morality." Naturally, the contradiction between the determination to shape republican consciences and the incessant invocation of the "neutral" school was quickly seized upon by the Catholic right, which insisted that all education was in some way "formative" and that educational neutrality was a contradiction in terms.[23]

The success of the republican project for cultural transformation ultimately depended upon the teaching corps. The maestro was "the soul of the school," whose principal task was "to convert the subjects of the Bourbon monarchy into citizens of the Spanish Republic" and "to forge the fighters that the Spanish Republic needs."[24] To equip teachers to bear the portentous responsibilities entrusted to them, the republicans consolidated and radically restructured teacher training. Henceforth, the bachillerato would be a prerequisite for admission to the normal schools, whose three-year curriculum would be devoted entirely to course work in progressive pedagogy.[25] Normal school professors and

---

[19] Llopis, *Revolución*, 239.
[20] OC of 12 January 1932, signed by Llopis.
[21] D of 6 May 1931; C of 13 May 1931; O of 12 January 1932.
[22] Law of Religious Congregations of 2 June 1933.
[23] Pedro Sainz Rodríguez, in *DSC*, no. 106 (26 June 1934): 4036–39.
[24] Marcelino Domingo, quoted in Llopis, *Revolución*, 86, 22.
[25] D of 29 September 1931. The syllabus for the normal school course on the History of Pedagogy, which appeared on 15 July 1933, suggests the progressive orientation given to pedagogy by the ministry.

state inspectors would henceforth be trained in the University of Madrid.[26] By raising entry-level salaries for maestros to three thousand pesetas (four thousand for those graduating with the new degree), they hoped to raise the status of the profession and attract competent personnel.[27]

The existing teacher corps, especially those in isolated village schools, presented a dilemma; unwilling (and unable) to dismiss them, the republicans instead endeavored to select the most promising for new schools and to overcome the negative effects of defective training and oppressive environments through "pedagogic weeks" and "pedagogic missions," short courses, professional journals, and continuing education by an expanded state inspectorate.[28] It is difficult to gauge the reception of the republican reforms among the state teacher corps. Some, enthusiastic supporters of the republican project, joined the Socialist and anarchosyndicalist teachers' syndicates after 1934 to protest the obstructionist policies of the right. Others, however, retained their Catholic and conservative loyalties, if we are to judge by the large numbers who escaped serious reprisals in the Nationalist zone after the start of the civil war. The determining factor was often contextual; urban maestros were more inclined to sympathize with the left than were those in rural areas, where republicanism confronted the forces of tradition. But even in the select ranks of the state inspectorate, a vocal minority of Catholic traditionalists objected to republican aims. Available case studies indicate that most maestros preferred to maintain a cautious distance from both innovation and extreme reaction and did not join parties or unions.[29]

[26] D of 27 January 1932, creating the Pedagogy section in the Faculty of Philosophy and Letters in the University of Madrid, and abolishing the Escuela de Estudios Superiores del Magisterio and the Chair of Higher Pedagogy created in 1904.

[27] Even at three thousand pesetas a year, maestros were among the lowest paid state employees. See the comparisons in *El Ideal del Magisterio* 9, no. 328 (28 November 1932): 1.

[28] A decree of 2 December 1932 reorganized the Inspection of Primary Education and ordered each province to publish a monthly bulletin of information and education for teachers and local councils.

[29] Adolfo Iniesta, *Garra marxista en la infancia* (Burgos: Hijos de Santiago Rodríguez, 1939), 219–32, contains a list of 115 state inspectors removed from office for their reactionary views by the "reds" in 1936 and puts the membership of the Spanish Federation of Educational Workers (FETE, the Socialist teachers' syndicate) at five thousand in 1934, thirty thousand in 1936–39. Castro Marcos, *Ministerio*, 55–113, also contains information on purges of the educational establishment in the Popular Front zone. For purges on the Nationalist side, see Jesús Crespo Redondo et al., *Purga de maestros en la guerra civil: La depuracion del magisterio nacional de la provincia de Burgos* (Valladolid: Ediciones Ámbito, 1987); Wenceslao Álvarez Oblanco, *La represión de postguerra en León: Depuración de la enseñanza, 1936–1943* (León: Santiago García, 1986); and Ramón Navarro

One way to compensate for the ideological and professional diversity of the teaching corps was to regulate the books that maestros used in their classrooms. In May 1932 the ministry asked the Council of Public Instruction to authorize a list of textbooks for use in the public schools. To allow teachers some freedom of choice, the list was to include at least twelve books for each subject in the primary curriculum.[30] It took the Council two years to review the books submitted by authors and publishers and to issue the first list of approved books; a second list appeared in February 1936.[31] Not surprisingly, these initial lists were short, especially in those disciplines like history and the sciences where "memoristic" textbooks and encyclopedias had long dominated the market. Many of the readers most popular with teachers were rejected because of politically inappropriate content or stylistic mediocrity. Thus, in many subjects, fewer than the minimum of twelve books received approval.

It was one thing to publish a list, and another to enforce it. The evidence suggests that many teachers kept on using prohibited books, either because their schools could not afford new ones or because the size of many classes discouraged even sympathetic teachers from adopting the time-intensive active methods promoted by the ministry.[32] Others resisted out of inertia or ideological hostility.[33] In any case, compliance was voluntary after July 1935, when a right-wing cabinet relieved maestros of the obligation to heed the lists.[34] The right objected to the ideological content of the approved books, not to the concept of state control, as the imposition of rigorous ministerial censorship under the Franco regime would amply demonstrate.

Other republican initiatives to impose uniform state standards on primary education were similarly thwarted by the accession to power of the center-right coalition in late 1933. A comprehensive bill to restructure and integrate primary and secondary schooling submitted to the Cortes by Fernando de los Ríos in December 1932 fell victim to the

---

Sandalinas, *La enseñanza primaria durante el franquismo (1936–1975)* (Barcelona: PPU, 1990).

[30] O of 28 May 1932.

[31] O of 17 May 1934 and 5 February 1936. *BOMIP*, no. 25 (17 May 1934): 1004–5, and no. 27 (21 February 1936): 477–85.

[32] See María Sánchez Arbós, "Los problemas de nuestra escuela," *BILE* 57, no. 873 (31 January 1933): 1–3.

[33] According to Romualdo de Toledo, the ministry notified inspectors of reported violations and instructed them to enforce the measure "with the greatest severity." *DSC*, no. 212 (27 June 1935): 8614. On teacher compliance, see the comment in *Avante* 7, no. 73 (July-August 1934): 110.

[34] O of 8 July 1935. The right argued that teachers had no obligation to comply until all subject lists contained at least twelve books.

change,[35] as did the planning for uniform curricula, methods, and policies for the public primary schools. When progressive educational journals charged the right with playing politics with purely technical decisions, Catholics retorted that republican pedagogy was nothing less than an assault on the foundations of national life.[36]

Although the general tendency of republican policy was to centralize and nationalize the educational system, an exception was made in the case of Catalonia. Marcelino Domingo, the first minister of public instruction, was himself a Catalan, but owing to the opposition of centralizers across the political spectrum, including the Socialists, concessions on educational matters were limited. The Constitution of 1931 acknowledged the right of the autonomous regions to teach in their local languages, but it also defined Castilian as the official language of the Republic, required its use as a co-official language in regional schools, and reserved to the central state the right to create schools, to set uniform standards and objectives, and to award degrees. The Catalan home-rule statute finally approved in September 1932 did not extend but only confirmed these provisions (although it granted autonomy to the University of Barcelona).[37]

Within the limits imposed by the constitution and inadequate financial resources, both the city of Barcelona and the regional Generalitat attempted to "Catalanize" primary and university education "in language and in spirit."[38] Non-Catalan maestros received instruction in Catalan at the normal schools; until age eight all children were taught exclusively in Catalan; new textbooks on Catalan history, language, and geography were published. By 1934 three-quarters of the courses at the University of Barcelona were taught in Catalan.[39] The "Catalanization" of the educational system received a mixed reception in Catalonia itself, especially among the Castilian-speaking elites and the non-Catalan working class.[40] Potential conflicts with Madrid were minimized during

[35] *DSC*, no. 273, app. 2 (9 December 1932); Llopis, *Revolución*, 249–68.

[36] "La reforma escolar," *RP* 14, no. 166 (October 1935): 483–84; "La ofensiva de las derechas contra la escuela nacional," *Escuelas de España* 2, no. 22 (October 1935): 477–80; speech of Sainz Rodríguez, *DSC*, no. 106 (26 June 1934): 4036–39.

[37] Law of 15 September 1932; D of 1 June 1933.

[38] Estatut interior de Catalunya of 25 May 1933, in Jordi Monés i Pujol-Busquets, *La llengua a l'escola (1714–1939)* (Barcelona: Barcanova, 1984), 275. See also his *El pensament escolar i la renovació pedagògica a Catalunya (1833–1938)* (Barcelona: Edicions de La Magrana, 1977); Joan Gay, *Societat catalana i reforma escolar* (Barcelona: Laia, 1973); and Cèlia Cañellas and Rosa Toran, *Política escolar de l'Ajuntament de Barcelona, 1916–1936* (Barcelona: Barcanova, 1982).

[39] According to the hostile commentator Castro Marcos, *Ministerio*, 122. See also the discussion in Monés, *Llengua*, 195–202.

[40] Cañellas and Toran, *Política escolar*, 146.

the first biennium by the political congruity between the national and regional governments, but once the right had come to power, it seized the opportunity provided by the Catalan declaration of independence in October 1934 to revoke a statute that in its eyes threatened both national unity and traditional values.[41]

The republican emphasis on primary education during the first biennium was understandable, given the correlations that both middle-class republicans and Socialists presumed to exist among literacy, educational access, progressive pedagogy, and political democracy. Secondary school reform proved more problematic, however, because of divergent aims among coalition members. Left republicans did not question the essential elitism of the bachillerato; they merely wished to democratize access and to make the curriculum more formative and challenging. Most Socialists, while not disagreeing, were more concerned with the "unified school"—that is, with fully integrating primary and secondary education under state control and creating post-primary alternatives to the traditional bachillerato.[42] Depending on whether one defined secondary schooling as an extension of the primary school, as an intermediate level of general culture accessible to intellectually able citizens from all classes, or as preparation for university studies, the preferred methodology and curriculum might vary considerably. Furthermore, reform proposals faced a greater degree of resistance, not only from the Catholic right, but also from the professional association of catedráticos, which was protective of its members' traditional rights, interests, and "dignity." By September 1932, the ministry was forced to acknowledge that the National Council of Culture had not yet reached consensus on a new plan.[43]

In the meantime, the institucionistas in the ministry, led by Domingo Barnés, had enacted by decree "formative" measures they had long advocated: student residences and preparatory primary schools in the institutos; coeducation; university training in pedagogy for future instituto catedráticos; new Institutos-Escuela in Barcelona, Seville, and Valencia.[44] They also substantially increased the number of institutos in anticipation of the demand generated by the closure of the religious colegios and the requirement of the bachillerato for normal school ad-

---

[41] See the remarks of Castro Marcos, *Ministerio*, 122–26.

[42] See Domingo, prologue to *Escuela en la república*, reproduced in *BILE* 56, no. 864 (30 April 1932): 97–107; and the speech of Llopis in *DSC* no. 59 (20 October 1931): 1820–24.

[43] D of 13 May 1931; O of 21 and 26 September 1932.

[44] Residence halls: D of 8 September 1931; preparatory schools: 25 September 1931; coeducation: 28 August 1931; Institutos-Escuela: 2 March 1932 (installed in buildings confiscated from the Jesuits).

mission. To recruit sufficient numbers of pedagogically sensitive and ideologically congenial catedráticos, the ministry organized short courses of professional orientation and selection for interested university graduates in 1933.[45] In response to this increased supply of school places, the number of secondary students rose by 72 percent between 1930 and 1934.[46]

In December 1932 Fernando de los Ríos was finally ready to present an omnibus bill for the reorganization of primary and secondary education to the Cortes. Institucionista elitism had clearly prevailed over Socialist concerns to democratize access when it came to the bachillerato, which the minister defined as an "intellectual formation that provides an historical and current vision of culture that equips [the student] for a spiritually distinguished existence." The proposal did not address the class-based vertical segmentation of Spanish education; it would still not be possible to transfer from one track to another by applying course work taken in the upper primary grades toward the bachillerato, even though the decree redefined the bachillerato as "the end of the process of generic human education" in which the emphasis should be on active learning and simplified course content.[47] The new curriculum did not propose to dispense with elite classical education, but rather to make it more effective by extending and rationalizing the course of study. The responsibility of the state for national culture was affirmed by reinstating the exclusive right of the instituto catedráticos to administer exams for the degree.

The republicans asserted state authority over secondary education in other ways as well. In September 1932 Domingo Barnés ordered all instituto catedráticos to cease using textbooks.[48] Students henceforth were to take notes and submit them for correction. In November the Council ordered each instituto to submit a report on its teaching methods, extracurricular activities, and attendance.[49] At the same time, the ministry published official syllabi and pedagogical guidelines for a "transitional bachillerato" that it had implemented pending approval of the omnibus reform bill in the Cortes.[50] On 30 December 1932 the ministry established the General Inspection of Secondary Education to provide closer supervision of the institutos. The following spring the minis-

---

[45] D of 23 June 1933.

[46] Lozano, *Educación*, 129; Pérez Galán, *Enseñanza*, 346. For the relative size of the institutos in the peninsula, see *Minerva* 10, no. 300 (5 November 1935): 4–6.

[47] *DSC*, no. 273, app. 2 (9 December 1932).

[48] See also previous D of 8 September 1931, asking the faculties of each instituto to review the books in use.

[49] O of 5 November 1932.

[50] O of 24 September 1932 and I of 28 November 1932

try asked for copies of all textbooks in print in preparation for a review and selection of the best, but gave up when the resulting submissions filled an entire room in the ministry.[51]

Instituto catedráticos, whose professional association was now meeting regularly, reacted with hostility to the reforms emanating from the ministry. If some measures reinforced their authority, others diminished their prestige and autonomy, at least in their own eyes. The majority of catedráticos—men in their forties or early fifties with fifteen to twenty years of experience—did not welcome the tendency of some in the ministry to refer to the *"magisterio de segunda enseñanza"*; they recognized that reconceptualizing the instituto as an extension of the primary school rather than as a gateway to the university threatened their traditional equality with university catedráticos.[52] The recruitment of *"cursillistas"* to occupy cátedras after a few improvised short courses and the publication of uniform syllabi and pedagogical guidelines confirmed their fears of professional demotion.[53] Active methods, in addition to undermining the aloof majesty of the cátedra, were also difficult to apply in classrooms where class sizes of sixty students were the rule.[54] Thus, catedráticos were not mollified by the promise of the new state inspection office to respect "legitimate interests and the procedures justified by long years of experience."[55]

Catedráticos who had written textbooks were especially outraged by the Council's criticism of their excessive cost and scholarly defects. Textbooks had been under attack from the Catholic right for years. Now they were under assault in the pages of the influential daily *El Sol* by leading republican intellectuals like the philologist Américo Castro, who attacked the "business of bad textbooks" as "the goblin that rouses the syndicalist spirit of the professoriate."[56] In response, the Association of Instituto Catedráticos began to mobilize against the "politicians" on the Council in defense of "their morale, their scientific credit, their honorability in short."[57] Feeding their discontent was *Minerva*, a

---

[51] See *Minerva* 8, no. 183 (11 May 1933): 1; *ES*, 7 February 1936, 1.

[52] *Escalafón de los catedráticos numerarios de Institutos Nacionales de Segunda Enseñanza* (Madrid: Imp. de L. Rubio, 1934–36) contains data on birthdates, salaries, and professional service.

[53] *Minerva* 8, nos. 181 and 196 (25 April and 29 August 1933): 1.

[54] In contrast, in the French lycées in this period, seventeen students per class was the average. Prost, *L'Enseignement*, 259.

[55] D of 30 December 1932.

[56] See *Minerva* 8, nos. 175 and 176 (8 and 14 March 1933): 1, and no. 184 (18 May 1933): 1–3. The average catedrático received a relatively meager salary of nine thousand pesetas a year, the same as a major in the Spanish army; textbooks provided an important source of extra income.

[57] *Minerva* 8, no. 183 (11 May 1933): 1, and 182 (4 May 1933): 1.

professional journal published by an integrist Catholic civil servant in the ministry, Miguel de Castro Marcos. The final straw came in April 1934, when the interim minister of public instruction, Salvador de Madariaga, took the unprecedented step of prohibiting the use of history textbooks written by two of the most senior catedráticos, Marcos Martín de la Calle and Juan Fernández Amador de los Ríos. Despite the patent defects of their books, which were carelessly written, poorly organized, and out of date, the elderly catedráticos quickly became martyrs to the cause of professional dignity.[58]

As a concession to the catedráticos, the next minister in the center-right coalition, Filiberto Villalobos, authorized the use of textbooks, subject to review and approval by an ad hoc committee appointed by the ministry, and issued new syllabi that did not infringe on their claim to be scholars, not teachers.[59] He also enacted a reform of the bachillerato by decree that partially addressed their curricular concerns, although it respected the general outlines of the plan proposed by De los Ríos eighteen months before, including the provisions that restored the state institutos' monopoly over examinations. As a result, Villalobos earned the enmity of the Catholic right, which forced his resignation when the Spanish Confederation of Autonomous Rightist Groups (C.E.D.A.) entered the cabinet in October 1934.[60]

In fact, the position of Catholic secondary schooling was scarcely altered during the Republic. By government estimates there were 20,684 secondary students and 352,000 primary students enrolled in Catholic schools at the end of 1932, a number that changed little during the next biennium.[61] As in so many areas of republican policy, the threat of change was much greater than the reality and served primarily to heighten animosity. Because the center-right government refused to enforce the implementing legislation, only the Jesuit colegios actually

[58] An O of 20 April 1934 prohibited the use, on scholarly grounds, of *Historia universal* by Juan Fernández Amador de los Ríos, and *Geografía e historia* by Marcos Martín de la Calle. Amador de los Ríos was catedrático in Zaragoza. Martín de la Calle, the catedrático at the Liceo Balmés in Barcelona who had attracted the particular scorn of Américo Castro, issued a bizarre public retort to the government. *Minerva* 8, no. 198 (12 September 1933): 3.

[59] D of 26 July, 29 August, and 12 October 1934. The review committees were appointed in O of 10 January and 13 February 1936. See *Minerva* 11, nos. 309–16 (11 January–25 February 1936): 1.

[60] D of 29 August 1934. Villalobos was a member of the Liberal Democratic party, headed by Melquíades Álvarez, who, like the Radical Republicans, had always defended state educational prerogatives against the church. See the educational programs issued by the party in *BILE* 52, no. 705 (31 December 1918): 363–64, and 45, no. 737 (31 August 1921): 247–49. Villalobos resigned on 29 December 1934. His successors in the ministry, Joaquín Dualde Gómez and Ramón Prieto Bancés, were also *melquiadistas*.

[61] Pérez Galán, *Enseñanza*, 172–75.

closed their doors; the remaining schools of the religious orders continued to operate, technically administered after 1934 by the Sociedad
Anónima de Enseñanza Libre (SADEL), a front organization of the
Catholic Confederation of Fathers of Families. Meanwhile, the Jesuits
from the elite Colegio San José in Valladolid had moved their opera-
tions across the Portuguese border, where they paired intensive religious
practice with active educational methods and sports to train a self-disci-
plined and motivated elite for battle against the Republic. In the process, "the Colegio went from being a factory of more or less Christian
bachilleres to being a novitiate of apostles." The students, all Spaniards,
were examined annually at the Instituto in Zamora until 1937, when
they returned to Valladolid.[62]

The Catholic strategy during the Republic was thus not merely defensive; it continued the offensive against state education that had originated in the Restoration and had finally begun to bear fruit during the
dictatorship. Although the Catholic right was increasingly divided between the "possibilist" CEDA and an intransigent right that included
the new National Catholic organization Acción Española, all agreed
on the need for constitutional revision to restore traditional Catholic
prerogatives over education. Insofar as the constitution was held to be
synonymous with the Republic, this amounted to a proclamation of
Catholic incompatibility with the basic principles of the regime. In the
campaign to mobilize Catholic opinion against the Republic, political
and intellectual leaders from the CEDA and Acción Española were
joined by the church hierarchy and such components of Acción Católica
as the ACN de P, the Fathers of Families, and the FAE, which rallied to
"reconquer the school for God" at numerous conferences, assemblies,
meetings, and "pedagogic weeks."[63] As Ángel Ayala, the founder of the
ACN de P, argued in a book written for Catholic youth, the advent of a
society of masses forced the church to embrace modern methods of organization, mass communications, and popular participation.[64]

In seeking to overturn republican educational legislation, the Catholic
right had at its disposal a wide variety of organs of public opinion,
including the publishing houses of the ACN de P; *Atenas*, the pedagogical journal published by the FAE; the venerable *El Magisterio Español*,
independently published but conservative and Catholic; *La Enseñanza
Católica*, which had promoted Catholic interests since 1910; and *Avante*,
a social Catholic professional journal. Against a "failed, disastrous and

[62] Luis Fernández Martín, S.J., *Historia del Colegio San José de Valladolid, 1881–1981*
(Valladolid: Colegio San José, 1981), 218–31, 202.

[63] Pérez Galán, *Enseñanza*, 283–304.

[64] Ángel Ayala Alarcó, S.J., *Formación de selectos*, vol. 2 of *Obras completas* (Madrid:
Atenas, 1940), was written during the Republic.

demoralizing laicism," they defended the "religious confessionality of education . . . and the school as a prolongation of the home."[65] The laic schools, in their view, were the product of an outmoded Jacobinism that was both immoral and incompatible with Spanish cultural traditions. Such schools were not, as they claimed, "neutral," but rather a platform for "socialist" maestros throughout Spain.[66]

The preferred target of Catholic vituperation was the Institución Libre de Enseñanza, a convenient and not inappropriate symbol of republican educational policy. On the one hand, the right accused the institucionistas of exploiting the educational budget for personal gain—an unfair accusation that deliberately ignored the ideological and professional reasons why republican governments favored progressive educators in official posts. On the other hand, they convicted the ILE of promoting educational theories incompatible with the Spanish national character.[67] As an alternative, Catholic educators defended "Spanish" pedagogy, whose tenets were allegedly adapted to the special "racial psychology" and national identity of Spaniards. "Spanish schools" were in philosophy and practice the antithesis of the Institución Libre de Enseñanza. In contrast to the "naturalism," "rationalism," and "materialism" of progressive pedagogy, the Catholic right proposed "Christian spirituality," spontaneity, and intuition; in opposition to its "judeo-masonic" internationalism and pacifism, they offered ardent patriotism and the "social peace" of the Gospel.[68] Catholic educators decried the ministry's abolition of textbooks, because it had encouraged "indifference or dislike of work, ignorance, indiscipline"—dangers particularly threatening in a race inherently individualistic and insubordinate.[69] Respect for textbooks in the "Spanish school" was a corollary of the Spanish respect for "ideas," just as the "thing-oriented" methodology of the New School was the product of the materialistic cultures of northern Europe and America.

Alongside these defenders of a "traditionally Spanish" pedagogy, another, smaller group of Catholic educators recognized the advantages to be gained from fusing the principles of active education and Catholicism. Going beyond the memory-based rhyming games and dramatic

[65] Romualdo de Toledo, in *DSC*, no. 106 (26 June 1934): 4025.

[66] Pedro Sainz Rodríguez, in *DSC*, no. 106 (26 June 1934):4036–39.

[67] See, for example, FAE, *Anuario de la educación católica. Curso 1934–1935* (Madrid: 1934), 12.

[68] Ibid., 12–13; Teodoro Rodríguez, *Infiltraciones judío-masónicas en la educación católica* (El Escorial: Imprenta del Monasterio, 1934); Agustín Serrano de Haro, "La enseñanza de la historia," *Avante* 7, nos. 70, 72, and 73 (April–August 1934): 50–51, 82–83, 100–101.

[69] Jaime Calzada, "Los libros en la escuela," *Atenas* 5, no. 38 (March 1934): 214–15.

dialogues popularized by Manjón and Siurot, they expressed real sympathy for the philosophical premises of the new pedagogy, rejecting only its secular worldview. In contrast to the traditionalists, whose view of human nature was essentially pessimistic, they conceded greater autonomy to the child in his quest for spiritual development. In the journal *Avante* they found a receptive outlet for their ideas, especially after 1932, when the editorial offices moved to Madrid from Barcelona. The editorial board of *Avante* included conservative and social Catholics, as well as a few progressives like Félix Martí Alpera, and accepted articles from a diverse group of contributors.[70] The prevailing tone was modestly democratic and assertively, but not aggressively, Catholic; collaborators conceptualized teaching in terms of patriotism and spiritual renovation and avoided the overt antirepublicanism of the traditionalists. By recognizing the legitimate goals of child-centered pedagogy and educational democracy, they hoped to win the competition for the hearts and minds of the majority of maestros in the public schools, whose professional awareness and political allegiance were still embryonic.

Although the republicans liked to claim that their victory represented a revolutionary break with the past, they were no less inclined to justify their regime in terms of Spanish history than were their interlocutors on the right. The invocation of historical precedent was an established convention of Spanish political discourse; to turn one's back on history was to concede to one's adversaries a potent instrument of argumentation that allowed appropriation of the past for partisan ends. It is not surprising, then, that a master of political dialectic like Manuel Azaña frequently resorted to history to justify the Republic and the new path upon which the nation was embarked.

Azaña's line of historical argumentation rested on the premise that the "quality of being Spanish and Spanish nationality do not depend on the political regime, nor on the structure of the state"—that is, the conventions of conservative discourse notwithstanding, Spanish nationality was not consubstantial with the "monarchical principle."[71] A single definition of "*lo español*" was impossible; to attempt one was to abandon history for metaphysics. History revealed the vast range of Spanish experience in the past and thus legitimated a variety of paths toward the future. But even without historical precedents, any opinion or any political regime capable of being imagined by Spaniards was no less "Span-

---

[70] *Avante* 5, no. 46 (January 1932) announced the beginning of a new stage in its history. The director of the journal was Anicet Villar; the editor, Federico Torres. A list of the board of editors was also included.

[71] Speech in the Cortes, 2 June 1932, in OC 2:289.

ish" than opinions or regimes already shared or experienced historically. History otherwise became a prison, a barrier to forward movement, whereas intelligent politics was necessarily based on a fusion of past practice and new ideas—"tradition corrected by reason."[72]

Somewhat in contradiction to this case for an infinity of possible "Spains," Azaña also invoked a "true" Spanish tradition of regional decentralization and urban democracy that had been derailed by the "caesarism" of the Habsburgs. The Republic was thus a "rectification" of Spanish history, a recovery of the popular pluralism of the Renaissance, as well as the only form of government fully consonant with that national tradition in its present stage of development. Azaña proclaimed himself to be "the most traditionalist Spaniard that there is in the Peninsula."[73] The task of the Republic was to teach Spaniards the truth that had "maliciously" been denied them as children: that "Spain has not always been an inquisitorial nation, nor an intolerant nation, nor a fanaticized nation, nor a nation in pursuit of a madness." The Republic was a "revenge against our own history," the restoration of "Spanish history to its true self."[74]

Above all, Azaña did not want history to be a source either of self-satisfaction or of anguish. Both the triumphalism of the right and the pessimism of the left had immobilized Spaniards by seeming to absolve them of personal responsibility for the future. The same theme had been struck by the literary historian Américo Castro a few years earlier, when he recalled his childhood education: "Our vision of history thus oscillated between a feeling of pride before the greatness of the sixteenth and seventeenth centuries and a limitless sadness before the disaster that followed. . . . From this careless education . . . are born the two attitudes that the Iberian citizen generally adopts: one of unlimited confidence in his country, together with the conviction that outside of ourselves there is nothing of excessive value; or one of bitter pessimism, disconsolate and infertile."[75] The goal of republican educational policy was to transform historical study into a positive inspiration for civic responsibility and republican virtue; by discovering a past that could be shared by all Spaniards, republicans hoped to lay the foundation for a collective national project oriented toward the future.

Rafael Altamira's dual program of historiographical and pedagogical reform provided the inspiration for republican policy makers. On the one hand, they expanded state financial support for historical research,

---

[72] Speech in the Cortes, 27 May 1932, OC 2:259.
[73] Speech to Acción Repúblicana, 28 March 1932, in OC 2:227.
[74] Speech at "El Sitio" in Bilbao, 9 April 1933, OC 2:693, 695.
[75] Américo Castro, "Las polémicas acerca de España," quoted in Pedro Sainz Rodríguez, *Testimonios y recuerdos* (Barcelona: Editorial Planeta, 1978), 354–55.

in the belief that entrenched political values were best combated by recovery of neglected dimensions of the Spanish past; for example, the pathbreaking work on the *mozárabes* of Toledo, published in 1926 by the Arabist Ángel González Palencia, suggested a culturally diverse, tolerant alternative to the traditionalist interpretation of national identity.[76] Accordingly, they created new research centers for Arabic and American historical studies at the universities in Seville, Madrid, and Granada and allocated additional resources to the Center for Historical Studies. To give students better grounding in both national and world history before launching them into a teaching career at the institutos, they extended the university degree in history by an additional year.

On the other hand, republican educators agreed with Altamira that the dissemination of historical knowledge was politically more significant than historical research. Symbolic of their commitment to historical pedagogy was the appointment of a Spanish national commission under the auspices of the International Conference on the Teaching of History, which celebrated its first assembly in Geneva in February 1932. With Altamira as president, the Commission made plans to hold the next international congress in Spain. (With the victory of the right in 1933, the invitation was retracted.)[77]

For the institucionistas in the ministry, the course seemed clear. The first step was to weed out the pernicious methods and textbooks that encouraged passivity and conservatism, character traits they deemed incompatible with democratic civic culture. The second was to create republican alternatives to entrenched habits and to disseminate them to teachers through continuing education programs, the progressive press, and the normal schools. As always, it was easier to identify the problem than to remedy it. A new syllabus provisionally developed for the normal school course on historical pedagogy was more certain of what to condemn—"verbalism," "external history," and textbooks—than of what to prescribe.[78] The authors of the syllabus—normal school professors and representatives from the Junta and the Museo Pedagógico—

---

[76] Ángel González Palencia, *Los mozárabes de Toledo en los siglos XII y XIII*, 4 vols. (Madrid: Instituto de Valencia de Don Juan, 1926).

[77] *El Ideal del Magisterio*, 16 January 1933, 3, lists the members of the Spanish national commission, most of whom were closely identified with Altamira and/or the ILE: Ángel Llorca (director of the Grupo Escolar Cervantes and in representation of the Junta's Residencia de Estudiantes); Francisco Barnés; José Giner Pantoja (ILE); Eladio García (Asociación Nacional de Inspectores de Primera Enseñanza); José de Deleito; Alfredo Jara (a normal school professor from Albacete): Carmelo Viñas Mey (a social Catholic catedrático of medieval history at the University of Madrid); Cayetano Alcázar; and Pedro Aguado Bleye.

[78] C of 5 October 1932, signed by Llopis. The cuestionarios were produced during a Short Course of Methodological Information held in the ministry in June 1932.

spoke assuredly of the value of history as a mental and "normative" discipline that exercised the memory, imagination, and comparative sense, while nurturing altruism, pacifism, internationalism, "true" patriotism, moral and civic virtue, social discipline, and a belief in progress. The "dominant idea" in history education, they asserted, should be "universal peace." But they offered little practical guidance on how to structure history teaching to achieve this outcome. Apart from the teachers' manuals published by the *Revista de Pedagogía* during the previous decade, like those by Sanjuán and Martí Alpera,[79] there were few resources to aid struggling teachers accustomed to relying on textbooks and rote learning. Pedagogical journals often published queries from maestros about acceptable textbooks and reference works. To aid them in lesson planning, the state inspectorate organized lending libraries that included recommended manuals as well as collections of legends, romances, and other popular literary sources.[80]

Gradually, help arrived, in the form of new teachers' guides and articles in progressive pedagogical journals.[81] Republican educators explained that history should focus on the pueblo and its progressive mastery of the physical and social environment. To make abstract ideas concrete, teachers should organize field trips, hands-on activities like autobiography or genealogy, and storytelling, thereby enlisting the familiar world of the child in the process of learning about the unfamiliar, distant world of the past. Likewise, older children should relate what they already knew to what they wanted to learn; composition and note taking should replace reading, a passive activity. Active methods like these were the primary school equivalents of Altamira's critical scholarship; the process of historical inquiry would nurture socially and politically constructive habits of engagement, cooperation, and objectivity.

The benefits of active methods seemed obvious, even if difficult to implement; the content of primary school history was more problematic. The dilemma was not only what to teach, but more subtly, how to reconcile a disinterested pursuit of knowledge about the past with its instrumentalization in the consolidation of the republican polity. As we have seen, Altamira's allegiance to positivism had restrained the inter-

---

[79] See chap. 5.

[80] Castellón, Inspección de Primera Enseñanza, *Boletín de Educación* 1 (December 1934–January 1935).

[81] See, in addition to Martí Alpera and Sanjuán, Ángel Llorca y García, *Libros de orientación escolar: Cien lecciones prácticas de todas las materias y para niños de todos los grados de la escuela primaria,* 3d ed. (Madrid: Caro Raggio, 1933); and Julio Fuster García, *Didáctica de la historia desarrollada en lecciones* (Madrid: Publicaciones de la Revista de Pedagogía, 1936). Among the new journals were *Escuelas de España* and the publications of the anarchosyndicalist and Socialist teachers' unions.

pretative and thus—in the eyes of some republicans—the "formative" value of his textbooks. Eager to remedy this defect, republicans failed to recognize its roots in the contradictory aims of his project. Instead, they chose to ignore historical complexity and ambiguity in the interest of a morally and politically coherent approach to the past.

What republicans wanted children to learn from history was diametrically opposed to what the Catholic right wanted them to learn. Whereas integrists emphasized providentialism, Spanish "difference," and filiopiety, republicans accentuated human agency, the brotherhood of peoples, and nationhood as a collective projection toward the future. Republican educators endorsed the resolutions condemning nationalistic textbooks that had been adopted at the postwar international congresses attended by Altamira.[82] "To establish geographical barriers by means of history when the majestic dirigible can cross them by air is madness. To pretend to be the conquerors of peoples and races because our dislocated and fraudulent history taught us so is utopian."[83] Children should learn that "all peoples are links in a endless chain,"[84] united by their similarities rather than separated by their differences. Socialists added to these pacifist sentiments their faith in the mission of the international proletariat. Accordingly, most republican teachers' guides stressed the history of European civilization, whose theme was the progressive conquest of the material, social, and spiritual obstacles to human solidarity.

National history, on the other hand, posed major problems for the republican left, partly because the heterogeneity of the republican coalition made unanimity of purpose difficult. For doctrinaire Socialists, national history was a "bourgeois" invention that intentionally obfuscated the historical reality of class conflict. The bourgeois left, however, was unwilling to dispense with national history altogether. National history, with its focus on public life, was a natural vehicle for giving citizens a sense of belonging to an ongoing, juridically and territorially defined community for whose well-being all were accountable. Properly structured, national history could lend solidity and veracity to abstract principles of civic and social responsibility.[85]

[82] In addition to the sources cited in chap. 5, nn. 121–27, see M. P. Capra, "La enseñanza de la historia en las escuelas primarias," *BILE* 56, no. 866 (30 June 1932):161–67; no. 867 (31 July 1982): 193–97; and no. 872 (31 December 1932): 361–64. Also League of Nations, International Institute of Intellectual Cooperation, *School Textbook Revision and International Understanding*, 2d ed., rev. (Paris: author, 1933).

[83] Fuster, *Didáctica*, 105.

[84] Andrés Ovejero, *El evangelio de la república: La constitución de la segunda república española comentada para niños*, in *Historia de la educación en España* 4:337. See also *RP* 14, no. 158 (February 1935): 80; and no. 166 (October 1935): 487–88.

[85] See the remarks of the institucionista Manuel García Morente at the Catalan summer school of 1932, quoted in Monés, *Pensament escolar*, 325.

The problem facing republicans was how to establish collective responsibility for a political community from whom most Spaniards had until only recently been consciously excluded. Taken as a whole, Spanish history offered little in support of republican political values. The centuries of greatest national glory were associated with empire, absolutism, warfare, and religious intransigence; modern history offered a dubious ancestry of civil war, caciquismo, imperial loss, and social conflict. Sympathy for American republicanism made it difficult to share the right's enthusiasm for Spain's colonial past, just as identification with the French Republic discouraged excessive celebration of the War of Independence. At the same time, the internationalism and pacifism of both republicans and Socialists ruled out establishing a national identity based on difference or military rivalry.

An alternative to interpreting national history as an epic struggle against external enemies was to internalize "the other," structuring the past as a domestic struggle between the forces of progress and those of tyranny. The Republic could thus be depicted as the triumphant embodiment of a popular national identity that had been denied expression by the absolutism and fanaticism of earlier regimes. The institucionista Ángel Llorca, the director of a laboratory school in Madrid, suggested starting with republican principles and working backward through time in order to contrast and distance the democratic present from the corrupt institutions and values of the past.[86] The problem with this approach was that it cut young Spaniards off from their own history and implicitly challenged the assumption that knowledge of national history and identity was essential to the growth of healthy patriotism. How could youth feel part of an ongoing community if the historical record of that community was so deplorable? The only reasonable solution to this dilemma appeared to be the one championed by Altamira: to situate Spanish history within a broader context of human progress and to demonstrate that the present was the outcome of past collective achievement.

The ideals set out in teachers' guides and professional journals were hard to realize, as the Council of National Culture discovered when it began approving history books for use in the public schools. The first list of authorized books published in May 1934 was brief; the second, issued in February 1936, was a bit longer, not only because new books had been written, but because the Council applied more "benevolent" criteria in order to reach the specified minimum of 12 books per sub-

---

[86] Llorca, *Libros de orientación*. Llorca, a member of the Socialist FETE, had studied with Cossío at the Museo Pedagógico and with Giner and Ortega at the Escuela de Estudios Superiores del Magisterio. He had been director of the Grupo Escolar Cervantes, a project of the Patronato Escolar of Madrid, since 1920.

ject. Approved history books fell into three categories: (1) collections of primary and secondary sources, (2) collections of historical readings written expressly for children, and (3) biographies. (In a separate category was the popular edition of the *Episodios Nacionales*, by Pérez Galdós.)

Although institucionistas praised the virtues of a direct encounter with primary documents, the most widely admired collection of sources, edited by Gloria Giner de los Ríos, exemplified the difficulties with the genre: the vocabulary, style, and subject matter of older sources were too difficult or too abstract for most elementary students to apprehend. Despite these drawbacks, the collection was approved as a classroom reference work in 1936, along with the award-winning, but equally sophisticated, collection of national epic poems paraphrased by Ángel Cruz Rueda.[87] More appealing to teachers and students were collections of historical readings, whose style and vocabulary could be calibrated to suit the intended audience and which permitted a selective approach to the past. The few ideologically and pedagogically acceptable historical readers then in print, however, were hybrids that were not so much collections of stories as episodic narratives strung together with transitional passages to provide a sense of historical continuity.[88]

One new reader that won immediate approval was *Mi primer libro de historia*, by Daniel González Linacero, a Socialist history professor at the Palencia normal school. Adapted to the "cyclical" method, this was the first in a series of three graded readers, each of which covered the entire history of human civilization in a few pages. The first grade text, written for children eight to ten years old, boasted large type, a rudimentary vocabulary, simple line drawings, and an intimate tone that addressed children directly in the familiar *tú*. In the second grade reader, for children ten to twelve years old, the vocabulary expanded along with the length of the text and the level of sophistication, but the structure was the same.[89] Beginning with the family and expanding outward to the human family and its social organization, the author adhered closely to Cousinet's prescriptions for "lessons of things" (plate 4). The implicit thesis was that human conquest of the physical environment had created the material conditions for the progressive evolution of reli-

---

[87] Gloria Giner de los Ríos, *Cien lecturas históricas* (Madrid: Espasa-Calpe, 1935); Ángel Cruz Rueda, *Las gestas heroicas castellanas contadas a los niños* (Madrid: Biblioteca Nueva, 1931).

[88] Gerardo Rodríguez García, *Historia de España en lecturas para los niños* (Madrid: Sucs. de Hernando, 1915); Alberto Llano, *Historia universal en lecturas amenas*, 4 vols. (Barcelona: Editores Seix y Barral, 1926).

[89] Daniel González Linacero, *Mi primer libro de historia*, 2d ed. (Palencia: Imp. de "El Diario Palentino," 1935); and *Mi segundo libro de historia* (Palencia: Artes Gráficas Afrodisio Aguado, 1934).

— 16 —

— 17 —

II

Queriendo los hombres vivir, no donde la Naturaleza les brindaba casa, sino donde a ellos les convenía, empezaron a construir con troncos y ramas de árboles,

Aldea de chozas

chozas y cabañas a su gusto, formando pueblecitos.

Cuando lasfieras abundaban muchopor aquellos alrededores, el miedo noles dejaría vivir tranquilos, ¿y sabéis lo que se les ocurrió?. Pues hicieron las cabañas en medio de lagunas, apoyadas en fuertes estacas para que no se hundieran, y así, rodeadosde agua, se encontraron bien seguras sus casas y sus familias.

Un palafito

III

Palacio asirio

Han pasado muchos cientos de años. Los hombres ya no viven en cavernas, ni en chozas. Han aprendido muchas cosas y entre ellas, a construir casas de piedra y de ladrillo; unas grandes, lujosas; otras pequeñas, humildes. Desde hace muchísimos años los ricos han tenido moradas suntuosas y los trabajadores, habitaciones reducidas y pobres. Mirad en los dibujos dos palacios. Allí vivía el señor con su familia, 'sus servidores y sus esclavos. Todo el pueblo le pagaba grandes contribuciones y le temían y adoraban como si fuera un dios...

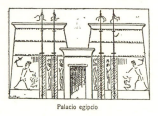

Palacio egipcio

Plate 4. "Lessons of things"—in this case, the history of human shelter—from Daniel González Linacero, *Mi segundo libro de historia*, 2d ed. (Palencia: Artes Gráficas Afrodisio Aguado, 1934). The text and illustrations in this chapter trace human housing from the caves of Antequera to the skyscrapers of New York. The themes of this reader are, on the one hand, the march of human progress and, on the other, the persistence of social and economic inequalities.

gious, political, and social ideas. While a clear sense of progress dominated each of the chapters (devoted to shelter, clothing, games, work, cooperation, etc.), González Linacero provided no sense of a concrete human community in a particular space, no connection between the separate categories of human activity, minimal coverage of public life, and no drama or personalities. Only occasionally in the second grade reader did children encounter historically situated, popular heroes of "universal" significance, like Gutenberg, Jacquard, Edison, and Pablo Iglesias. But if the sense of national values and purpose was weak, social values permeated the text. González Linacero censured the "ambition" that led men to war, the idleness and frivolity of "the rich," and the backwardness of peoples overly wedded to tradition, like the Arabs. And he pointed out the vast superiority of the present over the past, as a consequence of humanity's acquisition of the values of tolerance, cooperation, and productive labor.

The weakness of a reader like González Linacero's was its neglect of specifically Spanish themes, a deficiency republican educators sought to remedy by sponsoring competitions to encourage aspiring authors. The National Literature Prize of 1932 was awarded by the ministry to *Estampas de España*, a book of patriotic historical readings for older children by Fernando José de Larra, a descendent of the nineteenth-century liberal journalist. Larra's brilliant sketches, full of life despite their didactic purpose, focused on Spanish heroes selected to exemplify both a specific politico-cultural context and an enduring civic virtue. Although some of these heroes also figured in the Catholic pantheon, Larra assigned them very different historical and civic valences: the Numantian Retógenes represented not independence, but sacrifice; the Cid, not martial valor, but honor; the *comuneros*, not xenophobia, but liberty. Other sketches resurrected neglected historical figures to illustrate republican values: the caliph Abd-el-Rahman III symbolized *convivencia* and "good taste"; James the Conqueror, of Aragon, disinterest; and the social critic Larra, patriotism. The inclusion of two women—Isabel I and Agustina of Aragon, the heroine of the siege of Zaragoza—was a gesture in the direction of sexual equality. Larra was not reticent about drawing conclusions from his material; the values of freedom, justice, socialism, and the "holy spirit of rebellion" were insistently pressed on his young readers, as were the importance of decentralization, orderly administration, and civic duty. Where historical accuracy and political utility failed to coincide, he unhesitatingly chose the latter. Belief was more important than "cold foreign research" when vital national myths were at stake, he insisted: all peoples believe in their myths "if they desire to be something in the world, because they are beautiful, because they have the grandeur and the necessary fantasy to become the epic of the race, the *geste* of its immortality."[90] Ultimately, Larra's message was one of individual responsibility and freedom to "choose for yourself the truth you wish to choose": "It is necessary to know everything . . . but it is not necessary to believe everything and limit yourself to repeating what others have created. It is necessary oftentimes to deny, other times to affirm, and always to investigate, with your sights set on the desire to create a new science, a new art, a new politics, and new law; a better world."[91]

Faced with a shortage of suitable Spanish history readers, republicans looked abroad. In 1934 the Council approved *Historia anecdótica del trabajo*, by the French Socialist and League of Nations functionary Albert Thomas, which had been translated and adapted for a Spanish audience by Rodolfo Llopis in 1930.[92] Through a series of vignettes and thumbnail biographies, Thomas depicted the changing conditions of labor and the progressive growth of human liberty. Historical material in the sketches was based on documentary sources (like the *Odyssey*, Plutarch's *Lives*, medieval guild charters, and contemporary strike manifestos), which Thomas dramatized and converted into dialogue without violating the spirit of the originals. The rather wooden anecdotes written for the Spanish edition by Llopis—on the condition of shoemakers in medieval Burgos, the "tyrannicide" of Fuenteovejuna, and the life of Pablo Iglesias—lacked Thomas's verve, but they were apt and faithful reflections of the documentary sources on which they were based.

Despite its socialist themes and purpose, the reader was generally nonconfrontational in tone. Although Thomas and Llopis included violent episodes like the French subsistence riots of 1792 and the Spanish general strike of 1917, the brief interpretative remarks that concluded each reading spoke serenely to issues of equity and justice rather than to resentment and class conflict. To a remarkable degree, Thomas's book fulfilled the pedagogic and ideological requirements of the Socialists in the ministry—it was a social history with a social democratic message and a solid historical base. It proved to be popular with many maestros, as well.

Another translation approved by the Council was *Una historia del mundo para los niños*, by the American educator V. M. Hillyer.[93] More encyclopedic in coverage than Thomas's book, it was perhaps less well adapted to the Spanish milieu, for it was saturated with specifically North American political and cultural values. Nevertheless, its underlying purpose—to give young children a rudimentary sense of historical duration, process, and chronology, as well as of material and moral progress—endeared it to the republicans.

Nearly 60 percent of Hillyer's text was allocated to the prehistoric and ancient worlds. Old Testament Bible stories and admiring descriptions of Greek law and culture occupied a prominent place in this section. While his main emphasis was on daily life and technological advance, Hillyer remarked on the rise and fall of civilizations (which he referred to as successive "championships" of the world) and promoted moral values through well-worn anecdotes about George Washington

[92] Albert Thomas, *Lecturas históricas: Historia anecdótica del trabajo*, trans. and adapted by Rodolfo Llopis (Madrid: Juan Ortiz, 1930). Original title: *Histoire anecdotique du travail: Lectures historiques* (Paris: Bibliothèque d'éducation, 1900; 2d ed. 1925).

[93] V[irgil] M[ores] Hillyer, *Una historia del mundo para los niños*, trans. and adapted by Fernando Sáinz (Madrid: Juan Ortiz, n.d.). Original title: *A Child's History of the World* (1915). New editions were published well into the 1950s.

and the cherry tree and Columbus and the egg. His familiar tone and homely comparisons between current and past events suggested the continuity of human nature beneath the appearance of historical change.

Hillyer's liberal democratic, pacifist, and pluralistic religious values permeated the text, which presented the American Revolution and industrial progress as the culminating achievements of human civilization. In this schema, of course, there was little room for Spain. To compensate, the Spanish translator added brief sections on major episodes and figures in the Spanish past, like the Inquisition and Philip II. Although they provided an opportunity to denounce the evils of religious intolerance and bad government, these additions tended to discredit the Spanish past rather than to celebrate it. Unfortunately, Spain's role in histories that celebrated freedom of belief, material prosperity, and democratic government was necessarily marginal. Either Spain must be consigned to the periphery of human civilization or she must serve as a counterexample of the benighted, impoverished past that human progress had left behind.

For this reason, civics readers that combined ethical and political training with selected historical anecdotes were in some ways more attractive to liberal republicans than were narrative histories.[94] Civics readers were something of a novelty in Spain. Under the parliamentary monarchy the political oligarchy had displayed little enthusiasm for teaching children about their political rights and responsibilities; during the dictatorship, patriotic exhortation substituted for civics training. For republicans, however, civics education was an article of faith, the foundation of their conception of the nation as a juridically defined community of citizens enjoying equality before the law. Whereas civics readers had appeared only occasionally earlier in the century, after 1931 their numbers increased dramatically.

Civics readers usually presented the Republic as timeless, rather than historically conditioned, and they were by definition normative. Moreover, they permitted authors to focus on positive symbols of national identity, without having to cope with those parts of the national past incompatible with republican values. History thus became a cupboard to ransack freely in search of appropriate myths and exemplars to sup-

[94] The three civics readers approved by the Council in 1934 were Gervasio Manríquez, *Educación moral y cívica: (Libro de lectura)* (Barcelona: Editorial Ruiz Romero, 1933); Gerardo Rodríguez García, *Lecturas escolares de sociología* (Madrid: Lib. Sucs. de Hernando, 1923); and Victoriano Fernández Ascarza, *Lecturas ciudadanas: (Educación cívica)*, 2d ed. (Madrid: Editorial Magisterio Español, 1933). See also Joaquín Seró Sabaté, *El niño republicano: (Cuarto libro de lectura)*, 4th ed. (Barcelona: Salvador Santomá, 1933); and Alejandro Manzanares, *Ciudadanía: (Lecturas sobre el civismo)* (Gerona: Dalmáu Carles, Pla, 1935).

port a program of civic nationalism. Civics readers introduced a galaxy of new national symbols: the Cortes of Cádiz, the First Republic of 1873, the republican flag, the Himno de Riego, and the Constitution of 1931 itself, as well as a pantheon of national heroes. Special favorites were Mariana Pineda, Francisco Pi y Margall, Emilio Castelar, Joaquín Costa, Francisco Giner de los Ríos, Pablo Iglesias, and the martyred republican rebels Captains Galán and García Hernández—models chosen not for their representativeness as *Spaniards*, but as *republicans*. The fundamental moral and civic values they embodied were not peculiar to Spanish identity, but honored for their "universality." Spanish heroes and heroines who exemplified duty, conscience, justice, courage, dignity, moderation, and discipline not only legitimated the Republic's claim to membership in the community of civilized nations, but they were also worthy of a place in world history alongside other eminent republicans like Danton, Washington, and Bolívar. The resemblance to nineteenth-century Catholic representations of history as a moral guide was striking; only the cast of historical icons and the virtues they were said to represent had changed.

Republican efforts to transform the secondary school history curriculum, which De los Ríos labeled one of "the great pillars of a formative secondary education,"[95] ran up against the determined resistance of both the instituto catedráticos and the Catholic right. The De los Ríos reform proposal of 1932 required all students to study history and geography for five years, beginning in the first year of study. A Socialist with institucionista roots, De los Ríos once defined history as "a process of spiritual biology"; he envisioned history education as a cyclical, progressively more sophisticated exposure to historical processes that traced the gradual enlightenment of the Spanish spirit through time. The cuestionarios drafted by the Council of National Culture for the "transitional bachillerato" in late 1932 took a global approach to course content in the early grades: "a total vision of the Earth and of Humanity in the present moment and an idea of how men have lived through time." Since children began the bachillerato at age ten, the ministry also suggested using the same active methods that institucionistas prescribed for the primary school. Predictably, however, instituto catedráticos were not pleased to read that the task of the "enthusiastic maestro" (sic) was to make "the past come alive in the potent childish imagination."[96] While syllabi for the upper grades would presumably have been more sophisticated in approach, their preparation was curtailed by the electoral defeat of the republican coalition in 1933.

[95] *DSC*, no. 106 (26 June 1934): 4044.
[96] Report of 28 November 1932.

The Radicals and Liberal Democrats who occupied the ministry during the next biennium were more sensitive to the professional dignity of the catedráticos, as well as to the ideological objections of their Catholic coalition partners to the progressive thrust of the 1932 syllabi. An ad hoc committee of catedráticos was appointed to write new syllabi for the five-year history curriculum decreed by Villalobos in 1934. These cuestionarios omitted the active methods so repellent to the catedráticos and settled for lengthy lists of prescribed topics.[97] For the initial course, the committee mandated a survey of the traditional heroes and myths of the Spanish past, like Viriatus and Numancia, the Spanish Christian martyrs, Saint Isidore, Covadonga, the conquest of America, and the second of May. Each of the next four courses was dedicated to the four "ages" of Spanish history, broadly situated within European history. Although conventionally encyclopedic and superficially "factual," beneath the welter of reigns, wars, and conquests, the syllabi consecrated the national Catholic view of the Spanish past.

Catedráticos had no trouble adapting their old textbooks to the new structure of the bachillerato; in most cases, all that was necessary was to publish the chapters corresponding to the conventional periodization of Spanish history as separate volumes, one for each year of the syllabus. The net result was more books and higher prices; meanwhile, the content of the books did not substantially change since the center-right government did not at first require ministerial approval. Instituto textbooks thus continued to reflect the wide range of ideological commitments among the professoriate. Even though integrist Catholic opinion was well represented by such catedráticos as José Ibáñez Martín at the Instituto of San Isidro in Madrid, the Catholic right soon resumed its campaign against the textbooks written by progressive professors like Pedro Aguado Bleye, whose volumes allegedly provoked "nervous exhaustion" in the nation's youth. The right made plans to authorize only a limited number of texts, but this project was scrapped when the republicans returned to office in February 1936.[98]

The attempt to create a new "republican" culture through the schools had limited impact because significant segments of the educational system remained outside the reach of the state. In a society where consensus in civil society was lacking and state power limited, the schools were not uncontested agents of cultural hegemony, but rather sites from which to challenge the legitimacy of the state. The inability of the re-

[97] See *Cuestionarios para los estudios del bachillerato (Plan de 1934). Primero, segundo y tercer cursos* (Barcelona: Bosch, 1934).

[98] A series of articles highly critical of the textbooks by Gonzalo R. Lafora, "El desorden en la instrucción pública," appeared in *ES* on 17 and 26 January and 7 February 1936.

publicans to retain political control in a conflicted democratic polity and thus to direct state power against the enemies of the Republic or the unitary state, not only condemned their project to failure, but also confirmed the right's conviction that democracy and freedom of speech were incompatible with national unity.

A major source of fragmentation was Catalonia, where regional and municipal authorities subsidized schools whose aim was to create a Catalan, rather than a Spanish, civic culture. In the absence of new national curricular directives for the primary grades, Catalans were able to substitute the study of Catalan history for Spanish history in the primary schools governed by the Generalitat. By 1933 Catalan educators were beginning to produce Catalan-language textbooks, encyclopedias, and readers that dealt exclusively with Catalan history and culture. Since Catalanist schools had embraced progressive pedagogy early in the century, these books contained copious illustrations, simplified language and content, and suggestions for classroom activities.

History textbooks reflected the ideological divisions within the Catalanist movement.[99] The majority professed the federal republican values of the dominant party in the region, values basically compatible with those of the national republican parties and, more precariously, of the Socialists. But the outline of the Catalan past they presented was a mirror reflection of national history as it was generally structured by Spanish historians, whether on the left or the right. To begin with, Catalan authors scarcely made reference to "Spain" at all; insofar as it was necessary to refer to the rest of the peninsula, they spoke of "other Iberian lands," "Hispanic peoples," or "Hispania." The "natural" historical unit with which they were concerned was of course Catalonia, whose ethnic and territorial distinctiveness was, according to the eminent Catalan archaeologist Pere Bosch Gimpera, identifiable from prehistoric times.[100] Viewed from the Catalan perspective, familiar historical milestones in the national past took on a different coloration. The unification of the Visigothic kingdom was not a major step toward national unity, but merely one of many infringements of the autonomy and identity of Catalonia. The Reconquest was not a religious crusade, nor a

---

[99] The following discussion is based on Joaquím Pla Cargol, *La terra catalana: Libre quart*, 6th ed. (Gerona: Dalmáu Carles, Pla, 1932); and Raimon Torroja i Valls, *Història de Catalunya per a nois e noies* (Barcelona: Imprenta Elzeviriana, 1933); *Iniciació a l'estudi de la geografia i de la història de Catalunya* and *La nostra terra i la nostra història* (Barcelona: Imprenta Elzeviriana, 1933). For a full list of Catalanist textbooks published during the 1930s see Rosa Mut i Carbasa and Teresa Martí i Armengol, *La resistencia escolar catalana en llibres (1716–1939): Bibliografía* (Barcelona: Ediciones 62, 1981).

[100] See Pere Bosch-Gimpera, *La España de todos* (Madrid: Seminarios y Ediciones, 1976).

project for national unification, but a territorial conflict among competing sovereignties. Catalan nationality had reached its apogee in the thirteenth century under the leadership of a native dynasty that had extended Catalan hegemony through a successful program of peninsular and overseas expansion and had begun its decline with the advent of the Castilian Trastámara dynasty. Instead of viewing the union of Isabel and Ferdinand as the culmination of national history, Catalans saw it as a prelude to four centuries of absolutist assaults on Catalan liberties; the discovery of America was dismissed with the observation that it had damaged Catalan prosperity by shifting the focus of trade to the Atlantic. The textbooks passed quickly over the Habsburg and Bourbon eras, pausing only to recount the glorious defense of Catalan traditions in 1640 and 1714. But a new era of national recovery began with the reemergence of the Catalan national spirit in the nineteenth century, the movement for political autonomy in the early twentieth, and the full restoration of Catalan national identity under the democratic Republic. Punctuating these narratives were the Romantic poems and illustrations commemorating the Catalan Middle Ages that had been produced during the Catalan "Renaixença," along with biographies eulogizing republican heroes like Francisco Pi y Margall and Francesc Macià.

If the history textbooks written by the Catalan left emphasized the vicissitudes of Catalan political sovereignty, those written by the Catalan right focused on Catalan culture. Although the conservative Lliga Regionalista had ceded its hegemony in the region, there was still a substantial bourgeois audience for the conservative Catholic version of Catalanism that had dominated the origins of the movement.[101] That nationalism was primarily linguistic and cultural, rather than political. *Terra i ánima*, a reader published in 1934 by Anicet Villar, the editor of the Catholic pedagogical journal *Avante*, adopted the popular travelogue format to introduce children to the geography, history, and culture of the four Catalan provinces.[102] Readings highlighted artistic monuments like churches and castles, economic activities like viticulture, textiles, and shipping, traditional cultural products like folklore and pious legends, and the Romantic poetry of the Renaixença. Biographies commemorated Catalan artists, musicians, and scholars, conservative politicians like Prat de la Riba, and industrial giants like Güell. In this version, Catalanism was largely dissociated from its contemporary political

---

[101] See Josep M. Fradera, *Cultura nacional en una societat dividida: Patriotisme i cultura a Catalunya (1838–1868)* (Barcelona: Editorial Curial, 1992).

[102] Anicet Villar de Serchs, *Terra i ánima. Lectures sobre coses de Catalunya*, 2d ed. (Barcelona: Miquel A. Salvatella, 1935).

configuration and implicitly rendered more compatible with conservative and clerical alternatives to the regime in power.

Also beyond the reach of the state were the religious colegios, saved from closure by the accession of the right to power in 1933. Catholic educators used their freedom to subvert the Republic, making Azaña's observation that closing the schools of the orders was a "question of public health" less extravagant than it sounded. To set against the dominant figure of Altamira in the teaching of history, they canonized Menéndez y Pelayo (the "Fichte of Spain," according to Pedro Sainz Rodríguez, one of the founders of Acción Española). In 1934, Acción Española published a history of Spain composed entirely of excerpts from Menéndez y Pelayo's historical writings, in order to give the public "an idea of what a Spanish *History of Spain* ought to be, a thing radically different from the progressive interpretations with which the pedantry, when not the bad faith, of the majority of our historians has been poisoning us."[103] At the same time, Catholic educational journals, which regularly reviewed new schoolbooks, were quick to alert maestros to the dangers lurking in the history books approved by the National Council of Culture. Predictably, their main complaint against the history readers was their "anti-Spanish" character; under the republican regime, Spain was suffering "a deep crisis of patriotism." Partisan, sectarian interests had replaced disinterested love of the patria, and negativism had supplanted pride.[104] For Catholics the remedy was clear: "It is urgent that we react against the anguished consciousness of Spanishness morbidly cultivated by the generation of '98 if we wish to raise the spirit of Spain, which is now decayed, weak, and as if ashamed of itself."[105]

The epithet "anti-Spanish" encompassed a multitude of sins: internationalism, pacifism, contempt for or indifference to the "saints, martyrs, and colonizers" responsible for Spanish greatness, materialism, naturalism, and *extranjerismo*—that is, preference for foreign over indigenous models of state and society. The Catholic reviewer of Larra's *Estampas de España*, for example, could not contain his indignation over Larra's

[103] Prologue by Jorge Vigón, in Marcelino Menéndez y Pelayo, *Historia de España, seleccionada de la obra del maestro por Jorge Vigón*, 4th ed. (Madrid: Cultura Española, 1941) (1st ed. 1934), xv. See also Miguel Artigas, *La España de Menéndez Pelayo: Antología de sus obras, selección y notas*, 2d ed. (Valladolid: Cultura Española, 1938) (1st ed. 1933).

[104] *Atenas* 5, no. 33 (1933): 21–22. See also FAE (Federación de Amigos de la Enseñanza), *Nuestro patriotismo* (Madrid: Colección Atenas, 1933).

[105] Adolfo Maíllo, *Apuntes de pedagogía*, quoted in *Atenas* 5, no. 34 (November 1933): 62.

assertion that in 1808 "the triumph of the *afrancesados* would probably have benefited the country."[106] Ramiro de Maeztu, another founder of Acción Española, lamented the eclipse of the heroes around whom Spanish history had traditionally been structured, "as in the opera, where all revolves around the tenor and the soprano. But now they want the principal figure to be the chorus, the gentlemen or ladies of the troupe."[107] The Catholic press was especially incensed by the aggressive secularism of the republican history books, which were invariably mute on the religiosity of great Spaniards like Isabel I, Hernán Cortés, or Velázquez. The lack of "spirituality," "warmth," and patriotic pride in these books was, in the Catholic view, the worst sort of treason.

Not surprisingly, then, the rightist coalition suspended the Council's list of authorized books in July 1935 and explicitly prohibited maestros from using the histories by Thomas and Hillyer, which were allegedly saturated with "socialist, syndicalist, and communist" values.[108] Of course, this prohibition had the predictable effect of arousing the curiosity of many maestros, who hastened to purchase the outlawed books.[109] In the end, these two readers by foreign authors came to symbolize the struggle for cultural hegemony in Spain. Immediately after the elections of February 1936, the Popular Front government lifted the prohibition against them; when the civil war began, the Socialist teachers' syndicate, which had seized the conservative Catholic publishing house El Magisterio Español, assumed responsibility for their continued publication.[110]

Since private schools were under no obligation to adopt the books authorized by the Republic, Catholic publishing houses, which had expanded during the 1920s, continued to publish the old-fashioned history textbooks and encyclopedias abolished in state primary schools. Two of the largest publishers were Ediciones Bruño, for the LaSallean schools, and F.T.D. and Edelvives, trade names employed by the Marist Brothers. The methodological conservatism of their textbooks, which,

---

[106] Larra, *Estampas*, 168. The review was in *Atenas* 5, no. 36 (January 1934): 163–65.

[107] Ramiro de Maeztu, "Anticultura," *Atenas* 5, no. 38 (March 1934): 235–36.

[108] O of 8 July and 28 August 1935. See the remarks of Romualdo de Toledo in *DSC*, no. 212 (27 June 1935): 8614.

[109] *Escuela Española* 2, no. 22 (October 1935): 485.

[110] O of 13 March 1936. José Luis Sastre, *El Magisterio Español: Un siglo de periodismo profesional* (Madrid: Editorial Magisterio Español, 1966), 33–34; Castellón, *Boletín de Educación* 10 (March 1938), número extraordinario dedicado al nuevo plan de estudios de la escuela primaria. For educational policy in the Republican zone during the civil war, see Ricardo Safón, *La educación en la España revolucionaria (1936–1939)*, trans. María Luisa Delgado and Félix Ortega (Madrid: Ediciones de La Piqueta, 1978); Juan Manuel Fernández Soria, *Educación y cultura en la guerra civil. (España, 1936–39)* (Valencia: NAU Llibres, 1984); and Hipólito Escolar Sobrino, *La cultura durante la guerra civil* (Madrid: Editorial Alhambra, 1987).

save for the addition of short readings or poems, were still structured catechistically, may have been attributable in part to the social niche occupied by the schools of these orders. Both catered to a lower-middle- and working-class clientele in whom it was presumably still thought desirable to inculcate passive obedience to authority. In any case, they followed none of the modern trends in history teaching, cleaving to the chronologies of reigns and battles and the colorless enumeration of not-able events.

In religion these books were integrist; in politics, not merely monar-chist, but Carlist. In the first grade *Historia de España* published by Edelvives in 1934, for example, D. Carlos was said to "defend his rights according to the laws of succession," while the Cortes of Cádiz were faulted for "ignoring the secular laws of Spain" by adopting a constitu-tion "that contained revolutionary ideas from France."[111] The lengthy second-grade history published by Bruño included a pious anecdote that described how the liberal General Riego had confessed his errors and received holy communion before his execution in 1823.[112] The history section of the third grade *Enciclopedia escolar* published by Edelvives concluded by summarizing "the importance of the church in our his-tory," especially in the Middle Ages, when "it dominated everything, but without oppressing: it was a domination solicited and loved by all, as is that of a mother." Under the Bourbons, however, the church had fallen under the tyrannical "protection" of the throne, while in the con-stitutional period, "protection became a license for usurpation and ruin." A generous sprinkling of quotations from Menéndez y Pelayo, in a forty-two-page outline that contained few other quotes or anecdotes, further bolstered the theocratic framework.[113]

Like their predecessors, the integrist histories published in the 1930s freely mixed legend, myth, and prejudice: Bruño's history for ten to twelve year olds introduced the biblical Túbal and Tarsis as the first settlers of Spain, while Edelvives assured its readers that "almost all Arab culture was borrowed from the Spaniards."[114] The Bruño text expanded on this theme, pointing out that the Arabs did not deserve the credit they were generally given because they made their (overly praised) contributions "when they were no longer Arabs, but rather

[111] Edelvives, *Historia de España. Primer grado*, 10th ed. (San Sebastián: Editorial F.T.D., n.d.) (1st ed. 1934), 65, 67.
[112] Ediciones Bruño, *Historia de España. Segundo grado*, 7th ed. (Zaragoza: La Instruc-ción Popular, n.d.) (1st ed. 1934?), 220–22.
[113] Edelvives, *Enciclopedia escolar. Tercer grado*, 4th ed. (Barcelona: Editorial Luis Vives, 1940) (1st ed. 1933), 313.
[114] Edelvives, *Historia*, 24.

entirely Spaniards."[115] Most offensive to republican sensibilities, however, were the short, begrudging commentaries on the Republic and the
republican tradition, associated exclusively with "disorder," "anarchy,"
"laicism," and church burnings. Ignoring the republican flag, the Bruño
text concluded with an analysis of the coat of arms of the Spanish monarchy and a paean to nobility and social hierarchy.

If mainstream Catholic educators hewed to traditional methodologies, a minority attempted to challenge the institucionistas on their own
turf of active pedagogy. Although Manjón had died a decade before, his
Escuelas del Ave María still flourished, and his publishing house produced new editions of his stridently antiliberal pedagogical writings. In-
structions for a *tableau vivant* of Spanish history published in 1932, for
example, concluded with a mysterious figure, "X, the unknown," whose
final speech was far more anguished than any of the much criticized
laments of the regenerationists: "The future is today darker than ever,
and it is rash to make predictions. Nevertheless, one can feel the rum-
bles of communism which wishes to give battle to everything that signi-
fies order, religion, and property. The so-called elements of order cannot
unite. Battle must be given. Who will triumph?"[116] A few practicing
Catholics in the state teaching corps, as well as educators from the elite
orders, also attempted to modernize Catholic historical pedagogy in order to compete for the allegiance of state inspectors and teachers. Recognizing the limitations of traditional history education, journals like
Avante and, to a lesser extent, *Atenas* welcomed articles describing
strategies for realizing history's potential as a formative discipline.

In 1933 the FAE published a *Metodología de la enseñanza de la historia* by Agustín Serrano de Haro, that was virtually indistinguishable in
most of its methodological prescriptions from those of Altamira, whom
the author cited with approval on multiple occasions. The author, a
state inspector from Jaén, advocated cyclical programs, active methods,
and the study of art and folklore to understand and appreciate the spirit
of the pueblo whose creative activities were the essence of national life.[117]
A healthy patriotism, he argued offered soil in which to cultivate "fraternity, collaboration, and peace."[118] In *España es así*, a generously illustrated history textbook for upper primary students, Serrano de Haro

---

[115] Bruño, *Historia*, 59

[116] Andrés Manjón, *Gráficos aplicables a la escena* (Granada: Imprenta-Escuela de Ave-
Maria, 1932), 89–90.

[117] Agustín Serrano de Haro, *Metodología de la enseñanza de la historia* (Madrid: FAE,
1933). For a summary, see *Avante* 7, nos. 70, 72, 73 (April, June, July–August 1934): 50–
51, 82–83, 100–101. The lessons were originally delivered as a series of lectures at the
third Week of Pedagogical Studies sponsored by the FAE.

[118] Serrano de Haro, *Metodología*, 13.

attempted to put these principles into practice.[119] His paternalistic authorial voice invited children into the narrative on every page. Interesting information about daily life and social customs, artistic achievements, capsule biographies, dramatic set pieces, and patriotic commentary replaced the tedious accounts of reigns and battles. At the end of each chapter the author included suggestions for student activities and class discussions.

The similarities with the child-centered texts promoted by the republican left ended there, however. In Serrano de Haro's hands, the history of civilization was not the record of humanity's collective triumphs over the physical environment, but rather that of "the life-giving breath that Christ instilled in the civilization of the world."[120] More importantly, Serrano de Haro's mission was to cement national identity, not international solidarity. His text traced the history of Spanish identity since Celtiberian times, an identity he located in the traditional culture and spirituality of the Spanish pueblo. In the eighteenth century, Spanish elites had chosen "a dangerous path: to wish to be what one is not," but fortunately "the pueblo retained, integral and vibrant, its Spanish air and spirit."[121] Among the many suggestions for classroom activities was one to "reward the essay that most energetically and accurately condemns all attempts to deform the authentic spirit of the patria."[122]

España es así offered a stirring defense against the calumnies of the Black Legend; it represented triumphalism and exclusivity at their most exalted. "Spain has never been a backward country," Serrano insisted; indeed, Spain's contributions to world civilization were unparalleled.[123] In the Middle Ages Castile was populated by the "best" (i.e., the most Romanized) barbarians, and later "gave the world admirable lessons of Christian democracy." Its churches were unsurpassed in beauty, its people were the first to appreciate hygiene, and its culture "was very superior to that of other countries." The Spanish Renaissance produced Queen Isabel and Columbus ("the greatest Queen there has been in the world and the greatest man that the centuries have seen"), as well as Saint Teresa, "the premier [woman] writer in the world"; Velázquez, the "greatest painter"; the *Quijote*, "the premier novel"; and the Escorial, "the eighth wonder of the world."[124] Nor had Spanish genius flagged

---

[119] Agustín Serrano de Haro, *España es así*, 6th ed. (Madrid: Editorial Escuela Española, 1942) (1st ed. 1933; 14th ed. 1952).

[120] Serrano de Haro, *Metodología*, 31.

[121] Serrano de Haro, *España es así*, 235, 238.

[122] Ibid., 261.

[123] Ibid., 19.

[124] Ibid., 99, 102, 145, 153.

since the days of imperial greatness: of the 3,395 patents registered in the entire world in 1933, 2,381 were Spanish inventions.

What made this little history book so subversive was not its triumphalism, but the reactionary political values behind the author's conception of the "historical architecture" of Spain.[125] Although critical of monarchical absolutism, Serrano de Haro did not disguise his belief in the illegitimacy of Spain's constitutional history ever since the popular classes, exposed to the "contagion" of the French Revolution, had thrown themselves, "without secure ideals and without restraints, into revolutionary agitation." Children were invited to share "the sorrow and the bitterness that republican ideas, so alien to our tradition, have cost Spain."[126] Nevertheless, the ultimate message of the book was positive: Spaniards possessed a glorious national tradition that might be disregarded by evil or foolish leaders, but that could never be wholly eclipsed. The spiritual superiority that had guaranteed Spanish dominance in the sixteenth century still made Spain a great nation in the twentieth. The past should provoke neither nostalgia nor shame, but optimism, since Spanish traditions had lost none of their virtuality and relevance.

In *España es así*, and in a small but growing number of history books like it, Catholic educators explored the potential of modern historical pedagogy for mobilizing the masses. The integrist interpretation of the national past, combined with a modernized teaching method that respected and persuaded children rather than merely repressing them, presented a formidable barrier to the republican project for cultural transformation. The republicans lacked the time and the consensus to pursue their goals under conditions of maximum liberty, and the resources, both political and financial, to impose their vision by force. It was not only the active resistance of the right that they had to overcome, but the massive inertia built into the educational system. Teachers who had traditionally greeted directives from the ministry with apathy or a sense of déjà vu, found their skepticism reinforced by the swings of the political pendulum during the brief life of the Republic. Compliance with ministerial directives was discretionary: as one educator remarked, "Aren't we convinced that tomorrow or the day after a minister will enter the ministry who will order and command in the *Gaceta* just the opposite?"[127] In any event, harnessing state power to impose a cultural canon consistent with the republican political agenda also legitimized attempts by

---

[125] The phrase is Antonio Fernández's, in his review of Serrano de Haro's book in *Avante* 7, no. 76 (November 1934): 160.

[126] Serrano de Haro, *España es así*, 267, 266.

[127] *Escuela Española* 2, no. 22 (October 1935): 485.

political opponents to do the same thing and came perilously close to the censorship that the left had so bitterly opposed under the dictatorship.[128]

Furthermore, the left republicans' instrumentalization of the national past was hampered by the profound ambivalence with which they approached it. To the extent that they identified themselves in opposition to the "other" Spain, it was in opposition to their own history. Unable to define the Republic in terms of a continuous national tradition, they tended to marginalize the Spanish past when they did not deplore it. The community they imagined was one of republicans, rather than Spaniards; the moral links they sought to forge were intentionally transcendent of national boundaries, whether internal or external. True patriots, they nonetheless unintentionally invited the charges of antipatriotism that the right, so comfortable within the confines of traditional history, leveled against them.

Thus, despite repeated professions of faith in the efficacy of history as a wellspring of civic nationalism, the republican intelligentsia failed to create a sense of shared history that might have cemented the republican project. On the contrary, as political conflict mounted, the persistent fragmentation of the educational system only exacerbated the confrontation of opposing versions of the national past. Perhaps symbolic of the republican failure was the retirement of Altamira from his university chair on 10 February 1936. As Spaniards went to war with one another five months later; they were fighting not only to determine the future of the nation but also to define the meaning of its history.

---

[128] The republicans refused to acknowledge this similarity, however. See "El texto único en las escuelas," *RP* 14, no. 166 (October 1935): 484–85.

CHAPTER 8

History as Therapy: The Franquist Dictatorship, 1936–1953

> The History of Spain must be the *second*
> *religion* of Spaniards, without fear of idolatry,
> since, by the superior design of God, in our
> Spain the religion of the Patria is the same as
> the religion of Religion.
> (*José Pemartín Pemartín*)[1]

THE CIVIL WAR that erupted in 1936 registered the determination of Spain's privileged classes to resist the process of social, political, and cultural modernization unleashed by the proclamation of the Second Republic. Arguably, it was the threat posed by the republican cultural project that most frightened the right. The democratic constitution could be rescinded, social reforms and regional autonomy reversed, political parties and syndicalist organizations outlawed, and their leaders neutralized by death, imprisonment, or exile. But the support extended to the Republic by the urban middle and working classes suggested that the real threat lay deeper, in the inroads that modern values, aspirations, and behavior had made in Spanish culture. Accordingly, the coalition of parties and interest groups that exercised and disputed power within the Franquist regime placed a high priority on eradicating those tendencies and inculcating Spaniards with attitudes and comportments congruent with the reactionary political and social program of the "New State." Not surprisingly, the church, whose cultural hegemony had been most directly challenged by the Republic, and whose members bore the brunt of revolutionary fury in the first months of the war, took the lead in articulating and disseminating an ideology that legitimated both its own interests and those of the ruling elites.[2] The principal agent of social reproduction and political socialization would be the school,

---

[1] José Pemartín, the head of Secondary and Higher Education Services, quoted in *Atenas* 9, no. 81 (May 1938): 165.

[2] Over six thousand three hundred priests and members of religious orders were killed during the war. Juan Linz, "Religion and Politics in Spain: From Conflict to Consensus above Cleavage," *Social Compass* 27, nos. 2–3 (1980): 256.

whose organization and curricula would be drastically restructured to eliminate all traces of the ideological and structural reforms introduced during the Republic.

The nature of the Franco regime and its ruling ideas have been the object of considerable debate.[3] For the purposes of this study, however, it is sufficient to note that the regime was a counterrevolutionary response to the social and political reformism of the Second Republic by groups otherwise divided by class, goals, and ideology. Holding the disparate "families" of interests in balance would prove to be the greatest political talent of Francisco Franco. For at least the first twenty-five years of his dictatorship, however, his task was eased by their shared opposition to the liberal democratic and socialist currents that had battled for dominance in Spanish society during the 1930s and by their perception that "the red revolution was forged in the field of education . . . and the new Spain will not triumph if it does not conquer the School."[4]

The policies of the Franco regime in its first decade have been extensively studied and need only be summarized here. Until the death of General Franco in 1975 the cultural and educational policies—and the ideology that shaped them—were determined primarily by a succession of Catholic interest groups.[5] The Catholic monarchists of Acción Cató-

[3] For an introduction to the Franco regime, see Stanley G. Payne, *The Franco Regime, 1936–1975* (Madison: University of Wisconsin Press, 1987); Raymond Carr and Juan Pablo Fusi, *Spain: Dictatorship to Democracy*, 2d ed. (London: George Allen and Unwin, 1981); and Paul Preston, *Franco: A Biography* (New York: Harper Collins, 1993). The classic definition of Franquism is provided by Juan Linz, "Spain: An Authoritarian Regime," in Stanley G. Payne, ed., *Politics and Society in Twentieth-Century Spain* (New York: New Viewpoints, 1976); a rebuttal is Paul Preston, *The Politics of Revenge: Fascism and the Military in Twentieth Century Spain* (Boston: Unwin Hyman, 1990).

[4] Luis Ortiz Muñoz, *Glorias imperiales: Libro escolar de lecturas históricas*, 2 vols. (Madrid: Editorial Magisterio Español, 1940) 1:7.

[5] See especially Gregorio Cámara Villar, *Nacional-catolicismo y escuela: La socialización política del franquismo, 1936–1951* (Jaén: Editorial Hesperia, 1983), and "El adoctrinamiento político en la escuela del franquismo: Nacional-catolicismo y textos escolares, 1936–1951," in José Luis López-Aranguren et al., *Infancia y sociedad en España* (Jaén: Editorial Hesperia, 1983), 159–200; Alicia Alted Vigil, *Política del Nuevo Estado sobre el patrimonio cultural y la educación durante la guerra civil española* (Madrid: Ministerio de Cultura, Dirección General de Bellas Artes y Archivos, 1984); *Historia de la educación en España: Textos y documentos*, vol. 5, *Nacional-catolicismo y educación en la España de posguerra* (Madrid: Servicio de Publicaciones del Ministerio de Educación y Ciencia, 1990); Ramón Navarro Sandalinas, *La enseñanza primaria durante el franquismo (1936–1975)* (Barcelona: PPU, 1990); Victor García Hoz, *La educación en la España del siglo XX* (Madrid: Rialp, 1980); Jordi Monés i Pujol-Busquets, *L'escola a Catalunya sota el franquisme* (Barcelona: Edicions 62, 1981); and more briefly, Hipólito Escolar Sobrino, *La cultura durante la guerra civil* (Madrid: Editorial Alhambra, 1987); and Juan Manuel Fernández Soria, *Educación y cultura en la guerra civil: (España, 1936–*

lica seized the initiative during the opening weeks of the civil war and consolidated their position in October 1936 by monopolizing the newly created Commission for Culture and Education in the first Nationalist governing junta. In February 1938 a founding member of the group, Pedro Sainz Rodríguez, became the first minister of national education. With his resignation at the end of the civil war, leadership within the Catholic camp passed to the ACN de P; a propagandista, José Ibañez Martín, decisively shaped the regime's educational policy during his ten-year tenure at the head of the ministry. Meanwhile, the Opus Dei, a Catholic lay institute founded by a Spaniard, José María Escrivà Balaguer, in 1928, had staked out a preserve in the Consejo Superior de Investigaciones Científicas (CSIC), which usurped the functions and resources of the Junta para Ampliación de Estudios and the ILE, and, somewhat later, in the universities.[6] During the regime's "technocratic" phase in the 1960s, the Opus would capture the ministry as well. Between 1936 and 1945, however, the momentary prestige of international fascism enabled the Falange Española—or the "Movement," as it was later known—to press its own ideological and political claims with partial success.[7] In consequence, the ideology of the so-called New State in its opening phase was substantitively the "National Catholicism" elaborated in the 1920s and 1930s by the intellectuals of Acción Española overlaid with a veneer of fascist rhetoric, symbology, ritual, and organization. National Catholic ideologues continued to define Spanish nationality in terms of religion, history, and culture, but Falangist influence heightened the quotient of militant, authoritarian nationalism in their rhetoric.[8]

---

39) (Valencia: NAU Llibres, 1984). A profusely illustrated, triumphalist account by the minister of national education between 1939 and 1951 is José Ibáñez Martín, *Diez años de servicios a la cultura española, 1939–1949* (Madrid: Ministerio de Educación Nacional, 1950). For the role of the church in the Franco regime see Frances Lannon, *Privilege, Persecution, and Prophecy: The Catholic Church in Spain, 1875–1975* (New York: Oxford University Press, 1987), 198–257; and Juan José Ruiz Rico, *Papel político de la iglesia católica en la era de Franco (1936–1971)* (Madrid: Editorial Tecnos, 1977).

[6] O of 18 April and 17 May 1940 transferred the resources of the Junta to the CSIC and of the ILE to the state.

[7] On the Falange Española, see Stanley G. Payne, *Falange: A History of Spanish Fascism* (Stanford, Calif.: Stanford University Press, 1961); José-Carlos Mainer, *Falange y literatura* (Barcelona: Editorial Labor, 1971); and Elías Díaz, *Pensamiento español en la era de Franco (1936–1975)* (Madrid: Tecnos, 1983).

[8] A formal statement of National Catholic ideology may be found in José Pemartín Sanjuán, *¿Qué es 'lo nuevo'?: Consideraciones sobre el momento español presente* (Seville: Álvarez Zambrano, 1938). For the origins of National Catholicism, see chap. 6. The argument that National Catholicism was an ideology rather than a mentality is made by Cámara Villar, *Nacional-catolicismo y escuela* and "Adoctrinamiento política"; and Fernando Urbina, "Formas de vida de la iglesia en España, 1939–1975," in *Iglesia y*

As noted in chapter 6, the defining principle of National Catholic discourse was its claim that Spanish nationality had been definitively determined in the sixteenth-century fusion of the "Catholic ideal" with the "military monarchy."[9] Recourse to this historical ideal was a mode of legitimation, cultural definition, and political socialization. By codifying and sacralizing a particular interpretation of a particular moment in the Spanish past, National Catholicism invalidated divergence from that model as heretical and "anti-national." An immutable and immanent national tradition (what in nineteenth-century discourse had been called the "internal constitution") could not be affected by temporal changes in opinion or fashion. As Ibáñez Martín observed before the Cortes in 1945, Franco's rule was sanctioned by that tradition, not by popular consent: "If, for Spain today, Franco represents the continuity of History, and not the contingency of political circumstance, it is because he has known how to incorporate into the historical vocation of our Patria at the present moment the spirit of those traditional ambitions that gave our undertakings the[ir] metaphysical character."[10]

The distinction between the "traditional" and the "popular" was a crucial one in defining cultural policy: tradition not only conferred legitimacy, but it also permitted greater selection and control of the cultural components of the national identity that the regime claimed to embody. The popular culture consecrated as "traditional" distilled and authenticated values and customs supportive of a hierarchical and reactionary social order and a unitary state, while marginalizing those deemed inconsonant with the "purest and most traditional national essences."[11] The model of "traditional culture" against which both popular and elite culture were measured was Castilian, Catholic, rural, and, in the opening phases of the regime, imperial. To the extent that individual Spaniards or modern popular culture did not conform to this model, they were targeted for "Hispanization."

National Catholic historical discourse, intentionally exclusionary with regard to the "other Spain," also harbored ambiguities that revealed the internal tensions within the Franquist coalition. While both

---

sociedad en España, 1939–1975 (Madrid: Editorial Popular, 1977). For the argument that it was a "mentality," see Linz, "Spain: An Authoritarian Regime"; and Ruiz Rico, *Papel político.*

[9] Pemartín Sanjuán, *¿Qué es 'lo nuevo'?* 46–48.

[10] Speech of 14 July 1945, in Ministerio de Educación Nacional, Dirección General de Primera Enseñanza, *Ley de educación primaria de 17 de julio de 1945: Textos legales* (Madrid: 1952), 24.

[11] See Luis Díaz, "La manipulación de la cultura popular en España: Entre el folklorismo homogeneizador a la búsqueda de señas de identidad," in Richard Herr and John H. R. Polt, eds., *Iberian Identity: Essays on the Nature of Identity in Spain and Portugal* (Berkeley: Institute of International Studies, 1989), 98–111.

Catholics and Falangists constantly invoked the imperial age, Catholics spoke as if the intervening passage of time could be disregarded; the sixteenth century was not just a source of inspiration and rededication, as it seemed to be for Falangists, but a still viable model for contemporary social and political life. Whereas Falangists exulted in the "will to empire," Catholics stressed that empire was but a means toward spiritual ends. Catholics swore fealty to the patria—that is, to national spirit and tradition—and to the "Caudillo," Francisco Franco, as its savior and reincarnation. Falangists, in contrast, stressed obedience to the New State because "the nation and the State have once again met each other at the end of three centuries."[12] The Catholic right, which valued a strong state not as an end in itself, but as a necessary evil, demanded the "nationalization of the state," not the "'statification' of the nation."[13] Similarly, while Falangists spoke of a "revolution" in Spanish political life, the Catholic right preferred to speak of "rebirth," "resurgence," and "resurrection"—terms clearly counterrevolutionary in orientation and more congruent with the center of gravity of the Franquist coalition. Although both the Catholic right and the Falange professed allegiance to corporatism as a remedy for the conflicts inherent in liberal capitalism and democracy, the ideals of work, discipline, and social justice were taken seriously only by an handful of youthful Falangist intellectuals, who drifted away as the essentially reactionary character of the regime became apparent after the end of the war.[14]

As might be expected, the Catholic right was particularly suspicious of Falangist efforts to subordinate education to the state.[15] Nevertheless, their fundamental assumptions about the purposes of education were similar. Whether referring to "nationalization" or "Hispanization," both Catholics and Falangists saw in education the instrument with which to inculcate Spaniards with a sense of patriotism, social discipline, and national solidarity. The great crusade of the civil war had been undertaken to redeem the nation from the "original sin" of liberalism;[16] the sacrifice of the fallen would be justified only "when intense

[12] José Corts Grau, *Motivos de la España eterna* (Madrid: Instituto de Estudios Políticos, 1946), 11.

[13] Pemartín Sanjuán, *¿Qué es 'lo nuevo'?* 153.

[14] On the intellectual trajectory of these "sincere" Falangists, see Mainer, *Falange*; and Elías Díaz, *Pensamiento español.*

[15] See the rebuttal of Falangist pretensions in Pemartín Sanjuán, *¿Qué es 'lo nuevo'?* and Teodoro Rodríguez, *Nueva reconquista de España: (Caminos equivocados)* (Valladolid: Librería Santarén, 1936).

[16] Mariano Lampreave, "El concepto del deber," in Ministerio de Educación Nacional (hereafter MEN), *Curso de orientaciones nacionales de la enseñanza primaria celebrado en Pamplona del 1 al 30 de junio de 1938. Segundo año triunfal* (Burgos: Hijos de Santiago Rodríguez, 1938), 2:167.

commitment to the values and duties of the national community super-
sedes individual desire and suicidal factionalism."[17] Education, in other
words, must be formative, not merely instructional; its goal was not the
liberation of the individual, but the subordination of individual or partisan interest to the larger ends of the patria. Both Catholics and Falangists emphatically rejected a free market in ideas, which in their view
was responsible for the national crisis. Social harmony and national
strength could not be recovered through persuasion or debate, but only
through the reimposition of the eternal national values forged during
Spain's Golden Age.[18]

Unified in their appreciation of the importance of education and shar-
ing an elitist, hierarchical model of social relations, the Catholic right
and the Falange competed strenuously for control of the school system,
beginning with the universities, the incubator of the nation's "select minorities." Approved in 1943 at the height of Falangist influence, the
university reform law made substantial concessions to the Falange in
the areas of political socialization and syndicalization, but otherwise
conformed to the Catholic project for the re-Catholicization of Spanish
culture.[19] The law of 1943 dedicated the university not to free inquiry
but to the transmission of a national culture at once revolutionary and
traditional, "a Spanish, totalitarian humanism," whose purpose was to
shape not only the intellect but "the heart."[20] Research, teaching, and
training were explicitly subordinated to "dogma, Catholic morality and
canon law" and to the "programmatic points of the Movement." By
returning to the "unitary atmosphere of Catholic science," the Spanish
university would turn its back on the "unpardonable and chaotic inertia" and "de-Hispanization" of the previous two centuries, recapturing
instead the spirit "by which it was possible to dominate the globe with
the greatest Empire in History."[21]

Not surprisingly, historical studies occupied pride of place in the new
hierarchy of humanistic sciences. If the official patron saint of the new
Spanish university was Saint Thomas Aquinas, its effective patron from

[17] Adolfo Mailló, *Educación y revolución: Los fundamentos de una educación nacional* (Madrid: Editora Nacional, 1943), 8–9.
[18] These assumptions are evident in D 66 of 8 November and the C of 7 December 1936.
[19] The Ley de Ordenación Universitaria of 29 July 1943 is in *Historia de la educación* 5 (2): 607–65. A decree of 29 March 1944 established courses of "political formation" in the universities under the control of the National Movement. See the discussion in Cá-mara Villar, *Nacional-catolicismo*, 212–34.
[20] José López Ibor, *Discurso a los universitarios españoles* (1938), and Isidoro Martín, *Concepto y misión de la universidad* (1940), quoted in *Historia de la educación* 5 (1): 194, 225.
[21] Ley de Ordenación Universitaria of 29 July 1943, articles 3 and 4 and preamble, in *Historia de la educación* 5 (2): 607–26.

the beginning of the civil war was Menéndez y Pelayo, "the true spiritual father of the New Spain."[22] Hailed as the "Spanish Fichte" by the Instituto de España and as the founder of "Revolutionary Nationalism" by the Falangist Onésimo Redondo, Menéndez y Pelayo's lifelong dedication to the vindication of "traditional" Spanish science and letters made him the historical authority from whom no higher appeals could be contemplated.[23] By 1941 the condensation of his historical writings published by Acción Española in 1934 was in its fourth edition. New editions of the other foundational texts of National Catholicism by Menéndez y Pelayo's acolytes—especially Julián Juderías and the martyred Maeztu, killed in the opening weeks of the civil war—also appeared. From 1936 on, a flood of historical essayists in the Nationalist zone elaborated further on the peculiarities of the national spirit and the universality of its values. Two of the most influential were *El destino de España en la historia universal*, a recapitulation of the integrist view of the national past by the Jesuit historian Zacarías García Villada (another victim of leftist reprisals), and *Idea de la hispanidad*, by Manuel García Morente, an apostate from the Institución Libre whose principal contribution was the crystallization of Spanish identity into the transcendent figure of the "Christian *caballero*."[24] The common theme in this literature was its messianic definition of Spanish nationality, or hispanidad. Spaniards were a chosen race with a distinctive "style of life" and "unity of destiny" whose historical mission since Covadonga had been the defense of Christian civilization against materialism, atheism, and barbarism. The Spanish "difference" that progressives had lamented and sought to remedy was instead to be nurtured and celebrated. The international ostracism of the Franquist regime after 1945 only confirmed its contention that the Black Legend was the invention of hostile and uncomprehending foreigners to whom Spain owed neither accommodation nor apology.

Joining the essayists were the historical positivists in the tradition of the mature Menéndez y Pelayo. Biographies of imperial statesmen,

[22] Ediciones Bruño, *El libro de España* (Madrid: author, 1943), 12–13.

[23] On 16 September 1937 General Francisco Gómez Jordana dedicated university short courses to "the great Spanish polygraph." See also Instituto de España, *Menéndez y Pelayo y la educación nacional* (Santander: Aldus, 1938), 5; Ibáñez Martín, *Diez años*, vii; Pedro Sainz Rodríguez, *Testimonios y recuerdos* (Barcelona: Editorial Planeta, 1978), 193. Sainz Rodríguez ordered the publication of Menéndez y Pelayo's complete works on 19 May 1938. For a discussion of Menéndez y Pelayo's influence, see Fernando Valls, *La enseñanza de la literatura en el franquismo (1936–1951)* (Barcelona: Antoni Bosch, 1983), 24–28.

[24] Zacarías García Villada, S.J., *El destino de España en la historia universal*, 2d ed., rev. (Madrid: Cultura Española, 1940) (1st ed. 1936); Manuel García Morente, *Idea de la hispanidad*, 2d ed. (Buenos Aires: Espasa-Calpe, 1939) (1st ed. 1938).

saints, and military caudillos, compilations of data proving the perdurability of the Spanish national character, and triumphalist refutations of the Black Legend dominated historical discourse in the academies, the universities, the scholarly journals and the CSIC during the 1940s.[25] Those whose research focused on less exalted aspects of the Habsburg centuries were either removed from their chairs, like Altamira's disciple José de Deleito in Valencia, or denied the professional recognition their scholarship deserved; the pathbreaking social historian Antonio Domínguez Ortiz labored unrewarded in institutos in Granada and Madrid until 1979.[26]

A regime that boasted constantly of its fidelity to the national past nevertheless found it convenient to neglect large portions of it. A profound silence engulfed the themes that had preoccupied progressive historians: contemporary history, regional history outside Castile, and social history. Well-intentioned efforts, like that of the Falangist intellectual Pedro Laín Entralgo in *España como problema* (1947), to make room in the national past for the "other Spain" defeated in 1939, were rejected by Opus Dei integrists like Rafael Calvo Serer. In *España sin problema* (1949), Calvo Serer repudiated the metaphor of the "two Spains"; the victory of 1939 was "above all the victory of a particular cultural conception." To compromise now with heterodoxy—whether political, cultural, or religious—was to repeat the errors of the Restoration monarchy. Attempts to assimilate elements "unassimilable to national unitary and orthodox tradition" would lead inexorably to another "bloody cycle" of civil wars, whereas fidelity to the Spain of Menéndez y Pelayo would enable the nation to march confidently into the future.[27]

[25] On historiography in the 1940s, see José María Jover Zamora, "El siglo XIX en la historiografía española contemporánea (1939–1972)," in *Once ensayos sobre la historia* (Madrid: Ríoduero, 1976); and "Corrientes historiográficas en la España contemporánea," in Jover Zamora, *El siglo XIX en España: Doce estudios* (Barcelona: Editorial Planeta, 1974); and Gonzalo Pasamar Alzuria and Ignacio Peiró Martín, *Historiografía e ideología en la postguerra española: La ruptura de la tradición liberal* (Zaragoza: Universidad, 1981); and *Historiografía y práctica social en España* (Zaragoza: Secretariado de Publicaciones de la Universidad, 1987).

[26] While on permanent "research leave" in Madrid after the war, Deleito (1897–1957) published a series of monographs on the religious and social history of the seventeenth century. Domínguez Ortiz (1909–), whose early research focused on the *judeoconversos* and the social structures of the Old Regime, was denied a cátedra at the University of Seville. See Peter Bakewell, "An Interview with Antonio Domínguez Ortiz," *Hispanic American Historical Review* 65, no. 2 (1985): 189–202; and "Homenatge a Antonio Domínguez Ortiz," *L'Avenç* 14 (March 1979): 4.

[27] Rafael Calvo Serer, *España sin problema* (Madrid: Rialp, 1949), 140, 154. See also Pedro Laín Entralgo, *España como problema*, 2 vols. (Madrid: Aguilar, 1962), and the discussion in Elías Díaz, *Pensamiento español*, 52–58.

While scholars and pundits labored to purge national history of the distortions introduced by foreigners and perfidious Spaniards, educational reformers, viewing history as a "fundamental resort in the resurgence of patriotism," placed it at the center of the curriculum in both secondary and primary schools.[28] Even the Falangist "civics" course, Formation of the National Spirit (required for primary students in 1945 and for secondary students in 1953), was basically an immersion in National Catholic truths about the imperial past.[29] For progressives like Altamira (in exile in Mexico until his death in 1951), the educational value of history in a backward country like Spain lay in its empirical approach to questions of social and political process. In the Franco regime, history education was conceived as therapy—a wellspring of inspirational and community-building assertions about national values and purposes that could cure the unjustified inferiority complex from which Spaniards had suffered since the eighteenth century. The secondary school reform decree enacted by Sainz Rodríguez in 1938 dedicated the seven-year history curriculum to the "revaluation of Spanishness, the definitive extirpation of anti-Hispanic and philo-foreign pessimism" in order "to make manifest the moral purity of Spanish nationality; the superior universalist category of our imperial spirit, of hispanidad."[30]

Saturation in the principles of hispanidad through historical study was only part of a major restructuring of secondary education, which the Catholic right continued to perceive as "the most efficient instrument to influence, rapidly, the transformation of a society and the intellectual and moral formation of its future ruling classes."[31] The law of 20 September 1938 reforming the bachillerato was based on the Catholic conception of "formative" education. At the core of the single-track, humanistic "university bachillerato" was the intensive cyclical study of religion, classical languages (seven years of Latin, four of Greek), Castilian, geography, and history. But it also retained the hodgepodge of "modern" subjects—sciences, mathematics, philosophy, modern languages—that had traditionally characterized the Spanish bachillerato.

[28] Sainz Rodríguez, quoted in Alted Vigil, *Política del Nuevo Estado*, 227. On history in Franquist schools, see Rafael Valls Montés, *La interpretación de la historia de España y sus orígenes ideológicos en el bachillerato franquista (1938–1953)* (Valencia: Instituto de Ciencias de la Educación de la Universidad Literaria, 1984); Manuel Tuñón de Lara, "La interpretación 'policial' de la historia," *CP*, suppl. no. 3 (1976): 35–37; Cámara Villar, *Nacional-catolicismo*, 293–396; and Valls, *Enseñanza de la literatura*, 61–72.

[29] See FET y de las JONS, *Formación del espíritu nacional: Manual de iniciación político-social para enseñanza primaria* (Madrid: Ediciones de Frente de Juventudes, 1947); and Manuel Álvarez Lastra and Eleuterio de Orte Martínez, *Formación del espíritu nacional. (Curso 2°, 3°, 4° y 5°)*, 5 vols. (Madrid: Gráficas Canales, 1955).

[30] Law of 20 September 1938, signed by Sainz Rodríguez.

[31] Law of 20 September 1938. See Sainz Rodríguez, *Testimonios*, 255–60; and Alted Vigil, *Política del Nuevo Estado*, 189–210.

The result was a substantial augmentation of the course load, which amounted to ten courses a week in the upper forms. Coeducation was abolished (thus obliging the regime to open twenty-two new institutos for women). In complementary legislation published in 1940, the internal regimen of the institutos was assimilated to that of the Catholic colegios by the addition of study halls, proctors, spiritual exercises, and dormitories. Studying libre was not permitted until 1942. Sainz Rodríguez's goal was to transform a flaccid and incoherent system of elite education into an academically and spiritually rigorous one. Only then would Spain see the "return to the valorization of the authentic Being of Spain, of the Spain . . . which produced that pleiad of statesmen and warriors—all with a religious, classical and humanistic formation—of our imperial epoch."[32] This was not merely snobbism or nostalgia, but a political program for the future based on the conviction that most of Europe had taken a wrong turn in the sixteenth century. The restoration of classical, Catholic humanism would vindicate Spain as a nation with a "vocation of mission and exemplarity."[33] No longer condemned to bringing up the rear in Europe's march toward modernity, Spain would instead provide moral leadership in a materialistic world of demonstrably bankrupt values; indeed, Spain would defend Europe "against Europe herself."[34]

Conceived as an incubator of elites committed to the preservation of national values, the bachillerato was limited to those preparing for university study and the professions. Technical and vocational alternatives were neglected until the belated—and very modest—appearance of the *bachillerato laboral* in 1950.[35] Women students pursuing the classical bachillerato were obliged to follow an extended complement of courses in the domestic arts—a reflection of the traditionalist conception of gender roles that permeated the educational system, particularly in the colegios.[36] These restrictions braked the rapid expansion of the second-

---

[32] Law of 20 September 1938. For a defense of the classical bachillerato, see José Pemartín, *Formación clásica y formación romántica: Ideas sobre la enseñanza* (Madrid: Espasa-Calpe, 1942); and Carlos Alonso del Real, "Valor político de la enseñanza del latín," *Revista Nacional de Educación* 1 (July 1941): 43–50.

[33] Law of 20 September 1938.

[34] Pedro Sainz Rodríguez, "La escuela del Nuevo Estado," in MEN, *Curso de orientaciones* 1:80.

[35] D of 23 December 1949, creating Centros de Enseñanza Media y Profesional. The plan of studies for the four "modes" (agriculture and livestock, industrial and mineral, maritime and fishery, and feminine) was published on 24 March 1950. For an early complaint against the neglect of professional and vocational schooling, see Antonio Martínez García, "La orientación de nuestros adolescentes," *Atenas* 12, no. 115 (November 1941): 365–67.

[36] See I. Errandonea, "El bachillerato feminino" in *RyF* 43, nos. 456–57 (July–August 1943): 96–106.

ary school population that had begun during the 1920s and accelerated under the Republic; in the academic year 1949–50, fewer than 215,000 students were matriculated nationwide.[37]

Further limiting access to the bachillerato was the swing toward privatization. After eliminating fifty-two of the newer institutos as "superfluous," Sainz Rodríguez removed nearly all state controls on Catholic colegios. Students educated in *colegios reconocidos* (those whose faculties met minimum state standards) could pass to the next year of study on the basis of positive evaluations from their own professors; annual examinations in the institutos were abolished. After seven years of study, degree seekers faced only a single, extensive state examination administered by university catedráticos.[38]

Under this regime the schools of the religious orders flourished, as intended. While the number of institutos stagnated at fewer than 120, by 1948 there were nearly 700 private colegios—nearly three-fourths of them operated by religious congregations—enrolling close to 50 percent of all secondary students. Approximately another fifth of all students studied as libres, leaving only 30 percent officially matriculated in the state schools.[39]

Although the Falange objected to this radical decentralization of the school system, privatization was well suited to the reactionary social purposes of the dictatorship and the class interests it served. In the colegios the traditional hidden curriculum based on silence, obedience, emulation and class distinctions complemented the "character-building" discipline of the classics. In the retrospective view of one disillusioned graduate of the elitist Jesuit Colegio de Areneros in Madrid, the most lasting imprint was fear—fear of sin, of hell, of "communism," of anarchy, and thus, of freedom. The colegios in this fashion shaped not the "imperial warriors and statesmen" of national Catholic rhetoric, but a privileged youth conditioned "for integration, not for liberty."[40]

---

[37] On women's education, see Oficina de Información Diplomática, *Fifteen Years of Spanish Culture, 1938–1952* (Madrid, 1952), 81–82; for total enrollments, García Hoz, *Educación*, 126.

[38] As originally written, the law of 1938 allowed parents to conduct annual student evaluations, a procedure so open to abuse that it was abolished in 1945. The rules for official recognition of private colegios were approved on 7 December 1938. Decrees permitting parental evaluation and establishing the format of the state examination were approved on 24 January 1939. For an overview, see Enrique Frutos, "La enseñanza media en España en la primera mitad del siglo XX," *Bordón* 3, nos. 17–18 (1951): 119–36.

[39] Figures from Ibáñez Martín, *Diez años*, 197. This volume also lists the religious orders with schools in Spain and describes the most prestigious Catholic colegios.

[40] Javier Domínguez Martín-Sánchez, *Enseñanza católica para una generación: Víctima y testigo* (Madrid: Editorial Popular, 1979), 43. The author took his final vows as a member of the Society of Jesus in 1965. See also the memoirs by Luis Goytisolo and Nuria Pompeia published in *CP*, suppl. no. 3, "Fascismo y educación" (Sept. 1976): 45–49.

The autonomy granted the colegios was balanced by the enhancement of the power of the state to impose ideological uniformity through regulation of course content and textbooks. The Catholics' instinctive distrust of state-mandated syllabi and textbooks was mitigated by their control of the ministry. Consequently, for the first time since the passage of the Ley Moyano in 1857 the state's theoretical claim to regulate the content of textbooks and teaching became a reality.

The syllabi, or cuestionarios, prepared in May 1939 for the new bachillerato were far more prescriptive than the fundamentally descriptive lists of topics issued during the Primo de Rivera dictatorship and the Republic. They specified not only the topics to be covered in each course, but also their correct interpretation.[41] Following Menéndez y Pelayo, the history syllabi portrayed Spanish history as the struggle of a spiritual collectivity—the patria—to achieve and maintain its unique identity and universal mission in the face of internal division and external hostility. The national drama was a saga of triumph, betrayal, and eventual redemption; its center of gravity lay in the centuries of imperial greatness, from the "formation of one Spain" under the Catholic Kings through the valiant defense of Catholic orthodoxy by Philip II. The exclusive subject of study during the last two courses was the history and significance of Spanish imperialism in its spiritual and territorial dimensions. The syllabi attributed the political and cultural achievements of the patria to quintessential embodiments of the racial virtues like the Cid, Cardinal Cisneros, and the duke of Alba. They likewise attributed the decline from imperial glory to treacherous, heretical, or misguided Spaniards like the pious but irresponsible monarchs of the seventeenth century, the treasonous afrancesados of the eighteenth, and the "ambitious and brazen pseudo-intellectuals" of the twentieth. In contrast, they reduced the historical agency of the Spanish pueblo to that of spectator and repository of the national virtues betrayed by antipatriotic elites.

The cuestionarios grew longer and more prescriptive with each year of the curriculum. In addition to covering international diplomacy, the

---

[41] The seven-year history curriculum was structured as follows:
1° Geography and History of Spain
2° Amplification of Geography and History of Spain
3° Notions of World Geography and History
4° Amplification of World Geography and History of Culture
5° Amplification of History and Geography of Spain
6° History of the Spanish Empire. Its historic content. Formation. Institutions
7° History and significance of the Spanish Empire. Value of Hispanidad.

The cuestionarios for these courses were published in an O of 14 April 1939 (*BOE* 4, suppl. to no. 128 (8 May 1939): 17–25.

task of the two-year sequence on universal history and culture was to contrast the "moral purity of the Spanish nationality" with the "selfishness," "dissolvent rationalism," and "hypocritical puritanism" of the European nations and to compare their "materialism and anti-human demoralization " with the "national, spiritual, historical significance" of fascism, which "respects the dignity of the human person."[42] This course was to conclude with "the United States, the inferior materialist meaning of North American civilization, the lack of seriousness and moral unity, financial immorality, its unjust aggression against Spain and the Hispanoamerican countries . . . the materialization of Europe as a consequence of rationalism and the Reformation . . . the need for a basic renovation of European civilization, now at a dead end, and Spain and its exemplary mission."

In the fifth year the syllabus subtly shifted the emphasis from history as celebration to history as cautionary tale. Appropriately, the subject was Spain in the nineteenth and twentieth centuries. The domestic conflicts of the recent past could no longer be swept under the rug, as they had been during the Restoration, because the aim of the dictatorship was not transaction, but total victory. In order to inoculate students against the antinational heresies of the contemporary age, the cuestionario devoted considerable attention to the "liberal errors" of the parliamentary monarchy and to the two "disastrous" experiments with republicanism, especially the "anti-Catholic, antimilitarist, and anti-Spanish" Second Republic, which had delivered Spain to the "Judeo-Masonic international conspiracy, the socialist International, and the Comintern."[43]

Other subjects in the curriculum were similarly politicized in the official cuestionarios. Teachers of literature, for example, were cautioned "to flee from authors who may have literary merit, but who are dangerous for the moral formation and integrity of the Catholic Faith of the students." (Particularly problematic was Benito Pérez Galdós, whose notorious anticlericalism was difficult to reconcile with the obvious "*españolismo*" of the *Episodios nacionales*.)[44] In the scientific disciplines, theories incompatible with Catholic doctrine were ignored; as one Catholic educator remarked at a congress in 1947, "physical causalities are not sufficient to orient man in a world of moral causalities."[45] In philosophy Thomist scholasticism enjoyed a monopoly, and in all

---

[42] "Moral purity . . . Puritanism," in third year syllabus; "Communism . . . human person," in fourth year syllabus, ibid.

[43] Ibid., fifth year syllabus.

[44] Ibid. See also the discussion in Valls, *Enseñanza de la literatura*, 160–61.

[45] Consejo Superior de Investigaciones Científicas, Instituto San José de Calasanz, *Cuestiones de enseñanza media* (Madrid: C. Bermejo Impresor, 1947), 26.

fields the contributions of Spaniards to each field of knowledge, no matter how trivial, took precedence over those of foreigners, no matter how eminent.

To guarantee that the values prescribed by the cuestionarios were actually transmitted to students, the regime also monitored textbooks. As immutable distillations of received wisdom, textbooks embodied the authoritarianism of the new regime, which labeled them "a necessary instrument of work" in the decree appointing an ad hoc textbook review committee in July 1938. But the decree stopped well short of the texto único championed by the Falange; instead, it acknowledged the value of "an effective, though restricted liberty" that guaranteed "a level of pedagogic, scientific and political quality that responds to the ideals of the New State."[46] This formula was expected to protect church autonomy and publishing interests while equipping the state to impose conformity on the corps of catedráticos.

In practice, textbook censorship proved to be more effective in eliminating heterodoxy than in creating a uniform outlook and tone among approved texts. Composed of nine distinguished and politically orthodox university catedráticos, the committee vetted existing textbooks for religious and patriotic orthodoxy, scientific accuracy, presentation, stylistic felicity, length, and price.[47] History textbooks were evaluated by Juan Contreras y López de Ayala, marqués de Lozoya, a poet and professor of history and art history at the University of Valencia. Since the corps of instituto catedráticos had been purged of republican sympathizers at the end of the war,[48] it is perhaps not surprising that only a handful of the textbooks submitted to the committee for review were judged to be irredeemably impregnated with values incompatible with the National Movement. In one instance, Contreras rejected a text by Antonio Bermejo de la Rica, a long-time catedrático in Ávila and currently a Falangist provincial chief, for failing to exalt the Inquisition, Cardenal Cisneros, Charles V, and Philip II or to insist on the "unpopularity and antitraditionalism" of the Cortes of Cádiz. In another case, he disapproved the widely used geography texts by Joaquín Izquierdo Croselles, in spite of what he called their "extraordinary merit," be-

[46] O of 7 July 1938 in *BOE* 3, no. 12 (12 July 1938): 173–74.

[47] The records of the Comisión Dictaminadora de Libros de Texto de Segunda Enseñanza (1938–41): Geografía y Historia are in AGMEC, caja 7005 and 7008, leg. 9839 and 9840. Members of the Comisión included Juan Contreras, the marqués de Lozoya, for history and geography; José Pemartín, foreign languages; Francisco Cantera, Latin; Eloy Montero, law and political economy; and Joaquín Entrambasaguas, Spanish literature and language.

[48] According to Díaz, *Pensamiento español*, 20, there were 118 university professors, 200 secondary school professors, and 2,000 maestros in exile at the end of the war.

cause of liberal and "positivistic" tendencies that might prove "dangerous" for secondary students. Contreras also rejected the texts of the long-resident catedrático in León, Vicente Serrano Puente, for mentioning Blasco Ibañez and the Declaration of the Rights of Man. (More seriously, Serrano Puente was himself denounced to the local "purge commission" for his irregularity and unpunctuality in attending class and his frequent changes of textbook. Undeterred, Serrano survived the investigation and went on to publish new, politically correct versions of his old texts.)[49]

On the other hand, some books commended for their "perfect orthodoxy" were disapproved on scientific or pedagogical grounds. Contreras rejected nearly all of the eighteen textbooks submitted by Juan Fernández Amador de los Ríos, the seventy-year-old professor at the Zaragoza instituto, whose books had been prohibited on scholarly grounds during the Republic. At that time, the Catholic right had hastened to declare him a martyr to republican "sectarianism"; six years later, however, Contreras decided that the author's strident nationalism and Catholicism could not sufficiently compensate for the absence of critical judgment, "the picturesque and even grotesque details and the impassioned opinions," the organizational incoherence, and the garbled prose. "It is lamentable," Contreras concluded, "that Spanish students have been obligated to study such things." The committee also disapproved such long-standing pillars of Catholic education as the outdated manuals by the Jesuit Ramón Ruiz Amado and the primers published by the LaSallean editorial house, Bruño. Whereas the former were merely incompatible with the "pedagogical guidelines" of the new regime, the latter were "written by someone who . . . knows nothing about the subject."[50]

But these were the exceptions. Most existing textbooks were approved pending very minor revisions. Several authors were asked to redraw maps to reflect "recent changes" in the boundaries of the European states—references, presumably, to the Anschluss—and one or two overzealous patriots had to be told to remove demands for the annexation of Portugal from their books. But most texts passed muster if the committee found "nothing opposed to the principles of the National Movement"—hardly a ringing endorsement, but a true reflection of the bachillerato history texts, whose basic conservatism and narrative anemia had scarcely been touched by the political and educational progressivism of the Republic.

[49] On Serrano Puente, see Wenceslao Álvarez Oblanca, *La represión de postguerra en León: Depuración de la enseñanza, 1936–1943* (León: Santiago García 1986), 35–40.
[50] Comisión Dictaminadora, AGMEC, leg. 9840.

As a result of this initial review, the more egregiously defective history textbooks were finally banished, and the style and accuracy of others were modestly improved. For the most part, however, Contreras approved books whose scholarly and/or pedagogical merits he frankly acknowledged to be thin.[51] In fact, Contreras seemed to accept mediocrity as circumstantially unavoidable—if not, indeed, traditional. The list of approved history books ultimately contained 50 titles—most of them only superficially restructured and edited to avoid a major ideological offense.[52]

By 1941, cuestionarios for the bachillerato were written, catedráticos had been ideologically fortified by attendance at patriotic "professional orientation" courses, and the vacancies created by the purges had been filled, making it safe to disband the review committee and transfer its censorship duties to the Council of National Education.[53] Gradually, enterprising catedráticos began to write new textbooks conforming to the cuestionarios—although not in the numbers that had prevailed when their control of the annual examinations had guaranteed a captive market for their product. But there was little to distinguish the new texts, stylistically or substantively, from the encyclopedic, positivistic manuals long criticized by both left and right. In part this was owing to the conventionality of the cuestionarios themselves, which despite their ideological overlay were otherwise traditional in their chronological coverage of political and military history. Even more responsible was the institutional inertia that had insulated classroom culture in Spain from change for decades.

Although lacking the autonomy and prestige of their predecessors, instituto professors still viewed themselves as scholars, not teachers, and they were thus largely indifferent to directives that they make their teaching and textbooks more "formative." The explicit university orientation of the degree encouraged them to display their erudition, even though the cyclical structure and overt politicization of the curriculum

[51] For example, a third-year text by the Jesuit educator Enrique Herrera Oria, *Nociones de historia de España*, 2d ed. (Burgos: Ediciones Antisectarias, 1938), received grudging approval despite reservations about its "excessive simplification." Herrera Oria, an advocate of "active pedagogy," considered this a virtue, not a vice.

[52] Lists were published on 21 October, 4 November, and 29 December 1938; 23 January, 14 March, 27 October, 4, 8, and 9 November, 18 and 30 December 1939; 15 October 1940; and 24 and 28 January 1941 by the Comisión Dictaminadora. José Vázquez Riesco, *Bachillerato: Guía del alumno para el año académico 1939–40* (Madrid: Lib. de Enrique Prieto, 1940), 57–59, contains a list of the books approved for the academic year.

[53] O of 28 December 1939 prescribed the short courses; a law of 26 January 1940 set aside 80 percent of teaching positions in the institutos for excombatants, war orphans, and other politically privileged groups. Oposiciones were announced on 5 September 1940. The Comisión Dictaminadora was dissolved on 9 May 1941.

seemed to demand a more child-centered, affective approach. Further-more, the reform of 1938 did not alter the credentialist function of the bachillerato. Ministerial rhetoric about an end to "memorism" notwith-standing, student success was still measured by a state examination, and textbooks and teaching methods accordingly remained structured with that end in view. Indeed, during the 1940s memorization became more important than ever, since award of the degree depended on a single examination at the end of a seven-year course of study. Not surprisingly, the global failure rate was around 60 percent throughout the 1940s (even higher for students studying independently), and familiar complaints were soon heard about the length of the cuestionarios and textbooks.[54]

Because of the cuestionarios, the textbooks approved during the 1940s and 1950s were similar in organization, content, and style. Nevertheless, censorship could not entirely eliminate modest but noticeable variations in coverage, tone, and interpretation. Among those written by instituto catedráticos, only a handful exhibited the fervent militancy that characterized the official discourse of the regime. One author who did was Rafael Montilla y Benítez, catedrático at the Granada institute, who sacrificed scholarship to pursue catechization in integrist values. While tracing the development of the "One, Great, and Free" Spain, Montilla uncritically reported the miraculous intercession of the apostles and saints during the Reconquest and detected the "omnipotent hand of Divine Providence" in the development of the historical mission of the patria.[55] A few other catedráticos managed to convey a point of view without sacrificing either scholarship or sensitivity to their audience. Most notable were two professors from Barcelona: Santiago Sobrequés Vidal, whose sympathy for regionalism and liberalism subtly shaped his narrative, and José Asián Peña, who combined brevity, simple language, excellent maps, supplementary readings, restrained but persistent Catholic moralizing, and accurate scholarship in books that were probably as pleasing to children as they were broadly acceptable to the (admittedly narrow) range of political opinion in Franquist Spain.[56]

---

[54] Alfonso Guiraum Martín, "Algunas consideraciones en torno a los exámenes de grado," *Enseñanza Media* 15, no. 17 (March 1958): 146–51; García Hoz, *Educación*, 65–66. An order of 5 March 1940 initiated the process of reducing the cuestionarios.

[55] Rafael Montilla y Benítez, *Nociones de geografía e historia. Primer curso de bachillerato* (Granada: Imprenta Editorial Urania, 1938) and *Nociones de geografía e historia. Segundo curso de bachillerato*, 2d ed. (Granada: Imprenta Editorial Urania, 1939).

[56] Salvador Llobet and Antonio Pla, *Hesperia: Curso de geografía*; and Santiago Sobrequés Vidal, *Hispania: Curso de historia* (Barcelona: Ediciones Teide, 1944) (2 bks. in 1 vol.); José Luis Asián Peña, *Elementos de geografía general e historia de España. Primer curso de bachillerato*, 2d ed. (Barcelona: Bosch, 1940).

Most catedráticos, however, opted for the relative neutrality of the traditional positivistic narrative. Sparsely illustrated and cheaply produced, they were usually detached in tone, more or less critical of legend and traditional belief, and reluctant to moralize or celebrate. An order from Ibáñez Martín in 1942 deploring the lack of attention to the "incalculable merits" of Spanish science in most textbooks suggests the degree to which their authors had failed to respond to the triumphalist intent of the ministry.[57] Conformity to the new cuestionarios was necessarily approximate in the case of professors who merely refurbished textbooks written years earlier; in the case of books originally written to comply with republican cuestionarios, for example, pre-history, medieval civilizations, and the history of art received far more attention, and the Habsburg centuries far less, than was mandated in the 1941 syllabi.[58] Although all authors repeated the judgments and phrases prescribed by the cuestionarios, in many cases these were reproduced with little conviction or elaboration. On occasion, they were printed in small type, as if to distinguish "interpretation" from "fact."[59] For that matter, many of these prescribed conclusions differed little from the conventional platitudes of nineteenth-century Moderado textbooks: allusions to the national character, neglect of regions other than Castile, references to Columbus's voyage as the "most transcendent event that history has known," and emphasis on national unity had characterized Spanish textbooks for decades.

In their chapters on contemporary history, however, the instituto professors matched the apocalyptic tone of the official cuestionarios. Even the most relentlessly positivistic authors unleashed a torrent of abuse against liberalism, socialism, and the two republican experiments of 1873 and 1931. The image of liberalism that emerged was one of partisan squabbling and endemic anticlericalism, while the generally brief sections on the Second Republic mentioned only convent burnings, disorder, social conflict, separatism, and "communism."[60] Despite the

[57] O of 17 August 1942, in *BOE* 7, no. 237 (25 August 1942): 6452.

[58] The many books published through several changes of regime and curriculum by Fernando Arranz Velarde, catedrático in Santander, and Vicente Serrano Puente, in León, are almost indistinguishable from one another.

[59] See, in addition to the textbooks already cited, Ramón Castro Álava, *Geografía e historia. Primer curso de bachillerato* (Zaragoza: Librería General, 1945); and *Geografía e historia. 5° curso de bachillerato*, 3d ed. (Zaragoza: Librería General, 1940); Ciriaco Pérez Bustamante, *Síntesis de historia de España*, 8th ed., rev. (Madrid: Ediciones Atlas, 1959) (1st ed. 1939); Santiago Andrés Zapatero, *El imperio español: (Historia y geografía)* (Barcelona: Editorial Delta, 1942); Antonio Bermejo de la Rica, *La España imperial*, 8th ed. (Madrid: Gráfica Administrativa, 1952) (1st ed. 1942); Cristóbal Pellejero Soteras, *Geografía e historia. Segundo curso*, 2d. ed. (Madrid: Imprenta Helénica, 1940).

[60] See José Antonio Álvarez Osés, et al., "La historia en los textos de bachillerato

proximity and profundity of the tragedy of the civil war, Spanish youth were denied knowledge about the historical circumstances that had produced it. Measured in terms of emotional power, however, the "formative" value of these history texts lay precisely in the few pages assigned to contemporary history. Their lesson was clear and unmistakable: modern political forms were not merely deviations from the historical trajectory of the nation, but absolutely incompatible with its very identity.

The bachillerato textbooks used in Catholic colegios showed similar variations in form and function, but they were more consistently informed by integrist Catholic values. Some, like those published for the Piarist schools, settled for strict fidelity to the published syllabus with no concern for the "formative" qualities of the narrative. In contrast, the textbooks and readers for younger students by the Jesuit educator Enrique Herrera Oria, like those published by the Marianistas, were written without regard for the cuestionarios.[61] Instead of fact-driven narrative, they offered a mélange of vivid anecdotes, religious and patriotic poetry, maps, dramatic or sentimental illustrations, and extracts from the works of Menéndez y Pelayo, Maeztu, and other National Catholic luminaries. The result was a vision of national history in which past and present were partners within a single, seamless tradition.

In textbooks for the upper grades, however, the imminence of the final state exam set limits on experimentation with content and methodology. Most authors tried to combine accurate chronological narration with an insistence on the "parallelism or conjunction of the Catholic spirit and our history" but usually lacked the skills to breathe life and vigor into the straitjacket imposed by the cuestionarios. An exception was Feliciano Cereceda, professor at the Jesuit Colegio del Apóstol Santiago in Vigo. In his textbooks, events, movements, and institutions were not only fully described but also evaluated against the implacable standard of traditional Spanish values. Lavish in his use of adjectives, unwavering in his judgments (which echoed those of Menéndez y Pelayo), and thorough in his historical analyses, Cereceda presented a parade of monarchs, statesmen, artists, and philosophers whose virtues had taken Spain to great heights and whose errors had brought her to

---

(1938–1975). Proyecto de investigación y análisis de un tema: La Segunda República," *Revista de Bachillerato* 2, no. 9 (January–March 1978): 2–18.

[61] Textos E.P., *Historia de España. Segundo curso* (Madrid: Bibliografía Española, n.d.); S.M. [Antonio Martínez], *Manual de historia de España y lecturas históricas*, 3d ed. (Burgos: Hijos de Santiago Rodríguez, [1948?]); S. M., *Madre España: Libro de lectura. Grado medio y superior*, 4th ed. (Burgos: Hijos de Santiago Rodríguez, 1948); Herrera Oria, *Nociones de historia*, and *España es mi madre: Libro de lectura* (Valladolid: Imprenta Católica, 1939).

ruin. However schematized and Manichaean his system of values, his texts nevertheless engaged the reader to an extent infrequently realized in typical textbooks. History here acquired its full "formative" value as a repository of lessons about national identity and purpose without completely disregarding the obligations of historical scholarship.[62]

One way to illustrate the range of ideological saturation among bachillerato textbooks of the 1940s is to compare three textbooks written for the sixth year course on the Spanish empire. *La España imperial*, by the Santander catedrático Fernando Arranz Velarde, was merely a reedition of a textbook on modern Spanish history that he had written to comply with the republican cuestionarios of 1934. Like all his books, it was a short descriptive narrative devoid of "imperialistic" theorizing or National Catholic rhetoric.[63] Somewhat more interpretative in its approach was a text written specifically for the 1938 curriculum by Antonio Bermejo de la Rica, a Falangist catedrático in Ávila during the war and, later, in Madrid. Bermejo began with a theoretical discussion of empire, which he defined as "authority, power, sovereignty, concentration of force capable of imposing itself and expanding." An imperial people, he affirmed, "launches itself to carry its spirit and its dominion to other countries which it unites in its orbit."[64] After this bravura opening, however, Bermejo lapsed into a conventional political narrative of Spanish territorial expansion and collapse in Europe and America. Perhaps because the author was a chastened victim of the censor,[65] he kept editorializing to a minimum. Nevertheless, his argument that imperial decline could be traced to neglect of economic productivity was an implied rebuke to the antimodern ethos of the Catholic right.

Most emphatically interpretative was Feliciano Cereceda, who abandoned the conventions of bachillerato textbooks altogether in order to offer a systematic gloss on Ramiro de Maeztu's *Defensa de la hispanidad*.[66] In Cereceda's view, Spanish imperialism was "not characterized so much by the extent and power of its dominions as by the spirit that sustained it;"[67] accordingly, he scanted geopolitics in favor of religious

[62] Feliciano Cereceda, *Historia y geografía de España: (Acomodadas al cuestionario oficial señalado para quinto curso de bachillerato)* (Madrid: Ediciones FAX, 1941); *Historia del imperio español y de la hispanidad*, 2d ed. (Madrid: Razón y Fé, 1943).

[63] Fernando Arranz Velarde, *La España imperial (Siglos XV–XVIII)*, 3d ed., rev. (Madrid: Imprenta Góngora, 1951) (1st ed. 1938).

[64] Antonio Bermejo de la Rica, *La España imperial*, 8th ed. (Madrid: Gráfica Administrativa, 1952) (1st ed. 1942), 7.

[65] See the earlier discussion of textbook censorship.

[66] Feliciano Cereceda, *Historia del imperio español y de la hispanidad*, 2d ed. (Madrid: Razón y Fé, 1943). See the review by Enrique Herrera Oria in *Atenas*, 12, no. 107 (January 1941): 31.

[67] Cereceda, *Historia del imperio*, 8.

and cultural themes. His book traced Spain's vigorous defense of the true faith against foreign heresy, materialism, and atheism until her corrosion from within by these same forces. The triumphalist tenor of his essay reached a climax in its concluding paeans to the glorious past whose recovery now pointed to an equally glorious future:

> The future of Spain united, after three centuries, to the destiny of the past! Because our current desires coincide with past realities, we proclaim the historical continuity of today's imperialism with that which filled the glorious days of Philip II. . . . The ancient procession has not ceased; on the contrary it is once again in full flood. Along its path advance the dead and the living. As banners they carry the national glories, laden with universalism, bursting with Christianity, in which a world disoriented and in catastrophic convulsions centers and anchors itself. . . . This is the grand task that God has saved for the Spain of today . . . An exceptional destiny, but of immense responsibility, labor, specialization, firm thought and dense ideas, that subjugates minds and gives us souls docile to our voice and obedient to the watchword of command: Through the Empire, to God!![68]

The essential message in this text was the isomorphism of the past and the present: "Our past waits for us to create the future. The future we had lost we have found again in the past."[69] This negation of three centuries of history was counterrevolution with a vengeance; indeed, Cereceda made the socioeconomic implications of his conclusions explicit in arguing that the return to traditional ideals would "transfer man to the infinite horizons necessary in order to resign himself to the limitations of daily life."[70] Divine law transcended history, as Spaniards had once again come to recognize; disillusioned by the vanities of modernity, the rest of the world would now look to Spain for the true meaning of "civilization."

The disparities in values, tone, and structure among the textbooks assigned in institutos and colegios suggest one explanation for the paradox that has confronted historians—and survivors—of Franquist education in the 1940s. Given its high degree of centralization and professed commitment to political socialization, why did the regime fail to create a generation of impassioned standard bearers for National Catholicism? It is clear that the state review process did not guarantee uniform or effective implementation of the regime's educational objectives; censorship was exercised in primarily negative ways, to eliminate unorthodox views without necessarily insisting on ideological fervor or

[68] Ibid., 273–74.
[69] Ibid., 272.
[70] Ibid., 268.

pedagogical efficacy. More to the point, the essence of Franquist National Catholicism was negative—its real purpose was not to inspire a new Spain, but to legitimate the old one. As wartime vigilance and Falangist dynamism receded, the credentialist function and memoristic conventions of the Spanish bachillerato reasserted themselves. The stirring slogans, rituals, and chants of National Catholic discourse were mindlessly repeated, taken seriously by no one, and implicitly undermined by indifference, skepticism, or ridicule.[71]

In fact, what the right seemed to want from education was fundamentally contradictory: the effective mobilization of youth behind the banner of National Catholicism in combination with the passive conformity that derived from rote learning. The complaint of the director of the instituto in Ciudad Real that history education was failing to achieve its only real purpose—"the formation of a specific maturity or mental agility that enables the student to understand for himself the life and political and cultural actions of men"—was justified only if the Spanish state were interested in encouraging independent thought and civic participation.[72] After the regime stabilized, however, it asked no more of the bachillerato than what Spanish elites had always asked— that it adequately perform its social function of sorting and preparing Spanish youth for their roles in an agrarian, authoritarian society. Under these conditions, mobilization of the nation's youth was neither necessary nor desirable.

Another explanation for the paradox must lie in the contradictions of the official ideology itself. As portrayed through the history curriculum at all levels of the school system, National Catholic Spain was a nation of heroes whose imperial past had bequeathed them a legacy of spirituality, martial vigor, and universal exemplarity. But everyday life in the actual Spain of the 1940s was the reverse image of this uplifting vision. Poor, stagnant, and internationally ostracized, it bore little resemblance to the triumphant hegemon of political rhetoric. Of its privileged youth it asked only conformity, superficial piety, and silence, not heroism; the more sensitive could not help noticing the gap between the "empty

[71] Testimony corroborating this view may be found in Rafael Abella, *Por el imperio hacia Dios: Crónica de una posguerra (1939–1955)* (Barcelona: Editorial Planeta, 1978); Carlos Barral, *Años de penitencia* (Madrid: Alianza Editorial, 1975); and Domínguez Martín-Sánchez, *Enseñanza católica*. See also the memoirs in *CP*, suppl. 3 (September 1976): 45–49.

[72] José María Martínez Val, *La finalidad de la historia en la enseñanza media: Comunicación presentada en el Congreso Internacional de Pedagogía, Santander-San Sebastián, julio de 1949* (Ciudad Real: Publicaciones del Instituto de Estudios Manchegos, 1949), 14. See also Delegación de Distrito de Educación Nacional de Zaragoza, *La enseñanza media: Nuestra visión sobre el problema* (Zaragoza: Departamento de Publicaciones, 1947).

phrases" and the mediocre "reality of a country losing its ideological and spiritual values."[73] To be an effective explanation of the world, an ideology must bear some resemblance to the reality of those asked to subscribe to it, and if it is based on a particular reading of the past, that history must be linked in some plausible way to the problems and concerns of the present and future. Measured against this standard, National Catholicism was a dismal failure. That failure in turn limited the ability of the state to impose its ideology, despite its monopoly over the agencies of cultural transmission.

A triumphalist version of the national past also provided the substance for ideological reconstruction in the primary schools, although here the gap between the invocations of empire and the misery and limited horizons of the working-class children in the public schools was even wider.[74] After the experience of revolution and civil war, it was clear to the Catholic right that the passive docility of the uneducated could no longer be taken for granted. Furthermore, the Falange's ambition to become a mass party made it an active rival in the arena of primary education. Thus, Catholics now acknowledged the value of primary education as an instrument of "nationalization" and moved quickly to provide ideological orientation to the primary schools in the Nationalist zone.[75] On 19 August 1936 the Junta of National Defense ordered the opening of Spanish schools on schedule in order to begin "the Hispanization of the youth of the future," and charged town mayors with the responsibility for monitoring classroom activities for signs of "weakness or orientation opposed to the heathy and patriotic attitude of the Army and the Spanish people."[76] As a first step, coeducation was abolished and religion and sacred history were made obligatory in primary and secondary schools, as well as in normal schools.[77] This was followed by a purge of school libraries and teaching personnel to remove "the poisoners of the popular soul."[78] Over the next two years the purge was extended to public libraries, private school teachers, and normal school students. By the end of the war up to 30 percent of the teaching corps

[73] Abella, *Por el imperio*, 158. On the irrealism of the heroic ideal, see also Francisco Umbral, *Memorias de un niño de derechas* (Barcelona: Ediciones Destino, 1972), 128–29; and Domínguez Martín-Sánchez, *Enseñanza católica*, 31.

[74] Umbral, *Memorias*, 50–51; Rafael Abella, *La vida cotidiana en España bajo el régimen de Franco* (Barcelona: Argos Vergara, 1985).

[75] See Mailló, *Educación y revolución*, for a statement of Falangist educational aspirations; see Pemartín Sanjuán, *¿Qué es 'lo nuevo'?* 184–87, for the Catholic case for a central educational role in a "Catholic Fascist Spain."

[76] O of 19 August 1936.

[77] O of 4, 21, and 22 September and 10 November 1936.

[78] O 13 of 4 September 1936; D 66 of 8 November 1936; C of 7 December 1936.

had been dismissed, transferred, or demoted.[79] In Catalonia, where many teachers were sympathetic to both Catalanism and the left, the purge was especially rigorous. Schools belonging to the Generalitat and the municipality of Barcelona either were closed or reverted to the state.[80] Catalan language and culture disappeared from the schools, along with a large number of progressive maestros. Among them was the revered head of the municipal laboratory school in Barcelona, Félix Martí Alpera, who was accused of "leftist tendencies," "separatism," and "bragging, if not about being a declared atheist and Mason, about his regard for Rotarians and Quaker Friends, [and of] praising their philanthropy and Protestant spirit as superior to that of Catholics."[81]

The main target of the repression was of course the Institución Libre de Enseñanza, whose doctrines had allegedly molded the "incredulous and anarchic generations" and "revolutionary hordes" of the Popular Front.[82] What was new was not the litany of charges—of naturalism, atheism, materialism, and antipatriotism—but rather the virulence of the attack. For the Catholic right, the Institución was a tangible symbol of the modernizing forces that had challenged their world; accordingly, it became the scapegoat in their campaign to eradicate the conspiracy of foreigners, Masons, Jews, and "pseudo-intellectuals" bent on the destruction of the "true Spain." Invested with an infinite capacity for evil and an almost supernatural power to infect the body politic, the ILE was compared to an "ultravirus" whose deleterious effects were so pervasive that only the most strenuous "detoxification" would be successful against it.[83] Indeed, the stringent measures now required to eradicate the poison were the predictable result of a tragic lack of resolution in the past: "If the Inquisition had existed in the last half of the stupid nineteenth century and had given the handful of pretentious and pomp-

---

[79] D of 14 September and 7 October 1937; D of 14 March and 29 April 1937. See the discussion in Navarro Sandalinas, *Enseñanza primaria*, 66–76.

[80] O of 29 January 1939.

[81] Charges from the purge committee cited in Juan Benimeli, "Notas biográficas de D. Félix Martí Alpera," in Pedro Cuesta Escudero, ed., *Félix Martí Alpera (1875–1946): La seva contribució a l'escola pública. En motiu del seu homenatge* (Barcelona: GRAO, 1979), 35–36.

[82] C of 7 December 1936.

[83] The attacks on the ILE are too numerous to cite. Two of the most extended and vituperative are Enrique Suñer, *Los intelectuales y la tragedia española* (Burgos: Editorial Española, 1937); and [Miguel Artigas and Miguel Allué Salvador], *Una poderosa fuerza secreta: La Institución Libre de Enseñanza* (San Sebastián: Editorial Española, 1940), where the "ultravirus" metaphor appears on p. 22. For a review of this literature, see Elías Díaz, "La Institución Libre de Enseñanza en la España del nacional-catolicismo," *Historia Internacional*, no. 16 (July 1976): 69–78; and Mariano Pérez Galán, "La Institución Libre de Enseñanza en los comienzos del franquismo," *CP* 2, no. 22 (1976): 17–19.

ous Krausists and the Institución Libre de Enseñanza what they deserve, . . . we surely would have avoided this terrible Spanish civil war, a true war of religion that has arrived three centuries late."[84]

A tenet of National Catholicism was that the pueblo was the un-sullied repository of traditional Spanish values that would flourish once liberated from alien influences. In practice, however, the Franquist re-gime put little trust in the spontaneous regeneration of tradition, prefer-ring instead to "Hispanize" Spaniards by main force. Starting in July 1937 with the organization of "formative" short courses for maestros who had survived the purge, the regime, especially in its early "fascistiz-ing" phase, endeavored to impose ideological uniformity by strictly pre-scribing curricular content and methods. At a short course in Pamplona, Sainz Rodríguez reminded maestros that the purpose of the Movement was "to revive Spanish national feeling." Revolutionary pedagogy had destroyed "the idea of the Patria as a moral entity in the consciousness of Spaniards"; the pedagogy of the New State would restore it by teach-ing Spaniards to cherish their past and to strive to be worthy of it.[85]

New syllabi for the history curriculum in the primary grades were organized under the dual mottos of "Spain One, Great and Free" and "Hispanidad." Beginning with simple biographies and legends for young children, they culminated in the "imperialist Renaissance" of Primo de Rivera, José Antonio, and Franco.[86] In September 1937, the ministry announced a competition for a "Book of Spain" to "ensure that children in the future will definitively take the side of Spain." The opening phrase of the decree intoned that "the schools of the New Spain must be the ideal continuation of the trenches of today." Its in-structions to aspiring authors summarized succinctly the instrumental character assigned to history: "The history part [of the book] must at-tend especially to the simple and valiant refutation of those passages in our History that have been most tenaciously calumniated by the Black Legend. . . . It must accentuate the uninterrupted contribution of Spain to universal civilization, and preferably, the coincidence of these civiliz-ing efforts with the current Movement in which its history and grandeur is prolonged, and, as an alternative to absurd separatist tendencies, pro-pose the lofty idea of the union of all the regions within the great Span-ish Patria."[87]

---

[84] Pemartín Sanjuán, ¿Qué es 'lo nuevo'? 192–93.

[85] Sainz Rodríguez, "La escuela y el Nuevo Estado," in MEN, Curso de orientaciones 1:58.

[86] In Antonio Martínez García, S.M., "La metodología en la escuela primaria," in MEN, Curso de orientaciones 1:438–51.

[87] O of 21 September 1937. For an earlier conservative attempt to adopt a "Book of the Patria," see chap. 2.

The following spring, at Falangist urging, Sainz Rodríguez asked the newly created Institute of Spain (a cultural "senate" created by the fusion of the six scientific and literary academies) to write official textbooks for the schools.[88] When this drew an outcry from book publishers and Catholic groups, the minister withdrew his proposal, but warned that privately published books would have to be reviewed and approved by a ministerial committee to ensure the transmission of "that healthy doctrine, saturated with religious and patriotic spirit, that constitutes the essence of our National Movement."[89] In early 1939 the ministry ordered the renaming of primary schools to remove the names of those who had contributed to the "de-Christianization" of Spain or to the "gestation and development of the evil revolution."[90] The first school to be renamed was the Giner de los Ríos grade school in Madrid, which became the D. Andrés Manjón grade school on 20 April.

Despite this early interest in ideological cleansing, a new law defining the purpose and structure of primary education was not approved by the Cortes until April 1945. The delay measured not only the wartime strength of the Falange, which opposed concessions to the church, but also the lower priority assigned to popular education by the new regime. Low rates of schooling, and thus of literacy, confirmed the regime's lack of interest in primary education during the 1940s. School attendance was required only until a child reached age twelve. Official figures in 1949 revealed that 30 percent of school-age children lacked school places; without the substantial contribution of private schools, lay and religious, which educated 27 percent of the total enrollment nationwide, the situation would have been even more dire. Modest programs for school building did not even get underway until the early 1950s.[91]

According to the law of 1945, the principal objectives of primary education were "to form the will, conscience and character of the child toward the fulfillment of his duty and his eternal destiny" and "to infuse the spirit of the student with the love and the idea of service to the

---

[88] D of 11 April 1938. The Institute of Spain was created on 8 December 1937, the feast day of the Immaculate Conception. See *Las Reales Academias del Instituto de España* (Madrid: Alianza Editorial, 1992).

[89] O of 20 August 1938. See Alted Vigil, *Política del Nuevo Estado*, 220–24, for a discussion of this process. The Comisión Dictaminadora de los Libros de Texto dedicados a la Primera Enseñanza, appointed 29 August 1938, was composed of four instituto catedráticos: José María Albareda, José Oñate Guillén, José Ibáñez Martín, and José Rogerio Sánchez, all of them affiliated with the integrist right. The first list of approved books was signed on 1 March 1939.

[90] O of 20 April 1939.

[91] Ibáñez Martín, *Díez años*, 328–30; Navarro Sandalinas, *Enseñanza primaria*, 79–81, 143, 156–59.

Patria, in accordance with the inspiring principles of the Movement."
Cultivation of individual intelligence or development of practical skills
ranked farther down the list of objectives. Religion, Castilian language,
geography, and history were the primary vehicles for this educational
mission. Although a weekly class in "political formation" was entrusted
to the Movement, Ibáñez Martín emphasized that "the law is Catholic
. . . because our Regime is [Catholic]."[92]

The law laid particular stress on the maestro, an "apostle" whose
vocation and spirit of service to God and patria validated his claim to
"authentic aristocracy." Like their republican predecessors, Franquist
educators were sensitive to the central role of the teacher in the transmission of values; unlike the republicans, they were less concerned with
intellectual and professional competence than with ideological reliability.[93] The teacher training program outlined in the law of 1945 (but
not implemented until 1950) boasted of its high standards but actually
lowered them in comparison with the republican program of 1931. Admission to the new Escuelas del Magisterio required only four years of
secondary schooling; training was still primarily religious and patriotic;
and methods courses remained hostile to most twentieth-century techniques and theory.[94] Religious, political, and physical education comprised over a quarter of the prescribed course work. Abysmally low
salaries ensured that recruits to teaching were increasingly female and
drawn from those social groups with the least education and fewest
professional possibilities.[95]

The cuestionarios of 1938 ordered maestros to practice the "traditional Spanish pedagogy" of Luis Vives, San José de Calasanz, and Andrés Manjón, whose foundation was the "classic" system of repetition.
The reiteration of a limited number of received ideas was best suited for
primary education, according to the regime ideologue, José María Pemán: "Primary intelligences—children and the masses—are governed
by the law of 'minimum effort.' . . . The catechism or book of proverbs,

[92] MEN, Dirección General de Enseñanza Primaria, *Ley de Educación Primaria de 17 de julio de 1945: Textos legales* (Madrid, 1952).

[93] In 1940 Nationalist war veterans with a bachillerato were given teaching positions after completion of a small number of methods courses; in 1942 a new cadre of maestros began to receive training in the normal schools. Taking students as young as age twelve, the new course was little more than a watered-down three-year bachillerato followed by a year of training in "traditional Spanish pedagogy."

[94] See the two principal manuals: Enrique Herrera Oria, *Historia de la educación española desde el renacimiento* (Madrid: Ediciones Veritas, 1941); and Francisca Montilla Tirado, *Historia de la educación*, 5th ed. (Madrid: Graf. Andrés Martín, 1962).

[95] In 1948, salaries were 10 percent lower, in real terms, than in 1913. Women com-prised 73.4 percent of all normal school students in 1950. Navarro Sandalinas, *Enseñanza primaria*, 149, 165.

that speak in affirmations, are more believed than the philosophy professors who speak in arguments."[96] More precise methodological guidance was provided by Catholic professional journals like *Atenas*, *El Magisterio Español*, and its offshoot, *Escuela Española*.[97] Competition between the Falangist and the Catholic press was initially intense, but even in those journals nominally controlled by the Movement, like *Servicio* and *Consigna*, the Catholic outlook prevailed.[98] In these journals and in new pedagogical manuals, teachers were advised on how to apply the principles of "Spanish pedagogy" to the various disciplines in the curriculum, particularly ideologically charged subjects like history.

Despite their endless encomiums to Vives and Calasanz, Franquist educators did not really try to replicate the Catholic pedagogy of the sixteenth century, but instead tailored traditionalism to the political climate of the 1940s. While continuing to affirm the existence of original sin and the perils of unrestrained passion,[99] they defined education as not merely the *subjugation* of human passions and will, but also as their *redirection* into politically constructive channels. Harnessed in service to religion and patria by a pedagogy adapted to the national psyche, such "typically Spanish" characteristics as intuition, enthusiasm, willfulness, and idealism could regenerate the nation. National Catholic pedagogy aimed "to galvanize" the soul of the child; the rhetoric of pedagogical discourse in the 1940s was aflame with references to "warmth," "vibrancy," "sentiment," "will," "lyricism," "fervor," and even "madness." In contrast, the "alien," "cold," and "deadening" intellectualism of "rationalist pedagogy" was rejected as the creation of the methodical, scientific, but less idealistic races of northern Europe.[100] Although Germans and Britons might excel at mathematics and science, Spain's contribution to world civilization was its spiritual exemplarity.

Applied to the history curriculum, this methodology aimed to "achieve a strong and united national spirit" and to "install joy and pride in the

[96] Quoted in Alted Vigil, *Política del Nuevo Estado*, 182.

[97] See "¿Qué es 'El Magisterio Español?'" in Sastre, *El Magisterio Español*, 36–38.

[98] Influential pedagogical publications in the 1940s included the *Revista Nacional de Educación* (Ministerio de Educación Nacional); the *Revista de Educación Española* (FET y de las JONS); *Servicio* (Servicio Español del Magisterio, the official teachers' syndicate, controlled by the Movement); *Consigna* (Sección Femenina); and the *Revista Española de Pedagogía* (CSIC, Instituto San José de Calasanz).

[99] Sainz Rodríguez, "La escuela y el Nuevo Estado," in MEN, *Curso de orientaciones* 1:58.

[100] See, among many possible examples, Antonio J. Onieva, *La nueva escuela española: (Realización práctica)* (Valladolid: Librería Santarén, 1939); Valentín Aranda et al., *Hacia la escuela hispánica* (Madrid: Editorial Magisterio Español, 1936); or Josefina Álvarez de Cánovas, "Psicología del niño español," *Atenas* 13, no. 128 (December 1942): 227–38.

Patria in the soul of future generations."[101] History education was to be both therapeutic and prophylactic; but for this to occur, national history had to be internalized as an ineluctable legacy of instincts, behaviors, and obligations. To eradicate any lingering vestiges of the "declinist, defeatist, slanderous, or merely skeptical tendencies" allegedly inherited from the generation of '98 and the institucionistas,[102] every issue of the professional journals included uplifting vignettes from Spanish history, capsule biographies of pious monarchs, saints, and warriors, and essays on the national character, mission, and trajectory, all carefully chosen to exemplify the messianic and imperialist destiny of the patria: "to be great through the Faith in order that through the Faith, the other peoples of the globe might become great."[103] The point was not merely to reintroduce figures and epochs neglected or maligned by progressives, but to *virtualize* Spanish tradition, to instill in maestros a moral presentiment of Spanish genius and character, and to stimulate in them "a biological vibration" that they might subsequently transmit to their students by appealing to their innate sense of justice, their longing for heroism, their religiosity, idealism, and chivalry.[104] In encouraging identification with a series of Christian caballeros from the Cid and the *conquistadores* to Generalísimo Franco, teachers would hispanize their pupils, teaching them to "think in Spanish, feel in Spanish, desire in Spanish and act in Spanish."[105] From intimate knowledge would come love; as children loved and acknowledged the unconditional love of their mothers, so would they love "mother Spain" and share with her children on both sides of the Atlantic the fraternal bonds of hispanidad.[106] At the same time, children had to understand "the exact parallel be-

[101] MEN, *Ley de Educación Primaria de 17 de julio de 1945*, art. 6.

[102] Onieva, *Nueva escuela*, 184.

[103] Ibid., 185. For an example of the articles aimed at teachers, see Manuel Ballesteros Gaibrois, "Historia de España y doctrina del Movimiento," serialized in *Servicio* 1, nos. 1–28 (26 February through 3 September 1942), passim.

[104] For a typical example, see the biography of Philip II ("the most Spanish king of all") in *Servicio* 2, no. 65 (20 May 1943): 3. After describing Philip as the personification of the Spanish soul—"austere, intimate, cloistered soul, but also fugitive, generous, missionary soul, made to create and live the epic of the impossible"—the author urged maestros to teach about the imperial period so that "the new youth burns with the desire to be as in those days."

[105] Luis Igualada, "Hay que españolizar a los españoles," *Boletín de Educación de Zaragoza* 2, no. 7 (June-July 1937): 7–8.

[106] G. Ginés Grao, "España: Una, grande y libre," and José León Domínguez, "Símbolos ejemplares de nuestra raza: El Cid y el Conde Fernán González," *Atenas* 13, nos. 120–21 (April–May 1942): 100–105.

tween the development of Spanish nationality and the Catholic religion," in order to avoid the perils of statism or materialism.[107]

To engage hearts rather than minds, Catholic educators recommended a variety of techniques, some of them based on the memoristic "active methods" of Father Manjón, whose publications were again reedited and widely circulated. Mock battles between Romans and Carthaginians, Phoenicians and Greeks, and Reds and Nationalists persisted in both private and public schools. As a way of internalizing Spanish virtues, students memorized patriotic sayings and anecdotes drawn mainly from the imperial age.[108] One cynical survivor recalled that "Spaniards had memorable phrases for everything. After a battle, after a victory or a defeat, at the hour of death, Spaniards always had to spout a memorable phrase, as if they were in the theater, the Theater of History."[109] At the same time, children continued to memorize, as they had always done, the lists of Visigothic kings and martyred Spanish saints. Songs and choral responses ("Who are you? We are don Juan de Austria, we are the Duke of Alba, we are San Quentin, we are Lepanto, we are Spain")[110] were popular with the Falange, whose political socialization courses recapitulated the history of the imperial past in order to awaken the "vocation of Spain."[111] The Falange also invented a series of secular feast days commemorating important milestones in the history of the Movement:

12 October	Day of Hispanidad
29 October	Day of Faith (founding of the Falange)
20 November	Day of Sorrow (execution of José Antonio)
8 December	Mother's Day (Immaculate Conception)
9 February	Day of Fallen Youth (death of young Falangist Matías Montero)
1 April	Day of Song (end of civil war)
2 May	Independence Day

[107] José María Martínez Val, "La formación del sentido histórico en el niño," *REP* 3, no. 11 (July–September 1945): 177–210.

[108] See Antonio J. Onieva, *Frases célebres entresacadas de nuestra historia*, 3d ed. (Burgos: Hijos de Santiago Rodríguez, 1958) (1st ed. 1947).

[109] Umbral, *Memorias*, 50.

[110] Domínguez Martin-Sánchez, *Enseñanza católica*, 26–27.

[111] FET y de las JONS, *Formación del espíritu nacional*.

30 May	Day of Youth (St. Ferdinand, patron of the Youth Front)
18 July	Day of Courage (start of civil war)
4 August	Day of Gibraltar

The intent of this new calendar of holidays was not only to draw children and youth into ritual commemorations, but also to compete with the church in the arena of public festivals.[112]

Visual representations reinforced rote learning and dramatics. Suggested classroom activities for children often included copying the elaborate symbology of the regime (crosses, the yoke and arrows, the national coat of arms, etc.) and its slogans into a notebook. Graphics like that in plate 5 were not meant to aid children in conceptualizing historical time but to represent visually the regime's scheme of values.

Spain: One, Great, and Free, the dominant motto of the Franquist state, also summed up the tripartite periodization of Spanish history offered to primary students in textbooks, readers, and encyclopedias. In the first period (from the first settlers until the reign of the Catholic kings), Spaniards had gradually achieved religious, territorial, and political unity; in the second (the Habsburg centuries), unity had provided the conditions for imperial greatness; in the third (since the advent of the Bourbons), a community internally divided and demoralized by alien ideas had struggled to recapture its unity and freedom. Redeemed and restored to its true self by Franco's Crusade, Spain could now look forward to a new era of world leadership.[113]

The obvious appeal of textbooks to a government obsessed with ideological control, as well as to poorly trained teachers, made them the keystone of "traditional Spanish pedagogy."[114] Only books used in the public schools required state review and approval.[115] Primary schoolbooks ran the gamut from the most traditional, fact-driven compilations of "notions" to the most expressive and politicized evocations of epic figures and events. Unlike the texts written for the bachillerato by

[112] "Formación del Espíritu Nacional," in "Antonio Onieva and Federico Torres, *Enciclopedia Hernando: Segundo ciclo del período de enseñanza elemental. Niños* (Madrid: Lib. y Casa. Ed. Hernando, 1954).

[113] G. Ginés Grao, "España: Una, grande y libre," *Atenas* 13, no. 120–21 (April–May 1942): 101.

[114] See the defense of textbooks in Francisca Montilla Tirado, *Selección de libros escolares de lectura* (Madrid: Consejo Superior de Investigaciones Científicas, Instituto San José de Calasanz, 1954), 9–14.

[115] Primary school books were reviewed by an ad hoc ministerial review commission until 1941 and thereafter by the Council of National Education. O of 20 August 1938, 6 May 1940, and 8 May 1941.

Plate 5. "España: Una, Grande y Libre," blackboard illustration to ac-
company a lesson on Spanish history by G. Ginés Grao, in *Atenas* 13,
no. 120–21 (April–May 1942): 100–103. The high point of the Ancient
Age is the evangelization of the peninsula by Saint James, or Santiago
(symbolized by his cross and the pillar marking his encounter with the
Virgin Mary in Zaragoza). The religious and political unification of the
peninsula in the Middle Ages is symbolized by the cross of Reccared
and the yoke and arrows of the Catholic Kings. Columbus, Charles V,
and Philip II represent Spanish grandeur during the Modern Age. During the Contemporary Age, Spain is freed from two centuries of mis-
government and foreign oppression by the sword of General Franco.

instituto professors, they suffered from none of the tensions between scholarly methods and formative goals, uniformly sacrificing the former to the latter when ideological considerations required. Foremost was the need to inoculate the masses against the twin viruses of "separatism" and "communism" by defining these as alien to the Spanish tradition of religious and political unity. The cultural pluralism that progressives had praised as a source of national strength was now denied or condemned; accordingly, the Inquisition and the expulsion of Jews and *moriscos* were praised as prophylactic measures necessary to eliminate "crimes," disunion, and heresy. Even linguistic diversity was challenged; in one civics text, the peninsular languages (except for Basque) were demoted to the status of Castilian "dialects."[116] To discourage reflection on political and social issues, primary school books omitted most contemporary history altogether, leaping from the Carlist defense of "tradition" to the salvation of Spain from impiety and disorder by General Franco. Although the same distortions were also imbedded in many of the bachillerato textbooks, the disparities in the quality and quantity of historical information made a pointed statement about the class bias of Franquist schooling.[117]

If the ideological substratum of these textbooks was virtually uniform, their scope and style differed according to their authorship, date of publication, and intended audience. From the point of view of the architects of the new regime, the *Manual de historia de España*, published by the Instituto de España, represented the ideal narrative history.[118] Written by José María Pemán for upper primary students, it was

---

[116] Albino Menéndez-Reigada, *Catecismo patriótico español*, 3d ed. (Salamanca: Est. Tip. de Calatrava, 1939), 11–12.

[117] Among the primary grade manuals consulted for this study are Ediciones Bruño, *Historia de España. Segundo grado*, 7th ed. (Zaragoza: La Instrucción Popular, n.d.) (republished as *Tercer grado*, 12th ed. [Madrid: Editorial Bruño, 1949]); Cartillas Montana, *Historia de España* (Barcelona: Editorial Miguel A. Salvatella, [1940]); Edelvives, *Cartilla moderna de historia de España*, 5th ed. (Zaragoza: Editorial Luis Vives, 1939); *Historia de España. Primer grado*, 10th ed. (Zaragoza: Editorial Luis Vives, n.d.); *Historia de España. Segundo grado* (Zaragoza: Editorial Luis Vives, [1944]); and *Geografía e historia. Tercer curso* (Zaragoza: Editorial Luis Vives, 1951); Victoriano Fernández Ascarza, *Historia de España. Segundo grado* (Madrid: Magisterio Español, 1941); S.M. [Antonio Martínez], *Manual de historia de España*; Textos E.P., *Historia de España: Curso primero* (Madrid: Bibliografía Española, n.d.), and *Segundo curso*; Ricardo Ruiz Carnero, *Historia de España* (Madrid: Editorial Hernando, 1943); and María del Pilar Ibáñez de Opacua, *El libro de España* (Madrid: Publicaciones de la Institución Teresiana, 1941).

[118] Instituto de España [José María Pemán], *Manual de historia de España. Segundo grado* (Santander: Aldus, 1939), also published in a slightly longer and more attractive edition as José María Pemán, *La historia de España contada con sencillez para los niños . . . y para muchos que no lo son* (Cádiz: Est. Cerón, 1939). For a similar upper primary manual, written for girls, see Ibáñez de Opacua, *Libro de España*.

distinguished by the warmth of its tone, the prodigality of its moral judgments, and the accentuated teleology of its structure. To demonstrate that "all the best [in the] History of Spain comes together and is summed up in the Nationalist Zone," he alerted his readers to certain recurring themes: the providential emergence of caudillos in times of danger or disorder, the continuous struggle to repulse alien ideas and invaders, the national mission to universalize the true faith, the repeated treachery of bad Spaniards and foreigners. The line that divided the two Spains between 1936 and 1939 was the "eternal line of [Spanish] history: it was the frontier line against the invaders; it was the rigor of the Inquisition and the authority of Kings against heretics; it was the line of ships against the Turk at Lepanto: the day before yesterday it was the Carlist frontier; yesterday it was the prison bars around Sanjurjo."[119]

The aspirations of the new regime to inspire "a halo of emotion, a shuddering of heroism, a longing . . . for virtue"[120] among the young were even better realized in historical readers. In the early stages of the regime, Falangist imperial ambitions led to a new edition of *El muchacho español*, by José María Salaverría, and inspired works like *Glorias imperiales* by Luis Ortiz Muñoz, a history catedrático who served in a series of high-ranking positions in the Ministry of National Education in the 1940s.[121] Aimed at ten-to-twelve-year-old pupils and distributed at no charge to schools and colegios throughout the country, *Glorias imperiales* was the reader most often mentioned in an official survey of maestros, grade school directors, and school inspectors taken in the early 1950s.[122] Ortiz Muñoz's theme was the imperial vocation of Spain. The national story began with the spiritual and political conquest of Rome by the "Hispanic race" (represented by Seneca and the Roman emperors), the evangelization of Spain by Saint James, and the alliance of the Spanish caesar, Theodosius, with the Spanish pope, Saint Damasus. Led by the first "caudillo of Spain," don Pelayo, and later by "Castile, mother of Spain," Spaniards in the Middle Ages improvised a

---

[119] Instituto de España, *Manual*, 283. General José Sanjurjo had been imprisoned after an abortive coup against the Republic in August 1932. A leader of the conspiracy of 1936, he was killed in a plane crash in Portugal in the first days of the revolt.

[120] Agustín Serrano de Haro, *Yo soy español. El libro de primer grado de historia* (Madrid: Editorial Escuela Española, 1943), 6.

[121] Luis Ortiz Muñoz, *Glorias imperiales: Libro escolar de lecturas históricas*, 2 vols. (Madrid: Editorial Magisterio Español, 1940). Ortiz Muñoz, a member of both the ACN de P and the Falange, was successively general technical secretary, director general of secondary education, director general of university education in the ministry, and vicedirector of the Institute San José de Calasanz in the CSIC. There is a biography in the *Revista Nacional de Educación* 20 (August 1942): 80.

[122] Montilla Tirado, *Selección de libros*, 70–72. It should be noted that the ministry received only 773 responses to its questionnaire, which casts doubt on their typicality.

"religious militia" that saved Europe for Christianity. The first volume closed with the territorial unification of the peninsula after the conquest of Granada and looked ahead to the advent of the "greatest of the world Empires," whose triumphs formed the subject of the second volume.

The same yoking of imperial power to spiritual ends animated other readers, like *Escudo imperial*, by Antonio J. Onieva, *España es mi madre*, by Enrique Herrera Oria, and *Nuevas lecturas patrióticas*, by Antonio Fernández Rodríguez. Paraphrasing José Antonio, the founder of the Falange, Onieva reminded his readers that "to be Spaniards and Catholics is today one of the few elevated things on earth, if not the first."[123] Especially during and immediately after the war, Catholic schoolbooks took on a militant cast; a race of heroes and saints, Spaniards were destined to disciplined combat "because virility and manliness survive in deeds and not in lives, in exemplary undertakings and not in mealy-mouthed humanitarianism."[124] Not surprisingly, biography was a favored genre: "The history of a people is that of its outstanding figures, because they define the system, the path, and the norm. Everyone follows them."[125] Biographies of knightly warriors and conquerors illustrated that "with the sword one wins both heaven and empire."[126] Alongside the perennial favorites—the Cid, Gonzalo de Córdoba, Saint Ignatius, Hernán Cortés, and the Carlist general Zumalacárregui—appeared the heroes of the second "Reconquest"—especially General Moscardó, who, like Guzmán el Bueno before him, had sacrificed his son in defense of the patria, and of course, General Franco, the latest and most providential of a long line of military caudillos, saviors of the race. Only a handful of those typically portrayed were women—queens, saints, and those courageous female warriors María Pita and Agustina de Aragón—an intentional oversight that was remedied by separate biographical collections for girls that illustrated such feminine attributes as piety, modesty, and determination.[127]

Heroism, virility, and militancy, however, could be double-edged vir-

---

[123] Antonio J. Onieva, *Escudo imperial: Libro escolar de lectura* (Burgos: Hijos de Santiago Rodríguez, 1937), 4.

[124] Antonio Fernández Rodríguez, *Nuevas lecturas patrióticas*, 3d ed. (Zaragoza: Librería La Educación, 1937), 88.

[125] Antonio J. Onieva, *Cien figuras españolas: (Biografías de figuras célebres). Libro escolar de lecturas*, 1st ser., 16th ed. (Burgos: Hijos de Santiago Rodríguez, 1962) (1st ed. 1954), 6.

[126] Ibid., 104.

[127] Onieva, *Cien figuras*, was a popular biographical collection. See also his *Florilegio de mujeres españolas: (Biografías de españolas célebres). Libro escolar de lectura*, 3d ed. (Burgos: Hijos de Santiago Rodríguez, 1958) (1st ed. 1953). For a list of other biographical collections, see Valls, *Enseñanza de la literatura*, 65–66 n. 137.

tues. However useful in defining the national character in opposition to non-Catholics, bad Spaniards, and foreign critics, they posed a potential domestic threat to a regime dedicated to restoring traditional social relations and "order." Furthermore, war was a luxury the regime could not afford. Thus, the religious militancy that saturated some of the early readers was often tempered in primary-level civics texts by equating patriotism in the "totalitarian Christian State" with respect for values of brotherhood, hierarchy, and service.[128] In *Así quiero ser: (El niño del nuevo estado)*, Antonio J. Onieva, a school inspector whose youthful connections to the institucionistas placed him temporarily under suspicion during the postwar purges,[129] stressed the Spaniard's duty to serve, obey, and work: "He who obeys never makes a mistake." Onieva's resurrected the traditionalist interpretation of Spanish history as a struggle for independence from foreign influence, rather than as an epic of militant expansion. His definition of empire was accordingly directed inward: empire was "absolute and indivisible power over the people who are governed"; the "Caudillo is responsible only to God and History."[130]

This introversion of imperial ambition became dominant as the regime consolidated itself and Falangist influence waned. Typical in tone and rhetoric was the elementary primer *Yo soy español*, by Agustín Serrano de Haro, whose influential *España es así* went through twenty-five editions after the war. In *Yo soy español* national history began with the expulsion of Adam and Eve from the Garden and ended with the benevolent regime of Franco. Each chapter concluded with a maxim for pupils to memorize, ranging from the moral ("The Romans were strong but cruel. It is better to be good than to be rich and powerful") to the triumphalist ("Spain civilized America. The American nations call Spain mother"). *Yo soy español* presented children with a Manichaean world of sinners and saints, of savages and missionaries, of traitors and patriots. Like Onieva's civics text, it forsook imperial posturing for

---

[128] Menéndez-Reigada, *Catecismo patriótico*, 48.

[129] Onieva began life as a Carlist, came under the influence of the ILE in his youth, migrated to the Reformist party, supported the Primo de Rivera dictatorship, and during the 1930s was active in the Radical Republican party. He was a chief inspector of primary education in Asturias and editor of *La Voz de Asturias* until his transfer in 1935 to Madrid, where he joined the staff of *El Magisterio Español*. Denounced as an advocate of pacificism, internationalism, and naturalism after the end of the war, he avoided military reprisals and eventually rehabilitated himself with a personal letter to Franco. *El Ideal del Magisterio* 11, no. 395 (5 November 1984): 1; Expediente Depuración. Inspector de Primera Enseñanza A. J. Onieva, in AGMEC; Salvador Ferrer C. Maura, *Una institución docente: La Escuela de Estudios Superiores del Magisterio (1909–1932)* (Madrid: Imp. CEDESA, 1973), 292–96.

[130] [Antonio J. Onieva], *Así quiero ser: (El niño del Nuevo Estado). Lecturas cívicas H.S.R.*, 2d ed. (Burgos: Hijos de Santiago Rodríguez, 1940), 33, 14, 11.

homely concerns; Spain's enemies were not powerful foreign heretics, but the internal foes of religious unity and domestic tranquility. To be faithful to their history, children had only to defend the church, obey the Caudillo, and work in peace with their brother Spaniards.[131]

Also designed to encourage patriotism and national solidarity were the "travel books," which had enjoyed constant popularity in Spain since the 1920s. After announcing a competition in 1938 to select an official *Libro de España*, the ministry never chose a winner, but private publishing houses released their own versions, along with reeditions of perennial favorites like *España, mi patria*, by José Dalmáu Carles, *La patria española*, by Ezequiel Solana, and *La emoción de España*, by Manuel Siurot.[132] The standard format for these books was a journey through the provinces of Spain, usually by a group of children and their wise and patriotic counselor. (In the version published by the Marist order, the protagonists are two boys orphaned when their Falangist father is killed at the outbreak of the civil war. Raised by a former governess in France, they accept an invitation from a mysterious stranger to return to their homeland because "the sons of a martyr of Spain can't become men outside of Spain.")[133] During their journey the travelers discover the excellence and diversity of local history, architecture, natural resources, economic activity, and favorite sons. Regional diversity is presented as a source of national pride, rather than of disunion or particularism. From these encounters children were expected to learn to identify the *patria chica* with the *patria grande* and to admire the virtues of their countrymen—ingenuity, laboriousness, piety, patriotism, and traditionalism.

Some educators distrusted the travel books, arguing that they tended to encourage "a pugilism of provinces" that strengthened feelings of differentiation and local pride rather than of solidarity.[134] Nevertheless, the travel books remained popular with teachers and students long after

[131] Serrano de Haro, *Yo soy español*, 20, 65.

[132] See above, chaps. 2 and 6. Travel books consulted for this discussion include José Dalmáu Carles, *España, mi patria. Libro quinto* (Gerona: Dalmáu Carles, Pla, 1918); Manuel Siurot, *La nueva emoción de España: Libro de cultural patriótica popular* (Burgos: Hijos de Santiago Rodríguez, 1937); S.M., *Madre España*; Ezequiel Solana, *La patria española: Trozos escogidos acerca de la grandeza de nuestra patria, características de sus comarcas y vitalidad de su pueblo*, 14th ed. (Madrid: Escuela Española, 1962); Federico Torres, *Viajes por España: Manuscrito*, 8th ed. (Barcelona: Salvatella, [1942]); Antonio J. Onieva, *Viajando por España*, 5th ed., rev. (Burgos: Hijos de Santiago Rodríguez, 1951); and Edelvives, *El libro de España* (Zaragoza: Editorial Luis Vives, 1944).

[133] Edelvives, *Libro de España*, 7.

[134] Ediciones Bruño, *El libro de España* (Madrid: author, 1943), 12; Adolfo Maillo, "La comunidad nacional," *Servicio* 2, no. 62 (29 April 1943): 2.

the triumphalist readers of the 1940s had faded into obscurity. By presenting readers with a familiar world peopled with recognizable men and women, these books struck a chord of recognition that history books populated by aristocratic saints and warriors could not match. Their enduring success suggested that the institucionistas were right in urging maestros to focus on the local as a way of bringing history to life. The travel books measured the continuing strength of local identities, as well as the limited penetration of the regime's crusade to establish national identity as the primary identity of Spaniards.

In the many schools where such readers were a luxury, children learned Spanish history from "encyclopedias." The most widely adopted of these one-volume digests in the 1950s was the *Enciclopedia intuitiva, sintética y práctica*, by Antonio Álvarez Pérez, published in three grades with an accompanying teachers' guide by the Jesuit publishing house Miñón.[135] Despite the inflated claims of its title, both the explicit and implicit curriculum in the *Enciclopedia Álvarez* discouraged independent judgment, initiative, and creativity. The section devoted to Spanish history in all three levels was brief (62 pages in the second grade text; 185 in the third) and stylistically and structurally chaotic. Short paragraphs suitable for memorization were followed by supplementary paragraphs set in a small font and accompanied by readings and biographies in italics, moral aphorisms in cursive, and simple line drawings that students were meant to copy into their notebooks. This jumbled presentation mirrored the book's underlying conceptualization of history as a grab bag of assorted facts, examples, and "truths." The valor and heroism of historic Spaniards were virtues less to be imitated than admired; in their own lives children were advised to persevere in the true faith and to defend religion and patria to the death. The accompanying teachers' guide suggested classroom activities that involved copying and memorization, not active thought.

Such encyclopedias dominated the primary school market in the 1940s and 1950s, when economic stagnation limited the purchasing power of many families. The Piarist fathers (Textos E.P.), the Marist Brothers (Edelvives), and the LaSalleans (Ediciones Bruño) continued to publish versions of the encyclopedias in use before the war, as did Dal-

[135] Antonio Álvarez Pérez, *Enciclopedia intuitiva, sintética y práctica (Ajustada al cuestionario oficial). Segundo grado*, 80th ed. (Valladolid: Miñón, 1962) (1st ed. 1955; 101st ed. 1964); *Tercer grado* (Valladolid: Miñón, 1957) (1st ed. 1954; 115th ed. 1966); *Sugerencias y ejercicios: Libro del maestro. Tercer grado* (Zamora: Tipografía Comercial, 1955). According to D. Mauricio Santos, the former president of ANELE (Asociación Nacional de Libros y Materiales de Enseñanza), the *Enciclopedia Álvarez* had 80 percent of the primary school market in the 1950s and early 1960s. I am grateful to Sr. Santos for the informative interview he granted me on 22 May 1985.

máu Carles in Barcelona, El Magisterio Español in Madrid, and HSR in Burgos, which issued a new, slightly revised edition of Martí Alpera's mildly progressive encyclopedia without mentioning the author's name.[136] What the encyclopedias had in common was brevity and economy; there was little room for the impassioned narratives and inspiring biographies that were supposed to prepare youth for a life of imperial heroics. One subject among many distilled into a single volume, history remained the lifeless collection of facts and arbitrary assertions that had for so long attracted the ire of educational reformers on all points of the political spectrum. In *Journey to the Alcarria*, Camilo José Cela recounts his visit to a poor one-room school in Guadalajara province, where the star pupil proudly responded to the question "Who was the best queen of Spain?" by parroting, "Isabel I, because she fought against feudalism and Islam, brought about the unity of our country, and carried our religion and our culture beyond the seas." Asked if she knew what "feudalism" and "Islam" were, she replied, "No, señor, we don't have to learn that."[137]

On the other hand, encyclopedias, textbooks, and readers varied considerably in their levels of sophistication, editorial presentation, ideological saturation, and pedagogy, suggesting that the vigilance of the ministry over primary textbooks was limited to the maintenance of religious and political orthodoxy. Indeed, an unscientific survey of inspectors, grade school directors, and teachers in the early 1950s revealed a wide diversity of preferences that suggested that the reach of the state into the classrooms of the nation was far from perfect. Familiarity and availability often determined the selection of readers and encyclopedias in remote areas with few resources; many of the militantly ideological readers never reached their intended audience—as the Franquist educator conducting the survey repeatedly had cause to lament—while older progressive textbooks specifically prohibited by the ministry were still in use.[138] Regional and class preferences for certain texts also created variations in the way children encountered their nation's past.[139] The social segmentation of Spanish primary schooling distributed the most reac-

---

[136] [Félix Martí Alpera], *Nueva enciclopedia escolar H.S.R. Grado segundo*, 16th ed. (Burgos: Hijos de Santiago Rodríguez, 1942); *Tercer grado*, 3d ed. (Burgos: Hijos de Santiago Rodríguez, 1941). Most of the encyclopedias listed in the bibliography went through multiple editions and remained in print through the 1950s.

[137] Camilo José Cela, *Journey to the Alcarria*, trans. Frances M. López-Morillas (Madison: University of Wisconsin, 1964), 108–9. I am grateful to James Boyden for this reference.

[138] This is confirmed by Montilla, *Selección de libros*, 25.

[139] In his interview with me D. Mauricio Santos pointed out that only the *Enciclopedia Álvarez* enjoyed a national market; the others tended toward regional distribution.

tionary and catechistic textbooks to the less privileged; encyclopedias and manuals with well-developed narratives, supplementary readings, and other accoutrements of "active" education were reserved for the more advantaged.[140]

By the early 1950s a number of processes had undermined the initial project to "nationalize and Hispanize" the masses through the schools. The essentially conservative character of the regime, which asserted itself after repression, exile, and purges had eliminated the sources of "contamination" in the schools, defeated Falangist plans to mobilize the nation behind the state. In any event, a weak economy and limited resources posed an obstacle to the rapid transformation and expansion of the school system; by 1950 state funding for education had risen very little in real pesetas since 1936, spending per capita was the lowest in Europe, and 30 percent of school-age children remained unschooled despite a policy of subventions to private schools.[141]

Even had the Franquist state been richer or more fully committed to its initial program of political socialization, that program harbored internal contradictions that would have hindered its success. Regime ideologues might try to harmonize the tensions between Catholic integrists and Falangists with formulas like "Christian totalitarianism," but these pious phrases counted for little in the Catholic colegios, where the religious orders quietly pursued policies of noncompliance with the statist elements in the curriculum. Numerous former pupils have recalled the minimal influence enjoyed by the FET delegates entrusted with "political formation" and physical education courses; in one Catalan colegio, the teaching brothers distributed the copies of *Glorias imperiales* they received from the state, but did not use them. Likewise, the nationalistic but ostentatiously secular feast days concocted by the Movement to compete with the traditional Catholic calendar never got off the ground. In the opinion of Luis Goytisolo, it was not a fascist education they received, but a Franquist one—"reactionary, ultramontane and hypocritical."[142]

The official pedagogy of the regime contained its own contradictions. Catechistic methods, particularly as traditionally employed in Spanish classrooms, were incompatible with the professed aim of arousing the "emotional fiber" of the child. Memorization of the formulaic rhetoric of National Catholicism produced the confusion of meaningless phrases and images captured so vividly in the memoirs of Francisco Umbral and

[140] In this regard the books published by Dalmáu Carles, Hijos de Santiago Rodríguez, and S.M. were clearly superior to those published by E.P. and Edelvives.

[141] Navarro Sandalinas, *Enseñanza primaria*, 156–57, 161.

[142] Luis Goytisolo, "Un recuerdo triste," *CP*, suppl. no. 3 (September 1976): 45–46. See also the other memoirs in this issue.

Nuria Pompeia.[143] By the early 1950s even the original advocates of "traditional Spanish pedagogy" were forced to acknowledge the circumstantiality of its creation; the schoolbooks with their high-flown language and stirring calls to militancy had to be shelved, quaint relics of an historical moment whose intensity could not be recaptured.[144]

Finally, the insistent dichotomizing of Franquist history education was irreconcilable with its attempt to overcome class and regional conflict with patriotism and national pride. The favored image of "mother Spain"—the benevolent symbol of unconditional love and filial respect—could not disguise the systematic exclusion from the "Hispanic family" of all those "bad" or "false" Spaniards who had supported the Republic. After 1945 the regime provoked a xenophobic, nationalist response by dismissing international ostracism as yet another example of foreign incomprehension of Spanish principles and identity. But the sense of a beleaguered community became more difficult to sustain after the diplomatic recognition of the regime in the 1950s, and there was nothing more positive in the Franquist conception of history to take its place as a source of national cohesion. As we shall see, rather than abandon the historical interpretation that legitimated its existence, the regime chose to adopt a policy of benign neglect.

---

[143] Nuria Pompeia, "Por Dios, por la Patria y por los oscuros años cuarenta," in *CP*, suppl. no. 3 (September 1976): 46–47; Umbral, *Memorias*, 51.

[144] See the comments of Montilla throughout *Selección de libros*.

CHAPTER 9

Historical Amnesia: The Franco Regime, 1953–1975

[History] is today considered to be more
a science of the present and the future than
of the past.
(*Teresa Pérez Picazo*)[1]

TO EXPLAIN the declining importance of history as a tool of political socialization in the 1950s and 1960s, one must turn to the Cold War climate that ended Spain's diplomatic isolation and, more importantly, to the decision among influential stakeholders in the regime to secure international recognition and internal stability through a policy of economic modernization and growth. The resulting need for a skilled and politically docile labor force—reinforced by pressure from the OECD and the World Bank to invest in "human capital"—thus lay behind the series of reforms encompassing all educational levels that culminated in the General Law of Education and Financing of Educational Reform of 4 August 1970. Contributing to this trend, which involved both democratization of access and modernization of structures and curricula, was the emergence of liberal currents in both the ACN de P and the Falange, whose influence in the ministry and the universities shaped the direction of reform.[2] The fading memory of the civil war among Spanish youth, the global disavowal of "ideology" in the 1950s, growing American influence, increasing international contacts among intellectuals and educators, the reforms of Vatican II, and the liberalization of Spanish censorship laws in the 1960s all hastened the retreat from the highly politicized atmosphere of the postwar period (a retreat symbolically captured by the renaming of the Ministry of National Education as the Ministry of Education and Science in 1965). The necessary, but ironic, result of

---

[1] Teresa Pérez Picazo, *Didáctica de la historia* (Burgos: Hijos de Santiago Rodríguez, 1970), 3.

[2] On liberalization in the church, see Frances Lannon, *Privilege, Persecution, and Prophecy: The Catholic Church in Spain, 1875–1975* (New York: Oxford University Press, 1987); and Javier Tusell, *La oposición democrática al franquismo, 1939–1962* (Barcelona: Editorial Planeta, 1977); in the Falange, see Elías Diaz, *Pensamiento español en la era de Franco (1936–1975)* (Madrid: Tecnos, 1983).

the decision to modernize the Spanish economy was the official adoption of the modern pedagogical methods that the right had always associated with impiety and antipatriotism.

The process of reform began tentatively in 1953 with the signing of the Concordat of 27 August, which reaffirmed the right of the church to monitor the orthodoxy and morality of all schools, teaching, and textbooks. The new minister of National Education was Joaquín Ruiz Giménez, a member of the liberal wing of the ACN de P (and later a prominent figure in the Christian Democratic opposition). Having reassured the church, Ruiz Giménez attempted to increase the state's presence in the educational system, as well as to reinvigorate Spain's sclerotic academic culture by encouraging greater intellectual flexibility in the Opus-controlled CSIC and in the universities, especially in Madrid, where he appointed the liberal Falangist Pedro Laín Entralgo as rector. His inability to control the student disorders that this modest liberalization eventually provoked led to his removal from the ministry in 1957. Resumption of liberalization in the mid-1960s, when university enrollments exploded, produced similar results.[3]

The most significant of Ruiz Giménez's initiatives was his reform of the bachillerato in 1953, the first of four successive attempts at restructuring before the death of Franco in 1975.[4] Beginning with its dispassionate preamble, the law of 1953 presented a striking contrast with its predecessor of 1938. Although it recognized the religious and patriotic purposes of secondary education, it stressed the formation of "a vigorous social conscience . . . among Spanish youth" and affirmed the state's responsibility to make secondary schooling useful and accessible to all Spaniards intellectually equipped to take advantage of it. To make this meaningful, Ruiz Giménez abandoned the elitist classical bachillerato in favor of a general purpose "elementary bachillerato" of four years. Those anticipating university study would then study an additional two years in letters or sciences. He also reduced and modernized

---

[3] The university population rose from 37,200 in 1940 to nearly 67,400 in 1956 and almost 126,000 in 1966. Víctor García Hoz, *La educación en la España del siglo XX* (Madrid: Rialp, 1980), 128–29.

[4] D of 12 June 1953; D of 31 May 1957; D 1106 of 31 May 1967; and D 160 of 23 January 1975. General studies of education in the "technocratic" phase of the Franquist regime include: García Hoz, *Educación*; Manuel de Puelles Benítez, *Educación e ideología en la España contemporánea (1767–1975)* (Barcelona: Editorial Labor, 1980); Ramón Navarro Sandalinas, *La enseñanza primaria durante el franquismo (1936–1975)* (Barcelona: PPU, 1990); and Jordi Monés i Pujol-Busquets, *L'escola a Catalunya sota el franquisme* (Barcelona: Edicions 62, 1981). The most informative critique, however, is the so-called Libro Blanco of 1969, published by Ministerio de Educación y Ciencia (MEC) Secretaría General Técnica, *La educación en España: Bases para una política educativa* (Madrid, 1969).

the curriculum in both degree programs and strengthened the state's supervisory role by adding two new state examinations (*examenes de grado*) for all students, public and private, at the end of the fourth and sixth years. After the completion of a "preuniversity course" in which students would supposedly learn the techniques of criticism and analysis, they would submit to a "test of maturity" (*prueba de madurez*) administered in the universities. (Persistent high failure rates on university entrance exams would lead to constant tinkering with the "*preu*" over the next fifteen years.) The decree also strengthened the state inspectorate, which was charged with ensuring, among other things, that precedence be given to "intense assimilation over extensive erudition, the cultivation of intelligence over memory, and active methods over passive ones."[5] A Center for the Didactic Orientation of Secondary Education was created in the ministry the following year to disseminate information and encourage pedagogical innovation among instituto professors.[6]

The elementary bachillerato, which was sufficient for entry into middle-level professional schools (such as normal, commercial, and technical schools), signaled Ruiz Giménez's commitment to the democratization of secondary education. So too did the introduction of new forms of post-primary vocational training schools for skilled workers, and the addition of a university bachillerato in the Institutos Laborales. Demand for these new options and the labor force needs of an expanding economy inspired additional reforms by his successors in the ministry, who now saw secondary education as the common educational denominator that would cement "a profound and active spirit of solidarity, of community that must be united in progressive aspirations while remaining faithful to an inescapable historic destiny."[7] From the mid-1950s, but especially after adoption of the First Development Plan in 1964, the ministry worked to extend secondary education by expanding the number of institutos, further simplifying and modernizing the plan of studies, shortening cuestionarios and textbooks, and correlating degree programs to permit transfer from the professional and technical schools

[5] Law of 26 February 1953.

[6] Centro de Orientación Didáctica de Enseñanza Media. O of 27 December 1954. The Center published a professional journal, *Enseñanza Media* (*EM*), from 1956 to 1971.

[7] "El bachillerato para todos," *EM* 4, nos. 50–52 (November–December 1959): 1485–86. Activists occupying the ministry after Ruiz Giménez were the Falangist Jesús Rubio García-Mina (1957–62); and two members of Opus Dei, Manuel Lora Tamayo (1962–68) and José Luis Villar Palasí (1968–73). Julio Rodríguez Martínez (1973–74) and Cruz Martínez Esteruelas (1974–75), members of the so-called bunker of Franquist intransigents, temporarily halted the process of educational reform until the death of Franco.

to the university bachillerato.[8] By May 1967, when the ministry announced the integration of the *bachillerato laboral* with the elementary bachillerato in the name of "the unity of the men of Spain, . . . the democratization of culture and social mobility,"[9] the number of students pursuing secondary schooling had increased by 425 percent to 1,125,000 students, or about 27 percent of the student-age population.[10] According to the ministry, the goal was eventually to reach all children between the ages of ten and fourteen.[11]

To be sure, these global figures hid a highly differentiated situation that was still far from democratic. In 1970 only 5 percent of Spaniards living in rural areas reported completing secondary studies, as opposed to nearly 15 percent of urban residents.[12] Few in the urban working class studied beyond primary school. The modest interest (reflecting their modest utility) in the institutos laborales, which graduated only 2,357 students in 1963–64, justified their abolition in 1967. The elementary bachillerato attracted lower-middle-class students seeking semi-professional training and, ultimately, salaried employment; the university bachillerato—like the university—remained elitist.[13] While total secondary enrollments quadrupled, university matriculation between 1950 and 1967 only doubled.[14]

The expansive policies of the state eroded but did not erase the importance of the private colegios (78 percent of which were run by the religious orders).[15] Adjusting to the shifting function of the bachillerato, the colegios aggressively recruited students from a broader social base

[8] By 1965 there were 172 institutos and 71 "delegate sections" (subsidiaries or affiliates of full service institutos).

[9] Law 16 of 8 April 1967.

[10] MEC, *Educación en España*, 61, table 18.

[11] D 1106 of 31 May 1967. For a contemporary critique of the bachillerato, see Nicolás Sartorius, "Historia del bachillerato en España," in *Triunfo* 21, nos. 246 and 247 (18 and 25 February 1967): 13–17, 16–19.

[12] MEC, *Educación en España*, 31, table 7. Forty percent of the population was classified as rural at the same date, as compared to 37.5 classified as urban dwellers. Josep María Bas, "Entre la crisis agraria y la crisis educativa: Datos y cifras sobre las escuela rural y su entorno," *CP*, suppl. no. 2 (May 1976): 15–21.

[13] MEC, *Educación en España*, 26–28, table 5. See also Fundación FOESSA, *Estudios sociológicos sobre la situación social de España, 1975* (Madrid: Euramérica, 1976).

[14] University enrollment was over 154,000, or 3 percent of the relevant age group, a third of whom were matriculated in Madrid. García Hoz, *Educación*, 126–29.

[15] In addition to the 243 state schools (institutos and their branches) there were 59 "preu" centers, l,312 *colegios reconocidos* or *autorizados*, and l,371 private academies in 1965. José Luis Sastre, "La reducción de libros de texto en la nueva legislación de enseñanza media," *El Libro Español* 11, no. 123 (March 1968): 243. See also MEC, *Educación en España*; the annual report of the FAE [later, FERE], *Anuario de la Enseñanza Católica*; Manuel de Puelles Benítez, *Educación*, 410–11 n. 17; and *CP* 1, no. 9 (September 1975): 40.

and in 1968 still enrolled almost 40 percent of all secondary students.[16] Another 30 percent of students studied as libres. This segmentation, which in good measure reflected class differences, had a real impact on educational outcomes. By the ministry's estimate, only two-thirds of those pursuing the bachillerato earned the elementary degree; only a little more than one-third achieved the advanced degree, and only half of these passed the "maturity examination" required for university entrance. Students educated in private colegios consistently outperformed students matriculated in the institutos on the state exams, and both passed at higher rates than did the libres.[17] Clearly, expanding access could not alone achieve equality of results. Indeed, it tended to exacerbate the social segmentation always characteristic of the Spanish educational system.

Beginning with Ruiz Giménez the ministry also tried to enhance the quality and content of education delivered to students in the institutos. After 1953, official syllabi were accompanied by "methodological orientations" to encourage catedráticos to pay more attention to pedagogy. From the pages of the ministry's professional journal, Enseñanza Media, professional educators exhorted professors to replace formal lecturing and class recitation with "active" methods such as essays, class discussions, and field trips. State textbook regulations eliminated the discursive, footnote-laden tomes by which catedráticos had traditionally augmented their prestige and their incomes. Length was strictly regulated, partly to keep prices low and thus accessible to the influx of new students to secondary schools, partly because official pedagogical theory now relegated textbooks to a secondary role in the classroom. To make room for the mandated graphics and study aids, the text had to be simple and succinct.[18]

The problem of quality control and uniform standards became more

---

[16] The Federación Española de Religiosos de la Enseñanza (FERE), and its professional journal, Educadores, replaced the FAE and Atenas in 1957 as representatives of the corporate interests of the colegios. By the 1960s 10–15 percent of students in religious colegios were at least theoretically on scholarship. For the impact of these changes on one Jesuit school, see Luis Fernández Martín, S.J., Historia del Colegio San José de Valladolid, 1881–1981 (Valladolid: Colegio San José, 1981), 249–68. For church/state relations in education in this period see the sources in chap. 8 n. 5, and Jordi Monés i Pujol-Busquets, "El pensamiento escolar de la iglesia oficial desde la guerra civil hasta nuestros días," CP 4, no. 63 (March 1980): 33–40.

[17] On success rates, see MEC, Educación en España, 24; MEC, DGEM, Cátedra: Prontuario del profesor (Madrid, 1962–63), 779.

[18] Bachillerato textbook regulations appeared in D of 1 July 1955; O of 4 June 1957; O of 28 March 1958. The last prescribed the number of pages and illustrations and set price limits for books in each school subject. See Instituto Nacional del Libro Español, Comisión de Editores de Libros de Enseñanza, Textos para la enseñanza media: Catálogo general. Curso 1958–59.

acute with the multiplication of institutos.[19] After 1967 aspiring catedráticos were urged to take training courses in special Institutes for Educational Sciences created for the purpose in the universities. The emphasis on teaching did not sit well with those who recalled the glory days when a cátedra in an instituto was as prestigious as one in a university and possession of the bachillerato was a mark of social distinction; they continued to measure professional prestige in terms of publications and other scholarly activities. The loss of autonomy, the "degradation" of the title of catedrático, the devaluation of the degree, all suggested the same trend—the gradual shift of the bachillerato away from its traditional elite status as preparation for university study and toward its redefinition as part of the general education of citizens of all classes.[20]

The greatest obstacle to pedagogical transformation in the bachillerato was not the professoriat, however, but the state examinations, which ultimately shaped what students learned and how they learned it, especially students studying libre. Those exams, conducted en masse in the institutos and universities each May and June, still encouraged memorization, not critical thinking; the addition of textual commentaries and practical exercises to the exams was a dead letter because of overcrowded exam schedules. Further complicating the challenge of weaning Spanish secondary schooling from its dependence on rote learning were the publishing houses and booksellers who strenuously resisted proposals to abolish textbooks or to decommercialize their distribution.

Owing to its total neglect during the 1940s, primary education stood in urgent need of reform. High levels of illiteracy (nearly 18 percent nationally), reflected the persistent deficit of schools (42,000 in 1957, counting schools needing renovation; at 40 pupils per classroom this meant 720,000 children without a school place). Other problems were the deficient preparation of the teaching corps and its resistance to pedagogical modernization.[21] Real progress got underway in 1957 with the appointment of a new minister, the Falangist Jesús Rubio García-Mina, and his director general of primary education, Joaquín Tena Artigas (a

---

[19] The number of tenured and adjunct faculty increased by 3,700 in 1968. Law 1 of 5 April 1968.

[20] See Asociación Provincial de Catedráticos de Instituto, Comision de Investigación y Estudios Docentes, Madrid, *Degradación de la enseñanza media oficial y del Cuerpo de Catedráticos de Instituto: Informe* (Madrid: author, 1975). For brief biographies of the instituto catedráticos in 1960, as well as a complaint against the dilution of the professoriat, see Ministerio de Educación Nacional, Dirección General de Enseñanza Media, *Cátedra: Prontuario del profesor* (1960–61).

[21] See especially Navarro Sandalinas, *Enseñanza primaria*, 86–90, 148–50, 164–68.

statistician without political affiliation who had previously worked for UNESCO). Together, they created 23,000 new schools, an achievement partially blunted by high birth rates and a mobile population that created new demand in urban areas even as newly served rural areas were depopulated.[22] After the adoption of the First Development Plan, an increasing pace of construction, in combination with subventions to private schools and an aggressive adult literacy campaign, produced results. By 1968 official figures put illiteracy at no more than 3 percent of those under age sixty (a global figure that masked persistent regional differentials).[23] As in the case of secondary education, private schools, many receiving state subsidies, contributed substantially to this achievement.[24]

Systematic effort to transform the quality of primary education also began with the First Development Plan. Between 1964 and 1967, when the law of 1945 was officially revised,[25] a series of measures raised the age of obligatory schooling to age fourteen, divided elementary schooling into eight grades, raised training standards for maestros, prescribed new curricular objectives, and mandated annual evaluations of student mastery. The Certificate of Primary Studies (created in 1949 but generally disregarded) now became a requirement for employment, receipt of public services, and the exercise of citizenship rights. As a step toward integrating primary and secondary schooling, the certificate also validated entry into the third year of the elementary bachillerato.

Efforts to standardize and modernize classroom instruction began tentatively in 1953 under Ruiz Giménez with the publication of cuestionarios that gave maestros general directions on how as well as what to teach. Reflecting the transitional moment in which they were written, the 1953 cuestionarios paid homage to the "genius of Spain" and other National Catholic verities, but at the same time explicitly repudiated the repetitive teaching and learning methods so recently canonized as "traditional Spanish pedagogy" in favor of the active methods dominant in primary schools abroad. Acknowledging that the new techniques might seem "excessively revolutionary," the ministerial team insisted that "all

[22] Ibid., 205–10. I am grateful to Sr. Tena for graciously consenting to discuss his years in the ministry with me in an informative interview in July 1992.

[23] Navarro Sandalinas, *Enseñanza primaria*, 228. Census figures in 1970 put illiteracy at 9 percent, reflecting the large numbers of people over age seventy, especially women, who were not targeted by the literacy campaigns. For statistics broken down by sex and region, see Joaquim Capellades, "El analfabetismo en España: distribución territorial," *CP* 1, no. 2 (February 1975): 8–9.

[24] The state provided over 44 million pesetas in subsidies to private education in 1968–69. MEC, *Educación en España*, 59.

[25] D 193 of 2 February 1967.

education will be concrete, alive and active." Child-centered and collaborative primary education would not provide "notions," but rather develop the mental disposition to learn through active engagement with the real world of people and things. This methodological reorientation implicitly revolutionized the purposes of primary education as set out in the law of 1945. Instead of indoctrinating the child in his duties to God and patria, education was now to prepare him to understand and function within the physical and social environment in which he would live and work.[26]

The "revolutionary" methods introduced in 1953 ignited no revolution because teachers received little training in how to implement them. Despite the efforts of the enlarged state inspectorate and a lively professional journal, *Vida Escolar*, edited by the Center for Documentation and Didactic Orientation of Primary Education created by Tena in 1958, the classroom practices of a demoralized and underpaid teaching corps were usually shaped by tradition and convenience rather than theory; a ministerial planning document in 1962 acknowledged that maestros "routinely followed the schoolbooks (encyclopedias), . . . using them as the sole text."[27] Moreover, the professoriat in the normals schools was not uniformly supportive of the new orientation toward "scientific pedagogy." One of the most widely used texts, a history of Spanish education published in 1959 by the influential Catholic integrist Francisca Montilla, continued to condemn pedagogic "naturalism" as antipatriotic and antireligious.[28] In the more conservative Catholic orders, the progressive trend was also viewed with suspicion. While grudgingly admitting the value of individualized instruction and a freer classroom environment, they warned that it was also important "to develop in the child the idea of duty, obedience, docility, and renunciation."[29] Progressive pedagogy found its warmest welcome in Catalonia, where rapid industrialization made educational modernization imperative and where progressive pedagogy was a part of Catalan national identity.[30] Beginning in 1965 in the Institut Rosa Sensat and its annual summer schools, Catalan educators trained local teachers in the active methods of the New School movement, creating cadres who would later work for a truly "Catalan" school.[31]

---

[26] MEN, Dirección General de Enseñanza Primaria, *Cuestionarios nacionales para la enseñanza primaria* (Madrid: author, 1953), 10.

[27] Quoted in Navarro Sandalinas, *Enseñanza primaria*, 211.

[28] Francisca Montilla Tirado, *Historia de la educación*, 5th ed. (Madrid: Graf. Andrés Martín, 1962) (1st ed. 1959).

[29] Edelvives, *Historia de la pedagogía* (Zaragoza: Editorial Luis Vives, 1965) 2:267.

[30] See the comments of Alexandre Galí in *Escola catalana d'ahir y avui* (Barcelona: Ediciones de Mall, 1979), 41–42.

[31] Ibid., 21–23; Monés i Pujol-Busquets, *L'escola a Catalunya sota el franquisme;*

The emphasis on creating "human capital" in the First Development Plan led to more determined efforts to modernize curricula and teaching methods. Cuestionarios published in 1965 offered teachers detailed plans for intellectual, manual, aesthetic, and physical learning activities designed to instill in the individual child "habits, abilities, attitudes, values, and ideals that . . . will lead to the actualization and maturity of his personality." The curriculum was selected with the "integral formation" of the child in mind and adapted to "the necessities of Spanish society today." Following the practice in European and American schools, the ministry abandoned the traditional compartmentalization of school subjects; in the early grades subjects were "globalized" into affinity groups to conform more closely to the psychology of the child (not, it should be noted, the "Spanish child") and to the interrelatedness of the real world.[32] Glossy new textbooks adapted to the cuestionarios presented up-to-date material, organized in interdisciplinary fashion, with accompanying photos, graphs, maps, and other visual aids. Teachers' guides explained how they were to be used to complement experiential learning. The church and the Movement, which were still responsible for developing and teaching the so-called special subjects—religion, "civic-social" education, physical education, and homemaking—also followed this didactic strategy. The irony of this triumph of institucionista pedagogy went unremarked, however, since the contributions of the Institución Libre de Enseñanza to Spanish education were still officially unacknowledged. The transfer of the colegio Estudio, which had kept the institucionista program and spirit alive, even in clandestinity, since the 1940s, to larger quarters in an affluent suburb of Madrid in the late 1960s was nevertheless another sign that time was giving the victory to Giner and his disciples.[33]

A reform of the normal schools in 1967 restored the higher professional standards for teachers introduced by the Republic thirty-five years before. By requiring the university bachillerato for admission, it was possible to remodel the curriculum to emphasize practice teaching and methods courses, in which Catholic educational values were tem-

---

Ramón Moragas, "La 'escola d'estiu' de Barcelona en la escuela de Catalunya," CP 1, no. 6 (June 1975): 29–30; Maite Ricart, "Biblioteca Artur Martorell, primera de Barcelona especializada en pedagogía," Comunidad Escolar, 12–18 January 1987, 9; and Joan Gay, Societat catalana y reforma escolar (Barcelona: Laia, 1973).

[32] D 6 July 1965. "Globalization," a term borrowed from the Belgian child psychologist and educator Ovide Decroly (1871–1932), referred to the tendency of the child to apprehend the world as an integrated totality, not as a series of compartmentalized disciplines. For a critique, see Jordi Monés i Pujol-Busquets, "Aspectos ideológicos," CP, suppl. no. 3 (September 1976): 13–16.

[33] See Marta San Miguel, "El colegio Estudio, casi medio siglo de libertad y tolerancia," Comunidad Escolar, 26 January–1 February 1987, 13.

pered with modern, child-centered pedagogy.[34] Of course, most practicing teachers, especially those in rural areas, were still unacquainted with active methods, and many did not appreciate the participatory, individualist value system that underlay them. (In a 1972 survey, 69 percent of teachers in the provincial city of Cuenca agreed with the statement that "Children should be silent when their elders speak," as opposed to only 38 percent in Madrid.)[35] Older teachers used the new textbooks adapted to the 1967 cuestionarios in old-fashioned ways—not as sourcebooks to be consulted, but as textbooks to be memorized. But for younger teachers, they introduced new ways of acquiring knowledge and conceptualizing the world.

The limited and uncoordinated implementation of these piecemeal reforms pointed strongly to the need for a global reconceptualization of the entire educational system, which was still officially governed by the Ley Moyano of 1857. An extensive and highly critical white paper prepared in 1969 at the behest of an activist minister, José Luis Villar Palasí, quantified and analyzed the dimensions of the problem, then outlined potential solutions in the context of the economic needs of the nation and the political, social, and personal aspirations of its citizens.[36] The result was the ambitious and controversial law of 1970, which in many ways fulfilled the progressive agenda for educational reform that, among other things, the regime had fought the civil war to defeat.

The General Law of Education (LGE) of 1970 broke with the past in two important ways.[37] First, it defined education as a public service, a right the state guaranteed to all Spaniards. Because it also acknowledged the rights of private education and the confessional monopoly of the Catholic church, a necessary corollary was the provision of subventions to private colegios. Second, it took a large step toward eliminating the separate and unequal tracks for children of different social classes by fusing the elementary bachillerato with the primary school to create a single course of study for all children ages six to fourteen: the basic general education, or EGB. At age fourteen, EGB graduates could enter a relatively brief course of secondary schooling—the *bachillerato unificado y polivalente* (unified, polyvalent bachillerato, or BUP), a three-year, single track but internally differentiated degree program that would prepare them not exclusively for university study, but also for

---

[34] D of 8 June 1967. For methods, see the textbook by Isabel Gutiérrez Zuloaga, *Historia de la educación española*, 4th ed. (Madrid: Narcea de Ediciones, 1972) (1st ed. 1968).

[35] Amando de Miguel, "La transmisión de las ideologías autoritarias a través de los textos escolares," *CP*, suppl. no. 3 (September 1976): 32–34.

[36] MEC, *Educación en España*.

[37] MEC, *Ley general de educación y financiamiento de la reforma educativa y disposiciones complementarias*, 2d ed. (Madrid, 1976).

technical careers or the world of work. Those fourteen year olds unable or unwilling to study the BUP were to enroll for two years in a school of "Professional Formation."

Continuous evaluation was to replace the long-dominant system of centralized state exams (although access to the BUP and the university was still regulated by entrance examinations). At all levels the LGE proposed curricular and didactic reforms and mandated improved teacher training (elevating the normal schools to the status of university colleges, for example) to ensure their implementation. And in an effort to appease rising nationalist sentiment in Catalonia and the Basque provinces, it included in its mission statement "the incorporation of regional peculiarities, which enrich the unity and the cultural patrimony of Spain."[38]

Attacked by the right as "communist," by the church as "statist," and by the left as authoritarian and hypocritical, the law of 1970 was nevertheless a meaningful, if still partial, advance toward educational democratization. Implementation of its provisions—some of them ambiguous or contradictory—was slow and difficult, for a variety of reasons that cannot be discussed here.[39] In the years immediately after its passage, the final, reactionary governments of the dictatorship drew back from the plan, perceiving that the habits of independent thought and action deemed essential to rising productivity would also generate unwelcome demands for greater political and cultural freedom. Since the transition, democratic governments have gradually replaced the LGE with comprehensive reforms at all levels of instruction. In the interim, however, the LGE provided a functional framework for educational modernization that would have been impossible under the previous system.

The social and economic evolution of the 1950s and 1960s that was both cause and effect of educational reform also transformed the way that national history was conceptualized and taught. Although the National Catholic interpretation of the Spanish past never lost its "official" standing, it was gradually shorn of its hyperbolic rhetoric and removed to the margins of official political discourse. This demotion suggests

[38] Ibid., titulo preliminar 1.3.
[39] The General Law of Education of 1970 is discussed in Jaume Carbonell i Sebarroja, "Marco legal y política educativa," in *CP* suppl. no. 3 (September 1976): 24–29; Juan González-Anleo, *El sistema educativo español* (Madrid: Instituto de Estudios Económicos, 1985); José María Maravall, *La reforma de la enseñanza* (Barcelona: Editorial Laia, 1984); Mariano Fernández Enguita, *Reforma educativa, desigualdad social e inercia institucional: La enseñanza secundaria en España* (Barcelona: Editorial Laia, 1987); and MEC, *Libro blanco para la reforma del sistema educativo* (Madrid, 1989).

that history had lost its utility as a legitimizer of Francoism, which now began to justify itself not as the savior of an imperiled national tradition, but as the agent and guarantor of orderly economic growth and social mobility. In this context, rhetoric celebrating Spaniards' spiritual incapacity for modern life and disdain for material progress became dysfunctional. In addition, as Spain escaped the isolation of the 1940s, the gradual liberalization of intellectual life allowed alternative discourses on the national past to emerge. By the 1960s critics began to demand the incorporation of new historical interpretations and methods into history teaching in the schools. Rather than encourage historical approaches that might undermine its legitimacy, however, the regime preferred to relegate history to the backwaters of the curriculum. By the 1970s a new generation avid for the historical knowledge to which it had been denied access created a lively market for historical material of all kinds.

The initial cracks in the monolithic facade of postwar historical writing in Spain appeared in the late 1940s. In the prologue to volume 1 of his monumental *Historia de España*, Ramón Menéndez Pidal called for the reintegration of the "two Spains" in a "common Hispanic yearning," in order to cut short "the depressions and interruptions in the historical curve of our pueblo" and to "strike a firm course towards our high national destiny."[40] Two years later, in *España como problema*, Laín Entralgo echoed his appeal for an inclusive definition of "Spanishness" that would acknowledge the positive contributions of liberals to the secular dialogue on the meaning and future of the nation.[41] The work with the greatest impact, however, was a 1948 essay by Américo Castro, a philologist whose ties to the Institución and service to the Republic had led to his exile in the United States. In *España en su historia* Castro challenged the National Catholic credo by arguing that Spain and the Spanish national identity were the product of the seven centuries of conflict and coexistence (*convivencia*) among the three "castes" of medieval Spain—Christians, Muslims, and Jews. Relying heavily on literary sources, Castro emphasized the "Semitic" contributions, both positive and negative, to Spanish culture and argued that the subsequent repudiation of this pluralistic national identity by the dominant Christian caste—a tendency he labeled *vivir desviviéndose*, or a state of de-

[40] Ramón Menéndez Pidal, *Los españoles en la historia* (Madrid: Espasa-Calpe, 1982), 237. See the introduction to this edition by his grandson, Diego Catalán; and José María Jover Zamora, "Historia e historiadores españoles en el siglo XX," in *El legado cultural de España al siglo XXI*, vol. 1, *Pensamiento, historia, literatura* (Barcelona: Colegio Libre de Eméritos y Círculo de Lectores, 1994), 107–70.
[41] Pedro Laín Entralgo, *España como problema*, 2 vols. (Madrid: Aguilar, 1962).

nial—had condemned Spain to permanent spiritual crisis and historical inadaptation.[42]

The reply to Castro was quick to appear. From his exile in Argentina, the distinguished medievalist Claudio Sánchez Albornoz published *España: Un enigma histórico*, a massive critique of Castro's work that insisted on the continuous Latin and Christian foundations of Spanish culture, as well as on the continuous existence of an identifiable *homo hispanicus* from pre-Roman times onward.[43] From this perspective the Muslim occupation appeared as an alien interruption with unfortunate consequences for the later development of the nation. Less in tune with National Catholic notions was Sánchez Albornoz's argument that the Columbian discoveries and Habsburg succession also marked episodes of radical discontinuity in the Spanish past. The repercussions of the Castro–Sánchez Albornoz debate were immediately felt. On the one hand, it provoked another round of metaphysical speculation about Spanish identity; more fruitfully, it encouraged scholars to return to the archives for a closer look at the cultural and social foundations of medieval and early-modern Spain and their relation to the rest of Europe. The result was the recuperation of hitherto suppressed or forgotten voices with an equal claim to "Spanishness" and a new sense of possibility about the course of Spanish history.[44]

Within the historical discipline, other currents of scholarship were beginning to have an impact—especially, the French historical school associated with the journal *Annales*, and Marxist analysis. Returning from the Ninth International Congress of Historical Sciences in Paris in 1950, the Catalan medievalist Jaime Vicens Vives became an influential proselytizer for the transformation of the subjects, methods, and purposes of historical study. A professor at the Instituto-Escuela in Barcelona during the Republic, he was also a born teacher whose interest in pedagogic renovation was as strong as his dedication to archival research. In his "historical credo" published in 1951, Vicens outlined an ambitious program of historical renovation whose guiding principle was to be "History is life, in its complete diversity."[45] Instead of metahistori-

[42] Américo Castro, *España en su historia: Cristianos, moros, y judíos* (Buenos Aires: Losada, 1948). Castro expanded his ideas in *La realidad histórica de España* (México, D.F.: Porrúa, 1954) and in eleven subsequent iterations.

[43] Claudio Sánchez Albornoz, *España, un enigma histórico* (Buenos Aires: Editorial Sudamericana, 1953).

[44] For the gradual liberalization of Spanish scholarship in the postwar period, see Elías Díaz, *Pensamiento español en la era de Franco (1936–1975)* (Madrid: Tecnos, 1983); and Jover Zamora, "Historia e historiadores," in *El legado cultural de España*, 107–70.

[45] Jaime Vicens Vives, "Presentación y propósito," *Estudios de Historia Moderna* 1 (1951): i–xii (quote on p. xi). On Vicens Vives, see Mariano Peset and José Luis Peset, "Vicens Vives y la historiografía del derecho en España," in *Vorstudien zur Rechthistorik*

cal definitions of the national spirit, he proposed the quantitative analysis of serial data extracted from the archives. In place of the political
and diplomatic history of the empire, he advocated the study of the
geographical, economic, social, and mental structures that had constrained the behavior of individuals and social groups. Far from rejecting the modern world and its values, Vicens insisted on studying the
recent past. During the 1950s, the focus of his own scholarship shifted
away from the Catalan Middle Ages to the social and economic history
of nineteenth-century Catalonia. By making a case for history as a social science, Vicens offered an alternative to both triumphalist propaganda and empirically unverifiable assertions about national identity.
Together with his disciples at the University of Barcelona (who carried
on his work and attracted new practitioners after the master's untimely
death in 1960), Vicens set an example of scholarship that was methodologically rigorous and intellectually liberating in its redirection of historical focus on "the totality of the life of the common man."[46]

The perspectives of Marxist historians, particularly the French Hispanist Pierre Vilar, also sparked new interest in the social and economic
determinants of human activity, especially in the recent past. Like the
annalistes, Marxists sought to identify the structural similarities among
human societies, rather than the "superstructural" differences that distinguished one national context from another. The academic discovery
of Gramsci in the 1960s stimulated discussion of the relationship between intellectual production and social context. The Marxist critique
unmasked the legitimizing function of official historiography and de-
constructed the "nation" into a dynamic society of individuals and
groups with conflicting interests and values. It also encouraged historians to perceive the past as a servant of the present, rather than the
other way around.[47]

The historiographical currents imported from France, along with the
Spanish translation of a series of works by British and American historians, began to have an impact on young historians reaching professional maturity in the mid-1960s. At least through the 1970s, the dominant "conceptual triad" in progressive historiography was "feudalism,

---

(Frankfurt: Vittorio Klosterman, 1977), 176–262; and Stanley G. Payne, "Jaime Vicens
Vives and the Writing of Spanish History," *Journal of Modern History* 34, no. 2 (June
1962): 119–34.

[46] Jaime Vicens Vives, *Historia social y económica de España y América* (Barcelona:
Editorial Vicens-Vives, 1972) 1:xx.

[47] See José Luis López-Aranguren, *Moral y sociedad: Introducción a la moral social
española del siglo XIX*, 2d ed. (Madrid: EDICUSA, 1966); and Josep Fontana, *Historia:
Análisis del pasado y proyecto social* (Barcelona: Editorial Crítica, 1982).

bourgeois revolution, and capitalism."[48] Whether Spain had experienced the transition from feudalism to capitalism, whether it had undergone a bourgeois revolution, and if so, where, in which sectors, and under what conditions, were not merely matters of academic interest, but questions whose answers held implications for present political praxis. Because the models against which the Spanish experience was measured were borrowed from European historiography, much of the new historical literature involved explanations of Spanish failure to match the pace and scope of political, economic, and cultural modernization elsewhere in Europe. Nevertheless, the effort to place the Spanish case in comparative perspective registered a determination to deliver Spain from the ghetto of "difference" to which it had been consigned by National Catholic ideology. The emerging paradigm shift was yet another hint that the old trope of the "two Spains" was fast becoming an anachronism. It would take the successful transition to a stable democracy and a fully modern economy in the 1980s, however, to lay the notion of Spanish difference completely to rest.

The renovation of historical scholarship, which began to penetrate the universities in the 1960s, had no immediate impact on primary and secondary education. From the early 1950s, however, the general trend toward a controlled economic and educational modernization meant the devaluation of "all those sciences . . . not directly linked to the productive process and [of] those that might subvert traditional postulates."[49] The abandonment of the classical bachillerato was accompanied by a gradual, if unacknowledged, transformation of the mission and conceptualization of history in the curriculum. The most dramatic change was the reduction of the time allotted to history in the bachillerato, from seven years in the 1938 curriculum to one general course in the fourth year and a cultural history course in the sixth year of the 1957 plan of studies. An additional year was added in 1967, but even so, history had slipped far from the privileged place it had occupied in the early years of the dictatorship.

History declined in importance in the official curriculum because it was no longer expected to bear the burden of political socialization, a responsibility now relegated to the civics classes entitled Formation of

---

[48] Juan Sisinio Pérez Garzón, "La revolución burguesa en España: Los inicios de un debate científico, 1966–1979," in Manuel Tuñón de Lara, ed. *Historiografía española contemporánea: X Coloquio del Centro de Investigaciones Hispánicas de la Universidad de Pau. Balance y resumen* (Madrid: Siglo XXI, 1980), 91–138. See also Ignacio Olábarri Gortázar, "La recepción en España de la revolución historiográfica del siglo XX," in V. Vázquez de Prada, I. Olábarri, and A. Floristán Imizcoz, eds., *La historiografía en Occidente desde 1945* (Pamplona: EUNSA, 1985), 87–109.

[49] Monés i Pujol-Busquets, "Aspectos ideológicos," 15.

the National Spirit. To be sure, the syllabus and textbooks written for this course by the Movement were devoted almost entirely to "the characteristics of Spain's historical mission; her service to the high values of the Catholic conception of life; the significance that her men and representative deeds have had in world history; Spain's action in America and the value of the community of the Hispanic peoples."[50] But thus quarantined, National Catholic discourse on history no longer acted as a totalizing explanation of national life and purpose. Instead, it was an increasingly anachronistic and much-derided artifact of an earlier stage of the regime, whose strategy for political survival had now shifted from ideological mobilization to the promotion of work discipline and consumerism.

Stripped of its "formative" function, history became just one among several natural and social sciences in a utilitarian curriculum. The official cuestionarios for the bachillerato after 1953 were gradually purged of the normative rhetoric so abundant in the 1938 syllabi. Whereas the 1938 curriculum had privileged national history, the new plans combined Spanish with "universal"—that is, European—history. The fixation on the Habsburg empire gave way to more balanced coverage of the four historical "ages," and the previous exaltation of hispanidad was replaced with more modest references to "Spanish colonization." Befitting the regime's emphasis on economic modernization, the prescribed curriculum now included discussion of enlightened despotism and an introduction to the social organization and value systems of modern Europe: capitalism, industrialization, liberalism, the workers' movement, and nationalism. Restoration of a two-year Spanish history curriculum in 1967 permitted the addition of "the history of civilization," or what the syllabus called "the soul of peoples: their political, social and religious institutions and their economic, cultural and social development." Accompanying methodological guidelines instructed professors to "analyze with clarity the causes and consequences of historical deeds and events . . . and to emphasize the characteristics that have given former Societies their individual physiognomy and their contribution to the common cultural fund of Humanity."[51] Little difference separated this formulation from the much-maligned prescriptions of Rafael Altamira thirty years before.

The depoliticizing and Europeanization of the history curriculum was part of the regime's strategy for reinsertion into the European community after fifteen years of ostracism and autarky. Immediately after the Second World War the United Nations (echoing the efforts of the

[50] D of 12 June 1953.
[51] D 336 of 4 September 1967. Bachillerato general: Cuestionarios.

League of Nations twenty years earlier) had encouraged, through the auspices of UNESCO, the revision of history textbooks to promote world peace. This task was taken up enthusiastically by the Council of Europe in a series of conferences on history teaching held during the 1950s, which in turn produced several bilateral and regional agreements on textbook revision. When finally invited to the sixth (and last) of these conferences in 1959, Spanish representatives were eager to point out the absence of bellicosity and national prejudices in Spanish secondary school textbooks.[52]

The French historians who negotiated an accord on textbook revision with their Spanish counterparts in 1962 did not contest this claim.[53] For one thing, the textbooks submitted by the Spanish government to the bilateral commission had been chosen for their scrupulous scholarship and objective tone.[54] But the principal reason why the French historians found Spanish history textbooks to be innocent of national stereotyping or warmongering was that the books scarcely mentioned France (or any other nation) at all. In 1958 the maximum authorized length for a textbook covering the entire span of European and Spanish history was 304 pages; given the encyclopedic nature of the syllabi and the space consumed by required illustrations, study questions, summaries, glossaries, and brief readings, authors could not dilate on any topic and hope to stay within the prescribed limits.[55] Although the French delegates complained of the excessively reductionist treatments of essential events in French history, they recognized the structural impossibility of a remedy within the constraints of a curriculum in which history was increasingly an afterthought.

The physical transformation of bachillerato history books began in 1958 with the publication of state rules governing length, graphics, and price. Although this did not completely discourage prospective authors—there were twenty-two fourth-year history books on the ap-

[52] See United Nations, UNESCO, *A Handbook for the Improvement of Textbooks and Teaching Materials as Aids to International Understanding* (Paris, 1949); C. Peter Hill, *L'Enseignement de l'histoire: Conseils et suggestions* (Paris: UNESCO, 1953); Ramón Ezquerra Abadía, "La sexta conferencia para la revisión de los textos de historia" and "Revisión de los textos de historia," *EM* 4, nos. 33–36 (January–February 1959): 50–54, and 5, no. 67–69 (October–November 1960): 1565–79.

[53] *Conversaciones franco-españolas para la revisión bilateral de los manuales escolares de historia* (Madrid: Instituto Jerónimo Zurita, 1962).

[54] The fourth year texts were by Jaime Vicens Vives, José Luis Asián Peña, and Álvaro Santamaría. The Spanish members of the delegation were distinguished historians: José Antonio Maravall, Antonio Rumeu de Armas, Manuel de Terán Álvarez, Miguel Artola, Felipe Ruiz Martín, Ramón Ezquerra Abadía, Antonio Domínguez Ortiz, and Elisa Bermejo.

[55] O of 28 March 1958.

proved list in 1965–66—the expense and expertise required to meet the official guidelines made it impossible for the individual catedrático to write his own textbook and publish it locally.[56] In the 1960s no single book dominated the national market, but only larger firms were in a position to produce attractive books adapted to the new pedagogical requirements and to build market share through advertising, discounted bulk sales, and other strategies. Most larger concerns dominated regional markets, like Teide (founded by Vicens Vives before his death) and Bosch in Barcelona, or the ECIR consortium in Valencia, although a few, like El Magisterio Español and a newcomer, Anaya, sold books nationwide. Among the religious publishers, well-established enterprises like Bruño, Edelvives, Razón y Fe, and Marfil were overtaken in the 1960s by the rapidly expanding S.M., owned by the Marianistas.[57]

Because of the fragmentation of the bachillerato market, significant economies of scale were not possible; consequently, prices, although officially regulated, were still relatively high, triggering familiar demands from parents for a texto único. This time, however, their anger was directed at publishers, profit margins, and discounting practices, not at the ideologies of the authors. In response, the ministry first froze prices, and then, when this proved incompatible with its goal of improving quality, restricted the list of approved books to eight for each discipline.[58] The resulting consolidation of the industry produced some positive results: the best of the new books were lavishly illustrated with maps, charts, drawings, and photographs, thoughtfully laid out to ease reading and retention, and enriched with study question, summaries, primary sources, and, in the case of the S.M. manual, crossword puzzles.[59]

[56] Instituto Nacional del Libro Español, *Libros y material de enseñanza, 1965–66. Enseñanza media* (Madrid: Comisión Asesora de Editores de Libros de Enseñanza, 1965).
[57] Interview with D. Mauricio Santos, 22 May 1985.
[58] See the discussion in *El Libro Español* 21, nos. 123 and 124 (March, April 1968): 236–43, 334–38; and Mercedes Rivas, "La venta de libros de texto," *CP* 1, no. 5 (May 1975): 37–39. A defense of the new books is in José-María Martínez Val, "Los libros de texto," *EM* 4, no. 50–52 (November–December 1959): 1562–64.
[59] Books reviewed for this summary include the following: Santiago Andrés Zapatero, *Curso de historia*, 5th ed., 2 vols. (Barcelona: Élite, 1958) and *Historia de España y sus relaciones con la universal en las edades modernas y contemporáneas* (Barcelona: Librería Élite, 1965); Fernando Arranz Velarde, *Nociones de historia universal y de España: (Edades antigua y media)* (Madrid: Imprenta Góngora, 1958); José Luis Asián Peña, *Historia universal y de España* (Barcelona: Bosch, 1960); Antonio Bermejo de la Rica, *Historia. Tercer curso: Edades antigua y media* (Madrid: AGESA, 1954); Juan Blasco Cea, *Historia antigua y media universal y de España, tercer curso* (Madrid: Editorial Bruño, 1969); Manuel Capel Margarito, *Historia universal y de España. Tercer curso: Edades antigua y media* (Jaén: Unión Tipográfica, 1958); María Comas de Montañez, *Breve historia universal y de España* (Barcelona: Ediciones Sócrates, 1961); Juan M. Grima Reig, *Historia. 4º curso de bachillerato* (Valencia: ECIR, 1960); S.M. [J. J. Arenaza Lasagabas-

Particularly innovative was the historical atlas of maps drawn by Vicens Vives and published by Teide, which stressed the spatial dimension to the dynamics of invasion, conquest, settlement, and expansion in the Spanish past.[60]

Although these physical changes were intended to support active teaching and learning, the content of the official cuestionarios and the persistence of centralized examinations undercut this objective. Topics in political history, especially the battles, reigns, and alliances that led to the unification of the state, still predominated over social and cultural themes in the syllabi, and because of space limitations, authors could not devote more than a sentence or two to any topic.[61] While inevitably reducing everything to the same order of (in)significance, this also eased memorization and rapid testing and discouraged authorial editorializing beyond the addition of a reductionist phrase or adjective. Even though the cuestionarios included more contemporary history, the condensation of all of human history into one or two years of study meant that teachers seldom reached the end of the prescribed curriculum, leaving students better acquainted with the Greeks and the Romans than with events of the recent past. In fact, except for cosmetic improvements and the drastic reduction in their length and density, the new history manuals still strongly resembled the much-maligned narratives of one hundred years before.

Despite the compression of text, variations in tone, language, and emphasis persisted. At the liberal end of the spectrum were the splendid books published by Teide in Barcelona. Popular in private colegios that catered to the professional middle classes, Teide's history books were progressive in tone and oriented toward the comprehension of the con-

---

ter and Fermín Gastaminza Ibarburu], *Historia de España y universal, 4° curso. Plan 1967. Bachillerato elemental* (Madrid: Ediciones S.M., 1970); Antonio Rumeu de Armas, *Historia de España moderna y contemporánea. Curso preuniversitario*, 2 vols. (Salamanca: Anaya, 1969) and *Historia universal y de España. 3°. Edades antigua y media* (Salamanca: Anaya, 1969); Álvaro Santamaría Arandez, *Historia moderna y contemporánea. 4° curso*, 6th ed. (Madrid: Prensa Española, 1959); Santiago Sobrequés Vidal, *Hispania: Historia política y cultural de España*, 9th ed. (Barcelona: Ediciones Teide, 1960); Oriol Vergés, *Cives: Historia moderna y contemporánea. 4° curso de bachillerato*, 4th ed. (Barcelona: Editorial Teide, 1972); Jaime Vicens Vives, *Cives: Historia universal y de España*, 8th ed. (Barcelona: Editorial Teide, 1967) and with Sobrequés Vidal, *Orbe: Geografía e historia universal. Formación profesional industrial, 2° curso de iniciación profesional* 4th ed. (Barcelona: Editorial Vicens-Vives, 1962).

[60] Jaime Vicens Vives, *Atlas histórico de España*, 5th ed. (Barcelona: Editorial Teide, 1965).

[61] Another constraint on authors was that the ministry specified that the survey of history should be completed by April, in order to leave a month for review before the examination period.

temporary world. The treatment of the liberal constitution of 1812 in Teide's fourth year textbook illustrates its approach to the past. The author, Oriol Vergés, remarked that the Constitution of Cádiz was well drafted but "not understood by the pueblo, which did not have sufficient political and intellectual preparation for it, since it is estimated that 94 percent of the Spanish population at that time was illiterate."[62] Vergés thus resurrected the liberal tradition from the disrepute into which it had been cast, and offered an empirically verifiable structural explanation of why it had not received popular support. In contrast, the Marianistas' fourth year textbooks retained the integrist concept of a national tradition betrayed by the collusion of denaturalized Spaniards and foreign conspirators. The liberalism of the constitution, it averred, was the result of "the encyclopedist and *afrancesado* majority that attended the Cortes and [of] the influence of secret Masonic societies."[63] Generally speaking, however, bachillerato history texts in the 1960s were more similar than they were different. The prescribed textbook format offered no scope within which to develop differences in values and perspective into a coherent explanation of the Spanish past. Even the ordering of topics prescribed by the cuestionarios—which segregated topics in Spanish history from those in general European history—discouraged any inclination to see national history in relative terms or to compare its development to paths taken elsewhere.

Having embraced economic and social modernization and thus no longer dependent on its peculiar reading of the national past to justify Spain's "difference" from Europe, the regime now seemed determined to deny history any functional educational role whatsoever. To be sure, ministerial publications justified the study of history in terms of its ability to hone critical thinking skills. But official cuestionarios, textbooks, and exams combined to reduce it to the mindless memorization of an assortment of seemingly incontestable, but also unintelligible and apparently irrelevant facts. The regime that in 1964 celebrated "25 years of peace" instead of its victory over the "anti-Spain" now found it preferable to cover "the rancors and animosities of other times, perhaps bathed in blood . . . with a discreet veil of transcendence and forgetfulness and better, with the tunic of solidarity and Christian fraternity."[64]

Primary-school history, like primary education in general, did not undergo major changes until the mid-1960s. As noted earlier, a modest reform of methods began in 1953 with the publication of new cuestionarios that paid implicit homage to the institucionistas by recom-

---

[62] Vergés, *Cives*, 201.
[63] S.M., *Historia de España y universal*, 196.
[64] Ibid., 7.

mending storytelling, excursions, short readings, and biographies to bring history to life. Otherwise, however, the 1953 syllabus echoed the National Catholic rhetoric of the 1940s: "National history is not a dead series of *notions*, but, on the contrary, the contagious transmission of an ensemble of *values*, in whose deployment consists the historical justification of our pueblo."[65] Although cautioning against a "messianic" conception of the nation, the ministry still insisted on Spain's unique vocation for spiritual leadership. By some mysterious alchemy, however, the official definition of that spirituality had now come to embrace both Menéndez y Pelayo and Américo Castro: "Other countries might demonstrate, perhaps, superior pedigrees in terms of material progress. . . . Spain, in contrast, can be teacher of the world in terms of that *vivir desviviéndose* that made her a discoverer and missionary, 'hammer of heretics, light of Trent and sword of Rome.' "[66]

The 1953 curriculum had little impact in Spanish classrooms, where poorly trained teachers, limited resources, and low expectations were persistent obstacles to innovation. Over the mounting disapproval of younger educators, most children continued to learn national history from inexpensive encyclopedias like the *Enciclopedia Álvarez*; in better endowed schools patriotic travel books and biographical collections, many of them only slightly updated editions of those published decades earlier, supplemented the traditional manuals. The principal change in these schoolbooks, apart from the dilution of their National Catholic rhetoric, was their noticeable conceptual and linguistic simplification. Authors and publishers were not only more sensitive to the findings of developmental psychology, but they also now sold books to a larger and more diverse market. Thus, manuals and encyclopedias originally written in the 1930s and 1940s for children under age ten were now recommended for use by older children.[67]

With history no longer conceptualized as the instrument for inculcating a providential national identity, its utility and methodology became problematic. Ministerial guidelines for elementary encyclopedias allocated proportionally much less space to history than to language, science, and mathematics.[68] As nationalist and imperialist themes declined in primary school readers, purely religious themes increased.[69] A selec-

[65] O of 6 February 1953.

[66] Ibid. *Vivir desviviéndose* is, of course, an allusion to Americo Castro; the quoted material is from Menéndez y Pelayo.

[67] For example, the second grade encyclopedia by Félix Martí Alpera was reclassified as a third grade encyclopedia in the 1950s.

[68] O of 23 March 1960.

[69] According to Clementina García Crespo, *Léxico e ideología en los libros de lectura de la escuela primaria (1940–1975)* (Salamanca: Ediciones Universidad, Instituto de Ciencias

tion of minibiographies published in 1963 by Aniceto Villar (an editor of *Avante* during the Republic) was strikingly similar to the traditionalist readers published in the nineteenth century in its approach to history as a source of moral instruction. Gone were the aristocratic warriors and saints of the 1940s texts, whose superior will and courage had enabled Spain to rule the world. Villar's vignettes illustrated virtues desirable in a stable, orderly community: the sincerity of Solon, the charity of Ferdinand the Saint, the humility of Cardinal Cisneros, and the patriotism of that modern Guzmán el Bueno, Colonel Moscardó. Other readers marshaled history in support of the regime's ideology of economic growth. A prize-winning collection of readings for working-class children pointed out that the labor of millions of unknown men made possible the heroic deeds of explorers, kings, and inventors. If God's plan did not include liberation from the obligation to work, it was nonetheless leading men toward an era of greater unity and cooperation: the "Earth is the great patria of all men."[70]

When the primary school curriculum was modernized and reconfigured into eight separate grades in 1965, history was "globalized" into the social sciences.[71] To conform to Jean Piaget's model of child development, the new social studies programs were minimalist in content and organized "concentrically"—that is, they began with the daily activities, objects, and institutions in children's lives and gradually moved outward to abstract concepts of political and social organization, much as Cousinet had recommended in his "lessons of things." Presentist and functionalist in orientation, the experientially based curriculum found room for history only with difficulty. In the lowest grades, children studied how people had lived and worked in the past. In the syllabi for children in the middle grades, isolated historical symbols and events, like the Cid, the Catholic Kings and the Second of May, were somewhat arbitrarily distributed among the lessons on geography, civic duties, and social life. Only in the fifth grade did history recover an independent existence, in the form of a cyclical, highly schematized chronology of Spanish history, in which the fundamental principles of Catholicism and national unity determined the selection of topics. In a curriculum that emphasized practical skills, social discipline, and political demobilization, extended historical knowledge or a strong sense of national identity was not a priority. Relatively detailed, "factual" political narrative

---

de la Educación, 1983), 120–21, the percentage of exclusively Catholic themes rose sharply in the 1950s and early 1960s. Questions about the author's methodology, however, suggest that her conclusions should be accepted with caution.

[70] Patricio Grenier, ed., *Aventuras del hombre sobre la tierra* (Madrid: Magisterio Español, 1963), 69.

[71] O of 6 July 1965.

only reasserted itself in the seventh and eighth grade curricula, which were intended to articulate with the elementary bachillerato.

In reorienting its legitimating claims from the past to the present, the dictatorship dampened its National Catholic rhetoric about Spanish history and identity without attempting to invent or disseminate a more functional set of myths about the past. But the "veil of forgetfulness" with which the regime attempted to shroud historical consciousness did not have the intended effect. Instead, the content of national history, and the method of its transmission to the young, took center stage in a debate on educational means and ends in which political liberalization was the subtext. Conservative Catholic educators mourned the loss of normative content in the history textbooks at the same time that they warned against "culturalist progressivism"—internationalist and evolutionary postulates that were neither intelligible to children nor properly "formative": "Only nationalist conceptions, grounded in eternal values that surround all historical events with a sense of Providence and of maintenance of tradition, can be justified."[72] The marginalization of history and the reductionism of the new textbooks was equally alarming to a new generation of progressive university professors and their students. As it was taught in institutos and universities, history was not a stimulus to a "spirit of observation and reflection," but rather "an anarchic accumulation of unconnected or artificially treated events." The verdict of the young is final, observed the secondary school inspector and history catedrático Felipe Ruiz Martín: "History is a drag."[73]

Practitioners of the "new history" called for the reconceptualization of content and methods to make history more relevant to current concerns. By analyzing social and economic structures or "historical habitats" in the past, students would be better equipped to understand the social and economic transformations underway in the nation. If history were presented as "a necessary tool in the struggle for the material and moral progress of man,"[74] it could recover its rightful place at the center of an education that aimed not merely to adjust students to existing society, but to render them informed critics of its problems and potential for growth.[75]

[72] José Fernández Huerta, "El progresismo culturalista en la enseñanza de la historia," *Escuela Española* 17, no. 892 (11 January 1958): 3–4.

[73] Felipe Ruiz Martín, "La enseñanza moderna de la historia," in MEN, DGEM, *Cátedra* (1960–61), 139–46.

[74] Carlos Martínez Shaw, reviewing *Historia: Análisis del pasado y proyecto social*, by Josep Fontana, in *CP* 1 (January 1975): 19–21.

[75] See the essays on history in MEC, Centro de Orientación Didáctica de Enseñanza Media, *Didáctica de historia y geografía: (Estudios monográficos)*, vol. 1 (Madrid, 1965); and in *Vida escolar* 6, no. 44–45 (December–January 1962–63).

The contrast between the sterile narratives of the textbooks and the domestic and international upheavals of the late 1960s and early 1970s, together with the publication of new historical works by Spaniards and foreigners, clarified for young Spaniards the extent to which they had been denied access to their own past. At the same time, growing discontent in Catalonia and Euzkadi expressed itself as a cultural and ethnic nationalism that disavowed all links with "Spanish" national identity. The sense that history was the "genealogy of the present" fed the seemingly insatiable demand for historical knowledge that supported a growing number of professional journals and popular periodicals from the late 1960s onward; no less than five popular historical magazines could be found in the newsstands by 1978.[76] At last, the professional historians and Altamira's "man in the street" had come to share an interest in their common past as a way of resolving the political crisis of the present.

Echoes of this preoccupation could be found in the "orientations" developed for the new EGB in 1970, in which history emerged partially from the eclipse it had suffered in the 1950s and 1960s. As in earlier curricular reforms, the function of social studies was to socialize children to the world in which they lived; the ultimate goal, explained the ministry, was "to educate the group civically" by explaining the "distinct forms of relation and interdependence among men, in order to arrive at a necessary comprehension of our participation in public life through diverse organizations." In the lower grades, this presentist orientation meant that history was a very marginal component of an "area" that focused on geography, social organization, and civic responsibilities. For grades six through eight, however, history now provided an organizing principle, a window into past forms of human society, whose didactic value lay in the contrast they presented to the modern, harmonious, and stable world of the 1960s. The new programs, clearly shaped by the emerging scholarly enthusiasm for "structures," retained few reminders of the hallowed themes of National Catholicism, apart from occasional unembroidered references to "*lo hispánico*" or "*lo español*." Completely gone was the dichotomizing, exclusionary rhetoric of the past; the "Reconquest" had given way to "convivencia," the "Crusade" had become the "war of 1936," and the characteristic mentality of the present was alleged to be "the desire for peace; rapprochement of all men."[77]

[76] *Historia y vida* (1968) was followed by *Tiempo de Historia* (1974), *Historia Internacional* (1975), *Historia 16* and *Nueva Historia* (1976), and *L'Avenç* (1978). Several new scholarly historical journals also appeared in the early 1970s.

[77] MEC, Comisión Ministerial de Planes, Programas de Estudio y Evaluación, "Educación General Básica: Nueva orientación" (Madrid, 1970), 3.

Although superficially responsive to the demands of the "new historians," the 1970 EGB programs did not provide the promised foundation for a critical perspective on the past and the present. On the contrary, they were profoundly conservative in their implications. Although a large proportion of the syllabus was devoted to the twentieth century, the focus was not on the political and social crisis that led to civil war, but rather on the postwar period, when Spain enjoyed international acceptance, political stability, and prosperity. In the 1970 cuestionarios, the past was no longer the source of national identity, but merely a distant set of "structures" and "civilizations" whose relevance to the present was not specified. The responsibility of Spaniards was now to a "continuous present," an imagined community of workers and consumers without antecedents and without destination.[78]

The cuestionario published in 1975 for the social sciences in the new "unified and polyvalent bachillerato" (BUP) was a similar mixture of modern historiographical precepts and conservative educational goals. The stated role of geography and history in the curriculum was to help students "understand in depth the culture of the society in which they live, contribute to its perfection and development and facilitate *convivencia* and collaboration with others." During the first year, students surveyed the historical evolution of "civilizations," each characterized by "a space, a society, and a mentality," and allegedly destined to culminate in a "universal civilization" based on Western culture. After a second year course devoted to the human and economic geography of the contemporary world, the curriculum of the third and final year returned to the history and geography of Spain and the Hispanic nations. In this syllabus traditional periodization appeared under a new guise: topics in medieval history were grouped under the rubric "the historical differentiation of Spain"; topics in modern history fell under "universalization"; and those in contemporary history were labeled "difficulties of modernization." As in the EGB programs, the principal theme was the positive resolution of these "difficulties" under the benevolent and competent management of General Francisco Franco.[79]

Despite their inherently conservative bias, the new cuestionarios for the EGB and BUP provided a framework within which democratic reformers might hope to transform history into an instrument for change. A number of structural obstacles stood in their way, however, the most important of which was the disinclination or inability of professors and teachers to understand the interdisciplinary foundations of "total his-

[78] See José Luis López-Aranguren, *La cruz de la monarquía actual* (Madrid: Taurus, 1974), 105.
[79] O of 22 March 1975.

tory" or to implement pedagogical reforms. In the institutos the problem was primarily generational. Although older catedráticos clung to their familiar habits, recent graduates from the universities were comfortable with social and economic history, frequently more engaged politically, and eager to introduce interdisciplinary and critical methods to their students.

At the level of the EGB, however, the problem was both more intractable and more pressing, given that most children did not continue their studies beyond age fourteen. Although state normal schools were incorporated into the universities after 1970, their personnel and textbooks were minimally affected by the new historiographical and pedagogical currents. Normal school methods courses, for example, were not interdisciplinary, leaving graduates unprepared to implement the "globalized" primary curriculum mandated in 1965. The required course on historical pedagogy was strikingly old-fashioned, both in its conceptualization of history and in its pedagogy. With few exceptions textbooks for this course paid lip service to the totem of "total history" but in practice offered conventional political narratives.[80] Moreover, typically no more than 15 percent of these texts was devoted to methodological questions.[81]

The lapse into conventional historical approaches in most didactic manuals was of course magnified in the classroom, where the inertia and ignorance of older teachers prevailed over the efforts of young, urban-based maestros. In particular, weaning ill-prepared teachers from excessive reliance on reading and recitation proved problematic. Although the memoristic encyclopedias were finally banned after the adoption of the curricular reforms of 1965, many teachers used the textbooks developed to support the new programs in old-fashioned ways, aided in some cases by teachers' manuals that conveniently provided a catechism of questions and answers for each unit.[82]

This tendency was also unconsciously encouraged by the way in which some innovative publishers interpreted the principles of active pedagogy, particularly in areas not easily adapted to operational learning, like history. Santillana, a progressive publishing house founded in 1960, set an example followed by many others. Santillana's social

[80] José Sánchez Adell, *Cronos: Didáctica de la historia*, 4th ed. (Barcelona: Editorial Vicens-Vives, 1971); Salvador Aldana Fernández, *Didáctica de la historia. 2° curso. Plan 1967*, 2d ed. (Alcoy: Márfil, 1970); Pérez Picazo, *Didáctica*; Luis Coronas Tejada, *Didáctica de la historia*, 2d ed. (Salamanca: Anaya, 1971); Montserrat Llorens, *Didáctica de la historia*, 3d ed. (Barcelona: Editorial Vicens-Vives, 1965).
[81] An exception is Aldana Fernández, *Didáctica*.
[82] María Viñé Marcellán, *Guía didáctica de geografía e historia. 6° curso. Libro del maestro* (Burgos: Hijos de Santiago Rodríguez, 1969).

studies texts were written by groups of historians, developmental psychologists, and reading specialists who strove for brevity, accuracy, intelligibility, and objectivity. Extensive narration or interpretation was rejected in favor of short factual summaries, vivid graphics, and suggestions for independent study and group activities. Accompanying teachers' manuals guided the teacher through the text with suggestions on how to define objectives, lead class discussions, and organize collaborative projects. The emphasis on individualized work in the law of 1970 motivated the development of workbooks, or *fichas*—packets of exercises that required students to conduct research in large classroom reference books also supplied by the publisher. Underlying these innovations was the conviction that history textbooks should have no personality or point of view; they should merely present raw data, the interpretation of which was the responsibility of student-historians themselves. In writing their own histories, young people would acquire the critical skills, historical perspective, and objectivity that were the chief fruits of historical study.[83] It was the program of Altamira and Giner—updated, but still aimed at the creation of a democratic civic culture.

The results of these experiments were less than satisfactory, however. In many instances, the most innovative texts were rejected by teachers unwilling or unable to implement the new methods, or by parent advisory groups who objected to the additional cost of the expensively illustrated texts, workbooks, and reference works. Publishers like S.M., whose books were written for Catholic colegios, found additional markets among these groups. Publishers seeking to capitalize on a fad, but who did not understand the philosophy of active learning, produced workbooks that merely asked students to locate and copy facts, not to analyze or interpret them. Even where innovative textbooks were introduced, teachers often used them in traditional ways, asking students to memorize or copy from dictation the short descriptive paragraphs of factual material, just as they had done with the encyclopedias.

Advocates of the new critical methods of social and economic history were less eager to confront the objections raised by developmental psychologists, who argued that many historical concepts were too abstract for children under the age of sixteen to grasp.[84] Lacking the mental tools

[83] I am grateful to D. Emiliano Martínez, director of Santillana publishers, for the insights into the recent history of Spanish textbook publishing that he shared with me in an interview on 13 June 1985.

[84] For a summary, see Roy Hallam, "Piaget and the Teaching of History," *Educational Research* 12 (1969): 3–12; Mario Carretero, Juan Ignacio Pozo, and Mikel Asensio, "Comprension de conceptos históricos durante la adolescencia," *Infancia y aprendizaje* 23 (1983): 55–74; and Pozo and Carretero, "Enseñar historia o contar 'historias'?" *CP 9*, no. 111 (1984): 45–50.

to understand or critique social structures like feudalism or capitalism or to situate them in chronological time, children merely memorized terminology, much as they had done with the lists of Visigothic kings in an earlier day. On the other hand, adolescents in the last year of the BUP, while ostensibly mature enough psychologically, were unfamiliar with the social science concepts intrinsic to the new history, and again, resorted to memory to see them through the exams. A ministerial survey in 1984 confirmed that secondary school students were most attracted to contemporary history and displayed little comprehension of or interest in historically remote civilizations and social structures. (The exceptions were Greece and Rome, which came first in the syllabus and were treated more conventionally). The same survey indicated that textbooks still played an important role in 40 percent of classrooms and that examinations were by far the most frequent method of student evaluation.[85]

These difficulties pointed to what was perhaps the most serious obstacle to the transformation of student expectations and behavior—Spain's deeply rooted authoritarian culture. Stimulating historical imagination and critical understanding was not just a question of sending students in search of data; an entire system of family, social, and political values based on passive obedience, conformity, and credentialism militated against an easy transformation of the way history was taught.[86] In a society in which 51 percent of a sample of the active population harbored political attitudes that could be classified as "authoritarian,"[87] history education continued to reinforce old habits of deference to received opinion as often as it inculcated new habits of critical inquiry or disinterested judgment.[88]

Nevertheless, the changes in how history was conceptualized and taught that arose in the late 1960s and early 1970s signaled larger transformations in Spanish society. The disarticulation of the National Catholic paradigm, the emergence of alternative theoretical perspectives and investigative methods, and the embrace of active pedagogy and new themes by educational theorists, teachers, and policy makers were

[85] MEC, Inspección de Bachillerato del Estado, "Profesores y alumnos ante la enseñanza de la geografía y de la historia en el bachillerato," Documentos de Trabajo n° 15 (January 1984). I am grateful to the Servicio de Publicaciones for allowing me to consult this survey. In a survey of EGB professors in 1981, 53 percent responded that textbooks were "very important" in teaching. "El consumo de libros de texto, estancado," Nuestra Escuela 33 (June 1981): 5–11.

[86] See Amando de Miguel, "Transmisión de las ideas autoritarias," and 40 millones de españoles, 40 años después (Barcelona: Grijalbo, 1976), 179–91;

[87] Fundación FOESSA, Estudios sociológicos, 1201.

[88] See Onofre Janer, "En torno a la enseñanza de la historia," CP 1, no. 6 (June 1975): 48.

symptomatic of social and cultural processes whose significance would be fully realized only after the death of the dictator in 1975 and the transition to a stable parliamentary democracy. Integral to the cultural evolution that made the transition possible was the shift in the way that Spaniards understood national history and identity. As the metaphor of the "two Spains" faded away, the foundation was laid for the creation of a new imagined community better adapted to Spain's present and future.

History and National Identity

SINCE THE EIGHTEENTH CENTURY, European nationalisms, whether of the civic, ethnic, or authoritarian variety, have typically resorted to the national past, real or "invented," to establish the legitimacy of their claims in the present and future, especially where they have had to contend with strong particularist loyalties and cultural traditions. Nationalism has been strongest where nationalists have been able to create popular belief in a unique national personality and shared historical trajectory by using modern agencies of mass communication and socialization, especially the schools. In Spain, however, a weak oligarchic state, a fragmented and inadequate system of mass schooling and a divided political class produced a situation in which national history and identity were contested by groups seeking to capture and strengthen the state. These ranged from "civic nationalists" like Altamira and the institucionistas, whose goal was a juridical nation whose citizens shared common rights, freedoms, and responsibilities, to counterrevolutionary, authoritarian nationalists for whom religious and national identity were synonymous and whose vision of national identity was a shield against political and cultural modernization. The unitary nationalism of these groups was in turn challenged by Catalan and Basque nationalists, whose sense of separate identity was based on a distinct linguistic, cultural, and historical tradition and whose growing strength measured the incapacity of the Spanish state to develop mechanisms of political, economic, and cultural integration.

Each of these nationalist groups enlisted its version of national history in defense of its political and cultural project; all viewed secondary schooling as an opportunity to enlist the allegiance of elites and the primary schools as a mold for shaping the pueblo into the "nation" it desired. The parliamentary monarchy, which was unable to make the transition to mass politics and consequently was indifferent to the "formative" potential of mass schooling, eventually collapsed as economic and social modernization created tensions that the traditional mechanisms of control could no longer master. Thereafter, first the authoritarian right and then the democratic left seized the state in order to create a nation in its own image.

Neither the Primo de Rivera dictatorship nor the Second Republic lasted long enough to inculcate a common sense of national history and identity in the pueblo. But the experience of the long-lived and much more determined Franquist dictatorship illustrates what those regimes had begun to discover in their much shorter existence—that at least in Spain, the schools were not an infinitely pliable instrument with which to impose and maintain hegemony. Far from responding instantly to the commands of the state, the public schools comprised a semiautonomous sphere in which institutional inertia, classroom culture, and textbooks changed only under considerable pressure, whether from above or below, and then only gradually and incompletely. Furthermore, the state was far from enjoying an educational monopoly; on the contrary, its inability to meet the demand for schooling made it possible for opposition groups to challenge the dominant culture by creating an alternative system of schools. Thus, the strength of the religious colegios acted as a constant impediment to the creation of a liberal civic culture, first under the parliamentary monarchy (when the state's efforts to do so were admittedly halfhearted) and, more importantly, under the Republic. When the church finally relaxed its antiliberalism in the 1960s and began to distance itself from the dictatorship, an important obstacle to the eventual transition to democracy was removed. In similar fashion, the progressive educational movement spearheaded by the Institución Libre de Enseñanza prevented conservative elites from monopolizing national discourse on political and cultural values throughout the period, while in Catalonia (except during the repressive phase of the Franco regime), local governments took advantage of the limited reach of the state to nurture a sense of Catalan identity based on Catalan language, history, and culture.

Civic and authoritarian nationalists alike viewed history as an important element in cementing national solidarity. But as this study has shown, the determination to harness history to their respective political projects converted the Spanish past into a arena of cultural conflict. Radically different conceptions of the meaning of Spanish history produced equally divergent definitions of national identity and purpose, which rival groups attempted to transmit through their schools. Thus, what Spanish children learned about their past was in part a function of where, how, and by whom they were educated. But this study has also tried to suggest that children did not necessarily learn what their educators wanted them to know. Traditional teaching methods and textbooks proved to be poorly adapted to instilling the internalized knowledge, habits, and sentiments that both democratic reformers and the National Catholic right associated with the ends of "education" as opposed to "instruction." Thus, conflicting messages about the past were often only partly assimilated by their intended audiences, if at all.

The experience of the Franco regime suggests that not only the medium but the message itself was an obstacle to the development of Spanish nationalism. National Catholic ideology tried to resurrect a nation of imperial warriors and saints in a society battered by hunger, isolation, and bitterness. Furthermore, its definition of national identity was divisive, rather than communitarian, because it rested on dichotomies internal to the nation (good Spaniards/bad Spaniards) as well as external to it (spiritual Spaniards/materialistic foreigners). A definition of the nation that justified the victory of one-half of its members over the other half, and that elevated misery and humiliation to the status of national virtues could not hope to set deep roots.

Moreover, the Spanish identity promoted by early Franquism was increasingly dysfunctional once the regime made the decision to modernize economically and to pursue European integration. The dilemma was that the regime itself was anachronistic in the context of modernization; it could not invent an updated model of national character without endangering its raison d'être. Unable to construct a new past better suited to the changing horizons of the society, from the mid-1950s onward the regime simply abandoned history altogether, trusting in rising prosperity in a "continuous present" to legitimate its existence.

With the liberalization of the intellectual climate, this abdication of state supervision over the past left the field open to professional historians, whose scholarship became a tool of political subversion. By exploring the social and economic foundations of political power and locating Spain within general European patterns of historical change, they helped expose the gap between a modern society and a retrograde state. Once historical scholarship had questioned the empirical reality of Spanish "difference," the myth of Spanish inaptitude for modern political and economic life, which had helped legitimize the Franquist dictatorship, could no longer be easily sustained. By the time of Franco's death in 1975, the ideological barricades erected to prevent a return to constitutional democracy had thus been substantially eroded.

During the transition to democracy, Spaniards began the process of redefining themselves as a state and a nation. That process led to the Constitution of 7 December 1978, which established "the indissoluble unity of the Spanish Nation, common and indivisible patria of all Spaniards," and also "recognizes and guarantees the right to autonomy of the nationalities and regions that compose it and the solidarity among them all."[1] This transactional formula, which ensured the necessary consensus between the nationalist right and the democratic left, left many questions deliberately unanswered. Nearly twenty years later, Spaniards

---

[1] Constitution of 7 December 1978, article 2.

are still debating the relationship between the state and the autonomous communities and, more problematically, the relationship between "Spain" and the "nations" of which it is composed. Is Spain a "nation"? a "nationality"? or merely "a State formed by a group of nations"?[2] Across the political spectrum, and in the autonomous communities of Spain, "Spaniards" provide remarkably divergent answers to these questions. As Francesc Mercadé has observed, the "great variety of processes of internalization of national reality put obstacles in the way of the fundamental legitimation of the State."[3] At the same time, the oppositional character inherent to the formation of national identities (the us-versus-them phenomenon) raises serious questions about the viability of "Spain" as an "imagined community."

A 1981 study of Spanish and regional stereotypes provides empirical corroboration of the inverse relationship between local and national identities among Spaniards. Respondents were asked to list the traits most characteristic of (1) Spaniards, (2) the regional group to which they belonged, and (3) the other regional groups in Spain (Andalusians, Catalans, Castilians, Gallegans, and Basques). What was surprising about the results was not the tendency of each group to evaluate itself more positively than the others, but rather the small degree of overlap between the self-description of each group and the traits most frequently attributed to "Spaniards" in general. The adjectives most often applied to "Spaniards" by all respondents included repressed, religious, proud, and passionate, adjectives that no group applied to itself (although, significantly, some groups also applied them to Castilians). Only a single characteristic was uniformly applied by all groups to Spaniards, to other groups, and to themselves: *amantes de su tierra"* — that is, lovers of their homeland, or *patria chica*. Clearly, local identities still played a stronger role in many Spaniards' sense of themselves than did their identities as Spaniards. What is more, Spanish national identity was associated with negative qualities that most Spaniards preferred not to ascribe to themselves.[4] This suggests that National Catholic rhetoric convinced most Spaniards to define themselves in opposition to the identity promoted by the regime; the *caballero cristiano* became the re-

---

[2] Barrera in the Constituent Cortes, May 1978, quoted in Francesc Mercadé, "El marco ideológico de los nacionalismos en España (Siglos XIX, XX)," in Cristina Dupláa and Gwendolyn Barnes, *Las nacionalidades del estado español: Una problemática cultural* (Minneapolis: University of Minnesota, Institute for the Study of Ideologies and Literature, 1986), 41.

[3] Ibid., 35.

[4] José Luis Sangrador García, *Estereotipos de las nacionalidades y regiones de España* (Madrid: Centro de Investigaciones Sociológicas, 1981).

pressed, religious, proud, and passionate Castilians and Spaniards with whom no one else felt any affinity.

It seems unlikely that a survey taken today would produce substantially different results. The manipulation of history in the service of hyperbolic nationalism in the 1940s and 1950s so sensitized democratic reformers to the potential for abuse that they have refrained from creating a new, more functional and more inclusive identity and history for the nation apart from its constitutional expression. History textbooks written for the BUP since 1978 are studiously neutral, chronological narratives that respect the pluralistic cultural and political history of the peninsula, analyze the structural causes and the social and political consequences of its heterogeneous economic development, and shun metahistorical theorizing about national character and destiny.

But however satisfying to professional historians and to those in the autonomous communities, the recent reluctance to make a case for Spain as a national community with a common past has its drawbacks. On the one hand, it raises the familiar question of history's place in the curriculum. A flood of ministerial studies, model curricula, didactic guides, and journal articles on history teaching have appeared since 1975, addressing the same difficulties that confronted Altamira and his progressive colleagues at the turn of the century. The methods of professional history, which sharpen critical thinking skills, are difficult to put into practice in the typical secondary school classroom, and even more difficult to operationalize in the elementary grades. Moreover, the research questions that have engaged professional historians during the last thirty years, such as the price of wheat in the eighteenth century, property relations under feudalism, or popular concepts of death in the sixteenth century, are of limited appeal and beyond the intellectual grasp of many students, who frequently question their relevance to contemporary concerns, just as they previously questioned the educational benefits of memorizing the list of the Visigothic kings.[5] If history no longer defines nationhood, flees from patriotism, and fails to develop practical knowledge or skills, why is it in the curriculum at all?

The answer takes us back to the question of whether Spain is a state, a nation, a multi-national state, or all three. At a time when nationalism is on the rise throughout Europe and is threatening or has destroyed the integrity of other multi-national states, Spaniards concerned to preserve Spanish unity are searching for ways to build a sense of national iden-

[5] See Instituto de Ciencias de la Educación, Universidad de Zaragoza, *La enseñanza de la historia en BUP y COU: Visión del profesorado* (Zaragoza: author, 1983); and MEC, Inspección del Bachillerato del Estado, "Profesores y alumnos ante la enseñanza de la geografía y de la historia en el bachillerato," Documentos de Trabajo no. 15 (Madrid: author, January 1984).

tity that can peacefully coexist with the strong nationalist sentiments of Catalans, Basques, and other emerging nationalities within the Spanish state. On its face, this is not a utopian project; people can and do perceive themselves as having plural identities, to which they can feel similar loyalties, depending on context. But allegiance to a Spanish national identity cannot be taken for granted. As this study has shown, over the last century a succession of political regimes have largely failed in their attempts to instill a common understanding of national history and purpose. The terrain is thus relatively empty. But as M. A. Bastenier observed several years ago in the influential Madrid daily *El País*, Spanish governments since the transition have failed "to reoccupy the territory of our history as a civil ideology." In the meantime regional governments in Catalonia and Euzkadi have filled the vacuum with history schoolbooks in which "Spain" is ignored altogether. If the new Spanish democracy cannot invent for itself a national history that is more than the sum of the separate histories of its component nationalities, then it may lose the battle to maintain the balance between integration and autonomy. Bastenier's warning has not lost its relevance: "What one cannot do is make a gift of the past to others. For they will keep it."[6]

[6] M. A. Bastenier, "España y el uso del pasado," *El País Internacional*, 10 August 1992, 8.

Bibliography

Primary Sources

Unpublished Sources

ORAL INTERVIEWS

D. Emiliano Martínez, 13 June 1985
D. Mauricio Santos, 22 May 1985
D. Joaquín Tena Artigas, July 1992

MANUSCRIPT SOURCES

Archivo General de la Administración del Estado
Archivo del Ministerio de Educación y Ciencia
Ministerio de Educación y Ciencia, Comisión Ministerial de Planes, Programas de Estudio y Evaluación. "Educación General Básica: Nueva orientación." Madrid, 1970.
Ministerio de Educación y Ciencia, Inspección de Bachillerato del Estado. "Profesores y alumnos ante la enseñanza de la geografía y de la historia en el bachillerato." Documentos de Trabajo no. 15. Madrid, January 1984.

Published Sources

PERIODICALS

Anuario de la Enseñanza Católica
Atenas: Revista de orientación e información pedagógica
Avante: Revista mensual de pedagogía
Boletín de Educación
Boletín de la Institución Libre de Enseñanza (BILE)
Boletín de la Real Academia de la Historia (BRAH)
Boletín Oficial del Estado (BOE)
Bordón: Revista de la Sociedad Española de Pedagogía
Comunidad Escolar: Periódico semanal de información educativa
Consigna: Revista de la Sección Femenina dedicada a las maestras
Cuadernos de Pedagogía. Revista mensual de educación (CP)
Educadores: Revista de la Federación Española de Religiosos de Enseñanza
La Enseñanza: Revista educativa y de información (LE)
La Enseñanza Católica: Órgano de la Federación Católica de los Maestros Españoles
Enseñanza Media: Revista del Centro de Orientación Didáctica (EM)
Escuela Española
Escuelas de España: Revista pedagógica
Gaceta de Madrid
El Ideal del Magisterio: Órgano de la Confederación Nacional de Maestros
El Liberal (EL)
El Libro Español

El Magisterio Español: Periódico de instrucción pública
Minerva: Información sobre enseñanzas superior, segunda y especiales. Edición semanal
Nuestra Escuela: Revista de los trabajadores de la enseñanza. Unión General de Trabajadores
Razón y Fé (RyF)
Revista de Bachillerato
Revista de Educación (RE)
Revista de la Institución Teresiana
Revista de Pedagogía (RP)
Revista de Segunda Enseñanza (RSE)
Revista Española de Pedagogía (REP)
Revista Nacional de Educación
Servicio: Publicación de la Delegación Nacional de Educación FET y de las JONS
El Siglo Futuro
El Sol (ES)
Vida Escolar: Revista del Centro de Documentación y Orientación Didáctica
Vida Nueva

TEXTBOOKS, MANUALS, READERS, "ENCYCLOPEDIAS," AND OTHER SCHOOLBOOKS

Aguado Bleye, Pedro. *Compendio de historia de España.* 4th ed. 2 vols. Madrid: Espasa-Calpe, 1933.

———. *Manual de historia de España.* 4th ed. 2 vols. Bilbao: Editorial Eléxpuru Hmnos., 1925 (1st ed. 1915).

———. *Resumen de historia de España.* Bilbao: Imp. y Lib. Hijos de Pérez Malumbres, 1914.

Aldana Fernández, Salvador. *Didáctica de la historia. 2° curso. Plan 1967.* 2d ed. Alcoy: Márfil, 1970.

Alfaro y Lafuente, Manuel Ibo. *Compendio de la historia de España.* 11th ed., rev. Madrid: Lib. de la Viuda de Hernando, 1889 (1st ed. 1853).

Altamira y Crevea, Rafael. *Epítome de historia de España: (Libro para los profesores y los maestros).* Madrid: Ediciones de La Lectura, 1927.

———. *Historia de la civilización española.* Barcelona: Manuales Soler, 1902.

———. *Historia de España y de la civilización española.* 3d ed., rev. 4 vols. Barcelona: Herederos de Juan Gili, 1913.

———. *Manual de historia de España.* Vol. 14 of *Obras completas de D. Rafael Altamira.* Madrid: M. Aguilar, 1934.

Álvarez Lastra, Manuel, and Eleuterio de Orte Martínez. 5 vols. *Formación del espíritu nacional. (Curso 2°, 3°, 4°, y 5°).* Madrid: Gráficas Canales, 1955.

Álvarez Pérez, Antonio. *Enciclopedia intuitiva, sintética y práctica (Ajustada al cuestionario oficial). Segundo grado.* 80th ed. Valladolid: Miñón, 1962 (1st ed. 1955).

———. *Enciclopedia intuitiva, sintética y práctica (Ajustada al cuestionario oficial). Tercer grado.* Valladolid: Miñón, 1957 (1st ed. 1954).

———. *Sugerencias y ejercicios: Libro del maestro. Tercer grado.* Zamora: Tipografía Comercial, 1955.

Amicis, Edmundo de. *Corazón: (Diario de un niño)*. Madrid: Hernando, 1956 (1st Spanish ed. 1887).

Andrés Zapatero, Santiago. *Curso de historia*. 5th ed. 2 vols. Barcelona: Librería Élite, 1958.

————. *Historia de España y sus relaciones con la universal en las edades modernas y contemporáneas*. Barcelona: Librería Élite, 1965.

————. *El imperio español: (Historia y geografía)*. Barcelona: Editorial Delta, 1942.

Área de ciencias sociales. 8°. Fichas de trabajo. E.G.B. Madrid: Santillana, 1974.

[Arenaza Lasagabaster, J. J., and Fermín Gastaminza Ibarburu]. *Bachillerato elemental. 4° curso. Historia universal y de España*. Madrid: Ediciones S. M., 1961.

————. *Historia de España y universal. 4° curso. Plan 1967. Bachillerato elemental*. Madrid: Ediciones S.M., 1970.

Arranz Velarde, Fernando. *La España imperial. (Siglos XV–XVIII)*. 3d ed. rev. Madrid: Imprenta Góngora, 1951.

————. *La hegemonía de España: (Nociones de historia universal y de España)*. Santander: Tall. Tip. J. Martínez. 1935.

————. *Nociones de historia universal y de España: (Edades antigua y media)*. Madrid: Imprenta Góngora, 1958.

Artigas y Feiner, Juan. *Compendio de historia de España*. 7th ed. Barcelona: A. López Robert, 1901 (1st ed. 1878).

Asián Peña, José Luis. *Elementos de geografía general e historia de España. Primer curso de bachillerato*. 2d ed. Barcelona: Bosch, 1940.

————. *Historia universal y de España*. Barcelona: Bosch, 1960.

————. *Manual de historia de España*. Barcelona: Bosch, 1942.

Atlas histórico elemental. Zaragoza: Editorial Luis Vives, 1958.

Avendaño, Joaquín, and Mariano Carderera. *Curso elemental de pedagogía*. 7th ed. Madrid: Gregorio Hernando, 1878. (1st ed. 1850).

Ballester y Castell, Rafael. *Clio: Iniciación al estudio de la historia*. 5th ed. 4 vols. Tarragona: Editorial R. Ballester, 1933, 1935 (1st ed. 1913).

————. *Curso de historia de España*. 2d ed. Barcelona: Talleres Gráficas Lux, 1921.

Ballesteros Beretta, Antonio. *Síntesis de historia de España*. 3d ed., rev. Barcelona: Salvat, 1936.

Ballesteros Gaibrois, Manuel, and Roberto Ferrando Pérez. *Historia universal y de España. 4° curso*. Madrid: Ediciones La Ballesta, 1960.

Baró, Teodoro. *Historia de España*. 4th ed., rev. Barcelona: Lib. de Antonio J. Bastinos, 1891 (1st ed. 1876).

Beltrán y Rózpide, Ricardo. *Compendio de historia de España*. 5th ed. Madrid: Imp. del Patronato de Huérfanos de Intendencia e Intervención Militares, 1915 (1st ed. 1889).

Bermejo de la Rica, Antonio. *La España imperial*. 8th ed. Madrid: Gráfica Administrativa, 1952 (1st ed. 1942).

————. *Historia. Tercer curso. Edades antigua y media*. Madrid: AGESA, 1954.

————. *Historia. 4° curso. Edades moderna y contemporánea*. Madrid: AGESA, 1957.

Blasco Cea, Juan. *Historia antigua y media universal y de España. Tercer curso.* Madrid: Editorial Bruño, 1969.

Bosch Cusi, Juan. *Historia de España. Grado medio.* Rev. ed. Gerona: Dalmáu Carles, Pla, 1943 (1st ed. 1904).

Bruño, G. M. *Epítome del párvulo.* Madrid: Administración Bruño, 1915.

Calleja y Fernández, Saturnino. *Nociones de historia de España.* 65th ed. Madrid: Editorial Saturnino Calleja, 1915 (1st ed. 1886).

———. *Un viaje por España: Las regiones, su formación, su riqueza, sus costumbres, su historia.* Madrid: Editorial Saturnino Calleja, 1922.

Capel Margarito, Manuel. *Historia universal y de España. Tercer curso: Edades antigua y media.* Jaén: Unión Tipográfica, 1958.

Cartillas Montana. *Historia de España.* Barcelona: Editorial Miguel A. Salvatella, [1940].

Castro Álava, José Ramón. *Geografía e historia. Primer curso de bachillerato.* Zaragoza: Librería General, 1945.

———. *Geografía e historia. 5° curso de bachillerato.* 3d ed. Zaragoza: Librería General, 1940.

Cejador y Frauca, Julio. *Tierra y alma española.* Madrid: Sucs. de Rivadeneyra, [1924].

Cereceda, Feliciano. *Historia y geografía de España: (Acomodadas al cuestionario oficial señalado para quinto curso de bachilllerato).* Madrid: Ediciones FAX, 1941.

———. *Historia del imperio español y de la hispanidad.* 2d ed. Madrid: Razón y Fé, 1943.

Chico, Martín. *Patria: Lecturas nacionales.* 5th ed. Madrid: Editorial Hernando, 1933 (1st ed. 1898).

Colchero y Grande, Virgilio, and Virgilio Colchero y Arrubarrena. *Historia universal.* 5th ed. Madrid: Nueva Imprenta Radio, 1934 (1st ed. 1930).

Comas de Montañez, María. *Breve historia universal y de España.* Barcelona: Ediciones Sócrates, 1961.

Coronas Tejada, Luis. *Didáctica de la historia.* Salamanca: Anaya, 1971.

Cruz Rueda, Ángel. *Las gestas heroicas castellanas contadas a los niños.* Madrid: Biblioteca Nueva, 1931.

Dalmáu Carles, José. *Enciclopedia cíclico-pedagógica. Grado elemental.* Gerona: Editorial Dalmáu Carles, Pla, 1922.

———. *Enciclopedia cíclico-pedagógica. Grado medio.* 9th ed. Gerona: Dalmáu Carles, Pla, 1936.

———. *España, mi patria. Libro quinto.* Gerona: Dalmáu Carles, Pla, 1918.

Delegación Nacional de la Sección Femenina de FET y de las JONS. *Enciclopedia elemental.* 5th ed. Madrid: E. Giménez, 1959 (1st ed. 1951).

———. *Formación político-social. 2° curso de bachillerato.* 4th ed. Madrid: author, 1966.

Diego, Pedro de. *Lecciones familiares de historia de España: Libro de lectura.* Madrid: Librería de Hernando, 1878.

Edelvives. *Cartilla moderna de historia de España.* 5th ed. Zaragoza: Editorial Luis Vives, 1939.

————. *Enciclopedia escolar. Segundo ciclo.* Zaragoza: Editorial Luis Vives, 1958.

————. *Enciclopedia escolar. Tercer grado.* 4th ed. Barcelona: Editorial Luis Vives, 1940 (1st ed. 1933).

————. *Geografía e historia. Tercer curso.* Zaragoza: Editorial Luis Vives, 1951.

————. *Historia de España. Grado preparatorio (Cartilla).* Zaragoza: Editorial Luis Vives, 1957.

————. *Historia de España. Primer grado.* 10th ed. San Sebastián: Editorial F.T.D., n.d. (1st ed. 1934).

————. *Historia de España. Segundo grado.* Zaragoza: Luis Vives, [1944].

————. *Historia de la pedagogía.* 2 vols. Zaragoza: Editorial Luis Vives, 1965.

————. *Historia sagrada. Primer grado.* Zaragoza: Luis Vives, 1946.

————. *Historia sagrada. Segundo grado.* Zaragoza: Luis Vives, 1947.

————. *El libro de España.* Zaragoza: Editorial Luis Vives, 1944.

————. *Pedagogía general.* Zaragoza: Editorial Luis Vives, 1955.

Ediciones Bruño. *Enciclopedia. Primer grado.* 4th ed., rev. Madrid: author, n.d. (1st ed. 1934).

————. *Historia de España. Segundo grado.* 7th ed. Zaragoza: La Instrucción Popular, n.d. (1st ed. 1934?). Reprinted as *Historia de España. Tercer grado.* 12th ed. Madrid: Editorial Bruño, 1949.

————. *El libro de España.* Madrid: author, 1943.

Enciso Villanueva, Gabino. *Mi patria: Lo que ha sido, lo que es, y lo que puede ser España.* Burgos: Hijos de Santiago Rodríguez, [1920, 1929].

E.P. *Enciclopedia de la enseñanza primaria dispuesta por los PP. de las Escuelas Pías de España. Grado tercero.* Valencia: Editorial Saber, 1941.

————. *Enciclopedia de la enseñanza primaria dispuesta por los PP. de las Escuelas Pías de España. Segundo grado.* Valencia: Editorial Saber, 1942.

Estévanez, Nicolás. *Resumen de la historia de España.* Barcelona: Publicaciones de La Escuela Moderna, 1904.

Fernández, Antonio, Montserrat Llorens, and Rosa Ortega Canadell. *Área social. Historia contemporánea. Orbe. 8° curso de EGB.* Barcelona: Editorial Vicens-Vives, 1974.

Fernández Amador de los Ríos, Juan. *España en la edad media.* Pamplona: Imp. lib. y enc. de Nemesio Aramburu, 1911.

————. *Historia moderna y contemporánea de España.* 4th ed. Zaragoza: Imprenta Editorial Gambón, 1933 (1st ed. 1912).

Fernández Ascarza, Victoriano. *Historia de España. Segundo grado.* Madrid: Magisterio Español, 1941.

————. *Lecturas ciudadanas: (Educación cívica).* 2d ed. Madrid: Editorial Magisterio Español, 1933.

Fernández Rodríguez, Antonio. *España emocional: Lecturas e indicaciones alrededor de la esencia geográfico-espiritual de España.* Gerona: Dalmáu Carles, Pla, 1936.

————. *Nuevas lecturas patrióticas.* 3d ed. Zaragoza: Librería La Educación, 1937 (1st ed. 1930).

FET y de las JONS, Delegación Nacional del Frente de Juventudes, Jefatura Central de Enseñanza. *Formación del espíritu nacional: Manual de iniciación político-social para enseñanza primaria*. Madrid: Ediciones de Frente de Juventudes, 1947.

Franganillo y Monge, Manuel. *Lecturas cívicas comentadas*. Gerona: Dalmáu Carles, Pla, 1918.

F.T.D. *Historia de España*. Barcelona: Editorial F.T.D., 1932.

———. *Historia de España. Segundo grado*. 2d ed., rev. Barcelona: Librería Católica Pontificia, 1916.

———. *Primer grado. Historia de España*. Barcelona: author, 1912.

García Martínez, Eladio, and Modesto Medina Bravo. *Historia de España*. Madrid: Espasa-Calpe, 1934.

García Purón, Juan. *La moral en ejemplos históricos*. 2d ed. New York: D. Appleton and Company, 1902.

García Tolsa, Jesús. *Historia de los pueblos hispánicos: Libro de lecturas*. Barcelona: Editorial Vicens-Vives, 1961.

Gil Muñiz, Alfredo. *Hispania mater: Lecturas escolares escogidas*. 3 vols. Burgos: Hijos de Santiago Rodríguez, 1923–31.

Giner de los Ríos, Gloria. *Cien lecturas históricas*. Madrid: Espasa-Calpe, 1935.

González-Blanco, Edmundo. *Cincuenta españoles ilustres: Biografías compuestas y acopiadas para su lectura en las escuelas*. Madrid: Editorial Yagües, [1929].

González Linacero, Daniel. *Mi primer libro de historia*. 2d ed. Palencia: Imp. de "El Diario Palentino," 1935.

———. *Mi segundo libro de historia*. Palencia: Artes Gráficas Afrodisio Aguado, 1934.

Grenier, Patricio María, ed. *Aventuras del hombre sobre la tierra*. Madrid: Magisterio Español, 1963.

Grima Reig, Juan M. *Historia. 4° curso de bachillerato*. Valencia: ECIR, 1960.

Gutiérrez Zuloaga, Isabel. *Historia de la educación española*. 4th ed. Madrid: Narcea de Ediciones, 1972 (1st ed. 1968).

Herrera Oria, Enrique. *España es mi madre: Libro de lectura*. Valladolid: Imprenta Católica, 1939.

———. *Historia de la educación española desde el renacimiento*. Madrid: Ediciones Veritas, 1941.

———. *Nociones de historia de España*. 2d ed. Burgos: Ediciones Antisectarias, 1938.

Hillyer, V[irgil] M[ores]. *Una historia del mundo para los niños*. Translated and adapted by Fernando Sáinz. Madrid: Juan Ortiz, n.d. (1st American ed. 1915).

Ibáñez de Opacua, María del Pilar. *El libro de España*. Madrid: Publicaciones de la Institución Teresiana, 1941.

Instituto de España [José María Pemán]. *Manual de historia de España. Segundo grado*. Santander: Aldus, 1939.

Izquierdo Croselles, Juan, and Joaquín Izquierdo Croselles. *Compendio de historia general*. 2 vols. Granada: Urania, 1941–42.

Jaén Morente, Antonio. *Historia de España.* 3 vols. Seville: Imp. de Eulogio de las Heras, 1923.

――――. *Nociones de historia de América.* Edición oficial. Madrid: Imprenta Clásica Española, 1929.

Lafuente Vidal, José. *Compendio de historia de España.* 2 vols. Salamanca: Est. Tip. de Calatrava, 1924.

Larra, Fernando José de. *Estampas de España: Libro de lectura para muchachos y muchachas.* Barcelona: Editorial Montserrat, 1933.

Larrosa Barbero, Tomás. *Guía didáctica de geografía e historia. 5° curso: Libro del maestro.* Burgos: Hijos de Santiago Rodríguez, 1970.

Lillo Rodelgo, José Eusebio. *Primeras lecturas civiles.* Madrid: Espasa-Calpe, 1934.

Llach Carreras, Juan. *A través de España.* New ed. Gerona: Dalmáu Carles, Pla, 1935 (1st ed. 1912?).

Llano, Alberto. *Historia universal en lecturas amenas.* 4 vols. Barcelona: Editores Seix y Barral, 1926.

Llobet, Salvador and Antonio Pla, and Santiago Sobrequés Vidal. *Hesperia: Curso de geografía. Hispania: Curso de historia.* Barcelona: Ediciones Teide, 1944 (2 bks. in 1 vol.).

Llorens, Montserrat. *Didáctica de la historia.* 3d ed. Barcelona: Editorial Vicens-Vives, 1965.

López, A. R. *Historia de España.* Madrid: Casa Ed. Enciclopedia de las Escuelas, [1906?].

Luis-André, Eloy. *Nociones de educación cívica, jurídica, y económica.* Madrid: Imp. de los Hijos de M. G. Hernández, 1921.

Machiandiarena, Rufino. *Ensayo de historia de España.* San Sebastián: Imp. de Pozo, 1893 (1st ed. 1884).

Manjón, Andrés. *Gráficos aplicables a la escena.* Granada: Imprenta-Escuela del Ave-María, 1932.

――――. *Hojas catequísticas y pedagógicas del Ave María. Libro 3°.* Granada: Imprenta-Escuela del Ave-María, 1921.

――――. *Hojas históricas del Ave María.* Granada: Escuela del Ave-María, 1915.

Manríquez, Gervasio. *Educación moral y cívica: (Libro de lectura).* Barcelona: Editorial Ruiz Romero, 1933.

Manuales Manjón. *Historia de España: Breve resumen con dos gráficos.* 14th ed. Granada: Imprenta-Escuela del Ave-María, 1940.

Manzanares, Alejandro. *Ciudadanía: (Lecturas sobre el civismo).* Gerona: Dalmáu Carles, Pla, 1935.

Martí Alpera, Félix. *Nueva enciclopedia escolar. Grado primero.* 2d ed., rev. Burgos: Hijos de Santiago Rodríguez, 1931.

――――. *Nueva enciclopedia escolar. Grado tercero.* Burgos: Hijos de Santiago Rodríguez, 1935.

[――――]. *Nueva enciclopedia escolar H.S.R. Grado segundo.* 16th ed. Burgos: Hijos de Santiago Rodríguez, 1942.

[――――]. *Nueva enciclopedia escolar H.S.R. Tercer grado.* 3d ed. Burgos: Hijos de Santiago Rodríguez, 1941.

Martín de la Calle, Marcos. *Compendio de geografía e historia. (Segundo curso)*. Madrid: Imprenta de Jesús López, 1933.

———. *Compendio de historia de España*. Logroño: Imp. y Lib. de Carlos Gil, 1906.

Martínez Muñoz, Enrique. *Una escuela de la patria: Cartas de un maestro a un niño*. Cartegena: 1924.

Menéndez-Reigada, Albino. *Catecismo patriótico español*. 3d ed. Salamanca: Est. Tip. de Calatrava, 1939.

Merry y Colón, Manuel, and Antonio Merry y Villalba. *Compendio de historia de España: Redactado para servir de texto en los seminarios y colegios católicos*. Seville: Imp. y Lit. de José María Ariza, 1889.

Monreal y Ascaso, Bernardo. *Curso de historia de España*. 2d ed., rev. Madrid: Aribau (Sucesores de Rivadeneyra), 1875 (1st ed. 1867).

Montilla y Benítez, Rafael. *Nociones de geografía e historia. Primer curso de bachillerato*. Granada: Imprenta Editorial Urania, 1938.

———. *Nociones de geografía e historia. Segundo curso de bachillerato*. 2d ed. Granada: Imprenta Editorial Urania, 1939.

Montilla Tirado, Francisca. *Historia de la educación*. 5th ed. Madrid: Graf. Andrés Martín, 1962 (1st ed. 1959).

Morales, María Luz. *Algunas mujeres*. 2d ed. Gerona: Dalmáu Carles, Pla, 1934.

Moreno Espinosa, Alfonso. *Compendio de historia de España distribuído en lecciones y adaptado a la índole y extensión de esta asignatura en la segunda enseñanza*. 12th ed., rev. Barcelona: Tip. el Anuario de la Exportación, 1912 (1st ed. 1871).

[Onieva, Antonio J.]. *Así quiero ser: (El niño del Nuevo Estado). Lecturas cívicas H.S.R.* 2d ed. Burgos: Hijos de Santiago Rodríguez, 1940.

Onieva, Antonio J. *Cien figuras españolas: (Biografías de figuras célebres). Libro escolar de lecturas*. 1st. ser. 16th ed. Burgos: Hijos de Santiago Rodríguez, 1962 (1st ed. 1954).

———. *Escudo imperial: Libro escolar de lectura*. Burgos: Hijos de Santiago Rodríguez, 1937.

———. *Florilegio de mujeres españolas: (Biografías de españolas célebres). Libro escolar de lectura*. 3d ed. Burgos: Hijos de Santiago Rodríguez, 1958 (1st ed. 1953).

———. *Frases célebres entresacadas de nuestra historia*. 3d ed. Burgos: Hijos de Santiago Rodríguez, 1958 (1st ed. 1947).

———. *Viajando por España*. 5th ed. rev. Burgos: Hijos de Santiago Rodríguez, 1951.

Onieva, Antonio J., and Federico Torres. *Enciclopedia Hernando. Segundo ciclo del período de enseñanza elemental. Niños*. Madrid: Lib. y Casa Ed. Hernando, 1954.

———. *Enciclopedia Hernando. Segundo ciclo del período de enseñanza elemental. Niñas*. Madrid: Lib. y Casa Ed. Hernando, 1954.

Orberá y Carrión, María. *Nociones de historia de España*. Valencia: Imp. de R. Ortega, 1878.

Orodea e Ibarra, Eduardo. *Curso de lecciones de historia de España*. 6th ed. Valladolid: Imp. y Lib. de Hijos de Rodríguez, 1875 (1st ed. 1867).

Ortiz Muñoz, Luis. *Glorias imperiales: Libro escolar de lecturas históricas*. 2 vols. Madrid: Editorial Magisterio Español, 1940.

Paluzie Cantalozella, Esteban. *Historia de España para los niños*. Barcelona: Hijos de Paluzie, 1908 (1st ed. 1871).

Parravicini, Luigi A. *Juanito: Libro de lectura*. Barcelona: Imprenta Elzeviriana y Librería Camí, 1948 (1st Spanish ed., 1848).

Pascual de Sanjuán, Pilar. *Flora, o la educación de una niña*. Barcelona: Imp. y Lit. de Faustino Paluzie, 1881.

————. *La moral de la historia: Colección de cuadros históricos con su aplicación moral al alcance de los niños*. 6th ed. Barcelona: Lib. de Juan y Antonio Bastinos, 1881.

Pellejero Soteras, Cristóbal. *Geografía e historia. Segundo curso*. 2d ed. Madrid: Imprenta Helénica, 1940.

Pemán, José María. *La historia de España contada con sencillez para los niños . . . y para muchos que no lo son*. Cádiz: Est. Cerón, 1939.

Pérez Bustamante, Ciriaco. *Síntesis de historia de España*. 8th ed., rev. Madrid: Ediciones Atlas, 1959 (1st ed. 1939).

Pérez Picazo, Teresa. *Didáctica de la historia*. Burgos: Hijos de Santiago Rodríguez, 1970.

Picatoste Rodríguez, Felipe. *Compendio de historia de España*. Madrid: Librería de la Viuda de Hernando, 1884.

Pla Cargol, Joaquím. *La terra catalana. Libre quart*. 6th ed. Gerona: Dalmáu Carles, Pla, 1932.

Rastrilla Pérez, Juan. *Geografía e historia. E.G.B. 7°*. Madrid: S.M., 1973.

Real Academia de la Historia [Rafael Altamira]. *Historia de España, para uso de las escuelas primarias. Primer grado*. Madrid: Cía. Gral. de Artes Gráficas, 1930.

————. *Indicaciones a los maestros para la enseñanza de la historia de España*. Madrid: author, 1930.

Rodríguez García, Gerardo. *Historia de España. Grado elemental*. Madrid: Hernando, 1928.

————. *Historia de España en lecturas para los niños*. Madrid: Sucs. de Hernando, 1915.

————. *Lecturas escolares de sociología*. Madrid: Lib. Sucs. de Hernando, 1923.

Roig, Juan, Montserrat Llorens, and Antonio Fernández. *Area social. Geografía e historia. Orbe. 7° curso de E.G.B.* Barcelona: Editorial Vicens-Vives, 1973.

Ruiz Amado, Ramón. *Compendio de historia de España desde las más remotas épocas hasta la guerra europea de 1914*. Barcelona: Librería Religiosa, 1916.

————. *Historia de la educación y de la pedagogía*. 5th ed. Barcelona: Gustavo Gili, 1930 (1st ed. 1911).

Ruiz Carnero, Ricardo. *Historia de España*. Madrid: Editorial Hernando, 1943.

Ruiz Romero, Juan, and María de los Ángeles Muncunill. *Virtud y patria. Primer grado de lectura manuscrita*. Barcelona: Editorial Ruiz Romero, 1935 (1st ed. 1904).

Rumeu de Armas, Antonio. *Historia de España moderna y contemporánea. Curso preuniversitario*. 2 vols. Salamanca: Anaya, 1969.

————. *Historia universal y de España. 3°. Edades antigua y media.* Salamanca: Anaya, 1969.

Salaverría, José-María. *El muchacho español.* Madrid: Editorial Calleja, 1917.

Sánchez Adell, José. *Cronos: Didáctica de la historia.* 4th ed. Barcelona: Editorial Vicens-Vives, 1969.

Sánchez Casado, Félix. *Prontuario de historia de España y de la civilización española.* 16th ed. Madrid: Lib. Hernando, 1896 (1st ed. 1867).

Santacruz Revuelta, Pascual. *España sobre todo: Páginas patrióticas para la infancia.* Madrid: Imp. Viuda y hijos de Jaime Ratés, 1926.

Santamaría Arandez, Álvaro. *Historia moderna y contemporánea. 4° curso.* 6th ed. Madrid: Prensa Española, 1959.

Saz, Bernardo del. *Historia de España. Curso elemental.* 3 vols. Málaga: Tip. de Manuel Cerban, 1898.

Seró Sabaté, Joaquín. *El niño republicano. (Cuarto libro de lectura).* 4th ed. Barcelona: Salvador Santomá, 1933.

Serrano de Haro, Agustín. *España es así.* 6th ed. Madrid: Editorial Escuela Española, 1942 (1st ed. 1933).

————. *Yo soy español. El libro de primer grado de historia.* Madrid: Editorial Escuela Española, 1943.

Serrano Puente, Vicente. *Historia de España.* 2d ed. 2 vols. Valladolid: Librería Santarén, 1940 (1st ed. 1925).

Siurot, Manuel. *La emoción de España: Libro de cultura patriótica popular.* Madrid: Talleres Voluntad, 1927.

————. *La nueva emoción de España: Libro de cultura patriótica popular.* Burgos: Hijos de Santiago Rodríguez, 1937.

S.M. *Historia de España y universal. 4° curso.* Madrid: Ediciones S.M., 1970.

————. *Madre España: Libro de lectura. Grado medio y superior.* 4th ed. Burgos: Hijos de Santiago Rodríguez, 1948.

————. *Manual de historia de España y lecturas históricas.* 3d ed. Burgos: Hijos de Santiago Rodríguez, [1948] (1st ed. 1944).

Sobrequés Vidal, Santiago. *Hispania: Historia política y cultural de España.* 9th ed. Barcelona: Ediciones Teide, 1960.

Solana, Ezequiel. *Lecciones de historia de España. Primer grado o curso preparatorio.* Madrid: Magisterio Español, 1907.

————. *La patria española: Trozos escogidos acerca de la grandeza de nuestra patria, características de sus comarcas y vitalidad de su pueblo.* 14th ed. Madrid: Escuela Española, 1962.

————. *Tratado elemental de historia de España.* 8th ed. Madrid: El Magisterio Español, 1931 (1st ed. 1914).

Solís y Miguel, Prudencio. *Nociones de historia de España, para uso de escuelas y colegios.* Valencia: Libs. de Juan Mariana y Sanz, 1875.

Terradillos, Ángel María. *Prontuario de historia de España.* 18th ed. Madrid: Librería de la Viuda de Hernando, 1890 (1st ed. 1846).

Textos E.P. *Enciclopedia. Grado tercero.* 3d ed. 2 vols. Madrid: Editorial Bibliografía Española, 1948.

————. *Historia de España. Curso primero.* Madrid: Bibliografía Española, n.d.

————. *Historia de España. Segundo curso*. Madrid: Bibliografía Española, n.d.

Thomas, Albert. *Lecturas históricas: Historia anecdótica del trabajo*. Translated and adapted by Rodolfo Llopis. Madrid: Juan Ortiz, 1930.

Torres, Federico. *La historia del mundo contada a los niños*. 4th ed. Barcelona: Editorial Salvatella, 1942 (1st ed. 1934).

————. *Progreso: Lecturas históricas sobre el mundo, la vida, y las civilizaciones*. 2d ed., rev. Barcelona: Miguel A. Salvatella, 1941 (1st ed. 1935).

————. *Viajes por España: Manuscrito*. 8th ed. Barcelona: Salvatella, [1942].

Torroja i Valls, Raimon. *Història de Catalunya per a nois e noies*. Barcelona: Imprenta Elzeviriana, 1933.

————. *La nostra terra i la nostra història: Iniciació a l'estudi de la geografia i de la història de Catalunya*. Barcelona: Imprenta Elzeviriana, 1933.

Vázquez Gómez, José, et al. *Ciencias sociales. Fichas para trabajo individualizado del alumno. 6º EGB*. Barcelona: Prima Luce, n.d.

Vergara Martín, Gabriel María. *Apuntes de geografía e historia. (Primer año)*. Madrid: Hernando, 1934.

————. *Nociones de historia de España*. 3d ed. Madrid: Hernando, 1927.

Vergés, Oriol. *Cives: Historia moderna y contemporánea. 4º curso de bachillerato*. 4th ed. Barcelona: Editorial Teide, 1972.

Vicens Vives, Jaime. *Atlas histórico de España*. 5th ed. Barcelona: Editorial Teide, 1965.

————. *Cives: Historia universal y de España*. 8th ed. Barcelona: Editorial Teide, 1967.

Vicens Vives, Jaime, and Santiago Sobrequés Vidal. *Geografía e historia universal. Formación Profesional Industrial. 2º curso de Iniciación Profesional*. 4th ed. Barcelona: Editorial Vicens-Vives, 1962.

Villar de Serchs, Aniceto. *Anécdotas ejemplares: Episodios famosos de la historia de España. Dichos y hechos de personajes célebres*. Valladolid: Miñón, 1963.

————. *Terra i ánima: Lectures sobre coses de Catalunya*. 2d ed. Barcelona: Miquel A. Salvatella, 1935.

Viñé Marcellán, María. *Guía didáctica de geografía e historia. 6º curso. Libro del maestro*. Burgos: Hijos de Santiago Rodríguez, 1969.

Xandri Pich, José. *Del solar hispano: (Notas geográficas e históricas, costumbres y folklore)*. Palencia: Ediciones Justicia y Caridad, n.d.

————. *España legendaria: Narraciones históricas, tradiciones, leyendas y romances*. Madrid: Tip. Yagües, 1934.

Yela Utrilla, Juan Francisco. *Historia de la civilización española en sus relaciones con la universal*. Edición oficial. Madrid: Talleres Voluntad, 1928.

Yeves, Carlos. *Programas de primera enseñanza: Historia de España*. 8th ed., rev. Madrid: Lib. de los Sucesores de Hernando, 1908.

Zabala y Lera, Pío. *Historia de España y de la civilización española en la edad contemporánea*. 2 vols. Barcelona: Sucesores de Juan Gili, 1930.

Zabala Urdániz, Manuel. *Compendio de historia de España*. 17th ed., rev. 2 vols. Madrid: Imp. de Jaime Ratés Martín, 1922 (1st ed. 1883).

BOOKS AND ARTICLES

Abeledo, Amaranto A. *La enseñanza de la historia*. Buenos Aires: Librería y Editorial "El Ateneo," 1945.

Alonso del Real, Carlos. "Valor política de la enseñanza del latín." *Revista Nacional de Educación* 1 (July 1941): 43–50.

Altamira y Crevea, Rafael. *Cuestiones modernas de historia*. Madrid: Daniel Jorro, 1904.

———. *La enseñanza de la historia*. 2d ed. Madrid: V. Súarez, 1895 (1st ed. 1891).

———. *Ideario pedagógico*. Madrid: Editorial Reus, 1923.

———. *Psicología del pueblo español*. 2d. ed., rev. Barcelona: Editorial Minerva, [1917] (1st. ed. 1902).

———. *Temas de historia de España*. Vol. 8 of *Obras completas de D. Rafael Altamira*. Madrid: Compañía Ibero-Americana de Publicaciones, 1929.

American Historical Association, Committee of Seven. *The Study of History in the Schools: Report to the American Historical Association*. New York: Macmillan, 1899.

Anuario estadístico de la ciudad de Barcelona. Barcelona: Ayuntamiento, 1905.

Apalátegui, Francisco, S.J. "Del estudio de la historia en la segunda enseñanza." In *Asociación Española para el Progreso de las Ciencias. Congreso de Valladolid*. Madrid: Imp. de Eduardo Arias, 1917, 8:309–30.

Apostolado de la Prensa. *La segunda enseñanza en España y fuera de España: Algunas consideraciones sobre los últimos decretos del Ministerio de Fomento*. Madrid: Agustín Avrial, Imp., 1899.

———. *La verdadera regeneración de España*. Madrid: Agustín Avrial, Imp., 1898.

Aranda, Valentín, Alfonso Barea, and Antonio J. Onieva. *Hacia la escuela hispánica*. Madrid: Editorial Magisterio Español, 1936.

Arco y Garay, Ricardo. *La idea de imperio en la política y la literatura española*. Madrid: Espasa-Calpe, 1944.

Artigas, Miguel. *La España de Menéndez Pelayo: Antología de sus obras, selección y notas*. 2d ed. Valladolid: Cultura Española, 1938 (1st ed. 1935).

[Artigas, Miguel, and Miguel Allué Salvador]. *Una poderosa fuerza secreta: La Institución Libre de Enseñanza*. San Sebastián: Editorial Española, 1940.

Asociación Provincial de Catedráticos de Instituto, Comisión de Investigación y Estudios Docentes. *Degradación de la enseñanza media oficial y del Cuerpo de Catedráticos de Instituto: Informe*. Madrid: author, 1975.

Ayala Alarcó, Ángel, S.J. *Formación de selectos*. Vol. 2 of *Obras completas*. Madrid: Atenas, 1940.

Azaña Díaz, Manuel. *El jardín de los frailes*. Madrid: Alianza Editorial, 1982.

———. *Obras completas*. Edited by Juan Marichal. 4 vols. México, D.F.: Ediciones Oasis, 1966.

Barea, Arturo. *The Forging of a Rebel*. Translated by Ilsa Barea. New York: Viking Press, 1972.

Barral, Carlos. *Años de penitencia*. Madrid: Alianza Editorial, 1975.

Becerro de Bengoa, Ricardo. *La enseñanza en el siglo XX*. Madrid: Edmundo Capdeville, Librero, 1900.

Bello, Luis. *Viaje por las escuelas de España*. Vols. 1 and 2. Madrid: Magisterio Español, 1926–27; vol. 3. Madrid: Espasa-Calpe, 1927; vol. 4. Madrid: Compañía Ibero-Americana de Publicaciones, 1929.

Benot, Eduardo. *Errores en materia de educación y de instrucción pública*. 4th ed. Madrid: Librería de Hernando, 1899 (1st ed. 1859).

Blanco y Sánchez, Rufino. *Bibliografía pedagógica de obras escritas en castellano o traducidas a este idioma*. 5 vols. Madrid: Tip. de la Revista de Archivos, Bibliotecas y Museos, 1907–12.

Bosch-Gimpera, Pedro. *La España de todos*. Madrid: Seminarios y Ediciones, 1976.

Calvo Serer, Rafael. *España sin problema*. Madrid: Rialp, 1949.

Cánovas del Castillo, Antonio. *Historia de la decadencia de España desde el advenimiento de Felipe III al trono hasta la muerte de Carlos II*. 2d ed. Madrid: Librería de Gutenberg de José Ruiz, 1910 (1st ed. 1854).

Carretero, Mario, Juan Ignacio Pozo, and Mikel Asensio. "Comprensión de conceptos históricos durante la adolescencia." *Infancia y aprendizaje* 23 (1983): 55–74.

———. "La comprension de la historia en la EGB: Una asignatura pendiente." Manuscript.

Castillejo, José. *The War of Ideas in Spain*. London: H. Milford, 1937.

Castillo, Santiago, ed. *La historia social en España: Actualidad y perspectivas. Actas del I Congreso de la Asociación de Historia Social*. Madrid: Siglo XXI, 1991.

Castro, Américo. *España en su historia: Cristianos, moros, y judíos*. Buenos Aires: Losada, 1948.

———. *La realidad histórica de España*. México, D.F.: Porrúa, 1954.

Castro Marcos, Miguel de. *Legislación de Instrucción Pública referente a los institutos generales y técnicos*. Madrid: Tip. de la Revista de Archivos, 1921; 3d ed., Imp. del Rubio, 1927.

———. *Legislación vigente de Instrucción Pública referente a los institutos de segunda enseñanza*. 4th ed. Madrid, 1934.

———. *El ministerio de Instrucción Pública bajo la dominación roja: Notas de un espectador imparcial*. Madrid: Lib. Enrique Prieto, 1939.

———. *Vademecum del catedrático y del opositor*. Madrid: Imp. de G. Hernández y Galo Sáez, 1923.

Cela, Camilo José. *Journey to the Alcarria*. Translated by Frances M. López-Morillas. Madison: University of Wisconsin, 1964.

Chousa, Camilo. *La reforma de la segunda enseñanza*. Antequera: Imp. de Francisco Ruiz, 1930.

Colección legislativa de España. Parte 1a, *Legislación y disposiciones de la Administración Central, 1857–1936*.

Comisión Episcopal de Enseñanza y Educación Religiosa. *La iglesia y la educación en España, hoy*. Madrid, 2 February 1969.

Comisión de Reformas para el Mejoramiento de la Clase Obrera. *La clase obrera a finales del siglo XX*. 2d ed. Bilbao: Zero, 1975.

Consejo Superior de Investigaciones Científicas, Instituto San José de Calasanz. *Cuestiones de enseñanza media*. Madrid: C. Bermejo Impresor, 1947.

Conversaciones franco-españolas para la revisión bilateral de los manuales escolares de historia. Madrid: Instituto Jerónimo Zurita, 1962.

Corts Grau, José. *Motivos de la España eterna.* Madrid: Instituto de Estudios Políticos, 1946.

Cossío, Manuel B. *De su jornada: (Fragmentos).* Madrid: Imp. de Blass, 1929.

Costa y Martínez, Joaquín. *Maestro, escuela y patria: (Notas pedagógicas).* Vol. 10. Madrid: Biblioteca Costa, 1916.

———. *Tutela de pueblos en la historia.* Madrid: Imp. de Fortanet, 1917.

Cuestionarios del bachillerato elemental y normas sobre el establecimiento del nuevo plan. Madrid: Escuela Española, 1967.

Cuestionarios nacionales de enseñanza primaria. 4th ed. Madrid: Editorial Magisterio Español, 1968.

Cuestionarios para los estudios del bachillerato. (Plan de 1934). Primer, segundo y tercer cursos. Barcelona: Bosch, 1934.

Cuestiones actuales de pedagogía. 4 vols. Madrid: Federación de Amigos de la Enseñanza, 1934–35.

Delegación de Distrito de Educación Nacional de Zaragoza. *La enseñanza media: Nuestra visión sobre el problema.* Zaragoza: Departamento de Publicaciones, 1947.

Deleito, José de. *El aislamiento de España en el pasado y el presente: Conferencia dada en el Círculo Instructivo Reformista de Valencia el día 17 de marzo de 1915.* Valencia: n.p., 1915.

———. *La enseñanza de la historia en la universidad española y su reforma posible: Discurso leído en la solemne apertura del curso académico de 1918 a 1919 en la Universidad Literaria de Valencia.* Valencia: Tip. Moderna, 1918.

Delgado, Jesús. *Cuestiones pedagógicas de actualidad: Texto único. Objecciones y ventajas. El estado, el catedrático y el alumno ante el texto único oficial.* Madrid: Imp. del Asilo de Huérfanos del S.C. de Jesús, 1927.

Dewey, John. *Democracy and Education: An Introduction to the Philosophy of Education.* New York: Macmillan, 1916.

Diario de las sesiones de las Cortes. Congreso de los Diputados. Madrid, 1890–1923, 1933–36.

Diario de las sesiones de las Cortes Constituyentes de la Republica española, 14 julio–3 octubre 1933. Madrid, 1931–33.

Díaz Barea, Julio. *Prontuario del estudiante de bachillerato.* El Ferrol del Caudillo: La Latina, 1960.

Domingo, Marcelino. *La escuela en la república: La obra de ocho meses.* Madrid: M. Aguilar, 1932.

Domínguez Berrueta, Mariano. *Ante una campaña injusta: Notas para la defensa de la enseñanza oficial, de la libertad de enseñanza y del profesorado de los institutos nacionales.* Ávila: Tip. y Enc. Senén Martín, 1925.

Domínguez Martín-Sánchez, Javier. *Enseñanza católica para una generación: Víctima y testigo.* Madrid: Editorial Popular, 1979.

Dozy, Reinhardt. "Le Cid d'après de nouveaux documents." In *Recherches sur l'histoire et la littérature de l'Espagne pendant le moyen age.* 3d ed. Leiden: E. J. Brill, 1881 (1st ed. 1849).

Errandonea, Ignacio. *El plan de bachillerato actual.* Madrid: Editorial Razón y Fé, 1943.

Escalafón de los catedráticos numerarios de Institutos Nacionales de Enseñanza Media: Situación en 1° de octubre de 1941. Madrid: Información Universitaria, 1941.

Escalafón de los catedráticos numerarios de Institutos Nacionales de Segunda Enseñanza. Madrid: Imp. de L. Rubio, 1934–36.

Escolano Benito, Agustín, ed. *Historia de la educación: Diccionario de las ciencias de la educación.* 2 vols. Madrid: Anaya, 1985.

Escuela Española. Contestaciones al cuestionario para las oposiciones a plaza de más de 10,000 habitantes, convocatoria 1964: Temas de historia. Madrid: Editorial Escuela Española, 1965.

E.T.L. *En la dictadura. Por pueblos y aldeas: De las memorias de un delegado gubernativo.* Madrid: Editorial Católica Toledana, 1928.

FAE (Federación de Amigos de la Enseñanza). *Anuario de la educación católica: Curso 1934–1935.* Madrid, 1934.

————. *¡Bachillerato! Gráficos y números.* Madrid: Delegación Técnica de la F.A.E., 1931.

————. *En torno al ministerio de Instrucción Pública: (Actuación técnica de la F.A.E.).* Madrid: Editorial Voluntad, 1931.

————. *Nuestro patriotismo.* Madrid: Colección Atenas, 1933.

Fernández Huerta, José. "El progresismo culturalista en la enseñanza de la historia." *Escuela Española* 17, no. 892 (1958): 3–4.

Ferrer Canto, Ángel, and José Ángel Taverner Linares. *Programas graduados para una escuela unitaria.* Alicante: Modernas Gráficas Gutenberg, 1934.

Ferrer Guardia, Francisco. *La Escuela Moderna.* Gijón: Ediciones Júcar, 1976 (1st ed. 1912).

Figueroa y Torres, Álvaro, conde de Romanones. *Notas de una vida.* 2 vols. Madrid: Renacimiento, 1928–29.

————. *Las responsabilidades del antiguo régimen.* Madrid: Imp. Cervantina, 1924.

Fontana, Josep. *Historia: Análisis del pasado y proyecto social.* Barcelona: Editorial Crítica, 1982.

————. "Para una renovación de la enseñanza de la historia." *Cuadernos de Pedagogía* 1, no. 11 (1975): 10–13.

F.T.D. *Guía del maestro para uso de los Hmnos. Maristas de la Enseñanza: Redactada según las reglas y enseñanzas de su venerable fundador.* Barcelona: Editorial F.T.D., 1928.

Fundación FOESSA. *Estudios sociológicos sobre la situación social de España, 1975.* Madrid: Euramérica, 1976.

————. *Informe sociológico sobre el cambio social en España, 1975–1983.* Vol. 2. Madrid: Euramérica, 1983.

Fuster García, Julio. *Didáctica de la historia desarrollada en lecciones.* Madrid: Publicaciones de la Revista de Pedagogía, 1936.

Galiño, María Ángeles. "Metodología de la historia." *Bordón* 5, no. 39 (1953): 699–710.

Gálvez Carmona, Gonzalo. *Nuestra pedagogía: Cartas a un maestro.* Granada: Ed. y Lib. Prieto, 1938.

Ganivet, Ángel. *Idearium español. El porvenir de España.* 11th ed. Madrid: Espasa-Calpe, 1981 (1st ed. 1895).

García Martínez, Eladio. *La enseñanza de la historia en la escuela primaria.* Madrid: Espasa-Calpe, 1941.

García Morente, Manuel. *Idea de la hispanidad.* 2d ed. Buenos Aires: Espasa-Calpe, 1939.

García Villada, Zacarías, S.J. *El destino de España en la historia universal.* 2d ed., rev. Madrid: Cultura Española, 1940 (1st ed. 1935).

Gaziel [Agustín Calvet]. *Tots el camins duen a Roma.* Madrid: Editorial Aedos, 1959.

Gil de Zárate, Antonio. *De la instrucción pública en España.* 3 vols. Madrid: Imprenta del Colegio de Sordomudos, 1855.

Giménez Caballero, Ernesto. *Genio de España.* 3d ed. Zaragoza: Ediciones Jerarquía, 1938.

Giner de los Ríos, Francisco. *Educación y enseñanza.* Vol. 12 of *Obras completas.* Madrid: Espasa-Calpe, 1933.

González Palencia, Ángel. *Los mozárabes de Toledo en los siglos XII y XIII.* 4 vols. Madrid: Instituto de Valencia Don Juan, 1926.

Groizard y Coronado, Carlos. *La instrucción pública en España: Discursos y notas.* Salamanca: Ramón Esteban, 1897.

Gual Villalbí, Pedro. *Memorias de un industrial de nuestro tiempo.* Barcelona: Sociedad General de Publicaciones, 1922.

Guía del estudiante, 1918–19. Madrid: S.I., 1918.

Guía oficial de España (1873–1930).

Guibert, Jean. *A los maestros cristianos. El educador apóstol: Su preparación y ejercicio de su apostolado.* Trans. R.P. Antolín Saturnino Fernández. 14th ed. Barcelona: Imp. Moderna de Buinart y Pujolar, 1908.

Hallam, Roy. "Piaget and the Teaching of History." *Educational Research* 12 (1969): 3–12.

Hernández y González, Luis [Eloy Luis-André]. *Un espíritu nuevo en la educación: Un informe y un voto sobre el Instituto-Escuela. Reformas urgentes en la segunda enseñanza.* Madrid: Sucesores de Rivadeneyra, 1926.

Herrera Oria, Enrique, S.J. *La asamblea de catedráticos de instituto.* Madrid: Editorial Razón y Fé, 1931.

———. *Educación de una España nueva.* Madrid: Ediciones FAX, 1934.

———. *La enseñanza de la historia en el bachillerato: Orientaciones sobre planes y métodos. El material escolar y los museos escolares.* Valladolid: Tip. de Andrés Martínez Sánchez, 1926.

———. *Modernas orientaciones en la enseñanza superior y secundaria.* Madrid: Editorial Razón y Fé, 1929.

———. *¿Sabe educar España?* Madrid: Ediciones FAX, 1935.

Herrero García, Miguel. *Ideas de los españoles del siglo XVII.* 2d ed. Madrid: Editorial Gredos, 1966 (1st ed. 1927).

Hill, C. Peter. *L'Enseignement de l'histoire: Conseils et suggestions.* Paris: UNESCO, 1953.

Ibáñez Martín, José. *Diez años de servicios a la cultura española, 1939–1949.* Madrid: Ministerio de Educación Nacional, 1950.

Ibarra, Eduardo. "Cómo debe ser enseñada la historia." In *Asociación Española para el Progreso de las Ciencias. Congreso de Zaragoza. (1908)*. Madrid: Imprenta de Eduardo Arias, 1910, 6:59–74.

———. *Meditemos: (Cuestiones pedagógicas)*. Zaragoza: Biblioteca Argensola, 1908.

———. *Los problemas fundamentales de la segunda enseñanza*. Madrid: Huelves y Cía., [1929].

"Informe sobre los libros de texto." *Nuestra Escuela* 33 (June 1981): 5–11.

Iniesta, Alfonso. *Garra marxista en la infancia*. Burgos: Hijos de Santiago Rodríguez, 1939.

Instituto de Ciencias de la Educación, Geneva. *El espíritu internacional y la enseñanza de la historia: Estudios presentados al tercer Congreso Internacional de Educación Moral*. Madrid: Ediciones de La Lectura, Espasa-Calpe, 1932.

Instituto de Ciencias de la Educación, Universidad de Zaragoza. *La enseñanza de la historia en BUP y COU: Visión del profesorado*. Zaragoza: author, 1983.

Instituto de España. *Menéndez y Pelayo y la educación nacional*. Santander: Aldus, 1938.

Instituto Nacional del Libro Español. *Libros y material de enseñanza*. Madrid: Comisión Asesora de Editores de Libros de Enseñanza, 1961–78.

———. *Textos para la enseñanza media: Catálogo general. Curso 1958–59*.

Janer, Onofre. "En torno a la enseñanza de la historia." *Cuadernos de Pedagogía* 1, no. 6 (1975): 48.

Jara Urbano, Alfredo. "La historia en la escuela. (Notas y sugestiones)," *Revista de Pedagogía* 6, no. 71 (1927): 515–23, and no. 72 (1927): 558–66.

Jorro de Miranda, José. *Nuestros problemas docentes*. Vol. 1., *La Administración*. Madrid: Sucesores de Hernando, 1919.

Juderías Loyot, Julián. *La leyenda negra: Estudios acerca del concepto de España en el extranjero*. 13th ed. Madrid: Editora Nacional, 1954 (1st ed. 1914; 2d ed., rev. 1917).

———. *La reconstrucción de la historia de España desde el punto de vista nacional. Discursos leídos ante la Real Academia de la Historia en el acto de su recepción pública por . . . y por el Excmo. Sr. D. Jerónimo Becker y González el día 28 de abril de 1918*. Madrid: Imp. Clásica, 1918.

Junta para Ampliación de Estudios e Investigaciones Científicas. *Un ensayo pedagógico: El Instituto-Escuela de segunda enseñanza de Madrid. (Organización, métodos, resultados)*. Madrid: author, 1925.

Lafuente, Modesto. *Historia general de España, desde los tiempos más remotos hasta nuestros días*. 30 vols. Madrid: Establecimiento Tipográfico de Mellado, 1850–67.

Laín Entralgo, Pedro. *España como problema*. 2 vols. Madrid: Aguilar, 1962.

League of Nations, International Institute of Intellectual Cooperation. *School Textbook Revision and International Understanding*. 2d ed., rev. Paris: author, 1933.

Leo XIII. *Aeterni Patris* (1879).

Llopis, Rodolfo. "La enseñanza de la historia." *Revista de Pedagogía* 1, no. 1 (1922): 47–52.

————. *La revolución en la escuela: Dos años en la Dirección General de Primera Enseñanza.* Madrid: M. Aguilar, 1933.

Llorca y García, Ángel. *Libros de orientación escolar: Cien lecciones prácticas de todas las materias y para niños de todos los grados de la escuela primaria.* 3d ed. Madrid: Caro Raggio, 1933.

Llorens, Montserrat. *Metodología para la enseñanza de la historia.* 3d ed. Barcelona: Editorial Vicens-Vives, 1965 (1st ed. 1960).

Luis-André, Eloy. *La educación de la adolescencia: Estudio crítico del estado de la segunda enseñanza y de sus reformas más urgentes.* Madrid: Imp. de "Alrededor del Mundo," 1916.

————. *Españolismo. Prasologio. Pueblo y conciencia nacional.* Madrid: Sucesores de Rivadeneyra, 1931.

Luzuriaga, Lorenzo. *El analfabetismo en España.* Madrid: J. Cosano, 1926.

————. *Diccionario de pedagogía.* Buenos Aires: Editorial Losada, 1960.

————. *Historia de la educación y de la pedagogía.* 12th ed. Buenos Aires: Editorial Losada, 1977.

————. *Pedagogía social y política.* Buenos Aires: Editorial Losada, 1954.

Macías Picavea, Ricardo. *El problema nacional: (Hechos, causas y remedios).* Edited by José Esteban. Madrid: Fundación Banco Exterior, 1992 (1st ed. 1899).

Maeztu, Ramiro de. *Defensa de la hispanidad.* 4th ed. Madrid: Gráfica Universal, 1941 (1st ed. 1932).

————. *Hacia otra España.* Madrid: Fernando Fé, 1899.

Mailló, Adolfo. *Educación y revolución: Los fundamentos de una educación nacional.* Madrid: Editora Nacional, 1943.

————, ed. *Enciclopedia de didáctica aplicada.* 2 vols. Barcelona: Editoral Labor, 1971.

Mallada, Lucas. *Los males de la patria y la futura revolución española.* Madrid: Tip. de M. Ginés Hernández, 1890.

Marín Martínez, Tomás. *Historia: Orientaciones metodológicas.* Madrid: Instituto de Ciencias de la Educación, Universidad Complutense, 1973.

Martí Alpera, Félix. *Historia.* Madrid: Publicaciones de la Revista de Pedagogía, 1925.

Martínez Baselga, Pedro. *Sociología y pedagogía.* Zaragoza: Tip. de Emilio Casañal, 1909.

Martínez Val, José María. *La finalidad de la historia en la enseñanza media: (Comunicación presentada en el Congreso Internacional de Pedagogía, Santander-San Sebastián, julio de 1949).* Ciudad Real: Publicaciones del Instituto de Estudios Manchegos, 1949.

————. "La formación del sentido histórico en el niño." *Revista Española de Pedagogía* 3, no. 11 (1945): 177–210.

Marvaud, Angel. *La Question social en Espagne.* Paris: Félix Alcan, 1910.

Memoria para la apertura del curso académico de ——— *en el Instituto Provincial de Segunda Enseñanza de Barcelona* (1862–95).

Memoria sobre el estado del Instituto de Segunda Enseñanza de Lérida durante el año escolar de ——— (1859–92).

Menéndez Pidal, Ramón. *La España del Cid*. 2 vols. Madrid: Editorial Plutarco, 1929.

——. *Los españoles en la historia*. Madrid: Espasa-Calpe, 1982.

——. *Spaniards in Their History*. Translated by Walter Starkie. New York: W. W. Norton, 1950.

Menéndez y Pelayo, Marcelino. *Historia de España, seleccionada de la obra del maestro por Jorge Vigón*. 4th ed. Madrid: Cultura Española, 1941.

——. *Historia de los heterodoxos españoles*. 3 vols. Madrid: Librería Católica de San José, 1880–81.

Ministerio de Educación Nacional (MEN). *Boletín oficial del Ministerio*. Madrid, 1939–65.

——. *Curso de orientaciones nacionales de la enseñanza primaria celebrado en Pamplona del 1 al 30 de junio de 1938. Segundo año triunfal*. 2 vols. Burgos: Hijos de Santiago Rodríguez, 1938.

Ministerio de Educación Nacional, Dirección General de Enseñanza Media. *Cátedra: Prontuario del profesor*. Madrid, 1960–61, 1962–63.

Ministerio de Educación Nacional, Dirección General de Enseñanza Primaria. *Cuestionarios nacionales para la enseñanza primaria*. Madrid: Sección de Publicaciones de la Secretaría General Técnica, 1953.

——. *Ley de Educación Primaria de 17 de julio de 1945: Textos legales*. Madrid: Servicio de Publicaciones del Ministerio, 1952.

Ministerio de Educación y Ciencia (MEC). *Boletín oficial del Ministerio*. Madrid, 1965–75.

——. *Ley general de educación y financiamiento de la reforma educativa y disposiciones complementarias*. 2d ed. Madrid, 1976.

——. *Libro blanco para la reforma del sistema educativo*. Madrid, 1989.

Ministerio de Educación y Ciencia, Centro de Orientación Didáctica de Enseñanza Media. *Didáctica de historia y geografía: (Estudios monográficos)*. Vol. 1. Madrid, 1965.

Ministerio de Educación y Ciencia, Secretaría General Técnica. *La educación en España: Bases para una política educativa*. Madrid, 1969.

Ministerio de Fomento, Dirección General de Instrucción Pública. *Boletín Oficial: Contestaciones de los rectores a las Reales Ordenes circulares de 19 y 20 de mayo de 1893, referentes a los libros de texto de los catedráticos* 2, no. 2 (1894).

——. *Boletín Oficial: Reforma de la segunda enseñanza* 2, no. 3 (1894).

Ministerio de Fomento, Inspección General de Enseñanza. *Anuario legislativo de Instrucción Pública*. Madrid: Joaquín Bafuedano, 1891–1900.

Ministerio de Instrucción Pública y Bellas Artes. *Anuario legislativo de Instrucción Pública*. Madrid, 1900–1910.

——. *Boletín oficial del Ministerio*. Madrid, 1910–73.

——. *Colección legislativa de Instrucción Pública*. Madrid, 1910–72.

Ministerio de Instrucción Pública y Bellas Artes, Sección de Informaciones, Publicaciones y Estadística. *Escuelas normales de maestros y maestras: Estado actual de la enseñanza en España*. Madrid, 1925.

——. *Institutos nacionales de segunda enseñanza. La reforma de 1926: Estado actual de la enseñanza en España*. Madrid: Talleres Espasa-Calpe, 1928.

Ministerio de Instrucción Pública y Bellas Artes, Subsecretaría, Sección de Estadística. *Escalafón de antigüedad de los catedráticos numerarios de los institutos generales y técnicos.* Madrid: Est. tip. Sucesores de Rivadeneyra, 1908, 1923.

Miró, Ignacio Ramón. *La enseñanza de la historia en las escuelas.* Barcelona: Antonio J. Bastinos, 1889.

Montilla Tirado, Francisca. *Selección de libros escolares de lectura.* Madrid: Consejo Superior de Investigaciones Científicas, Instituto San José de Calasanz, 1954.

Morayta de Sagrario, Miguel. *Historia general de España desde los tiempos ante-históricos hasta nuestros días.* 9 vols. Madrid: González Rojas, 1886–96.

Morote, Luis. *Los frailes en España.* Madrid: Imp. de Fortanet, 1904.

———. *La moral de la derrota.* Madrid: G. Juste, 1900.

Muñiz Vigo, Acisclo. *El generalísimo Franco en la escuela española.* Oviedo: Editorial FET, 1939.

Museo Pedagógico Nacional. *La enseñanza de la historia en las escuelas.* Vol 1. Madrid: Imp. de E. Maestre, 1934.

Oficina de Información Diplomática. *Fifteen Years of Spanish Culture.* Madrid, 1952.

Onieva, Antonio J. *Metodología y organización escolar.* Madrid: Ediciones Afrodisio Aguado, 1940.

———. *La nueva escuela española: (Realización práctica).* Valladolid: Librería Santarén, 1939.

Ortega Canadell, Rosa. *Metodología de la geografía y de la historia en el bachillerato.* Madrid: Dirección General de Enseñanza Media, n.d.

Ortega y Gasset, José. *España invertebrada: Bosquejos de algunos pensamientos históricos.* 6th ed. Madrid: Ediciones de la Revista de Occidente, 1971 (1st ed. 1921).

———. *Obras completas.* Madrid: Alianza Editorial/Revista de Occidente, 1983.

———. "La pedagogía social como programa político" (1910). *Boletín de la Institución Libre de Enseñanza* 40, no. 678 (30 September 1916): 257–68.

Ortega y Rubio, Juan. *Historia de España.* 8 vols. Madrid: Bailly-Baillière, 1908–10.

Orwell, George. *Collected Essays, Journalism and Letters of George Orwell.* Edited by Sonia Orwell and Ian Angus. Vol. 4. New York: Harcourt, Brace and World, 1968.

Parral Cristóbal, Luis. *Elementos de pedagogía redactados conforme al programa oficial para el ejercicio escrito de oposiciones a escuelas públicas elementales y de párvulos dedicados a los maestros y maestras.* 3d ed. Tarragona: Est. Tip. de F. Aris e Hijo, 1902.

Pemán, José María. *El hecho y la idea de la Unión Patriótica.* Madrid: Imprenta Artística Saez, 1929.

Pemartín, José. *Formación clásica y formación romántica: Ideas sobre la enseñanza.* Madrid: Espasa-Calpe, 1942.

Pemartín Sanjuán, José. *¿Qué es 'lo nuevo'?: Consideraciones sobre el momento español presente.* Seville: Álvarez Zambrano, 1938.

————. *Los valores históricos en la dictadura española.* 2d ed. Madrid: Editorial Arte y Ciencia, 1929.

Pérez, Dionisio. "Cuentos de ayer, realidad de hoy." *Nuevo Mundo* 26, no. 1300 (6 December 1918): n.p.

Pérez de Ayala, Ramón. *A.M.D.G.* In Vol. 4 of *Obras completas.* Madrid: Editorial Pueyo, 1931.

Pijoán, J. *Mi don Francisco Giner (1906–1910).* San José de Costa Rica: Repertorio Americano, 1927.

Pius XI. *Divini Illius Magistri* (31 December 1929).

Posada, Adolfo. *Política y enseñanza.* Madrid: Daniel Jorro, 1904.

Poveda Castroverde, Pedro. *Itinerario pedagógico.* Madrid: Consejo Superior de Investigaciones Científicas, Instituto de Pedagogía Aldus, 1964.

Pozo, Juan Ignacio, and Mario Carretero. "El adolescente como historiador." *Infancia y Aprendizaje* 23 (1983): 75–90.

————. "Enseñar historia o contar 'historias'?" *Cuadernos de Pedagogía* 9, no. 111 (1984): 45–50.

Pozo, Juan Ignacio, Mario Carretero, and Mikel Asensio. "Cómo enseñar el pasado para entender el presente: Observaciones sobre la didáctica de la historia." *Infancia y Aprendizaje* 24 (1983): 55–68.

Primer Congreso Nacional de Educación Católica, Madrid, 21–26 de abril de 1924. Madrid: Tipografía de la "Revista de Archivos," 1925.

Programa de enseñanza para las escuelas elementales. Sarriá-Barcelona: Escuela Tipográfica y Librería Salesiana, 1904.

Ribera, Julián. *La superstición pedagógica.* 2 vols. Madrid: Imp. Ibérica, 1910.

Rodríguez, Teodoro. *La enseñanza en España.* Madrid: Imprenta Helénica, 1909.

————. *Infiltraciones judío-masónicas en la educación católica.* El Escorial: Imprenta del Monasterio, 1934.

————. *Nueva reconquista de España: (Caminos equivocados).* Valladolid: Librería Santarén, 1936.

————. *La segunda enseñanza.* Madrid: Imp. de la Viuda e Hija de Gómez Fuentenebro, 1901.

Rojí de Echeñique, Ángel. *El educador en acción.* Pamplona: Imp. de la Viuda de Román Velandia, 1910.

Rubio, Federico. *Mis maestros y mi educación: Memorias de niñez y juventud.* Madrid: Imp. y encuad. de V. Tordesillas, 1912.

Ruiz Amado, Ramón. *Educación cívica.* Barcelona: Librería Religiosa, 1918.

————. *La educación intelectual.* 3d ed., rev. 2 vols. Barcelona: Editorial Librería Religiosa, 1942. (1st ed. 1909).

————. *El patriotismo.* Madrid: Razón y Fé, 1910.

Ruiz Martín, Felipe. "La enseñanza moderna de la historia." In Ministerio de Educación Nacional, Dirección General de Ensenanza Media, *Cátedra: Prontuario del profesor.* Madrid, 1960, 139–45.

Ruiz de Obregón Retortillo, Juan. "Nuevas orientaciones de la historia." *La España Moderna* 26, no. 307 (1914): 5–17.

Sainz Rodríguez, Pedro. *Evolución de las ideas sobre la decadencia española y otros estudios de crítica literaria.* Madrid: Ediciones Rialp, 1962.

————. *Testimonios y recuerdos.* Barcelona: Editorial Planeta, 1978.

Salaverría, José-María. *La afirmación española: Estudios sobre el pesimismo español y los nuevos tiempos.* Barcelona: Gustavo Gili, 1917.

Sales y Ferré, Manuel. "Psicología del pueblo español." *Nuestro Tiempo* 2, no. 13 (1902): 9–20.

Sánchez Albornoz, Claudio. *España: Un enigma histórico.* Buenos Aires: Editorial Sudamericana, 1953.

Sánchez Sarto, Luis, ed. *Diccionario de pedagogía.* 2 vols. Barcelona: Editorial Labor, 1936.

Sanjuán, Teófilo. *Cómo se enseña la historia.* Madrid: Publicaciones de la Revista de Pedagogía, 1923.

Sastre, José Luis. "La reducción de libros de texto en la nueva legislación de enseñanza media." *El Libro Español* 11, no. 123 (March 1968): 243.

Seignebos, Charles, Ch.-V. Langlois, L. Gallouedec, and M. Tourneur. *L'Enseignement de l'histoire: (Conférences du Musée Pédagogique, 1907).* Paris: Imprimerie Nationale, 1907.

Sela y Sampil, Aniceto. *La educación nacional: Hechos y ideas.* Madrid: Librería General de Victoriano Suárez, 1910.

Serrano de Haro, Agustín. "En torno a la enseñanza de la historia." *Bordón* 5, no. 39 (1953): 711–17.

————. *Metodología de la enseñanza de la historia.* Madrid: F.A.E., 1933.

Shaw, Rafael. *Spain from Within.* London: T. Fisher Unwin, 1910.

Silió Cortés, César. *La educación nacional.* Madrid: Francisco Beltrán, 1914.

Silva Giménez, David. *Los textos escolares de EGB: Encuesta al profesorado.* Madrid: INCIE, Departamento de Prospección Educativa, 1976.

Siurot, Manuel. *Cada maestrito: Observaciones pedagógicas de uno que no ha visto en su vida un libro de pedagogía.* Seville: El Correo de Andalucía, 1912.

Suñer, Enrique. *Los intelectuales y la tragedia española.* Burgos: Editorial Española, 1937.

Ubierna y Eusa, J. A. *La función docente del estado: Legislación vigente en España.* Madrid: Hijos de Reus, 1917.

Umbral, Francisco. *Memorias de un niño de derechas.* Barcelona: Ediciones Destino, 1972.

Unamuno, Miguel de. *Obras completas.* Madrid: Escelicer, 1968.

United Nations, UNESCO. *A Handbook for the Improvement of Textbooks and Teaching Materials as Aids to International Understanding.* Paris, 1949 (Spanish ed. 1952).

United States Department of the Interior, Bureau of Education. *Biennial Survey of Education, 1916–1918.* Washington, D.C.: Government Printing Office, 1921.

Utande Igualada, Manuel, ed. *Planes de estudio de enseñanza media.* Madrid: Ministerio de Educación Nacional, Dirección General de Enseñanza Media, 1964.

Vázquez Riesco, José. *Bachillerato: Guía del alumno para el año académico 1939–40.* Madrid: Lib. de Enrique Prieto, 1940.

————. *Libro del alumno de segunda enseñanza.* Madrid: Lib. de Enrique Prieto, 1938.

Vega y Relea, J. "La enseñanza de la geografía y la historia en las escuelas." *Revista de Pedagogía* 1, no. 10 (1922): 381–82.

Vicens Vives, Jaime. *Historia social y económica de España y América.* 5 vols. Barcelona: Editorial Vicens-Vives, 1972.

———. "Presentación y propósito." *Estudios de Historia Moderna* 1 (1951): i–xii.

Vila Seima, José. "De la enseñanza de la historia." *Revista Española de Pedagogía* 29, no. 116 (1971): 369–92.

Vincenti y Reguera, Eduardo. *Política pedagógica (Treinta años de vida parlamentaria): Discursos relativos a los presupuestos de Instrucción Pública, mensajes de la Corona, interpelaciones, proposiciones de ley, etc.* Madrid: Imp. de los Hijos de M. G. Hernández, 1916.

Xandri Pich, José. *Programas graduados de enseñanza primaria, divididos en seis grados con instrucciones didácticas para su desarrollo.* Madrid: Tip. Yagües, [1925?].

Yeves, Carlos. *Programas de primera enseñanza: Historia de España.* 8th ed., rev. Madrid: Hernando, 1908 (1st ed. 1879).

Secondary Sources

Abella, Rafael. *La vida cotidiana en España bajo el régimen de Franco.* Barcelona: Argos Vergara, 1985.

———. *Por el imperio hacia Dios: Crónica de una posguerra (1939–1955).* Barcelona: Editorial Planeta, 1978.

Abellán, José Luis. *Sociología del 98.* Barcelona: Ediciones Península, 1974.

Ahier, John. *Industry, Children and the Nation: An Analysis of National Identity in School Textbooks.* London: Falmer Press, 1988.

Alberola, Armando, ed. *Estudios sobre Rafael Altamira.* Alicante: Instituto de Estudios "Juan Gil-Albert," Caja de Ahorros Provincial de Alicante, 1988.

Albisetti, James C. *Secondary School Reform in Imperial Germany.* Princeton: Princeton University Press, 1982.

¡Alça la voz pregonero! Homenaje a Don Ramón Menéndez Pidal. Madrid: Corporación de Antiguos Alumnos de la Institución Libre de Enseñanza y Cátedra-Seminario Menéndez Pidal, 1979.

Alonso, Dámaso. *Menéndez Pidal y la cultura española.* La Coruña: Instituto "José Cornida" de Estudios Coruñeses, 1969.

Alted Vigil, Alicia. *Política del Nuevo Estado sobre el patrimonio cultural y la educación durante la guerra civil española.* Madrid: Ministerio de Cultura, Dirección General de Bellas Artes y Archivos, 1984.

Althusser, Louis. "Ideology and the Ideological State Apparatuses." In *"Lenin and Philosophy" and Other Essays,* translated by Ben Brewster. New York: Monthly Review Press, 1971.

Álvarez Bolado, Juan. *El experimento de nacional-catolicismo, 1939–1975.* Madrid: EDICUSA, 1976.

Álvarez Junco, José. "Ciencias sociales e historia en los Estados Unidos: El nacionalismo como tema central." *Ayer* 14 (1994): 63–80.

———. *La ideología política del anarquismo español.* Madrid: Siglo XXI, 1976.

————. "La invención de la Guerra de la Independencia." *Studia Histórica: Historia contemporánea* 12 (1994): 75–100.

————. "El nacionalismo español como mito movilizador." In R. Cruz and Manuel Pérez Ledesma, eds. *Cultura y acción colectiva en la España contemporánea.* (forthcoming).

Álvarez Oblanco, Wenceslao. *La represión de postguerra en León: Depuración de la enseñanza, 1936–1943.* León: Santiago García, 1986.

Álvarez Osés, José Antonio, Ignacio Cal Freire, María Carmen González Muñoz, and Juan Haro Sabater. "La historia en los textos de bachillerato (1938–1975): Proyecto de investigación y análisis de un tema: La Segunda República." *Revista de Bachillerato* 2, no. 9 (January–March 1978): 2–18.

Anderson, Benedict. *Imagined Communities: Reflections on the Origins and Spread of Nationalism.* London: Verso, 1983.

Andrés Gallego, José. "Una escuela rural castellana: Fuencaliente del Burgo, 1847–1901." *Revista Española de Pedagogía* 120 (1972): 401–15.

————. *La política religiosa en España, 1889–1913.* Madrid: Editora Nacional, 1975.

Apple, Michael W. *Ideology and Curriculum.* Boston: Routledge and Kegan Paul, 1979.

Araya, Guillermo. *El pensamiento de Américo Castro: Estructura intercastiza de la historia de España.* Madrid: Alianza Editorial, 1983.

Archer, Margaret S. *Social Origins of Educational Systems.* London and Beverley Hills, Calif.: Sage Publications, 1979.

Balcells, Albert. *Cataluña contemporánea, 1900–36.* 2 vols. Madrid: Siglo XXI, 1976.

Bakewell, Peter. "An Interview with Antonio Domínguez Ortiz." *Hispanic American Historical Review* 65, no. 2 (1985): 189–202.

Barreiro Rodríguez, Hector. *Lorenzo Luzuriaga y la renovación educativa en España, 1889–1936.* La Coruña: Ediciós do Castro, 1989.

————. *Primeras jornads de educacíon: "Lorenzo Luzuriaga" y la política educativa de su tiempo. Ponencias.* Ciudad Real: Diputación Provincial, Área de Cultura, 1984.

Batanaz Palomares, Luis. *La educación española en la crisis de fin de siglo: (Los congresos pedagógicos del siglo XIX).* Córdoba: Diputación Provincial, 1982.

Batllori, Miquel. "Maravall, renovador de la historia socio-cultural d'Espanya." *L'Avenç* 102 (March 1987): 56–59.

Beattie, Nicholas. "Sacred Monster: Textbooks in the Italian Educational System." *British Journal of Educational Studies* 29, no. 3 (1981): 218–35.

Beltrán Reig, José María. *La enseñanza en la ciudad de Alicante: Primer tercio siglo actual.* Alicante: Instituto de Estudios Alicantinos, Diputación Provincial de Alicante, 1981.

Ben-Ami, Shlomo. *Fascism From Above: The Dictatorship of Primo de Rivera in Spain, 1923–1930.* New York: Oxford University Press, 1983.

Berger, Peter, and Thomas Luckmann. *The Social Construction of Reality.* New York: Doubleday, 1966.

Berkowitz, H. Chonon. *Pérez Galdós: Spanish Liberal Crusader.* Madison: University of Wisconsin Press, 1948.

Bernad Royo, Enrique. *La instrucción primaria a principios del siglo XX: Zaragoza, 1898–1914*. Zaragoza: Institución "Fernando el Católico," 1984.

Bernstein, Basil. *Class, Codes and Control*. Vol. 3, *Towards a Theory of Educational Transmissions*. Boston: Routledge and Kegan Paul, 1975.

Bhabha, Homi, ed. *Nation and Narration*. New York: Routledge, 1990.

Blas Guerrero, Andrés de. *Sobre el nacionalismo español*. Madrid: Centro de Estudios Constitucionales, 1989.

Blasco Carrascosa, Juan Ángel. *Un arquetipo pedagógico pequeño-burgués: (Teoría y praxis de la Institución Libre de Enseñanza)*. Valencia: Fernando Torres, 1980.

Blinkhorn, Martin. "Conservatism, Traditionalism and Fascism in Spain, 1898–1937." In *Fascists and Conservatives: The Radical Right and the Establishment in Twentieth-Century Europe*. London: Unwin Hyman, 1990.

———. "Spain: The 'Spanish Problem' and the Imperial Myth." *Journal of Contemporary History* 15, no. 1 (January 1980): 5–25.

Bly, Peter, ed. *Galdós y la historia*. Ottowa: Dovehouse Editions, Canada, 1988.

Boerne, Peter, ed. *Concepts of National Identity: An Interdisciplinary Dialogue*. Baden-Baden: Nomos Verlagsgesellschaft, 1986.

Bonilla y San Martín, Adolfo. *Marcelino Menéndez y Pelayo (1856–1912)*. Madrid: Est. Tip. de Fortanet, 1914.

Botrel, Jean-François. *Libros, prensa y lectura en la España del siglo XIX*. Translated by David Torra Ferrer. Madrid: Fundación Germán Sánchez Ruiperez, 1993.

Botti, Alfonso. *Cielo y dinero: El nacional-catolicismo en España (1881–1975)*. Madrid: Alianza Editorial, 1992.

Bourdieu, Pierre, and Jean-Claude Passeron. *The Inheritors: French Students and Their Relation to Culture*. Translated by Richard Nice. Chicago: University of Chicago Press, 1979.

———. *Reproduction in Education, Society and Culture*. Translated by Richard Nice. London and Beverley Hills, Calif.: Sage Publications, 1977.

Boyd, Carolyn P. "The Anarchists and Education in Spain, 1868–1909." *Journal of Modern History* 48 (1976): 125–72.

———. "'Mother Spain': Patriotic Travel Books in Spain, 1900–1950." Manuscript, 1995.

Brenan, Gerald. *The Spanish Labyrinth*. New York: Cambridge University Press, 1961.

Breuilly, John. *Nationalism and the State*. Manchester: Manchester University Press, 1982.

Breve reseña histórica de la Compañía de María (Religiosos marianistas). Madrid: n.p., 1935.

Bush, John W. "Education and Social Status: The Jesuit College in the Early Third Republic." *French Historical Studies* 9, no. 1 (1975): 125–40.

Caballero, Valentín. *Aportaciones pedagógicas de las Escuelas Pías*. Madrid: Consejo Superior de Investigaciones Científicas, Instituto San José de Calasanz, 1950.

Cacho Viu, Vicente. *La Institución Libre de Enseñanza*. Madrid: Rialp, 1962.

Cámara Villar, Gregorio. *Nacional-catolicismo y escuela: La socialización política del franquismo, 1936–1951.* Jaén: Editorial Hesperia, 1983.

Camporesi, Valeria. *Para grandes y chicos: Un cine para los españoles, 1940–1990.* Madrid: Ediciones Turfan, 1993.

Cañellas, Cèlia, and Rosa Toran. *Política escolar de l'Ajuntament de Barcelona, 1916–1936.* Barcelona: Barcanova, 1982.

Capel, Horacio, et al. *Ciencia para la burguesía: Renovación pedagógica y enseñanza de la geografía en la revolución liberal española, 1814–1857.* Barcelona: Universitat, 1983.

Capel Martínez, Rosa María. *El trabajo y la educación de la mujer en España (1900–1930).* Madrid: Ministerio de Cultura, Dirección General de Juventud y Promoción Cultural, 1982.

Carnoy, Martin. "Education and Theories of the State." *Education and Society* 1, no. 2 (1983): 3–25; 2, nos. 1–2 (1984): 3–19.

Caro Baroja, Julio. *El mito del carácter nacional: Meditaciones a contrapelo.* Madrid: Seminarios y Ediciones, 1970.

Carr, Raymond, and Juan Pablo Fusi. *Spain: Dictatorship to Democracy.* 2d ed. London: George Allen and Unwin, 1981.

Caruthers, Mary J. *The Book of Memory: A Study of Memory in Medieval Culture.* New York: Cambridge University Press, 1990.

Castells, José Manuel. *Las asociaciones religiosas en la España contemporánea: Un estudio jurídico-administrativo (1767–1965).* Madrid: Taurus, 1973.

Caudet Roca, Francisco. *Vida y obra de José María Salaverría.* Madrid: Consejo Superior de Investigaciones Científicas, 1972.

Chancellor, Valerie E. *History for Their Masters: Opinion in the English History Textbook, 1800–1914.* New York: Augustus M. Kelley, 1970.

Cheyne, George J. G. *Joaquín Costa, el gran desconocido: Esbozo biográfico.* Barcelona: Ariel, 1972.

Cirujano Marín, Paloma. "Aproximación sociológica al panorama historiográfico español, 1844–1874." In *Estudios de historia social: Homenaje a Manuel Tuñón de Lara,* 2:697–711. Madrid: Universidad Internacional Menéndez Pelayo, 1981.

Cirujano Marín, Paloma, Teresa Elorriaga Planes, and Juan Sisinio Pérez Garzón. *Historiografía y nacionalismo español, 1834–1868.* Madrid: Consejo Superior de Investigaciones Científicas, Centro de Estudios Históricos, 1985.

Clark, Linda L. *Schooling the Daughters of Marianne: Textbooks and the Socialization of Girls in Modern French Primary Schools.* Albany, N.Y.: SUNY Press, 1984.

Crespo Redondo, Jesús, José Luis Sáinz Casado, José Crespo Redondo, and Carlos Pérez Manrique. *Purga de maestros en la guerra civil: La depuración del magisterio nacional de la provincia de Burgos.* Valladolid: Ediciones Ámbito, 1987.

Cuesta Escudero, Pedro, ed. *Félix Martí Alpera (1875–1946): La seva contribució a l'escola pública. En motiu del seu homenatge.* Barcelona: GRAO, 1979.

De Miguel, Amando. *40 millones de españoles, 40 años después.* Barcelona: Grijalbo, 1976.

————. "La transmisión de las ideas autoritarias a través de los textos escolares." *Cuadernos de Pedagogía*, suppl. no. 3 (1976): 32–34.

Dendle, Brian J. *Galdós: The Early Historical Novels*. Columbia: University of Missouri Press, 1986.

Díaz, Elías. *La filosofía social del krausismo español*. Madrid: EDICUSA, 1973.

————. "La Institución Libre de Enseñanza en la España del nacional-catolicismo." *Historia Internacional*, no. 16 (July 1976): 69–78.

————. *Pensamiento español en la era de Franco (1936–1975)*. Madrid: Tecnos, 1983.

Díaz de la Guardia, Enrique. *Evolución y desarrollo de la enseñanza media en España de 1875 a 1930: Un conflicto político-pedagógico*. Madrid: Ministerio de Educación y Ciencia, CIDE, 1988.

Díaz Mozaz, José María. *Apuntes para una sociología del anticlericalismo*. Madrid: Editorial Ariel, 1976.

Diorio, Joseph A. "The Decline of History as a Tool of Moral Training." *History of Education Quarterly* 25, no. 2 (spring-summer 1985): 71–102.

Dorado Soto, María Ángeles. *El pensamiento educativo de la Institución Marista*. Barcelona: Nau Llibres, 1984.

Dupláa, Cristina, and Gwendolyn Barnes, eds. *Las nacionalidades del estado español: Una problemática cultural*. Minneapolis: University of Minnesota, Institute for the Study of Ideologies and Literature, 1986.

Dupuy, Aimé. "Les livres de lecture de G. Bruno." *Revue d'histoire économique et sociale* 31, no. 2 (1953): 128–51.

Durkheim, Émile. *Education and Sociology*. Translated by Sherwood D. Fox. Glencoe, Ill.: Free Press, 1956.

Eggleston, J. *The Sociology of the School Curriculum*. Boston: Routledge and Kegan Paul, 1977.

Elorriaga Planes, María Teresa. "Evolución temática de la historiografía española de 1844 a 1874." In *Estudios de historia social: Homenaje a Manuel Tuñón de Lara*, 2:713–22. Madrid: Universidad Internacional Menéndez Pelayo, 1981.

Elwitt, Sanford. *The Making of the Third Republic: Class and Politics in France, 1868–1884*. Baton Rouge: Louisiana State University Press, 1975.

Escola catalana d'ahir y avui. Barcelona: Ediciones de Mall, 1979.

Escolano Benito, Agustín. "Las escuelas normales, siglo y medio de perspectiva histórica." *Revista de Educación* 30, no. 269 (1982): 55–99.

Escolar Sobrino, Hipólito. *La cultura durante la guerra civil*. Madrid: Editorial Alhambra, 1987.

Esenwein, George R. *Anarchist Ideology and the Working-Class Movement in Spain, 1868–1898*. Berkeley and Los Angeles: University of California Press, 1989.

Esteban Mateo, León. *Boletín de la Institución Libre de Enseñanza: Nómina bibliográfica (1877–1936)*. Valencia: Departamento de Educación Comparada e Historia de la Educación de la Universidad, 1979.

————. *La Institución Libre de Enseñanza en Valencia*. Valencia: Editorial Bonaire, 1974.

Fagg, John E. "Rafael Altamira (1866–1951)." In S. William Halperin, ed., *Essays in Modern European Historiography*. Chicago: University of Chicago Press, 1970.

Fentress, James, and Chris Wickham. *Social Memory*. London: Basil Blackwell, 1992.

Fernández Clemente, Eloy. *Educación y revolución en Joaquín Costa y breve antología pedagógica*. Madrid: EDICUSA, 1969.

Fernández Enguita, Mariano. *Reforma educativa, desigualdad social e inercia institucional: La enseñanza secundaria en España*. Barcelona: Editorial Laia, 1987.

Fernández Martín, Luis, S.J. *Historia del Colegio San José de Valladolid, 1881–1981*. Valladolid: Colegio San José, 1981.

Fernández Soria, Juan Manuel. *Educación y cultura en la guerra civil: (España, 1936–39)*. Valencia: NAU Llibres, 1984.

Ferrer C. Maura, Salvador. *Una institución docente española: La Escuela de Estudios Superiores del Magisterio (1909–1932)*. Madrid: Imp. CEDESA, 1973.

Ferro, Marc. *The Use and Abuse of History, or How the Past Is Taught*. Boston: Routledge and Kegan Paul, 1984.

Fey, Eduardo. *Estudio documental de la filosofía en el bachillerato español (1807–1957)*. Madrid: Consejo Superior de Investigaciones Científicas, Instituto de Pedagogía San José de Calasanz, 1975.

Fletcher, Richard. *The Quest for El Cid*. New York: Alfred A. Knopf, 1990.

Foard, Douglas W. *The Revolt of the Aesthetes: Ernesto Giménez Caballero and the Origins of Spanish Fascism*. New York: Peter Lang Publishing, 1989.

————. "The Spanish Fichte: Menéndez y Pelayo." *Journal of Contemporary History* 14, no. 1 (January 1979): 83–97.

Fox, Edward Inman. *La crisis intelectual del 98*. Madrid: EDICUSA, 1976.

Fradera, Josep M. *Cultura nacional en una societat dividida: Patriotisme i cultura a Catalunya (1838–1868)*. Barcelona: Editorial Curial, 1992.

Freyssinet-Dominjon, Jacqueline. *Les Manuels d'histoire de l'école libre, 1882–1959: De la loi Ferry à la loi Debré*. Paris: Armand Colin, 1969.

Frutos, Enrique. "La enseñanza media en España en la primera mitad del siglo XX." *Bordón* 3, nos. 17–18 (1951): 119–36.

Fusi, Juan Pablo. "Center and Periphery, 1900–1936: National Integration and Regional Nationalisms Reconsidered." In Frances Lannon and Paul Preston, eds., *Elites and Power in Twentieth-Century Spain: Essays in Honor of Sir Raymond Carr*. Oxford: Clarendon Press, 1990.

Gallego, Saturnino. *Sembraron con amor: "LaSalle," centenario en España (1878–1978)*. San Sebastián: Industria Gráfica Valverde, 1978.

Gamero Merino, Carmela. *Un modelo europeo de renovación pedagógica: José Castillejo*. Madrid: Consejo Superior de Investigaciones Científicas, Instituto de Estudios Manchegos, 1988.

García Camarero, Ernesto, and Enrique García Camarero. *La polémica de la ciencia española*. Madrid: Alianza Editorial, 1970.

García Cárcel, Ricardo. *La leyenda negra: Historia y opinión*. Madrid: Alianza Universidad, 1992.

———. "Maravall i la història del pensament." *L'Avenç* 102 (March 1987): 60–61.

García Crespo, Clementina. *Léxico e ideología en los libros de lectura de la escuela primaria (1940–1975).* Salamanca: Ediciones Universidad, Instituto de Ciencias de la Educación, 1983.

García del Dujo, Ángel. *Museo Pedagógico Nacional (1881–1941): Teoría educativa y desarrollo histórico.* Salamanca: Ediciones Universidad, Instituto de Ciencias de la Educación, 1985.

García Delgado, José Luis, ed. *La crisis de la Restauración: España entre la primera guerra mundial y la II República.* Madrid: Siglo XXI, 1986.

———, ed. *España entre dos siglos: Continuidad y cambio.* Madrid: Siglo XXI, 1991.

———, ed. *España, 1898–1936: Estructuras y cambio. Coloquio de la Universidad Complutense sobre la España contemporánea.* Madrid: Universidad Complutense, 1984.

———, ed. *La España de la Restauración: Política, economía, legislación y cultura.* Madrid: Siglo XXI, 1985.

———, ed. *Los orígenes culturales de la II República.* Madrid: Siglo XXI, 1993.

———, ed. *La II República española: Bienio rectificador y Frente Popular, 1934–1936.* Madrid: Siglo XXI, 1988.

———, ed. *La II República española: El primer bienio.* Madrid: Siglo XXI, 1987.

García de Valdeavellano, Luis. "Don Rafael Altamira, o la historia como educación." In García de Valdeavellano, ed., *Seis semblanzas de historiadores españoles.* Seville: Publicaciones de la Universidad, 1978.

García Hoz, Víctor. *La educación en la España del siglo XX.* Madrid: Rialp, 1980.

García i Sevilla, Lluis. "Lengua, nació i estat al diccionario de la Real Academia Espanyola." *L'Avenç* 16 (May 1979): 50–55.

García Puchol, Joaquín. *Los textos escolares de historia en la enseñanza española (1808–1900): Análisis de su estructura y contenido.* Barcelona: Publicacions Universitat de Barcelona, 1993.

García Regidor, Teódulo. *La polémica sobre la secularización de la enseñanza en España (1902–1914).* Madrid: Fundación Santa María, 1985.

García y García, Matilde. "Los examenes de bachillerato en España, desde 1900 a 1950." *Bordón* 10, no. 74 (1958): 89–109.

———. "La Inspección de Enseñanza Media en medio siglo de legislación española (1900–1950)." *Bordón* 10, no. 73 (1958): 21–27.

———. "Orientaciones legislativas de las enseñanzas del bachillerato en el presente siglo." *Educadores* 6, no. 30 (1964): 855–85.

Gay, Joan. *Societat catalana i reforma escolar.* Barcelona: Laia, 1973.

Geertz, Clifford. *The Interpretation of Cultures: Selected Essays.* New York: Basic Books, 1973.

Gellner, Ernest. *Nations and Nationalism.* Ithaca: Cornell University Press, 1983.

Gildea, Robert. *The Past in French History.* New Haven: Yale University Press, 1994.

Gillis, John R., ed. *Commemorations: The Politics of National Identity*. Princeton: Princeton University Press, 1994.

Giner, Severiano. *Escuelas Pías: Ser e historia*. Madrid: Ediciones Calasancias, 1978.

Giroux, Henry A. "Hegemony, Resistance and the Paradox of Educational Reform." *Interchange* 12, nos. 2–3 (1981): 3–26.

———. *Ideology, Culture and the Process of Schooling*. Philadelphia: Temple University Press, 1981.

———. "Theories of Reproduction and Resistance in the New Sociology of Education: A Critical Analysis." *Harvard Educational Review* 53, no. 3 (1983): 257–93.

Gómez García, María Nieves. *Educación y pedagogía en el pensamiento de Giner de los Ríos*. Seville: Publicaciones de la Universidad, 1983.

Gómez Mendoza, Josefina, and Nicolás Ortega Cantero. "Geografía y regeneracionismo en España (1875–1936)." *Sistema* 77 (March 1987): 77–89.

Gómez Molleda, Dolores. *Los reformadores de la España contemporánea*. Madrid: Consejo Superior de Investigaciones Científicas, Escuela de Historia Moderna, 1966.

Gómez-Navarro, José Luis. *El régimen de Primo de Rivera: Reyes, dictaduras y dictadores*. Madrid: Ediciones Cátedra, 1991.

González-Anleo, Juan. *Catolicismo nacional: Nostalgia y crisis*. Madrid: Ediciones Paulinas, 1975.

———. *El sistema educativo español*. Madrid: Instituto de Estudios Económicos, 1985.

González Calbet, María Teresa. *La dictadura de Primo de Rivera: El directorio militar*. Madrid: Ediciones El Arquero, 1987.

González Rodríguez, Encarnación. *Sociedad y educación en la España de Alfonso XIII*. Madrid: Fundación Universitaria Española, 1988.

Gooch, George Peabody. *History and Its Historians in the Nineteenth Century*. Boston: Beacon Press, 1959.

Gramsci, Antonio. *Prison Notebooks*. Edited by Joseph A. Buttigieg, translated by Joseph A. Buttigieg and Antonio Callari. New York: Columbia University Press, 1991.

Greenfeld, Liah. *Nationalism: Five Roads to Modernity*. Cambridge: Harvard University Press, 1992.

Grew, Raymond, and Patrick J. Harrigan. "The Catholic Contribution to Universal Schooling in France, 1850–1906." *Journal of Modern History* 57, no. 2 (June 1985): 211–47.

Grillo, R. D., ed. *"Nation" and "State" in Europe: Anthropological Perspectives*. New York: Academic Press, 1980.

Guasch Borrat, Juan María. *"El Debate" y la crisis de la Restauración (1910–1923)*. Pamplona: Ediciones Universidad de Navarra, 1986.

Guereña, Jean-Louis, and Alejandro Tiana, eds. *Clases populares, cultura, educación: Siglo XIX y XX. Coloquio hispano-francés (Casa de Velázquez, Madrid, 15–17 junio de 1987)*. Madrid: Casa de Velázquez and Universidad Nacional de Educación a Distancia, 1990.

Guerrero Salom, Enrique. "La Institución, el sistema educativo y la educación de las clases obreras a finales de siglo." *Revista de Educación* 23, no. 243 (1976): 64–81.

Halperin, S. William, ed. *Essays in Modern European Historiography*. Chicago: University of Chicago Press, 1970.

Harrigan, Patrick J. "The Social Appeals of Catholic Secondary Education in France in the 1870s." *Journal of Social History* 8 (spring 1975): 122–41.

Hernández, Francesc, and Francesc Mercadé. *Estructuras sociales y cuestión nacional en España*. Barcelona: Ariel, 1986.

Hernández Díaz, José María. *Educación y sociedad en Béjar durante el siglo XIX*. Salamanca: Ediciones Universidad, Instituto de Ciencias de la Educación, 1983.

Herr, Richard. *The Eighteenth-Century Revolution in Spain*. Princeton: Princeton University Press, 1958.

Herr, Richard, and John H. R. Polt, eds. *Iberian Identity: Essays on the Nature of Identity in Spain and Portugal*. Berkeley, Calif.: Institute of International Studies, 1989.

Hillgarth, Jocelyn N. "Spanish Historiography and Iberian Reality." *History and Theory* 24, no. 1 (1985): 23–43.

Hiner, N. Ray. "Professions in Process: Changing Relations between Historians and Educators, 1896–1911." *History of Education Quarterly* 12, no. 1 (1972): 34–42.

Hinterhauser, Hans. *Los "Episodios Nacionales" de Benito Pérez Galdós*. Madrid: Editorial Gredos, 1963.

Histoire et historiens depuis cinquante ans: Méthodes, organisation et résultats du travail historique de 1876 à 1926. New York: Burt Franklin, 1971 (1st ed. 1927–28).

Historia de la educación en España: Textos y documentos. 5 vols. Madrid: Servicio de Publicaciones del Ministerio de Educación y Ciencia, 1979–91.

Hobsbawm, Eric. *Nations and Nationalism since 1780: Programme, Myth, Reality*. New York: Cambridge University Press, 1990.

Hobsbawm, Eric, and Terence Ranger, eds. *The Invention of Tradition*. Cambridge: Past and Present Publications, 1984.

Holtby, David. "Society and Primary Schools in Spain, 1899–1936." Ph.D. diss., University of New Mexico, 1978.

"Homenaje a Galdós." *Cuadernos Hispanoamericanos: Revista mensual de cultura hispánica* 250–52 (1970–71).

"Homenatge a Antonio Domínguez Ortiz." *L'Avenç* 14 (March 1979): 4.

Hroch, Miroslav. *Social Pre-Conditions of National Revival in Europe: A Comparative Analysis of the Social Composition of Patriotic Groups among the Smaller European Nations*. New York: Cambridge University Press, 1985.

Hutchinson, John. *Modern Nationalism*. London: Fontana, 1994.

Jackson, Gabriel. *The Spanish Republic and the Civil War*. Princeton: Princeton University Press, 1965.

Jenkins, Brian. *Nationalism in France: Class and Nation since 1789*. Savage, Md.: Barnes and Noble Books, 1990.

Jiménez Díez, José Antonio. "Ideología y política en la historiografía española de 1844 a 1874." In *Estudios de historia social: Homenaje a Manuel Tuñón de Lara*, 2:679–95. Madrid: Universidad Internacional Menéndez Pelayo, 1981.

Jiménez-Landi, Antonio. *La Institución Libre de Enseñanza y su ambiente.* Madrid: Taurus, 1973.

Jobit, Pierre. *Les Éducateurs de l'Espagne contemporaine: Les krausistes.* Paris: E. de Boccard, 1936.

Jover Zamora, José María. "Ante una hegemonía frustrada." *Saber leer* 7 (1987): 1–2.

———. "Caracteres del nacionalismo español, 1854–1874." *Zona Abierta* 31 (1984): 1–22.

———. *La civilización española a mediados del siglo XIX.* Madrid: Espasa-Calpe, 1991.

———. "Corrientes historiográficas en la España contemporánea." In *El siglo XIX en España: Doce estudios.* Barcelona: Editorial Planeta, 1974.

———. *La imagen de la primera república en la España de la Restauración: Discurso leído el día 28 de marzo de 1982 en el acto de su recepción pública; y contestación del Excmo. Sr. D. José Antonio Maravall Casenoves.* Madrid: Real Academia de la Historia, 1982.

Juliá, Santos. *Azaña: Una biografía política.* Madrid: Alianza Editorial, 1990.

Jutglar Bernaus, Antoni. "La enseñanza en Barcelona en el siglo XX." *Anales de Sociología* 2, no. 3 (1967): 7–39.

———. "Notas para el estudio de la enseñanza en Barcelona hasta 1900." In Ayuntamiento de Barcelona, *Materiales para la historia institucional de la ciudad.* Vol. 16. Barcelona: Instituto Municipal de Historia, 1966.

Kappeler, Andreas, ed. *The Formation of National Elites: Comparative Studies on Governments and Non-Dominant Ethnic Groups in Europe, 1850–1940.* Vol. 6. New York: New York University Press, European Science Foundation, 1992.

Keylor, William R. *Academy and Community: The Foundations of the French Historical Profession.* Cambridge: Harvard University Press, 1975.

Kiernan, Victor G. "Class and Ideology: The Bourgeoisie and Its Historians." *History of European Ideas* 6, no. 3 (1985): 267–86.

Koon, Tracy H. *Believe, Obey, Fight: Political Socialization of Youth in Fascist Italy, 1922–1943.* Chapel Hill: University of North Carolina Press, 1985.

Kramer, Lloyd, Donald Reid, and William L. Barney. *Learning History in America: Schools, Cultures, and Politics.* Minneapolis: University of Minnesota Press, 1994.

Lannon, Frances. *Privilege, Persecution, and Prophecy: The Catholic Church in Spain, 1875–1975.* New York: Oxford University Press, 1987.

———. "The Socio-Political Role of the Spanish Church—A Case Study." *Journal of Contemporary History* 14, no. 2 (April 1979): 193–210.

El legado cultural de España al siglo XXI. Vol. 1, *Pensamiento, Historia, Literatura.* Barcelona: Colegio Libre de Eméritos y Círculo de Lectores, 1994.

El legado de Costa: Huesca, septiembre de 1983. Madrid: Ministerio de Cultura, Subdirección General de Archivos, Diputación General de Aragón, Departamento de Cultura y Educación, 1983.

Lerena Alesón, Carlos. *Escuela, ideología y clases sociales en España: Crítica de la sociología empirista de la educación*. Barcelona: Ariel, 1976.

Lewis, Bernard. *History Remembered, Recovered, Invented*. Princeton: Princeton University Press, 1975.

Lida, Clara E. "Educación anarquista en la España del ochocientos." *Revista de Occidente* 97 (1971): 33–47.

Linehan, Peter. *History and the Historians of Medieval Spain*. New York: Oxford University Press, 1993.

Linz, Juan J. "From Great Hopes to Civil War: The Breakdown of Democracy in Spain." In Juan J. Linz and Alfred Stepan, eds., *The Breakdown of Democratic Regimes*. Baltimore: Johns Hopkins University Press, 1978.

———. "Religion and Politics in Spain: From Conflict to Consensus above Cleavage." *Social Compass* 27, nos. 2–3 (1980): 255–77.

———. "Spain: An Authoritarian Regime." In Stanley G. Payne, ed., *Politics and Society in Twentieth-Century Spain*. New York: New Viewpoints, 1976.

López, Miguel A. *La Escuela Normal de Granada, 1846–1970*. Granada: Universidad, 1979.

López-Aranguren, José Luis. *La cruz de la monarquía actual*. Madrid: Taurus, 1974.

———. *Infancia y sociedad en España*. Jaén: Editorial Hesperia, 1983.

———. *Moral y sociedad: Introducción a la moral social española del siglo XIX*. 2d ed. Madrid: EDICUSA, 1966.

López Martín, Ramón. *Ideología y educación en la dictadura de Primo de Rivera*. Vol. 1, *Escuelas y maestros*. Valencia: Universitat de València, Departamento Educación Comparada e Historia de la Educación, 1994.

López-Morillas, Juan. *Hacia el 98: Literatura, sociedad, ideología*. Barcelona: Ariel, 1972.

———. *The Krausist Movement and Ideological Change in Spain, 1854–1874*. Translated by Frances M. López-Morillas. New York: Cambridge University Press, 1981.

———. *Racionalismo pragmático: El pensamiento de Francisco Giner de los Ríos*. Madrid: Alianza Universidad, 1988.

Lozano Seijas, Claudio. *La educación republicana, 1931–1939*. Barcelona: Universidad, Departamento de Pedagogía Comparada e Historia de la Educación, 1980.

Mainer, José-Carlos. *La edad de plata (1902–1931): Ensayo de interpretación de un proceso cultural*. Barcelona: Ediciones Asenet, 1975.

———. *Falange y literatura*. Barcelona: Editorial Labor, 1971.

———. "De historiografía literaria española: El fundamento liberal." In *Estudios de historia social: Homenaje a Manuel Tuñón de Lara*, 2:439–72. Madrid: Universidad Internacional Menéndez Pelayo, 1981.

Maingueneau, Dominique. *Les Livres d'école de l'école libre, 1870–1914: (Discours et idéologie)*. Paris: Le Sycomore, 1979.

Malagón, Javier, and Silvio Zavala. *Rafael Altamira y Crevea: El historiador y el hombre*. México, D.F.: Universidad Nacional Autónoma de México, 1971.

Maravall, José Antonio. "Ganivet y el tema de la autenticidad nacional." *Revista de Occidente*, 2d ser., 3, no. 33 (1965): 389–409.

————. *Menéndez Pidal y la historia del pensamiento.* Madrid: Ediciones Arion, 1960.

Maravall, José María. *La reforma de la enseñanza.* Barcelona: Editorial Laia, 1984.

Marcos Oteruelo, Alfredo. *El pensamiento de Gumersindo de Azcárate.* León: Institución Fray Bernardino de Sahagún, 1985.

Marichal, Juan. *El intelectual y la política en España, 1898–1936.* Madrid: Consejo Superior de Investigaciones Científicas, Publicaciones de la Residencia de Estudiantes, 1990.

Martínez Bonafé, Ángels. *Ensenyament, burgesía i liberalisme: L'ensenyament secundari en els orígins del País Valencià contemporani.* Valencia: Diputació Provincial, 1985.

Martínez Martín, Jesús A. *Lectura y lectores en el Madrid del siglo XIX.* Madrid: Consejo Superior de Investigaciones Científicas, 1992.

Mateos Pérez, P. "¿La revolución de Saturnino Calleja?" *Leer* 8 (1987): 36–39.

Maura Gamazo, Gabriel, duque de Maura. *Bosquejo histórico de la dictadura, 1923–1930.* 5th ed., rev. Madrid: Tip. de Archivos, 1930.

Maynes, Mary Jo. *Schooling in Western Europe: A Social History.* Albany, N.Y.: SUNY Press, 1985.

Mérida-Nicolich, Eloisa. *Una alternativa de reforma pedagógica: "La Revista de Pedagogía" (1922–1936).* Pamplona: Ediciones Universidad de Navarra, 1983.

Mews, Stuart, ed. *Religion and National Identity.* New York: Oxford University Press, 1982.

Millán Sánchez, Fernando. *La revolución laica: De la Institución Libre de Enseñanza a la escuela de la República.* Valencia: Fernando Torres, 1983.

Monés i Pujol-Busquets, Jordi. *L'escola a Catalunya sota el franquisme.* Barcelona: Edicions 62, 1981.

————. *La llengua a l'escola (1714–1939).* Barcelona: Barcanova, 1984.

————. *El pensament escolar i la renovació pedagògica a Catalunya (1833–1938).* Barcelona: Edicions de La Magrana, 1977.

————. "El pensamiento escolar de la iglesia oficial—desde la guerra civil hasta nuestros días." *Cuadernos de Pedagogía* 4, no. 63 (March 1980): 33–40.

Monés i Pujol-Busquets, Jordi, Pere Solà, and Luis Miguel Lázaro. *Ferrer Guardia y la pedagogía libertaria: Elementos para un debate.* Barcelona: Icaria Editorial, 1977.

Moreno Alonso, Manuel. *Historiografía romántica española: Introducción al estudio de la historia en el siglo XIX.* Seville: Servicio de Publicaciones de la Universidad, 1979.

————. *La revolución francesa en la historiografía española del siglo XIX.* Seville: Servicio de Publicaciones de la Universidad, 1979.

Morodó, Raúl. *Los orígenes ideológicos del franquismo: Acción Española.* Madrid: Alianza Universidad, 1985.

Morón Arroyo, Ciriaco, et al. *Menéndez Pelayo: Hacia una nueva imagen.* Santander: Sociedad Menéndez Pelayo, 1983.

Mosse, George. *The Nationalization of the Masses.* New York: Fertig, 1975.

Mujer y educación en España, 1868–1975: V Coloquio de Historia de la Educación. Santiago de Compostela: Departamento de Teoría e Historia de la Educación de la Universidad, 1990.

Müller, Detlef K., Fritz Ringer, and Brian Simon. *The Rise of the Modern Educational System: Structural Change and Social Reproduction, 1870–1920.* New York: Cambridge University Press, 1987.

Murillo Ferrol, Francisco. *Estudios de sociología política.* Madrid: Tecnos, 1963.

Mut i Carbasa, Rosa, and Teresa Martí y Armengol. *La resistencia escolar catalana en llibres (1716–1939): Bibliografía.* Barcelona: Ediciones 62, 1981.

Navarro Sandalinas, Ramón. *La enseñanza primaria durante el franquismo (1936–1975).* Barcelona: PPU, 1990.

Ninyoles, Rafael. *Madre España.* Valencia: Prometeo, 1979.

Nora, Pierre, ed. *Les Lieux de mémoire.* Vol. 1, *La République,* and Vol. 2, *La Nation.* Paris: Gallimard, 1984–86.

Nuccio, Richard Anthony. "The Socialization of Political Values: The Content of Official Education in Spain." Ph.D. diss., University of Massachusetts, 1977.

Núñez, Clara Eugenia. *La fuente de la riqueza: Educación y desarrollo económico en la España contemporánea.* Madrid: Alianza Universidad, 1992.

Núñez, Clara Eugenia, and Gabriel Tortella, eds. *La maldición divina: Ignorancia y atraso económico en perspectiva histórica.* Madrid: Alianza Editorial, 1993.

Núñez Encabo, Manuel. *Manuel Sales y Ferré: Los orígenes de la sociología en España.* Madrid: EDICUSA, 1976.

Olábarri Gortázar, Ignacio. "La recepcion en España de la *revolución historiográfica* del siglo XX." In V. Vázquez de Prada, I. Olábarri, and A. Floristán Imizcoz, eds., *La historiografía en Occidente desde 1945.* Pamplona: EUNSA, 1985, 87–109.

Ollero Tassara, Andrés. *Universidad y política: Tradición y secularización en el siglo XIX español.* Madrid: Instituto de Estudios Políticos, 1972.

Once ensayos sobre la historia. Madrid: Ríoduero, 1976.

Ortega Berenguer, Emilio. *La instrucción pública en la II República, Málaga, 1931.* Málaga: Diputación Provincial, 1982.

Ozouf, Mona. *L'École, l'Église et la République, 1871–1914.* Paris: Armand Colin, 1963.

Palacio Atard, Vicente. *Menéndez Pelayo y la historia de España.* Valladolid: Escuela de Historia Moderna del Consejo Superior de Investigaciones Científicas, 1956.

Palacio Lis, Irene. *Rafael Altamira: Un modelo de regeneracionismo educativo.* Alicante: Publicaciones de la Caja de Ahorros Provincial, 1986.

Palacios Bañuelos, Luis. *Castillejo, educador.* Ciudad Real: Diputación Provincial, 1986.

———. *Instituto-Escuela: Historia de una renovación educativa.* Madrid: Ministerio de Educación y Ciencia, Centro de Publicaciones, 1989.

Parsons, Talcott. *The Social System.* Glencoe, Ill.: Free Press, 1959.

Pasamar Alzuria, Gonzalo, and Ignacio Peiró Martín. *Historiografía e ideología en la postguerra española: La ruptura de la tradición liberal.* Zaragoza: Secretariado de Publicaciones de la Universidad, 1981.

———. *Historiografía y práctica social en España.* Zaragoza: Secretariado de Publicaciones de la Universidad, 1987.

———. *Los inicios de la profesionalización historiográfica en España.* Zaragoza: Secretariado de Publicaciones de la Universidad, 1987.

Payne, Stanley G. *Falange: A History of Spanish Fascism.* Stanford, Calif.: Stanford University Press, 1961.

———. *The Franco Regime, 1936–1975.* Madison: University of Wisconsin Press, 1987.

———. "Jaime Vicens Vives and the Writing of Spanish History." *Journal of Modern History* 34, no. 2 (June 1962): 119–34.

———. "Nationalism, Regionalism, and Micronationalism in Spain." *Journal of Contemporary History* 26, nos. 3–4 (September 1991): 479–91.

———. *Spain's First Democracy: The Second Republic, 1931–1936.* Madison: University of Wisconsin Press, 1993.

———. *Spanish Catholicism: An Historical Overview.* Madison: University of Wisconsin Press, 1984.

Pérez Bustamante, Ciriaco. *Primer centenario de la muerte de Don Modesto Lafuente: Discurso leído en la junta solemne conmemorativa del 29 de enero de 1967.* Madrid: Imprenta y Editorial Maestre, 1967.

Pérez de la Dehesa, Rafael. *El pensamiento de Costa y su influencia en el 98.* Madrid: Sociedad de Estudios y Publicaciones, 1966.

Pérez Galán, Mariano. *La enseñanza en la segunda república española.* Madrid: EDICUSA, 1977.

———. "La Institución Libre de Enseñanza en los comienzos del franquismo." *Cuadernos de Pedagogía* 2, no. 22 (1976): 17–19.

Pérez González, Eugenio. *El magisterio sevillano a comienzos del siglo XX.* Seville: Servicio de Publicaciones del Ayuntamiento, 1982.

Perz, John R. *Secondary Education in Spain.* Washington, D.C.: Catholic University, 1934.

Peset, José Luis, Santiago Garma, and Juan Sisinio Pérez Garzón. *Ciencias y enseñanza en la revolución burguesa.* Madrid: Siglo XXI, 1978.

Peset, Mariano, and José Luis Peset. *La universidad española (Siglos XVIII y XIX): Despotismo ilustrado y revolución liberal.* Madrid: Taurus, 1974.

———. "Vicens Vives y la historiografía del derecho en España." In *Vorstudien zur Rechtshistorik.* Frankfurt: Vittorio Klosterman, 1977, 176–262.

Phillips, Carla Rahn. "Sources for the Life of Christopher Columbus." Society for Spanish and Portuguese Historical Studies *Bulletin* 17, no. 1 (1992): 13.

Pike, Frederick B. *Hispanismo, 1898–1936: Spanish Conservatives and Liberals and Their Relations with Spanish America.* Notre Dame, Ind.: University of Notre Dame Press, 1971.

Plumb, J. H. *The Death of the Past.* New York: Houghton Mifflin, 1971.

Pozo Andrés, María del Mar del, Manuel Segura Redondo, and Alejandro R. Diez Torre. *Guadalajara en la historia del magisterio español, 1839/1939: Cien años de formación del profesorado.* Alcalá de Henares: Universidad, 1986.

Pozo Pardo, Alberto del. "Año 1898: Llamada de esperanza a una regeneración pedagógica de España." *Revista Española de Pedagogía* 36, no. 140 (1978): 103–16.

Prellezo García, José Manuel. *Manjón, educador: Selección de sus escritos pedagógicos*. Madrid: Editorial Magisterio Español, 1975.

Preston, Paul. *The Coming of the Spanish Civil War: Reform, Reaction and Revolution in the Second Republic, 1931–1936*. New York: Harper and Row, 1978.

———. *Franco: A Biography*. London: Harper Collins, 1993.

———. *The Politics of Revenge: Fascism and the Military in Twentieth Century Spain*. Boston: Unwin Hyman, 1990.

Prieto, Alberto. "El franquisme i la història antiga." *L'Avenç* 18 (1979): 75–77.

Prost, Antoine. *L'Enseignement en France, 1800–1967*. 2d ed., rev. Paris: Librairie Armand Colin, 1968.

Puelles Benítez, Manuel de. *Educación e ideología en la España contemporánea (1767–1975)*. Barcelona: Editorial Labor, 1980.

Rafael Altamira (1866–1951). Alicante: Diputación Provincial, Instituto de Estudios "Juan Gil-Albert," 1987.

Ramírez, José Luis, ed. *Estudios sobre la Segunda República*. Madrid: Tecnos, 1975.

Ramírez, José Luis, et al. *Las fuentes ideológicas de un régimen: (España, 1939–1945)*. Zaragoza: Pórtico, 1978.

Ramos, Vicente. *Palabra y pensamiento de Rafael Altamira*. Alicante: Caja de Ahorros de Alicante y Murcia, 1987.

———. *Rafael Altamira*. Madrid: Alfaguara, 1968.

Ranum, Orest, ed., *National Consciousness, History, and Political Culture in Early-Modern Europe*. Baltimore: Johns Hopkins University Press, 1975.

Las Reales Academias del Instituto de España. Madrid: Alianza Editorial, 1992.

Rey Carrera, Juan, S.J. *El resurgir de España previsto por nuestros grandes pensadores: Donoso, Balmes, Aparisi, Menéndez y Pelayo, Vázquez de Mella*. San Sebastián: Editorial Española, 1938.

Rial, James. *Revolution from Above: The Primo de Rivera Dictatorship in Spain, 1923–1930*. Fairfax, Va.: George Mason University Press, 1986.

Riemenschneider, Rainier. "L'Enseignement de l'histoire en Allemagne sous le IIIe Reich." *Francia, Forschungen zur westeuropaischen Geschichte* 7 (1979): 401–28.

Ringer, Fritz K. *Education and Society in Modern Europe*. Bloomington: Indiana University Press, 1979.

———. *Fields of Knowledge: French Academic Culture in Comparative Perspective, 1890–1920*. New York: Cambridge University Press, 1992.

Robinson, Richard A. H. "Political Conservativism: The Spanish Case, 1875–1977." *Journal of Contemporary History* 14, no. 4 (1979): 561–80.

Romero Maura, Joaquín. *La rosa de fuego: El obrerismo barcelonés de 1899 a 1909*. Barcelona: Grijalbo, 1975.

Ruiz Berrio, Julio, ed. *La educación en la España contemporánea: Cuestiones históricas. Libro homenaje a Ángeles Galiño*. Madrid: Sociedad Española de Pedagogía, 1986.

——. *Política escolar de España en el siglo XIX (1808–1833)*. Madrid: Consejo Superior de Investigaciones Científicas, 1970.

Ruiz Miguel, Alfonso. "La Junta para Ampliación de Estudios." *Historia 16* 5, no. 49 (May 1980): 85–93.

Ruiz Rico, Juan José. *El papel político de la iglesia católica en la España de Franco*. Madrid: Tecnos, 1977.

Rulon, Henri-Charles, and Philippe Friot. *Un siècle de pédagogie dans les écoles primaires (1820–1940): Histoire des méthodes et des manuels scolaires utilisés dans l'Institut des Frères de l'Instruction chrétienne de Ploermel*. Paris: J. Vrin, 1962.

Safón, Ricardo. *La educación en la España revolucionaria (1936–1939)*. Translated by María Luisa Delgado and Félix Ortega. Madrid: Ediciones de La Piqueta, 1978.

Sahlins, Peter. *Boundaries: The Making of France and Spain in the Pyrenees*. Berkeley and Los Angeles: University of California Press, 1989.

Sainz Rodríguez, Pedro. *Marcelino Menéndez Pelayo, ese desconocido*. Madrid: Fundación Universitaria Española, 1975.

Samaniego Boneu, Mercedes. *La política educativa de la Segunda República durante el bienio azañista*. Madrid: Consejo Superior de Investigaciones Científicas, 1977.

Samaniego Boneu, Mercedes, and Valentín del Arco López, eds. *Historia, literatura, pensamiento: Estudios en homenaje a María Dolores Gómez Molleda*. 2 vols. Salamanca: Narcea, 1990.

Sánchez Agesta, Luis. *Historia del constitucionalismo español (1808–1936)*. 4th ed., rev. Madrid: Centro de Estudios Constitucionales, 1984.

Sánchez Pascua, Felicidad. *El instituto de segunda enseñanza de Badajoz en el siglo XIX (1845–1900): (Orígenes, tratamiento estadístico del alumnado y bibliométrico de los profesores)*. Badajoz: Diputación Provincial, 1985.

Sangrador García, José Luis. *Estereotipos de las nacionalidades y regiones de España*. Madrid: Centro de Investigaciones Sociológicas, 1981.

Sanz Díaz, Federico. *La segunda enseñanza oficial en el siglo XIX*. Madrid: Ministerio de Educación y Ciencia, Dirección General de Enseñanzas Medias, 1985.

Sartorius, Nicolás. "Historia del bachillerato en España." *Triunfo* 21, no. 244 (4 February 1967): 47–53, and no. 246 (18 February 1967): 13–17.

Sastre, José Luis. *"El Magisterio Español": Un siglo de periodismo profesional*. Madrid: Editorial Magisterio Español, 1966.

Seco Serrano, Carlos. *Militarismo y civilismo en la España contemporánea*. Madrid: Instituto de Estudios Económicos, 1984.

Simón Palmer, Carmen. *La enseñanza privada seglar de grado medio en Madrid, 1820–1868*. Madrid: Instituto de Estudios Madrileños, 1972.

Sirera Oliag, María J. *Las enseñanzas secundarias en el País Valenciano*. Madrid: Fundación Juan March, 1979.

Smith, Anthony D. *National Identity*. Reno: University of Nevada Press, 1991.

Solà Gusiñer, Pere. *Las escuelas racionalistas en Cataluña (1909–39)*. Barcelona: Tusquets, 1976.

——. *Francesc Ferrer i Guardia i l'escola moderna*. Barcelona: Curial, 1978.

Surtz, Ronald E., Jaime Ferrán, and Daniel P. Testa. *Américo Castro: The Impact of His Thought. Essays to Mark the Centenary of His Birth.* Madison: The Hispanic Seminary of Medieval Studies, 1988.

Talbott, John E. *The Politics of Educational Reform in France, 1918–1940.* Princeton: Princeton University Press, 1969.

Teich, Mikulas, and Roy Porter, eds. *The National Question in Europe in Historical Context.* New York: Cambridge University Press, 1993.

Tiana Ferrer, Alejandro. *Maestros, misioneros, y militantes: La educación de la clase obrera madrileña, 1898–1917.* Madrid: Centro de Publicaciones del Ministerio de Educación y Ciencia, CIDE, 1992.

Tierno Galván, Enrique. *Costa y el regeneracionismo.* Barcelona: Editorial Barna, 1961.

Tombs, Robert, ed. *Nationhood and Nationalism in France: From Boulangism to the Great War, 1889–1918.* New York: Harper Collins, 1991.

Totosaus, José María. "Presencia de la iglesia en el sector escolar." In *Iglesia y sociedad en España, 1939–1975.* Madrid: Editorial Popular, 1977.

Tuñón de Lara, Manuel. "La interpretación 'policial' de la historia." *Cuadernos de Pedagogía*, suppl. no. 3 (1976): 35–37.

———. *Medio siglo de cultura española (1885–1936).* Madrid: Tecnos, 1973.

———. *La II República.* 2 vols. Madrid: Siglo XXI, 1976.

———, ed. *Historiografía española contemporánea: X Coloquio del Centro de Investigaciones Hispánicas de la Universidad de Pau. Balance y resumen.* Madrid: Siglo XXI, 1980.

Turin, Yvonne. *La educación y la escuela en España de 1874 a 1902: Liberalismo y tradición.* Translated by Josefa Hernández Alfonso. Madrid: Aguilar, 1967.

———. "1898, el desastre, ¿fue una llamada a la 'educación'?" *Revista de Educación* 23, no. 240 (September–October 1975): 23–29.

Tusell, Javier. *La oposición democrática al franquismo, 1939–1962.* Barcelona: Editorial Planeta, 1977.

Ucatescu, Jorge. *Ideas maestras de la cultura española.* Madrid: Reus, 1977.

Ullman, Joan C. *La Semana Trágica: Estudio sobre las causas socioeconómicas del anticlericalismo en España (1898–1912).* Barcelona: Ariel, 1972.

———. "The Warp and Woof of Parliamentary Politics in Spain, 1808–1939: Anticlericalism versus 'Neo-Catholicism.'" *European Studies Review* 13, no. 2 (April 1983): 145–76.

Urbina, Fernando, "Formas de vida de la iglesia en España, 1939–1975." In *Iglesia y sociedad en España, 1939–1975.* Madrid: Editorial Popular, 1977.

Utande Igualada, Manuel. "Un siglo y medio de segunda enseñanza," *Revista de Educación* 30, no. 271 (1982): 7–41.

Valls, Fernando. *La enseñanza de la literatura en el franquismo (1936–1951).* Barcelona: Antoni Bosch, 1983.

Valls Montés, Rafael. *La interpretación de la historia de España y sus orígenes ideológicos en el bachillerato franquista (1938–1953).* Valencia: Instituto de Ciencias de la Educación de la Universidad Literaria, 1984.

Varela Ortega, José. *Los amigos políticos.* Madrid: Alianza Editorial, 1977.

Vaughn, Michalina, and Margaret S. Archer. *Social Conflict and Educational*

Change in England and France, 1789–1848. New York: Cambridge University Press, 1971.

Vázquez de Knauth, Josefina. *Nacionalismo y educación en México.* México, D.F.: El Colegio de México, 1970.

Vélez, Diana. "Regeneration and Pacification: Modernization and the Agents of Social Control, Spain, 1895–1917." Ph.D. diss., Princeton University, 1977.

Vilanova Ribas, Mercedes, and Xavier Moreno Julià. *Atlas de la evolución del analfabetismo en España de 1887 a 1981.* Madrid: Centro de Publicaciones del Ministerio de Educación y Ciencia, CIDE, 1992.

Vilar, Pierre. "Patria y nació en el vocabulari de la Guerra contra Napoleó." In *Assaigs sobre la Catalunya del segle XVIII.* Barcelona: Curial, 1973.

Villacorta Baños, Francisco. *Burguesía y cultura: Los intelectuales españoles en la sociedad liberal (1808–1931).* Madrid: Siglo XXI, 1980.

Viñao Frago, Antonio. "Espacios masculinos, espacios femininos: El acceso de la mujer al bachillerato." In *Mujer y educación en España, 1868–1975: V Coloquio de Historia de la Educación.* Santiago de Compostela: Departamento de Teoría e Historia de la Educación de la Universidad, 1990.

———. "Historia y educación en y desde Murcia: Un análisis contextual." In *Historia y educación en Murcia.* Murcia: Universidad de Murcia, ICE, 1983.

———. *Innovación pedagógica y racionalidad científica: La escuela graduada pública en España (1898–1936).* Madrid: Ediciones Akal, 1990.

———. *Política y educación en los orígenes de la España contemporánea: Examen especial de sus relaciones en la enseñanza secundaria.* Madrid: Siglo XXI, 1982.

Weber, Eugen. *Peasants into Frenchmen: The Modernization of Rural France, 1870–1914.* Stanford, Calif.: Stanford University Press, 1976.

Williams, Raymond. *The Long Revolution.* New York: Columbia University Press, 1961.

Willis, Paul. "Cultural Production Is Different from Cultural Reproduction Is Different from Social Reproduction Is Different from Reproduction." *Interchange* 12, nos. 2–3 (1981): 48–67.

Yetano, Ana. *La enseñanza religiosa en la España de la Restauración (1900–1920).* Barcelona: Anthropos, 1988.

Yllán Calderón, Esperanza. *Cánovas del Castillo: Entre la historia y la política.* Madrid: Centro de Estudios Constitucionales, 1985.

Young, Michael F. D., ed. *Knowledge and Control: New Directions for the Sociology of Education.* London: Collier-Macmillan, 1971.

About the Author

Carolyn Boyd is Professor of History at the University of Texas at Austin. She is the author of *Praetorian Politics in Liberal Spain*.